Scripts of Blackness

RaceB4Race

RACEB4RACE: CRITICAL RACE STUDIES
OF THE PREMODERN

Geraldine Heng and Ayanna Thompson, series editors

A complete list of books in the series is available from the publisher.

Scripts of Blackness

Early Modern Performance Culture and the Making of Race

Noémie Ndiaye

PENN

UNIVERSITY OF PENNSYLVANIA PRESS

PHILADELPHIA

Published by
University of Pennsylvania Press
Philadelphia, Pennsylvania 19104-4112
www.upenn.edu/pennpress

Printed in the United States of America on acid-free paper
10 9 8 7 6 5 4 3 2 1

Hardcover ISBN 9781512822632
Ebook ISBN 9781512822649

A catalogue record for this book is available from the
Library of Congress.

"On February 6, 1628, a very old Black woman from Las Cruces
was buried in this church.

She was free and over a hundred years old. People called her the
Marquess.

Alms paid for her burial, and her memorial
mass took place two days later."
Burial records of San Bernardo Church, Seville

This book is for the Marquesses,
Who knew a thing or two about performance;

For the late Dr. Julie Renee Butler,
Who really wanted to read these pages;

Et pour tous ceux qui sauront entendre.

CONTENTS

Plates follow page 136

Performative Blackness
in Early Modern Europe

Scene 1

January 4, 2016. Seville, Spain. Following a tradition that originated, we are told, in the mid-nineteenth century, thousands of spectators gather in the streets to attend the annual Parade of the Magi, *la cabalgata de reyes.* At dusk, some thirty pageant wagons start moving, laden with music equipment, multicolored neon lights, and costumed children who shower spectators with fistfuls of candies. The kings' wagons arrive last: this year, King Balthazar is performed by the president of the Sevilla FC soccer club, in blackface, as always. He is attended by local volunteers, most on foot, some on white horses, all in dazzling North African white garb, with white cheches on their heads sharply contrasting with the black gloves on their hands, black makeup on their faces, and bright red lipstick applied within the natural contour of their lips. They laugh, dance to the tambourines, strike a pose for the cameras, and throw candies at spectators. The ground is sticky with crushed candies. You look around; you are the only visibly Black person in this crowd.

Scene 2

March 2019. Paris, France. An upcoming performance of Aeschylus's *The Suppliants* is advertised on the website of your alma mater, Paris-Sorbonne University, with photographs from a rehearsal featuring white actresses playing the Libyan Danaids in blackface. Students and antiracist organizations protest and get the performance canceled. Outrage over the cancellation ensues from academic, cultural, and governmental institutions denouncing censorship, attacks on creative freedom, and the misguided importation of American cultural sensibilities and performance history into French society. You read the press: antiracist protesters are accused of misunderstanding the director's intentions, Aeschylus's intentions, and the universalist values of a color-blind republic. The production will be performed two months later, with actresses sporting golden masks this time, in the presence of the minister of culture, the minister of higher education, diplomats, congressmen, and the Parisian academic establishment.[1]

Scene 3

Spring 2008. Paris, France. In her office, your formidable acting teacher (a senior white woman) gives you (a young Black woman) feedback on your performance in *Salina*, an unremarkable African fantasy play by a popular contemporary playwright that she added to your portfolio. She is trying to steer you in the right direction the best way she can— the way her own training, culture, and experience have taught her to. She is trying to help. "This scene is not working, Noémie. It's not working because you are not being African enough for the part. You need to find it. I don't know. Maybe we could—" (she gestures toward her own face while looking at you. The gesture is vague but unmistakably evocative). She will not complete her sentence, perhaps because she caught the expression on your face, or because she can hear herself now. You look at the shelves of classic European drama covering the walls around the two of you.

Those three scenes of formation constitute the affective substrate of *Scripts of Blackness: Early Modern Performance Culture and the Making of Race* and offer a unique experiential shortcut to some of the core ideas of this book.

Performative blackness—a type of racial impersonation that brings into being and fashions what it claims to mimic—haunts the memory of the Western theatre industry far beyond the confines of the Anglo-American world to which its study has so often been limited.

Performative blackness is tied to the use of prosthetic techniques of embodiment that include but are not limited to masks and makeup.

Performative blackness rubs up against lived Blackness historically and politically in ways that have informed the lives of Black professional performers to this day.

Many European countries suffer from forms of cultural amnesia that either erase performative blackness from their history altogether (like France), or erase the early modern roots of performative blackness, making it appear more recent than it is (like Spain).

Performative blackness holds bodies politic together: it is a conduit for communities to tell the fictions they need to hear about themselves, in conflict and in celebration alike.

Those three scenes drive my commitment to understand the appeal that participation in the economy of performative blackness has held across space and time since its inception. In this book, I ask: what did performative blackness do for early modern Europeans? I explore the invention of performative blackness in Renaissance Europe with the hope that uncovering the ideological operations of that racial technology in early modernity might yield insights for the present—a hope that the broken, recursive, and lacunar history separating our moment and early modernity but also linking them might generate theoretical traction.

In this book, I consider the material practices of racial impersonation in use in early modern Western Europe. I reconstruct three specific techniques— black-up (cosmetic blackness), blackspeak (acoustic blackness), and black dances (kinetic blackness)—in order to map out the poetics of those techniques by tracking metaphorical strains regularly associated with them in performance. Those metaphorical strains, the titular *scripts of blackness* of this book, were not simply ornamental: operating across national borders, they constituted resources, as they provided spectators and participants with new ways of thinking about the Afro-diasporic people who lived or could live in their midst, and conceptually brought blackness into being as a racial category organizing power relations. All early modern European nations whose colonial aspirations involved Afro-diasporic populations found in performative blackness a most useful instrument. By putting into conversation expansive early modern English, French, and Spanish archives that are seldom discussed and never discussed in relation to one another, in this book, I attempt to grasp the stories Europeans told themselves through performative blackness, and the effect of those fictions on early modern Afro-diasporic subjects. This attempt proceeds from first-person knowledge that the history of early modern performative blackness is ongoing (as Sylvie Chalaye puts it, "it is as if racialized actors and actresses today had to become the perennial African ambassador, that comedic figure of French baroque theatre inherited from court masquerades"), and from a hope that historical consciousness might foster a greater awareness of the scripts permeating the multimedia terrain of performative blackness in our own moment.[2]

To provide a synthetic introduction to *Scripts of Blackness*, in this opening chapter, I first define some the project's key words: I explain what the word race meant in early modernity, and I provide an account of the early modern racial matrix that is simultaneously historicized and informed by Critical Race Theory. With those indispensable conceptual premises in place, I proceed to set up the geographical bounds of this project and show that the emergence of blackness as a racial category was a glocal phenomenon that took place in an intercolonial space following the development of de facto color-based slavery in the Atlantic world starting in the mid-fifteenth century. I then unfold the central argument of this book: I explain what early modern scripts of blackness were, where they can be located for historiographic purposes, what the phrase "performative blackness" means in the context of early modern performance culture, and how the scene of ideological production where scripts of blackness coalesced functioned. Finally, I disclose and justify the transverse, transnational, and "reparanoid" investments and methodologies that animate this book, and I discuss choices I made regarding periodization, racial terminology, and translation, before providing a map of the book's chapters.

The Racial Matrix: Rank, Religion, and Phenotype in Early Modernity

Race, I contend, is a concept best modeled as a matrix, in the full etymological sense of the word: as a womb-like space producing and nurturing paradigms that differ from each other yet share the bulk of their genetic material, and whose lives remain inextricably interconnected.[3] Here I use the word *paradigm* simultaneously in its lay sense, to refer to "a pattern or model, an exemplar" of the concept of race, and in its linguistic sense, to refer to a "set of units which are linguistically substitutable in a given context, especially a syntactic one" (*OED*). If concepts are, as Timothy Harrison puts it, "shared cultural products . . . visible in the interstices between idea and word,"[4] then the lexical deployment of the word "race" indicates that, in Europe, the primary paradigms in the racial matrix were degree, or rank, and religion until the end of the sixteenth century. In France, as Guillaume Aubert notes, "the idea of race rapidly became an essential feature of the early modern French ethos," as the old military aristocracy, the *noblesse d'épée*, had a strong impetus to devise an ideological apparatus to prevent the new aristocracy appointed by the king, the *noblesse de robe* or *nouveau nobles*, from encroaching on their inherited privileges.[5] Across the Channel, in late sixteenth-century England, this system corresponded to what Jean E. Feerick describes as the then-dominant "race-as-blood" system.[6] For Ivan Hannaford, within that racial paradigm, "to belong to a race was to belong to a family with a valorous ancestry and a profession of public service and virtue."[7] In Spain, the religious paradigm was stronger: since the promulgation of the statutes on the purity of blood (*limpieza de sangre*) starting in 1449, blood had been used as a tool to racialize religious difference (Judaism and Islam), which was imagined as hereditary.[8] I will return shortly to and engage more expansively with the various historical contexts invoked in this paragraph. My point for now is theoretical: the racial matrix is characterized by its fertility, that is, its ability to keep generating new paradigms without terminating older ones.[9]

At the end of the sixteenth century, stimulated by the age of discovery and the material incentives of colonization, the racial matrix produced a new paradigm: the word *race* came to refer to phenotypical differences for which skin tone quickly became a shorthand. Across Europe, phenotype, which had hitherto functioned as one type of difference among others, became a type of racial difference: the emergent paradigm of race-as-phenotype joined the dominant paradigms of race-as-degree and race-as-religion. Degree, religion, and phenotype are all racial paradigms: exemplars of the concept of race and substitutable sets of units in the grammar of intercultural power relations called *race*. Indeed, understood in the light of Critical Race Theory, race is not a form of human difference but a system of power falsely packaged as a system of knowledge. Race is what happens when, in a given society, the dominant group defines a population group on the basis of an arbitrary criterion and begins seeing that criterion as an embodied, essential, and hereditary trait that justifies the specific positioning of the target population group in the social order. As Geraldine Heng luminously puts it, in race making, features are "selectively essentialized as absolute and fundamental, in order to distribute positions and powers differentially to human groups. . . . Race is a structural relationship for the articulation and management of human differences, rather than a substantive content."[10]

I add "hereditary" to Heng's "absolute and fundamental" because heredity delimits a certain domain of power relations. It is, for instance, what keeps gender distinct from race, coconstitutive as gender and race might be. Indeed, only in (usually misogynistic) discursive contexts fantasizing about uninterrupted genealogies of women are women invoked as a race.

The "structural relationship of race" is, as Stuart Hall puts it, always an interested one, as it effects "the distribution of symbolic and material resources between different groups and the establishment of racial hierarchies."[11] In early modernity, that interested discourse served a nascent economic system, capitalism, which, in Immanuel Wallerstein's words, "needs all the labour-power it can find," and embraces the subordinating logic of racism rather than the ejecting logic of xenophobia. "Racism is the magic formula" allowing the system "simultaneously to minimize the costs of production . . . and minimize the costs of political disruption."[12] Understood as an interested economic mechanism, race can refer to something different at different points in time and space, while its primary sociopolitical function remains stable. Emphasizing the purpose of racialization allows us to break away from what Ian Smith calls "the terminological obsession" that informs attempts at relegating the invention of race to the post-Restoration era, and "obscures race's strategic, opportunistic, negotiating purpose."[13] Race is not the same thing in the fifteenth and in the twenty-first centuries, or in Spain and in India, but it *does* the same thing: it hierarchizes difference in service of power.

There are many ways to map the multitude of meanings covered by that deceptively transparent word, *race*, both in early modernity and in the present. Scholars devise models that best reflect their own investments in the study of race. My choice to use the matrix metaphor and to bring within the fold of that metaphor what others might read as the entirely different notions of class and religion (largely setting aside, to do so, the lexical deployment of the word *race* in early modern contexts) reflects my investment in thinking about race as a dynamic structure of power relations that is systemic, future oriented, and constantly in movement. The modern use of the term *matrix* in the domains of mathematics, logic, computing, and technological reproduction (printing, sound recording, photography) clearly inscribes matrices into the realm of the synthetic and so should, I hope, prevent the organic side of the metaphor from ever fully naturalizing the racial logic. At the same time, the matrix model, with its ever-threatening fertility, calls for vigilance, as it signals that race-as-phenotype is neither the first nor the last racial paradigm that will emerge: it is interlocked with race-as-religion and race-as-rank, and when a new racial paradigm emerges (as it will), race-as-phenotype will be interlocked with that new paradigm too.[14] The logic of interconnectedness at the core of the racial matrix ultimately resonates with Ann Laura Stoler's observation that racisms cite one another: that since "racial discourses draw on the past as they harness themselves to new visions and projects," we can never truly know whether we are "witness to a legacy of the past or the emergence of a new phenomenon all together."[15]

Racial paradigms are always at work within one another and against one another, perpetually ready for reactivation as needed, simultaneously past, present, and future. That sense of dormant liveness, of fertility, of cyclical repetition, and yet of limited predictability drives my use of the matrix metaphor to explain the inner workings of the concept of race. The expansive conceptual articulation of race in early modernity has proved particularly hard to grasp because the modern understanding of race that we bring to archives is limited to bodily surfaces; acknowledging this, I seek to displace that partial phenotypical understanding of race. Grasping race in its expansiveness should help put to rest critical impulses to set *race* narrowly construed in opposition to religion and class as distinct concepts vying for primacy as the central form of Othering in early modernity. All three belong to and in the field of early modern critical race studies.[16]

Matrices are always already racial, for, whether they be organic, synthetic, or both, matrices all have the same purpose: reproduction, the very instrument of race in its most elementary sense, that of common descent and lineage. This may explain why race features so prominently in the Wachowskis' acclaimed science-fiction trilogy that will already have come to mind for many readers: *The Matrix*.[17] Given its versatile symbolism, these movies have been enlisted in service of various ideological projects, yet I mention them here because this trilogy uniquely illuminates the racial matrix's relation to reality and time.[18] Centering on a multiracial coalition of rebels' messianic quest to free a vegetative mankind from its enslavement to intelligent machines, *The Matrix* critiques late capitalism in the West by rereading the Gospel and the Platonic allegory of the Cave through the lens of transatlantic slavery. In this allegory, the importance of Black protagonists such as the Oracle, the Prophet (Morpheus), and the fearless Captain (Niobe), together with the appearance of philosopher, activist, and race scholar Cornel West himself as Counselor in the last human city, Zion, are not coincidental. They signal the centrality of race and of Blackness to the movie's understanding of human history in the West at the turn of the millennium, as well as the centrality of race to the matricial concept itself—a concept that the movie revamps and recirculates but does not invent.[19]

In response to frustratingly recurrent dismissals of conversations about racism on the grounds of race's scientific inexistence, Critical Race Theory has had to explain over the years, with various analogies, that just because something does not exist does not mean the notion of it cannot affect our lives in concrete, tangible, and tragic ways.[20] Given its resemblances to the racial matrix, the Wachowskis' matrix offers another such useful analogy. Like the Wachowskis' matrix, the racial matrix is a neural-interactive simulation—a web of beliefs that holds no tangible reality—and just like one's real body can die if their avatar dies in the Wachowskis' matrix, the beliefs and behaviors we engage in in the racial matrix have very real, often deadly, effects. The racial matrix also instantiates particular relations to time: like any reproductive apparatus, matrices make us live in the past, much like the Wachowskis' matrix recreates a two-hundred-year-old historical reality. In addition, as in the films, the racial matrix needs to reboot regularly. A constantly rebooting racial matrix voids the idea of racial time as forward motion and deploys itself as a structure for which space and time are not singular. Race, in other words, is a flexible and canny conceptual continuum: it bends, moves, and changes with the times, as best serves its purpose of hierarchizing difference in the service of power in whichever context it operates.

With the concept of the racial matrix in hand, I zoom in, within this immense mobile structure, onto one specific node at the key moment of its formation: racial blackness. In *Scripts of Blackness*, I argue that early modern theatre and performance culture at large played a decisive role in the formation of blackness as a racial category, as phenotype entered the racial matrix. In early modernity, performance was a privileged cultural site for what Michael Omi and Howard Winant famously called "racial formation," that is, "the process by which social, economic and political forces determine the content and importance of racial categories and by which they are in turn shaped by racial meaning."[21]

The Bounds of Blackness:
Intercolonial, Global, and Glocal Spaces

To be sure, Europeans did not discover dark-skinned Africans in the Renaissance. Geraldine Heng has shown that in the Middle Ages "a hierarchical politics of color, centering with precision on the polarity of black and white, existed and is evidenced across the multitude of texts, sacred and secular, that descends to us." Although the hierarchical politics of color did affect the ways Europeans thought of Africans, the "signifying field had stabilized" to the extent that color could be played with "under specific hermeneutic conditions, to switch between alternate valencies."[22] Similarly, Cord Whitaker, while striving to "keep in the foreground the material ramifications of medieval race-thinking . . . with their implications for real bodies," has mostly brought to light the symbolical play of color in medieval English literature, or "the extent to which blackness in the Middle Ages was a metaphorical vehicle whose engagements with imagination and interpretation were exceedingly flexible."[23] Heng and Whitaker signal that the evolution of European thought about Africans between the Middle Ages and early modernity was less a rupture than a shift: in the early modern age, the material ramifications of race thinking for real bodies started outweighing the possibilities of symbolic play. That is what Whitaker sees as the medieval "black metaphor" losing its "shimmer," and what I call the production of blackness in the racial matrix.[24]

The development of de facto color-based slavery in the mid-fifteenth century precipitated the irruption of a sizeable population of sub-Saharan descent in European societies and cultures, a watershed for the purposes of periodization within premodern critical race studies. In this book, I might focus on the mindset of white Europeans and the stories they told themselves by performative means, but the realities of Afro-diasporic life form the horizon against which the shape of that mindset and those stories begin to register and become intelligible. Given the glaring whiteness of the archives, I fully recognize the impossibility, with few exceptions, of recovering the early modern Afro-diasporic perspective in any authentic form. But I do not need to recover traces of that perspective in white sources to know it existed. In other words, we may never be able to look at early modern Afro-diasporic subjectivity directly, but—in this book—like the sun, it casts a light that makes everything else visible in early modernity.

The historical, political, and socioeconomic contexts accounting for the production of blackness as a racial category were colonial and slaving contexts. *Scripts of Blackness* surveys—between England, Spain, and France—a space bound by particularly strong colonial drives. These three countries were major players, allies, and competitors in the development of color-based slavery in the Atlantic world. That is not to say that they were the only players: two European countries colonized by Spain, namely, Portugal (whose influence over Spanish theatre is unmistakable) and the Low Countries, were crucial to this process, and the future development of early modern critical race studies in the direction of Portuguese and Dutch archives will further enrich our understanding of early modern European racial formations.[25] If, I argue, color-based slavery was a transnational practice involving sustained exchanges between colonial powers, so was the production of blackness as a racial category. English, French, and Spanish racializing discourses of blackness, while distinct, were intertwined and, as early modern dictionaries suggest, mutually constitutive: the production of blackness as a racial category was a transnational European endeavor. The conceptual frame of this book is thus, to use Robert Stam and Ella Shohat's term, "an intercolonial frame."[26]

It is my contention that early modern performance culture did not passively reflect the intercolonial emergence of blackness as a racial category but actively fostered it. This becomes visible when one compares the fate of blackness on stage and in lexicographic culture. The lexicons that early modern Spaniards, Frenchmen, and Englishmen used at the beginning of the seventeenth century signal that, with various degrees of decisiveness, early modern Europeans were starting to think of blackness as the basis for a new identity category distinct from the older paradigms that had so far defined sameness and difference.

In Iberia, the new category emerged clearly and early. In his dictionary *Tesoro de la lengua castellana o española* (1611), Sebastián de Covarrubias defines a *negro* as "an Aethiop whose color is black."[27] For Covarrubias, *negros* differed from Muslim *moros* phenotypically: he defines the color "tawny" (morena) as a "color that is not completely black—like the color of the *moros*, whence the name of the color, unless it comes from blackberry (mora)."[28] Covarrubias defines *moros* on the basis of geographic origin, as "people from the province of Mauritania."[29] *Negros* have a different geographic origin, for Covarrubias defines "Guinea" as "the land of the *negros*, or Ethiops, in Africa, where the Portuguese enslave people."[30] In Covarrubias's rendition of early seventeenth-century Spanish racial lexicon, then, there was a group of people called *negros* who were defined by the darkness of their skin, their sub-Saharan geographic origin, and their frequent subjection to enslavement—and those people were clearly distinct from *moros*. Of course, there were people who belonged to both categories— enslaved *moros* whose skin was darker, and *negros* who were Muslims—but they are not mentioned by Covarrubias. That such exceptions hardly appear on stage in the *Siglo de Oro* attests to the role of theatre in actively constructing blackness as an independent identity category.[31] In Spain, both sites of knowledge production, lexicography and performance, worked in synchrony to develop blackness as an identity category that could intersect with other categories precisely because it stood on its own.

The clarity and earliness with which blackness emerged as a racial category in Iberian culture are directly connected to the pioneering role of Iberians in the development of color-based slavery. The Portuguese, having first established trading posts (*feitorias*) all along the western African coast, changed the traditional dynamics of slave trade in Mediterranean Europe, which for so long had been not color-based but religion-based. They started enslaving sub-Saharan Africans en masse and sold them in the urban port centers of Lisbon and Seville in the middle of the fifteenth century.[32] From those two cities, enslaved Afro-diasporic people spread over the Iberian Peninsula. A 1565 census had Afro-Spaniards as approximately 13.5 percent of the total population in Seville, commonly known as the "blackest" city in Europe, and Fernández Alvarez estimates that there were forty-four thousand enslaved Afro-diasporic people in Spain by the end of the sixteenth century.[33]

Colonization quickly made the dynamics of slave trade more complex. When Iberians started transporting enslaved people to their American colonies in 1501, that new circuit involved only enslaved people of sub-Saharan descent. Indeed, in a 1543 edict, Charles V expelled from the Spanish colonies "all male and female slaves from Barbary, or Moors recently converted to Catholicism, as well as their children," in order for them not to "infect" the New World with the powerful threat of Islam.[34] Such provisions were reiterated throughout the second half of the sixteenth century: because enslaved Muslim were de facto prohibited in the colonies, Iberians increasingly resorted to enslaved pagans, usually from sub-Saharan Africa. Seville and its Casa de contratación, being the heart of the Spanish colonial administration and the home of many prominent slave owners in the empire, became a point of connection between the old and the new slavery systems. Some enslaved Afro-Spaniards were sent to the colonies from Seville, although laws were passed to limit the influence that enslaved *ladinos*, who were familiar with Spanish culture and thus able to navigate it to their own benefit, could have over enslaved Africans from the 1520s onward.[35] Conversely, seventeenth-century plays increasingly reflect the historical reality of enslaved Afro-diasporic characters traveling from the colonies to the metropole. Across the empire, the slave trade intensified in the first decades of the seventeenth century, as the Iberian Union between Spain and Portugal formed and thrived (1580–1640).

Lexicography reveals a slower emergence of blackness as a racial category in early modern France and England, where involvement in colonialism and de facto color-based slavery was mostly aspirational at the end of the sixteenth century and solidified throughout the seventeenth century. There, performance culture seems to have been one step ahead of lexicographic culture: scripts of blackness effected the ideological work that lexicography would register only later.

While there was no such thing as a regulated slave trade in Tudor England, the Afro-British community grew in the sixteenth century as a result of diplomatic and commercial exchanges between England and Iberia. Enslaved people were offered as gifts; English merchants such as John Lok, the Gonsons, the Winters, and the Hawkins family participated in the slave trade and brought some enslaved people home with them; Iberians who settled in London, such as the Portuguese Marrano community, often imported their lifestyle with them, including an enslaved domestic workforce. Gustav Ungerer estimates that the Afro-British population amounted to 0.5 percent of the London population in the 1590s.[36] On the basis of extensive research into early modern English records, Imtiaz Habib argues that precisely because slavery was not legally recognized in England, Afro-diasporic people who had been smuggled into the country found themselves in a legal limbo that, together with linguistic and cultural alienation, made them vulnerable to the whims of their clandestine buyers. This resulted, for most of them, in lives of "unspoken chattel bondage."[37]

The Afro-diasporic presence was nowhere near as great in numbers in England as it was in Spain, and the archives reflect that imbalance, but it was noticeable enough to cause Queen Elizabeth to issue edicts of deportation against the Afro-diasporic population at the turn of the century.[38] The fact that, in those edicts, Queen Elizabeth used both the terms "Negars" and "Blackamoors"— a word coined in the 1580s to distinguish dark-skinned Moors from white-passing Moors, and which boomed in the 1590s—suggests that those two words were not exactly synonymous: there was enough referential distance between them for them to be productively juxtaposed in that legal document. In that sense, Elizabeth's terminology aims at a level of preciseness that exceeds what we find in most early seventeenth-century lexicons, which consistently conflate blackness with Moorishness, a religious identity category.[39] To see blackness explicitly differentiated from, if sometimes overlapping with, Moorishness, we have to turn to the English stage. Only theatre, the commercial expansion of which coincided with the development of the racial lexicon in the 1590s, repeatedly disambiguated blackness, race-as-phenotype, from Moorishness, race-as-religion.[40]

The situation was similar in France, where racial lexicons remained highly ambiguous throughout the seventeenth century, most often conflating North and sub-Saharan Africans under the Muslim *More* label, while defining *Mores* as black.[41] While Lucette Valensi and Simone Delesalle mistakenly state that the word *Nègre* did not feature in early seventeenth-century French dictionaries, I agree with them that those dictionaries were shaped by "an embarrassment at the existence of *Nègres* as people and as slaves," and I suspect that the widespread conflation between *Nègre* and *More* in French lexicographic culture had the convenient effect of hiding the embarrassing connection between *Nègres* and slavery.[42] The archival work that Imtiaz Habib, Gustav Ungerer, Rosalyn L. Knutson, and others have conducted to unearth the Afro-diasporic presence in early modern England has, to this day, no equivalent in French studies. Even the work of historians who specialize in the history of Blackness or race—such as Erick Noël or Pierre Boulle—hardly touches on the Afro-French community prior to the middle of the eighteenth century.[43] Yet, there may very well have been such a community in early modern France, for there is no reason to believe that France had fewer cultural, diplomatic, and commercial contacts with the slave-trading Iberian Peninsula than England did. At any rate, we know that there had been regular contacts between Rouen merchants and the west coast of Africa in the second quarter of the sixteenth century, when Norman merchants tried to breach the Portuguese monopoly over the region.[44] Merchants brought back *malagueta* spice to be sold on the Rouen markets. Is this the only commodity they smuggled from a region that had an infrastructure ready for selling human beings to Europeans?

Even if we construe the absence of evidence as evidence of absence and thus assume that there was no substantial Afro-French population at the beginning of the seventeenth century, there were many representations of sub-Saharan people in early modern France, and we can read those representations in the light of Allison Blakely's claim that "the existence of color prejudice in a predominantly 'white' society does not require the presence of racial conflict or even of a significant colored population."[45] The mechanisms through which France came to develop an interest in Afro-diasporic subjects would then resemble the mechanisms through which what is now Germany developed colonial fantasies about South America in the early modern period, centuries before it had any colony of its own, as described by Susanne Zantop. Zantop underlines the importance of the Black Legend in the formation of a sensibility that imagined colonization conducted by Germany as an ideal mode of colonization contrasting with the ethically failed Iberian experience.[46] Similarly, I argue that early seventeenth-century France—a country that entered the colonial competition fairly late because of the crippling effect of the wars of religion until the end of the sixteenth century—understood Atlantic expansion through the Iberian experience, which had involved color-based slavery for over a century and a half.

One interesting example supporting this reading of the French situation is Jean Nicot's definition of the word *More* in his *Thrésor de la langue francoyse*, which he began in the 1570s:

> Properly speaking, a *More* is man or a woman from the province of Mauritania in Africa. *Maurus, Maurusius.* Spaniards and Italians also say *Moro*. A *More* is tawny, or olive, unlike the *Negro* whom we call *More* when we put him on tavern signs. But that is a misuse of the word, because the *Negro*, whom we may call black, is perfectly black in color, usually with a short flat nose, thick lips, of pagan and gentile creed—he lives in the heartland and on the coast of Africa. By contrast, the *More* is of a tawny color, with a common face, and a Muslim creed. It is because of Islam that the term *More* has been used outside of its initial boundaries and extended to all those who share that faith—except the Turks, whom we still call Turks although they are Muslims.[47]

This definition shows how much early seventeenth-century French people were looking to the Iberian lexicon and culture for thinking about identity categories and race. Nicot does not define a *Noir* or *Nègre*—those words do not even feature in his dictionary. Rather, he defines a *negro*: he defines a Spanish word through a French contextual lens. Not surprisingly, Nicot knew Iberian racial cultures and languages firsthand: he had served as French ambassador in Lisbon from 1559 to 1561. Nicot's turn to the Iberian racial lexicon illustrates one of the fundamental premises of this book: that racial formation in the early modern period was a transnational process characterized by the circulation of racial tropes and ideas across European borders, often—but not always—northward. For a man like Nicot familiar with southern European racial discourses, *negros* and *moros* were two distinct conceptual categories that remained lexically conflated in French only because of intellectual blunder and inertia. As I will show, one major site of knowledge production that bypassed lexical inertia early on was performance.

Analyzing early modern performative blackness within an intercolonial framework in *Scripts of Blackness*, I take up Africanist and performance scholar Catherine Cole's invitation to rethink our perception of blackface not as "a quintessentially American form" but as "a quintessentially colonial one."[48] Cole brings to light the meanings that blackface minstrelsy took on as it spread through colonial empires in the nineteenth century, and I propose to extend her insight further: I argue that all early modern European nations with strong colonial aspirations deployed, worked with, and worked through performative blackness. The intercolonial space of this book is a global space: the performances studied here all took place in metropolitan Europe, but they are informed by the core-periphery dynamics of the fantasized, coalescing, thriving, and deliquescent colonial empires that spanned the early modern globe. By choosing that globally inflected metropolitan space in which to explore the racial politics of performative blackness, I seek to bridge the growing divide between race scholars who center Blackness and those who advocate for a global ambit sensitive to different racial articulations, often resenting what they perceive as an American imperialism at work in the field.[49] In *Scripts of Blackness*, I center Blackness in a global framework, and I explore the racialization of Blackness as interconnected with other paradigms and tropes within the racial matrix.

The political impetus at the core of race scholarship mandates that it reflect on its own political moment of production, whether that political moment be the culture wars of the Reagan era in the foundational works of early modern critical race studies such as Kim F. Hall's *Things of Darkness*, or the Obama presidency and the illusions of postracialism in the works published over the last decade or so. I am completing this book in 2022 in the wake of a historical uprising and in the heat of a conservative backlash against Critical Race Theory that made one thing abundantly clear: we will not move beyond white supremacy without collectively centering the Black/white binary and relentlessly deconstructing it with the best tools at our disposal.

Like any pandemic, white supremacy is a global threat; addressing it requires global thinking. The movements of global solidarity—in Amsterdam, Tunis, Tokyo, Seoul, London, Rio de Janeiro, Madrid, Pretoria, Rome, Sydney— that followed the murder of George Floyd often brought to light forms of anti-Black racism specific to the countries that produced them. To take but one example, in France, it is a standard rhetorical move, in order to discredit and silence antiracist activists who protest blackface or seek to draw attention to profound societal issues, to accuse them of importing American sensibilities and operating as agents of American cultural imperialism. Relational thinking is thus framed as the problem, while it actually is the solution. Indeed, in June 2020, protests of unprecedented size took to the streets against police brutality and systemic racism in Paris and across the country. Protesters paired the murder of George Floyd in Minneapolis with the murder of Adama Traoré, a twenty-four-year-old

French man of Malian descent who was killed by police in the Parisian suburb of Beaumont-sur-Oise in 2016. The Traoré family had demanded justice for the last four years, but never had their movement gained much traction until the response to the murder of George Floyd.

The French protesters who demanded "Justice pour Adama" while chanting "Black Lives Matter" were not the pawns of American cultural imperialism. Rather, they brought to light the glocal nature of racism against Afro-descendants and of the struggle for Black Liberation. Those phenomena's glocality means that they have been historically shaped by global forces and are experienced in the present as highly localized yet bound in futurity by a sense of joint destiny across locales.[50] As Katherine McKittrick and Clyde Woods put it, "Black geographies," those lived by Black subjects, necessarily "reconfigure classificatory spatial practices" and "allow us to consider alternative ways of imagining the world."[51] The dichotomy between global-mindedness and Black-centrism in early modern critical race studies is a false one. This book rejects it and embraces Blackness as a global analytic by unearthing the early modern roots of glocal racism against Afro-descendants with a keen awareness that such nefarious multinational invention calls for a multinational response.

Scripts of Blackness, Racecraft, and the Ways of Ideology

In *Scripts of Blackness*, I argue that the scripts projected onto the material techniques used by white actors—professional and amateurs—in various loci of early modern European performance culture shaped new habits of mind, new ways for spectators to think of the Afro-diasporic people who lived or could live in their midst. My ambition is not to account for the entire regime of representation of early modern blackness, what Stuart Hall calls "the whole repertoire and imagery of visual effects through which 'difference' is represented at any one historical moment."[52] Rather, I aim to explore some of the scripts that animated three specific performance techniques often but not always used simultaneously: black-up, blackspeak, and black dances. I aim to reconstruct how early modern Afro-diasporic characters looked, sounded, and moved in various performance settings, in order to reassemble the racializing scripts of blackness that such cosmetic, acoustic, and kinetic impersonation yielded. Because scripts of blackness far exceed the techniques of impersonation that they animate, recovering them requires more than a focus on material practices—it requires a capacious approach grounded in literary and performance studies that uses material culture only as a starting point. The technical names I use to refer in English to those three techniques are necessarily anachronistic, because they had no set names in early modern England (archives do not yield such names, at least). While I discuss in detail the multilingual terminologies of impersonation that were available to the early moderns in each chapter of this book, I avoid the term *blackface*, not for fear of anachronism, but because nineteenth-century minstrelsy, which coined the term *blackface*, synthesized cosmetic, acoustic, and kinetic blackness: the term thus proves too blunt of an instrument for the analysis of performative blackness intended here.

I use the term *racecraft* as an allusion to *stagecraft*, to flag in no uncertain terms the role that performative practices played in shaping new racial formations in the early modern world. However, I use that term very differently from historians and race scholars Karen and Barbara Fields, who pun on *witchcraft* to comment on the hold of racial thinking on our minds, defining racecraft as "one among a complex system of beliefs, also with combined moral and cognitive content that presuppose invisible, spiritual qualities underlying and continually acting upon the material realm of beings and events."[53] As my account of the racial matrix should make clear, unlike the Fieldses, I do not see racial thinking as shoving class-based thinking "out of the vocabulary available for public debate," for, in early modernity, conversations about phenotype and rank (as well as religion) used the same vocabulary and were part and parcel of the same racial concept.[54] I am, however, moved by a desire similar to the Fieldses' to understand how racial thinking can "hijack the mind" to foster a sense of "obviousness."[55] I see early modern performative scripts of blackness as doing just that. Scripts of blackness shaped a European structure of feeling about Afro-diasporic people: scripts of blackness captured and fostered affective social experiences of an emergent racial formation "in solution," as Raymond Williams would say, and gave them semantic and material articulations.[56]

Early modern scripts of blackness are varied, for they animate techniques of performance that hold no single or definite meaning per se. The meaning of black-up, blackspeak, and black dances in a given production was determined by what Stuart Hall calls "indexical" signs, that is, literary cues that helped close or "fix" the free-floating meaning of the "iconic" signs of cosmetic, acoustic, or kinetic blackness into ideologically inflated "dominant," or "preferred," meanings.[57] In this book, I reconstruct the encoding and decoding, the hermeneutic process through which playwrights, performers, and spectators collaboratively produced performative blackness. In that process, material practices attached to white performing bodies were indexically inflected to produce a conceptual blackness that could then be attached to real Afro-diasporic bodies. That conceptual blackness, born from a dance between the bodily and the abstract registers, was malleable in that it had no clear borders (it did not stipulate who was or was not black) and no stable substantial content (it did not articulate what it meant to be black in any unified or systematic manner). That malleability is precisely what gave that concept its purchase for the purposes of race making, as it enabled strategic redefinitions of the concept's scope and substance on the basis of glocally articulated needs. This book captures a selection of such redefinitions under the rubric of scripts of blackness.

Racialization has always been a performative process: to cite Xavier Jonathan Inda, the racial body does not exist in nature any more than the gendered body does, and "racial performativity is a matter of reiterating the norms through which a racial body is constituted."[58] By exposing how early modern techniques of racial impersonation could shape the meaning of blackness by virtue of their repetitiveness, citationality, and expectedness, I suggest that theatre and performance culture at large offered an early space for modeling and thinking about the larger ideological mechanisms that racialize human bodies.[59] In light of this analogical structure, I use the phrase "performative blackness" to refer to the techniques of racial impersonation studied in this book, rather than "performed blackness." By calling such affected blackness "performative," I do not mean that early modern cosmetic, acoustic, or kinetic blackness was perceived as efficacious beyond what the limits of spectators' engagement with a propositional "what if?" temporarily permitted. I mean that those techniques of impersonation and the scripts of blackness that animated them "constituted" the black body "as an effect of discourse" in its absence.[60] I mean that they publicly "constituted the identity they are said to express or reveal."[61] If the term *performative* aptly captures the work of early modern scripts of blackness in fashioning and upholding oppressive racial constructions, I do not see early modern scripts of blackness as the site for the potential politics of emancipation that many thinkers of gender and racial performativity are invested in—except in the cases, which I consider briefly at the end of Chapter 2 and at length in Chapter 4—when Afro-European performers themselves got to partake in racial performativity.[62]

Scripts of blackness have a particular ontology, which draws on and reworks Diana Taylor's classic distinction between the archive and the repertoire. Cosmetic, acoustic, and kinetic performance techniques are part of what Taylor calls "the repertoire of embodied practice/knowledge," which is not as ephemeral as one might think, transmitted as it is through "spoken languages, dance, sports, and rituals."[63] However, as previously mentioned, the flexible meaning of those early modern performance techniques was constantly redefined ad hoc by indexical signs: literary cues preserved in the "archive of supposedly endur- ing materials (i.e. texts, documents, buildings, bones)."[64] In other words, mean- ing emerged from the interaction between material practices belonging to the repertoire and poetic cues belonging to the archive. I chose the metaphor of the script in part to signal the hybrid nature of the racializing hermeneutics of performance as equally material and textual. Yet my debt to the archive goes further, since, in this book, which is informed by but not limited to the meth- odologies of literary studies, I look for the repertoire-*in*-the-archive.[65] The early modern archive certainly does not capture the whole repertoire of racial imper- sonation, but it gives us a good glimpse. Stage directions in playtexts, acting companies' receipts, and various testimonies help us reconstruct the looks of black-up and black costumes; playtexts, broadside ballads, and Christmas carols script black accents; dictionaries, stage directions, dance treatises, and iconog- raphy describe and depict black dances. Without a doubt, a large part of the repertoire is forever lost to us, but the archive is more generous than one might think.

Scripts of blackness help account for what Ayanna Thompson powerfully identifies as the contradictory construction of race as simultaneously essential and performative on stage: "I am arguing that early modern performance cre- ated race in a contradictory fashion precisely because it was an act. Thus race ends up being constructed in the contradictory terms of 'discursivity and cor- poreality': it is a performance, a discourse, but a performance in which the body is privileged. The audience's gaze upon the racialized characters' bodies licenses the materiality of those bodies, but the performance—white actors in costume and make-up—simultaneously deconstructs that materiality."[66] Scripts of black- ness help us understand the illogic or contradictory effect of racial imperson- ation on stage. The artificiality of cosmetic, acoustic, and kinetic blackness was never lost on spectators, but the scripts of blackness that their flexible herme- neutic configuration produced found their way to spectators and acquired, through reiteration, the solid sense of obviousness that makes for essential con- structions of race. Thus, I see scripts of blackness as contributing to the integra- tion of blackness into the racial matrix more than resisting such integration, and, in that sense, I depart from a scholarly tradition that tends to construe the material practices of the stage as a site enabling resistance to the dominant strands of ideology articulated in dramatic playtexts.[67] I argue that early modern scripts of blackness—albeit unstably and self-consciously—overwhelmingly constituted blackness as a racial category, thereby providing, in performance, a steady counterpoint even to the playtexts that we see as most complex and progressive in their portrayal of blackness. Racecraft matters precisely because it enabled plays to enact contradictory impulses, to lend themselves to opposite interpretations, and thereby cater to the largest possible audience.

The ideological efficacy of early modern racecraft relied on distributed agency in the scene of hermeneutic production. Grasping that distributed agency requires that we suspend the scholarly reflex to foreground the unique contours of specific playwrights' or actors' engagements with racecraft: that we pay less attention to innovations, ruptures, and canonicity, and rather embrace Foucault's idea that it is not "necessary or possible to distinguish between what is new and what is not," for racecraft "is not a field of inert areas broken up by fecund moments; it is a domain that is active throughout."[68] The historiography of racecraft has little use for the singular, all the less since its domain is not limited to drama, but spans a vast culture of performance whose agents have turned anonymous and whose events have often become fungible in the historical record. In that sense, writing a history of racecraft supposes that, in Judith Butler's words, we "untether the speech act from the sovereign subject" and think of scripts of blackness as *conventional*, to the extent that the racecraft practitioner "speaks *conventionally*, that is, . . . speaks in a voice that is never fully singular. The subject invokes a formula (which is not quite the same as following a rule), and this may be done with little or no reflection on the conventional character of what is being said. The ritual dimension of convention implies that the moment of utterance is informed by the prior and, indeed, future moments that are occluded from the moment itself. Who speaks when convention speaks? In what time does convention speak? In some sense, it is an inherited set of voices, an echo of others who speak as the 'I.'"[69] Butler's account of the speaking subject's agency models how I think in this book about the agency of individual playwrights and performers in the scene of hermeneutic production called racecraft.

The other key participant in this schema of distributed agency, is, of course, the spectator, for, as reception theorist Susan Bennett cogently puts it, "a performance can activate a diversity of responses, but it is the audience which finally ascribes meaning and usefulness to any cultural product."[70] Audience responses are neither uniform nor entirely predictable. The metaphor of the script, obviously drawn from theatrical culture, is meant to convey a sense of openness to contingency: a script is the basis for improvisation for the *commedia dell'arte*. To produce a script is to abdicate claims to control over a performance. To think of scripts of blackness is to acknowledge that early modern spectators were "emancipated" in Jacques Rancière's sense:

> The spectator also acts, like the pupil or the scholar. She observes, selects, compares, interprets. She links what she sees to a host of other things that she has seen on other stages in other kinds of place. She composes her own poem with the element of the poem before her. She participates in the performance by refashioning it in her own way by drawing back for example, from the vital energy that it is supposed to transmit in order to make it a pure image and associate this image with a story which she has read or dreamt, experienced or invented. They are thus both distant spectators and active interpreters of the spectacle offered to them.[71]

Rancière's thinking might be rooted in Enlightenment ideals, but his description of spectating mechanics has a transhistorical reach. Rancière compares a fantasy of theatre in which the director would control the message spectators receive to the delusions of the "stultifying pedagogue" who believes they directly control what students learn. Educators know better than this. But we also know that, however agency flows and gets distributed in our classrooms and in the network of spaces that extend the classroom, learning will happen. Rancière's analogy thus provides a useful model for thinking holistically about the scene of ideological production that is racecraft in early modernity. Agency was distributed in ways we cannot perfectly grasp or systematize, yet ideological production clearly happened. The scene of ideological production had many moving pieces: *Scripts of Blackness* imagines what could happen in a scenario of maximal cooperation between playwrights, performers, and consumers of performative blackness in the moment of its production. Such maximal cooperation was not systematic (ideology never works perfectly or seamlessly), but that scenario is necessary from a historiographic perspective to render scripts of blackness intelligible and mappable.

To ask how the scene of ideological production functions in terms of agency is, ultimately, to ask whose interests it serves or can serve. Jean E. Howard's magisterial study of theatre's participation in ideological production in a time of massive social change, *The Stage and Social Struggle in Early Modern England*, demonstrates that the models of Gramscian hegemony and of Althusserian ideological State apparatus do not apply in an early modern theatre that regularly eschewed royal censorship, and whose commercial interests led it to cater to diverse viewpoints and interests in its representation of class and gender. "It does not seem to me true," Howard writes, "that these texts always served established power, whether one defines established power as the monarchy, the aristocracy, the Anglican Church, or the male sex. . . . The drama enacted ideological contestation as much as it mirrored or reproduced anything that one could call the dominant ideology of a single class, class faction, or sex."[72] The difficulty Howard identified in pinpointing a stable set of interests that early modern theatre could have served turns into a clear impossibility when we widen the corpus, as I do in this book, and understand public theatre within a larger performance culture. Black-up, blackspeak, and black dances moved among sites of performance that were open to elite audiences (court entertainments such as English masques, French ballets, Spanish *teatro palaciego*), to spectators with disposable income (commercial theatres in London, Madrid, Rouen, and Paris), or to anyone (free street theatre accompanying religious processions, pageants celebrating aristocratic entries into big cities, civic parades such as the London Lord Mayor's pageant, religious services including carols in blackspeak, and any setting for social dances, from revels to block parties).

The risks to which Howard alerts us of reading the ideological work of an entire performance culture through the lens of a single class, faction, or sex are palpable in as classic a study as Eric Lott's *Love and Theft: Blackface Minstrelsy and the American Working Class*. Indeed, Lott's commitment to reading minstrelsy as a cultural form that was not "devised simply to reinforce social hierarchy in [a society] whose every act proclaims it" led him to produce a resistance reading and to construe blackface as a medium that primarily enabled working-class white men to figure issues of class through race, occasionally expressing racial sympathy in the process, as they "precariously lived their whiteness."[73] *Love and Theft* signals that the impulse to read theatre as something more than the mere instrument of established hegemonic power can prove a double-edged sword in the study of racial impersonation. In *Scripts of Blackness*, I seek to handle that double-edged impulse with care. Ultimately, I do not see a contradiction between the claim that early modern performance culture constituted blackness as a racial category and the impossibility of pinning down the stable beneficiaries of such ideological production. In *Scripts of Blackness*, I argue that early modern performance culture produced blackness as a conceptual resource available to all European spectators via techniques of racial impersonation and scripts of blackness that, in their multiplicity, could cater to various classes, factions, and sexes.

Baroque Investments: A Transverse, Transnational, and Reparanoid Project

Much scholarship has been devoted to studying the racialization of blackness in early modern English theatre by focusing on individual plots, authorial psychology, and character typologies; *Scripts of Blackness* attempts something different by foregrounding the hermeneutic animation of performance techniques.[74] Thus I have structured this book around performance techniques, rather than geography, genre, tropes, or authors, as one might expect. I have also resisted the temptation to organize the book by degrees of artificiality, which would have yielded chapters dedicated, respectively, to early modern Black performers playing black characters (rare), to white performers playing black characters (numerous), and to white performers playing the roles of white characters who themselves play black characters (their number increases over time). More often than not— and I flagged exceptions—scripts of blackness move transversally across those three levels of artificiality; instances from the last category, with their heightened metatheatricality, thus help bring to light the scripts that animate instances from the other two categories.

Organizing chapters around specific performance techniques allows me to engage with the repertoire-in-the-archive and to curate collections of exhibits across languages, media, and centuries that rub up against each other, and in that rub, acquire evidentiary density. Those collections draw on a large corpus of plays from England, Spain, and France, some well known and some forgotten: late miracle plays, mystery plays, *autos*, interludes, plays produced for the commercial theatre, ballets and masques produced at court, and processional dances performed throughout the period. The majority of French and Spanish plays and documents I study have not been translated into English (unless otherwise noted, all translations are my own), and many have not been reprinted since the sixteenth and seventeenth centuries. I also mobilize iconographic documents (woodcuts in playtexts, illuminated manuscripts, engravings, professional paintings, costume sketches), musical documents (broadside ballads, music sheets), treatises (on cosmetics, anatomy, dance, theatre, ethnography), dictionaries, poems, chronicles, travel writings, parish registers, religious

edicts, royal decrees, and legal documents (hiring contracts, theatre companies' receipts, complaints).

This book's transverse structure also allows me to bring to the fore two regimes of racialization—the acoustic and the kinetic—that have received hardly
any scholarly attention in early modern performance studies, because the Western understanding of theatrical performance relies so heavily on the supremacy
of the visual, or scopic, regime. Without a doubt, much remains to be said about
cosmetic blackness in early modern Europe—especially around the figuration
of gender and sexuality in that tradition, and I attend to this historiographic
lacuna. Yet blackspeak and black dances did some of the most interesting performative work of racialization in early modernity, and I have structured this
book in an effort to make their distinct ideological operations perceptible. Although the sequence of chapters might suggest that the repertoire of performative blackness expanded from the cosmetic to the more actorly domains of vocal
and kinetic virtuosity, lacunar early modern archives lend themselves to that
claim only tentatively. It might very well be the case that, in England and in
France, the development of professional acting and celebrity culture occasioned
the expansion of performative blackness in the direction of blackspeak and
black dance over time. However, in Spain, the three techniques developed
simultaneously, and future findings in French and English archives might surprise us. I overwhelmingly perform in this book what Eve Sedgwick calls a "paranoid" reading, seeking "to expose the ruses of power," even when—as is the
case with scripts of blackness—the agents of power are indistinct, the uses of
power varied, and its reception open-ended.[75] Yet I want to emphasize the less
immediately visible "to and fro movement" between paranoid and reparative
critical stances that informs this book.[76] The reparative approach is clearest in
the last chapter, where I assemble available traces of Afro-diasporic agency, as
Afro-Europeans engaged with, responded to, and used for their own benefit the
culture of kinetic blackness that was coined and wielded against them. Reparative leanings also inform the historiographic principle that I call *recording*,
which I use at various points to reconstruct transnational genealogies of racial
performance in the subjunctive mode when lacunar archives curtail the use of
the indicative.[77] In early modern English, while the noun *record* was attached to
the legal domain (meaning a witness, a testimony), the verb *to record* was attached to the domain of memory (meaning to remember, to rehearse, to go over
in one's mind) and to the domain of performance (meaning to sing in counterpoint).[78] *Recording* thus denotes a way of singing based on dialogue between
two melodic lines. The contrapuntal structure does not undermine but enhances

both melodic lines with a high degree of sophistication. As a historiographic metaphor, recording happens when theatre historians allow their work to operate on more than one mode, weaving a contrapuntal song that hinges on *évidence*— that luminous sense of presence—into their evidentiary work.

No field has thought with more depth, complexity, and urgency than Black studies about the ethics of care that must drive historiographic inquiries into racial archives. By proposing the historiographic model of baroque recording, I am suggesting that the conceptual resources of early modernity may have something to contribute to that ongoing critical conversation.[79] I see contrapuntal recording as a practice that resonates with "critical fabulation," a method driven by Saidiya Hartman's hope that "by advancing a series of speculative arguments and exploiting the capacities of the subjunctive (a grammatical mood that expresses doubts, wishes, and possibilities), in fashioning a narrative which is based upon archival research," she could "tell an impossible story and amplify the impossibility of its telling."[80] Recording also has affinities with what Audre Lorde calls "biomythography," which C. Riley Snorton invokes as a practice of invention for recounting Black Trans lives lost in the archives, a prosthetic "practice of symbolic surrogation, not as a supplemental thing, but through supplementarity," which "is not about completion" and "does not perform or propose reconciliation."[81]

Recording as I construe it uses the openness to changes, surprises, and hope proper to the reparative stance in order to support the paranoid drive toward exposure that is at the core of my inquiry. Such hybridity is pervasive, compounding what I playfully call this book's *reparanoia*: its wide and conflicted range of affective responses to the early modern racial archives. *Scripts of Blackness*'s self-avowed reparanoia is grounded simultaneously in a reparative desire (shared with many) to account for an early modern Afro-diasporic life that exceeded the painful heinousness of racial formations, and in a paranoid distrust of the comfort and complacency that such accounts of early modern Black life can easily elicit among twenty-first-century readers prepared for any number of reasons to minimize the transhistorical reality of antiblackness.

Scripts of Blackness moves across fields, but also across space. This book heeds Barbara Fuchs's important warning that "no field is an island" by integrating early modern critical race studies—a field that originated in early modern English studies and, more specifically, in Shakespeare studies—vertically within the expanded temporal reach of Black studies and horizontally within the emerging field of transnational early modern race studies.[82] Pushing beyond the limits of Anglophone archives to study the mechanisms through which early

modern culture constituted blackness as a racial category is not a luxury but a
necessity, if we are to understand a phenomenon that was in itself transnational.
While comparative approaches seek to identify "commonalities, differences,
and points of contact," transnational or "intersectionist" approaches, in Sharon
Marcus's words, "focus on concrete interactions between national literatures,
studying influences, circulations, reprints, and translations, to show how literary developments depend on transnational contacts."[83] In the early modern period, only in rare cases can we trace the direct influence of one cultural unit
(performance technique, hermeneutic configuration, lexeme, or playtext) on a
unit from a different culture. And yet, similar things, different in their sameness, happen in different places across a relatively short time span, evidencing a
rhizomatic dissemination of racial concepts, performance techniques, and racialized theatregrams in early modern Europe.[84] *Scripts of Blackness* takes both
approaches, the transnational and the comparative, in an effort to reveal cultural idiosyncrasies that mononational approaches structurally enshroud.

Doing transnational early modern critical race studies does not mean simply collating knowledge currently disseminated in various fields: it means generating knowledge and finding new evidence for all those fields. Blackness has
hardly been studied as form of difference in the theatre of the *Siglo de Oro*,
mostly because scholars of Spanish theatre have traditionally focused on religion as the dominant paradigm of difference in Iberia, inherited from the medieval period. Building on the pioneering work done in theatre studies by Baltasar
Fra-Molinero and more recently by John Beusterien, Nicholas R. Jones, and
Emily Weissbourd, in conversation with the work done by historian Aurelia
Martín-Casares and visual culture scholars Erin Rowe, Larissa Brewer-García,
and Carmen Fracchia, this book studies the emergence in early modern Spanish
theatre of phenotype-as-race, a newly established paradigm distinct from religion-
as-race in the racial matrix.[85] *Scripts of Blackness*, however, departs from most
recent scholarship on early modern Afro-Europeans in Iberian and Hispanic
studies, in that, guided by a reparanoid ethos, it queries the reparative turn that
field has taken in the last decade. *Scripts of Blackness* puts pressure on the argumentative grammar now in vogue, which too often construes black oppression
as a mere qualifying clause to a main clause foregrounding Black resistance and
self-emancipation.

While the representation of Afro-diasporic people in French fiction and
drama in the eighteenth century has recently been studied, an entire corpus of
earlier materials remains overlooked.[86] Studies of race in the ancien régime, focusing on a rich production of *récits de voyage*, ethnography, and anatomy trea-

tises, have overlooked theatrical productions. This omission has reinforced the prevailing assumption that sub-Saharan Africans and slavery were absent from the stage prior to the eighteenth century. Christian Biet, Sylvie Chalaye, and Toby Wikström recently started expanding the archive by looking at the early modern intersections of race and theatre; my work is indebted to theirs and demonstrates that focusing on performance can significantly advance this urgent line of inquiry.[87] Such silences in early modern French studies are due in part to the fragmentary nature of the French early modern dramatic archive, which, just like Spanish theatre, has only recently started benefitting from systematic recuperation, digitization, and indexing. I would however argue that those silences are also due in large part to what Doris Garraway calls "historical abjection," the silencing of colonial slavery in French historiography that started during the Enlightenment and influenced the constitution of what we have come to know as the canon of classical French theatre.[88]

Because the early modern period saw the rise of nation-state formation and a literary golden age in several European countries including France, England, and Spain, the canon from the period plays a special role when those countries reflect on their identity and history today. It is a starting point where collective imagination, reflected in syllabi and cultural politics, begins to define ideas of national identity in those parts of Europe. I seek to open up those ideas by locating an Afro-diasporic presence in English, French, and Spanish cultures at that time, and by showing that interracial negotiations and white supremacist leanings and practices, as well as minoritarian resistance to those leanings and practices, have long been part of European identity. Such reckoning is long overdue and much needed in the climate of identitarian xenophobia that has recently settled over many parts of Western Europe.

Moving across time, space, and fields ultimately requires rethinking traditional periodization. In many ways, the temporal reach of *Scripts of Blackness*, from the beginning of the sixteenth century to the very end of the seventeenth century, is unorthodox, because reckoning with the different chronologies of different national and regional literary traditions demands unorthodoxy. I am thus concerned with the period called the *baroque*. The baroque is a moment of stylistic departure from Renaissance classicism, which follows different timelines and takes different forms in different countries. Probably derived from the Portuguese word *barocco*—which designates an irregularly shaped pearl that could be fitted to make gorgeous eccentric jewelry in the early modern period—the term denotes an aesthetic based on beautiful irregularity and characterized by complexity, surprise, dizzying folds, metamorphoses and illusions, perpetual movement, self-referentiality, and a lavish profusion of carefully contrived ornaments. While, as a cultural project, the baroque is usually associated in scholarly discourse with Counter-Reformation efforts in Catholic countries (and thus shunned in English studies), baroque aesthetics actually operated across early modern Western Europe. Black dramatic characters are native to those aesthetics, and it is those characters' development, their continuities, and their transformations that ultimately drive my periodizing choices, delineating a long baroque arc.

A final note on terminology and translation. As mentioned earlier, early modern performance culture strategically produced blackness as a malleable racial category, the substantive content of which could be redefined with each script of blackness to suit specific needs, and the boundaries of which could be renegotiated ad hoc to include or exclude, for instance, mixed-race, North African, and South Asian characters. In other words, blackness was produced in early modern Europe as a prescriptive identity, not a descriptive one. Consequently, a reparanoid recording of racecraft must tread on the grounds of racial terminology with care and purpose. When I use the word *Black*—for instance, to talk about myself—I am expressing a political commitment, a choice, the same choice that French Africana studies scholar of Ivorian descent Maboula Soumahoro so eloquently describes:

> I decide to be Black. Not because history has defined and fashioned me as such on the basis of my body. I am Black because bodies that look like mine have for a very long time reacted, fought, contested, resisted, and escaped from recurring organized attempts at making them inferior. By resisting and affirming their humanity, the bodies and minds that were construed as black have gifted the world a multitude of treasures. I define myself as Black as I decide it, because I know history. It is a choice. By deliberately entering a transnational community bound by arts, letters, and by the spirituality so deeply ingrained in the intellectual traditions I have evoked throughout this book, I am performing an act of political solidarity.[89]

In this book, when my use of the term *Black* or *Blackness* is informed by such empowering dynamics of politico-cultural self-identification, I capitalize the word to signal it. However, as Kim F. Hall remarks, we can no longer grasp the self-determined cultural identity of the Afro-diasporic people who were racialized by early modern processes of racecraft: their subjectivity escapes us.[90] It is impossible for us to know whether they would have wanted to appropriate and politically reclaim the prescriptive racializing identity imposed on them by white supremacy. To avoid making that choice for them (by calling them Black), or reenacting the violent act of racialization they suffered (by calling them black), I follow a set of guidelines. When I cite early modern texts, I abstain from translating racial lexemes (i.e., terms that explicitly denote racial identities). Thus, whenever I translate French and Spanish texts into English, I depart from the conventions of the *Chicago Manual of Style*—which otherwise preside over this book—by leaving the original racial lexemes untranslated in italics, for "the same words, due to different histories, carry very different connotations and intonations" in different cultures.[91] When I speak from my own perspective—that of the modern historiographer and critic—of the people, real and fictional, who were racialized by scripts of blackness, then I use the terms *Afro-diasporic*, *African*, *Afro-European*, *Afro-descendant*, and sub-Saharan, depending on context. I reserve the term *black* (lowercase) for the instances when I ventriloquize the perspective of early modern white supremacy. I trust readers, when they encounter those terms in my prose, to remember that *blackness* (lowercase) refers to an artificial prescriptive category created for strategic purposes, and to know the difference between *blackness* and *Blackness*. With these guidelines, I hope to produce a historiographic account of racecraft that deconstructs the prescriptive racial episteme of early modernity without reifying it.

Similar ethical considerations inform my use of glyphs as I translate passages of Spanish blackspeak into English. Indeed, I had to make decisions regarding the best way of rendering into English racially motivated phonetic deviations within a foreign language, and I came to the conclusion that this is a task to refuse. There is an ontological difference between racializing idioms artificially crafted for performative purposes and Afro-diasporic dialects organically developed and historically shared by real communities of speakers. Using the latter in order to translate the former into English would be a mistake, because it would give to blackspeak a touch of authenticity while giving authentic Afro-diasporic dialects a touch of comedy—neither of which is warranted. Most importantly, that approach to translation would turn me into a modern producer of blackspeak, and I have no wish to participate in the reproduction, recirculation, and revitalization of a racializing technique that always catches on all too easily amid readers and listeners, as early modern archives show us. Thus, in this book, the grammatical distortions of blackspeak are signaled to the anglophone reader with a star symbol immediately preceding the grammatically marked word or word group, and the phonetic distortions of blackspeak are signaled with a hash symbol immediately preceding the phonetically accented word or word group. With this protocol, I seek to point out deviations and to make the ideological inflections of early modern blackspeak intelligible without facilitating twenty-first-century blackspeak performances in classrooms, private studies, or public theatres.

Black-Up, Blackspeak, and Black Dances: A Map of This Book

Structured around performance techniques, this book explores sequentially the deployment of scripts of blackness through cosmetic, acoustic, and kinetic impersonation in the performance culture of early modern Europe. In the first two chapters, I reconstruct some of the major scripts attached to cosmetic blackness in Western Europe from the early sixteenth century to the late seventeenth century. Those two chapters form a diptych on the scopic regime of racialization and should be read as such, together. While the first panel of that diptych, stretching from the 1530s to the 1620s, focuses on the public theatre's negotiations of the legacy of medieval black-up, the second panel, stretching from 1604 to the end of the seventeenth century, explores the hermeneutic reconfigurations of black-up triggered by a new and sustained engagement with gender and sexuality in high baroque culture.

Chapter 1 sets up for the book the glocal dimension of the ideological needs to which scripts of blackness flexibly respond. In it, I argue that cosmetic blackness inherited a residual diabolism from its long-standing association with the devil in medieval performance culture, yielding exclusionary scripts of blackness that cast Afro-diasporic people as figures of the Enemy-Within threatening to tear apart the fabric of Christian societies. That exclusionary script—which the Shakespearean canon, with plays such as *Titus Andronicus* (1594) and *Othello* (1604), mobilizes and intensely scrutinizes—fed into the strong xenophobia and racial aversion that seized England in the late Tudor and early Stuart eras, as the Afro-British population started becoming visible.[92] The same exclusionary script of blackness functioned as a cautionary tale against the assimilation of Africans into the transoceanic French body colonial that certain parts of early baroque France such as Rouen, Normandy, fantasized about on stage. That script is apparent in plays such as *Les Portugaiz infortunez* (1608), *La tragédie françoize d'un More cruel* (1613), and *La comédie admirable intitulée la merveille* (ca. 1620).[93] In Spain, however, the exclusionary script of blackness hardly met the needs of a society that had practiced de facto color-based slavery since the mid-fifteenth century. In Renaissance Spanish theatre then, cosmetic blackness quickly shed its diabolical associations and shifted from producing scripts of black exclusion to producing scripts of black commodification in a wide corpus that ranges from Sánchez de Badajoz's *farsas* (1520–50) to Jímenez de Enciso's *Comedia famosa de Juan Latino* (1620–25), via Andrés de Claramonte y Corroy's *El valiente negro en Flandes* (1620–25), and Lope de Vega's black saint *comedias* (1599–1608).[94] By associating blackness with various types of commodities, those scripts could, for instance, exclude Afro-Spaniards from mankind and deny them fundamental rights, construe them as goods whose consumption was pleasurable and necessary to the health of a hungry body politic, and construe select Afro-Spaniards as exceptional, thereby helping pass a system of racial oppression as a system of racial meritocracy.

Chapter 2 argues that high baroque theatrical culture's elaboration of female black-up was driven by the need to cast doubt on the desirability of Afro-diasporic women. Scripts of female blackness were thus framed in erotic terms that obfuscated the fact that, in the brave new world shaped by early modern colonization and color-based slavery, white men very often perpetrated sexual violence against Afro-diasporic women that had little to do with eros. What I call the oblique aesthetics of Afro-diasporic women's desirability found its way into various scripts of female blackness, of which this chapter analyzes three. In France, the oblique aesthetics of Afro-diasporic women's desirability manifested itself through an absence—a silence. Indeed, starting in the mid-1620s, numerous baroque court ballets excluded Afro-diasporic women from their highly eroticized sphere of representation by unfurling scenarios of interracial desire that exclusively cast Afro-diasporic men and white women. Such scenarios were doubly effective for ideological purposes. On the one hand, by framing Afro-diasporic men as Petrarchan "slaves to love" who willingly surrendered their freedom to aristocratic French women, the wish-fulfilling script of black enslavement to love celebrated a noncoercive idea of color-based slavery that gracefully sidestepped thorny ethical issues. On the other hand, that script excluded from the dance of interracial desire on stage the enslaved people most often involved in coercive interracial sex offstage: Afro-diasporic women.

In England, the oblique aesthetics of Afro-diasporic women's desirability produced a succuban script that is particularly visible in plays such as John Webster's *The White Devil* (1612) and William Davenant and John Dryden's *The Tempest, or The Enchanted Island* (1667).[95] That script framed black women as succubae: dark gender-bending demons who carry the seeds of another race as they coerce Christian men into extramarital sex in their sleep, in an exculpatory

state of powerlessness, in the intimacy of their own houses, at the expense of
their own physical and spiritual health. Succuban scripts of blackness hinged
on fetishistic mechanisms of inversion and disavowal in relation to the rape of
Afro-diasporic women. Finally, in Spain, the oblique aesthetics of Afro-diasporic
women's desirability produced a colorist script in which the stock character of
the pretty and witty brown-faced *mulata* dialectically articulated the desirability
of all Afro-diasporic women. In the vast repertoire of Lope de Vega's Sevillian
comedias (1609–35), desirable *mulatas* are contrasted with undesirable *negras*.[96]
Yet they retain a strong hermeneutic kinship with blackness, in part because the
anxiogenic prospect of *mulatas'* unmoored, spreading, and ever-less-readable
brownness threatened the socioracial taxonomies and hierarchies of Hispanic
societies. Whether they are poetically moored in blackness or they deliberately
embrace their Blackness—as Elvira fiercely does in *Servir a señor discreto* (ca.
1618)—desirable *mulatas* function simultaneously as foils to and substitutes for
their mothers.

Chapter 3 turns away from the scopic regime of racialization and toward
the acoustic one, focusing on mock-African accents, or, blackspeak. In Spain
and in the Iberian world at large, blackspeak was extremely popular. From the
1530s onward, it circulated multidirectionally in a nexus of urban performance
spaces that included public churches, private houses, processions, public theatres, and court theatres. There, it disseminated scripts of black infantilization
that lent ideological support to the slavery-based social status quo. This mechanism is captured particularly well in interludes by Tirso de Molina (1617–35)
and Quiñones de Benavente (1660s), among others.[97] Blackspeak yielded other
popular scripts of blackness that promoted ideas of black animalization and degeneration. I call what is perhaps the most interesting acoustic script of blackness *the script of ethnic conjuration*. This script hinged on blackspeaking white
performers' ability, simply by virtue of their own whiteness, to conjure up
older traditions of ethnic stage accents and thereby strategically connect Afro-
Europeans to other racialized groups with a history of theatrical impersonation.
For instance, the script of ethnic conjuration serves, in Richard Brome's *The
English Moor, or The Mock-Marriage* (1637), to connect Afro-Britons with the
Irish, and thereby inscribe them on the same brutal colonial horizon whence
the racialized Irish stage accent had risen at the turn of the sixteenth century.[98]
The same script served, in Nicolas Du Perche's comedy *L'ambassadeur d'Affrique*
(1666), to connect sub-Saharan Africans with stage Turks, and thereby Orientalize them in ways that conveniently displaced issues of color-based slavery
onto a fantasized Ottoman East far from the French realm and ethos at the very

time when slavery boomed in the French Caribbean.[99] The script of ethnic conjuration is relational: it reveals the ever-interconnected lives of blackness and of
other nodes in the early modern racial matrix. The chapter concludes with Sir
Francis Fane's comedy *Love in the Dark, or The Man of Bus'ness* (1675), not only
to point out the conjunction and endurance of the various acoustic scripts of
blackness previously identified, but to think through the complementary dance
of blackspeak and black-up.[100]

Chapter 4 turns to the kinetic as a racializing regime per se, situated at the
intersection of the scopic and the acoustic. In this chapter, I argue that kinetic
culture in early modern Europe was a vast interactive terrain where dances construed as Afro-diasporic by white producers and consumers—often with the
collaboration of Afro-Europeans—functioned simultaneously as instruments
of racialization and self-emancipation. In Spain, Creole Andalusian *danzas de
negros* produced scripts of black sexualization associating Afro-Spaniards with
the lower bodily stratum; they featured in social dance settings, street processions, and commercial theatres alike from the sixteenth century onward. The
wild popularity of this choreographic style and its titillating scripts of sexualization encouraged Afro-Spaniards to claim those dances, transform them, and
use them to renegotiate the terms of their own enslavement, either symbolically,
as a way to reclaim their own mobility and bodily self-determination, or materially, as a way to earn enough money to buy their freedom or make a career. In
France, whether in popular dances such as the *moresque* or in elaborate baroque
court ballets, black dances produced scripts of black animalization that downgraded Afro-diasporic people in the Great Chain of Being and expropriated
them from ownership and self-ownership. Nevertheless, white male aristocrats
used that choreographic style and danced animalistically to protest what they
saw as their own expropriation from ownership and self-ownership at the hands
of the French king, which they experienced hyperbolically as a form of bondage.
In England, similar dynamics of appropriation by rebellious aristocrats informed
Queen Anne's kinetic performance in Ben Jonson's *Masque of Blackness* (1605),
as the queen consort hyperbolically experienced the racially informed patriarchal ideology promoted by James I as a form of bondage.[101]

The scripts of blackness that operated under the kinetic regime (sexualization and animalization) stand out not for their originality, but for their
affordances—for the acts of resistance or rebellion that their popularity enabled
dancers to perform through them. The chapter tracks the spread of black dances
and the scripts of blackness that animated them in Jacobean and Caroline commercial theatre where, in plays such as Philip Massinger's *The Bondman* (1623),

English "antics" started functioning as a conduit expressing unstable power relations between enslaved black characters and white enslavers.[102] Ultimately,
plays such as Molière's *Le malade imaginaire* (1673), William Davenant's *The
History of Sir Francis Drake* (1659), and William Wycherley's *The Gentleman
Dancing-Master* (1673) reveal that, as France and England's participation in the
slave trade intensified, their kinetic culture of racial impersonation followed in
the footsteps of danzas de negros, adopting the political configuration of Spanish footwork.[103]

*   *   *

"This scene is not working, Noémie." If my formidable acting teacher had
known some thirteen years ago about the long history of performative blackness in Western Europe—if the historical abjection that rules over academic
curricula in France and elsewhere had not deprived her of a crucial knowledge
of those traditions of racial impersonation—would she have thought for a second of black-up as an aid for me to "find" my character's Africanness? I doubt it.
If she had known that scripts of blackness, the performative mechanisms that
brought blackness into the world as a racial category, originated in the corpus of
early modern drama that is the basis of any classical actor's training—if she had
known that the transnational dramatic canon of the golden age is such stuff as
race is made on—what might have happened to the bust of Molière under
whose gaze and authority I rehearsed so often for three years? *Scripts of Blackness* is the book I wish she could have read at the time.

CHAPTER I

A Brief History of Baroque Black-Up

Cosmetic Blackness and Religion

Give the Devil his due.

Early modern English proverb

Performance techniques tell the stories spectators need to hear, and their history helps them do so. A fundamental premise of this book is that the meaning of performative blackness is always strategically defined by history and poetics in response to glocally articulated ideological needs that change based on social, cultural, political, and economic contexts. The history of early modern black-up in Western Europe is, to a large extent, a history of secularization in which various traditions slowly branch out and away from a core episteme of religious allegory inherited from the Middle Ages. The scripts of blackness that black-up, or cosmetic blackness, yielded in the early baroque period (which, for our purposes, extends from the 1530s to the 1620s) proceeded primarily from the public theatre's negotiations of black-up's religious legacy, inherited from medieval performance culture. First and foremost came, as a result of those negotiations, what I call *the diabolical script of blackness*, that is, a script of exclusion.

Across Western Europe, medieval drama represented the Devil in black-up. As Virginia Mason Vaughan notes, in English cycle plays, numerous episodes representing the Fall of Lucifer have him comment on his own transformation from white to black as divine punishment: he has become a "feende black" in the Chester cycle, "a devil ful derke" in the Coventry creation, and he has "waxen blacke as any coyll" in the Wakefield creation.[1] We know that those devils were performed in black-up from sources such as the records of professional guilds performing the Coventry cycle plays: for instance, referring to damned souls, the Drapers' Company records from 1561 to 1579 list extra costs for "the blacck-yng of the sowles' facys."[2] As Dympna Callaghan explains, actors may have used "charred cork mixed with a little oil" as minstrels would later do, some combination of soot and grease, or, more basically, charcoal.[3] A costlier option, more rarely used, was to burn walnut shells, or—even better—ivory, which was reputed to produce the most beautiful black.[4] The popularity of charcoal black-up in French religious theatre—explained in part by its cost-effectiveness compared to more lavish alternatives—is evident in a letter from Michel de L'Hospital to Cardinal du Bellay (ca. 1560), where he recalls attending a performance: "the most striking element was the character of Lucifer, with horns on his forehead, his face all smeared with charcoal, and his coiled tail."[5] Nondramatic literature suggests that the same technique was used in medieval Iberian performances, whose existence is attested to in the *Siete partidas* proclaimed by king Alfonso X of Castile in 1265. The same king, in *Cantigas de Santa María*, describes the devil as "a man black in color" (un omne negro de coor), "a tall man, thin, hairy, and black like pitch" (longo magro e veloso / e negro como pez).[6]

Medieval theatre practitioners have left no traces of black-up's materiality, but we have images that can help us visualize stage devils. Indeed, the fourteenth-century French manuscript of the *Miracles de Nostre Dame par personnages* comes with miniatures often read as renderings of the plays' performance.[7] In these miniatures, devils are represented with hairy black skin (along the same lines as devils in king Alfonso's *Cantigas*), wild hair, and pointed wings; they also have horns, and their goatish legs end with claws. The devils in the miniatures of the early fourteenth-century manuscript of the *Mystère du jour du jugement* (see Plate 1) can be described similarly, with one important variation: in this mystery play, the devils' skin tone could be black, grayish, or reddish-brown. The miniatures suggest that the cosmetics used for black-up could be more or less charged in various pigments to create nuances. Other powdered substances, such as walnut wood, or the fruit stones mentioned by Nicholas Hilliard in *The Arte of Limning*, could be used with grease to create different shades of black-up.[8]

On stage, the blacked-up medieval devil had a double epistemology: he was both, in Robert Weimann's words, a comedic folk figure providing "a subversive expression for class frustration and protest" and a theological figure that spectators truly believed in and feared most deeply.[9] As a result, the audience's disposition toward the Devil could fluctuate during performances, oscillating between sympathy, hilarity, and hostility. Constant through those oscillations, however, was the audience's perception of stage devils as a disruptive force. "Operating supportively within the bounds of traditional religion," writes John Cox, "stage Devils reveal communal values by default, illustrating (often satirically) what fifteenth century English society saw as most destructive of its sacral cohesion.... Where society was concerned, the devil's opposition defined community by default, illustrating emblematically what community was not by opposing what it was."[10] Medieval stage devils threatened to tear apart the fabric of Christian societies: that legacy is key to understanding the ideological work performed by the diabolical script of blackness—a script of exclusion that hinged on the hermeneutic overlap between the Devil and other beings performed in black-up in the eyes of Renaissance spectators familiar with the episteme of religious drama. When that hermeneutic lens was successfully activated, characters in black-up were scopically associated with dark entities threatening to destroy Christian European societies from within. The diabolical script of blackness was cultivated by theatre makers who wielded poetic cues to reactivate the preexisting demonic associations of black-up at strategic junctures.

There were, of course, differences between medieval diabolical black-up and Renaissance Afro-diasporic black-up. The latter did away with the animal components of the Devil's costume, added ethnically recognizable garments, and resorted to wigs in an attempt to render the texture of natural black hair: in England, performers used wigs made of stiff lambskin fur, while in Spain, a performance record from 1525 points toward the use of expensive wigs rendering the texture of African braids, twists, or locks.[11] The add-ons changed, but the basic technique of painting actors' faces and either painting or covering their limbs with black cloth remained.[12] The diabolical script of blackness led spectators familiar with the older uses of black-up to ponder in performance the presence of Afro-diasporic people in Christian European societies. The early modern stage was indeed haunted by a question: could Afro-diasporic people be absorbed into societies that imagined themselves as bodies politic whose members were implicitly linked by intimate and organic forms of collectivity? The stage answered the question with its own language, in this case, with black-up and its historically accrued semiotic leverage. On the secular stage, I argue, the diabolical script of blackness would mark black characters as outcasts who, like the Devil, could not be woven into the fabric of early modern European societies.

This chapter moves gradually away from the diabolical script of blackness and from a theatrical culture that would hold on to that script throughout the early modern period, to one that would relinquish it very early on in favor of other scripts. In the first section of this chapter, focusing on England, I read the popularity of the diabolical script of blackness and its exclusionary discourse, epitomized in *Titus Andronicus* (1594), in light of the late Tudor and early Stuart contexts of xenophobia and racial aversion. I then cross the Channel to read the deployment of the same script of blackness in French theatre in light of the unspoken colonial fears and desires of early baroque France. From the first mercantile itchings in port cities on the Atlantic coast to Richelieu's 1626 decision to form the Compagnie de Saint-Christophe, from Colbert's foundation of the Compagnie des Indes Occidentales in 1664 to the promulgation of the *Code noir* dictating in 1685 conditions for slavery in the colonies, France continuously fashioned itself as a colonial slave-trading power in the seventeenth century, and that self-fashioning required the country to renegotiate its relation to sub-Saharan Africans, slavery, and the racial matrix. Performance culture and stage-craft, I argue, were crucial sites for such cultural negotiations to take place. During the early baroque period, in Rouen, the diabolical script of blackness was integrated into local conversations about French colonial expansion in plays such as *Tragédie francoize d'un More cruel* (1613), *La merveille* (ca. 1620), and *Les Portugaiz infortunez* (1608). Most often, that integration reckoned negatively with the Iberian colonial experience, suggesting that a similar expansion would involve Afro-diasporic subjects that could not safely be assimilated into a transoceanic and colonial French body politic. Moreover, that integration sometimes hinged on the trope of the Devil's pact, which Christians have a duty to break by all means—legal obligations be damned. In such cases, the diabolical script of blackness construed Afro-diasporic people as fit to ensnare and cheat out of their labor with legal and moral impunity.

Returning to England, I argue that *Othello* (1604) reflects on the popularity of the diabolical script of blackness: by substituting a whitefaced woman for a blacked-up man as the iconic sign whose meaning is being indexically closed—by detaching the technique from blackness for a brief moment—the play renders the racializing technique visible; uncovers its uses, mechanics, and efficacy; and invites analysis. *Othello* exposes the demonizing rhetoric underlying the diabolical script of blackness as a tool wielded by the white male gaze against anyone it seeks to oppress. English theatre, unlike its Spanish and French counterparts, never relinquished the diabolical script of blackness in the early modern period; yet a play like *Othello* directed spectators' attention early on to the devastating effects of the diabolizing rhetoric at play.

The chapter ultimately progresses from a scenario in which the diabolical script of blackness is critiqued to one where it is rejected wholesale. Indeed, in the final section of this chapter, I use the case of Iberian theatrical culture to support my overarching claim: that scripts of blackness respond flexibly to glocally articulated ideological needs. A slavery-based society like early modern Spanish society did not need to hear exclusionary stories about blackness; its theatrical culture therefore drifted away from the diabolical script of blackness early on. Indeed, the support that Afro-diasporic subjects received from the Catholic Church across the empire during the sixteenth century and the first decades of the seventeenth century, with prominent figures such as the Jesuit Alonso de Sandoval, grounded the idea that Afro-diasporic Christians did belong in the body of the church, albeit in a subaltern position. The church's discourse was not disinterested but embedded in a colonial project supported by the crown and powered by a ruthless mercantilist ethos. Its transformative ideological push, necessitated by the imperatives of a slavery-based economy, correlates with the wane of the diabolical script of blackness on stage. The new script of blackness that thrived on stage in its place across genres—which I call *the commodifying script of blackness*—deployed strategic poetics to reframe spectators' perception of cosmetic and prosthetic blackness invoking various types of commodities, including animals, foodstuff, or luxury goods. In its own way, each of the poetic strands of the commodifying script of blackness told a story that upheld the institution of slavery. The animal paradigm excluded Afro-diasporic people from mankind, denying them fundamental rights and turning them into property; the foodstuff paradigm construed them as goods whose consumption was not only pleasurable but necessary to the health of a hungry body politic. The luxury paradigm served to distinguish Afro-diasporic subjects deemed exceptional from regular ones, carving a strategic space to express admiration for some people of color within the framework of color-based slavery. It thereby helped pass a system of racial oppression as a system of racial meritocracy. In short, the commodifying script of blackness was a spectrum of stories: the chilling efficacy of that racializing system derived precisely from the variety and combinability of its scopic narratives.

Some of the dramatic texts that this chapter and the next mine to unearth the early modern deployment of scripts of blackness are canonical, while others (often some of the most interesting ones) are virtually unknown. My ambition is not to exhaust the interpretive possibilities arising from such a rich and exciting new archive, but to uncover the specific hermeneutic layers, connections, and associations that coalesce when we read those texts through the logic of specific performative regimes of racialization—here the scopic. Such an effort required the deferral of many interpretive clues and paths, which the growing field of early modern critical race studies will no doubt set to elucidate in the future.

Introducing the Diabolical Script of Blackness

In the 1580s, English theatre makers started using cosmetic black-up to represent sub-Saharan Africans in plays such as Marlowe's *Tamburlaine* (1590), or maybe even earlier, in lost plays such as the anonymous *Theagenes and Chariclea* (1572) and *The Queen of Ethiopia* (1578).[13] The diabolical script of blackness quickly became a popular dramaturgic device in London: between 1590 and 1620, it was all the rage. George Peele introduced the device to the English stage in *The Battel of Alcazar* (1589), where he presents the villainous "Negro" Moorish king Muly Mahamet in terms that indexically activate the diabolical accents of black-up:

> Black in his look, and bloody in his deeds,
> And in his shirt stained with a cloud of gore,
> Presents himself with naked sword in hand,
> Accompanied as now you may behold,
> With Devils coated in the shapes of men.[14]

Peele's spectacularly diabolical black king launched a fashion that would last for more than thirty years. In *Titus Andronicus* (1594), Aaron actively contributes to the deployment of the diabolical script of blackness:

> *Lucius* Bring down the Devil for he must not die
>   So sweet a death as hanging presently.
> *Aaron* If there be Devils would I were a Devil,
>   To live and burn in everlasting fire,
>   So I might have your company in hell,
>   But to torment you with my bitter tongue. (5.1.145–50)[15]

In *Lusts Dominion* (1600), Eleazar the Moor is called "that fiend, / That damned Moor, that Devil, that Lucifer" by Cardinal Mendoza—at the cardinal's own risks, for "Who spurns the Moor / Were better set his foot upon the Devil."[16] In *Othello* (1604), Iago tries to make Brabantio fall for the diabolical script of blackness that he deploys around the Moor:

Arise, arise
Awake the snorting citizens with the bell,
Or else the Devil will make a grandsire of you. (1.1.92–94)

Even in a lighthearted comedy such as George Chapman's *The Blind Beggar of Alexandria* (1596), Porus, the king of Ethiopia, is called a devil when Elimine chooses him as her new husband:

Elimine In my eye now the blackest is the fairest,
     For every woman chooses white and red,
     Come martial Porus thou shalt have my love.
Bebritius Out on thee foolish woman thou hast chose a Devil!
Porus Not yet sir till he have horns.[17]

The gravity of the diabolical script of blackness is quickly deflated with a joke on cuckoldry, yet Bebritius's comment shows that he reads harmless Porus in the tradition launched by Peele. Finally, in Rowley's *All's Lost by Lust* (1619), when Jacinta refuses to marry the Moorish king despite her father's promise, she uses familiar rhetoric: "base African, / Thine inside's blacker then thy sooty skin"; she further calls him "a dragon" and a "hellhound."[18] Jacinta's rhetorical cues efficiently trigger the audience's performative memory and activate the diabolical script.

This sample of plays is by no means exhaustive, but it evidences a sustained craze across dramatic genres for the diabolical script of blackness on English commercial stages from 1590 to 1620. While the demonization of blackness across media was not new, this noticeable craze was, I argue, the response that the stage offered to contemporary changes in the social, demographic, and discursive landscapes of early modern London, the Afro-diasporic population of which amounted to 0.5 percent of the total in the 1590s, according to Gustav Ungerer. Surveying a large number of records including royal and aristocratic household accounts, government proclamations and legal records, parish registers, medical notations, and personal accounts, Imtiaz Habib draws a clear line between the Afro-diasporic people who arrived in England during the first half of the sixteenth century—usually Afro-Iberians who could occasionally exercise an "independent recognized public role" in England, and the Afro-diasporic people who arrived in the second half of the century. Those in the latter category arrived in a time of economic crisis, "as a result of England's expeditionary forays to Africa and the Western Atlantic in search of new commodities and markets. . . . Its effect on the English was to transform the African into a menial subject suitable for commercial exploitation through enslavement." Habib did not find a single record showing an African in an independent professional capacity. He concludes, "With a few exceptions, the living situations of black people revealed in the data span a range from menial work, albeit with skills, to chattel existence, including prostitution, with the last two categories constituting the clear majority."[19]

In other words, the rare exceptions to the rule should not blind us to the fact that, if Afro-diasporic people in Tudor and early Stuart England were not called slaves, they were nevertheless usually unfree. The fetishism of key words should not prevent us from examining actual power dynamics; interest in institutional slavery should not blind us to more subtle, insidious, and interesting forms of interracial power play in Elizabethan and Stuart England. Habib's ability to perceive shades of gray between freedom and institutional slavery is a productive direction to follow. The experience of "unspoken chattel bondage" that he describes is best understood when read along the lines of twenty-first-century human trafficking in the Western world, which teaches us that people live de facto in bondage in societies where slavery is illegal. Given the early modern legal vacuum on the subject, it is likely that, on the spectrum of unfreedom, some late Tudor Afro-Britons fell close to slavery, while others fell closer to indentured servitude like many lower-class white Englishmen, and others closer to servanthood. Habib's findings provide evidence that Afro-Britons were subjected to various forms of highly profitable economic exploitation—which explains their demographic increase over the period.

This economic exploitation came together with a discourse of denigration that implicitly justified positioning Afro-Britons at the bottom of the social hierarchy. That multifaceted discourse of denigration included, among others, the theatrical discourse scrutinized in this book, a religious discourse (Africans descend from Cham; their servitude was thus sanctioned by scripture), and a medical discourse, exemplified by George Best's well-known *A True Discourse of the Late Voyages of Discoverie for the Finding of a Passage to Cathaya*, which defines blackness as a form of transmissible "naturall infection."[20] This coalescent discourse of denigration received a boost in the early 1590s, when, Habib notes, the Afro-diasporic presence in England increased significantly because of the establishment of the Barbary Company in 1585 and the Privy Council's letter patents of 1588 and 1592 authorizing commercial excursions to Guinea and Sierra Leone respectively. This demographic increase worsened tensions about the distribution of material resources. Despite their position at the bottom of the social hierarchy, late Tudor Africans became perceived as competitors for resources in a context of "rising prices of essentials, food scarcities, popular dissension and riots, an increase in the proportion of the London poor greater than that of the city's population, collective xenophobia about aliens, and the 'obsessional' surveillance that was the response of the government to perceived challenges to its authority and to fears about infiltration and corruption of its national life."[21] Through age-old mechanisms of scapegoating, this situation resulted in the rise of English racism against Afro-diasporic people in London.[22] It is in this context of growing resentment toward the Afro-diasporic presence in England and gradual de facto, if not de jure, acceptance of Afro-diasporic unfreedom on English soil—both of which occasioned and called for a denigration of Afro-Britons—that I read the vogue of the diabolical script of blackness on the English stage between 1590 and 1620. This script was theatre's response to a new racial climate, and it signals its participation in a moment of new racial formation.

In *Titus Andronicus*, the first English play to deploy the diabolical script of blackness around an enslaved man, the connection to the racial climate of 1590s London is palpable. *Titus Andronicus* is not a religious play but, with the diabolical script of blackness, it repurposed a religious discourse for its own ends. I have argued at length elsewhere that Aaron, the enslaved Blackamoor, is a catalyst for contemporary English anxieties about immigration and fear of turning—under Iberian influence—into a nation foreign to itself.[23] Those anxieties crystallize on stage into the diabolical script of blackness, which is deployed quite transparently around Aaron, as he declares, with the most serpentine alliterations:

Aaron Some Devil whispers curses in my ear
    And prompts me, that my tongue may utter forth
    The venomous malice of my swelling heart.
Lucius Away, inhuman dog, unhallowed slave!
    Sirs, help our uncle to convey him in. (5.3.11–15)

Lucius Andronicus, vocalizing potential audience reactions, responds to the diabolical script of blackness that Aaron activates by reading the Moor as excluded from mankind ("inhuman dog"), from the Roman religious community ("unhallowed"), and from citizenship ("slave").

The exclusionary mechanisms inherent in the diabolical script of blackness become hereditary as they are extended to Aaron's innocent "Blackamoor child," who is introduced by his own nurse as "a Devil": "a joyless, dismal, black, and sorrowful issue . . . loathsome as a toad" later called a "black slave" and a "tawny slave" by his father (4.2.64, 4.2.66–67, 4.2.119, 5.1.27). The child's unstably dark complexion makes him diabolical in Lucius's eyes:

> *Lucius* Oh worthy Goth this is the incarnate Devil,
>   That robbed Andronicus of his good hand,
>   This is the pearl that pleased your Empress eye,
>   And here's the base fruit of her burning lust,
>   Say wall-eyed slave whither wouldst thou convey
>   This growing image of thy fiendlike face,
>   Why dost not speak? What deaf, not a word?
>   A halter, soldiers! Hang him on this tree,
>   And by his side his fruit of bastardy.
> *Aaron* Touch not the boy, he is of royal blood.
> *Lucius* Too like the sire for ever being good,
>   First hang the child that he may see it sprawl,
>   A sight to vex the father's soul withal.
>   Get me a ladder. (5.1.40–52)

Reading the baby's color as a promise of diabolism in "this growing image of thy fiendlike face," Lucius subjects the baby to the same forms of social exclusion as his father: he excludes him from citizenship and thus treats as enslaved a boy who was born free according to Roman law. Indeed, according to the Roman law famously captured as *partus sequitur ventrem*, children were to inherit their mother's status, regardless of their father's condition—and the play seems to reference this law at times.[24] This disposition of Roman law, however, ran contrary to English law until the Restoration. Thus, by determining the baby's social status based on his father's social status and complexion, Lucius is not thinking like a Roman, but like a late sixteenth-century Englishman. He reads the baby's blackness as Shakespeare's spectators would.

If, as Emily Bartels shows, English subjects resisted the three edicts that Elizabeth promulgated between 1596 and 1601 to deport "Negars and Blackamoors," the fates of Aaron and his son already suggested in 1594 that, for all the xenophobia and racial aversion in early modern London, Afro-diasporic people could not be excised from the fabric of English society so easily. Aaron and Tamora's mixed-race child is not killed or ejected but raised in the shadows of imperial Rome in a lowly position beneficial to a colonialist society that capitalizes on racial thinking in order to produce as much labor power as possible at a minimal cost.[25] Similarly, the punishment reserved for Aaron at the end of the play—"Set him breast-deep in earth and famish him, / There, let him stand, and rave, and cry for food" (5.3.178–79)—for all its raw cruelty, shows us a Blackamoor literally taking root in the English soil. *Titus Andronicus* is an aporetic play: it uses the diabolical script of blackness to scopically convey the idea that Afro-diasporic people could not fit into English society, while simultaneously intimating, through various dramaturgic moves, that, given the economic logic of empires past, present, and future, Afro-Britons could no longer be removed from that society either.

Black-Up and Atlantic Promises in Early Baroque France

In 1608, Samuel de Champlain was sent across the Atlantic to found the city of Québec, the most important permanent settlement in Canada and future seat of New France. The same year, Rouen-based playwright Chrétien des Croix wrote *Les Portugaiz infortunez*. The anonymous *Tragédie françoize d'un more cruel* followed in 1613, and *La merveille* closed in 1620 a decade of Rouen plays invested in scopic racecraft. These plays built the diabolical script of blackness into local conversations about French expansion in the Atlantic world. In this respect, they depart from early Renaissance uses of black-up to represent Afro-diasporic characters, which were not always filtered through a diabolical script in France.[26] The diabolical script irrupts in French plays with investments in the colonial question specifically. Indeed, *Les Portugaiz infortunez* might stage conquest in the Indian Ocean, and *Le More cruel* as well as *La merveille* might stage slavery in the Mediterranean, but, in the late 1600s, Rouen businessmen had the Atlantic on their minds. Robin Blackburn has shown that "in the long run, the French colonization effort was to depend more on the State and less on the spontaneous impulses of civil society than had been the case with England."[27] In the early seventeenth century, however, the French colonial model still oscillated between private enterprise and State control, and if one city in France had entrepreneurial impulses comparable to the English ones, it was Rouen. Champlain drew a large portion of his capital from Rouen merchants, whose investment in the Québec venture was probably motivated by the powerful local textile industry's interest in North American furs (Québec was founded as a fur post). Similarly, Rouen was the most important French port for trading with Brazil, whence it imported red brazilwood for dyes. In short, the mercantile city of Rouen had its eyes on the Atlantic earlier than the rest of the country did.

The importance of the Atlantic for Rouen shows in the city's theatrical output. In 1611, Rouen playwright Georges Duhamel wrote *Acoubar ou la loyauté trahie: Tragédie. Tirée des amours de Pistion et Fortunie en leur voyage de Canada*, the first European play to stage Canada and call for its colonization.[28] At the same time, the spread of the Black Legend, denouncing the ethically failed Iberian model of colonization, raised questions about how French colonization should be conducted. Theatre in Rouen became a platform for discussing the desirability, lawfulness, risks, and ideal modalities of a French expansion into the Atlantic.[29] The use of the diabolical script of blackness in Rouen plays such as *Les Portugaiz infortunez*, *Le More cruel*, and *La merveille* fueled ongoing local conversations on colonialism by provoking spectators to consider whether Afro-diasporic subjects could safely be woven into the fabric of a potential transoceanic and colonial French body politic.

This early concern with Afro-diasporic subjects in the Atlantic context may come as a surprise to the extent that, in 1613, France had not yet started its own expansion along the West African coast or in the Caribbean. However, blackness had already entered the discursive domain in France, for colonial fantasies had already started developing, and those fantasies were colored by the Iberian experience through which France understood Atlantic expansion. That Iberian experience—simultaneously defamed, decried, and envied—had involved color-based slavery for over a century and a half by 1608. *Le More cruel* stages Spaniards in Mallorca, an island over which Spain was struggling to maintain control against Barbary Corsairs throughout the early modern period, and *Les Portugaiz infortunez* stages Portuguese people in the Indian Ocean, a region in which Portugal sought to expand its dominion in the sixteenth century. The plays show two paradigmatic European colonial powers (united in the Iberian union when the plays were written) involved in empire making, and engaging with sub-Saharan Africans as they do so. Rouen merchants knew that the Atlantic empires with which they wanted to compete relied on enslaved Africans to function. Erick Noël's exploration of French archives in search of Afro-French people reveals the presence of "Nègres" in Normandy long before anything similar was recorded in Paris: in Dieppe for instance, one such person is recorded as early as 1567, and in Rouen, Africans enter the record in the late 1600s, precisely at the time where the repertoire of Rouen plays under consideration was being produced.[30] The Iberian experience had entangled the notions of expansion in the Atlantic and economic exploitation of Afro-diasporic people in French collective imagination—and the Rouen plays reflect this.

Let us take a closer look at these plays' strategic mobilization of the diabolical script of blackness. In 1613, Abraham Cousturier, a major publisher in Rouen—a city that, at the time, published twice as many plays as did Paris— published *La tragédie françoize d'un More cruel envers son seigneur nommé Riviery, gentil homme espagnol, sa damoiselle et ses enfans*. This anonymous play was based on a novella by Bandello that François de Belleforest had translated into French and embellished some fifty years earlier.[31] The domestic revenge tragedy has a simple plot: in Mallorca, an enslaved *More*, having received a particularly violent beating for no reason at the hand of his Spanish enslaver, decides to wait for the best moment to get his revenge. His enslaver, Riviery, realizing how unfair he has been, decides to make amends by freeing the *More* and keeping him as a free servant in his household. The *More* feigns gratitude. He waits for the day when Riviery goes hunting, leaving his wife and children in the care of his trusty servant. The *More* then sequesters the family inside the enslaver's castle and pulls up the drawbridge. He rapes Riviery's wife before her children's eyes. The eldest son calls for help and is heard by a messenger. Alerted by the messenger, Riviery rides back to the castle and begs the *More* to spare the life of his loved ones. From atop the castle's tower, the *More* promises to do so if the enslaver cuts off his own nose—a punishment traditionally reserved for runaway enslaved people. Desperate, Riviery does it. The *More* laughs at him and then breaks his promise by stabbing the mother and throwing both her and the children from the top of the tower. He then jumps into the sea, killing himself to escape punishment.

There is little doubt that the source text for this play, Bandello's novella about the Moor of Mallorca, also informs the scene in *Titus Andronicus* when Aaron cheats Titus into cutting his own hand, promising that the emperor shall spare his sons' lives for it. A father agrees to mutilate himself hoping, but in vain, to save the life of his sons. The connection between *Titus Andronicus* and Bandello's material is so clear that when English Restoration balladeers transmediated Bandello's novella, they saw Aaron in the Moor of Mallorca and changed the setting of the plot from Mallorca to Rome accordingly.[32] Aaron thus influenced the Moor of Mallorca's late reception in England; he may very well have influenced his early reception in France too. Indeed, *Titus Andronicus* was performed almost twenty years before *Le More cruel*, and during those years three quartos of the play, presumably based on Shakespeare's foul papers, had been published. Because of the dire lack of documentation about theatrical life in France in that period, we are forced to conjecture and to draw conclusions in the subjunctive mood—in other words, to "record." I record, then, that Cousturier, one of the most important publishers of playbooks in Rouen, the theatrical capital of France and a most important platform for Anglo-French trade at the time, got his hands on a quarto of *Titus Andronicus*. He may also have seen some English drama performed—if he had spent time in London between June and October 1594, he could have seen *Titus Andronicus* on stage, along with most of the plays that would resonate in his subsequent dramatic publications over the next twenty years.[33] Cousturier might also have seen some English plays at home, for English traveling actors toured France and came to Rouen in 1598–1599, thus popularizing the English repertoire.[34] The popularity of *Titus Andronicus* may thus very well have influenced Cousturier's decision to publish *Le More cruel*.

Both of the plays inspired by Bandello's novella across the Channel mobilize the diabolical script of blackness. *Le More cruel*, like several other plays published by Cousturier, was printed with five woodcuts representing key moments of the plot that have been understood as replicating moments of ideal performance.[35] They represent the *More* with pitch black skin (his facial features are drawn in white lines), as opposed to the white Spanish characters—which I read as a way of rendering in print the use of black-up, or *barbouillage*, during the play's performance (Figure 1).

Whether this play was performed before or after the text was printed is a question that cannot be answered in the present state of the archive. In the absence of documentation regarding the performance history of the play, recording means thinking of the relation between the printed text (with its woodcuts) and performance as dynamically as possible. In my reading, then, the woodcuts both reflect some of the performance dynamics of black-up and script future potential performances in black-up.[36]

Cousturier's decision to include the woodcuts was a strong intervention. When Belleforest had translated and embellished Bandello's story a few years after its original publication in 1566, he had characterized his protagonist, "a slave born on the Barbary coast, and a true Barbarian as he proved to be," as a "poor tawny man" (pauvre bazané).[37] The adjective *basané* derives from *la basane*, a word for sheep leather that could be red, black, and all shades of brown. When used metaphorically to describe human skin, the term refers to various complexions on a broad chromatic range. This term's flexibility enabled it to encompass a population as diverse as the North African population. In other

FRANCOISE.

ACTE DEVXIEME.
Le More, Riuiery, la Damoiſelle.

le More.

Vis que fortune à tant aidé à mon deſſain
Que ie ſuis deliuré d'vn iong tant inhumain
Et que ie ſuis dehors d'vn puis plain de miſeres

B

Figure 1. "Riviery Freeing the *More* Against His Wife's Advice" in *Tragédie françoize d'un More cruel*. Woodcut. 1613. Bibliothèque nationale de France.

words, Belleforest, just like Bandello's original, left the skin tone of the *More*
to his reader's imagination.[38] Cousturier, however, ended this tradition when
he adorned the playtext with woodcuts depicting the *More* as unambiguously
dark-skinned. That decision most probably was the publisher's response to the
play's deployment of a diabolical rhetoric all too often associated with black-up
in performance.

Indeed, when he has found the way to avenge his wrongs, the *More* calls on
the forces of Hell to assist him in his design:

> The hour is near when he [Riviery] shall pay with usurious interest
> For the ills I suffered. Come on in, Pluto,
> Megaera, Tisiphone and her sister Alekto,
> Hasten: I am calling on you all—you all!—
> To assist me in my righteous suit. . . .
> If you favor me, I ask you to come
> Quickly, with thunder and lightning—
> Stinking Megaera, are you lagging
> With your burning torch?
> Come to me too, you screaming ghosts,
> You demons, spirits, and howling dogs of Hell![39]

The antique hell divinities manifest the influence of humanism in the period,
but the performance techniques used to represent those divinities come from
Catholic theatre, making the distinction between devils and classical deities of
the underworld moot: the "screams" and "howls" as well as the group of devils
come from the tradition of mystery play performances. Similarly, "thunder,"
"lightning," and Megaera's "burning torch" echo the sound effects and pyrotech-
nics of the medieval *diableries* described by Rabelais and Jacques Thiboust.[40] Let
us imagine what the audience saw during this invocation: a *More* in black-up
surrounded by devils in black-up coming to aid him. In that moment, black-up
materialized the hermeneutic kinship between the vengeful African and the
devils around him. This kinship is strengthened a few lines later, when, after
first flinching at the thought of killing Riviery's innocent children to punish
their father, the *More* regains determination and exclaims:

> What, will this foul man
> Live unpunished for such a cowardly crime?

What, will he brag to everyone
That he subjected me to such ignominy
And I did not resent it? Ah! I will sooner turn
Whiter than milk and more crimson than coral![41]

Playing on the famed impossibility of washing the Ethiop white, the *More* asks spectators to take his blackness as guarantee that he will exact vengeance against the enslaver's innocent and beloved children, a course of action that likens him to the vengeful Lucifer exacting vengeance against the race of Man.

The *More*'s revenge unfolds, including rape, mutilation, child murders, and gruesome deaths. The play draws unambiguous conclusions from the *More*'s actions:

Lords and gentlemen, how blind are we
To hold as servants those nasty *Mores*,
Who are a hundred times more treacherous in their cruelty
Than tigers and lionesses![42]

In those final lines, Riviery questions the fitness of *Mores* for enslavement when it comes at the cost of a Moorish presence in Christian societies. Riviery follows the opinion expressed by Belleforest that Europeans, and Frenchmen in particular, should not use enslaved *Mores* but only resort to nationals as labor force.[43] Riviery echoes one of the hunters, who during a choric conversation on the soundness of Riviery's course of action, declares: "We should only trust people who share our own Law."[44] "Law" (loy) is to be understood in both religious and political terms: the Hunter implies that because the *More* is a Muslim, he cannot be trusted to follow the laws of Catholic Mallorcan society, and thus, he constitutes a threat to that society. The diabolical script of blackness uses the scopic regime to articulate an argument similar to Riviery's and to the Hunter's, insinuating that, just like the Devil in medieval theatre, the dark-skinned Muslim *More* threatens to tear apart the social fabric of a Catholic society. Collapsing religion and politics, the play reverberates with an event that was unfolding in the Iberian Peninsula at the very time when *Le More cruel* was written and performed (1609–14): the expulsion of *moriscos*, Spaniards of Muslim descent. As it underlines the risks inherent in having dark-skinned Muslims live in a Christian society, the play seems to register the traumatic contemporary events unfolding on the other side of the Pyrenees, and to import some Spanish concerns with the integrity of the national body politic into France—after all, the play is called *La Tragédie françoize d'un more cruel* (emphasis added).

The concern with Frenchness and French identity powering this theatrical engagement with Spanish racial and colonial history is evident in another anonymous play Cousturier published around 1620, a comedy entitled *La merveille*. In it, a distinctly French captain named Flodoar disembarks close to "the Cairo of Babylon" (3) and walks alone on the shore, eager to see "the great circuit of this vast universe."[45] He is immediately taken captive by two of the Egyptian Sultan's "Satrappes." Upon learning that Flodoar is a renowned architect who can build "big towers, triumphant palaces, grave castles, Arsenals, and Louvres," the Sultan orders him to build a palace in the French style on the Euphrate's banks in two years' time, on penalty of death (14).[46] Faced with this impossible deadline, Flodoar despairs, invokes the devil Pharos, and makes a pact. Pharos will complete the palace, kill the "Sattrapes," transport Flodoar back to France with all the Sultan's riches, and fulfill all his wishes for sixteen years—in exchange for Flodoar's soul. Flodoar refuses to sign any obligation unless Pharos signs one too. Flodoar is legally savvy, unlike his obvious English counterpart Dr. Faustus, but like many spectators in Rouen—which was the seat of the Norman Parliament. Should Pharos default on any part of his obligation, Flodoar's pact will be voided. Flodoar thus finds a way to make the devil default: he asks for an impossibility, a tower of gold that would bridge Heaven and Hell, the titular marvel.

I underline the legalistic dimension of this play because legalism is a recurrent feature of the early French baroque deployment of the diabolical script of blackness. Indeed, in the opening lines of *Le More cruel*, the Moor of Mallorca describes his own enslavement as a form of "extorsion." In 1613, this term did not mean extortion, but tort, justifying his "righteous suit" against Riviery's "cowardly crime."[47] By using a distinctly legal term to describe his own enslavement as an infringement on his natural rights, the *More* gives support to Toby Wikström's reading of the play as an attack on the institution of slavery. The recurrence of legal tropes and terms signals that the diabolical script of blackness construed Africans as figures always already involved in fraught legal negotiations with white Christians. Because, in the folklore traditions pervasive on the early modern stage, the Devil uses the legal apparatus of contract relations to steal Christian souls, it is only fair for Christians to use that same apparatus against him. As a French proverb from the fifteenth century goes: "'Tis fine to wrong the Devil" (Au diable l'on peut faire tort), and the French word "tort" here is to be heard with its full legal resonances.[48] The diabolical script of blackness thus could construe Afro-diasporic people as people fit to be ensnared by legal means: people whose labor could be stolen with moral impunity.

The comedic resolution of *La merveille* hinges on the French hero's success at escaping the grip of the Sultan and then the grip of Pharos—that is, his success at shrewdly disengaging twice from pacts that would prove lethal (physically or spiritually) if he carried them to term. In both cases, those relations entail dark-skinned antagonists. Indeed, when he first sees the Sattrapes, Flodoar remarks on their skin tone: he asks "Qui sont ces bazanés?" (10) and he later calls them "les Sattrapes Noirs" (32). Later on, Pharos describes himself as "un démon bazané citoyen du Tartare" (a tawny demon and a citizen of Hell), and the woodcut on the play's frontispiece depicts the demon's skin as pitch black (33). *La merveille* tells its spectators and readers that a wise and skillful Frenchman will find ways to break all contracts—even contracts that might seem beneficial at first—with dark-skinned enemies abroad (in Egypt) or at home (in France).

In Rouen's scopic regime of performative racialization, the integrity of the French body politic as a potentially transoceanic colonial body was threatened not only by a black Islamic presence (as is the case in *Le More cruel* and in *La merveille*) but by any non-Catholic Afro-diasporic presence. Indeed, we find the same ideological concerns and use of the diabolical script of blackness at work in another Rouen play staging sub-Saharan Africans, *Les Portugaiz infortunez*, by Nicholas Chrétien des Croix (1608), in which Islam is entirely absent. This play too is based on a historical anecdote and constitutes another French cautionary take on the colonial and racial history of Iberia. In February 1552, the rich Portuguese galleon of Don Manuel de Sousa y Sepulveda, captain-general of the island fortress of Diu, India, was shipwrecked off the Cape of Good Hope on its way back to Lisbon. Those who survived the shipwreck and could make it to the shore of Natal started walking northward in hope of reaching Mozambique, where their countrymen had established trading posts, and where they might be rescued by a Portuguese ship. The play shows them arriving in Manique, which is ruled by Mocondez, king of the Kaffir people. Of note here is the fact that the word *Kaffir* in Arabic means "nonbeliever," that is, a non-Muslim. Mocondez is hostile toward Europeans, whom he sees, understandably, as a threat. Despite the Portuguese pleas for help and hospitality, he remains firm in his belief that Portuguese colonizers, those "thieves with such white skin," are evil, dangerous, and deceitful: "they come from remote lands / to steal our goods and subjugate us too."[49] He tricks the Portuguese into yielding their weapons, orders his men to rob them, beat them, and leave them destitute, without food, shelter, or clothes. Sousa's wife, Leonore, buries herself waist deep in the ground to hide her shame, and she starves to death with her children. Sousa, looking for roots to eat in the forest, is devoured by African beasts. The dark continent refuses to feed Portuguese appetites and swallows them—like a medieval hellmouth—in this cautionary play against colonial greed.

The play mobilizes the diabolical script of blackness when the Kaffirs of Natal attack and strip the shipwrecked Portuguese. Desperate, Leonore de Sepulveda exclaims:

> Ah, diabolical race,
> Begotten by Pluto, excrements of the earth! ...
> Hateful people! Malicious race!
> A hundred times more brutal than a furious she-bear![50]

Until this point, probably under the influence of Montaigne's work, the play had depicted the Kaffirs with a refreshing amount of cultural relativism.[51] But Leonore's address—"diabolical race!"—puts an end to this humanist stance by activating the diabolical script of blackness. The scatological metaphor she uses plays directly into the exclusionary script's symbolism of social ejection. The pagan African priest Serif frames the attack against Portuguese colonial agents as an exemplum:

> They are fleeing!
> Strip them all and expose their whiteness! Run! Hurry!
> Let us present their spoils to the king:
> This punishment will set a law for others.[52]

Those "others" who might benefit from this "law" are the Rouen spectators, and the moral of the play is transparent: sub-Saharan Africans, even when they are emphatically *not* Muslims, are not to be trusted as allies in the process of colonization. The Portuguese who, for lack of options, made a pact and yielded their weapons to receive hospitality from the Kaffirs lost everything—goods, clothes, dignity, and life.[53] Whereas *Le More cruel* shows the dangers of having non-Christian Afro-diasporic people living among Christians, *Les Portugaiz infortunez*, just like *La merveille*, shows the dangers of entering contractual relations with non-Christian Afro-diasporic allies, cautioning against their integration into any potential transoceanic colonial French body politic. In the first two decades of the seventeenth century, the French embrace of colonization and slavery was not sealed, but even plays that rejected it used the diabolical script of blackness to do so.

Shakespeare's Invitation

The diabolical script of blackness was an extremely useful ideological tool. It was so useful, in fact, that at least one playwright wrote a play about its uses, portability, and lethal efficiency. *Othello* (1604) revolves around the possibility for an Afro-diasporic Christian man to become incorporate in Venice, to be woven into the fabric of a European society. In *Othello*, Shakespeare presents his audience with a dark-skinned Moor whose difficulties in joining the Venetian body politic cannot be blamed on religion: he is a Christian defending Venice and Cyprus against the Turks, even in death. The rejection that Othello— a man whose "thick-lips" (1.1.64) and "sooty" skin (1.2.71) signal sub-Saharan origins—faces from Iago and others within Venetian society is, rather, based on his phenotype. In a play asserting that Afro-diasporic integration into Venetian—read: English—society is not an issue of religion, the diabolical script of blackness, which frames the question of social inclusion in religious terms, is bound to come under scrutiny. *Othello* pressures the diabolical script of blackness and the religious rhetoric that underlies it by staging the operations, contradictions, and, ultimately, sheer power of the white male gaze using that hermeneutic lens. As Arthur Little observes, when watching black-up, Shakespeare's audience was "witnessing the work, the staginess of whiteness."[54] I would add that, during a performance of *Othello*, in addition to witnessing the self-conscious play of whiteness, spectators could witness—self-consciously or not—the white male gaze at work. Iago is uniquely skilled at orienting the white male gaze. The man who will "show out a flag and sign of love—/ Which is indeed but sign" (1.1.158–59) is an "ancient," that is, a sign bearer, a professional semiotician, and a gifted one. His power lies in his ability to anticipate and manipulate others' interpretation of signs, especially bodily signs. The first bodily sign that he frames is Othello's dark skin, when he directs Brabantio's gaze to read it as diabolical:

> Even now, now, very now, an old black ram
> Is tupping your white ewe. Arise, arise!
> Awake the snorting citizens with the bell,
> Or else, the Devil will make a grandsire of you. (1.1.90–93)

Characterizing Othello as a demonic ram and calling him the Devil's issue, Iago tilts Brabantio's hermeneutic frame, which helps the *magnifico* imagine that the dark-skinned Moor might have used witchcraft to seduce Desdemona. He confronts Othello head on with that charge:

> O, thou foul thief, where hast thou stowed my daughter?
> Damned as thou art, thou hast enchanted her!
> For I'll refer me to all things of sense,
> If she in chains of magic were not bound,
> Whether a maid so tender, fair, and happy,
> So opposite to marriage that she shunned
> The wealthy curlèd darlings of our nation,
> Would ever have, t' incur a general mock,
> Run from her guardage to the sooty bosom
> Of such a thing as thou—(1.2.63–72)

The rationale articulated by Brabantio is of an aesthetic nature, yet the religiously inflected comment "damned as thou art" manifests the success of Iago's attempt at framing Othello's "sooty bosom" as diabolical. That scopic framing leads Brabantio to suspect Othello of all activities associated with the diabolical, all "practices of cunning hell"—witchcraft, magic, and enchantments (1.3.104). Brabantio suspects Othello of witchcraft not solely because he is at a loss to understand his daughter's choice, but also because, within his tilted hermeneutic frame, regardless of attractiveness, whoever looks "sooty" is likely to be connected to the Devil.

During the trial scene that ensues, that likelihood is the only element that Brabantio can produce as evidence against Othello. The duke and the Senate thus have to weigh the evidentiary value of the diabolical script of blackness, and they find it wanting:

> To vouch this is no proof
> Without more wider and more overt test
> Than these thin habits and poor likelihoods
> Of modern seeming do prefer against him. (1.3.108–11)

The duke discards the association of black-up with the diabolical as insufficient, but not without commenting on its popularity first (it is "of modern seeming"). In other words, Iago does not invent the diabolical script of blackness; he simply orients Brabantio's white male gaze in that direction. By placing this skill in the hands of a Machiavellian character whose vengeful intentions are transparent to the audience, the play directs our attention to how easily the diabolical script of blackness can be mobilized for strategic purposes and nefarious ends. The Senate's verdict in favor of Othello counters Iago's scheme, and what is commonly regarded as the comedic section of the play, its first act, coincides with a debunking of the fallacious associative logic proper to the diabolical script of blackness.

The tragic section of the play is powered by Iago's shrewd redirection of his hermeneutic skills. Overcoming his failure at framing black-up as diabolical for the white male gaze in the Senate, Iago launches a successful attempt at framing whiteface—specifically, Desdemona's whiteface—as diabolical. The moment a skilled semiotician with theatrical flair redirects the preferred meaning that early modern English racecraft had given to blackness for the last twenty years toward a white woman, she dies. In that moment of transfer from a black man to white woman, in its fleeting detachment from the organic matter of bodies, the scopic branch of racecraft becomes visible, as if to invite analysis.

Iago flaunts his ability to orient the white male gaze in relation to blackness and whiteness alike in act 2, scene 1, when Desdemona asks him to praise her. Producing "old fond paradoxes" to demean women who are, respectively, "black and witty," "fair and foolish," "foul and foolish," and fair and witty, Iago programmatically implies that, with the right rhetorical tools, all women, be they fair or dark-skinned, ultimately can be construed as "whores" and treated as such. This interaction was intended by Desdemona as an interlude to distract her from worrying about Othello's fate at sea; it unveils the full extent of Iago's misogyny, but just as importantly, it discloses his ability to frame cosmetic whiteness and blackness as equally damnable. The interlude thus functions as a miniaturized *mise en abîme* of Iago's expert manipulation of the diabolical script of blackness and whiteface throughout the play.

From that scene onward, the play unfolds another trial, in which Desdemona, by acting as a "solicitor" defending Cassio's "cause" (3.3.37–28), unwittingly turns herself into a culprit. During her trial, her theatrical whiteface is weighed as evidence against her and found sufficient; Desdemona is condemned and executed as a "fair devil" (3.3.485). The irony of the situation is that, by successfully orienting Othello's gaze, Iago is having the Moor read the world through the same white male gaze that first scrutinized him. It is commonly accepted that Othello falls because he unwittingly internalizes a white male gaze, or as Ania Loomba puts it, "Othello is a victim of racial beliefs precisely because he becomes an agent of misogynist ones."[55] I would add that the continuity between racist and misogynist beliefs at the core of Iago's white male gaze shows in the continuity between the concrete forms of denigration to which Moors and women are subjected—first among them, the diabolical hermeneutics of cosmetics.

Iago uses a variety of tactics—such as producing false testimonies (about Cassio) and fabricating material evidence (the handkerchief)—to indict the innocent, but framing bodily signs is, without a doubt, his strongest suit. He frames Desdemona's bodily signs in general as deceitful, when he mentions to Othello that

> She did deceive her father marrying you;
> And when she seemed to shake and fear your looks,
> She lov'd them most . . .
> She that, so young, could give out such a seeming. (3.3.221–24)

The deceitfulness of Desdemona's bodily signs crystalizes in one particular body part: her fair skin, performed by means of cosmetic whiteface. As is well known, anticosmetic sentiment was an integral part of both misogynistic and antitheatrical discourses in early modern England. Not only was theatrical whiteface deceitful in that it helped boy actresses pass as girls; it also carried the heavy cultural perceptions associated with women's cosmetic practices offstage.[56] As Dympna Callaghan puts it, makeup was associated with sex workers, and "it was because of their power to beautify that the red and white were assumed to be a form of hypocrisy, misleading men by feigning a beauty that women did not really possess."[57] For boy actresses, as Andrea Stevens notes, "the habitual use of cosmetics did indeed permanently injure the skin" given the high toxicity of the chemicals involved, and we might "wonder whether actors were marked by their trade in the way that tanners bore the visual evidence of their profession even unto death."[58] In that case, whiteface gave boy actresses "a beauty they did not really possess" or soon would not possess any longer.

I would consider yet another source of deceitfulness: while the diluted red used on the boy actresses' cheeks could read as artificial blushing, the thick layer of white makeup used as foundation would hide the performer's blushing as efficiently as black-up. The obfuscation of the physical manifestations of shame by real or cosmetic blackness was often construed as an indication of African shamelessness in Renaissance drama; by the same logic, whiteface could also be construed as a sign of female shamelessness, a characteristic proper to "whores." It is no coincidence that the only other woman who is called "fair" in the play is a sex worker: Bianca, the "most fair Bianca" (3.4.165), whose very name evokes whiteface. *Othello*'s plot depends on the cosmetic techniques of the early modern stage in that the multiple forms of deceitfulness attached to the leading boy actress's whiteface are the foundations on which Iago can build his case against the fair Desdemona.

The "pearl" Desdemona is called fair at least ten times in the play (e.g., 5.2.357). Her fairness is a defining feature of her physical appearance: it saturates both the rhetoric of the play and the boy actress's makeup. Thus Iago does not even need to explicitly attack Desdemona's complexion for Othello's mind to immediately turn to it when her honor is in doubt:

> Exchange me for a goat
> When I shall turn the business of my soul
> To such exsufflicate and blown surmises,
> Matching thy inference. 'Tis not to make me jealous
> To say my wife is fair, feeds well, loves company,
> Is free of speech, sings, plays, and dances well.
> Where virtue is, these are more virtuous. (3.3.195–201)

Fairness passes the test for now, yet it is the very first element that Othello mentions as a bodily sign that could alert a jealous husband to his wife's potential infidelity. As Iago's poison works on him, the fairness of her skin becomes, in his mind, the main sign of her duplicity. As Farah Karim-Cooper perceptively notes, "the face paints," for which Venetian ladies were famous, "probably confuses the issue further for Othello, who finds her increasingly impenetrable. . . . Prior to Othello's suspicions, Desdemona was just a noblewoman who more than likely used cosmetics, but now the paints on her face become evidence of her guilt."[59]

Othello ponders Desdemona's whiteness when he contemplates murdering her ("A fine woman, a fair woman, a sweet woman!" [4.1.167]), just before he murders her ("Yet I'll not shed her blood, / Nor scar that whiter skin of hers than snow, / And smooth as monumental alabaster" [5.2.3–5]), and after he has murdered her ("Ill starred wench! / Pale as thy smock" [5.2.281–82]). Scrutinizing her case means scrutinizing her complexion. Confronting her, Othello demands:

—Turn thy complexion there,
Patience, thou young and rose-lipped cherubin,
Ay, there look grim as hell. . . .
O thou weed,
Who art so lovely fair . . .
Would thou hadst ne'er been born! . . .
Was this fair paper, this most goodly book,
Made to write "whore" upon? (4.2.64–74)

In Othello's tilted frame, Desdemona's fairness, materialized by means of paper-white foundation and lip red, has turned black in the moral sense:

Her name, that was as fresh
As Dian's visage, is now begrimed and black
As mine own face. (3.3.403–5)

That moral blackness is described as diabolical just like black-up ("grim as hell"): Othello is reading Desdemona's whiteface through a diabolical script. Reading Desdemona as demonic authorizes physical violence against this "young and sweating devil" (3.4.36): it is no coincidence that he calls her a devil just before striking her in public (4.1.231)—indeed, as the French put it, *'tis fine to wrong the Devil*. Ultimately, the diabolical hermeneutics of whiteface allows Othello to murder his wife:

I will withdraw
To furnish me with some swift means of death
For the fair devil. (3.3.493–95)

Demonizing Black people and demonizing white women are not mutually exclusive moves; on the contrary, they are continuous and, as Kim F. Hall shows in *Things of Darkness*, mutually dependent within the white male gaze. Given the antithetical symbolism of black and white, there is, however, a contradiction between demonizing blackness and whiteness. Thus, I suggest that, by expending his demonizing efforts indifferently around black-up and whiteface, Iago unwittingly alerts spectators to the fact that this demonizing rhetoric can be used to argue literally one thing and its opposite, and, by so doing, hints at some of its internal contradictions. In other words, if the diabolical script of face painting, applied to both black men and white women, manifests the presence of a unified white male gaze behind Iago, its indifferent treatment of the black and white antithesis suggests that major inconsistencies might be at work within that gaze. There, I believe, lies the play's potential critique of the white male gaze.

That critique, however, does not cast any doubt on the power of the white male gaze, whose domination over the rest of the play remains absolute. This is particularly visible in the scene when Emilia discovers Desdemona's corpse and demonizes Othello:

Othello She's, like a liar, gone to burning hell:

   'Twas I that kill'd her.
Emilia O, the more angel she,
      And you the blacker devil!
Othello She turn'd to folly, and she was a whore.
Emilia Thou dost belie her, and thou art a devil.
Othello She was false as water.
Emilia Thou art rash as fire to say
      That she was false. O, she was heavenly true! (5.2.133–40)

In this exchange, Othello is reading Desdemona through the diabolical script of whiteface, while Emilia (performed in whiteface) deploys the diabolical script of blackness around him. The stylistic devices that structure this stichomythic exchange, built on syntactical and rhythmic parallelisms, emphasize the parallelism between the two characters' opposite hermeneutic frames. This agonistic moment exposes the portability of the demonizing rhetoric and the lack of substance inherent in the diabolical hermeneutic lens. And yet, at the same time, it ironically shows both a white woman and a black man ventriloquizing demonizing discourses produced by a white male gaze that oppresses them both and, embodied in the person of Iago, ultimately destroys them both. No more than Othello does Emilia, the early modern incarnation of white feminism, succeed at perceiving the continuity between misogynistic and racist oppression.

Iago's downfall notwithstanding, the denouement of the play stages the triumph of the white male gaze that he has served and oriented all along. That gaze survives him. *Othello* suggested pessimistically yet prophetically in 1604 that the demonizing rhetoric and the diabolical scripts produced by the white male gaze would remain in circulation. Indeed, after Iago's machinations are discovered, Othello redirects demonization toward him:

Lodovico Where is that viper? Bring the villain forth.
Othello I look down toward his feet; but that's a fable
    If that thou be'st a Devil, I cannot kill thee. . . .
    Will you, I pray, demand that demi-Devil
    Why he hath such ensnared my soul and body? (5.2.293–310)

The performative affinities between Iago and the Vice character of morality plays are well known and often used to substantiate Othello's reading of Iago as diabolical. Yet are we to trust a man who accused his wife of being the Devil just a moment earlier? It would be so satisfying if Iago were the Devil: then Shakespeare's decision to place the demonizing rhetoric in the Devil's mouth would read as an ironical indictment of the diabolical script of blackness itself. And that might very well be the case. But another reading of that final moment, focused on the troubling displacement of the demonizing rhetoric, provides a more sinister vision of the play.

Indeed, Othello, it seems, has not learned much from what happened to him, from the trial he underwent and from the trial through which he put Desdemona. Othello's anagnorisis is a layered process, since he has to first recognize Desdemona and Cassio as innocent and Iago as a villain to recognize himself as guilty.[60] However, that process of recognition remains incomplete to the extent that, while he realizes what his tragic predicament is, he does not realize how it came to be. He does ask *why* Iago "thus ensnared [his] soul" (5.2.310) and, famously, never gets a real answer, but he does not ask the question he should be asking: *how*? Even in his last monologue, in which he tries to frame his own story, Othello merely designates himself as "wrought" and "perplexed in the extreme" and stops short of providing any real explanation (5.2.356). "What you know, you know," Iago frustratingly states; yet the most frustrating element of those final instants might very well be what Othello does *not* know. He does not know that Iago perplexed him by making him read Desdemona through a script produced by the white male gaze to demonize women and Afro-diasporic people alike. He does not know that Iago perplexed him by wielding racecraft. If Othello's anagnorisis had included the operations of racecraft, he would not wield the white male gaze's instrument against anyone at that point; he would stay away from the pernicious diabolical script that relies on thin "seemings," on purely associative logic, and that authorizes physical violence. Iago is bedeviled, and not only by Othello: as he orders for Iago to be tortured, Lodovico, who utters the final lines of the play and restores order, calls him a "damnèd villain" (5.2.325) and "a hellish villain" (5.3.379).

Surely, there is something diabolical about Iago. Still, his demonization is the final stroke in a larger pattern, and the continued circulation of diabolical hermeneutics by protagonists who should know better by the end of the play transfers the didactic onus from characters onto spectators. Ian Smith has shown that Othello's final monologue places the responsibility to speak of Othello as he is and "nothing extenuate" (5.2.352) onto spectators: "Othello understands that, given the play's imperial geopolitics, the members of his immediate audience will revert to seeing in his blackness the enemy "Turk" within, an identity and status that will require rigorous unpacking and thoughtful explanation. In the play's closing moments, therefore, unable to ultimately exercise his own narrative agency, Othello will have to delegate and entrust that responsibility elsewhere."[61] It seems to me that spectators are entrusted to "unpack" Othello's story for him not only because he is about to die, but also because he failed to unpack it rigorously himself. Spectators are trusted to draw the lessons that Othello could not, and to reflect on the diabolical scripts that caused his demise. The significance of that critique and of the interpretive responsibility it places on spectators and readers becomes manifest when we reckon with Anthony Gerard Barthelemy's observation that "between 1604 and 1687, *Othello* was in production no less than fourteen times" so that "no generation of seventeenth-century playgoers could not have seen the play in several revivals."[62] Othello and Smith remain skeptical about the outcome of that transfer—"among his white, Christian auditors, whom can [Othello] trust to tell his story or speak of him in a balanced way?"[63] I too wonder what or whether at all early modern spectators thought of the diabolical script of blackness or the white male gaze when they left the playhouse. Yet *Othello* was an invitation to reckon with the ideological efficacy and the lethal hermeneutic operations of scopic racecraft, and the present book means to answer Shakespeare's invitation.

Devil Begone: Black-Up, Commodities, and Slavery in Early Modern Spain

Othello's deployment of a diabolical script of blackness around an exceptional Afro-European Christian is uniquely English. Early baroque French drama does not dream of black Christians, and had Shakespeare's play been performed in Madrid in 1604, it would have given Spanish spectators pause, for the history of black-up in early baroque Spain consists in an active rejection of the diabolical script of blackness. Of the countries considered in this book, Spain was the first to associate performative blackness with the diabolical by scopic means, and also the first to relinquish that association. Early embrace and rejection are consistent with Spain's early involvement in color-based slavery and with the ideological needs specific to an economy that required the conditional inclusion of the enslaved into the enslaving body politic. In this final section, I account for the disappearance of the diabolical script of blackness in early modern Spain, and I explore the original script of blackness that thrived in its stead.

The *Códice de autos viejos* suggests that Spanish theatre scopically associated the diabolical with sub-Saharan identity decades before English and French theatres did. The *Códice* is the largest extant compilation of Castilian medieval theatre: ninety-six plays, most anonymous, compiled between 1550 and 1575, clearly early modern rewritings of medieval theatre (some of the plays allude to "Lutherans," for instance). In many of those plays, sixteenth-century theatrical practices are superimposed onto medieval dramaturgic traditions: such superimpositions apply in particular to the description of stage devils. For instance, in *Aucto de los hierros de Adan*, one lower-class demon is described as "black like jet" (negro como el azabache).[64] In one of the *Códice*'s plays, *Aucto de la paciencia de Job*, we see the inverted twin of the diabolical script of blackness: an Africanization of the blacked-up devils. As part of his efforts to ruin Job, the Devil tries to seduce his servant and take him into his service. The servant, a fool, is intrigued by his potential new master's appearance and asks:

> *Fool* Tell me, good sir, where were you born?
> *Satan* Why do you ask? Do I look bad to you?
> *Fool* Not so good either. You look all burned by
>   The sun or the air, and you don't mind
>   Walking around without a shirt.
> *Satan* Why shouldn't I, shepherd boy?
> *Fool* Ha, you're handsome, in truth! What short garments!
>   Are you from the court or from Guinea?[65]

The fool, whose foolishness is actually rooted in solid working-class common sense, immediately links the Devil's blackened skin, exposed by his short garments, to sub-Saharan Africans. By the second half of the sixteenth century, "Guinea" had become a synecdoche for West Africa, where Iberian traders enslaved people en masse. The term Guinea emerged as a result of fifteenth-century Iberian slave trade, and its insertion into the fool's mouth is one of the ways early modern culture inscribes itself over medieval materials in the *Códice*. As for the fool's allusion to "the court," it probably has to do with the fact that, in Madrid, most slave owners lived at court. Later in the same scene, the fool mentions Satan's horns: these make him kin with the devils of French medieval theatre. Yet this alignment of the Devil with his French medieval predecessors is disrupted by the racialized quality of the fool's perception of black-up:

> *Fool* And what is your name, good Sir?
> *Satan* I am Satan.
> *Fool* That's a fancy name: will I get a livery over there?
> *Satan* Serve me, brother, and you'll wear good clothes.
> *Fool* Brother? You, my brother? If my mother ever bore one like you
> Let me die with my clothes and boots on!
> My mother was white, and you are very dark
> She was perfect, and you are thick-lipped. . . .
> No, mister Satan, you have been deceived:
> I'd rather believe that a tailless cat bore you.[66]

The fool uses keywords such as "Guinea," "tapetado" (very dark), and the neologism "boquicumplido" (thick-lipped) to conflate the negatively inflected image of a sub-Saharan man with that of the Devil in the spectators' minds. Early modern conceptions of Africans permeate the *Aucto de la paciencia de Job* and inform its reconstruction of the medieval stage Devil.

The description of Africanized devils in the *Códice de autos viejos* illustrates the inseparability of Afro-diasporic characters from the social context of slavery in early modern Iberian culture. Indeed, María Luisa Mateo Alcalá has shown that the devils who are identified as "racially black" (de raza negra) in the *Códice* are often portrayed in a position of servitude: "in their hellish world, they function as servants to their diabolical lords, thus promising, perhaps, slavery to whoever yields to sin."[67] In *Farsa del triunfo del sacramento*, for instance, Pecado, Sin, is described by State of Innocence as a "negrillo" or "negrito." When he first appears onstage, Pecado is clearly described as the servant of Soberbia, Pride, who orders him to capture State of Innocence.[68] Pecado, however, is reluctant to fulfill the task, not out of moral qualms, but because, in his own words, he is "a timid coward with little heart." After upbraiding him copiously, Soberbia forces him to execute the mission by placing him under the surveillance of Engaño, Deceit.[69] Pecado the "negrillo" is thus described as a lazy subaltern devil who must be coerced into labor. The world of devils resembles the world of men. The play is not only injecting the early modern image of a man from *Guinea* into medieval material: it is also injecting the power structure in which enslaved Iberians lived in early modernity.

However, the Africanization of devils that we find in the *Códice* waned quickly, and—most importantly—its inverted twin, the scopic demonization of African characters, never took hold in Renaissance Spain. Devils are no longer Africanized in seventeenth-century religious theatre. One explanation for this is the evolution of the representation of the Devil in popular culture at large. Indeed, Teresa Ferrer Valls explains that, partly under the influence of the Trent Council, which banned the use of biblical materials for profane purposes, "the dimension of the Devil that was carnivalesque, popular, ugly, joking, amusing, playful, sometimes irreverential and also likeable was lost in seventeenth century drama."[70] Since early Afro-diasporic stock characters were conceived of as comedic characters because of their lower-class social status in Iberian societies, serious devils in seventeenth-century religious *autos* could hardly remain associated with them. As Peter Anthony Checca has shown, in Calderón's *autos sacramentales*, the Devil specializes increasingly in deceiving humans, rather than terrifying or amusing them. Seventeenth century Spanish religious theatre emphasized the idea that the Devil walks the earth among us, and, most of the time, we fail to recognize him. In this perspective, giving him the recognizable aspect of an Afro-diasporic man would have been counterproductive.[71] Arsenio Moreno Mendoza confirms that the Devil is not Africanized in commercial *comedias nuevas* either.[72] The disappearance of Africanized devils from Spanish theatrical culture around 1590 stands in stark contrast with France and England, where the diabolical script of blackness was just budding.

Another and more central explanation for the dissociation of blackness from diabolism at work in early modern Spanish theatre is the emphasis that the Catholic—first and foremost, the Jesuit—authorities put, continuously and increasingly throughout the *Siglo de Oro*, on the potential of Afro-Iberian Christianity across colonial empires. This vision built on *Las siete partidas*, which recognized the ensouled humanity of the enslaved (*siervos*) while sanctioning and regulating the institution of slavery; that code was still in effect in early modern Spain and its colonies. The importance of the Catholic Church's push in favor of integrating Afro-Spaniards into a religiously defined body politic registers early on in the sixteenth century, for instance in *Farsa teologal*, written by Diego Sánchez de Badajoz (a priest in addition to being a playwright) for Christmas celebrations at some point between 1520 and 1550. In *Farsa teologal*, a *negra* enters the stage "singing and drumming a jug" thereby interrupting a lengthy conversation between a shepherd and a theologian about points of

Catholic dogma.[73] The Afro-diasporic woman sings a Nativity hymn, to the great delight of the theologian, who marvels

> O sacred divine Word!
> O eternal mysteries!
> That you should reveal your ways
> even unto unschooled *negros* [*negros bozales*]![74]

The *negra*'s role is to manifest God's greatness. When, later in the play, her enslaver decides to change his ways and to become the good Catholic he should have been all along, he confesses to the theologian and the priest that he has failed to observe the duties of a Catholic master: his *negra* is not baptized.

> *Shepherd* [*To the negra*] Are you a Christian?
> *Soldier* Neither her nor he to whom she belongs.
> *Parish Priest* We have to talk about this.
>   This is unacceptable.
> *Soldier* I am a *moro* although I was baptized once.
>   As for her, I don't even know whether she is baptized.
> *Priest* But how does the Lord maintain you?! ...
>   She is not baptized?!
>   She lives among Christians, and yet she is a *mora*?!
>   [*To the negra*] Were you cleansed by water divine?
> *Negra* I have never *#washed myself with wine,
>   But with water, yes, sir, I *#have.[75]
> *Priest* We have to check this
>   To be absolutely sure,
>   Because that Sacrament
>   May not be bestowed twice.[76]

After giving the audience a refresher on how many times each sacrament may be administered, the priest orders the shepherd to teach the *negra* how to pray in Latin; and despite the shepherd's protestations that she speaks too poorly to learn anything, the priest insists: "I will teach her myself."[77] The resolution of this member of the Catholic clergy leads the shepherd to call her "my dark-skinned sister" (hermana prieta), and he even considers marrying her.[78] That moment dramatizes the influence of the Church's position vis-à-vis Afro-Spaniards. Sánchez de Badajoz's plays are peppered with gestures including

Afro-Spaniards within a religiously defined body politic; nowhere, however, is that gesture clearer than in *Farsa teologal*.[79]

A couple of decades later, in 1569, that concern expanded to the empire, as the king wrote to the archbishop of Lima that he had received certain reports from Peru according to which, in the colony, enslaved Afro-diasporic people were neither baptized nor catechized, and he asked the archbishop to attend to their religious education with as much zeal as he attended to the religious education of Indigenous subjects.[80] Berta Ares Queija hypothesizes that the reports received by the king came from Jesuits, who had focused their proselytizing efforts on the Afro-diasporic community as soon as they had arrived in Peru in 1568. Converting the enslaved was a necessity, for bringing true Faith to heathens was the official justification of slavery and imperial expansion. The importance of spreading Catholicism was often invoked as ethical cover for the economic imperative of replenishing the imperial labor force after Charles V and Pope Paul III forbade the enslavement of Indigenous Americans in the 1530s.[81] It is in the wake of this long-standing missionary activity that I read the famous repository of Jesuit rhetoric *De instauranda aethiopum salute* by Alonso de Sandoval, who spent his life baptizing and catechizing some forty thousand enslaved people in Cartagena, Colombia. The six-hundred-page compendium was completed by 1624, first printed in Seville in 1627, and reprinted in Madrid with significant changes in 1647.[82] Sandoval arrived in Cartagena in 1604 and started working in the "*negros'* ministry" (ministerio de los morenos) in 1607: *De instauranda aethiopum salute* formalizes twenty years of thinking and preaching, which developed not in a vacuum, but in a Jesuit missionary intellectual tradition that had started in the 1560s.[83] In other words, Sandoval's book was first published in 1627, but it was the culmination of a late sixteenth-century Jesuit sensibility. Sandoval belonged to a community concerned with the lack of proper Catholic education with which most enslaved Afro-diasporic people arrived in the Indies. Indeed, since Charles I of Spain, soon to become Charles V, had decreed in 1518 that enslaved people brought to the colonies directly from Africa (without transiting through the Iberian peninsula) had to become Christian by the time they reached the Indies, they had to be baptized before Iberians could purchase them, which often led slave traders to expedite baptisms in Africa in ways that emptied the sacrament of its meaning. *De instauranda aethiopum salute* was meant to solve that problem. The book compiles ethnographic, theological, and social data about Afro-diasporic people in the Iberian empire and offers a method for properly catechizing and baptizing enslaved Afro-diasporic people. Sandoval's goal is to save the souls of the enslaved by including them in the imperial Catholic community. In his prologue to the reader, he writes: "Our Lord Jesus Christ had great esteem for those people [*negros*], showing us that His majesty can and will set fire to charcoals and turn them into live coals that radiate light. . . . Since the souls of those black and miserable sinners are so black that they can easily compare with charcoals: it seems that His radiance and divine fire burn with more strength and efficiency when they inflame and convert those dark ugly coals into fine rubies."[84] Conversion is both a spiritual and an alchemical transformation here, from coal into rubies. Sandoval is running a baroque metaphor: because Afro-diasporic people are "charcoal," they can easily be set ablaze with God's flame. In order to promote the baptism and catechizing of the enslaved, Sandoval is suggesting that Afro-diasporic people will make exceptionally good members of the imperial Catholic community—if missionary readers apply the Jesuit method.

The cultural diffusion of that idea is evident when we compare Sandoval's phrase to an excerpt from Lope de Vega's saint play *El negro del mejor amo* (1599–1608). In this play, Antiobo, the son of the Moorish prince of Algiers and a dark-skinned Ethiopian princess, having had a Christian nurse as a child, takes pity on the Christian captives in Algiers, turns on his family and kingdom, and returns the Christian captives to Sardinia. There, he converts, becomes a saint, and sacrifices himself to save Sardinia from a Turkish invasion. Antiobo declares:

> [I am] not stained, but rather cleansed
> By the blood of One, who, despite my blackness
> Has paid the ransom for my redemption.
> God made me of coal
> So that even the tiniest spark
> Of His holy inspiration
> Might set my heart ablaze
> In an instant.[85]

Lope de Vega could not have read Sandoval's prologue when he wrote this scene, but the resemblance between the two passages signals that the metaphor of the blazing charcoal on which Sandoval drew was part of a discourse on the potential of Afro-diasporic Catholicism that preexisted his work and was popular enough by the end of the sixteenth century to find its way onto the stage.[86]

Concern for the value of Afro-diasporic Catholicism circulated fluidly between the colonies and the metropole. For instance, between 1613 and 1614, the archbishop of Seville, Pedro de Castro y Quiñones, who was also a jurist, asked for the testimonies of several slave-ship captains about how enslaved Afro-diasporic people were baptized along the Guinea River and the Cacheo River before being purchased. These testimonies led him to the same conclusions as Sandoval, with whom he may have corresponded at the time.[87] That is, enslaved Africans were baptized without giving their consent, without receiving catechism, and without receiving an explanation about the meaning of baptism in a language they understood. Thus, the archbishop published an edict ordering all the curates of his archdiocese to question the Afro-Spaniards in their parishes about their baptism. The edict came with a method for conducting the interrogation.[88] Many Afro-Spaniards received baptism anew based on the results of this investigation, and they came to be known as *rebautizados* (the rebaptized). The timing of the massive (re)conversion operation launched by the archbishop of Seville suggests that it may have had to do with anxieties generated by the rhetoric accompanying the ongoing expulsion of *moriscos*, but it was also informed by the sixteenth-century Jesuit discourse on *negros*.

An overwhelming majority of early modern commercial plays starring Afro-diasporic characters have their action set either in Spain or in the Spanish empire and show characters who have been baptized and thus are part of the same Catholic community as spectators, albeit in a subaltern position. The fact that Afro-diasporic characters emphatically belonged to the same religious community as spectators must have made it difficult to demonize them.[89] If the Devil cannot be assimilated and always threatens to tear the social fabric of a Christian society, Catholic Afro-Spaniards simply could not read as devils, and this manifested in the new scripts developed to reconfigure the hermeneutics of black-up on stage.

The process of conceptually dissociating blackness from the diabolical is explicitly dramatized in the genre of the black saint play popularized by Lope de Vega, which emphasizes the disconnection between Afro-diasporic people's skin color and the color of their souls. Undermining attempts at moralizing phenotype, this move preempts the use of the diabolical script of blackness. Lope makes this move most strikingly in *El sancto negro Rosambuco de la ciudad de Palermo* (ca. 1607), a play that dramatizes the life of St. Benedict the Moor, a well-known sixteenth century Sicilian saint and patron saint among African American Catholics today. In the early modern period, Sicily was part of the Spanish Empire. In Lope's play, Rosambuco, a Turkish Ethiop captured at sea, is enslaved and serves in the household of a Sicilian gentleman, Lesbio. Following supernatural injunctions by Christ and St. Benedict, he converts to

Catholicism. Signs suggest early on that he has been chosen by God to manifest His glory, and so, Rosambuco joins the Franciscan monastery Jesus del Monte. Following the pattern initiated in *El negro del mejor amo* by which all subsequent black saint plays would abide, *El sancto negro* disconnects its convert protagonist's phenotype from his soul.[90] Rosambuco is described as particularly dark-skinned, darker than the enslaved *negra* Lucrecia, who, her mistress comments, does not sport "as much soot and paint."[91] To achieve this visual effect, the actor must have been covered with a conspicuously thick and dark layer of cosmetics. Rosambuco is scopically constructed as particularly dark to emphasize the bleaching effect of grace following Catholic baptism:

> Already, within my breast I can feel
> The new delights that afford me bravery,
> Courage, and inspiration.
> Ah perverse Quran!
> I intend to abandon your lies:
> Now I seek my glory,
> Now I long to be a Christian,
> Now I rejoice with this new law.
> A white soul within a black body![92]

While at the beginning of the play the darkness of Rosambuco's skin aligned with the darkness of his Muslim soul, his conversion to Catholicism washes his soul white and thus disrupts the alignment between physical appearance and spirituality. Catholics can be of all skin tones because all Catholic souls are white, the play says. Indeed, after his baptism, Rosambuco prays, and God promises him via the stage musicians that "although you are black, one day, you will be fair, handsome, and white" (bello, hermoso y blanco)."[93] Commenting on the whiteness of Rosambuco's future heavenly body, God confirms that the saint's soul has just been whitewashed.

Lope de Vega's black saint plays use cosmetics in ways that echo the dominant Catholic perception of Afro-diasporic bodies and souls as disconnected upon baptism. In doing so, those plays could be seen, to use John Beusterien's terminology, as "de-narrativizing" black-up, that is to say, as disconnecting blackness from any historical, cultural, or religious etiology.[94] We get only a partial picture, though, by assuming that this perception, just because it did not moralize phenotype, was liberating. Denarrativization is always a renarrativization. The Catholic theology that informed this perception of dark skin as immaterial at

the end of the sixteenth century was coterminous with a strong investment in
the material sub-Saharan body in which Spaniards could indulge guilt-free
once that body was separated from its soul. Sandoval himself partook in the
obsession, by making in his treatise many references to the "ugliness" and
"deformities" of the very people he wanted to include in the imperial body
politic.[95]

This obsession with the fleshliness of the sub-Saharan body emerges in *El
sancto negro* when Rosambuco, tasked with exorcising the viceroy's daughter,
invokes God's power to free the young white girl from diabolical forces, and the
Devil answers through her mouth:

> You can't,
> You stupid sooty *negro*—
> You are so ugly that I want to run away. . . .
> Neither you, nor the heavens, nor God himself
> Suffice against me. Can't they see
> Your pig snout,
> Your jet, your smut,
> And the black frying pan that you are?
> "*I am a #*negro* *from Angola, and I *want to take you out
> Of #the little Miss" Ha! Why don't you take this instead!
> *(She gives him the finger.)*[96]

The ideological ambivalence of this paragraph is vertiginous. The passage proves
that Spaniards like Pedrisco who equate Afro-diasporic Catholics with the
Devil are wrong; it proves that Rosambuco has been chosen by God to be
His champion, but it also reinforces severe aesthetic prejudices against Afro-
diasporic bodies in a cruel comedic way. The audience most probably laughed at
the Devil's race jokes. This scene effaces the difference of the sub-Saharan body
and yet compulsively emphasizes it. The play is obsessed with the materiality of
Afro-diasporic bodies, comparing them to animal parts, cooking utensils, and
gemstones. The belief that dark skin is spiritually immaterial and the obsession
with the materiality of dark bodies are two sides of the same coin. The partition
between body and soul instated by the Catholic Church, by making the soul
the only important thing in God's eyes, left the earthly body prey to men's
rule and desires. In an age of slavery, this was not a neutral move. It left Afro-
diasporic material bodies available as commodities fit for desire, purchase, trade,
and consumption. Even at its most optimistic about Afro-diasporic souls, Spanish

theatre participated in the widespread reification of Afro-diasporic bodies. In light of this ambivalence and of the scripts of blackness it yields, I am less inclined than other scholars to read the black hagiographic tradition that Lope de Vega brings to the stage reparatively, as a force of liberation in the early modern racial struggle.[97]

None of this should come as a surprise, for the ideological inclusion of Afro-diasporic people into the religiously defined body politic was itself embedded in a larger cultural drive toward materialism. Indeed, the last few pages of the 1627 version of Sandoval's compendium are an important reminder that the cultural intervention of the Catholic Church in favor of Africans was not a disinterested humanitarian act. They articulate explicitly the mercantile ethos of the colonial project in which Jesuit missionaries—who were prominent slave owners in the colonies—participated.[98] There, Sandoval uses the metaphor of the pearl to describe enslaved Afro-diasporic people as simultaneously spiritual and commercial commodities: "The sovereign Merchant of the Gospel, whose urgent desire is to bring, in the East and the West, pearls of great value (who are souls redeemed with His blood) out of the coarse and ugly shells of black and Indian bodies, has put in the Indies religious men [Jesuits], who plunge like divers into the deep and into a sea of difficulties to collect them."[99] Depicting Jesus himself as a merchant, Sandoval—who, as Larissa Brewer-García has shown, was particularly invested in framing Africans as "spiritually venerable but enslaveable"—proudly lays out the mercantilist ethos that fuels his project.[100] The pearl metaphor that he uses fuses colonial economic interests and missionary zeal at the expense of nonwhite bodies—it merges the interests of white people and the interests of God. The church had a vested interest in including Afro-diasporic people in its fold, for it partook in the same mercantile practices and worldview that would propel the emergence of the next great hermeneutic configuration of black-up. That hermeneutic configuration hinged on a new script of blackness: no longer spiritual, the script was mercantile.

What I call *the commodifying script of blackness* pushed spectators to read black-up as indicative of the commodity status of a character, in line with the ideological demands of a slavery-based economy. Such an economy requires not the exclusion dynamics that the diabolical script of blackness rehearsed in early baroque France and England but rather a conditional inclusion of the enslaved into the enslaving society in a subaltern position. The slave-owning early modern Spanish society needed the discourse of racism as Immanuel Wallerstein defines it: "a mode of inclusion but of inclusion at inferior ranks ... [that] exists to justify the lower ranking, to enforce the lower ranking, and perversely even,

to make it somewhat palatable to those who have the lower ranking."[101] The
commodifying script of blackness was the performative arm of that discourse.
Across dramatic genres, animalizing metaphors, foodstuff metaphors, and luxury goods metaphors (three sub-scripts that all fall under the rubric of commodities) were deployed around Afro-diasporic characters. Those metaphors
were mixed, matched, and often wielded against one another to frame and reframe cosmetic blackness by different characters with different effects. Animal
and food metaphors often served to put Afro-diasporic characters with social
aspirations back in their place, while metaphors of luxury goods helped them
claim some privileges. This last sub-script is often strategically mobilized by
characters who understand the system in which they live and seek to exercise
their agency within it—characters who use the master's hermeneutic tools to
try and dismantle the master's house.

    In short, the commodifying script of blackness is a spectrum that ranges
from animals to food to luxury metaphors, and the racial struggle of early modern Afro-Spaniards maps onto that spectrum. Although the corpus I use to
bring this spectrum to light is necessarily limited, I contend that this analytical
model extends beyond this corpus, to Siglo de Oro theatre at large. Attending
to that spectrum is a critical gesture that can move the field of early modern
Hispanic race studies in new directions: rather than ask whether early modern
Iberian culture had room for positive literary and artistic representations of
Blackness (which of course it did: how could such a rich, nuanced, and capacious globalized culture *not* have room for them?), I ask instead, inspired by
Critical Race Theory: how did early modern Hispanic systemic racism—like
any systemic racism at any point in space and time—integrate positive representations of Afro-diasporic people and Black agency optimally for its own purposes? In part, through scripts of blackness.

    Animalization, as Robert Hornback recently showed, was one strategy
within overarching trans-European patterns of comedic representation that associated Afro-diasporic people with the stunted intellect of natural fools from
the mid-fifteenth century onward. Yet the connotations of animalization are
not restricted to the domain of rationality; they also articulate a narrative of
domestication justifying slavery.[102] Indeed, as Erica Fudge notes, in early modern anthropocentric thinking, "an animal (like most women) does not have the
right to own property; animals can only *be* property."[103] The implications of
that second clause are tremendous for early modern Afro-Spaniards. To be animalized is to lose one's claim to life, one's claim to freedom—to be to be turned
into property, or chattel. As Antonio Santos Morillo reminds us, in the inven-

tories compiled by Renaissance notaries, enslaved Afro-Spaniards were listed among animals.[104] Animalization dehumanizes Afro-Spanish characters, establishes an empathy gap, and inscribes characters whose real-life counterparts overwhelmingly lived in urban settings into the domestic sphere. The poetics of animalization deployed around black-up attaches Afro-Spaniards to households like black pets or pests.

Sánchez de Badajoz's *Farsa teologal*, as previously discussed, dramatizes the influence of the Catholic Church in the undemonization of Afro-Spanish characters and their real-life counterparts and, in the same breath, participates in the rise of the animalizing paradigm within the commodifying script of blackness. Indeed, passing allusions to the diabolical (undermined by the exasperation of the characters uttering them) soon yield to the pervasive script of animalization.[105] As soon as he enters, the soldier-master calls his *negra* "a bitch" (perra).[106] At the end of the play, the shepherd proposes to the *negra* with her enslaver's blessing, but she rejects his proposal (for she is already married and knows that, like or unlike baptism, that sacrament may not be bestowed twice). The vengeful shepherd asks the soldier and the priest

> You two, just for fun's sake,
> Would you mind doing me a favor?
> Let's toss up that lowlife![107]

The verb translated as "tossing up" here, *mantear*, referred to "a playful skit usually performed with dogs during Carnival," in which a dog was wrapped in a blanket and violently tossed up and down through the city's streets.[108] While that ritual could be inflicted on humans, it was defined in relation to dogs. By making this suggestion, the shepherd animalizes the *negra*, and she picks up immediately on the insult as she engages in a physical fight with him (which she comically wins). After the priest intervenes and commands them to reconcile, the shepherd agrees to embrace her, and—for the second time in the play—he calls her a "cockroach" (escarabajo) as he does so.[109] While the comparison with a dog includes the *negra* in the economy of domestic slavery, the final comparison with a cockroach allows the shepherd to construe the Afro-diasporic presence in the Iberian Peninsula as an infestation.

Sánchez de Badajoz launched a fashion: animalizing black women was all the rage in sixteenth-century Spanish theatre, for instance in works by Jaime de Huete or Feliciano da Silva.[110] Lope de Rueda, however, had the dubious privilege of solidifying and enriching the trope. In *Comedia llamada Eufemia*, the white servant Polo courts the *negra* Eulalla and tries to convince her to leave her enslaver's household, run away with him, and marry him. Eulalla, who is coquettish and has a couple of options besides Polo for marriage purposes, dreams of improving her social status and asks him to give her pets that would signal her new status as a well-off *señora* first: "*a parrot so I might *teach it how to speak in its cage, and a female monkey so I might *have it at my door, like #well-off ladies do."[111] Eulalla does not realize that Polo's intention, as soon as she follows him, is to "sell her first thing, pretending that she is my slave."[112] Calling her a "greyhound bitch" (galga) behind her back,[113] Polo makes it clear that Eulalla's dreams will not materialize: as an enslaved Afro-Spaniard, Eulalla can only *be* the exotic pets she aspires to own—whether it be a prattling caged bird or a monkey-in-waiting.[114]

The animalizing script of blackness coexisted in Siglo de Oro performance culture with other commodifying sub-scripts of blackness predicated on metaphors of food and luxury goods. In performance, these three sub-scripts were often mixed, matched, and contrasted. As early as Lope de Rueda's early sixteenth-century *Comedia llamada de los engañados*, an Afro-Spanish woman had been called "face of uncooked asparagus"—for deep purple asparagus turns green when cooked at length.[115] But in response to the intensification of the slave trade across the empire, seventeenth-century theatre made an exponential use of the burlesque foodstuff script that so vividly articulated dynamics of consumption and absorption. Indeed, by the time Lope de Vega wrote his most successful comedias, the Afro-diasporic presence in Spain, fueled by slavery, was increasing and would not drop before the middle of the eighteenth century.[116] The number of Afro-Spaniards was booming in Andalusian cities such as Granada, Cádiz, Malaga, and Seville. Spain and its empire consumed enslaved people voraciously, and the idea of consumption constitutes the ideological subtext of the foodstuff script that theatre often uses to indexically close the meaning of black-up. Likening body parts to delicious and exotic comestibles, food poetics, via the power of analogical thinking, narrativizes Spanish society's mechanisms of consumption, absorption, and elimination of enslaved people. Whether they strengthened or poisoned it, Afro-Spaniards became part of a body politic that could not sustain itself without them. Siglo de Oro theatre thus captured what Gitanjali Shahani calls "the colonial histories and racial formations by which people become food, by which subjects become edible objects."[117]

Diego Jiménez de Enciso provides a formidable example of that script of consumption in the final scene of *Comedia famosa de Juan Latino*, which he may have written in the early 1620s.[118] In this scene, Juan Latino, the exceptional Afro-diasporic scholar inspired by a historical figure, graduates in the presence of the archbishop, the Duke of Sesa, and Don Juan of Austria—who instantiate, respectively, religious, social, and political authority.[119] Juan receives his doctorate, which will allow him to take the prestigious position he has been awarded at the Cathedral of Granada. The ceremony includes a *vexamen*—literally, a vexation—that is, the public ritual early modern Spanish doctoral candidates had to undergo to receive their degree, during which a peer read a satire of the candidate's personal shortcomings. Castillo, Juan's good friend, thus offers a burlesque portrait of the graduate, which begins with scholarly themed furniture metaphors (comparing Juan to a desk and inkpot). Castillo gradually shifts his focus from Juan's intellect to his body. Castillo proceeds and soon uses comestible tropes:

> Listen to me, Proto-*negro*,
> The best of all your caste,
> Listen to me, you red wine decanter
> Listen to me, you rotten fig
> Listen to me, you stocking dye
> Listen to me, you prune,
> Listen to me, you Benedictine slipper
> Listen to my *merry jest*—and jest with me,
> Even if your color
> Is not *berry*, but *jest*-nut! . . . [120]
> Master Hood writes in
> His learned Miscellanies
> That, one day, as certain goddesses
> Of this region
> Were passing by,
> Dame Nature invited them in.
> It was a Saturday, and, to her chagrin,
> She had nothing to offer them,
> So she started cooking tripe—
> Some say it was beef tripe.
> In her wisdom, Nature
> Took a big sausage
> Into which she threw
> Letters, languages, and various essences,

Nominative cases, gerunds,
In short, all of Grammar,
Theology, and the arts.
But she threw in too much hot black pepper,
So when the sausage cooked,
It burst open like a horse blanket.
Minerva, the goddess of war,
Knowing that the fair Duke of Sesa
Is the king of arms,
Sent the sausage to his house.
There it has been hanging from the fireplace,
For as many years as you can see on that face,
Without ever being released,
For sausages can be enslaved too. . . .
O you Latinate *chorizo*![121]

The metaphor of Juan Latino as a "chorizo" peppered with humanistic knowledge and Black heat is the grandiose culmination of a list of dark-colored
foods—wine, fig, prune, chestnut, berry—that metaphorically turn both Juan's
mind and his body into delicious comestible commodities. The image of Juan
Latino as a tripe or blood sausage carries strong phallic connotations (especially
when the sausage "bursts open" under the effect of heat), as well as fecal ones.
Those phallic and fecal connotations endow the image with a grotesque dimension that, as Mikhail Bakhtin defines it, puts into play the body's lower stratum,
its processes of appetence, absorption, and elimination.

The commodifying foodstuff script was capacious: it contained ideologically meaningful subnarratives. For instance, it could narrativize who exactly
had the right to consume enslaved Afro-Spaniards. Calderón de la Barca, who
knew *Comedia famosa de Juan Latino*, wrote an interlude called *Shrovetide (Las
carnestolendas)*—performed between 1646 and 1652.[122] That interlude reminds
us that only Catholics were allowed to consume enslaved people in early modern Spain. In it a *gracioso* offers to perform the role of a *negro*. His costume is
ready: his face "looks like blood pudding," and he is wearing "burgundy bon-
net" as a wig.[123] The reference to blood pudding echoes the vexamen in *Juan
Latino* and turns the *negro* into a commodity that can be consumed only by
Christians—for blood pudding is made of pork blood. That cultural understanding ran deep enough for *Comedia famosa de Juan Latino* to publicly re-

hearse it: when the Duke of Sesa announces to the Muslim-descended *morisco* community the new cultural prohibitions formulated against them by the crown, he tells them that "they may not own male or female black slaves."[124] The food paradigm could also articulate a colonial narrative of black slavery. For instance, in *El yerro del entendido*—first performed in 1660[125]—a Creole *mulata* woman (criolla) from Caracas sees her "brown complexion" (color pardo) compared to "marmalade" and "cane in bright red wine," and her hard hands are compared to "sweet potatoes."[126] Hormigo reuses the wine image used by Castillo in his vexamen, but he compares the body parts of a *mulata* woman from Venezuela to distinctly American comestibles.

Different subscripts of blackness do different ideological work. In early modern Spanish theatre, while the animal script and the foodstuff script are often deployed to squash Afro-Spanish characters' social aspirations within a slave society, the luxury script frames black-up with the opposite effect. As was the case with animalizing and foodstuff metaphors, comedia nueva developed, multiplied, and popularized an interpretive paradigm sporadically present in sixteenth century *farsas* in response to socioeconomic and cultural changes—namely, in response to a new ideological need for racial success stories.[127] The luxury script likens dark skin to jet (*azabache*), gems (joya), or jasper and ebony (ebano y jaspe).[128] It is extended around characters of beautiful, virtuous, and allegorical Ethiopian queens untouched by slavery, as well as exceptional enslaved Afro-diasporic men whose distinction—spiritual, intellectual, or personal—is explicitly construed as a sign of internal whiteness. The latter often participate actively in their own commodification along the lines of the luxury paradigm in an attempt to seize on the privileges attached to this sub-script.[129]

The deliberate participation of those exceptional men in the deployment of the luxury paradigm is observable in Andrés de Claramonte y Corroy's *El valiente negro en Flandés*, which follows the itinerary of Juan, an Afro-Spaniard born in Merida, Extremadura.[130] Juan is an extremely ambitious young man who, born in slavery, refuses to follow the advice given by Doña Juana, his enslaver, to remain a water seller in Merida. Juan dreams of becoming a hero: he enlists in the army and leaves for the front in the Low Countries. In the army, he encounters deep-seated racism and fights his way to the top. On the front, he accomplishes great deeds; notably, he captures William of Orange, earning Spaniards one of their greatest victories. Impressed by his valor, the Duke of Alba takes Juan under his protection: he takes him to Madrid to meet the king, who thanks him personally for his service, gives him a competent pension, and

promotes him to "maestre de campo."[131] Juan is greeted as a hero at home,
where, in his new glory, he fixes the romantic subplot of the play, which involves
the honor of the white women in his household, Doña Leonor and Doña Juana.
He redresses the wrongs of the former and marries the latter, who, again, is his
former enslaver. Because it focuses on a formerly enslaved black military hero
who secures royal preferment and a white wife, *El valiente negro en Flandés* begs
for comparison with *Othello*. Yet there is a major difference between the Spanish protagonist and his English counterpart: while Othello tragically relin-
quishes any attempt at framing his own complexion and thereby leaves that tool
in the hands of Iago, Juan actively competes with his own Iagos to control the
hermeneutic configuration of black-up. Claramonte's play dramatizes its protagonist's successful apprenticeship as a semiotician of blackness: Juan's climb-
ing the social ladder coincides with his successful use of the luxury script of
blackness.

Like any apprentice, Juan fails at first. In the opening scene, he quickly discovers that his rational arguments in favor of racial equality (monogenesis, climate theory, social determinism) do not reach his white antagonists. The
response that Juan gets from soldiers who will not let him enroll in the army is
frustrating: "Look: a *negro* holding a philosophical discourse! Why don't you
try holding a frying pan instead?"[132] Juan tries to bring the conversation back to
the argumentative track, but in vain: "Juan: We originate from the sun which
embraces us. / Second lieutenant: So you are coal with a soul, basically?"[133] This
is a turning point for Juan: the moment when he understands that, to win
this battle and get what he wants, he has to fight the battle on the same field as
his opponents, that is, on the field of metaphors that script blackness. He starts
speaking the soldiers' language: poetics. Using the common metaphors encountered both in Sandoval's work and in Lope's black saints' plays, he responds,
"Coal yes, and the kind of coal which, once enflamed, turns every spark into a
beam of light."[134] Thus warmed up, Juan rehearses metaphors of luxury goods
to defend the beauty of his color: "Jet finds its place on the most beautiful
throats. . . . The beautiful porphyry is black, as is ebony. . . . Pentarb is black that
protects against burning fire."[135] Yet the soldiers tersely answer: "We know the
qualities of blackness: it's a vile color in the presence of ivory."[136] A fight ensues,
and Juan has to run away. His first hermeneutic battle is lost, yet incrementally,
he hones his skills. By the end of the play, Juan can use poetic commodification
to his own advantage. When, having captured the Prince of Orange, he is invited to dine with the Duke of Alba and his noble prisoner, he orchestrates the
conversation thus:

Juan I obey you, and I sit down.
    I will now look like black jet
    Between two crystals.
Orange I would prefer your jet, Captain,
    To all the ivory that enriches me.[137]

Implying that he would trade his own whiteness for Juan's blackness, the Prince of Orange reverses the hierarchy between jet and ivory established by the soldiers in the opening scene.

While this successful apprenticeship correlates with and facilitates Juan's rise through the ranks and through Spanish social hierarchies, Claramonte's play reminds us that the luxury script of black commodification is part of a spectrum designed as a whole to affirm the status quo of color-based slavery in early modern Spain. At the beginning of act 2, while Juan and his own servant Antonillo are waiting to be introduced to the king, three courtiers start mocking them:

Don Pedro Look at those *negros*: what conspicuous figures. . . .
Don Francisco I have seen them waiting in this antechamber for the
    last two days.
Don Martin Look how gravely the dog perambulates!
Don Francisco And his servant matches his steps.
Don Pedro They must be worth three thousand *reales*, servant and
    master together.[138]

The courtiers then sneeze and fart at the two Afro-Spaniards to provoke them, until Juan fights them. The courtiers receive help; Juan and Antonillo survive only because the duke and the king interrupt the scene. Because of its affinities with the genre of the *entremés* (interlude), this scene is invested with a critical function. Indeed, not only does this scene have the scatological dimension of an entremés (something Fra-Molinero points out); it also has the length of one, and its insertion at the opening of act 3 resembles the natural location of an entremés in a comedia.[139] *Entremeses* as a genre often functioned as counterpoints to the main plot of the comedia they interrupted: they contradict or comment comically on some aspect of the play, disrupting the possibility for the performance to issue a totalizing message. This scene thus articulates a critique of the play's denouement and of the wish-fulfilling image of Spanish society as affording social mobility to Afro-Spaniards on the basis of individual merit by reminding spectators that the commodification of blackness was systemic. Indeed, as Cedric J. Robinson notes in *Black Marxism*, Juan Valiente, the historical figure on whom Claramonte's protagonist was based, may have been the first Afro-Spaniard to receive an *encomienda* (as reward for his valor in the colonial war against the Indigenous Araucanians of Chile), but "significantly enough, when he died in 1553 (killed in action against the Arauca), his old master Alonso Valiente had begun legal action to reclaim him and any property he had amassed."[140] Juan Valiente simply could not beat an entire system.

The discourse of black commodification could maintain itself as an all-dominating and pervasive ideological system precisely because, as a spectrum that included seemingly positive representations such as the luxury script, it offered grounds for contention, hustle, and individual struggle. That system came with built-in pressure outlets, that is, with poster boys and success stories for allegedly exceptional black subjects that made a slaving society look like a fair system of racial meritocracy. By the 1620s, that was the story Spanish society needed to tell and hear about itself, much more than old demonic stories of exclusion, and new scripts of blackness emerged to answer those needs.

CHAPTER 2

A Brief Herstory of Baroque Black-Up

Cosmetic Blackness, Gender, and Sexuality

Think on me,
That am with Phoebus' amorous pinches black,
And wrinkled deep in time.

Antony and Cleopatra, 1607

The feminization of black-up in high baroque theatre—which, for our purposes, refers to theatre produced between 1604 and the end of the seventeenth century—constitutes the single most important turn in the history of black-up in the Western world. Yet few subjects have been erased in scholarly discourse more than blacked-up female characters in early modern drama. In an influential essay, Lynda Boose argued that early modern Afro-diasporic women were, unlike their male counterparts, "unrepresentable" because the Western anxieties attached to their wombs required their suppression. For Boose, early modern literature "suppressed" or "repressed" narratives of interracial romance between Afro-diasporic women and white men because those women's ability to pass darkness on to their children disrupted patriarchal fantasies of parthenogenic reproduction that could dispense with mothers: "It is in the person of the Afro-diasporic woman that the culture's preexisting fears both about the female sex and about gender dominance are realized. Through her, all free-floating anxieties about 'the mother's dark place' contaminating the father's design for perfect self-replication become vividly literal."[1] While Boose is right that Afro-diasporic women's wombs fed anxieties that conditioned their aesthetic representation, Joyce Green MacDonald makes a cogent critique: "Boose's explanation seems to subsume racial difference entirely within gender difference. I am not convinced that the barring of Afro-diasporic women from representation was entirely the result of male patriarchal anxiety."[2] Those anxieties had less to do with fantasies of parthenogenesis than with the place of mixed-race children—whose relation to whiteness and to freedom was in flux—in socioracial hierarchies.

The wealth of materials reviewed in the present chapter leads me to depart from the current doxa about "the removal of dark-skinned women from representation," whether that removal take the form of absence, as Boose suggests, or of an always imperfect whitening of ancient and modern African queens, as MacDonald argues.[3] Focusing on performance leaves us no choice: it demands that we pay attention to the simulacrum of presence. Across Western Europe, Afro-diasporic women *were* performed in black-up very frequently in the seventeenth century, and the scripts of blackness deployed around those characters told spectators the stories of Afro-diasporic womanhood that they increasingly needed to hear. Those stories grappled with a taboo that was, indeed, unrepresentable: not Afro-diasporic women themselves, but the fact that, in the age of colonial expansion, those women were often sexually assaulted by white men within social, political, and economic structures that rewarded such acts of sexual violence. This gruesome reality, I argue, was systematically obfuscated on stage, as plays featuring black female characters redirected spectators' attention toward irrelevant and vacuous interrogations of Afro-diasporic women's desirability. Thus, I concur with MacDonald that early modern theatre deployed a concern with "the extent of whiteness's reliance on, and concomitant obsession with the sexual and laboring bodies of black people—perhaps especially of the Afro-diasporic women who are so conspicuously rare in the canon of Shakespeare's works and so essential in the maintenance of colonialist fictions of gender and racial identity."[4] But in view of newly excavated performance archives, we must reconsider the idea that this obsession or taboo expressed itself primarily through erasure from the stage in the seventeenth century.

The terms *allusion* and *displacement*, which MacDonald uses to describe representations of Afro-diasporic womanhood that evoke ideas of blackness around the bodies of white characters, are the most useful critical tools currently available to us. To build expansively upon those terms, I offer the capacious notion of *the oblique aesthetics of Afro-diasporic women's desirability*. *Obliqueness*, referring to the quality of that which is "not explicit or direct; not going straight to the point; indirectly stated or expressed; indirect," semantically sits at the intersection of physiological discourse (obliques are human muscles), premodern moral discourse (as in "diverging from right conduct or thought; perverse, aberrant"), and a grammatical discourse focused on the object position (as in "designating any case of a noun other than the nominative or the vocative").[5] A muscular body whose gender performance is always already deemed perverse and aberrant in an episteme where she features exclusively as the object of discourse, the desirable Afro-diasporic woman was obliquely represented on the early modern stage, and that obliqueness was glocally defined.

This chapter moves toward visibility, as my focus in each section gradually shifts from a theatrical culture of quasi invisibility to one of hypervisibility for Afro-diasporic women. In French performance culture, the oblique angle of representation for desirable Afro-diasporic women falls most squarely under the paradigm of erasure established by Boose and MacDonald. Indeed, in high baroque France, as the State officially took a colonial stance in the 1620s, black-up became extremely popular in court ballets, where it was hermeneutically reconfigured to tell spectators new stories about the Afro-diasporic people in their midst. No longer the story of exclusion we encountered in early baroque theatre, it was a new story of subordination, in which Afro-diasporic male characters burning with love for the white ladies in the audience willingly turned themselves into Petrarchan slaves to love whose desire could never be gratified. That script allowed performance to celebrate color-based slavery while gracefully sidestepping the thorny ethical issue of what Susan Peabody calls the Freedom Principle, which French culture saw as central to its self-definition.[6] That story hinged on sexual dynamics that required the masculinization of black-up, yielding a configuration that excluded from the dance of interracial desire on stage the enslaved people most often coerced into interracial sex offstage: Afro-diasporic women. Some awareness of those dynamics transpires in a court ballet like *Grand bal de la douairière de Billebahaut* (1626), which stages Afro-diasporic women only to emplot the mechanics of their exclusion from the genre at large.[7]

In England, the oblique aesthetics of Afro-diasporic women's desirability took on a different shape. Given the comparatively rare longevity of the diabolical script of blackness in the Protestant nation, the sudden and sustained feminization of black-up that took place under James I's reign produced a number of new scripts, including what I call *the succuban script of blackness*. That specific script construed Afro-diasporic women as succubae, that is, as dark demons who coerce Christian men into extramarital sex in their sleep at night, when they are in an exonerating state of powerlessness. Succuban sex was imagined as located simultaneously inside and outside of the economy of familial reproduction—for those gender-bending creatures served as vehicles for the seed of another race—the human race, to which they did not belong. The succuban script hinged on fetishistic mechanisms of inversion that fantasized about the rape of desirable Afro-diasporic women while disavowing it. Thus obliquely represented, the desirability of Afro-diasporic women hid in plain sight on the English stage. Tracing the succuban hermeneutics of black-up in large performance archives from the 1610s to the 1670s and paying particular attention to *The White Devil* (1612) and *The Tempest, or Enchanted Island* (1667), I argue that the colonial black succuba's fraught relation to the seed she carries for another race became a fixation point on stage as the century progressed.

In the last section of this chapter, I turn to Spanish theatrical culture, where female black-up had dominated the stage since the beginning of the sixteenth century, but where the commodifying scripts of blackness explored in Chapter 1 had systematically excluded enslaved Afro-diasporic women, or *negras*, from the domain of beauty conjured up in performance by metaphors of luxury materials. That partition, however, was disrupted by the stock character of the desirable *mulata*, which Lope de Vega developed at the beginning of the seventeenth century. Indeed, the enslaved light-skinned woman and the luxurious scripts of brownface deployed around her were originally meant to tell a colorist story of desirability. And yet, as I show by close reading Lope's *mulata* repertoire with a particular emphasis on *Servir a señor discreto* (1610–18), the hermeneutic contours of the *mulata* adjusted to accommodate a powerful ideological need at odds with colorism: the need to anchor mixed-race Afro-descendants in blackness. *Mulatas'* colorist brownface could not shed its hermeneutic kinship with the black-up of *negras* largely because the anxiogenic prospect of *mulatas'* unmoored, spreading, and ever-less-readable brownness threatened socioracial taxonomies and hierarchies that were crucial to Hispanic societies. Ultimately, in performance, female brownface and its self-contradictory relation to black-up, as simultaneously same and other, tested the bounds of black womanhood while obliquely acknowledging the desirability of all Afro-diasporic women.

There are a few things this chapter does not purport to do. First, I do not aim to provide in this chapter a comprehensive account of the aesthetic strategies used to represent Afro-diasporic women in early modern performance culture. The three scripts that this chapter analyzes were not the only scripts available to French, English, and Spanish audiences for thinking about Black women, and I am well aware of scripts' tendency to hybridize and overlap with one another. I simply endeavor to make visible three powerful scripts of female blackness that have remained unnoticed to this day, and I offer them as particularly rich examples of the oblique aesthetics of Afro-diasporic women's desirability that permeated baroque theatrical culture at large in Western Europe. Second, I do not claim to capture all the ways in which sexuality informed the lives and theatrical representations of Afro-diasporic women. Reading aesthetic representations in dialogue with colonial and slaving contexts where Afro-diasporic women's sexuality mattered primarily for what it could yield has led me to focus here on heterosexual reproductive sexuality. Third, this chapter is not a romance: it does not reclaim or celebrate on the reparative mode what could erroneously read as a long-lost history of interracial desire. I foreground moments when aesthetic strategies crafted to uphold the taboo of Afro-diasporic women's desirability burst at the seams, and I care for the bursting mostly because it exposes the seams. What is interesting is not the oblique acknowledgment of those women's desirability (which is a nonquestion: Black women's desirability is always a given), but rather the strength of the taboo that conditioned such obliqueness. The latter originated from the horrors of sexual violence committed against Afro-diasporic women across colonial worlds—horrors that ultimately had less to do with desire than with power, greed, and slavery. Desire covers a multitude of sins in early modern performance culture. That the early moderns deliberately mistranslated such sins into the obfuscating language of eros does not mean I do in this book.

Exclusions: Looking for Afro-Diasporic Women in France

Boose's and MacDonald's arguments about the invisibility of Afro-diasporic women applies most convincingly to the French baroque archive, where it is hard to find Afro-diasporic women, hidden as they are behind abundant representations of their male counterparts. In 1613, at the invitation of the Italian-born French queen consort Marie de Medici, the Fedeli comici, a commedia dell'arte company led by Giambattista Andreini and Virginia Ramponi Andreini, came to France and stayed there for almost a year.[8] They performed, among other pieces, a black-up play called *Lo schiavetto* (The little slave). One of the play's plotlines follows Florinda, a Neapolitan white woman abandoned by her lover, who (foreshadowing the numerous abandoned maidens who would put on black-up to triumph over their unfaithful lovers in English Caroline drama a decade later) puts on black-up and pretends to be an enslaved Afro-diasporic man in order to track down her lover, poison him, and thereby avenge her honor. The attempted murder fails, and the lovers are happily reunited.[9]

Lo schiavetto advertised in Parisian circles the Neapolitan reality of domestic black slavery. Virtually all editions of the playtext emphasize that reality by featuring a striking close-up of the schiavetto's recognizable slave collar (Figure 2).

Emily Wilbourne insightfully argues that the disguise so vividly rendered on the play's frontispiece has a symbolical value, as it turns Florinda into "the material embodiment of a literary figure: a slave to love. As a slave to love, Florinda-as-Schiavetto is the outward impersonation of an inward state, her body becoming the legible surface from which her emotional turmoil can be read: 'Schiavetto' is less a disguise than a powerfully coherent manifestation of Florinda's lovesick identity."[10] The idea that enslaved blacked-up characters are Petrarchan slaves to love is the foundation of a script of blackness that would come to dominate French performance culture for the next six decades. That script and its erotic contours would develop and thrive first and foremost—but not exclusively— in the performance culture of the royal court, the same court that had welcomed the Fedeli comici and their blacked-up Florinda in 1613, and would welcome them again repeatedly in the 1620s.[11] In that cultural moment, the scopic script of black enslavement to love started telling spectators a new story about Afro-diasporic people, a story of voluntary servitude. The cross-dressing plot of *Lo schiavetto* resonates imperfectly yet evocatively with the gender mechanics of this script of blackness—namely, with this script's concealment of women's plight behind lustful black men.

The motif of the enslaved Afro-diasporic man as a Petrarchan slave to love vehicled by *Lo schiavetto* found a fertile terrain at the court of Louis XIII, for it fulfilled fast-growing local ideological needs. Indeed, although there was no such thing as a French colonial empire during most of the seventeenth century, the interest in Atlantic colonies that had developed early in Rouen spread to the rest of the country over the course of the following decades. In 1626, Richelieu appointed himself *grand maître et surintendant de la navigation*, a new position that granted him unprecedented control over the French Navy, and he launched a long-term multifronted program to strengthen it and take control of the seas. This revitalization originated from a desire to simultaneously increase State control over French citizens and impose Bourbon France onto the international stage. Indeed, by strengthening the royal navy, Richelieu hoped to crush the power of Huguenot fortified cities such as La Rochelle that controlled the French Atlantic coast with the help of their fellow Protestants from England, and to surveille French citizens who traveled between France and New France

LO
SCHIAVETTO
COMEDIA
DI GIO: BATTISTA
Andreini Fiorentino.

DEDICATA
ALL'ILLVSTRISS. SIG.
GIROLAMO PRIVLI
Meritiſſimo Figliuolo di ſua Serenità.

CON LICENZA, ET PRIVILEGIO.

IN VENETIA, M.DC.XX.
Nella Stamperia di Gio: Battiſta Ciotti.

Figure 2. Frontispiece of *Lo schiavetto*. Giovanni Battista Andreini.
Woodcut. 1620. Munich, Bayerische Staatsbibliothek, Res/P.o.it. 35, p. 4
urn:nbn:de:bvb:12-bsb10926110-2.

unbeknownst to the metropolitan authorities.[12] At the same time, Richelieu wanted to break the Dutch and English quasi-monopoly over maritime trade routes, to eliminate the acts of piracy that plagued low-performing French merchant ships, and, last but not least, to humble Hapsburg Spain by attacking it at the root of its wealth (and thus at the root of its imperialism in Europe): its American colonies.[13]

To reach those goals, building a new fleet was necessary, but not sufficient. Richelieu decided to charter private companies modeled after the English and Dutch joint-stocks companies. Historians often underline that while Richelieu had no colonial passion per se and did not imagine that Atlantic possessions would yield boundless riches to the kingdom, he thought of French expansion in the Atlantic as the only way for France to take its place on the European stage. Thus, he granted charters and trade monopolies to commercial companies targeting specific overseas areas, such as La Compagnie Rouennaise du Cap du Nord (which traded with the region between the North bank of the Amazon and the Orinoco) and La Compagnie du Cap Vert et du Sénégal (which traded with West Africa). The first truly colonial company was La Compagnie de St. Christophe, founded in 1626 to focus on the Antilles.[14] In short, in the late 1620s, the French State, in the person of Richelieu, embraced the colonial project and made no secret of it.[15] Forty enslaved Afro-descendants were brought to the French part of St. Kitts from other Caribbean islands that same year, and in 1629, French colonists started importing enslaved people directly from Africa.[16] There were five to six hundred enslaved Afro-diasporic people in the French part of St. Kitts in 1635.[17]

A growing awareness of the practice of slavery in French-controlled territories transpires in early modern popular culture. The gradual appearance of color-based slavery on the national horizon is palpable in public debates, visual culture, and, later in the century, colonial chronicles published in the metropole. For instance, during the public conference organized by the Bureau d'addresse on October 1, 1640, the topic assigned for debate was "On Negroes" (les Nègres).[18] Using the words *More* and *Nègre* as synonyms, the first orator speculated about what causes dark skin, "which is not an accident but an inseparable property distinguishing *Mores* from other men and constitutive of the *Nègre*'s nature."[19] The second orator depicted dark-skinned Afro-descendants as naturally suited for slavery:

> *Nègres* have many other particularities beyond their skin tone that distinguish them from other people, such as thick lips, flat noses, cotton-

like hair, eyes and teeth whiter than other men, . . . not to mention their minds, which are so ignorant that, while they have an abundance of flax, they lack cloth, for they are unable to manufacture it; they have sugarcane, and yet they don't make any use of it neither for themselves nor for trade purposes; they regard copper over gold (which they prize at the same rate as salt); they have plentiful game and yet will not hunt; they have neither laws nor medicine. Such ignorance makes those minds more abject and servile than other people's: they are born to be slaves, so much so that free-born Abyssinians, the worthiest people in Ethiopia, when they enter someone's service, expect to be whipped with cow whips.[20]

That conference—performed in a public space and circulated in various print formats and languages including English—attests to the presence of the colonial black condition on the Parisian cultural horizon as early as the 1640s.[21]

Visual culture confirms this permeation. In 1643, just one year after Louis XIII legalized the slave trade, Matthieu Le Nain painted *The Smokers, or The Guard* (*La tabagie*), which represents soldiers smoking tobacco, with a black servant waiting on them and looking at the spectators with a gentle smile (see Plate 2). Such a painting suggests that Afro-descendants were associated in collective imagination with the addictive colonial goods that Parisians craved, in this case, tobacco. A couple of years later, the same Mathieu Le Nain painted *The Children's Dance Lesson* (*Leçon de danse d'enfants*), in which little girls from a well-off family are learning how to dance to the sound of an Afro-diasporic musician's pocket fiddle (see Plate 3), pinpointing the integration of Afro-diasporic servants into the everyday life of metropolitan households. Finally, as early as 1647, in *Ballet des rues de Paris*, which playfully personifies the streets of Paris, the capital city has a Black Street (la rue des Mores).[22]

The development of slavery in the French colonies and its infiltration of metropolitan lifestyles posed a major political problem. Indeed, the practice of slavery blatantly contradicted France's self-image as the champion of what Sue Peabody calls the Freedom Principle, the old tradition according to which no one could be enslaved on French soil. The Freedom Principle originated in a 1315 ordinance in which Louis X enabled serfs to buy their own freedom and automatically freed enslaved people who would set foot in France, playing up the homophony between the name of the country and the idea of enfranchisement. It was reasserted in 1571, when a court of law in Bordeaux forbade a Norman merchant from selling enslaved black people because "France, the Mother of

Liberty, does not allow for slaves."[23] Embraced by Jean Bodin, it was recorded in the customary laws compiled by Antoine Loysel in 1607: "everyone is free in this realm, and as soon as a slave reaches it, upon baptism, he becomes free."[24]

The scripts of blackness we find in high baroque performance culture speak to France's unreconcilable aspirations as champion of the Freedom Principle and as a fledgling colonial power in the era of color-based slavery. Resolving the contradiction between old ideals and colonial realities was the fast-growing local ideological need that the script of black enslavement to love could and would fulfill so efficiently on stage for decades. While, as we saw in Chapter 1, the diabolical script of blackness was deployed in the early baroque period in cautionary tales against the inclusion of Afro-descendants in any potential colonial body politic, starting in the 1620s, the hermeneutic configuration of cosmetic blackness became erotic, circulating fantasies of consensual enslavement. This reconfiguration occurred in a context of radical transformation for France's theatre industry. As the theatrical scene moved to Paris, partly because of Richelieu's own patronage, the proximity between the stage and the siege of power increased, and the concentration of talented theatre professionals in the capital benefited the development of court theatre.[25] Afro-diasporic characters in black-up became a staple of court ballets in the 1620s. Court ballets responded to the court's stance on French expansion in the Atlantic and functioned as a laboratory, a space where black-up could be rethought, where its semiotics and its politics with relation to Afro-diasporic people and the French body politic could be reconfigured, and slavery embraced.[26] This laboratory's influence ultimately radiated far beyond court culture.

The operations of the script of black enslavement to love are exemplified in *The Happy Shipwreck (Ballet du naufrage heureux)*, a 1626 ballet written by Claude de L'Estoille (a member of the Société des Cinq Auteurs) and performed at the Louvre in the king's presence to celebrate the colonial policies launched that year. A merchant opens the ballet by explaining to the ladies in the audience, "les beaux astres de la cour," that his ship was wrecked:

> The riches of my ships
> Could not be saved
> From the wrath of the wind and the sea.
> Yet I am receiving more precious ware now,
> And I believe that, having found you,
> I have gained more than I have lost.

My pilot, my sailors,
And all their passengers will shortly
Come and pay homage to you.[27]

Directly addressing the ladies in the audience was a generic requirement of court ballets; in this piece, it serves as narrative thread. In keeping with the merchant's promise, characters enter, dance, woo the ladies, and exit, according to a serial logic of display. The passengers include "a tobacco user" (un preneur de tobac)—a staple that places the wrecked ship and the ballet as a whole in a colonial Atlantic space—some "bourgeois," and a "a worldly man (un mondain). Then, some of the fantastic inhabitants of the shore where all those people got shipwrecked decide to woo the Ladies too: we now see "ghosts" (des fantosmes), "a madman" (un furieux), "an umbrella carrier (un porteur de parasol), "Pandorians covered with mirrors" (des Pandoriens couverts de miroirs), "men with three faces" (des hommes à trois visages), "men dressed with the four elements" (des hommes vestus des quatre elements), "little monsters" (des petits monstres), and finally, "les Mores." We know that those *Mores* were performed in black-up from illustrations with which other ballets starring those stock characters were published, such as *Grand bal de la douairière de Billebahaut*, also performed in 1626. Such illustrations put to rest any doubts about how dark exactly *Mores* were in high baroque French performance culture. As we know from Claude-François Ménestrier's 1682 description of typical ballet costumes, "*Mores* have their hair short and frizzy, their face and hands black, they go bare-headed, unless they wear a gold diadem with pearls; they must have earrings."[28] The position of the *Mores* in this serial logic is ambiguous: they could belong to the list of monstrous creatures living on the shore where the ship got wrecked, but since travelers and natives mix on stage, they could also be part of the ship's cargo— especially given the presence on board of an "umbrella carrier," a character typically represented as black in early modern iconographic traditions.

Those *Mores*, in line with the Petrarchan aesthetic that permeated Renaissance court cultures, are "burning" with love for the ladies in the audience. Indeed, the libretto unfurls an obsessive poetics of burning, as the ballet's female spectators seem to set everyone on fire. This poetics explains the position of the *Mores* at the end of the series on display: they are the culmination of this chain, for they bear the material mark of burning on their face. In a symbolic system where to love is to burn, characters in black-up covered with soot are the ultimate lovers:

Unparalleled beauties,
Your eyes, more beauteous than the sun,
Have also wronged us more.
That star is more clement than you:
It only blackened our faces,
While you burnt our hearts.[29]

Not content with symbolically mobilizing the etymological understanding of
Aethiopian skin as burnt skin, the ballet revitalizes it by having those *Mores*
burn onstage. Indeed, immediately after the *Mores'* declaration, the Alchemist
enters, a charlatan and worthy character of the genre that Mark Franko calls the
burlesque court ballet:[30]

I distill night and day
Waters to make unguents
That can cure by night or day
Anyone it does not make sick.[31]

The Alchemist, moved by the *Mores'* plight, decides to help by recasting them:

I want to melt in my furnaces
Those miserable lovers,
And the beauty I will give to those *Mores*
Will be greater than their current ugliness.
I want for them to charm all eyes
And vanquish their mistresses:
Though they be no gods,
They shall possess those goddesses.[32]

"A dialogue between the Alchemist and the *Mores* he melts in his furnace" follows (Un dialogue de l'Alchimiste et des Mores qu'il fond dans son fourneau):
the *Mores* rejoice in the Alchemist's oven, anticipating the joys that will ensue
from such pains. Their death is not marked by any stage direction, but a "collier"
(le porteur de charbon) enters, his own face smeared with coal, who brings the
Mores' hearts on stage, and thusly concludes the ballet:

As I carry this coal, I keep trembling,
And suddenly, all pleasures run away from me,

For this coal is made of the lovers' hearts
That love burnt the way it burns me now.[33]

Claude de L'Estoille bases the poetics of his libretto on the idea that dark skin is
burnt skin, and he shows characters in black-up burning on stage, without ever
activating the diabolical script of blackness. The furnace is not a hellmouth; the
Alchemist is not Lucifer; the *Mores* are not devils. The language of the libretto
is unambiguous on this point. This would have been an unforgivable missed
dramaturgic occasion some fifteen years earlier, but in 1626 at the court of Louis
XIII, this scene did not read as a missed opportunity, because black-up was used
and understood differently, in response to emergent needs.

The new script was enabled by the relocation of the early baroque diabolical
script of blackness to a performance space where religion had no traction: the
gallant space of court ballets. In that new space, the lechery traditionally attrib-
uted to black devils was detached from its religious roots and took on a secular
life of its own. From then on, the strategic deployment of indexical signs ensured that, in the eyes of spectators, a blacked-up character was no longer black
because he was morally fallen, but because he had fallen for the white ladies in
the audience. This erotic framing, exemplarily articulated in *Ballet du naufrage
heureux*, features in most ballets with blacked-up *Mores*, in at least thirty libretti produced between 1620 and 1650.[34]

To perceive the ideological work performed by the erotic framing of black-
up, we must focus on the power structure linking the gallant *Mores* to the white
ladies in the audience. Emblematically, in the 1632 *Grand bal des effets de la nature* (*Nature's Effects*), a "neigre" tells his "mistress" (maîtresse):

If the color that I am wearing
Is as dark as a coffin
It is because my body is mourning
The loss of its freedom [*franchise*].[35]

The absolute submission of those Afro-diasporic characters to their "maîtresses"
is key. Indeed, the term *maîtresse* already had its sexual connotations in 1626,
but it also referred to a power structure folded into many court ballets: slavery.
While the gallant *Mores* use the rhetoric of courtly love to woo their potential
mistresses, they also offer themselves as slaves to the French aristocrats in the
audience: they are, like the blacked-up Florinda in *Lo schiavetto*, slaves to love.
In *Boutade des Mores esclaves d'Amour délivrés par Bacchus* (1609), for instance,

the *Mores* eventually conclude: "We are overjoyed and we love our shackles / when we have the honor to wear them for you."[36] This play on the ambiguity of the term *maîtresse*, ubiquitous in the ballets of that period, is not coincidental: rather, it constitutes a representational strategy.

Framing the white master-black slave relation in erotic terms is a sublimating representational strategy that bypasses the notion of coercion inherent in slavery. In that sense, it illustrates Stuart Hall's understanding of fetishism:

> Fetishism takes us to the field where fantasy intervenes in representation; to the level where what is shown or seen in representation can only be understood in relation to what cannot be seen, what cannot be shown. Fetishism involves the substitution of an object for some powerful but forbidden force. Fetishism . . . includes disavowal. Disavowal is the strategy by means of which a powerful fascination or desire is both indulged and at the same time denied. It is where what has been tabooed nevertheless manages to find a place of representation. As Homi Bhabha observes, "it is a non-repressive form of knowledge that allows for the possibility of simultaneously embracing two contradictory beliefs, one official and one secret, one archaic and one progressive, one that allows the myth of origins, the other that articulates difference and division."[37]

Fetishistic disavowal—or, the art of having one's cake and eating it too—was the core affective and psychological mechanism driving the script of black enslavement to love in high baroque France. That new hermeneutic configuration was informed by what Sylvie Chalaye insightfully, if passingly, identified as the French early modern "bad conscience" (la mauvaise conscience). For Chalaye, bad conscience precluded the development of realistic representations of Africans in early modern French performance culture. I hope to have made clear that the script of black enslavement to love that triumphed onstage during the high baroque period did indirectly address blackness, race, and slavery, and that the very indirection of it all is what matters.[38] Court ballet culture developed an erotic framing of black-up suffused with fetishistic disavowal and wish fulfillment that gracefully sidestepped ideological contradictions. The indirection of high baroque representations of colonial slavery laid the foundations for the "mechanisms of avoidance" and "displacement" detected by Madeleine Dobie later on in eighteenth-century French culture, where "there was a strong cultural disincentive to portray colonial slavery, a system considered economically advantageous, but which raised moral questions."[39]

As Julia Prest notes, most often, the verse printed in court ballet libretti were not uttered on stage (where they might have been drowned by the music): rather, they were meant to be read by spectators during and after the ballet, constituting "an essential guide to the performance," both lived and remembered.[40] Court ballet was thus a multimedia experience that did not stop when the performance ended: the libretti that spectators took home ensured the circulation of the new erotic hermeneutics of black-up beyond the appointed time, space, and circle of live performance. It is through such conduits that the aesthetics of court culture influenced the commercial stage. The influence of the script of black enslavement to love beyond court culture is palpable in the commercial plays that appropriated it. Thomas Corneille, for instance, in his comedy *L'inconnu* (1675), includes an *entrée* lifted from the aesthetics of court ballets, where, to seduce a countess, a viscount has a striking little tableau vivant performed at her place. A miniature proscenium-staged theatre is rolled onto the stage ("on fait rouler vers eux un théâtre") by "magnificently clad slaves" (des esclaves richement vêtus). The portable theatre represents a bedroom. Its furniture is played by performers who remain perfectly still: five gilded Cupids pretending to be statues ("On voit cinq statues toutes d'or représentant des Amours") and two blacked-up *Maures* pretending to be gueridons ("il y a deux guéridons faits en Maures").[41] At the end of the scene, the Cupids spring into motion while *Maures* sing a love song.[42] By associating the blacked-up *Maures* with enslavement (the magnificently clad slaves) and Eros (Cupids), and by turning them into commodities (the gueridons) while having them sing the praises of a spectating white lady, Thomas Corneille literalized and made visible in 1675 the ideological operations that had been at work in the script of black enslavement to love for decades.

To recapitulate, the script of black enslavement to love was an interactive ideological device that responded to the position of the court on the question of Afro-diasporic colonial subjects, and that interpellated spectators as protocolonial agents involved in the making of color-based slavery. The king who saw all those ballets eventually legalized slave trading in 1642. The script's permeation of French theatrical culture evidences its popularity—one heightened by its ability to respond to emerging ideological needs. Those needs were particularly well accommodated by a script that simultaneously construed black men as desiring their own enslavement and foiled its own interracial sex plot. Indeed, black men on stage had to willingly surrender their freedom to white ladies in the audience, but they also had to be denied those ladies' enjoyment.

In *Achille victorieux* (1627), for instance, playwright Vincent Borée drew on the court ballet tradition to create the character of Memnon, an African king and "a smoky Vulcan," who leads his Ethiopian armies to rescue Troy when Priam calls, and hopes to marry Polixene in return.[43] He activates the script of black enslavement to love when he imagines kissing Polixene and describes it as "taking a kiss from the very sun that is burning me to ashes"; he later refers to his love for her as a "humble slavery."[44] Achilles kills his African rival in the final scene, thereby rewriting the fall of Troy as a successful attempt to preempt interracial sex. A similar move features in the plot crafted by the Theban prince Ligdamis to seduce Orphise in Nicolas Mary's tragicomedy *Orphise ou la beauté persécutée* (1638). Ligdamis orders his men to disguise themselves as blacked-up *Mores* and try and abduct Orphise—who has so far scorned him—so he might foil their attempt, rescue Orphise, and frame himself as a hero.[45] Like most plots involving the specter of dark-skinned rapists in the Western world from early modernity onward, Ligdamis's devious plan works perfectly.[46]

The script of black enslavement to love thus assuaged simultaneously the moral malaise caused by the growing practice of color-based slavery on French soil and the anxieties attached to threats of interracial sex between black men and white women. Last but not least, that script excluded from the dance of interracial desire the people most likely to be coerced into interracial sex offstage: Afro-diasporic women. If, as Kim F. Hall established, Petrarchan tropes were used in early modern English lyric poetry to represent Afro-diasporic women and, through them, "the possibility of conquest and enrichment as well as the threat of potential destruction," in French performance culture, by contrast, Petrarchan tropes served to represent Afro-diasporic men and, through their obsession with white women, rendered Afro-diasporic women invisible.[47] At least half of the ideological work effected by the script of black enslavement to love therefore proceeds not from what it shows and imagines, but from whom it does not show, and what it refuses to imagine. The dearth of Afro-diasporic women on stage does not mean that they were absent from the French cultural horizon: it means that their absence results from compulsive acts of erasure triggered by anxieties regarding their all-too-well-known desirability. At the root of Afro-diasporic women's exclusion from the interracial erotic economy of the high baroque stage in France, we find shame and denial about colonial realities.

Indeed, the paucity of white women in French colonies notoriously led to a widespread tolerance of interracial unions in the early seventeenth century:

later colonial chronicles such as Jean-Baptiste Du Tertre's *Histoire générale des Antilles habitées par les François* seek to shame Frenchmen for their passion for Afro-diasporic women.[48] Metropolitans knew about the allure of Afro-diasporic women in the Caribbean colonies—how else could they understand, for instance, the burlesque *Epistre chagrine à M. de Rosteau* written by Paul Scarron, where the poet, bemoaning his poverty and the general misery of authors in 1650s France, considers moving to America and praises the beauty of "our Indian and Negro women" out there? "Their polished hue of black ebony / Deserves no less than white Yvory."[49] The prospect of interracial romance is, in this poem, one of the most appealing features of the American dream for white men. Doris Garraway notes that in the early modern French Caribbean, "sexual libertinage took many forms, from the traffic in Indian and European women and the taking of African slaves as wives and concubines to sordid attacks and sexual indulgences on the plantation and the libidinal excesses in colonial cities, where free women of color rivaled their white competitors for the richest white men."[50] French secular officials frowned on those unions not only because they passed moral judgment on libertinage, but, most importantly, because the children born out of wedlock from those unions muddled the color line separating the free from the unfree. From the official perspective, preserving and developing a colonial society founded on color-based slavery required turning Frenchmen away from Afro-diasporic women, and from 1665 onward, a multifronted legal and fiscal campaign was launched to that end—to little success.[51]

As Felicity Nussbaum suggests, "that Afro-diasporic women were largely erased from the theatre of empire even as they figured critically in the lives of Jamaican planters and slaveowners, soldiers in the French and Indian Wars, traders with the East Indies, and voyagers to the Pacific Islands suggests that Afro-diasporic women and their half-caste children, at least as much as white men's fear of the man of color, carried the power to unsettle colonial relations and narratives about them."[52] Yet what happened on the islands did not stay on the islands. Louis XIV's minister of finances, Colbert—who would later prepare the first version of the infamous *Code noir* (1685)—had in his service "two perfectly beautiful *négresses* who had wit and spoke French well."[53] The Sun King himself was rumored to have fathered a mixed-race daughter, Louise Marie-Thérèse, the "*Moresse* of Moret" (see Plate 4).[54] The vow of celibacy that Louise Marie-Thérèse had to take as a Benedictine nun secluded in the abbey of Moret-sur-Loing had the triply beneficial effect of removing her from public life and the public gaze, damming the mixed-race stream in the French royal bloodline, and removing the king's daughter from a racialized erotic economy that could only demean her and, by extension, her father. Afro-diasporic women's desirability all around the globe was the worst-kept secret of Parisian salons.

The colonial roots of Afro-diasporic women's erasure from the stage by means of exclusion become even more obvious when one considers that early baroque plays written before Richelieu initiated the French colonial turn had regularly featured desirable African queens. *Les Portugaiz infortunez* (1608), discussed in Chapter 1, features a tender-hearted Kaffir queen, Mélinde, whose name overbrims with melanin, and whose feminine physique is emphasized as the play insists on her "long and pointed" breasts.[55] *L'Ethiopique, ou les chastes amours de Théagène et de Chariclée* (1609), by Octave-César Génetay, another Rouen playwright, included another beautiful and magnanimous African queen: Persina, Chariclea's Ethiopian mother in Heliodorus of Emesa's Greek romance *Aethiopika*.[56] The same character featured in the cycle of *Les chastes et loyales amours de Théagène et Chariclée*, by Alexandre Hardy, presumably performed at the Hôtel de Bourgogne in Paris in 1601.[57] In 1598, Jean Boissin de Gallardon, in line with the Ovidian tradition, included a dark-skinned Andromeda in *La Perséene, ou la délivrance d'Andromède*.[58] The Ovidian tradition of female African beauty did not disappear from poetry in premodern France, but it was erased from performance culture at the dawn of the colonial era, and court ballets led the charge.[59] Indeed, between 1620 and 1736, to the best of my knowledge, the only Afro-diasporic woman to feature in a commercial play is the Moorish woman who sings a brief song in Thomas Corneille's previously mentioned *L'inconnu* (1675), and, in ballet culture, only two Afro-diasporic female characters are recorded for the second half of the century: the Moorish princess performed by Mlle. de Verpré in *Ballet d'Alcidiane* (1658), and the "Mauresse" performed by the Duchess of Nemours in a masquerade at St. Germain-en-Laye in 1679.[60] Exceptions are very few.

Grand bal de la douairière de Billebahaut (1626) makes explicit the exclusion of Afro-diasporic women from the economy of interracial desire that implicitly underlies all plays and performances mobilizing the script of black enslavement to love. In that ballet, the great *"Cachique"* king—who, despite his American name, is African—enters the stage perched on a mechanical elephant. His train includes "a squad of tawny men" (une escouade de basanez) with "short flat noses" (nez camus).[61] The detailed watercolors created by Daniel Rabel for this ballet show that this squad fell into two groups: on the one hand, drumming African musicians with ankle shackles and slave collars reminiscent of the one sported by Florinda on the frontispiece of *Lo schiavetto*, and, on the other hand, gallant African soldiers with rich outfits and long red swords (see

Plate 5). The latter group spoke the lines of "*les Africains*" in Bordier's libretto. As true *Mores galants*, these dashing soldiers dance and court the white ladies in the audience. One of them, played by Monsieur de Longueville, declares:

> Let me die o heavenly wonder,
> If the proudest African lady
> Compared to the beauty of your eyes
> Is anything but a quintain.[62]

A "quintain" was a mannequin set on top of a pole used as target for jousters to train upon—a dummy, most often gendered as male. The grotesque comparison between African ladies and quintains denigrates and dehumanizes those women by turning them into objects, and it offers a painful image of sanctioned violence against African women's bodies. Here, African men explicitly express their desire for white women by excluding African women from the spheres of humanity, femininity, beauty, and eroticism.

We cannot know how the white ladies in the audience took the compliment, but the libretto embeds the African women's response. Indeed, as soon as the African men are done dancing, "a troop of African women enters and attacks the African men with zagay lances; the men suffer it kindly and only protect themselves; then, all the Cacique's train goes back where it came from."[63] African women hear the insult and respond by turning male African offenders themselves into quintains as they attack them with zagays. This gesture, however, ironically reinforces their exclusion from the spheres of femininity, beauty, and eroticism. Zagays have obvious phallic connotations: this gesture masculinizes African women by putting them in the position of male jousters, and it feminizes African men as they suffer a good beating "kindly." The masculinization of African women is performatively reinforced by the fact that, in this ballet and in most burlesque court ballets (unlike in other genres and commercial plays), all performers were male, and the costumes worn by African women in Rabel's drawing exposed their arms, legs, and stomachs, thereby revealing the masculine musculature of the performers (see Plate 6). Such revealing costumes are rare in extant ballet iconography, suggesting that the costume designers wished to make a particular effect in displaying the blackened muscles of male performers in drag. Masculinization reinforces the very discourse that the African women rejected.

This discourse reeks of misogynoir, a critical term coined by Moya Bailey to "describe the co-constitutive antiblack and misogynistic racism directed at Afro-diasporic women" that specifically targets and polices "Afro-diasporic

women's desirability."[64] Widely used in Black studies and contemporary antiracist activism, the term gets at "the unique ways in which Afro-diasporic women
are pathologized in popular culture" by contrast with other women of color
who are not of sub-Saharan descent.[65] That pathologization hinges on "age-old
stereotypes of Afro-diasporic women's supposed unattractiveness and hypersexual nature."[66] In light of *Grand bal de la douairière de Billebahaut*'s plot,
"age-old" must mean 1626, if not earlier. An early instantiation of misogynoir
and of the trope of the "angry Black woman" that have persisted to this day,
Bordier's African women stood no chance in the erotic economy of French court
ballets. They are not given lines or a chance to voice their perspective. They disappear instantly. *Billebahaut* emplots the exclusion of Afro-diasporic women in
French performance culture with a cruel lucidity.

Inversions: The Succuban Script of Blackness in England

When it comes to representing Afro-diasporic women in their anxiogenic desirability, fetishistic aesthetics based on disavowal were not unique to high baroque France. English performance culture too developed oblique modes of
representation and new scripts of female blackness, among which one specific
script, exculpatory in nature, construed Afro-diasporic women as lustful gender-
bending creatures perpetrating sexual assault on white men. The succuban script
of blackness perversely inverted the real gender dynamics of interracial rape culture informing English colonial and—increasingly so—metropolitan realities.
Those realities transpire perhaps most clearly in a play like Philip Massinger and
John Fletcher's *A Very Woman* (1634), where, in a middle of a slave market scene,
a citizen purchases a couple of little girls:

> *Citizen* Twenty Chekeens for these two.
> *Master* For five and twenty take 'em.
> *Citizen* There's your money;
>   I'll have 'em, if it be to sing in Cages.
> *Master* Give 'em hard Eggs, you never had such Black birds.
> *Citizen* Is she a Maid, do'st think?
> *Master* I dare not swear Sir,
>   She is nine year old, at ten you shall finde few here:
> *Citizen* A merry fellow, thou say'st true. Come children.
>   *Exit with the Moors.*[67]

The short exchange between the Citizen and the Master leaves little doubt that those girls will be sexually assaulted within a year. It is in the light of their plight that I read the condition of the Zanches, Zanthias, Kates, Jacconettas, Fidellas, and other Afro-diasporic maidservants of the Jacobean, Caroline, and Restoration stages. The nine-year-old whose maidenhead is a titillating object of speculation and index of market value for the white men who sell and buy her is the real-life face of the theatrical black succuba whose presence I trace in the English archive.

Afro-diasporic women show up simultaneously in many areas of English performance culture around the same time as *Othello*, which, as we saw in Chapter 1, had redirected the diabolical script of blackness toward a white woman. They appear suddenly in closet drama (*The Tragedy of Mariam*, 1604), court masques (*Masque of Blackness*, 1605), and commercial theatre (the lost *Solomon and the Queen of Sheba*, 1606; *The Wonder of Women*, 1605; and Shakespeare's *Antony and Cleopatra*, 1607).[68] Jacobean drama is characterized by a sudden and sustained feminization of black-up. The succuban script of blackness was not made out of thin air: it is one of the main forms that the male script of diabolical blackness—which was ubiquitous in 1600s English theatre—took when characters of black women emerged on stage. Indeed, there are no records of the costumes worn by Afro-diasporic female characters; nonetheless, we can assume that, to perform Afro-diasporic women, boy actresses combined the wigs and prosthetic breasts they used to perform white women with the black-up cosmetics typically used to perform Afro-diasporic men. Materially construed as female devils, those characters invited spectators to read them as succubae and playwrights to write them as such.

In that respect, theatrical culture stands out from other domains of representation. Indeed, with a few exceptions, English early modern iconography and visual culture do not show succubae, and English demonological treatises, sermons, pamphlets, philosophical conferences, and nondramatic literature hardly ever describe the physical appearance of succubae.[69] By contrast, English plays regularly frame the succubae they allude to or put on full display as specifically dark-skinned.[70] For instance, in Philip Massinger and John Fletcher's *The Prophetess* (1622), Delphia conjures up a "she-devil" called Lucifera, whom the fool Geta describes as "a prettie brown devil," "marvellous and well-mounted." He immediately wishes to kiss her and have her sit on his lap, for he is instantly consumed with desire and "burnt to ashes."[71] Geta amorously shortens Lucifera to "Lucie," a nickname that, in this sexually charged context, may remind us of "Lucy Negro," the famous London madam who may have inspired Shakespeare's Dark Lady. I

read the distinctive blackness of theatrical succubae as an indication that the
dramaturgic emergence of that figure derived specifically from the feminization
of the black-up performance technique and the wildly popular script of diabolical
blackness that had accompanied it for two decades. In early modern England,
not all succubae were imagined as dark-skinned and not all dark-skinned women
were read as succubae, but on stage they very often were, because of the hermeneutic baggage of the performance technique used to bring them to life by white
male performers.

Most sixteenth-century lexicons define a succuba as a "whore," a "harlot,"
or a woman "lying with another woman's husband," yet the secular use of the
word as a sexual slur cannot be dissociated from the superstitious beliefs from
which the succuba originates. In those beliefs, the typical succuban rape plot
features a devil who takes on the form of a woman in order to have sex with a
male human who realizes only too late who his paramour was. Such forced encounters were often imagined as taking place while the man was asleep, which is
why early modern accounts often associate incubi and succubi with the medical
condition of the "night-mare," which Henry Fuseli would so famously illustrate
in 1781. Swiss theologian Ludwig Lavater puts it most succinctly in 1569: "*Ephi-
altae,* and *Hyphialtae,* that is *Incubi* and *Succubi,* (which we cal Maares) are
night spirits or rather Diuells, which leape vpon men in their sleepe. The phisitians do affirme that these are nothing else but a disease."[72] A psychoanalytical
reading easily construes this association of succuban sex with nightmares as a
sign that succuban rape plots subconsciously fulfilled repressed desires.

The succuban rape plot was popularized by early modern witchcraft literature. Indeed, as Walter Stephens has shown, the figure of the succuba, present
in the Bible and in the writings of St. Augustine and Thomas Aquinas among
others, received new attention at the beginning of the early modern period, as
the conceptualization of witchcraft and *maleficia* changed and became heavily
reliant on practices of demonolatry grounded in demonic copulation.[73] Succubae and incubi came to occupy an important place in popular imagination
when they became central to the definition of the witch qua witch. James I's
Daemonologie, in the Forme of a Dialogue (1597) devotes a whole section to
them. As Philomathes asks about the existence of those creatures, Epistemon
confirms: "that abhominable kinde of the Deuils abusing of men or women, was
called of old, Incubi and Succubi, according to the difference of the sexes that
they conuersed with."[74] These devils are lexically distinguished solely on the basis of the sexual positions—prone or supine—dictated by the gender of the
humans they assault. Moreover, James's use of a masculine ending rather than a

feminine one to refer to the supine companions of white men (succubi rather than succubae) grammatically materializes these creatures' fundamental absence of gender. (While the grammatically masculine form *succubus* is the most common, I use the acceptable feminine form, *succuba*, to mark the gender of the real-life people encoded through that figure on stage.) "Whereas yee inquire if these spirites be diuided in sexes or not, I thinke the rules of Philosophie may easelie resolue a man of the contrarie: For it is a sure principle of that arte, that nothing can be diuided in sexes, except such liuing bodies as must haue a naturall seede to genere by. But we know spirites hath no seede proper to themselues, nor yet can they gender one with an other."[75] Spirits have no "seed" and thus cannot "gender" with one another and reproduce their own race: while succubi occupy dead female bodies in order to tempt living males (and incubi do the opposite), these devils are essentially unsexed gender-bending creatures.

Yet they were imagined as partaking in human sexual reproduction, so much so that the *Malleus maleficarum* insists that incubi and succubi abstain from "vices of any sort against nature, meaning not only sodomy, but also any other sin whereby the act is wrongfully performed outside the proper channel (extra vas debitum)."[76] Succuban sex is always either reproductive or potentially reproductive. Jean Bodin notes that in Germany, "such copulation sometimes produces children, which they call *Wechselkind*, or changelings."[77] James I, however, more skeptical than Bodin, uses the unsexed nature of spirits to claim that sexual intercourse with incubi or succubi cannot lead to mixed births. When Philomathes asks about the "sundrie monsters" reputed to have been born from those ghastly unions, Epistemon answers:

> These tales are nothing but *Aniles fabulæ*. For that they [devils] haue no nature of their owne, I haue shewed you alreadie. And that the cold nature of a dead bodie, can woorke nothing in generation, it is more nor plaine, as being already dead of it selfe as well as the rest of the bodie is, wanting the naturall heate, and such other naturall operation, as is necessarie for working that effect, and in case such a thing were possible (which were all utterly against all the rules of nature) it would breed no monster, but onely such a naturall of-spring, as would haue cummed betuixt that man or woman and that other abused person, in-case they both being aliue had had a doe with other.[78]

In James's reasoning, if a child is born from a union between a man and a succuba, it was engendered by the corpse occupied by the succuba not by the succuba

herself—an unlikely yet "natural" case of generation preempting the production of cross-breed "monsters" (such as Caliban, born from a witch and a devil).
In that case, succubae partook in the process of human reproduction only as
sources of energy. Arguments similar to James's were rehearsed across Europe in
the *Malleus maleficarum* (1487).[79] In *The Discoverie of Witchcraft* (1584), Reginald Scot saw succubae less as sources of energy in human reproduction than as
fleshly demonic vehicles by which to transfer human male seed to human female wombs as succubae turn into *incubi*: "the Devil, in likeness of a pretty
Wench, lyeth prostitute as Succubus to the man, and retaining his nature and
seed, conveyeth it unto the Witch, to whom he delivereth it as Incubus."[80]

In other words, in the accounts of English demonologists, whether they are
energy sources or fleshly vehicles, succubae occupy a fraught place in the economy of human reproduction. They are perceived as vehicles for the seed of a
race—the human race—to which they do not belong and thus are located simultaneously inside and outside of the economy of the human reproduction.
Succubae emerge from demonological discourse as unsexed yet female-presenting
dark-skinned devils with whom Englishmen are forced to have sex in the dark,
against their own will, in an exonerating state of powerlessness, in the intimacy
of their own domestic space, at the expense of their spiritual and physical health,
simultaneously inside and outside the economy of familial reproduction.[81] The
figure of the succuba thus defined would prove a useful and long-lasting tool for
representing the desirability of Afro-diasporic women obliquely.

There is no doubt that Afro-diasporic women had been the object of sexual
fantasies in Europe long before the beginning of the colonial era. As early as the
twelfth century, philosopher Pierre Abélard had put some of those fantasies in
writing: "it often happens that the flesh of black women is all the softer to touch
though it is less attractive to look at, and for this reason the pleasure they give is
greater and more suitable for private than public enjoyment."[82] About a century
later, Albertus Magnus, the scientist and theologian, had agreed: "seed is found
in black women—who engage in sex more than all other women—more than in
white women. For black women are hotter, and most of all dusky women, who
are the sweetest to have sex with, so lechers say, and because the mouth of their
vulva is temperate and gently embraces the penis."[83] Yet the question of Afro-
diasporic women's desirability and involvement in interracial sex would acquire
a new urgency with the development of England's investments in Mediterranean and transatlantic trades and England's colonial aspirations at the end of
the sixteenth century.

Robert Gainsh, in his account of the second voyage to Guinea published in Hakluyt's *Principall Navigations* (1589), had already suggested that, among the Garamantes of Lybia, "women are common: for they contract no matrimony, neither have respect to chastity," and Leo Africanus had already written about "Negros" that "there is no nation under heaven more prone to venerie": "they have great swarmes of harlots among them."[84] Pieter de Marees's "description and historicall declaration of the golden Kingdome of Guinea, otherwise called the golden coast of Myna," was translated and published in *Purchas his Pilgrimes* in 1625, and shifted the focus in the perception of African women from general whorishness to a lustfulness directed at white men specifically:

> Of the native women of these parts, first I will tell you of their natures, complexions, and conditions: while they go with their privy members uncovered, as I said before, and as they had no shame at all, so when they begin to wear some thing on their bodies, they begin to express shamefastness, but then begin to be lecherous, which they naturally learn from their youth upwards. . . . They give themselves thereunto, that they might be beloved of us; for they esteem it to be good fortune for them to have carnal copulation with a Netherlander, and among themselves brag and boast thereof.[85]

Thomas Herbert also writes in *A Relation of Some Yeares Travaile Begunne Anno 1626* (published 1634) that "the savage inhabitants" of southwestern Africa / Zaire and Angola "are very ceremonious in thanksgivings, for, wanting requitals, if you give a woman a piece of bread, she will immediately pull by her flap and discover her pudenda."[86] Both de Marees and Herbert insist on the responsibility of the Dutch in depraving African women, yet such depictions contributed to circulating a popular image of the Afro-diasporic woman as unruly, libidinous, and preying upon virtuous white Englishmen.

It is against such a cultural backdrop that we must read the development of the succuban script of blackness on stage, a fetishistic structure accommodating taboo fantasies of coercive sex with Afro-diasporic women. Enslavement was structurally involved in the early modern understanding of succuban sex as the witch's submission to her demonic paramour.[87] By depicting Afro-diasporic women as demonic, the succuban script of blackness cast them in the role of rapists and enslavers, perversely inverting the realities of colonial life where the rape of enslaved Afro-diasporic women by white men was rampant. Succuban acts, rather than coercive ones, were convenient devices that enabled white men to indulge in desire for interracial sex, while exonerating them from responsibility and guilt. Of course, one of the implications of this libidinal structure is that the Englishmen involved in scenarios of succuban sex might be suspected of witchcraft. And yet, with the exception of the wizard Prospero in William Davenant and John Dryden's *The Tempest, or The Enchanted Island* (1667), to which I will return in a few pages, succuban plays most often redirect suspicions of witchcraft toward black women themselves.

The black succuba is perhaps most forcefully incarnated in the stock character of the Afro-diasporic maidservant, which first appeared in Marston's *The Wonder of Women* (1606) and was most famously instantiated in the character of Zanche in Webster's *The White Devil* (1612), launching what Celia Daileader felicitously calls "Zanchophilia."[88] When Zanche engages in sexual intercourse with a white man, she and her lover playfully describe their intercourse as having taken place "in a dream," as nightmarish succuban sex always does. Zanche's succuban dimension becomes visible at the intersection of that sexual encounter and her constant demonization in the play.[89] The deployment of the succuban script of blackness in *The White Devil* is all the more striking since the play does not mobilize the diabolical script of blackness around Afro-diasporic male characters. Indeed, when Mulinassar, the Moorish general performed in black-up by the Duke of Florence, arrives at Brachiano's court in Padua, Flamineo and Horatio function as embedded spectators and depict Mulinassar as a thinly veiled replica of Othello. Mulinassar is a Christian Moor, an experienced general defending Venice and Crete against the Turks; he is a knowledgeable man, presumably of a certain age, with little heat in the blood, and whose conversation seduces without fail—Othello *redux*. In this description as in the rest of the play, while Mulinassar is clearly identified as a Moor, and while he must have been performed in black-up in order to evoke his intertextual original, there is no single hint of diabolism in the imagery used to refer to him.

By contrast, Zanche, the maidservant performed in black-up, is bedeviled as soon as she sets foot on stage.[90] "Zanche brings out a carpet, spreads it, and lays it on two fair cushions": spectators' first encounter with Zanche consists in watching her prepare the bedroom where her mistress Vittoria is about to have an adulterous rendezvous, and the oriental décor reinforces the connections between the Moorish woman's cultural identity and the scene of lust about to unravel.[91] Just a few lines after Mulinassar is introduced to the spectators, Marcello greets Zanche's entrance by asking his brother Flamineo: "Why does this Devil haunt you?" (5.1.86).

The succuba effect unfolds, as Flamineo answers his younger brother's question:

I know not.
For by this light I do not conjure for her.
Tis not so great a cunning as men think
To raise the Devil: for here's one up already,
The greatest cunning were to lay him down. (5.1.86–90)

Flamineo, the master of the household, "lays down" regularly with this devil of a maid whom he has promised to marry. Like any succuban encounter, that relationship is fraught with power dynamics involving loathing and coercion. Such dynamics invert those most likely to have existed in real early modern households including Afro-diasporic maidservants:

Flamineo I'll tell thee, I do love that Moor, that Witch, very constrainedly: she knows some of my villainy; I do love her, just as a man holds a wolf by the ears. But for fear of turning upon me, and pulling out my throat, I would let her go to the Devil.
Horatio I hear she claims marriage of thee.
Flamineo 'Faith, I made to her some such dark promise, and in seeking to fly from't I run on, like a frighted dog with a bottle at's tail, that fain would bite it off and yet dares not look behind him. (5.1.152–60)

Zanche enters at this point, and spectators can see Flamineo courting her in order to assuage her doubts about his affection and to ensure her silence. Their bantering is interrupted by Marcello:

Marcello You're a strumpet,
          An impudent one. [*Kicks Zanche.*]
Flamineo Why do you kick her? Say,
          Do you think that she's like a walnut-tree?
          Must she be cudgell'd ere she bear good fruit?
Marcello She brags that you shall marry her.
Flamineo What then?
Marcello I had rather she were pitched upon a stake
          In some new-seeded garden, to affright
          Her fellow crows thence.

Flamineo You're a boy, a fool,
    Be guardian to your hound, I am of age.
Marcello If I take her near you I'll cut her throat.
Flamineo With a fan of feathers?
Marcello And for you, I'll whip
    This folly from you. (5.1.189–99)

"Strumpet": the word is out, and it is associated with physical abuse, since Marcello beats Zanche as he speaks, leading Flamineo to ask, "must she be cudgell'd?"

The comparison between Zanche and a walnut tree is not coincidental: walnut was a very common brown dyeing agent and might have been used to concoct the cosmetic paste on the faces of the actors playing Zanche and Mulinassar. Johann Jacob Wecker includes a walnut-based recipe for black-up into *Cosmeticks, or The Beautifying Part of Physick* at the end of the sixteenth century: "Of Waters That Black the Face: With Chymical instruments, extract a most clear water from green walnut-shells and gaules [dark tree resins], with which if you wet the face or hands, they grow black by degree, like to an Aethiopian; which afterwards if you would restore to their former whiteness, you must distill vinegar, juice of lemmons, and colophonia, and washing with that will take off the blackness."[92] Taking a close look at this recipe, Richard Blunt notes that walnuts clearly produced particularly resistant pigmentation; once covered with a top coat of egg base similar to tempera, this concoction was ideal for actors in black-up to avoid problems of smearing and smudging on stage, as it could be removed only with the right chemicals.[93] For that reason, this concoction, probably spread on Zanche's face, makes the metaphorical link between Zanche and a "walnut tree" particularly threatening to whiteness. Indeed, the image of the walnut tree "bearing fruit" suggests that Zanche might be pregnant by Flamineo, which would explain her eagerness to find a husband quickly in the person of Mulinassar, with whom she later has sexual intercourse "in a dream." Zanche might be in the same situation as the Afro-diasporic woman evoked in *The Merchant of Venice* (1596) when Lorenzo teases the lecher Launcelot for his "getting up of the negro's belly."[94] By bearing walnut-brown fruit, Zanche's womb has the power to stain Flamineo's family, if not literally, according to Blunt, then racially: she can brown Flamineo's family tree.

In response to Flamineo's provocative comparison, Marcello offers another metaphor that also binds the sexual and vegetal domains yet undermines the power of Zanche's womb:

I had rather she were pitched upon a stake
In some new-seeded garden, to affright
Her fellow crows thence.

The punishment he imagines for Zanche's offense is sexual ("pitched upon a stake" has phallic connotations), but it disconnects the Afro-diasporic women from the economy of generation and reproduction. Zanche is to stand as an exemplar scaring away her fellow "black crows," whose ravenous succuban appetites threaten the fertility of the rightfully "seeded" English gardens that are white women's wombs. Marcello, perceiving Zanche's sisters as sexual gluttons on whom good "seed" is wasted, mobilizes the succuban script to enforce his views and keep Zanche in her place, defined in terms of both phenotype and class.

Ultimately, spectators are posed to perceive a contradiction between Marcello's use of the succuban script of blackness and the play's larger shattering of the religious discourse underlying it. Indeed, as the title of the play suggests, nearly every character in Webster's play is a little bit of a devil. "O me! This place is hell," Vittoria ultimately realizes (5.3.179). As Flamineo puns in a flash of clear-sightedness:

As in this world there are degrees of evils:
So in this world there are degrees of Devils.
You're a great duke; I, your poor secretary" (5.2.58–60)

In this play, the proliferation of white devils who use the succuban script against Zanche undermines the dichotomy between good and evil that founds that hermeneutic lens. Most strikingly, in her last scene, just before she dies, Zanche simply flips the succuban script:

Gasparo Thou art my task, black fury.
Zanche I have blood
        As red as either of theirs; wilt drink some?
        'Tis good for the falling sickness: I am proud
        Death cannot alter my complexion,
        For I shall never look pale. (5.6.227–31)

While Zanche's last two lines, replete with Black pride, have been abundantly commented on, her offer to let Vittoria or the murderer (it is not entirely clear whom she is addressing) drink some of her blood has remained puzzling to specialists of the play. I argue that this strange offer reverses a trope attached to succubae who were imagined "during the sex act . . . to drain off a number of vital essences and fluids, such as blood, breath, life-energy, and semen to the point of their victims' death."[95] In that sense, succubae were similar to the witches with whom they had sex as incubi, and with whom they were inextricably associated in popular imagination: redirecting potential suspicions of witchcraft to Zanche herself, Flamineo called her "that Moor, that Witch" in a previously cited passage. According to Antonio de Torquemada in *The Spanish Mandeuile of Miracles* (1600), "sorcerers" go "sucking out the blood of men, when by any meanes they may, especially that of little children."[96] By offering to let any white person around her suck her blood, Zanche rewrites her imminent death as her victimization by the play's real succubi and incubi—its swarm of titular white devils.

The succuban script of blackness had a long life. It can help us understand, for instance, the wild popularity of interracial bed-trick scenes in late Jacobean and Caroline theatre: coercing men into having sex with them under the deceptive appearance of a fair woman, succubae are natural bed-trick queens. In Beaumont and Fletcher's *Monsieur Thomas* (1615), for instance, Mary tricks her wild suitor Thomas into bedding her Afro-diasporic maidservant, Kate (a name shared by many early modern Afro-European women).[97] In the dark, "a bed is discovered with a Blackamoor in it," and Thomas, delighted, comments on "how soft the rogue feels," until, desirous to see his lover, he lights a candle and finds out who is really in his bed: "Holy Saints defend me, / The Devil, Devil, Devil, O the Devil / . . . I am abus'd most damnedly, most beastly, / Yet if it be a she-Devil."[98] In 1632, just one year after the Queen Henrietta Maria's Men had revived *The White Devil* at the Phoenix theatre, Richard Brome evoked a similar scene in *The Novella*, in which a white woman, pretending to be a courtesan, has her Afro-diasporic maidservant, Jacconetta (actually an Afro-diasporic eunuch in disguise), lay in her stead and trick the lecherous Pantalone.[99] In the second part of *The Fair Maid of the West* (1631), Goodlack and Roughman paradoxically protect the color line and prevent Mullisheg, the blacked-up king of Fez, from making further advances on English Bess by promising Mullisheg and his wife, Tota, that they will get to participate (separately) in interracial bed tricks with the English people they respectively lust for.[100] Brome revisited this motif shortly after *Fair Maid Part 2* was performed, in *The English Moor, or The Mock-Marriage* (1637).

Brome's play signals the dynamics of inversion at work in the succuban script by making interracial sex an object of desire for white men. Indeed, while the jealous Quicksands puts black-up on his wife, convinced as he is that no man can be drawn to an Afro-diasporic woman, notable wencher Nathaniel Banelass is drawn to the woman in black-up not despite but because of her blackness. Banelass, who clearly has a fetish for Afro-diasporic women, eventually has a sexual encounter with the woman in black-up and is disappointed in no small measure to find out, at the end of the play, that this woman is none other than Phillis, an impoverished white woman whom he had undone and abandoned at the beginning of the play. His reaction—"The devil looks ten times worse with a white face, / Give me it black again" (5.3.1047)—confirms the role that succuban fantasies, a desire not just for Afro-diasporic women but for Afro-diasporic women imagined as demonic, played in his attraction to her. Phillis has many counterparts in late Jacobean and Caroline drama—all avatars of the Florinda theatregram we first encountered in *Lo schiavetto*.[101] Yet those characters of white women who all decide to go into black-up in order to make themselves invisible and thereby gain the social agency necessary to arrange their romantic situations and restore their imperiled honor seem immune to demonization, probably because those heroines are supposed to remain quintessentially white under their disguise so that spectators might sympathize with them. Temporarily framed as a *succuba*, Phillis is an exception to that rule, and that exception opens a space of visibility for the strength of the white male desire (Banelass's) fueling the succuban script.

The colonial subtext of the anxieties that subtend the succuban script of blackness is explicitly articulated in *The Knight of Malta* (1618).[102] On the island of Malta, a notorious site of interracial friction on the early modern English stage, Zanthia, an Afro-diasporic maidservant, betrays her white mistress, Oriana, in order to secure the affection of the villainous Frenchman Mountferrat. Like Flamineo and Zanche in *The White Devil*, Mountferrat does not care for Zanthia but uses sexual gratification to keep the Afro-diasporic woman silent, and promises of marriage to secure her help in raping Oriana: "she doth love me yet / and I must her now, at least seem to do" (72). Like most men involved in interracial sex scenarios, Mountferrat enjoys the sex, but, unlike most of his homologues (Banelass excepted), he acknowledges it:

Zanthia Mountferrat, know,
  I am as full of pleasure in the touch
  As ere a white fac'd puppet of 'em all,
  Juicy, and firm, unfledge'd 'em of their tyres,
  Their wires, their partlets; pins, and Periwigs,

> And they appear like bald cootes, in the nest;
> I can as blithly work in my loves bed,
> And deck thy fair neck, with these Jetty chains,
> Sing thee asleep, being wearied, and refresh'd,
> With the same organ, steal sleep off again.
> *Mountferrat* Oh my black swan, sleeker than Cignets plush,
> Sweeter than is the sweet of Pomander,
> Breath'd like curl'd Zephyrus, cooling Lymon-trees,
> Straight as young pines, or Cedars in the grove,
> Quickly discend lovers best Canopie
> Still night, for Zanthia doth enamour me
> Beyond all continence. . . .
> It is not love, but strong Libidinous will
> That triumphs o're me, and to satiate that,
> What difference twixt this Moore, and her fair Dame?
> Night makes their hews alike, their use is so,
> Whose hand is so subtle, he can colours name,
> If he do winck, and touch 'em? Lust being blind,
> Never in women did distinction find. (72–73)

To woo Mountferrat, Zanthia invokes the main domains in which Afro-diasporic women were valorized in early modern Mediterranean culture: the haptic (she is "full of pleasure to the touch") and the musical (she can sing, and not only like a "swan").[103] Yet those qualities are not sufficient for Mountferrat to be drawn to Zanthia: what arouses him is her exchangeability with her "fair Dame" in obscurity, her ability to pass for a white woman in the dark. What truly arouses him, in short, is the succuban sex plot. Created as she has been, according to Mountferrat, for sexual encounters in the dark, for "libidinous will" but not for "love," Zanthia is meant to be perceived through the succuban lens.

When he believes that Zanthia has poisoned Oriana out of jealousy, Mountferrat demonizes her, exclaiming that she is in her "black shape, and blacker actions . . . hels perfect character." He asks: "Why grinst thou, devil?" (88). He asserts that the Devil is her "black sire" and calls her a

> black swoln pitchy cloud, of all my afflictions:
> Thou night hag, gotten when the bright Moon suffer'd:
> Thou hell itself confin'd in flesh. (89)[104]

Dubbing his lover a "night hag," Mountferrat comes very close to calling her a succuba. That privilege, however, is reserved to Norandine, who rants in the final scene:

> Marry was it Sir; the only truth that ever issued out of hell, which her black jawes resemble; a plague o'your bacon-face, you must be giving drinks with a vengeance; ah thou branded bitch: do' ye stare gogles? I hope to make winter-boots o' thy hide yet; she fears not damning: hell fire cannot parch her blacker than she is: d'ye grin, chimney-sweeper.... We'll call [Mountferrat] Cacodemon, with his black gib there, his Succuba, his devils seed, his spawn of Phlegeton, that o'my conscience was bred o' the spume of Cocitus; do ye snarle you black jill? She looks like the Picture of America. (95)

In addition to calling her a succuba, Norandine animalizes Zanthia and uses a term—"branded bitch"—that can frame her as a sex worker or as a slave. In the colonial world where enslaved women were always vulnerable to sexual assault, those two terms overlapped, and, as we saw in *A Very Woman*, this overlap informed the popular perception of Afro-diasporic women. Moreover, Norandine's comment that "she looks like the picture of America" suggests that Zanthia, in line with the widely circulated anthropomorphic representations of America in early modern cartographic culture, might be scantily clad at that point in the play, reinforcing her association with sex work and sexual assault. This image, invoking Native American femininity, brings a different subparadigm from the racial matrix into Zanthia's imaginative makeup, reminding us of the connected lives of those paradigms. Yet our understanding of "the picture of America" need not be limited to the figure of the Indigenous woman. Indeed, the picture of America had included Afro-diasporic women for a long time by 1618. Maybe the "new-seeded gardens" threatened by ravenous black succubae that Marcello had in mind in *The White Devil* were not solely English gardens but also new plantations overseas.

The succuban script of blackness did not disappear with the Civil War—far from it. Because the story it told about blackness answered the needs of an English colonial project that was immune to the political turmoil of the Interregnum and advanced steadfastly throughout the century, the succuban script returned when theatre returned under the Restoration.[105] Indeed, contrary to what the scholarly doxa currently holds to be true, a rich corpus of woefully understudied plays strongly suggests that Restoration acting companies, especially the Duke's, did have a tradition of female black-up. The myth—long accepted in early modern critical race studies—that there were no Afro-diasporic women in Restoration drama, due primarily to some alleged distaste of Restoration actresses for black-up, can be explained to a large extent by the archival pull exercised in our field by canonical plays, especially tragedies, which mostly involve Afro-diasporic male characters.[106] Yet the recent development of large digital databases like EEBO containing fully searchable playtexts affords new possibilities for us to resist the centrifugal force of the canon and to consider more diverse texts—some of which do include dark-skinned Afro-diasporic women—such as Dryden's *An Evening's Love, or The Mock-Astrologer* (1668), Thomas St. Serfe's *Tarugo's Wiles, or The Coffee House* (1668), Edward Howard's *The Womens Conquest* (1671), Elkanah Settle's *The Empress of Morocco* (1673), or Thomas Otway's *The Atheist* (1684).[107] In addition to new black-up plays, Jacobean and Caroline classics featuring dark-skinned Afro-diasporic female characters were regularly revived on the Restoration stage, and it is unlikely that those revivals erased or whitewashed characters as iconic as Zanche or Zanthia.[108] Resisting the pull of the canon can open exciting critical avenues.

By the 1660s, the cultural background against which female black-up and its succuban script were deployed had changed, for the taboo desire for Afro-diasporic women that this trope had long enabled and fulfilled in the sphere of representation had, by then, been exposed and legally condemned—firmly, publicly, and repeatedly. Indeed, various laws passed in the 1660s that instituted chattel slavery in the colonies encouraged slave owners to use brutal means of control and incentivized planters to enslave even more people, not solely in the Caribbean but also in Virginia and in the mainland. Because implementing chattel slavery meant owning and controlling the wombs of enslaved women, concerns about the enslaved hinged primarily on the sexuality of Afro-diasporic women, who constituted a third of the enslaved people purchased in the English colonies during the seventeenth century.[109] A Virginia statute of 1662, for instance, made the *partus sequitur ventrem* rule a reality in the English colonies by ruling that all children born to an enslaved woman would be born in bondage. The same statute tightened regulations against racial mixing, stating that "if any Christian shall commit fornication with a Negro man or woman, he or she so offending shall pay double the fines imposed by the former act."[110] Those two laws were promulgated in two consecutive sentences suggesting that the acts of interracial "fornication" the assembly was trying to deter involved Afro-diasporic women rather than Afro-diasporic men. In sum, by 1660, that white men had sex with Afro-diasporic women was a well-known fact with which the law grappled, for interracial sex produced children who were of crucial interest to slave owners symbolically and financially.[111] In a society profoundly concerned, to quote Jennifer Morgan, with "the possibilities of [Afro-diasporic women's] wombs," the black succuba, who, as a reproductive vehicle for another race's seed, was always positioned simultaneously inside and outside of the economy of sexual familial reproduction, took the spotlight onstage, and her presence gradually intensified.[112]

Nowhere is Restoration drama's use for black succubae more visible than in John Dryden and William Davenant's rewriting of Shakespeare's *Tempest*, subtitled *The Enchanted Island* (1667), a tragicomedy that illustrates the stage's permeation with what Elizabeth Maddock Dillon calls "the colonial relation," a term that "concerns the way in which far-flung territories become entwined with the central site of English political and economic power—namely, London."[113] In their rewriting, Dryden and Davenant go to great lengths to curtail any possibility of interracial union: they excise the original plotline of Claribel's marriage and turn her father, Alonso, into a man more likely to "repulse the Moors of Spain" from Portugal "in defense of Christianity" than to marry his daughter to the king of Tunis.[114] They remove the queer scene in which Caliban and Trinculo find refuge under a gabardine and form a single "monster of the isle with four legs." Last but not least, they give Caliban a twin sister, called Sycorax like their late mother, whose name is vaguely reminiscent of a succuba.

Sycorax of 1667 is, like her brother, a "freckel'd-hag-born whelp not honoured with a human shape," and a slave whom Prospero "keeps in service" (10). Several textual clues point toward Sycorax's sub-Saharan aspect. Caliban first describes "mistress monster his sister" as "beautiful and bright as the full moon" (24). Once she appears on stage, Trincalo comments "she's monstrous fair indeed" but remains determined to marry her "for estate more than for beauty" (28). This ironic comment on her "fairness," comparable to the silvery whiteness of the full moon, suggests that Sycorax is the opposite of fair and white. Trincalo calls her "my fair fuss"—short for "fussock," a fat unwieldy woman—and "my dear blobber-lips" (38), a phrase that echoes the multiple references to Afro-diasporic men like Othello and Aaron as "thick-lips." Susan B. Iwanisziw acknowledges that Sycorax, whose mother was a Moor from Algiers, is "never labeled by race or ethnicity," yet she reads such textual clues as evoking, through the lens of virulent misogynoir, a "few identifiably 'African' traits," and I agree.[115] *The Enchanted Island* was extremely popular: frequently revived and revised throughout the century, it was performed every year from 1698 to 1735. At the Theatre Royal in Drury Lane, there were over 180 performances of the play or its operatic version amended by Thomas Shadwell (1674) in the first half of the eighteenth century.[116] Such longevity gave the play a crucial role in shaping late seventeenth-century English spectators' conceptions of Afro-diasporic femininity: *The Enchanted Island* was to Afro-diasporic women what *Othello* was to Afro-diasporic men. In the long run, Sycorax paved the way for the caricatures of enslaved black women of mid-eighteenth-century English operas.[117]

Sycorax has at her command "a hundred spirits to attend us, Devils of all sorts, some great roaring Devils, and some little singing Sprights" (61), bequeathed to her by her late witch of a mother: such touches deploy the succuban script of blackness around her. Sycorax is construed as a libidinous creature that lusts after white men and seeks as many of them as possible: "My Lord, shall I go meet'em? I'll be kind to all of 'em / Just as I am to thee" (60). Later on, Trincalo sees her "tippling yonder with the serving men" (63). Trincalo seems to be her favorite, though attraction is not mutual. If sexual intercourse happens, it will involve loathing and coercion, like any succuban encounter, as we learn from Sycorax's very first appearance on stage:

> *Caliban* He shall get thee a young Sycorax, wilt thou not, my Lord?
> *Trincalo* Indeed I know not how, they do no such thing in my
>   Country.
> *Sycorax* I'le shew thee how: thou shalt get me twenty Sycoraxes; and
>   I'le get thee twenty Calibans.
> *Trincalo* Nay, if they are got, she must do't all her self, that's certain. (39)[118]

Sycorax's enthusiastic evocation of reproduction suggests that the potential issues of her womb will—in line with colonial law—follow the nature and, by extension, status of their mother's race, not their father's: she will give birth to little Sycoraxes and Calibans, not little Trincalos.

This exchange also underlines the play's participation in the regime of representation identified by Jennifer Morgan in the early modern English-speaking colonial world, where "images of Afro-diasporic women's reproductive potential, as well as images of their voracious sexuality, were crucial to slaveowners faced with female laborers," because "erroneous observations about African women's propensity for easy birth and breast-feeding reassured colonizers that these women could easily perform hard labor in the Americas."[119] Morgan explains: imagined as giving birth without pain, Afro-diasporic women were no daughters of Eve, which enabled colonial societies to simultaneously deny them any claim to womanhood and justify their forced reproduction of the enslaved community. The denial of womanhood that, for most of Sycorax's real-life counterparts, led to lives of labor in the fields alongside Afro-diasporic men, translates into Sycorax's masculinization.[120] Indeed, introduced in the dramatis personae by the same epicoene label as her brother ("monster of the isle"), she is masculinized throughout. She is "bigger" than Prospero's daughters (38) and depicted as fighting with Caliban, "beating him off the stage" (64)—not unlike the African women featured in *Grand bal de la Douairière de Bille-bahaut* in 1626 Paris. Finally, as Iwanisziw points out, "in contradistinction to the sexual ingenu/e Hippolito whose role was usually performed by a woman, she was frequently played by a male actor."[121]

Simultaneously masculinized and hypersexualized, Sycorax is construed as unfit to become part of any civilized economy of gender and sexuality. While the three young white Creoles of the island—Miranda; her twin sister, Dorinda; and the future Duke of Mantua, Hippolito—undergo a sentimental and sexual education in which they learn temperance, monogamy, and exogamy in prepa-ration for their ultimate return to Europe, Sycorax fails on all counts. Her in-temperance is obvious; she fails at monogamy by leaving her husband, Trincalo, for Stephano; and she fails at exogamy by committing incest with her brother Caliban: "Why then I'le tell thee, I found her an hour ago under an Elder-tree, upon a sweet Bed of Nettles, singing Tory, Rory, and Ranthum, Scantum, with her own natural Brother" (63). Such behavior prevents her from finding her way into the erotic economy that leads to matrimony and family life. Despite her repeated attempts, Sycorax does not get to engage in sexual intercourse with any of the white sailors, and when she expresses the desire to follow her husband to England, he refuses, preventing her from bringing interracial lust to the metro-pole: "No my dainty Dy-dapper, you have a tender constitution, and will be sick a Shipboard. You are partly Fish and may swim after me. I wish you a good Voy-age" (82).[122] In the post-1670 editions of the play, Sycorax does not even try to make it to Europe—that possibility cannot be spoken out loud anymore, not even in the hypothetical mode.

The play, after toying with the prospect of an interracial marriage, fore-closes that path. That is not to say that the denouement forecloses the possibili-ties of Sycorax's womb, only that the play, espousing the ideological imperatives of the colonial relation, deploys the succuban script to construe Sycorax as a potentially efficient reproductive vehicle for another race, while denying her the status of woman and mother that only matrimony can guarantee. If, for Renais-sance demonologists, succubae had no claim over the issue of their wombs because neither their wombs nor the seed they carried were theirs de facto, *The*

Enchanted Island suggests that Sycorax will never have any claim over the issue of her womb, because neither her womb nor the seed it carries are hers de jure. At the end of *The Enchanted Island*, a laboring Sycorax who is childless yet infinitely fertile *in potentia* remains in the absolute power of the wizard Prospero, who, unlike the Shakespearean original, does not leave the colonial island with the newlyweds, does not drown his book of secrets, and does not break his phallic staff.

Contradictions: Brownface and Colorism in Spain

When is a black woman not a black woman? Long before the development of the "tragic mulatta" plot so familiar to American culture, Spanish theatre grappled with that question. The last script of blackness that I will recount in this chapter stars a stock character unique to high baroque Spanish theatre: the *mulata* maid developed first and foremost by Lope de Vega at the beginning of the seventeenth century. The *mulata*, I argue, was a theatrical experiment in colorism that backfired. Born in a culture that had long relished characters of enslaved Afro-diasporic women yet systematically denied them any claim to beauty and desirability, the light-skinned *mulata* character was designed to tell a colorist story of differential aesthetic and erotic value among enslaved Afro-diasporic women based on their proximity to whiteness. The *mulata* character, in other words, is a testimony to the advanced development of the phenotype-as-race paradigm within the early modern racial matrix and to the consequent recalibration of the cosmetic sensorium of Iberian theatre at the beginning of the seventeenth century. The experiment backfired, however, in that *mulata* brownface never shed its strong hermeneutic kinship to black-up. That hermeneutic retention responded, in part, to a cultural need, in an age of racial mixing, to anchor and stabilize in blackness a brownness that, unmoored, could undo socioracial hierarchies. In response to contradictory ideological needs, brownface scopically told spectators a story that construed mixed women of African descent as simultaneously foils to and substitutes for African women, their mothers and sisters. In its contradictions, that script obliquely acknowledged the desirability of enslaved Afro-diasporic women in their many hues.

From its inception, performative blackness was uniquely feminine in early modern Spain. The various commodifying scripts of blackness discussed in Chapter 1 developed primarily around female characters. Notoriously, many of Lope de Rueda's early sixteenth-century comedias and eclogues (*coloquios pasto-*

riles) feature *negra* characters. In each of them, the negra's intervention is concentrated in one dense self-contained comedic scene that functions as a detachable skit (*paso*) to be used ad hoc by acting companies. Such calculated portability suggests that *negra* scenes—which Cervantes describes as Lope de Rueda's dramaturgic signature—were a popular go-to option for his acting company.[123] Although *negro* characters too were used for comedic purposes as early as the middle of the sixteenth century, the canon of Renaissance black-up in Spain is dominated by female characters, in ways that contrast strikingly with the historical development of black-up in early modern England and France.[124]

The reliance of Spanish black-up on female characters is not fortuitous: black slavery in metropolitan Iberia was primarily urban and domestic, and the inscription of blackness in the sphere of urban domestic slavery coincides with its feminization both materially and symbolically, for, as C. Riley Snorton puts it, in the domestic sphere of the enslaver's home, "blackness-as-womanhood (regardless of sex) is depicted as the result of a compulsory labor of care."[125] Thus, there are, to the best of my knowledge, no cases of demonized Afro-diasporic women in early modern Spanish theatre: the triumph of the commodifying scripts of blackness at the expense of the diabolical script did not even need to happen for *negra* characters. Both on stage and offstage, Afro-diasporic women were always already commodities: harmless and comedically domesticated consumable goods.

As we saw in Chapter 1, the foodstuff narrative and the animalizing narratives were most lavishly deployed around *negra* characters in the Renaissance theatre of Lope de Rueda, Feliciano da Silva, Jaime de Huete, and others. No doubt, comedic *negra* characters often have strong personalities, vocal claims, and a healthy sense of self-worth, but ultimately, the comedies in which they feature enact plots that keep them in their place, limiting their agency and social aspirations to the rhetorical realm.[126] This emplotment of Afro-diasporic women's inability to contest color-based slavery coincides with the deployment of the foodstuff and animalizing scripts of blackness. While the foodstuff and the animalizing paradigms are associated with enslaved *negras*, the luxury paradigm, designed to confer some degree of privilege onto some Afro-diasporic characters strategically deemed exceptional, was exclusively deployed in baroque theatre around Afro-diasporic women who were not enslaved.

The luxury paradigm, which, in its feminine deployment, was of an aesthetic nature, attached to beautiful, virtuous, and—often—allegorical Ethiopian queens elevated through luxury metaphors. For instance, in *El negro del mejor amo*, the black saint's mother, Sofonisba, is the daughter of the king of Ethiopia: that beautiful and virtuous dark-skinned princess is described as "a gem" (joya).[127] Similarly, in Luis Vélez de Guevara's *Virtudes vencen señales* (ca. 1620), the king of Albania describes in detail a painting of "the queen of Ethiopia, Sheba, in which the white Belgian Timantes had given brilliance and spirit to jet,"[128] and in Calderón's auto sacramental *La sibila del Oriente* (1682), the queen of Sheba is described as having a complexion of "jasp and ebony."[129] The beauty conferred to African queens via those luxurious metaphors differs from the simulacrum of white beauty to which the enslaved *negra* Eulalla fruitlessly lays claim in Lope de Rueda's *Comedia de Eufemia*, as she expresses her desire to dye her hair blond and to use skin-lightening creams.[130] Ultimately, the exclusive association of the luxury hermeneutics of black-up and its aesthetic value with free African queens rendered the ideas of beauty and enslavement incompatible in relation to Afro-diasporic women. The particular deployment of the commodifying scripts of blackness on the Spanish stage thus preempted the appearance of beautiful and desirable enslaved Afro-diasporic women characters. Enslaved *negra* characters were ubiquitous on stage, yet, conspicuously, never desirable.

Enter the *mulata*. By contrast with *negras*, *mulata* characters, although they are enslaved, are often constructed through the lens of the luxury script. That choice bears the heavy imprint of colorism, a system of power attuned to chromatic nuances: in a colorist society, shades of skin tone correlate with specific amounts of social privilege, and proximity to whiteness is rewarded by all.[131] Colorism has a wide-ranging array of manifestations, yet it primarily manifests itself, for women, in the aesthetic realm. The colorist luxury-based hermeneutics of *mulata* brownface is a case in point, as we can see in the portrait of Esperanza, whom an enamored white suitor describes in Lope de Vega's *Amar, servir, y esperar* (1624–35) as

> A cute *mulata* slave
> With a cunning face
> (For you know those women are
> The beauty spots of Seville);
> She has nothing to envy ivory for,
> With her skin of shining ebony,
> Which is neater and smells sweeter
> Than almond blossoms in April.
> She can also be rougher than a grater,

Ignoring danger,
With a little hat on her forehead
Like a horse blinder,
And swift slippers
Covering her walnut feet.[132]

The enslaved Esperanza is construed through the animalizing script (she wears horse blinders) and the foodstuff script (she has walnut feet and she smells of almonds), but her beauty is conveyed through the luxury script (her skin is of shining ebony). Another example: Fabio, a white servant, tries to seduce the *mulata* Esperanza in *Amar, servir, y esperar* by promising:

I will give you a necklace
Made of emeralds and baroque pearls
So that you will soon be able to call ivory
this yoke-bearing neck of yours.[133]

Luxurious adornments—material or poetic—can turn an animalized *mulata* into a luxurious creature of creamy white ivory, he promises.

Not only does the range of indexical signs used to close the meaning of brownface differ from that used to close the meaning of black-up; in performance, enslaved *mulata* characters also looked and sounded different from enslaved *negra* characters. Stage directions never indicate that actresses playing *mulatas* should "put soot on their faces" (la cara tiznada), as they so often do for *negra* characters. Whatever cosmetic paste actresses used to create brownface, it was not soot. The same attention to hairstyle that we encountered in sixteenth-century archives of performative blackness informed the creation of the *mulata* archetype. In *Servir a señor discreto* (1610–18), when Lope introduces the *mulata* Elvira, the stage direction describes her hair as "a little topknot of black curly hair fitted on her head."[134] Similarly, in *El premio de bien hablar y volver por las mujeres* (1624–25), the *mulata* Rufina is described as wearing her hair as "loose curly ringlets."[135] Such curly wigs differ from those sported by *negros* a century earlier, in the 1525 Toledo performance, which tried to render the texture of African braids, twists, and locks, or from the headscarf sported by the *negra* Margarita on the frontispiece of Jaime de Huete's *Tesorina* (Figure 3).

Aurally, *mulata* characters are distinct from *negras* for they never speak in blackspeak, the comedic dialect reserved to enslaved Afro-diasporic characters on stage, which I discuss at length in Chapter 3. *Mulatas* speak unaccented

Figure 3. Frontispiece of *Tesorina* (dramatis personae). Jaime de Huete.
Woodcut. Circa 1530. Imágenes procedentes de los fondos de la Biblioteca
Nacional de España.

Castilian: they are enslaved, yet they "speak white," disrupting the alignment
between diction and enslavement.

   In the colorist aesthetics of high baroque Spanish theatre, not only were
negras construed by performative means as different from *mulatas*; they functioned as foils to *mulatas*. To give one example, in Lope's *La vitoria de la honra*
(1609–15), the *mulata* maid Dorotea, listed as "enslaved" (esclava) in the dramatis personae, is contrasted with the *negras* and *negros* performing in a street *baile*
that she is eager to see. Dorotea does not participate in the musical and choreographic performances of blackness; rather, she, along with white spectators,
consumes them. In that sense, there is irony at the end of the play, when, to

avoid the wrath of her mistress's husband, who has just discovered his wife's disloyalty, she hides in a large basket of flour and comes out of hiding "covered with flour" (llena de harina).[136] The brownfaced woman gets a top coat of white-face and thereby reveals on the burlesque mode what was imagined to be there all along in a colorist world: the whiteness within her.

And yet this colorist orchestration of a foil relation between *negras* and *mulatas* backfired in comedias nuevas. First, at a basic logical level, offstage and on stage, *mulatas* existed only because of interracial sex between—most of the time—white men and Afro-diasporic women. Thus, the very existence of that character tacitly acknowledged and reminded spectators of the desirability of enslaved Afro-diasporic women in early modern Spain, which the peculiar de-ployment of the commodifying scripts of blackness denied. Second, the herme-neutics of brownface never fully relinquished its strong kinship with the hermeneutics of blackness deployed around *negras*.

The ways in which the hermeneutics of blackness stuck to *mulata* brown-face are particularly apparent in *Servir a señor discreto*, one of Lope de Vega's thirty-something Sevillian plays, most of which he wrote after his stay in Seville between 1600 and 1604.[137] A major Iberian port since the fifteenth century, Seville had become the capital of Spanish imperial commerce at the beginning of the sixteenth century, when the Casa de Contratación was built: Lope often celebrates Seville as the "port and gate of the Indies" (puerto y puerta de Indias). It was the port through which enslaved Afro-diasporic people arrived in Spain, and it had the highest number of Afro-diasporic people, both free and unfree, in Europe. Contemporaries often compared Seville to a chessboard, with an even number of black and white pieces.[138] *Mulatos* were visible and numerous enough to have their own confraternity separate from the Hermandad de los Negritos, which participated in Corpus Christi processions under its own ban-ner.[139] Lope includes *mulata* "esclavillas" in most of his Sevillian plays, even when their dramatic arcs do not require it. *Mulatas* bring Sevillian couleur lo-cale to the stage.

Servir a señor discreto's subplot revolves around the relationship between a servant, Giron, and Elvira, the *mulata* maid of Leonor, the play's heroine, and possibly her illegitimate half sister, since both young women have an *Indiano* merchant father, and Leonor calls Elvira "sister" (hermana) at one point (97). Elvira's mother comes from Biafra, and her father from Lima, Peru (189). From the start, Giron describes Elvira as "a little *mulata* slave" (una cierta esclavilla mulata) "a *mulata*, who, I hear, is smart as a whip."[140] Like her *mulata* sister Leonor in *Los peligros de la ausencia* (1613–20), Elvira is very good at seeing and pursuing her own interests.[141] She is deemed attractive by many white men, including Giron, who promises to marry her, and Don Silvestre's men, whom Elvira scares away with a knife when they start taking liberties to check whether it is true that *mulatas* "have very soft skin."[142] Elvira attracts men and she knows it—she boasts: "I like my own color / Because, as they say, brown skin knocks men dead."[143] Giron has no intention whatsoever of marrying Elvira once he gets what he wants from her, yet Elvira is not to be trifled with. Ultimately, Elvira wins, as the Count, true deus ex machina, forces Giron to marry her in the last ten lines of the play in order to reward her services. Elvira is not an exception: more often than not, Lope's *mulatas* get their (white) man.

Commodifying hermeneutics are ruthlessly deployed around Elvira, not least by Giron, whose own racial ambiguity, often pointed out by Elvira, renders him fearful of turning socially black by marrying a woman of color. Indeed, Elvira repeatedly states that she does not consider Giron to be white. When she reveals Don Pedro's identity to Leonor's father, for instance, she states that "his servant [Giron] is a man of my own complexion, and very well-spoken."[144] Later on, when she wants Giron to taker her in his arms and he protests that she will stain him, she ironically asks: "Oh, is your highness so white?"[145] No other character in the play treats Giron as nonwhite or ever alludes to his physical appearance, so Elvira's statements might just be a strategy to bridge the divide between her lover and herself. However, we also have to consider the possibility that Elvira, whom we know to be "smart as a whip" and attuned to the ways of colorism, might just be right. Giron might be *passing* as white, and his obsessive fear of turning black might originate precisely from his own adjacency to whiteness in a colorist society.

Giron fluently deploys commodifying scripts around Elvira when he needs to keep her at bay—for instance, when he sets off for Madrid with his impoverished master, and tries to get some cash as parting present from her:

> *Elvira* Did you just say money?
> *Giron* Yes, money.
> *Elvira* How can you be short on cash
>   When you serve such a great master?
> *Giron* He's not short on cash, but I am.
> *Elvira* With him, you cannot lack anything.
>   Now, you can treat yourself
>   With memories of me.
> *Giron* That's it?

Elvira I want you to take my soul with you.
Giron I had rather take your body with me:
      That way I could sell it
      And make money out of it.[146]

Partitioning Elvira's soul and body immediately leads to the commodification of her body, through sex work, slavery, or both. A tiff ensues, and Elvira eventually gives Giron the money he asks for, but not before Giron has made it clear that he will never stop viewing Elvira's body as a precious commodity. When they are finally reunited in Madrid, Giron further confirms this:

Giron My little *negra*!
Elvira Unfortunately so.
      Giron, let us stop fighting: let me put my arms
      Around your neck, and, for the love of God,
      Let us look like a writing tool and its inkwell.
Giron That's nice jet I am putting around my neck.[147]

Beyond the sex joke, by referring to herself as an "inkwell" in which Giron can dip his "writing tool," Elvira is mobilizing commodifying metaphors that evoke a scrivener's trade, and more specifically, the process of drafting and signing a marriage contract, a subject that she successfully revisits in the final scene of the play. She is calling on a commodifying script to further her own agenda and re-configure her own position in Spanish society as a married woman—a move that Dryden and Davenant's Sycorax would have recognized. Giron, however, ignores her point and runs a stale metaphor instead: as he "puts her arms around his neck," he puts on a "jet" necklace (a metaphor prefiguring the "jetty chains" with which Zanthia would offer to "deck" Mountferrat's "fair neck" on the English stage about a decade later in *The Knight of Malta*). By using the luxury script attached to beautiful Ethiopian queens, Giron placates her, moves the conversation from the sphere of marriage back to the sphere of interracial amorous conquest, and exempts himself from commodification in the process. Elvira, quick-witted as ever, sees him and immediately snaps back "O, is your lordship so white?"

The beautifying luxury paradigm is lavishly deployed around Elvira throughout the play. At the end of the second *jornada* (Act 2), Elvira turns herself into a precious brown statue by promising, "I will be quiet as if I were made of bronze."[148] Similarly, when Don Pedro rehearses with Giron all the compliments he intends to pay to Leonor's trusted maid in order to ingratiate himself with her, he compares Elvira to quicksilver, which "purifies gold in the crucible."[149] The comparison pays homage to Elvira's transformative power over Leonor (whose name bursts with gold), and it inscribes her in a goldsmith's inventory. When Elvira enters, the flatterer performs fantastically: "Bless the gentleman who made love to your mother, for he set ebony into ivory so well!"[150] Elvira becomes a precious sculpture of ivory with ebony incrustations, espousing the often-feminized Renaissance aesthetics of beautiful contrasts. Unsurprisingly, he also describes her teeth as pearls ("boca de perlas") in the tradition of the Petrarchan blazon.

Yet even in that moment when Elvira is construed through a colorist script that gives her access, enslaved as she is, to a world of beauty and privilege her mother could not dream of, the older hermeneutics of *negra* black-up sticks to her. Indeed, just a few minutes before he praises her pearly teeth, Don Pedro makes a pun that collapses the luxury and the animalizing scripts:

> *Pedro* Plautus forgives
>   Lovers' flatteries best.
>   He says that they flatter
>   Even their ladies' dogs,
>   For their dogs often
>   Serve to excuse their faults.
>   Look how well I will flatter
>   The *mulata*.
> *Giron* You must really be in love,
>   If you already call her *mulata* a bitch.
> *Pedro* A bitch [perra], yes, and a pearl [perla] at the same time.[151]

By punning on the quasi-homophones *perra* and *perla*, Don Pedro reveals the unstable boundary between the animalizing script traditionally deployed on stage around enslaved Afro-diasporic women ("bitch") and the beautifying luxury script traditionally deployed around free African queens, and now around enslaved *mulatas* ("pearl").[152] Those two scripts are but one letter away from each other, and, as we will see in Chapter 3, that letter itself is an unstable boundary particularly likely to shift in the mouth of *negro* characters who often mispronounce [R] as [L]. Giron repeats the pun later on: "let me follow this sooty bitch—I mean pearl!"[153] Lope de Vega recycled that pun in *El premio de bien hablar y volver por las mujeres*, where the white servant Martín uses it against the *mulata* Rufina; in *La vitoria de la honra*, where Don Antonio, the gallant, also calls his mistress's *mulata* maid, Dorotea, "una perla"; and in *Los peligros de la ausencia*, where the white servant Martín calls the *mulata* Leonor "a pearl with two Rs" (perla con dos erres).[154] The *perra/perla* pun is one of the many ways in which the hermeneutics of blackness and its scripts stick to brownface across the repertoire of *mulata* plays.

Tropes central to the scripts of female blackness follow Elvira wherever she goes. I will not rehearse here the numerous occurrences when Elvira is animalized or discussed as foodstuff, but the moments when her brownface is alluded to as if it were black-up deserve special attention. When the servant Rosales tries to procure Elvira's favors, he calls her "my darling soot" (tizne mia); she calls herself "coal" (carbones); during a friendly fight, Leonor tells Elvira to "go scrub herself with soap" (vete a xabonar mulata); Giron, when he finally accepts to marry her, calls her "a sea of ink" (un mar de tinta).[155] When he first mentions her, he construes her, despite her mixed inheritance, as squarely African: "I am in love; my love has sailed from Guinea to Seville" and "to praise you, I will consult Ethiopian Muses, for it would be improper for me to invoke the Spanish ones."[156]

Moreover, whenever Elvira is given a choice, she chooses to identify with Blackness. When, in the scene previously cited, Don Pedro compares Elvira to "an ivory statue incrusted with ebony" (143) turning her into a white creature lightly spotted with blackness, Elvira sets Don Pedro straight "leave such jokes, sir: a tailor cut this little piece of flannel from my mother."[157] Elvira, who is compared to various textiles in the play, including velvet and chambray, references herself as a piece of flannel and affirms that she is cut of the same cloth as her Biafran mother. Elvira proudly self-identifies as Black and has every intention to spread Blackness. When Giron calls her a "magpie" (picaza), she, the self-identified "inkwell," retorts that she intends to kiss him and thereby literally put her Black mark on him, her new creation: "*Elvira me fecit*! That way I know no harlot will dare say anything to you—they will know my signature."[158] Elvira's Black pride overflows.[159] When is a Black woman not a Black woman? Never.

While the visual imagery deployed in this play to describe *mulatas* tends to awkwardly juxtapose blackness and whiteness without truly merging them—as in the case of the ivory statue incrusted with ebony, or in the moments when Giron compares his future mixed-race children to pieces on a chessboard, black *and* white, rather than brown—the desire to craft a new colorist hermeneutics of brownface occasionally registers more successfully in the repertoire.[160] In *Los peligros de la ausencia*, for instance, the *mulata* Leonor's forearms and hands are described by Martín, as "amber gloves" (guantes de ambar)—a metaphor that colors the luxury script as golden brown in line with the material practices of cosmetic brownface.[161] Indeed, even though the phrase "amber gloves" seems, at first, to refer to the early modern practice of using ambergris to scent gloves, its recurrent association with eroticized light-skinned people of Afro-diasporic descent forces us to parse its meaning differently. In the third jornada of Lope de Vega's *La dama boba*, for instance, a song personifies Love as a traveler who moved from Spain to the Indies and returned to the peninsula enriched: one of the sartorial marks of his newly acquired status is "gloves marinated in ambergris" (guante de ambár adobado).[162] The nouveau riche quality that this prop denotes cannot be untangled from its colonial quality, which proceeds from lands associated in popular imagination with the racial hybridization of its inhabitants and the production of *mulatos*: as the call and response song of *La dama boba* repeats no less than twenty times, the man with amber gloves "comes from Panama!" (viene de Panamá).

Starting in the 1630s, the existence of *mulata* actresses in Spain is well documented: actresses such as Josefa María Fernández, known as "la *Mulatilla*," and Francisca López, known, precisely, as "guantes de ámbar," acquired some fame.[163] Read in conjunction with the Lopescan network of associations between *mulatas* and amber gloves, Francisca López's choice of stage name cannot be coincidental. It demands that we read "amber gloves" not only as an olfactive, but also as a chromatic trope participating the colorist version of the luxury script of blackness from the beginning of the seventeenth century onward. The trope recurs in *Amar, servir, y esperar*, where Andrés calls the *mulata* Esperanza "amber."[164] Yet the metaphor coexists, in the very same scene, with older tropes attached to black-up such as "besmirched angel" (angel tiznado).[165] In other words, even at its apex, brownface could never shed blackness. Colorist brownface thus emerges as simultaneously other than *and* the same as its intended foil, blackness.

The hyper-sexualization of Spanish *mulatas*, both on stage and offstage, as well as their resistant hermeneutic association with blackness were strong enough for foreigners to see them. John Dryden, who read Spanish, even staged those Iberian dynamics in *An Evening's Love, or The Mock-Astrologer*, which was performed by the King's Company just one year after his *Enchanted Island*.[166] Actress Nell Gwyn, the king's mistress, played the role of Jacinta, a witty young Spaniard who falls in love with Wildman, "a guest of the English ambassador's retinue" in Madrid.[167] Wildman has a strong libido and harbors no wish whatsoever to curtail it; determined to tame her suitor into matrimony,

Jacinta first tests his fidelity by posing as alluring exotic women. The first disguise she picks is a veiled Moroccan lady, Fatyma, "a brunet of Afrique" whose skin color is not specified.[168] Her second disguise is that of an enslaved *mulata*.[169] The wild Englishman falls for Jacinta both times—with a clear preference for the second disguise, which involves brownface:

> *Jacinta* 'Tis impossible your love should be so humble, to descend to a Mulatta.
>
> *Wildman* One would think so, but I cannot help it. Gad, I think the reason is because there's something more of sin in thy colour then in ours. I know not what's the matter, but a Turky-Cock is not more provok'd at red, then I bristle at the sight of black. Come, be kinder to me.[170]

Wildman pays the enslaved mulatta to procure her favors; she accepts, and she informs him that, as a rule, a gentleman may only hope "to be admitted to pass my time with, while a better comes: to be the lowest step in my Stair-case, for a Knight to mount upon him, and a Lord upon him, and a Marquess upon him, and a Duke upon him, till I get as high as I can climb."[171] The *mulata* that Dryden stages smacks of the succuban script of blackness that was part of English performance vernacular (there is "sin in thy color"), but she is also typically Spanish in that white men undeniably desire her, poetics of blackness stick to her brown skin (the sight of her is "the sight of black"), and her erotic allure makes her socially mobile—which turns her into a threat to established socioracial hierarchies. There is no such scene of *mulata* impersonation in the Spanish text that inspired Dryden's play, Calderón de la Barca's *El astrologo fingido* (1632): Dryden invented it because *mulatas* denoted Spanish culture in English cultural imagination.[172]

Mulatas threatened the stability of Spanish socioracial taxonomies and hierarchies, and the need to assuage that threat in the realm of representation competed, in the crafting of the hermeneutics of brownface, with the initial drive toward colorism. The very competition of those conflicting ideological needs (the need to immobilize brownness and the need to uplift it at the expense of blackness) explains the tensions at work in a practice of brownface that aspires to coin a uniquely luxurious idiom of brownness while holding on to the foodstuff and animalizing scripts of blackness. Blackness stuck to brownface because unmoored brownness was a dangerous thing that had to be moored in blackness's artificial stability.

Spanish *mulatos* generated strong anxieties at the time. For Baltasar Fra-Molinero, early modern literary representations of *mulatos* and *mulatas* spring from "bad conscience shared by the audience," the awareness that *mulatos* "are the result of illegitimate unions"—unions overwhelmingly involving white men and enslaved Afro-diasporic women.[173] "Illegitimacy" is the keyword to understand the status and perception of *mulatos* in early modern Spanish society: it explains why "guilds, brotherhoods, universities and the Church approve one after the other, on both sides of the Atlantic, norms and dispositions to exclude *negros* and *mulatos* from those institutions."[174] Those cultural anxieties hinged specifically on *mulatas*, because they were the vector that exponentially increased the number of Afro-descended Spaniards. At the turn of the seventeenth century, the archives tell us that, because of their sexual allure in Spanish society, *mulatas* were disproportionately involved in legal cases of concubinage or prostitution. This reality transpires on stage, for instance, in *El premio de bien hablar*, where the *mulata* Rufina is described as "the quintessence of all the discreet roguishness that blackness breeds in this country," or, later on, in Vicente Suárez de Deza y Ávila's interlude *Bayle entremesado del galeote mulato* (1663), which features a *mulata*, La Chaves, who associates with sex workers.[175] Because sexual relations, consensual or not, were most often consummated illegitimately, *mulatas* "embodied the rupturing of the social, racial, and moral order."[176] Not only did *mulatas'* hypersexualization threaten the family structure on which social order relies: Alessandro Stella notes that the practice of abandoning children at the hospital (he studies in particular records of the Casa Cuna of Cadix), regardless of actual motivations, ensured that the children abandoned by their *mulata* mother would grow up free.[177] The hypersexualization of *mulatas* had the long-term effect of increasing the number of free Afro-diasporic people in the Iberian peninsula.

The anxieties attached to alluring *mulatas* in early modern Spanish culture were linked to the threat that they and their offspring posed to a culture obsessed with racial legibility and classification. The development of that sensibility was tied to the colonization of the Americas whence racial mixing was believed to proceed. In his 1495 Latin-Spanish dictionary, Antonio de Nebrija had included the term *negro de Guinea*, but not *mulato* or *mestizo*.[178] In 1609, El Inca Garcilaso de la Vega published in Lisbon his *Comentarios reales*, in which he devotes a whole chapter to the "new names used to call various generations," including *mulatos*.[179] Two years later, in 1611, Covarrubias included the terms *mulato* and *mestizo* in his *Tesoro de la lengua castellana o española*. And sixteen years later, Sandoval, in *De instauranda aethiopum salute*, reinforced the idea that racial mixing came from the empire, scrutinizing the shades of brown skin produced there: "Among white men, there are many kinds of whiteness, and, similarly, among black men, there are many kinds of blackness. Indeed, between white and vermillion, you will find shades such as pale and golden; and, similarly, between white and black, you will find shades such as ashen, swarthy, red, and tawny, like Indians in this New World who generally look tawny, or like cooked quince, or jaundiced, or chestnut brown—and that also applies to *negros*."[180] Sandoval mobilizes the foodstuff paradigm and adds some comestible shades to the list, such as "*mulato*-like or completely *mulato*, dun, black mixed with Indian, yellowish-brown, between *mulato* and black, chestnut brown, or toasted—for this nation has all of those colors, and many more."[181] Those lexical changes from Nebrija to Sandoval over 130 years reflect both the transformation of the racial makeup of the imperial population and the drive of the Spanish racial epistemology toward classification, even as the number of *mulatos* in the empire overtook the enslaved *negro* population.[182]

Such classifications had legal ramifications, and their undermining was a subject of concern for the authorities. In 1568 a letter sent by the king to the Real Audiencia of Mexico mentions that the numerous *mulatos* and *mestizos* who "only know their relatives on their mothers' side, stay with them," which could "over time, become a problem."[183] As Joanne Rappaport shows, in the New Kingdom of Granada, the designations for mixed-race people, *mestizos* and *mulatos*, were "no stable markers of identity" and, in legal records, "under particular circumstances [determined by power play] people classified as *mestizo* [and sometimes *mulato*] dropped out of the *mestizo* slot and into other categories," usually, the "*indio*" category.[184] The same year, a general law for the Indies extended to *mulatos* and *zamboigos* the interdiction to carry weapons.[185] Anxieties crystalized around *mulatos*' ability to claim allegiance to different communities, to claim the privileges of more than one socioracial group, to live performative lives akin to what Barbara Fuchs calls "passing." In other words, to quote Stuart Schwartz and Frank Salomon, "people of mixed birth formed not so much a new category as a challenge to categorization itself."[186] Or, as Monica Styles puts it, "Mulatto became a metaphor for the person who subverted racial categories."[187]

The slipperiness of the *mulato* category, the challenge it posed to categorization itself, is palpable in Garcilaso de la Vega's 1609 definition of *mulatos* as the children not of Caucasians and sub-Saharan Africans, but rather of *negros* and *indios*. In Iberia, this move toward a classification of imperial subjects was embedded in the ongoing process of national self-fashioning that mobilized all cultural spheres: a process in which, as Fuchs has shown, the self-fashioning of Spain as a fictitious Christian nation without African roots depended on policies of discrimination, exclusion, and expulsion based on a complex apparatus of statuses regarding the purity of blood (limpieza de sangre). Most importantly, "the possibility of making these distinctions depended on subjects being transparent and classifiable."[188] A general obsession with racial visibility, legibility, and indexability ensued.

The potential racial illegibility of *mulatos* played into the widespread pre-existing anxieties attached to the hybrid subjects that were *conversos* and *moriscos*. In particular, *moriscos* and *mulatos* seem to have been bound together in cultural imagination. For instance, Sandoval's observation that some *negros* (presumably mixed Afro-diasporic people) have the color of "cooked quince" echoes the phrase used in documents that inventory the sale and redemption of enslaved people during the Moorish rebellion in the Alpujarras (1569–71) to describe some *Moros*: "white tending to cooked quince."[189] *Mulatos* shared their brownness with some *moriscos*, and what they shared with all *moriscos* was their ability to trouble strict racial classifications, precisely because they could pass as other than *mulatos*. This was even more the case with their light-skinned children who could, especially when they were free, pass as white. That might have been the case for Giron in *Servir a señor discreto*, and that might have been what Elvira knew. Some of the most famous *pinturas de castas*, such as those painted by Miguel Cabrera, acknowledge the ability of children born from a white father and a *mulata* mother to pass as white, when they indicate, as Fuchs notes, that such children are called *moriscos*.[190] On Cabrera's painting, the white father strokes his daughter's face under the unimpressed gaze of the *mulata* mother, and the juxtaposition of the father's hand and his daughter's cheek underlines the difficulty of telling the father's complexion apart from his child's, whose gendering as feminine is no happenstance (see Plates 7 and 8). Associating those children with *moriscos*, pinturas de castas do not classify those children as white, but as anxiety-provoking *passers-as-white*.

In a culture so deeply invested in rendering legible invisible forms of racialized difference (in the case of *conversos* and *moriscos*), Afro-descendants of mixed heritage, with their innumerable shades of beige and brown skin, their ability to pass, and their tendency to multiply by virtue of their sexual allure in the eyes of white Spaniards, threatened to destabilize established socioracial hierarchies all around the Hispanic world. The very fact that some *mulatas*, such as the previously mentioned Josefa María and Francisca López "amber gloves," could become professional actresses illustrates my point: *mulatas* could infiltrate and potentially destabilize from within various institutions that *negras* could not. In that context, marking those characters' African heritage and making their heritage indissolubly visible, undeniable, and stable—making blackness *stick*—worked toward assuaging anxieties. I read the ways in which scripts of blackness stick to brownfaced *mulatas* on stage as gestures in that direction. If the hermeneutics of brownface ends up spanning the whole spectrum of the commodifying scripts of blackness, from foodstuff and animals to luxury goods, it is because stage *mulatas* were a nexus where conflicting ideological needs met—where colorism and its desire to uplift brownness clashed with the need to moor and anchor in blackness an all-too-mobile brownness that threatened to collapse subparadigms on the phenotypical axis of the racial matrix. If the colorist script of blackness that theatre deployed around Afro-diasporic women sounds self-contradictory, it is because the era had self-contradictory ideological needs.

Conclusion: *Wrinkles Deep in Time*

I opened this diptych of chapters on the history of baroque black-up with the metaphor of a tree, defining that history as one of "secularization in which various traditions slowly branch out and away from a core episteme of religious allegory inherited from the Middle Ages." The tree metaphor, with all its genetic implications and its involvement (beautifully explored by Jean E. Feerick) in the poetics of the early modern racial discourse, helps us understand the connected lives and itineraries of the diabolical hermeneutics of black-up in performance cultures as different as the English, French, and Spanish ones.[191] Yet to conceptualize the connected lives of female black-up in those cultures in the high baroque period, we need a new model, one closer to what Susan Lanser usefully calls "confluence." By contrast with influence, "rather than implying causality across surface evidence, confluence suggests a convergence of relatively simultaneous phenomena from a deeper common source, rather like symptoms of a systemic illness or surface water from an underground aquifer." The deeper common source, or "shared social, political, or cultural logic," that informed the connected hermeneutic lives of female black-up in early modern England, France, and Spain was the anxiogenic truth that, all around colonial worlds, white men engaged in coercive sex with Afro-diasporic women and were encouraged to do so by the social, political, and economic structures in which they lived.[192]

Aesthetic strategies were crafted to accommodate in erotic terms brutal realities that ultimately had little to do with desire. Early modern performance
culture obfuscated the issue of mass rape with an erotic framing foregrounding
the "question" of Afro-diasporic women's un/desirability. Geometrical exclu-
sions, fetishistic inversions, and glaring contradictions are just some of the
forms that the oblique aesthetics of Afro-diasporic women's desirability took
across early modern Europe, and the continued expansion of archives will, no
doubt, bring more scripts and oblique representational strategies to the surface.
Retrieving those is the task of intersectional feminists who refuse to replicate in
a scholarly mode the early modern urge to render Afro-diasporic women invisible. If we are to obey Shakespeare's Black, desirable, and powerful Cleopatra's
command to

> Think on me,
> That am with Phoebus' amorous pinches black,
> And wrinkled deep in time (1.5.27–29),

then we must remember that a wrinkle is, originally, a fold, crease, a ridge on
what should be a smooth surface: a wrinkle is an oblique line. Crucially, we
must remember that the nonquestion of Afro-diasporic women's un/desirabil-
ity written into the manifold racializing scripts of blackness deployed around
blacked-up female characters on early modern stages worked, first and foremost,
as a distraction.

Plate 1. "Satan Sending Devils to the Antichrist" in *Mystère du jour du jugement*. Parchment. 1326–50. Bibliothèque municipale de Besançon, Ms 579, f. 8v.

Plate 2. *The Smokers, or The Guard* (*La tabagie*). Mathieu Le Nain. Oil on canvas. 117 × 137 cm. 1643. © RMN-Grand Palais / Art Resource, NY.

Plate 3. *The Children's Dance Lesson* (*Leçon de danse d'enfants*). Mathieu Le Nain. Oil on canvas. 85.1 × 114.9 cm. 1645–48. The Menil Collection, Houston.

Plate 4. *La Mauresse* (Presumed daughter of Louis XIV). Pierre Gobert.
Oil painting. Late seventeenth century-early eighteenth century.
Bibliothèque Sainte-Geneviève, Paris. Cliché Charmet.

Plate 5. "The Cacique and His Train Enter" in *Grand bal de la douairière de
Billebahaut*. Daniel Rabel. Drawing. 1626. Bibliothèque nationale de France.

Plate 6. "The African Women Enter" in *Grand bal de la douairière de Billebahaut*. Daniel Rabel. Drawing. 1626. Bibliothèque nationale de France.

Plate 7. *De español y negra, mulata*. Miguel Cabrera. Oil on canvas. 148 × 117.5 × 5.5 cm. Circa 1763. Colección particular en custodia en el Museo de Historia Mexicana.

Plate 8. *De español y mulata, morisca*. Miguel Cabrera. Oil on canvas.
148 × 116.5 × 5.6 cm. Circa 1763. Colección particular en custodia en el
Museo de Historia Mexicana.

Plate 9. "Costume Design for the Cacique" in *Grand bal de la douairière de Billebahaut*. Daniel Rabel. Drawing. 1626. The New York Public Library.

Plate 10. *Chafariz d'el Rey* (King's Fountain in the Alfama district of Lisbon). Oil on wood. 93 × 163 cm. Circa 1570–80. Coleção Berardo / The Berardo Collection, Lisbon, Portugal.

Plate 11. "Black Slaves Dancing" in *Thierbuch*. Zacharias Wagener. Watercolor. 1640. Kupferstich-Kabinett, Staatliche Kunstsammlungen Dresden. Photo: Herbert Boswank.

L'afrique

A mes yeux les climats bruslés
Aux autres regions paroistroient preferables

Si les monstres affreux dont ils sont habités
Estoient a celuy ci semblables.

Chez Mariette au coq rue St Jacques

Plate 12. "L'Afrique" in *Recueil de modes.* Nicolas Arnoult et al. Engraving.
1750. Bibliothèque nationale de France.

CHAPTER 3

Blackspeak

Acoustic Blackness and the Accents of Race

(I'm just going to say this right now so we can get it over with:
I don't know what a real slave sounded like. And neither do you.)
Branden Jacobs-Jenkins, *An Octoroon*, 2014

In *Fragoa d'amor*, a tragicomedy written by Gil Vicente in 1525 to celebrate the wedding of João III of Portugal and the Spanish infanta Catherine of Austria, Cupid and Mercury decide to celebrate the arrival of the new queen by giving the Portuguese people the opportunity to be recast, remade, and hammered to perfection in their titular "Forge of Love." The first to seize upon the gods' offer is Fernando, an enslaved Afro-Portuguese man, who asks to be turned "white like a chicken egg" (branco como ovo de gallinha), with a "very thin nose" (fazer nariz mui delgada) and "thin lips" (faze me beiça delgada).[1] Disappointment ensues:

> *The Negro exits from the forge, looking like a white gentleman.*
> *Yet they could not hammer blackspeak out of him.*
> *Negro* Now my hand *is white,
>   And my leg *is white too
>   But . . . I still *talk black!
>   If I still *talk black,
>   What is the point of *looking white?
>   If I still *speak in blackspeak
>   And not in Portuguese,
>   What was all the *hammering for?

Mercury That's all we could do.
     You got what you asked for.[2]

Here, Gil Vicente, the prolific bilingual playwright who popularized *fala de preto* in Portuguese theatre and *habla de negros* in Spanish theatre—both of which I translate as *blackspeak*—draws attention to the efficacy of a performance technique that sonically marks Fernando, or "Furunando" as he calls himself, as irremediably black for spectators, even once black-up has been removed. That technique codifies the sound of Afro-descendants' speech forms for stage purposes. Eminently risible and thus specific to the genre of comedy widely defined, blackspeak relies on grammatical mistakes (incorrect conjugation, numbering, or gendering), foreign lexical imports (from various early modern African languages), and exaggerated phonetic distortions—three elements that coalesce to form a standardized, recognizable, and replicable black accent. To wash an Ethiop white, visuals are not enough, Vicente suggests, for, as Fernando discovers, what spectators hear can be as important as what they see. Vicente illustrates the idea that sound is, to quote Jennifer Lynn Stoever, "a critical modality through which subjects (re)produce, apprehend, and resist imposed racial identities and structures of racist violence. . . . [Sound is] a set of social relations and a compelling medium for racial discourse."[3]

To get a sense of the importance of sound and accent as a medium for racial discourse in early modern Europe, let us take a walk in the streets of Seville during Holy Week 1604, and let us listen. Dozens of Catholic confraternities solemnly carry superb floats laden with religious sculptures and wind through the city arteries, following the traditional procession itinerary that leads them all to the cathedral. Music everywhere the floats go. Yet, around El Salvador Church, there is a brawl, a commotion, and laughter—getting louder and louder. That year, the powerful confraternity of Nuestra Señora de la Antigua y Siete Dolores would lodge a complaint against the less affluent confraternity formed by Afro-Sevillians, both free and unfree, the Hermandad de los Negritos. They would accuse the Black confraternity of violently breaking protocol and decorum by attacking them in order to enter the Church of El Salvador out of turn. That accusation speaks to thinly veiled fears in the face of the pride, assertiveness, and social mobility championed by the Hermandad de los Negritos: fears that the slavery-based racial and social order might be disrupted by willful Afro-Spaniards who refuse to know their place and wait their turn. The confraternity of Nuestra Señora issued a grievance with the archbishop, asking that the Hermandad de los Negritos be dissolved, or at least forbidden to participate in the same processions as white confraternities (in other words, be segregated) in the future—under threat of excommunication.

In the memo preserved today in the archives of the archdiocese, Francisco de Acosta mentions that "every year their confraternity [los Negritos] takes part in the procession of the Holy Week, they have quarrels either with the respectable people of the other confraternities who march at the same time, or quarrels with people who mock them."[4] The memo includes several testimonies, one of which, delivered by presbyter Juan de Santiago, gives us more information about the specific "mockeries" that regularly infuriated the Black brothers: "Many people jeered and directed offending sounds at the *negros*, talking to them in blackspeak (guineo), and embarrassing them, with great disrespect for the procession and the representation of our Savior's Passion. And so the *negros* would disband and respond, swear, and insult those who were jeering at them, which made the whole thing more like a jest or an interlude (cosa de risa y entremés) than a Holy Week Procession."[5] This testimony signals that the injurious dimension of blackspeak (guineo) was obvious to all parties involved, since some Sevillians purposefully used blackspeak in combination with whistles and "offending sounds" (probably scatological and animalistic, like the sounds that we heard courtiers hurling at Juan and his servant in the king's antechamber in *El valiente negro en Flandés* in Chapter 1) to insult the members of the Hermandad de los Negritos. That 1604 altercation between white Spaniards speaking blackspeak (guineo) and Afro-Spaniards using authentic Afro-Spanish speech forms voiced linguistic differences that vividly exposed the artificiality and strategic nature of theatrical blackspeak. For a hot minute, the whiteness of blackspeak must have been deafening.

But this vignette also reveals, just as importantly, the triumph of self-aware artifice, the counterintuitive and yet undeniable power of a performative technique to condition auditors' perception of reality. Indeed, Juan de Santiago's final sentence eerily merges blackspeak and Afro-Spaniards' responses, despite the differences exposed during the altercation, by reading both linguistic entities as part of the same comedic entremés and aesthetic universe (the whole thing sounded "like a jest or an interlude"). The dynamics of street processions, which enable a theatricalization of the world, facilitated this merger. While the very altercation he witnessed exposed the artificiality of theatrical blackspeak to the naked ear, the witness could not help but hear the scene through the ideologically inflated filter of early modern stagecraft. This anecdote speaks to the central object of this book: what I call racecraft, that is, the ability of theatrical and performative stagecraft to foster habits of mind, to transform spectators' reading of the world offstage, and thereby participate in early modern racial formations.

I seek to radically expand our understanding of the scope, effect, and significance of blackspeak in early modern Europe. Iberian Blackspeak has been studied in depth by scholars such as Frida Weber de Kurlat, Edmond de Chasca, Paul Teyssier, and Nicholas R. Jones—a study facilitated by the abundance of scripted blackspeak in the extant archives of Iberian print culture.[6] However, the extant European archive of printed blackspeak located primarily in Iberia is only the tip of an iceberg of performative practices rendered largely invisible by the technical limitations of the scripting process itself. For instance, an unusual grouping or ungrouping of words can disrupt the flow of a sentence and betray the speaker as nonnative. Alain Fleischer notes that, "in some cases, an accent might have more to do with rhythm than with phonetic pronunciation."[7] Fleischer's observation is based on his experience as a French speaker, but for native speakers of a stress-based language—such as English or Spanish—detecting a nonnative speaker is even easier: nothing gives away a proficient ESL speaker like stressing the wrong syllable in a polysyllabic word. Similarly, the accent of an early modern Afro-European whose native language was tonal—as is the case of most Bantu languages—was likely to contain exotic-sounding variations in pitch, and actors familiar with them could easily caricature them in their version of blackspeak. But codifying such rhythm-based, stress-based, or tone-based accents would have required scripting systems that early modern European performance culture neither had nor developed for that purpose. Thus, printed scripts could neither dictate nor render the full sonic impact of blackspeak in performance. Scripts are suggestive, not prescriptive, in that respect. To repurpose Jennifer Linhart Wood's turn of phrase, in "the sonic laboratory of the early modern theatre," actors could increase the intensity of scripted blackspeak by using rhythm, stress, and tonal modulations according to their own skills and taste, and any insightful study of blackspeak must reckon with their agency.[8]

Under the umbrella of blackspeak, I include speech forms in which a black accent was applied to European vernaculars, but also speech forms in which a black accent was applied to various imaginary African languages that I generically refer to as "Africanese."[9] In this version of blackspeak, which early modern plays labeled "jargon" or "gibberish," sonic difference came across not through distortion but through novelty effects created, for instance, by variations in pitch and phonemes unheard of in the auditors' vernacular, by the use of voice inflections evoking emotions inappropriate for that specific dialogic situation in the auditors' vernacular, and by deliberately crafted imbalances whereby "jargons" express in two words what European languages express in two periodic sentences. Reading texts that script Africanese through a performative lens, we must keep in mind that actors did not pronounce those lines with the standard accent of their own vernacular but, most likely, with what they imagined to be a thick black accent, as did the actors who delivered black-accented European vernacular. In both versions of blackspeak, actors—cued or not—could connect pronunciation to visual caricature and to black-up by using the demands blackspeak placed upon their elocution as an opportunity to grimace: they could use their mouth, jaws, and lips in keeping with the perennial fixation of racial caricatures on the fuller lips of Afro-descendants, regardless of whether the words they uttered existed or not in European vernaculars.

The two versions of blackspeak, Africanese gibberish and black-accented European vernacular, could be combined in performance. They were combined, for instance, in the musical genre of Neapolitan *moresche* and, by extension, in the moresche routines of the influential commedia dell'arte repertoire that circulated throughout Europe. Indeed, in Orlando di Lasso's mid-sixteenth-century moresche titled "Alla pia calia," the lyrics mix black-accented Neapolitan vernacular with Africanese gibberish (Figure 4).

The irruption of gibberish ("cian cian, ni ni gua, gua") is palpable on the music sheet, when tablature interrupts itself and musical notation disappears to be replaced with a black-accented sentence, the meaning of which can be approximated as "What language have we down here! Bless the clamor, Gurgh!"[10] That metalinguistic comment ends on a nugget of guttural gibberish (gurgh!), which introduces a nonsensical sentence as musical notation resumes ("he he he he ha ha ha ho ho ho ho").[11] That sequence is an invitation: the interruption of tablature on the music sheet suggests that, in performance, singers were at liberty to improvise, pause, and expand on that moment of gibberish before returning to singing in accented Neapolitan. In sum, early modern blackspeak was a highly modular racializing device, and, here again, rare extant scripts such as Di Lasso's moresche must be regarded as the waterline of an iceberg of potential vocal modulations.

I coin the term *blackspeak* to emphasize the fact that, just like Orwell's Newspeak, this aesthetic code is an artificial language with real-life consequences, a limiting language that ultimately contains and controls the thoughts and aspirations of its fictional speakers on stage.[12] Its development was implemented, however, not in a top-down power structure such as the one imagined by Orwell but in a structure of distributed power requiring the active and

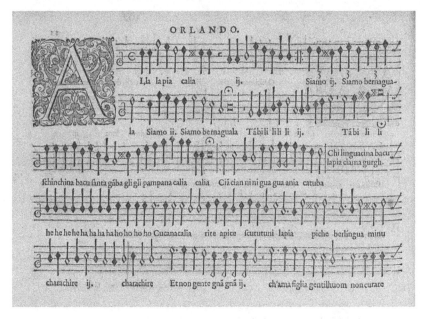

Figure 4. *Libro de villanelle, moresche, i altre canzoni*. Orlando Di Lasso.
Print. 1582. Munich, Bayerische Staatsbibliothek, 4 Mus.pr. 60, fol.11v.
urn:nbn:de:bvb:12-bsb00084745-7.

enthusiastic participation of various agents: playwrights, actors, and audience
members. Just as important, I call it *blackspeak*, rather than habla de negros,
media lengua, or *língua de preto*, the terms used by scholars of Iberian theatre,
because I seek to show that, although blackspeak was primarily an Iberian device, it came to operate across and beyond the borders of the Iberian Peninsula,
throughout Western Europe. Attentiveness to the various forms of blackspeak—
black-accented European vernaculars, Africanese gibberish, and modulations
of those two formulas—dramatically widens the scope of blackspeak studies, to
Italy, England, France, and probably other European traditions. By adopting
a transnational approach, I seek, as always, to break away from the Anglo-
centrism that has long characterized the field of early modern critical race studies, but I also wish to counter the assumption, common among race scholars in
Hispanic studies, that there was a gap between the Iberian Peninsula, which
produced literary representations of Afro-diasporic people based on real observation, and the rest of Western Europe, which, allegedly, produced literary
representations of Africans based on "purely literary notions from antiquity

and the Middle-Ages" disconnected from the social and historical realities of the moment.[13] Across early modern Europe, blackspeak was a major performative technique of racialization essentializing difference in the service of power to locate Afro-descendants at the bottom of social orders. Blackspeak contributed to establishing within an early modern trans-European framework what Stoever theorizes in the context of post–Civil War America as "the sonic color line," that is, "the process of racializing sound—how and why certain bodies are expected to produce, desire, and live among particular sounds—and its product, the hierarchical division between 'whiteness' and 'blackness.'"[14]

In the process of racializing sound, artifice, far from being an impediment, was the key dimension that enabled blackspeak to do its work. Indeed, all early modern performances of blackspeak were artificial and heavily highlighted their own artificiality. One Spanish interlude, *Entremés cantado de las dueñas*, written by Luis Quiñones de Benavente and performed in the royal palatial compound of Buen Retiro in 1645, is one of the rare documented performances that featured an authentic Afro-Spanish performer: an unnamed enslaved man who belonged to theatre company manager Andrés de la Vega.[15] In the playtext, the performer's lines are scripted in perfectly unaccented Castilian, suggesting that habla de negros worked best for theatrical purposes when performed by a white actor. Such dynamics are even more pregnant in English and French plays, where blackspeak is systematically performed not just by white actors but by white actors playing white characters who, in turn, pretend to be Afro-diasporic. That frequent mise en abyme of blackspeak's whiteness emphasizes—revels in— the core artificiality of blackspeak. In this chapter, I unfold the implications of such reveling by sounding the affordances of blackspeak's artifice and their ideological ramifications in the early modern racial struggle.

What was the purchase of systematically putting blackspeak in the mouths of white actors when gifted Afro-Europeans, free and unfree, would presumably have welcomed the opportunities of the acting profession? What did the actors' whiteness enable? Beyond the obvious pleasure of impersonation shared by actor and spectators, a large part of the answer is control. Artifice enabled theatre makers to control the final acoustic product: to develop blackspeak forms whose calculated sounds could infantilize and animalize Afro-Europeans at will. Yet control is only part of the answer. Indeed, white performers using blackspeak, simply by virtue of their own whiteness, could conjure up older traditions of stage accents and thereby connect Afro-Europeans symbolically and politically to other racialized groups with a distinct history of theatrical impersonation. What the performers' whiteness enabled was the activation of acoustic

racecraft's memory. Thus, it is blackspeak's very artificiality that gave it its racializing affordances via what I call *the script of ethnic conjuration*, an associative
script that connects blackness with other paradigms or subparadigms in the racial matrix. The ideological implications of such associations are varied, and in
that sense, the effects of the script of ethnic conjuration are open-ended. The
hitherto unexplored connective dimension of blackspeak highlights what David Theo Goldberg calls the "relational" nature of racial formations across space
and time, and the need for early modern race scholars to study racial formations
as mutually implicated.[16] By highlighting the interconnected lives of tropes and
paradigms within the racial matrix, I heed Goldberg's call.

My account of blackspeak departs significantly from the path-opening
scholarship written on early modern linguistic blackness over the last ten years,
primarily by Ian Smith, Robert Hornback, and Nicholas R. Jones. In *Race and
Rhetoric in the Renaissance: Barbarian Errors*, Ian Smith powerfully argues that
barbarism, the ancient mark of profound difference that had been understood as linguistic incapability—sometimes manifesting in ancient Greek theatre
through "stuttering, mumbling, malapropisms, grammatical errors"—was reaf-
fixed to Afro-descendants in Renaissance England, as the inhabitants of North
African Barbary became conveniently associated with barbarity.[17] Methodolog-
ically, Smith's study aligns with the concluding section that Bruce Smith dedicates to Shakespearean plays in *The Acoustic World of Early Modern England:
Attending to the O-Factor*, where he limits "aural marks of African identity" to
the domains of rhetoric and poetics.[18] The Shakespearean examples Ian Smith
uses to exemplify this process are only partially convincing, to the extent that
Aaron, Caliban, and Othello, if temporarily afflicted by barbarity (in the form of
silence, "gabbling," or collapse), perform more linguistic and poetic capability than
incapability overall. By using a wider array of plays and resisting Shakespeare-
centrism, I hope to reveal the full power of Smith's core argument in early modern
theatre, not only in England, but across Europe.

A comparative and transnational ambition similar to mine informs Robert
Hornback's *Racism and Early Blackface Comic Traditions: From the Old World
to the New*, which bridges the gap between Iberia and England, studying in
groundbreaking ways the use of "black dialects in derisive depictions of blackness." Hornback traces the recurrence of black "broken, ungrammatical, mis-
pronounced baby talk" that foreshadows the techniques of nineteenth-century
minstrelsy.[19] Hornback, however, grounds his study of early modern English
blackspeak in sixteenth-century morality plays, whose blacked-up protagonists
are constructed as allegorically, not racially, black. I take a different route by us-

ing a narrower and, I believe, stronger definition of what counts as acoustic early modern blackspeak.

My third and last central interlocutor is Nicholas R. Jones, who argues in *Staging Habla de Negros: Radical Performances of the African Diaspora in Early Modern Spain* that a number of representations of Afro-descendants authored by early modern white writers are not racist but, rather, "render legible the voices and experiences of black Africans in ways that demand our attention." For Jones, habla de negros "embodies a dialectical and performative masked truth that has the potential to disavow antiblack racism and stereotyping." Embarking on a self-avowed revisionist project, Jones does "not believe that the Renaissance Iberian composers, musicians, and playwrights caricaturized or denigrated Africanized speech forms conclusively."[20] Jones is committed to reading blackspeak as a medium that affords possibilities of resistance for Afro-Iberians and, consequently, finds subversion in the texts where he seeks to reclaim Black agency. I share Jones's project to understand performances of blackspeak within the social realities of early modern Spain, but I find that the dynamics of racial impersonation that are central to blackspeak foreclose most avenues for Black resistance.

In this chapter, I reconstruct some of the scripts of blackness that black-speak offered to auditors grouped in acoustic communities whose "identity is maintained not only by what its members say in common but what they hear in common," to quote Bruce Smith.[21] Each of the chapter's two halves focuses on a version of blackspeak (black-accented European vernaculars or Africanese gib-berish), moves comparatively or transnationally, and follows a chronological arc. In the first half of the chapter, which is focused on black-accented Euro-pean vernaculars on stage, I trace the development of blackspeak in early mod-ern Spain to reconstruct a very popular script of black infantilization. I use historical records to highlight blackspeak's circulation between real and theat-rical settings, with Spanish theatre at the center of a nexus of urban perfor-mance spaces including churches, private houses, and procession streets through which blackspeak moved multidirectionally and disseminated its ideological contents. I analyze the comic mechanisms of blackspeak, and I show how, in interludes by Tirso de Molina, Quiñones de Benavente, and many others, black-speak could make auditors perceive Afro-diasporic characters as childish, exces-sively physical, and intellectually deficient, thereby lending ideological support to the slavery-based social status quo.

Turning to the only extant English play mobilizing this version of black-speak, Richard Brome's *The English Moor, or The Mock-Marriage* (1637), I explore

other popular acoustic scripts of blackness: scripts of animalization or degeneration, and scripts hinging on the conjuration of other racialized groups. Indeed, I
posit that London playgoers may have heard the novelty of blackspeak through
the filter of older traditions of stage accents such as continental and Irish accents,
the latter signaling the appearance of Afro-diasporic people on the same colonial
horizon whence the racialized Irish stage accent had risen. That colonial horizon
was saturated with ideas of degeneration that would soon be linguistically associated with all English colonial subjects.

In the second half of this chapter, I focus on Africanese gibberish, to show
that acoustic scripts of animalization and ethnic conjuration obtained across
the Channel, in early modern France. French acoustic racecraft differed from
its English counterpart, however, in its strategic concealment of the colonial
modes of thinking in which blackspeak was embedded. The use of Africanese
"*jargon*" in Nicolas Du Perche's neoclassical comedy *L'ambassadeur d'Affrique*
(1666), inscribes Afro-descendants in an ongoing history of national formation,
and in an ongoing history of Orientalist representations that used Turkish jargon on stage. Du Perche's play activates the conjuration mechanisms of blackspeak in ways that Orientalize its African characters. This Orientalization of
blackness by acoustic means happened at the very time when the number of
enslaved Afro-diasporic French speakers boomed in the Caribbean, and I read
it as a manifestation of mechanisms of denial, displacement, and erasure triggered by deep metropolitan anxieties about the fate of the Freedom Principle.
Ultimately, I turn to Sir Francis Fane's little-known Restoration comedy *Love
in the Dark* (1675), not only to point out the long shelf life of the acoustic scripts
of blackness previously discussed, but also to explore the complementary interactions of blackspeak and its cosmetic counterpart, black-up.

Part 1. Vernacular Blackspeak

"Sew My Mouth from Side to Side, and My Tongue Too": habla de negros

In Spain, blackspeak developed, thrived, and survived in urban settings where
theatre makers and consumers lived and worked within earshot of Afro-Spaniards.
Blackspeak appears in Spanish theatre roughly a decade after it appears in Portuguese literary culture, in the early 1530s. It flourished immediately, in the
works of playwrights who had all lived in the vicinity of Afro-Iberians: playwrights from Portugal (the bilingual Gil Vicente); Andalusia (Lope de Rueda

was from Seville; Feliciano de Silva lived in Seville; Francisco Delicado hailed from Jaén); Extremadura, a commercially and culturally porous region between Spain and Portugal (Sánchez de Badajoz); and cities using an enslaved workforce (Gaspar Gomez de Toledo). Blackspeak as a theatrical technique boomed in the first decade of the seventeenth century. This boom coincided with the permanent return of the royal court from Valladolid to Madrid in 1607. Together with its thirst for entertainment, the court brought back an estimated fifty-five thousand persons to the city: aristocrats, administrators, servants—so many potential patrons for the *corrales* of Madrid. The return of the court to Madrid fixed the city's dire demographic situation, ensured its ascendency over its Castilian neighbors, and boosted its economy, including its entertainment economy. Doing so, it "increased the proportion of servants, menials, and marginals" in the city, among whom one would find enslaved Afro-descendants, a status symbol cherished by Iberian aristocrats.[22]

Toponymy attests to their presence in the soundscape of early modern Madrid. For instance calle de los Negros (black men's street), which corresponds to the upper segment of today's calle Tetuán, just above Puerta del Sol, was called so because there lived the people enslaved by the president of the Council of the Indies (who, given his charge and the symbolism attached to it, was likely to own one of the largest enslaved retinues in the city).[23] Not only does toponymy attest to the connection between aristocrats and high officials with the enslaved and to the presence of Afro-Spaniards in some of the most central streets of Madrid; it also reveals a contact zone between theatre makers and Afro-diasporic *madrileños*. Indeed, an examination of the legal documentation on theatre makers collected by Teresa Ferrer-Valls reveals that calle de los Negros was an important street for the theatre community in Madrid: between 1601 and 1630, many costume makers, sellers, renters, musicians, choreographers, and actor families lived and worked there, conducting their trade within earshot of Afro-Spaniards.[24] Moreover, as Mimma de Salvo notes, many documents show that successful actors and actresses owned enslaved people; that was the case for Micaela de Luján, for example, whose household—in which Lope de Vega spent many years—included an enslaved *negra* and her children.[25]

The drop in the Afro-diasporic population in Madrid and Seville in the 1640s correlated with a decrease of black characters in comedias on the public stage.[26] Black characters and blackspeak did not disappear; they were, in part, relocated and became a recurrent fixture of entremeses, a genre particularly popular at court, especially after the completion of the Coliseo theatre in the Buen Retiro compound built for Philip IV.[27] Performance culture was intense at Buen Retiro: as previously mentioned, this is where *Entremés cantado de las dueñas*, starring the man enslaved by Andrés de la Vega, was performed in 1645. This anecdote highlights the status of Buen Retiro as a place where aristocrats kept consuming enslaved Afro-Spaniards, interludes, and enslaved Afro-Spaniards in interludes after 1640.[28] It is in that little bubble that blackspeak survived in the second half of the century, and the conditions of its survival confirm that proximity to Afro-Spaniards was a key feature of blackspeak's ecosystem.

But this situation does not lead me to read blackspeak as an attempt to reproduce authentic Afro-Spanish speech forms.[29] Rather, it leads me to argue, based on the anecdote of the 1604 Holy Week altercation between Nuestra Señora de la Antigua y Siete Dolores and the Hermandad de los Negritos, that artificial blackspeak thrived in diverse urban soundscapes where its juxtaposition with authentic Afro-Spanish speech forms enabled it to do its ideological work. Blackspeak thrived in sites where audiences were conditioned to pick up its parodic dimension—sites where proximity to authentic Afro-Spanish speech forms highlighted its whiteness and artificiality, thereby alerting auditors to the intentionality of its acoustic effects. Indeed, it is a natural response, when we listen to someone speaking our language with an accent, to focus on the semantic content of their speech despite the accent; our minds work hard to grasp what the speaker means and to ignore the obstacle to comprehension that is the accent. Our cognitive response to authentic accents, in sum, is to try to unhear them. By contrast, virtuosic artificial accents like blackspeak demand our attention: their effects are impressed upon us and our imagination because of their self-avowed artificiality, not in spite of it.

To take the full measure of blackspeak's social energy in Spain, we must think of the stage as the center of an urban nexus of acoustic performance spaces—including churches, private houses, and procession streets—through which blackspeak circulated multidirectionally. Blackspeak entered Spanish culture through music and poetry, and more specifically through Rodrigo de Reynosa's late fifteenth-century *coplas* (popular songs), published as *cordel* literature in Seville and meant to be sung to a famous local tune. The coplas imagine a call-and-response dialogue between two enslaved people: Jorge, whose ethnic origin is *Gelofe Mandinga* courts Comba from Guinea. Blackspeak would never lose the musical coloration of its first instantiations in Spain; associated with religious celebrations, such songs often embed their own performative premises. For instance, in the "Christmas Carols and chansonettes that were sung in the choir of the Cathedral of Seville to celebrate the coming of the Holy Kings to Bethlehem when Jesus Christ was a newborn" in 1644, we can hear:

Brother, we the *#*negros* *have come
To *pledge #allegiance to the #King,
For we *are *vassals to His law
Just like #white #courtiers are.
I *swear to #holy #God,
To #his beautiful Virgin Mary,
Who is more #beautiful than a #white #rose,
And to the sovereign Child.
Gungulum gua!
Singing and #dancing
We *have come to *adore Him!
Gungulum gun,
Gungulum gua![30]

Inside the cathedral, the very place, physical and spiritual, that was supposed to effect the integration of enslaved Afro-diasporic people into the Spanish body politic, during celebrations that included them symbolically and physically, the voice of Afro-diasporic Catholics was distorted into blackspeak, and white churchgoers were encouraged to join the choir. None of this comes as a surprise when one remembers that the staircases of that cathedral were the primary stage that slave merchants used to display their wares and conduct their trade in Seville.

This Christmas carol is one among many. *Villancicos* in blackspeak were performed for Christmas, the Epiphany, and Corpus Christi from the 1630s (if not earlier) to the middle of the eighteenth century, first and foremost in the Cathedral of Seville but also in other Andalusian cities with important Afro-Spanish populations (such as Córdoba and Granada), in the cathedral of Toledo, the basilica-cathedral of Zaragoza, and the Royal Chapel in Madrid. The tradition of blackspeak *villancicos* was so popular that it spread throughout the empire and was performed in the cathedrals of Lima, Cuzco, La Paz, Bogotá, Mexico City, Puebla, and Guatemala City.[31] Blackspeak villancicos were printed on broadsheets that were offered to the powerful members of the parish and sold on popular markets to the less powerful ones, ensuring that blackspeak, which must have been in high demand given the number of broadsheets preserved at the Biblioteca Nacional de España today, would keep circulating after the celebrations, entering people's private homes.[32] Those printed villancicos found perhaps an even easier access to private houses when they were written by celebrated poets such as Luis de Góngora and Sor Juana Inés de la Cruz.[33] Printing religious and nonreligious villancicos lyrics on cheap broadsheets, combined with the spectacular development of the dramatic publishing industry in the early seventeenth century, maximized the circulation of a technique born nearly a century earlier. Blackspeak cannot exist outside of performance: to understand what a passage in blackspeak means, the reader has to vocalize the lines. Seventeenth-century readers, living in a culture where reading was very often an out-loud group experience akin to a private performance, were likely to read the blackspeak texts they owned *en voz alta* (out loud). By reading or singing those texts aloud, private readers became consumers and producers of blackspeak who could be imitated in turn, furthering its circulation. Blackspeak thus involved both theatre goers and theatre readers as active agents in the racialization of Afro-Spaniards.

El negro, an entremés by Tirso de Molina published in 1635 and presumably performed at some point between 1617 and 1635 in Madrid by Juan Bautista Valenciano's acting company, exemplifies the theatrical deployment of blackspeak and some of the scripts of blackness attached to it.[34] In *El negro*, sound and meaning work in concert: black speech, saturated as it is with physicality, construes Afro-Spaniards as obsessed with bodily appetites at the semantic level, while, at the acoustic level, blackspeak helps reinforce the audience's perception of Afro-Spaniards as supra-physical and infra-intellectual, thereby infantilizing them. The plot goes thus: by a beautiful midsummer night in Madrid, on an idyllic patch of green, white friends are listening to musicians singing a *romance*, a narrative ballad, called "Sin color anda la niña" (The pale wandering maid). An enslaved Afro-Spaniard, Domingo, enters. He breaks the law in doing so, since the enslaved were forbidden to leave their house or their enslaver's house and walk the streets at night in early modern Madrid. They risked severe corporal punishment for doing so. But Domingo is fearlessly taking a stroll, and he enters the stage, drawn—as his theatrical peers often are—to the sound of guitar:

> A #Guitar! What lovely sound!
> I don't know what the #devil it is
> About this *instrument,
> But I sure love #it:
> It #moves my soul.
> And here I am, listening like a #fool,
> While the sun is rising on me.[35]

Rapidly, Domingo shows himself determined to prick the white friends' idyllic bubble. He likes the sound of guitar, but he disapproves of this "old" ballad: he demands a more recent and danceable tune, and he criticizes its plot from a comically down-to-earth viewpoint. Indeed, for the heroine of the ballad, the "pale wandering maid" who, abandoned, pines away, pales away, and loses sleep over her lover's absence, Domingo—who has little patience for foolishness—has a prescription: a better diet and a better lover. Domingo interrupts the ballad six times and is ordered to be silent. After his sixth interruption, the white friends lose patience:

Argales
> Will you be quiet?

Domingo
> Yes #sir,
> I'll be #quiet like a duegna,
> Like a nun in the parlor,
> Like an eighty-year-old mother-in law,
> Like a child who gets butt-whipped,
> Like a sore loser,
> Like your blacksmith #neighbor,
> Like cats and dogs squeezed together,
> Like a woman in labor,
> Like a plaintiff who's been played,
> Like base characters getting mad
> In a bad play.
> I swear to #God and on my #conscience,
> To be #quiet like those are.

Argales
> Good Lord! If you don't
> Shut up, may God smash your skull!

Domingo
> #I wish I could, my good sir!
> I #wish #to God a #shoemaker would
> Sew my mouth, from side to side,
> And my #tongue too!
> But, given my #condition, I think that,
> Even if they sewed it,
> I *would have to speak #with my eyes,
> My hands, my ears,
> My feet, #with my #knees,

My #muscles, #with my legs,
#With my shoulders, and then again,
#With the one eye I have left.
Musician
Damned *negro*, shut up,
And we'll have a party for you right here.
Domingo
Fine, I'll be #quiet. With a #condition, though:
I want in.
See, I *know how to dance too!³⁶

Domingo compulsively interrupts the *romance* players out of his unwillingness
or inability to empathize with the love it celebrates, a love whose truest manifestation consists in the abdication of all bodily pleasures and necessities (such as
food, sex, and sleep—and, ultimately, life) on the "pale" maid's part. His discourse is fueled by what spectators would read as the stereotypical obsession of
Afro-diasporic characters with the body, which prevents him from understanding more refined forms of love.³⁷ Domingo's enthusiasm for bodily appetites is
self-evident when he recommends a healthier lifestyle to *la niña*:

To recover, #God *willing,
She should eat
#bacon, #beef, mutton,
#hen, #partridge, #rabbit,
#pigeon, #goose, #turkey,
#chicken and #cocks (but not coxcombs!)
#capon, #chorizo,
#sirloin, #gizzards,
#salami, #sausage,
And a whole pan of lard! . . .
You are losing sleep over one lover,
Yet, in every #street you could #find
A thousand kinds of lovers:
One with a red mustache,
One with a black #head of hair,
Another one with a big fat body
#And shapely legs,
Another one whose collar

Makes his Adam's #apple so #salient
That he could put #glasses on #it
As other do on their #noses;
Yet another lover who—[*They interrupt him.*]³⁸

Recommending a diet that consists exclusively of meat (with an emphasis on pork), punning that she should eat "cock but not coxcombs" before detailing the "salient" body parts of potential lovers, Domingo offers a solution based on a vision of the carnivalesque body as meat to be consumed in all ways—not surprisingly, that vision informed scopic constructions of the Afro-diasporic body itself on the Spanish stage, as we saw in Chapter 1. The idea he develops—that, should he be silenced, every part of his body will speak for him—reinforces the inextricable connection between speech and physicality: the black body is a speaking body, and black speech speaks only of the body. Domingo's victory over the *romance* partisans is marked by a merry dance, which consecrates the exulting triumph of the body.

This carnivalesque celebration of the body has a flipside: it is inseparable from a vision of tortured bodies. With some of the images that permeate the scene, whether it be the "butt-whipped" child, the woman giving birth, Argales's desire to see God smash Domingo's skull, or Domingo's own phantasmatic evocation of a shoemaker sewing his mouth from side to side, this interlude is suffused with a vision of the body in pain, the body whipped, beaten, cut, and torn open, as Domingo's enslaved body could be at any moment in this interlude, if an *alguazil* enters and discovers him roaming freely by night. That Domingo has only "one eye left" makes it impossible to ignore that such brutalization has already been perpetrated on his body, over and over and over again. (And it also helps us understand why Domingo's perception of the world so heavily leans on the acoustic mode.) In that sense, Tirso de Molina's comic interlude dramatizes the full range of early modern Spanish investments in Afro-diasporic bodiliness—and owns it. Such open acknowledgment of the brutality to which Afro-Spanish bodies were subjected aligns with larger aesthetic currents that scholars such as Carmen Fracchia have recently traced in Hapsburg visual culture.³⁹

The cultural obsession with physicality that fuels Domingo's black speech at the semantic level is central to the comic mechanisms of blackspeak on the acoustic level, which I understand in a Freudian light. Laughter, Freud argues, arises when we deem that someone has taken "too much trouble" to perform a physical function, or "too little trouble" to perform a mental or intellectual function: "A person appears comic to us if, in comparison with ourselves, he makes too great an expenditure on his bodily functions and too little on his mental ones; and it cannot be denied that in both these cases our laughter expresses a pleasurable sense of the superiority which we feel in relation to him."[40] Artificial phonetic distortions could easily be perceived by audience members as excessive expenditure, or effort, spent on a defective elocution. Indeed, it would have been hard not to notice the surplus of labor performed and deliberately exaggerated in ways that demanded attention by the blackspeakers' jaws, lips, and tongues. For any audience member sharing the opinion casually articulated by George Puttenham that one of the "fit instruments man hath by nature" to the purpose of speaking is "thin and movable lips," the fuller lips of Afro-Europeans must have appeared to be an obstacle to easy elocution.[41]

Bozal was the Spanish term used to refer to slaves who had recently arrived from Africa and had not yet perfectly mastered the Spanish language yet (by contrast with acculturated ladino slaves); etymologically derived from "muzzle," the term simultaneously animalized Afro-Spanish speakers and framed their speech forms as resulting from material obstacles to proper elocution. Nicholas R. Jones sees in that term a sign of "Spain's cultural and somatic fixation on big African lips."[42] This fixation informs theatrical representations of Afro-descendants' elocutionary challenges. It is likely that listeners laughed at how much work it took artificially blackened mouths to pronounce simple words. That cultural fixation on sub-Saharan lips certainly informed the presence of the built-in thick lips of the masks used during the previously mentioned 1525 danza de negros in Toledo, as well as Iago's decision to call Othello a "thick-lips" (1.1.66), or the nickname "morruda" (thick-lipped) given to the enslaved blackspeaking Margarita in Jaime de Huete's *Tesorina*.[43] Blackspeak thus derives some of its comic force from the clumsy surplus of physical labor that its production necessitates from the fictional Afro-diasporic character—to which the virtuosic labor produced by white performers draws attention.

Parallel to their excessive expenditure on physical elocutionary functions, blackspeakers also invited laughter with their insufficient expenditure on intellectual functions. The latter often makes an adult resemble a child, and Freud argues later on that we laugh most often when, at a preconscious level, we find the object of our laughter to remind us of a child.[44] The idea that laughter arises when we recognize an "infantile" element in someone illuminates the comic force of blackspeak: indeed, Paul Teyssier uses the phrase "childish syntax" to describe Portuguese blackspeak.[45] The infantile dimension of blackspeak manifests in various acts of simplification. In the previously cited scenes from Tirso de Molina's *El negro*, simplification operates phonetically in Domingo's *yeísmo* (delateralization), that is, his decision to ignore the distinction between *ll* and *y*. A drive toward simplification also manifests in the neologistic form *sabo* (I know), an invented regular form for the highly irregular verb *saber* (to know) that morphologically follows the logic of children and beginning language learners.[46] That Domingo's accent should affect and undermine the moment when he claims some kind of knowledge is no coincidence; rather, it miniaturizes the ideological work of blackspeak.

This acoustic construction of Domingo as excessively physical and intellectually deficient or childish via blackspeak complements his semantic construction as a character driven by bodily appetites. The association of *negros* with excessive physicality provided ideological support for the various forms of physical exploitations to which Afro-Spaniards were subjected, while their association with deficient intellect and childishness conveniently upheld the idea that white Spaniards had a moral mandate to educate them, to "force the black man out of the spiritual Africa in which he lives."[47] That "spiritual Africa" was a state of savagery, or spiritual and cultural misery, and could be corrected only by a Europeanization enforced through the practices of a slavery-based Catholic society. Via the script of black infantilization, blackspeak thus supported an ideology that positioned Afro-Spaniards at the bottom of the social order based on essentialized qualities.

Certainly, people did not go to the theatre driven by a desire to defend the institution of slavery: they went for pleasure, as we do. And yet, laughter theorists assure us, it matters little whether auditors consciously or deliberately participate in such exercises of power. They do not need to be aware for the comic accent to perform its ideological work. On the contrary, Henri Bergson explains, laughter pursues its goals "unconsciously, and even immorally in many individual instances."[48] Freud refines this idea when he argues that the cognitive processes conducive to the emission of laughter must remain "automatic":

> The comic process will not bear being hypercathected by attention; it
> must be able to take its course quite unobserved. . . . It would, how-
> ever, contradict the nomenclature of the "processes of consciousness"
> of which I made use, with good reason, in my *Interpretation of Dreams*,
> if one sought to speak of the comic process as a necessarily unconscious
> one. It forms part, rather, of the pre-conscious; and such processes,
> which run their course in the preconscious but lack the cathexis of at-
> tention with which consciousness is linked, may aptly be given the

name of "automatic." The process of comparing expenditures must remain automatic if it is to produce comic pleasure.[49]

In other words, the less aware audience members are of their own cognitive processes and of the racializing dynamics at play, the louder they laugh. In that
sense, blackspeak operates "unobserved." Acoustic racecraft thus relied on a
subtle formula of attention and inattention: the white artificiality of blackspeak
directed auditors' attention to its sonic texture, but blackspeak remained risible
only as long as auditors did not reflect too much on what made the texture of
"funny talk" funny. That formula of attention and inattention caught auditors
in its web. The acoustic scene of ideological production was one of distributed
agency between playwrights, performers, and audiences, but also one that was
very hard for auditors to opt out of.

   The strength of blackspeak as an ideological tool operating at the "preconscious level" to protect the economic foundations of Spanish society helps make
sense of a curious paradox. Indeed, one intriguing dimension of blackspeak is
that while it relies primarily on corrective responses and impulses, the correction, it seems, cannot—even must not—ever be fully carried out. Indeed, if
blackspeak were to disappear—that is, if Afro-diasporic characters were to
speak in unaccented Castilian (as must have been the case for many seventeenth-
century Afro-Spaniards), the stage would lose one of its finest racializing ideological tools. We get a glimpse of the importance of the persistence of blackspeak
on stage, uncorrected and unamended, in *El negro*, when Domingo emphatically delivers the final line of the interlude: "I cannot shut up, I swear #to God,
as hard as I try!"[50] He repeats several times that he desperately wants to remain
quiet but is unable to do so: he describes his own talkativeness as a medical
"condition," and this condition is a form of violence—yet another one—visited
on him by the comic dramaturgy of blackness. This dimension must have struck
Luis Quiñones de Benavente, the master of seventeenth-century *entremeses*,
who rewrote and expanded on Tirso de Molina's skit in the early 1660s.[51] In
Quiñones de Benavente's version, Domingo speaks even more, his accent is even
thicker, and he receives a fitting nickname: "el negrito hablador" (the chatty
little *negro*). In cases such as this one, it is tempting to read the persistence of
artificial black voices through a reparative lens, as a statement of Black resil-
ience. But not all speech is free. I suspect that blackspeak persisted because it
fulfilled more than it resisted the needs of the proslavery ideology in which it
participated. This ideology needed talkative little Domingos to keep talking in

order to racialize themselves without end: Afro-Spaniards had to remain perpetually in need of sonic correction, education, and exploitation.

This mechanism is particularly audible in an anonymous late seventeenth-
century interlude called *La negra lectora* (The Black Woman Who Would Fain
Read), in which three young clerks decide to play a cruel trick on Dominguilla,
an Afro-Spanish cook famous for her tripe stew, who dares take evening classes
to learn how to read and improve her pronunciation.[52] Such an initiative should
be praised in a society that values linguistic mastery and *ladino* identity over
bozal identity among the enslaved, yet the clerks seek to punish Dominguilla
for her ambition:

> Who is prompting *#negras*
> To become so learned?
> Cookbooks: that is all
> They should study![53]

They describe Dominguilla's crime and punishment in the following terms:

> I heard that this little *morena*
> Is learning how to read and write
> From schoolmaster
> Manuel Perez Botijon:
> After class, when children leave,
> He teaches that *negra*
> The alphabet book.
> Now, since she is a *bozal*,
> With our wits, we'll trick her
> Effortlessly—
> Willy-nilly.
> First, we'll bring the teacher
> Who is indoctrinating her
> So he might start the lesson
> And teach her our language.
> Once she is distracted
> We'll steal the bitch's tripe stew!
> And then, the three of us will
> Seize our guitars

And treat her with proverbs:
We'll joke about our prank
And tell her commonplaces
That she can neither say
Nor pronounce correctly![54]

The three lads perceive Dominguilla's desire to lose her accent and learn how to
read and write Castilian as an uppity transgression. Because her transgression
has to do with linguistic mastery, so does her punishment: aiming commonplaces and proverbs at her, they weaponize the parts of language in which
national culture is most sedimented, to show that the cultural community to
which those sayings are "common" does not include her. The denouement re-
places this fantasized scene of punishment with a scene of sonic humiliation, in
which the schoolmaster and the three clerks mock her pronunciation. The pleasure they take in her phonetic failures is only equal to their displeasure when
she succeeds:

> *Teacher* H.
> *Negra* Ache.
> *Teacher* H.
> *Negra* (Making a big effort to pronounce the letter correctly) H.
>> *At this point, the three lads sneeze loudly, saying "Achoo! instead of*
>> *"H," with much noise and mirth. The teacher does the same,*
>> *behind his spectacles.*
> *Francisco* Gee! See what a #fine reader
>> The #strumpet Mandingo #sister is![55]

Dominguilla pronounces a sound correctly, but the figures of white philological
authority bring her back to blackspeak. It is their real-life counterparts who
hurled blackspeak at the members of the Hermandad de los Negritos during
the Sevillian processions of Holy Week 1604.

Like the Afro-Spanish brothers whom Juan de Santiago could not help but
acoustically conflate with interlude characters as he witnessed the altercation,
Dominguilla cannot win this fight, for she inhabits an acoustic space where she
must keep making the mistakes that justify her oppression. She must inhabit
the space of childishness, excessive physicality, and deficient intellect that blackspeak sonically constructs. She must play out the scripts. Dominguilla's scene of
humiliation impels us to resist the temptation to read the sonic mode automati-

cally as a conduit for resistance in racializing regimes of performance. To do justice to the sonic, to give it its due, and to push against the hegemony of the scopic regime in Western epistemologies and in premodern critical race studies, we must resist the urge, common in sound studies, to place it in an oppositional relation to the oppressive scripts that cosmetic blackness delivered on early modern stages.[56] We must, instead, apprehend the ideological work that blackspeak and its acoustic scripts of blackness did on their own terms, violence and all.

"Broken English": Black Sonics in Jacobean and Caroline England

A fascination with acoustic blackness starts manifesting in Jacobean England as early as *The Tempest* (1611), in which, prior to his encounter with Europeans, Caliban, son to a Moorish witch and a dark devil, "would gabble like / A thing most brutish."[57] This gabbling might be what the satirical poet John Taylor aimed for when he composed in 1614 "certain verses written in Barbarian tongue, dropt out of a Negroes' pocket in honor of tobacco," or when he wrote in 1613 a gibberish "Epitaph in the Barmooda tongue, which must be pronounced with the accent of the grunting of a hogge."[58] The grunting epitaph is followed by its translation into the gibberish of "the Utopian tongue," followed by "the same in English, translated by Caleb Quishquash, an Utopian borne and principal Secretary to the great Adelantado of Barmoodoes," whose name is reminiscent of Caliban's.[59] Taylor's imaginary Afro-diasporic idioms, squarely located in a transatlantic space, ignore grammatical rules and complete the roots of English words with either Latinate or animalistic suffixes, breaking the English language in the process. As Hornback points out, Taylor's poetic experiment never became a literary convention, despite its cheeky conclusion that "if there bee any Gentlemen, or others that are desirous to be practitioners in the Barmoodo and Vtopian tongues: the Professor (being the Author hereof) dwelleth at the olde Swanne neere London Bridge, who wil teach them (that are willing) to learne, with agilitie and facility."[60] Nevertheless, Taylor's experiment outlined the conceptual map of blackspeak and its scripts of blackness in early modern England. On that map, we find topoi such as animalization and degeneration (the grunting of a hog), the conjuration of other people and other cultures destabilizing the identity and integrity of the English language (Latin suffixes), and new colonial spaces (Barmooda) peopled with "Calebs" and "Negroes."

The desire for sonic impersonation surfaces in Webster's *The White Devil* (1612), in which the Blackamoor maid Zanche, declares, as she first sees Mulinassar:

"That is my Country-man, a goodly person; / When hee's at leisure Ile discourse with him / In our owne language."[61] A decade later, in Philip Massinger's *The Parliament of Love* (1624), when the unfaithful Clarindor is caught red-handed making advances to a blacked-up maid believed to be Moorish, he pleads:

> I desired
> To hear her speak in the Morisco tongue;
> Troth, 'tis a pretty language.[62]

In each of these plays, the Afro-diasporic speech act is either already past or postponed to a future that never materializes. Such dynamics of deferral suck spectators into a shared economy of desire for sonic blackness left untouched by the imperfections that its actual deployment on stage would inevitably contain. That desire was first to be fulfilled by Richard Brome, a Caroline playwright known to resort to regional, social, and foreign accents. One of those playwrights with what Bruce Smith calls a particularly wide "speech network," Brome "intended the background of [early modern London] heteroglossia to be heard on stage."[63] Brome's city comedy *The English Moor, or The Mock-Marriage* was performed at Salisbury Court by Queen Henrietta's Men in 1637, and published some twenty years later. This is the only extant play to use black-accented vernacular blackspeak in early modern England.[64]

Brome's experiment with blackspeak may have been fueled by his firsthand observation of the Afro-British presence in the city. As Cristina Paravano notes, he did not travel extensively, nor did he study languages; his heteroglot dramaturgy of accents is, rather, the result of "a remarkable perceptiveness to the linguistic stimuli around him, by walking around London and in the playhouses."[65] This does not mean that Brome sought to put authentic Afro-British accents on stage, but rather that, like its Spanish counterpart, English blackspeak blossomed in a space where it was juxtaposed with authentic Afro-British accents— spaces where its whiteness and artificiality were particularly audible, enabling it to do its ideological work. Matthew Steggle connects the name of the imaginary Blackamoor maid in Brome's play, Catelina, to Imtiaz Habib's finding that several Afro-diasporic women living in Britain were called Catelina.[66] Additionally, the play's dedicatee-reader, William Seymour, had Afro-Britons in his household and probably had an illegitimate mixed-race granddaughter himself.[67] Could Brome have found himself within earshot of those Afro-Britons during one of the visits he paid to his patron? Quite possibly. Steggle also connects the fact that Quicksands lives in Market Lane to Imtiaz Habib's finding that this street was popular with successful merchants, the very class that had Afro-Britons in its service in early modern London.[68] The Afro-diasporic population amounted to 0.5 percent of London's population in the 1590s and kept growing in the first half of the seventeenth century, owing mostly to the acceleration of Anglo-African trade and to the end of the Anglo-Spanish War in 1604, which facilitated Anglo-Spanish trade, including the trade of enslaved people.[69] If, as Jean E. Howard argues, in city comedies, "through their place-based dramatic narratives, playwrights helped representationally to construct the practices associated with specific urban spaces," *The English Moor* uses Market Lane to negotiate the social tensions attached to the fantasized "urban problem" of the Afro-British presence in Caroline London.[70]

In England just as in Spain, artifice enabled blackspeak to do its ideological work: *The English Moor* revels in the artificiality and whiteness of blackspeak. Catelina is an Afro-diasporic role played by a white female character played in turn by a white boy actress. When Catelina speaks, she is linguistically contrasted with African characters who, unlike her, are constructed within the world of the play as authentically Moorish: Moors "hir'd to dance and to speak speeches" during Quicksands's private masque (4.1.883). Like the authentic Afro-Spanish performer in the *Entremés cantado de las dueñas* at *Buen Retiro* in 1645, those "authentic" Moors deliver their lines in perfectly unaccented English. Brome's Moorish performers sound like the Afro-British London stable boy who speaks fluently and without any accent in William Stepney's 1591 *The Spanishe School-Master*.[71] A close reading of *The English Moor* brings to light the key affordances of blackspeak's artifice, namely, the ability to associate Catelina with degeneration and to conjure up older stage accents and their ideological resonances.[72]

The English Moor focuses on the marriage of Quicksands, a Shylock-inspired old Jewish usurer who does commerce with Barbary and lived in the multiracial city of Venice at some point in his life, to Millicent, a young, smart, and beautiful Christian woman, who successfully avoids her husband's bed and, ultimately, exits the marriage. Quicksands is concerned, rightly so, that all the young men he has ruined in London might seek to avenge their wrongs by making him a cuckold. To avoid this, he disguises Millicent as a Blackamoor maid called Catelina, assuming that no Englishman could possibly be drawn to a dark-skinned woman. His assumptions fall flat before notorious wencher and fetish holder Nathaniel Banelass:

> *Nathaniel* It is the handsom'st Rogue
> I have ere seen yet of a deed of darkness;

> Tawney and russet faces I have dealt with,
> But never came so deep in blackness yet. . . .
> He keeps this rye-loaf for his own white tooth
> With confidence none will cheat him of a bit;
> Ile have a sliver though I loose my whittle. . . .
> Hist, Negro, hist.
> *Millicent* No see, O no, I darea notta.
> *Nathaniel* Why, why—pish—pox I love thee,
> *Millicent* O no de fine white Zentilmanna
>   Cannot a love a the black a thing a.
> *Nathaniel* Cadzooks the best of all wench.
> *Millicent* O take—a heed—a my mastra see—a.
> *Nathaniel* When we are alone, then wilt thou.
> *Millicent* Then I shall speak a more a.
> *Nathaniel* And Ile not lose the Moor-a for more then I
>   Will speak-a. (4.1.717–31)

A month later, to celebrate his imagined victory over the young men who would cuckold him and who now believe that Millicent is dead, Quicksands organizes a private masque to which he invites his enemies. The masque is to reveal who the Blackamoor maid really was all along.[73] Quicksands does not know that Millicent has traded places with her own white maid, Phillis, who was once undone by Banelass. Neither does Banelass when he uses the masque revels to make advances at Catelina now played by Phillis:

> *Nathaniel* Musick, play a Galliard,
>   You know what you promised me, Bullis.
> *Phillis* But howa can ita be donea.
> *Nathaniel* How I am taken with the elevation of her nostrils.
>   Play a little quicker—Heark you—if I lead you
>   A dance to a couch or a bed side, will you follow me?
> *Phillis* I will doa my besta. (4.1.808–11)

Banelass and Catelina/Phillis are caught, and a trial ensues, during which true identities are revealed. Quicksands is tricked into divorcing Millicent; Banelass is tricked into marrying Phillis.

Blackspeak is passed on from Millicent to Phillis like cosmetic blackness: as a disguise component that masks identity and makes the two women interchangeable as they work together. Blackspeak here entails inconsistent grammatical distortions (Catelina's failure to conjugate, when she says "no see" instead of "I will not see," does not carry over) and consistent phonetic distortions including the repetition of epenthetic [a] and the transformation of [ð] (an English sound notoriously hard to pronounce for nonnative speakers) into [z], of [dʒ] into [z], and of "master" into "mastra," which is evocative of future "massa" developments. To a Caroline English ear, Catelina's accent could have recalled various traditional stage accents: it was probably replete with what Wood calls "the sonic uncanny—the odd experience that something is alien and yet strangely familiar."[74] Her Spanish name suggests that, like most Afro-Britons at the beginning of the seventeenth century, the imaginary maid Catelina either was born in Iberia or had spent time in Iberian cultures prior to coming to England. Logically, we would expect Catelina's blackspeak to smack of Spanish (the way Spanish blackspeak often smacked of Portuguese). There lies the rub: while strong traditions of scripted French, Italian, and Dutch accents exist in early modern English drama, there is no equivalent for Iberian accents. Iberian accents may have been (and probably were) used by individual actors, but they are not scripted in extant playtexts as evidence of standard practice.[75]

Having no standard model of Spanish stage accent to imitate, Brome seems to have borrowed some features from the French and Dutch stage accents: Catelina pronounces the definite article "the" as "de," a feature also used by the French *The Damoiselle*, and by the Dutch in William Haughton's *Englishmen for My Money* and Thomas Dekker's *The Shoemaker's Holiday*.[76] Catelina's accent also draws on West Country regional English accents: "zentilmanna," for instance, is reminiscent of the "z" words used by Edgar in *King Lear* when he counterfeits a West Country peasant accent. However, Catelina's epenthetic "a," which immediately strikes Banelass, is Brome's own invention; for that reason, it may have read as carte blanche to the boy actress in charge of those lines. To script blackspeak, Brome used something foreign, something British, something new. This motley of connections is meaningful. By conjuring the French and Dutch accents, Brome's blackspeak connects Catelina to Europeans who were involved in the Atlantic slave trade (in addition to the Iberians who christened her). Conjuring a rustic regional English accent also connects her to the lower class within a traditional English social geography. Understood in relation to foreign European stage accents, blackspeak gives Catelina a double set of coordinates that positions her and the Afro-Britons she stands for as simultaneously outside and inside of the English nation.

The preexisting stage accent most likely to be conjured up by Catelina's blackspeak bits, however, was the Irish accent, which, together with other accents from the British Isles had been staged for over thirty years. Indeed, although scripted Celtic accents bear little resemblance to Catelina's, given the prominence in popular culture of a racial discourse that blackened Irish identity, audiences in the presence of the blackspeaking white boy actress likely connected blackspeak to the older tradition of Irishspeak. Unlike the conjuration of the French, Dutch, and West Country accents, the conjuration of Irishspeak hinged not on actual phonetic resemblances, but on a shared history of sonic impersonation on stage combined with a shared history of symbolical association in blackness. Just three years before Brome wrote *The English Moor,* Thomas Herbert had included in his *Relation of Some Yeares' Travaile* (1634) a short lexicon of the African language spoken by the "savage inhabitants" of the Cape of Good Hope with their "blubberd lips."[77] He had noted that "their words are sounded rather like that of apes than men, whereby it is very hard to sound their dialect, the antiquitie of it whether from Babell or no. . . . Their pronunciation is like the Irish."[78] Herbert's thought does not follow a logic of gradation moving toward the greater or lesser of three evils as much it follows a logic of deduction: this African language sounds animalistic and nonhuman (a pre-Babel origin points toward inchoate polygenetic thinking), ergo, it sounds like the Irish language. It is safe to assume that Irish Gaelic and the African language spoken at the Cape of Good Hope have little in common: Herbert found their pronunciation similar because Africans and Irishmen occupied a similar place in his perception of the world, and that place was defined by colonial interests. On stage, the mouth of the white boy actress voicing artificial blackspeak enabled the colonial linkage of the African and the Irish to materialize in the ears of Brome's auditors.

Celtic accents derived their *vis comica* from scripts very similar to scripts of blackness: it portrayed Celticspeakers as childish, intellectually deficient, and excessively physical in plays such as *The Famous History of the Life and Death of Captain Thomas Stukely* (1605), Shakespeare's *Henry V,* and Ben Jonson's *Irish Masque at Court* (1613). Unlike Continental accents, Gaelic stage accents constituted, as David J. Baker puts it, "ludicrous caricatures" that participated in "the colonizers' typology" and were informed by dynamics of conquest and racialization.[79] By integrating the new population group of Afro-Britons into that tradition, Brome recuperates its power dynamics, extends it to blackspeak, and comments indirectly on the place of Afro-Britons in the nation.

Early modern European political thinking consecrated the importance of linguistic unity for any nation with colonial aspirations.[80] In Britain, efforts to promote and impose the king's English as linguistic standard—in which writers and especially playwrights were instrumental—correlated with efforts to suppress Welsh, Scottish, and Irish languages from the political and legal spheres, as the gradual annexation of those territories unfolded. Paula Blank reads the appearance of Welsh, Scottish, and Irish accents on stage (distinct from regional English accents, which are older yet participate in the same hegemonic enterprise) around 1603 as directly connected to the growing linguistic and political imperialism of the English crown in those regions.[81] By directing this performance technique toward Afro-Britons, Brome underlines the role of Africa in "the rise in English travel and trade and the consequent emergence of England as a naval power" fit to serve imperial projects.[82] The fact, pointed out by Kim F. Hall, that the Anglo-African trade was characterized as early as the mid-sixteenth century by English attempts at breaking the Iberian monopoly on slave trafficking places Afro-diasporic bodies within the protocolonial sphere of English concerns.[83] Brome's redirecting of the imperialist linguistic dynamics of British accents toward Africans via blackspeak speaks to this positioning of their bodies and transfers to Afro-diasporic characters a relational mode predicated on fantasies of conquest. Indeed, in the two blackspeak scenes of *The English Moor*, the only character who listens and responds to Catelina's blackspeak, Banelass, aggressively and successfully seeks to conquer her black(ened) body. In those two scenes, sexual and colonial conquest overlap, and the gendering of the Afro-Briton enhances the political dimension of the new British accent that is blackspeak. English blackspeak proceeds from a colonial mode of listening—Banelass embodies that mode, and the audience is implicated in it.

Because of its colonial background, the theatrical technique of the Irish accent evoked specific fantasies of racial degeneration, which Brome recuperates quite heavy-handedly via the script of ethnic conjuration and redirects toward Afro-Britons. Indeed, sustained Anglicizing attempts at suppressing the use of Gaelic in Ireland, were, according to Paula Blank, fueled by anxieties not so much concerning Irish cultural resistance as concerning a possible "Gaelicization of the English" who lived in "Dublin and . . . two rural provinces, the baronies of Forth and Bargy in County Wexford, and to Fingall, a region north of Dublin." It is the accent of those Gaelicized Englishmen that was caricatured on stage as "Irish" by Ben Jonson and others. Spenser's *A View of the Present*

State of Ireland (1596) transparently reads questions of language politics in racial terms, as he articulates that "the notion that speaking Irish had adulterated the lifeblood of the English stock."[84] According to Spenser, for the English to intermarry with the Irish and let Gaelic-speaking wet nurses suckle their children entailed severe risks of "infection" that would make the English stock "degenerate" into wild Irishmen, or, for Sir John Davies in 1612, into beasts.[85] When they staged Anglo-Irishmen's accents, Blank explains, early seventeenth-century playwrights drew on this racial understanding of language in the British Isles: the accent functioned as auditory markers of the Anglo-Irish racial degeneration caused by physiological and linguistic mixture. Those anxieties about English racial degeneration, first coined in the Irish context, easily extended to Afro-Britons, given the common positioning of Afro-British women like Catelina—or the mother of William Seymour's mixed-race granddaughter—as sex workers, sexually assaulted maids, and wet nurses.

In *The English Moor*, the "degenerative" dimension of blackspeak is emphasized by the acoustic parallelism established between Catelina and Quicksands's intellectually disabled son, Timsy, an illegitimate child born long before Quicksands married Millicent. A "simple child" born from the interracial union of a Jewish man and a Christian Englishwoman, Timsy was entrusted by Quicksands to Matthew Hulverhead:

> for a certain sum
> Which I did pay, 'twas articled that I should ne'er be
> Troubled with it more. (4.1.853)

Some of Quicksands's young enemies convince Buzzard, a servant he unjustly dismissed, to disguise himself as Timsy so that they might crash Quicksands's masque. The operation is a success. Buzzard's Timsy disguise includes "long coats," a spinning "rock and a spindle" (spinning constitutes Timsy's main occupation in Norfolk), and a linguistic element: 90 percent of his lines consist in "Hey toodle loodle loodle loo," which, based on the definition of the word "toodle" (an onomatopoeia imitating the sound of a musical pipe), Steggle interprets as "an instruction to make noise rather than a set of words to be spoken."[86] Timsy's condition is thus largely constructed on the sonic mode, through his inability to speak English other than in broken bits and strange noises. When Buzzard and his crew crash Quicksands's masque, the disguised Buzzard's voice erupts a mere nine lines after Catelina's delivers her last line in blackspeak, dramaturgically reinforcing the bond between blackspeak and the speech of a man whose disability is presented as a form of permanent infancy reminiscent of the acoustic script of infantilization.

Quicksands thinks of his son's condition in degenerative terms. Degeneration, the idea that the child is lesser than his parents, that the family's blood—one of the meanings of "race" in the early modern period—has been affected and that qualitative change is happening for the worse, is patent even in Timsy's nickname: the "Changeling." When Buzzard's crew threatens to leave "Timsy" in his father's care, Quicksands replies: "My grief and shame is endless" (5.3.1086). The question of degeneration is made even more urgent by Arnold's statement that he is bringing Timsy back to his father because

> we are not bound
> To keep your child, and your child's children too.
> . . . He has fetched up the bellies of sixteen
> Of his thrip-sisters. (4.1.857–60)

"Thrip" is a Norfolk term for "spin," a verb metaphorically coding sexual intercourse. The Changeling is fathering more changelings; degeneration is gaining traction. Not surprisingly, Timsy's comic force resembles that of the *negros* characters we encountered in the Spanish tradition. Timsy derives his raw comic effect from what Freud would identify as his (perpetual) childishness, his (clinically) deficient expenditure on intellectual matters, and his excessive expenditure on physical (sexual) matters. The parallel that is set up for the audience between Timsy's broken speech forms and Catelina's blackspeak reinforces the racializing dimension that blackspeak inherited from the stage Irish accent. Understood as connected to the Irish stage accent and to Timsy's speech forms, blackspeak constructs Catelina as a subject fit to be conquered, possessed, and racialized—but also as a subject likely to make the English body politic "degenerate" in that very process.

With blackspeak, *The English Moor* mobilizes a linguistic trope that would become central to English colonialism at large throughout the seventeenth century, namely, the trope of "broken English." While the phrase "broken English" was premiered by playwright Thomas Heywood in 1612 to convey the idea that English was historically constituted as a hybrid language, "part Dutch, part Irish, Saxon, Scotch, Welsh, and indeed a gallimaffry of many" Continental languages, it was quickly recuperated and ascribed to the subjects of English colonial rule.[87] Absent from early English chronicles depicting the New World and its inhabitants (Thomas Harriot, John Smith, and others), the phrase appears in colonial writings starting in the early 1620s, at the moment when Anglo-Indian relations became strained, and when, in the wake of the 1622 Jamestown Massacre, colonists used Native American violence as a pretext to further advance the land-grab project.[88] In 1649, Edward Terry would mention that East Indians too spoke "broken English."[89] In collective imagination, the rapid and systematic ascription of "broken English" to colonial subjects—be they Irish, Native American, or from the Indian subcontinent—conferred to metropolitan English a reparative sense of integrity vulnerable to degeneration, like the race of its native speakers.[90]

In 1655, Edward Terry included in his *Voyage to East India* the story of Cooree, a young boy from the Cape of Good Hope who, forty-three years earlier, had been abducted by British sailors, "brought to London, and there kept, for the space of six months, in Sir Thomas Smith's house (then Governour of the East-India Company)."[91] There, "when he had learned a little of our Language ... [Cooree] would daily lye upon the ground, and cry very often thus in broken English, *Cooree home goe, Souldania goe, home goe!*"[92] By including the African boy in the linguistic sphere of English colonialism as a speaker of "broken English," the mid-seventeenth-century writer was not reading a 1612 episode anachronistically. Rather, he merely stated in explicit terms what Brome had sensed and implicitly voiced via the script of ethnic conjuration produced by acoustic racecraft some twenty years earlier: that from the beginning of the seventeenth century onward, speaking "broken English" had been the sonic badge of all the racialized subjects who found themselves in the way of English colonialism.

Part 2. Africanese Blackspeak

Mind the Scratches: African Ambassadors, Jargon, and French Orientalism

Blackspeak was a two-headed monster whose mouths both spouted the same scripts of blackness. Indeed, Africanese blackspeak too deployed scripts of infantilization, animalization, degeneration, and ethnic conjuration. The stories it told early modern French audiences resembled those conveyed by Brome's vernacular blackspeak, with a major difference: French blackspeak did not disclose—it actually hid—the colonial horizon whence it arose.

On paper, French blackspeak seems to have developed late, but transnational routes winding through Italy suggest that French audiences may have

become familiar with blackspeak long before it entered French dramatic archives. Indeed, one major platform for the dissemination of blackspeak across
Europe in the late sixteenth century was Naples, where the musical genre of the
moresche was born, here again, within earshot of Afro-Neapolitans, since in
Italy "by the seventeenth century, the two largest enslaved populations were
found in Livorno on the Ligurian coast and in Naples."[93] The influence of the
Iberian social model in Spain's outposts and the numerous cultural, literary, and
theatrical exchanges that imperial circulation availed help account for the development of Neapolitan blackspeak.[94] Moresche was "an offshoot of a genre vari-
ously called *canzone villanesca*, *villotta*, *villanella* or *napolitana*, all of these
describing a secular song in the Neapolitan dialect," a genre that was popularized in the 1530s, around the same time as Iberian blackspeak.[95] Moresche songs
dramatize comic courtship scenes within the Afro-Neapolitan community:
they unfurl profanity-laden dialogues between the stock characters of Giorgio
and Catalina (or Lucia), who sing with a thick mock-African accent and pepper
their Neapolitan vernacular with words lifted from Kanuri, a language spoken
in the Bornu Empire (now northeastern Nigeria).

Moresche blackspeak spread throughout Europe via commedia dell'arte
performers. Indeed, Eric Rice notes in hitherto unpublished research that, on
the frontispiece of his well-known 1622 series titled *Balli di Sfessania*, which
theatre historians use as a primer on the visual culture of commedia dell'arte,
French engraver Jacques Callot associated lyrics lifted from Orlando di Lasso's famous moresche songs with commedia dell'arte's own stock characters
(Figure 5).

"Lucia mia!" one grotesque-looking character lovingly exclaims, while
Lucia peeps at him through the curtain; "Cucurucu!" another continues;
"Bernoualla!" another responds while playing the tambourine. "Bernoualla":
a distinctly French distortion of the Italian word "bernoguala," that is, "Bornu
people," the same fictional people singing in the 1568 collection of moresche
composed by Orlando di Lasso. During his years of training in Italy, Callot saw
much theatre; since *Sfessania* is a Neapolitan term, it is fair to assume that the
1622 series was inspired by performances Callot saw in Naples, and the frontispiece shows that, in Naples, moresche songs from the mid-sixteenth century
had found their way into commedia dell'arte routines. None of the *zanni* on
Callot's frontispiece is represented as blacked-up, which suggests that blackspeak was autonomous in that repertoire. In other words, to Hornback's important finding that early modern commedia dell'arte performers disseminated
Africanist stereotypes via the black-masked Harlequin character as they toured

Figure 5. Frontispiece of *Balli di Sfessania*. Jacques Callot. Etching and engraving. Circa 1622. The Art Institute of Chicago / Art Resource, NY.

Europe, we should add that commedia actors also disseminated blackspeak through their moresche routines.[96] It is likely, then, if we believe Callot, that Italian actors introduced European audiences to blackspeak long before English or French playwrights scripted the technique in their own plays.

Moresche songs, modular as they were, combined the black-accented vernacular version of blackspeak and the Africanese version of blackspeak. In early modern France, it is the Africanese component that took hold first.[97] Africanese blackspeak quickly resorted to scripts of black animalization, as we can see in *Grand bal de la douairière de Billebahaut* (1626). The ballet mobilizes acoustic racecraft: "Enters the African Narrator, his flat nose first, followed by a squad of *Basanés* who dance before the elephant on which the Great Cacique appears to his people. The Cacique babbles and warbles [ramage], and his subjects answer him in such excellent gibberish [excellent jargon] that the audience can understand none of them."[98] The libretto does not describe that "excellent jargon" in any way: with that stage direction, René Bordier delegated to performers (professional dancers and aristocratic amateurs) the responsibility of crafting that gibberish, engaging their own racial imaginations in the process. That stage direction gave performers license to incorporate animalizing sounds, such as the cacique's "warbling" (ramage), into their sonic performance of blackness. Such "warbling" effect might have sought to convey the impression made by a tonal language onto the speaker of a nontonal one. The stage direction, nonprescriptive in its vagueness, also gave performers the freedom to extend that comic scene of linguistic chaos longer than we imagine when we read the libretto. The "excellent jargon" stage direction gave a sonic blank check to the energetic performers' ensemble.

At work in stage "jargon" were scripts of animalization, but also scripts of ethnic conjuration evoking other marginalized groups with a history of sonic impersonation. Indeed, jargon, like "broken English" in the Anglophone context, is a dense and deceptively transparent term that captures a long history of French language politics. Derived from the onomatopoeic root [garg-], which mimics garbling throat operations, the word referred to the singing of birds (like the cacique's "ramage") as early as the twelfth century, and to the secret language of the underworld, soon to be associated with Romani people under the "Gypsies" label, as early as the thirteenth century.[99] Because jargon refers to speech forms that sound human yet are not intelligible to the listener, Furetière's *Dictionnaire universel* (1690) records two additional meanings: *jargon* can refer to "ancient or foreign languages we cannot understand" or to "the vicious and corrupted language of the people and peasants that is extremely hard to understand" in the countryside.[100] Even though the State would not actively work to eradicate French regional dialects until the Revolution, the crown saw it as its political interest to promote the *langue d'oïl* as the standard for administrative and literary purposes from the 1539 edict of Villers-Cotteret onward.[101] That slow yet steady process—facilitated by the advent of print culture and professional theatre—turned regional dialects into jargons.

French theatre had a long tradition of staging regional jargons through an ambivalent lens that simultaneously mocked and celebrated its object. That tradition was at least as old the *Farce de maître Pathelin et son jargon* (1485), in which the protagonist, pretending to be mad, comically performs scripted dialects from Brittany, Limousin, Normandy, and Picardie, among others.[102] The tradition climaxed in the 1660s, largely under the influence of playwrights such as Raymond Poisson, Nicolas du Perche, and Molière, who, in *Monsieur de Pourceaugnac* (1673), staged regional jargons under the synonymous label of "baragoin."[103] *Baragouin*—a term that first appeared in the fourteenth century and might be etymologically connected to "barbarity"—refers, in the *Dictionnaire de l'Académie Française* (1694) to "imperfect and corrupted French" as well as "foreign languages one does not understand."[104] Thus, both versions of black-speak, black-accented vernacular and Africanese, could be labeled jargon or bara-gouin interchangeably.[105] I insist on the synonymy between jargon and baragouin not out of philological zeal but out of a keen awareness that on this very synon-ymy hinges a network of French *politique de la langue* as wide and capacious as the transatlantic colonial space. Suffice it for now to say that the use of the term *jargon* to refer to Africanese blackspeak in *Grand bal de la douairière de Billeba-haut* (1626) inscribed African characters into an older performative tradition historically bound up with forceful politics of nation building.

Neoclassical drama would uphold that legacy. In 1666, little-known play-wright Nicolas Du Perche wrote *L'ambassadeur d'Affrique*, a comedy heavily based on the first two acts of an equally little-known *comédie à l'espagnole* writ-ten four years earlier by Edmé Boursault, *Le mort Vivant*.[106] The plots of those two plays start similarly: a worthy young man (Fabrice/Lélie) loves a young woman (Stéphanie/Lucresse), and he must overcome the opposition of her father figure, the *senex*, who wishes to marry her off to the wrong suitor (in the earlier play, himself, or, alternatively, another young man who is ultimately re-vealed to be the young woman's natural brother; in the latter play, Ariste, an old professor suspected of being Jewish). The young man has a plan. He has his smart *zanni*-type servant (Gusman/Crispin) use black-up to disguise himself as the powerful "African ambassador" currently in town and claim Stéphanie/Lucresse's hand in order to scare his rival away. Unlike *Le mort vivant*, *L'ambassadeur d'Affrique* is set in 1666 Paris, and in Du Perche's play, Crispin uses blackspeak in addition to black-up to counterfeit the African ambassador.

To the jargon of Ariste—the learned Jewish suitor who cannot help but spout Latin (23–26)—and to the jargon of *L'Allemand*—the manservant who speaks French with a heavily scripted German accent (45–46)—Crispin, alias the African ambassador, opposes the jargon of Africanese blackspeak.[107] Crispin enters with a train of blacked-up Africans, whom the maid calls "little devils" (diablotins).[108] While he speaks to French characters in unaccented French, Crispin talks to his African retinue in jargon:

> *Crispin* Tirbautes.
> *A servant in African habit Ben d'harleK.*
> *Crispin Gooth dan kem cum vir,*
>   *Salkardy bucdemeK satir*
>   *Et voldrecam.*

The professor (to Lélie) What is he singing now?
Lélie He says he is growing restless
  To see Lucresse,
  So he is sending for her. (37)[109]

Stage directions do not label the technique used by Crispin, yet the professor's choice of words ("what is he singing now?") evokes the avian dimension of jargon's original meaning. Crispin also breaks into Africanese jargon when he pretends to be angry:

Crispin Leave at once, or *Kamdem S Koreille*
  Horleam scanem tourtoury
The Professor What is he saying?
Lélie He is upset you were so bold,
  And he wants you out of here immediately. (31)[110]

Du Perche's creative use of capitalization for guttural sounds is an experimental attempt at sketching a scripting system for French Africanese blackspeak. These scenes, however, are the only moments of blackspeak in the play, and later rewritings of the play did not conserve them.

In *L'ambassadeur d'Affrique*, the ubiquitous acoustic script of ethnic conjuration connects the African ambassador to a learned Jew and to an immigrant worker (Germans formed the largest immigrant group in early modern France)—two figures marginalized in national imagination. The African ambassador's juxtaposition with them in the play's dramatic arc makes that connection particularly audible in the playhouse. Unlike in *The English Moor*, acoustic conjuration works here, I argue, to obfuscate the colonial context whence the desire for acoustic blackness came. That obfuscation results from the ambassador's acoustic association with domestic Others (Jews, German immigrants, Romani "Gypsies"), and it also results from his acoustic Orientalization. Indeed, the script of ethnic conjuration connects Du Perche's African ambassador to a tradition of sonic impersonation that was all the rage in neoclassical France: Turkish stage *jargon*.

The first occurrence of Turkish jargon on the French stage may have been in Jean Rotrou's comedy *La soeur* (1647), a play based on Giambattista della Porta's late sixteenth-century *La sorella*, which was popular enough to be reworked by Tristan Lhermitte in *Le parasite* (1654).[111] In the influential *La soeur*, a smart manservant, Ergaste, pretends to know Turkish in order to prevent

Horace—a Frenchman who grew up as a captive in Ottoman Turkey and thus knows Turkish but not French—from revealing truths that would hinder his master's matrimonial projects (71–75). Ergaste's mock-Turkish, "*Carigar camboco, ma io ossansando?*" (72), is exposed as "a fake jargon no one uses" (79) by the only character in the play who knows both French and Turkish (Horace's lines, directly lifted from Della Porta, are written in authentic Ottoman Turkish).[112]

Du Perche took his cue from the tradition of Turkish stage jargon when he rewrote Boursault's original *Le mort vivant* (1662), which did not feature blackspeak, into *L'ambassadeur d'Affrique* (1666). Dramaturgic similarities suggest that Du Perche drew specifically on Antoine de Montfleury's masterful Turkish jargon comedy, *L'école des jaloux ou le cocu volontaire* (1664).[113] In *L'école des jaloux*, a group of Spaniards puts together a stratagem to cure the overjealous Santillane of his condition, and this stratagem involves disguising themselves as Turks. The manservant, also called Gusman, plays the part of the Great Turk and lays claim to Santillane's wife in that capacity. Gusman, alias the Great Turk, speaks in jargon when he speaks to his own Turkish train, and he breaks into a Turkish jargon that particularly emphasizes guttural sounds when he plays angry. "How dare you jest in my presence? I will be avenged! *Biradam fourk dermak galera gourdini*!"[114] Du Perche's blacked-up Gusman spouting Africanese jargon was inspired by Montfleury's Oriental Gusman spouting Turkish jargon. That filiation was not lost on Molière who, in *Le bourgeois gentilhomme*, just a few years later, lifted the marriage plot of Du Perche's play and turned the disguised ambassador back into a Turk, as he was in Montfleury's play.[115] We may have only two scenes of blackspeak in the extant archives of French neoclassical drama, but the technique was at the center of conversations between the key playwrights of the time, suggesting that scarce archival traces are the waterline of an iceberg of unrecorded performative practices and experiments.

In Du Perche's play then, a script of conjuration Orientalized the African ambassador, and I see in that acoustic Orientalization of blackness the same mechanisms of displacement and erasure discussed in Chapter 2. Indeed, the Orientalization of blackspeak, and by extension of blackness, manifests what Madeleine Dobie sees as a large-scale repression of the ethical issues posed by the boom of color-based slavery in the French Caribbean starting precisely in the 1660s and the exculpatory displacement of slavery practices onto the despotic Oriental world that reigned supreme in eighteenth-century French culture.

In a costume sketch created by Daniel Rabel for *Grand bal de la douairière de Billebahaut*, the African king is called "Cacique, king of the Americans"

(Cachique, roy des Amériquains), but strikingly the word "Amériquains" was scratched out and replaced with "Affriquains" (see Plate 9). That scratch, which we may read as an impressive *acte manqué* or as the material mark of denial preserved in the archive, simultaneously reveals and silences the true cultural and political space to which the blackspeaking character belongs as early as 1626: a transatlantic American space already marked by a long history of color-based slavery. French denial runs deep; thus, in both *Billebahaut* and *L'ambassadeur d'Affrique*, blackspeaking Africans are only temporary visitors, passing delegates who do not originate from, belong to, or remain on French soil. The transient nature of blackspeakers in French drama bespeaks a conflict between the desire to experience and use sonic blackness, and the denial-fueled need to distance blackness from the French sphere. Baroque and neoclassical drama were adept at reconciling those incompatible racial desires, and blackspeak participated fully in that effort.

The denial that drives the Orientalization of blackspeak becomes deafening when heard in counterpoint to French colonial chronicles, which, precisely in the 1660s, start using the terms jargon and baragoin to refer to the French spoken by racialized subjects in the Caribbean: native "sauvages" but also, and even more often, "Nègres."[116] In other words, in neoclassical France, the notions of *jargon* and *baragoin*—the pillars of French politique de la langue, which had long been bound up with French forceful nation building—were explicitly extended in colonial writings to a transatlantic colonial space where Afro-descendants were becoming Francophone perforce. As a play like *L'ambassadeur d'Affrique* reveals, it is not true that colonialist desire and use for acoustic blackness did not register on the neoclassical stage. Rather, archives, incomplete and limited as they are (yet in a state of perpetual becoming), sketch a history of performative desire, denial, shame, and displacement that leaves the historian with evidence of erasure—with scratches to record. Techniques of racial impersonation tell the stories some need to hear, and, sometimes, they silence the stories some need to silence.

"So Many Black Moors and Frenchmen in the Nation":
Restoration Soundscapes

Sir Francis Fane's *Love in the Dark* (1675), a Restoration comedy surprisingly neglected in early modern race scholarship, self-consciously rehearses the major tropes of blackness that had developed over time in the canon of early modern

English drama.[117] This play is a dense anamorphic reckoning with the legacy of artifice at the core of performative blackness on the English stage. Its use of Africanese gibberish signals that sound was perceived in seventeenth-century England as a more important medium for racial engagement than what extant dramatic archives might suggest. *Love in the Dark* alerts us to the long shelf life in England of the various transnational acoustic scripts of blackness previously discussed.

Set in Venice, the play features an Othello-type Milanese general, Sforza, who saves the island of Candia from the Turks on behalf of the Venetian senate and happily elopes in the middle of the night with the doge's daughter. The doge's daughter, inspired by Desdemona, is a smart, eloquent, virtuous, and self-possessed young woman who, using black vizards for her own purposes, is not afraid of symbolically blackening her own face. When the doge discovers their marriage, he "grieve[s] at the dishonor of his spotless race" (68). The play's subplot revolves around a libidinous senator and "old banker" (2) reminiscent of Quicksands in *The English Moor*: ominously named Cornanti, he always fears that one of the young men he has ruined might try to cuckold him and, as a result of his jealousy, lets a blacked-up character enter his claustrophobic household.

Cornanti's wife, Bellinganna, in an attempt to secure Trivultio as husband for her smitten cousin, desires to speak with him and invents a stratagem to that end: "my Husband fears no Devils but your White ones: therefore for the security of his Person, he has just now sent out his servant Jacomo to buy a Negro Slave: put yourself into that Colour and Habit, and find means to be sold to him, and you shall be assur'd of a kind Reception" (17). The device of embedded black-up, lifted from *The White Devil* (1612), had become ubiquitous in Caroline drama and had been resurrected in earlier Restoration comedies such as *The Marriage Broaker, or The Pander* (1662), and *Emilia* (1672).[118] Francis Fane took the artifice of that device one step further and created a black-up triple-decker: in his play, a white actor (John Lacy) performs a white character (Intrigo), who pretends to be yet another white character (Trivultio) who himself pretends to be a black character (the "Negro slave").

The play includes two scenes of blackspeak. Intrigo, described in the dramatis personae as "a curious formal coxcomb," intercepts a letter that Bellinganna intended for Trivultio, and, following her advice, he puts on black-up to gain access to her. When the manservant Jacomo introduces the new enslaved member of the household to his master, Cornanti, linguistic issues immediately arise:

Cornanti Where had you this Black?

Jacomo I bought him at the Porto Santo.

Cornanti Methinks he is a better favour'd Moor than ordinary.

Jacomo I, Sir, his Nose is not so flat as most of theirs, and he has not altogether such a black Mossy Pate.

Cornanti I like him never the better for his good Features: but speaks he not our Language?

Jacomo Not a word, Sir.

Cornanti Oh, then 'tis well enough. But, a pox, these strait-chin'd Moors will make plaguy signs to a Woman. Didst thou ever hear him speak?

Jacomo I, and understand him too. *Aside.*—My Master, I'm sure, speaks no Morisco; I'll pass for a Learned Man.

Cornanti How didst thou come to learn their Language?

Jacomo Oh, Sir, I was a Slave fourteen months at Algiers. I was taken in Cavalier Strozzi's Ship, about twenty years ago, and learn'd their Language so perfectly, that I was made Interpreter to the Ambassadors that came to the Governor: Oh, Sir, you shall hear. Have at you, Sir. *Andiboron hoblicon hu.*

Intrigo Aside pausing. Now for some hard words or I'm undone. *Tirenatum tenoch comti.*

Cornanti What's that now?

Jacomo Why, marry Sir, I told him, that you said he should be well us'd; and he made an answer, that shew'd a great deal of Respect, but little manners: in fine, 'tis a great compliment in their Countrey.

Cornanti Come, come, what is it?

Jacomo Why, Sir, the Sence of it is, He takes it to be an Honor to be employ'd in your most contemptible Offices.

Cornanti Come, you're a Rogue: this is no humane Language; but the Dialect of the Barbary Stallions. Say that over again.

Jacomo Dilloron losicon hu.

Cornanti You Rogue you, that's not the same.

Jacomo Aside scratching his Head. Pox o' this dull memory of mine. 'Tis very near the same, Sir. I confess I cannot now speak it so well; but never a man in Italy understands it better.

Cornanti You're a bold Knave, Sirrah. I'll go in, to my Wife, and bring her to see her new Servant. (28–29)

A white servant who needs to prevent the spread of sensitive information from a foreigner's mouth pretends to act as translator: he speaks gibberish to the foreigner and translates what he truly pleases to his own countrymen. He is at liberty to do so because the foreigner is unable to communicate in the local vernacular.

This scene makes liberal use of what I would call the "lost in translation" motif: the transnational theatregram that, first initiated in della Porta's previously mentioned comedy *La sorella*, found its way into various national dramatic canons, from Jean Rotrou's *La soeur* (1645) to Thomas Middleton's *No Wit, No Help Like a Woman's* (1611?) some sixty years before Fane wrote *Love in the Dark*.[119] Marjorie Rubright has convincingly argued that in *No Wit*, by contrasting the authentic stage Dutch of the monolingual Dutch boy with the gibberish Dutch of the mock translator, Middleton prompted spectators to note the difference between the two and to recognize the proximity between correct Dutch and English, thereby encouraging cross-cultural conversations and complicating the notion that stage accents always marginalize foreigners.[120] And yet, *Love in the Dark* shows that this generous framework for understanding the ideological work effected by stage accents hardly applies to non-Northern Europeans—and certainly not to Africans. In Fane's Africanese blackspeak experiment, the linguistic control group that was Middleton's Dutch boy disappears, replaced by yet another pretender. We get gibberish against gibberish in a moment of complete imaginative unleashing, which, to Cornanti, sounds like the neighing "Dialect of the Barbary Stallions."

There is no reason not to take Cornanti at his word here, and in case we do not, the Blackamoor is explicitly animalized later in the play in ways that mobilize the specter of degeneration we encountered in *The English Moor*. Indeed, when the blacked-up Intrigo, now fitted with Venetian clothes, is asked to look into a mirror, he is compared to various beasts:

> *Jacomo* Your Negroship is rarely well adjusted.
> You want nothing but a white Peruig:
> Oh, 'twould set off your sweet Westphalian Hogs-face. (*Intrigo looks for his Face o'th backside of the Glass; and does many Apish things.*) Oh, do you want your scurvy Wainscot chops? I, there they are, my pretty sweet Baboon.
> *Intrigo* (*Intr. whispers to Jack.*) You might use some moderation in your abuse.

Jack You look like an ass and you don't want to be told on it.

Cornanti What's that he says? The poor fool's afraid I should understand his gibberish. (30–31)

Dressing enslaved Afro-descendants with European garments was all the rage in Restoration England. In the second half of the seventeenth century, as sugar culture soared in the English colonies and especially after the creation of the Royal Adventurers into Africa, soon to become the Royal African Company— which was dedicated to slave trading—colonials and travelers brought enslaved people to London with them, and "having a black slave or two in one's household soon became a craze for all who could afford it."[121] This phenomenon transpires in Pepys's *Diary*, in visual culture, where Afro-British pages feature in their enslavers' portraits, and in the ever-increasing number of hue-and-cry advertisements in metropolitan newspapers. Once dressed in the likeness of Europeans, Intrigo is explicitly likened to a "hog" and to a "baboon" doing "apish things." This gives a new meaning to the moment in act 5 when the servant Circumstancio seeks to utter the word "nigromancy," and his tongue slips and lands on ideas of black monstrosity: "I think your Worship's a Strologer, or a Negromonster, that can make two people of one" (86). Blackamoors are construed in the play as hominids whose subhumanity manifests through their chattering— their human-sounding yet unintelligible jargon. Picking up on Fane's clues, an actor who knew his trade—and John Lacy certainly did—could easily have included animalizing sounds in his performance of Africanese gibberish.

Africanese blackspeak here is informed by scripts of animalization, but also by scripts of ethnic conjuration. Indeed, once Cornanti exits, Intrigo and Jacomo discover their real identities to each other, and Intrigo temporarily buys Jacomo's silence. When Cornanti finds his enslaved servant, supposedly ignorant of the vernacular, courting his wife's *duegna*, Jacomo jumps ships:

> *Intrigo seeing Cornanti nods at Jacomo, who winks, and nods at him again.*
> *Intrigo cries out in a lamentable Gibberish.*
> *Intrigo Queki sini baski. Ahi puli tinderis.*
> *Cornanti* Did not I observe this Rascal talking to my Wife and Vigilia?
> *Intrigo Cajiski oli melan. Ahi poluki, Ahi.*
> *Nodding and winking at Jacomo, who nods and winks again.*

Jacomo Alas, good Signior Intrigo, this is worse than *A hone, Ahone.*
No, Sir, I scorn to betray my Master. To come a spy thus from
Taffaletta, Under the Rose, it was not welle.
Intrigo Aside. Oh the false knave!
Cornanti Bless me! Is this Intrigo?
Jacomo It must needs be he by his way of speaking. Never any man
was so deceiv'd by a Rogue. (45)

As this scene's opening stage direction signals, the operative term for tracking Africanese blackspeak in English theatre is "gibberish," a term that Cornanti himself uses to refer to Intrigo's blackspeak later on in the play, and one replete with older ethnic and racial connections (31). Indeed, in his 1611 dictionary, Cotgrave illuminatingly translates the English word "gibbridge" into the French "jargonnois, patois, bagois, jargon de galimatias."[122] Here, translation signals a set of fraught associations that goes beyond the laconic monolingual definition of the word given by John Wilkins in 1668 as "speech not intelligible." Translation gives us access to the racial implications of that word.[123] The word "gibberish" appears often in sixteenth- and early seventeenth-century lexicons as a synonym for "pedler's French, fustian, rogues' language," defined more explicitly as "the barbarous language used among those cheating and filching vagabonds, that call themselves Aegyptians, or Bohemians," better known as Romani "Gypsies."[124] Jacomo's statement that Intrigo is a "rogue" alludes to the deceitfulness of his course of action, but also to the sedimented association of gibberish with English Roma. "Rogue," applied to the blackspeaking Intrigo, activates the racial discourse pertaining to Romani people or, rather, conjures it.[125]

In *Love in the Dark*, acoustic ethnic conjuration accomplishes a lot of its racializing work via yet another route, that is, via the strong parallelism that the play establishes between Intrigo—a character whose disguise includes black sonics—and Visconti—a character whose disguise includes French sonics. Indeed, in order to gain access to his own lover, Melinda, Visconti disguises himself as a Frenchman with a heavily scripted accent; as he notes at the end of the play in a metadramatic moment, "I am not the first French-Master, that has run away with a Gentleman's Daughter" (82). The parallelism between French accent and blackspeak is established in dramatic terms (since Visconti and Intrigo use the same device for the same purpose), but also, quite possibly, in performative terms. Indeed, John Lacy, the actor who played Intrigo, was famous for performing and writing parts that used a heavy French accent—for instance in his own evocatively titled play *Monsieur Raggou*.[126] There is a chance, then, that his French accent technique informed his black-accented African gibberish in performance.

The genealogy of the play, too, connects French accent and Africanese gibberish. Indeed, while English Africanese blackspeak was, as extant printed archives suggest, a novelty in 1675, the use of gibberish to represent exotic Others was not. Three years prior to *Love in the Dark*, Edward Ravenscroft had adapted Molière's *Le bourgeois gentilhomme* for the English stage, and in appropriating and transforming Molière's Turkish *jargon* in *The Citizen Turn'd Gentleman* (1672), he had imported to England the stage tradition that was, as we saw, at the core of *L'ambassadeur d'Affrique*.[127] Unlike Molière, Ravenscroft had included some "Blacks" in the Turkish train of his play.[128] I record that the conjunction of black characters and Turkish gibberish orchestrated by Ravenscroft in *The Citizen Turn'd Gentleman* might have inspired Fane's experiment with Africanese blackspeak three year later. In that scenario, the fantasies of invasion that bind Frenchmen and Blackamoors in *Love in the Dark* ironically echo the potentially transnational genealogy of the play.

The acoustic parallelism between Frenchmen and Africans in Fane's play is explicitly articulated in xenophobic terms when Intrigo's servant, Circumstancio, boxes his own blacked-up master and smugly declares: "I need none of your teaching, Goodman Black, 'Twas never a good World, since there were so many Black moors and Frenchmen in the Nation" (35). Frenchmen and dark-skinned Afro-Europeans are perceived as invaders by the white servant who voices popular commonsense and class resentment. By virtue of the parallelism that the play works so hard to make obvious, the xenophobic vitriol spilled against the French is implicitly directed, at least in part, toward Blackamoors too.

The French presence in Venice is constructed as an invasion. When the doge finds the play's lovers—including Sforza and his own daughter—together at night in his own palace, masked, ready to elope, and armed (in breach of Venetian law), he reads the situation as a "Spanish plot," for Sforza and Trivultio are Milanese, and thus subjects of the king of Spain.

The Case is plain, these strangers have design'd
To whore our Daughters, cut our Throats, and put
A Spanish Yoak upon this free-born State. (69)

Visconti manages to escape, but he is soon found again, and fantasies of invasion are immediately redirected from Spain to France:

Enter a Watchman, with many of the Rabble about him. Visconti passes by hastily in his French Habit: the Watchman comes up to him.

Watchman Stand; Whither so fast? Are not you one of the Conspirators?

Visconti Me be povré Estranger.

1 Man A Frenchman, a Frenchman.

2 Man A French Dog; all the Plots come from thence.

3 Man Knock him down.

4 Man Brain him. This is he that set my House o' fire. 'T could be no body but a Frenchman.

6 Man This is he that got my Daughter with Child. That was a French trick too.

Watchman Keep the Peace neighbors, and let us bring him before the Senate. He was in as much haste, as if he had been coming from Candia or Gygery.

All I, I, away with him, away with him. A Plot, a Plot: the French, the French.

1 Man They'll burn the City.

2 Man They'll worry our Wives and Children.

3 Man They'll let in the Sea, and drown us.

5 Man Twas they that brought the Plague into Venice.

7 Man I, and the Pox too, formerly.

Watchman What's your name?

Visconti Me be Metre de Language to Signior Grimani. Me be no Frenchman, me be Italieen.

1 Man No matter, you shall be hang'd for looking like one.

2 Man I, for clipping the true Language.

3 Man You shall be hang'd Al-a-mode de France.

Watchman Come, come away.

All Away with him, away with him.

Boys follow him crying: A Mounsire. A Mounser. A Munchir. A Mister Mownseer.

Exeunt all in a hurry, haling him away. (71–72)

The motif of invasion is here articulated as a destructive penetration: that of the city itself with seawater as French invaders open the dams, but, most obsessively, that of the Venetian body politic, as the French invaders threaten to impregnate

Venetian women and to contaminate them with diseases (pox and plague). French invasion is couched in sexual terms, as a form of predation whose specter was introduced earlier, when Trivultio had decreed that "Lying with another Man's Wife, is like invading an Enemies Countrey" (20), or when Grimaldi, hearing the mock-French Visconti say that he could "sing as well as de Eunuch Italien," had answered, "I would he were one too, then I might securely admit him into my Family" (28). The framework of invasion helps us understand why, when Cornanti deplores the cultural influence of France in Venice—understand: Restoration England—he complains that his customers are all "airy Bankrupt, gawdy Butterflies, / The Apes of chattering Frenchmen" (8). "Chattering" is the term Cotgrave uses to define the speech of birds, grasshoppers, and apes.[129] For Cornanti, Frenchmen, just like hominid Blackamoors, are apes, and by imitating them, Venetians (understand: Londoners) turn into simian creatures themselves. Invasion induces degeneration.

It is in that context that we must understand the deployment of a comedic French accent that might otherwise have seemed innocuous. The sexual invasion of the Venetian body politic is mirrored by the acoustic invasion that the French accent represents in the soundscape of the play. Thus, the distortions of the French word "Monsieur" by English speakers at the end the scene quoted above might sound playful, but they are actually retaliatory in an acoustic context where accents perpetrate symbolical violence. When Visconti denies being French with a mock Italian accent ("Me be no Frenchman, me be Italieen"), we face the absurdity of a Milanese faking an "Italian" accent for a Venetian crowd while he spoke in an unaccented manner right until this point, making the question of regional dialects moot. This absurd moment foregrounds the fact that the play's entire soundscape is built for English ears: the "true language" that is being "clipp'd" here—an alternative to "broken"—both by the French accent and by blackspeak is the English language. The metaphor of "clipping the true language" that the rabble uses uncannily connects, here again, the French accent and its twin, blackspeak, to older English racial formations. Indeed, coin clipping was a capital crime in medieval and early modern England: that crime was invoked to justify "the greatest massacre of Jews in English history" when, in 1278–79, "perhaps as many as half the country's adult Jewish males were executed" for alleged crimes such as coin clipping and counterfeiting.[130] Currency is the common value guaranteed by the king that founds all social transactions, and thus holds the body politic together—so is the English tongue. Clipping the country's currency or its tongue constitutes a debasing attack on the body politic perpetrated by racializable Others: Jews, Romani "Gypsies," foreigners, and, from then on, Blackamoors.

Conclusion: Blackspeak and Black-Up

The black-accented vernacular version of blackspeak that was ubiquitous in early modern Iberia and its dependences gained popularity in France and in England in the late eighteenth century. In England, that strand of blackspeak boomed in the late 1760s, just when the abolitionist movement took flight, which supports David West Brown's point that plays resorting to blackspeak were often "produced at a time of roiling debates about race and empire."[131] Similarly, in France, blackspeak soared in the early 1790s, in the wake of the French Revolution, the Haitian Revolution, and the first abolition of slavery (1794).[132] I argue that the recurrent popularity of blackspeak in commercial drama at times when the legitimacy of slavery was hotly debated is due to the fact that blackspeak structurally enables race plays to perform ideological ambivalence; to enact self-contradictory impulses by balancing plotlines that can be sympathetic to Afro-diasporic characters with a sonic stagecraft that keeps those characters in their place. In that sense, the contexts in which blackspeak was mobilized in eighteenth-century France and England shed light retrospectively on its deployment in early modern Iberia.

To conclude, let us return one last time to *Love in the Dark*. Intrigo's itinerary as an enslaved Afro-diasporic man throughout the play asserts the centrality of sound to early modern racecraft. After being arrested, released, and then mistaken for a vizard-wearing lady, Intrigo, still in black-up and still desirous to "dive into the fresh intrigues and cabinet councils"—for he is the eponymous Man of Business of the play and loves nothing better than gossip—hides in the great "Trunk of Records" of the senate house (76). The door keeper did "get a hole made on purpose to put out [his] head and hands" (76), and Intrigo witnesses from there the happy resolution of the play, as lovers, throughout act 5, convince the authorities to let them marry one another. While Intrigo remains invisible to the characters on stage, spectators can see him peeping out and taking notes. When the senators decide to open the trunk to look for a precedent in the city's legal records, Intrigo rises, "his face as black as mummy" with a white peruke on top, and the assembly takes him for the ghost of Ordelafo, the twelfth-century doge who established the very law that the lovers broke (91). Yet as soon as he opens his mouth and starts using the ridiculous idiosyncratic turns of phrase he has been using throughout the play, the assembly recognizes him. This final scene foregrounds the centrality of acoustic markers of identity. *Love in the Dark* plays with the materiality of prosthetic blackness and the various identities it could construe, as the blacked-up Intrigo is read at various points in the play as a Blackamoor, a vizarded lady, and a decaying corpse, or a ghost.[133] The playful hermeneutic instability of scopic blackness in that play draws attention to the efficacy of acoustic blackness, which often threatens to—and ultimately does—reveal identities that scopic impersonation obfuscates.

Love in the Dark thus impels us to grapple with the relation between cosmetic blackness and acoustic blackness in early modern performance. Fundamentally, acoustic blackness depends on the scopic regime. Indeed, what enabled blackspeak to do its ideological work was its artificiality: blackspeak could infantilize blackness, animalize it, and conjure up profound connections with other racialized groups in performance because it was performed by white actors—and for audiences to grasp the performers' whiteness, they had to see it. They had to see the greasy materiality of cosmetic blackness, or, more simply, they had to see the exposed white skin of the performers, as was the case in the Italian tradition of moresche. It would, however, be inaccurate to model the relation between blackspeak and black-up as asymmetrical or supplemental, for, as we saw in Chapters 1 and 2, the hermeneutic reception of black-up was conditioned by indexical poetic cues, which are necessarily voiced. There was a fundamental mutual dependency between the scopic and the acoustic regimes in early modern racecraft.

This does not, however, necessarily imply a mutual dependency between the specific techniques of blackspeak and black-up, which could and often did function on stage without each other. Moresche singers used blackspeak sans black-up, and in Gil Vicente's *Fragoa d'amor*, "Furunando" much laments the ability of blackspeak to convey performative blackness sans black-up. Reciprocally, until the late eighteenth century, English and French performance archives mostly attest to black-up's ability to operate on stage without blackspeak. The strength and popularity of those various performance traditions suggests that neither performance technique was in any way lacking: for the purposes of race making, blackspeak and black-up were autonomous, complete, and deadly effective techniques. When they operated in conjunction, most often, they complemented each other, reinforcing each other's scripts of blackness. For instance, in Spanish theatre, the elite black characters (saints, exceptional male scholars and soldiers, *mulatas*) around whom the luxury script of blackness is deployed all speak in unaccented Castilian—as opposed to the nonelite enslaved

black characters, around whom foodstuff and animalizing scripts of blackness
are deployed, who usually speak in blackspeak. Scopic and acoustic stories of
blackness could also deepen and heighten one another. For instance, still in
Spain, the commodifying scripts of blackness operated as a shortcut form of
racialization, getting spectators accustomed to thinking about Afro-descendants
as commodities, but it did not explain why those *negro* characters deserved to
be treated as commodities. By contrast, blackspeak framed those characters as
childish, intellectually deficient, and excessively physical, three characteristics
that made them particularly suited for slavery. The script of black infantilization delivered by acoustic means articulated a rationale for the script of black
commodification delivered by scopic means.

For this complex web of entanglements—which comprises the dependency
of blackspeak on the scopic regime, the dependency of black-up on the acoustic
regime, blackspeak and black-up's independence from each other, and their exponential efficacy when they operated in conjunction—there can hardly be a
better metaphor than dance, the love child of the scopic and the acoustic regimes. It is probably not a coincidence that the scenes of *The English Moor*
where Catelina is performed in black-up and blackspeak at the same time involve intense kinetic and choreographic action. Ultimately, dance is not only a
metaphor for our purposes: rather, it is the key to yet another regime of early
modern racecraft, to which I will now turn.

CHAPTER 4

Black Moves

Race, Dance, and Power

OK, Ladies, now let's get in formation.

Beyoncé, "Formation," 2016

Thomas Tryon's *Friendly Advice to the Gentlemen Planters* (1684) presents readers with a vivid dialogue between Sambo and his enslaver, a West Indian planter eager to see him dance:

Master I call'd you to make us some Sport, let us see one of your
Dances, such as are used in your own Country, with all your
odd Postures and Tricks, for Diversion; I have heard you are the
best at it of all my People.

Slave Boon Master! If you will have me Dance upon mine Head, or
Caper on the top of the House, I must do it, though I break my
Neck; for you are become Lord both of my Feet, and every part
of me, but I fear I shall not be able at present to answer your
Expectation handsomly, I am so much out of humour, and unfit
for Feats of Activity.

Master Why? What's the matter Sirrah! I'll warrant, you have been
frollicking so long amongst your Companions that now you'll
pretend you are Weary.

Slave Truly, Sir! This being the only Day in the Week you spare us
from hard labour, and allow us for Recreation, we do a Sundayes
amongst our selves, endeavour to forget our Slavery, and skip

about, as if our Heels were our own, so long sometimes, till our
Limbs are almost as weary with that as with working.[1]

Tryon's dialogue captures the well-known ambivalent power dynamics of slave
dances recorded across the Atlantic world from the 1660s onward.[2] As Saidiya
Hartman has shown, Atlantic slave dances, including slave ship dances and
plantation dances, historically functioned as ambivalent sites for enslavers to
exercise their power over black bodies through "innocent amusements" and for
the enslaved to build communities, retain African cultural practices, and mock
their enslavers through "the subterranean politics of the enslaved." As Hartman
luminously puts it: "these performances constituted acts of defiance conducted
under the cover of nonsense, indirection, and seeming acquiescence. By virtue
of such tactics, these performances were sometimes turned against their instrumental aims; at the same time, the reliance on masquerade, subterfuge, and indirection also obscured the small acts of resistance conducted by the enslaved."[3]
In Tryon's dialogue, the West Indian enslaver exercises his authority over Sambo's
body by demanding a dance, since he is "Lord of both his feet and every part of
him," while the enslaved use dance as a way of reclaiming self-determination
and ownership over their own bodies, dancing "as if [their] heels were their
own." In the 1680s, white colonists such as Tryon were acutely aware of the ambivalent power dynamics of Afro-diasporic slave dances.

Yet those well-known power dynamics did not originate either in the Atlantic world or in Tryon's day and age. I locate the origin of those kinetic power
dynamics in sixteenth-century metropolitan Europe. During the Renaissance,
a multidirectional circulation of emerging racial ideas and performance techniques across porous national borders led to the development of a particularly
vivid trans-European kinetic idiom of blackness. I refer to this idiom as *black
dances* for the sake of brevity. In this chapter, I bring to light the black dances
performed in early modern metropolitan Europe, and I show that black dances
were perceived as a medium expressing ambivalent interracial power relations
from the very moment sub-Saharan Africans were brought to the Iberian Peninsula, long before Thomas Tryon's time. Tracing black dances in sixteenth- and
seventeenth-century Spanish, French, and English performance cultures, I argue that renderings of dances that were perceived as African in the public sphere
helped crystalize emerging notions about blackness and conceptualize black
dances as a practice steeped in interracial power play.

A quick look at the basic structure of early modern European dance culture
helps explain why dance was a particularly efficient medium for racializing

Afro-diasporic people. Today, much more is known about court dances than about the rest of early modern dance culture, because court dances, embedded as they were in the world of power and politics, were more abundantly described and documented than any other dances at the time. Dance was part of the daily life of European courts, and it was deployed most lavishly and memorably on any occasion of State. Overrepresented in the archive, then, courtly dances should not blind us to the pervasiveness of dance in early modern European societies at large. The growing number of dancing masters advertising their services all across Europe throughout the period confirms the ubiquity of dance.[4] Dance was a major form of entertainment: available to all, it grew steadily in popularity throughout the early modern period. From marketplaces to bourgeois houses, city halls, parliaments, and aristocratic mansions in the countryside—not to mention religious pageants or festivals, wedding celebrations, baptisms, and, of course, commercial playhouses—dance was everywhere.[5] Dances circulated across national borders, creating a rich array of regional variations on the same choreographies, and they circulated across class borders. Indeed, while many popular social dances (such as *pavanes*, *branles*, *courantes*, and *voltas*) were performed at court and integrated into masques, ballets, or *mascarades*, recipro-cally, dances that had first been designed for court performances were often adapted and integrated into the repertoire of social dances available to all.[6] As for commercial theatre, it enthusiastically cannibalized all dances in existence for its own benefit. Communication between the various social settings of early modern dance culture enabled black dances to permeate all the loci of that cul-ture, thereby maximizing the spread of the racial discourse that moved them forward.

Dance had triumphed across Renaissance Europe as a practice that simul-taneously shaped gender performance (women's and men's dancing styles obeyed markedly different aesthetic codes) and class performance.[7] A pillar of aristocratic education, an indispensable social grace, and a major asset for court-iers in their endeavor to secure royal preferment, dancing expressed the social rank of any dancer. Even when aristocrats performed popular social dances, Castiglione tells us, decorum had to be observed: aristocrats had to use a spe-cific kinetic style, based on *sprezzatura*, in order to mark their noble pedigree.[8] At a time when class distinctions constituted the dominant paradigm in the racial matrix, dance had shaped race performance. Quite naturally then, when the epistemological shift that is of interest to us took place, that is, when race-as-phenotype joined the dominant paradigms of race-as-degree and race-as-religion within the early modern European racial matrix at the turn of the sixteenth century, dance was well positioned to shape bodily performance along the lines of the emergent racial paradigm. Dance's long-standing entanglement with the gendered racial matrix had turned the kinetic medium into an efficient essentializing machine.

As some early modern scholars (such as Sebastián de Covarrubias or Thoinot Arbeau) themselves suspected, black dances, while imagined and labeled as quintessentially African, may or may not have derived from the authentic African and Afro-diasporic dances imported and developed by Afro-Europeans in Spain, England, and France. Thus, I use the term *black dances* to refer to dances that, regardless of authenticity, were defined as black in the imagination of the dominant segment of European populations that enthusiastically consumed and replicated them. Those dances were often performed by white actors in black-up, but also by professional Afro-diasporic dancers who may have delivered what spectators paid for—at least in some cases—for it is not hard to imagine that Afro-Europeans may have resorted to kinetic code-switching for different audiences, leading to the development of different sets of kinetic blackness. While they can hardly be suspected, as we saw in the preceding chapters, of participating in the production of black-up and blackspeak, Afro-Europeans often performed black dances in public for a living, with, perhaps, the perverse effect of increasing the authenticity capital of those dances over time.

In many respects, the following entry, performed in 1649 in Avignon, France, in the burlesque *Ballet des divers entretiens de la fontaine de Vaucluse*, allegorically captures the main features of early modern European black dances: "Two eunuchs, slaves to the Emperor-of-the-lands-that-have-not-been-discovered-yet, and who, on a whim of nature, were born half-white and half-black, while waiting for their master, made an entry that was so entertaining, with steps and postures so unknown in our regions, that they left spectators enraptured to a degree that cannot be expressed."[9] To translate: black dances are aesthetically foreign, indissolubly attached to the practice of slavery in lands begging to be colonized, characterized by genital fixation, and performed perhaps half of the time by Afro-diasporic people and half of the time by white people. Most importantly, enraptured audiences cannot get enough of them. The French ballet entry truly captures the popularity of early modern black dances, which moved between performance sites: from Andalusian street processions and public squares to commercial corrales in Spain, from village feasts to court ballets and Parisian theatres in France, from royal pageants in Edinburgh to court masques and London theatres in Britain. Black dances took the different loci of early modern European performance culture by storm. Their racializing effect influenced a wide range of spectators, all "enraptured to a degree that cannot be expressed."

Black dances are a core component of the racializing discourse deployed around Afro-diasporic people in early modern European popular culture, and they have yet to receive sustained critical attention. Indeed, in early modern critical race studies, interest in *Masque of Blackness* has not yet blossomed into a more systemic inquiry into the kinetic performance of blackness in English theatre, while English early modern dance studies, which has produced fascinating accounts of the reception and reimaginings of Native American dances, has not yet extended its attention to Afro-diasporic dances.[10] In early modern French studies, very few race scholars include ballets in their corpus, and those who do, like Sylvie Chalaye, tend to treat libretti as pure drama without factoring in the unscripted element of dance. Meanwhile, French ballet scholars reckon very little with race, and those who do tend to turn their attention predominantly to "Turqueries" or Native American dances (a notable exception is Mark Franko, whose work on "Mores galants" was pivotal for mine).[11]

Finally, early modern Hispanic studies have produced detailed accounts of ethnic dances involved in street processions, which have recently been put in conversation by Nicholas R. Jones with danzas de negros performed on stage.[12] I depart from Jones's thought-provoking work in that, as previously mentioned, I do not read the black dances recorded in white archives as instances of authentic Afro-diasporic dances evidencing a retention of African aesthetics and subjectivity.[13] Rather, I acknowledge the epistemological limitations imposed by the whiteness of the archives, and I find that those limitations reinforce the uncertainties voiced by Arbeau and Covarrubias about the ontology of early modern black dances. Simply put, the white gaze that filtered black dances into the archives makes it impossible to know whether they were authentically Afro-diasporic dances. Black dances refer to knowable perceptions of unknowable dances. Like Jones, I am committed to reclaiming an early modern Black agency erased from the record, but I locate that agency elsewhere: in Black performers' documented bids for control over black dances' cultural sites of production.

Providing a sustained account of European black dances as early modern racial technology involves looking at several kinds of theatre (processional, commercial, private) and several national traditions together. Naturally, the quantity of sources recording black dances varies drastically from country to country, reflecting differences between Black demographics in Iberia and in the rest of early modern Europe. However, giving weight to the available English and French sources on black dances reveals important transnational commonalities. It reveals that, in the three countries under consideration, black dances operated as racializing tools that construed Africans as endowed with various essential qualities justifying their positioning at the bottom of the social order, while, at the same time, they were used for purposes of self-emancipation by various groups that either were or perceived themselves to be oppressed. A racializing technique used to claim or reclaim mobility, agency, and self-determination, early modern European black dances channeled social energies into performances of power relations. In other words, what is most original about early modern black dances is not so much the scripts of black sexualization and animalization that they share with black-up and blackspeak but the political affordances of those scripts in their wildly popular kinetic forms: performers used black dances and their scripts of blackness to claim their right to ownership and self-ownership. In various contexts, the "injurious" kinetic speech act of black dances could, to cite Judith Butler, "be 'returned' to its speaker in a different form, . . . be cited against its originary purpose, and perform a reversal of effects."[14] Early modern performance archives register such reversals as well as white resistance to and ruthless appropriations of those reversals.

In this chapter, I seek to give a sense of the vast interactive terrain in which black dances emerged, traveled, and operated in early modern Europe. To do so, I move chronologically, from the middle of the sixteenth century to the end of the seventeenth century, and northward, from Spain to England via France. In Spain, danzas de negros, Creole Andalusian black dances subsumed in the strenuous priapic dancing style called *guineo*, deployed a script of black sexualization. Featured in social dance settings, street processions, and commercial theatres alike from the sixteenth century onward—in keeping with the increase of the Afro-Spanish population and the development of color-based slavery— guineo sexualized Afro-diasporic people in popular perceptions, associating them with the lower bodily stratum. Yet these black dances were also used and transformed by Afro-Spaniards to renegotiate the terms of their enslavement, either symbolically, as a way of reclaiming mobility and ownership over their own bodies, or very materially, as a way of earning money to buy their own freedom, or of ingratiating the controversial Black confraternities with the Spanish population. In short, the ambivalent power dynamics of late seventeenth-century Atlantic black dance were already in place in sixteenth-century metropolitan Spain.

In the second section, I bring to light an early seventeenth-century choreographic tradition that was not limited to but was particularly potent in France and heavily features scripts of black animalization. Spanning different dances, that tradition animalized the body language of Afro-diasporic people in social dance settings, popular culture, and court ballets alike. In a culture that read movement as an expression of the soul, infusing black body language with animal forms downgraded Afro-diasporic people in the Great Chain of Being, giving them a liminal position at the bottom of mankind that could only translate as a lowly position in the social order. In court ballets, aristocrats used that choreographic tradition to declass their own bodies and subversively contest aspects of the royal authority that they experienced as tyrannical. They danced animalistically to protest what they saw as forms of expropriation from ownership and self-ownership: they danced black to renegotiate their condition in relation to the king, which they experienced hyperbolically as a form of bondage. Black dances remained long in vogue in court ballets, and they infiltrated forms of commercial theatre that retained strong affinities with court culture in neoclassical France, such as *pièces à machines*, operas, and *comédies-ballets*, whose participation in racial discourse has remained staggeringly underappreciated to this day.

The French and the Spanish traditions, as different as they were from each other, can illuminate the early modern English tradition of black dances. In the last section of this chapter, I first read Queen Anne's kinetic performance in *Masque of Blackness* (1605) in the light of the French ballet tradition, as a privileged aristocratic act of rebellion vis-à-vis the racially informed patriarchal ideology that ruled at the court of James I, which Anne experienced as a form of bondage. I hypothesize that the script of animalization infiltrated the kinetic discourse of *Masque of Blackness*, and I reveal its pervasiveness in the fashionable "antics" of late Jacobean commercial theatre, which underwent a process of Africanization in the Caroline period. In that period, black dances were reconfigured as a site of contestation not so much for white aristocratic performers as for Afro-diasporic characters. Philip Massinger's *The Bondman* (1623) illustrates how English theatrical "antics" started functioning as a conduit expressing unstable power relations between fictional enslaved Afro-diasporic characters and white enslavers, in ways that resembled the power structure of early modern Spanish black dances. The tradition of black antics not only survived the Civil War; it throve in Interregnum and Restoration theatrical cultures. That development—particularly evident in Davenant's *The History of Sir*

Francis Drake (1659) and Wycherley's *The Gentleman Dancing-Master* (1673), coincides with an intensification of color-based slavery in the Atlantic, where, increasingly, enslaved people like Thomas Tryon's Sambo danced as if their heels were indeed their own.

Guineo or Kineo? Dance, Slavery, and Mobility in Early Modern Spain

The travel literature available to early modern Europeans spread the notion that dancing was second nature to sub-Saharan Africans, starting with Leo Africanus's statement that, in contrast to his fellow North Africans, "The *Noirs* know how to live the good life. . . . They do all they can to have all the pleasures possible, always merrily dancing, always engaged in parties, feasts, and various other merriments. . . . Of all Africans, they know how to have the best time."[15] In Spanish cultural imagination, Afro-diasporic people's love for dancing was strong, and if the witnesses of the time are to be believed, Spaniards' love for watching Afro-diasporic people dance was even stronger. In a letter dated June 1582, Philip II writes to his daughters that he rushed to the window to see black dances performed by Afro-Portingals in the streets of Lisbon.[16] Portugal was rivaled only by Andalusia in that respect: in the interlude *Entremés de los mirones*, Cervantes mentions the "little square in front of Saint Mary-the-White where crowds of *negros* and *negras* would gather" to dance in Seville.[17] As chronicler Diego Ortiz de Zúñiga cynically explains in 1677, in Andalusia "*negros* had been treated with benignity since the time of King Henry III, and they were allowed to gather and have dances and parties on resting days: that way they showed up for work willingly and tolerated captivity better."[18] Andalusians' fascination with dances defined as African is evoked in the ever self-referential medium of theatre: in Simón Aguado's interlude *El platillo* (1602), for instance, instead of pursuing—as he should—the thieves who just robbed a rich colonial (*indiano*), the bailiff follows a group of Afro-Spanish dancers performing a Canary dance in the streets of Granada without realizing that those dancers are not really Afro-Spaniards but the very thieves that he seeks, in black-up. He gently excuses himself in front of the audience: "I'm enjoying this so much that I'm going to follow them."[19]

What could such dances have looked like on stage? Covarrubias, in *Tesoro de la lengua castellana* (1611), defines guineo thus: "Guineo, or *negro* from Guinea, is a certain dance with quick and hurried movements; it may be that it was brought from Guinea and *negros* were the first to dance it, or it may come from the Greek verb *kineo* (to move) *moveo, incitor*, because of the agility and rapidity of this dance."[20] Imagining a Greek origin for guineo, Covarrubias sees in black dances an incarnation of the kinetic principle itself—condensed kinesis. His uncertainty about the authenticity of guineo as an African dance bespeaks a possible awareness of the indissoluble entanglement of black dances' genesis in contexts of interracial mixing and frictions in the slave-owning region of Andalusia. Lope de Vega highlights the same uncertainty when he exposes black dances as Andalusian fabrications masquerading under authentic African guise in *La limpieza no manchada* (1618). When the allegory of Ethiopia enters the stage to pay homage to Spain with a "baile de negros" performing Ethiopian "parties and merriments," Spain interrupts her: "You come under a disguise, / But I recognize you, Andalusia!"[21] Covarrubias and Lope de Vega were probably not the only early modern Spaniards to doubt the provenance and authenticity of black dances, but it is the nature of essentializing dances— and of the whole set of performative practices studied in this book under the rubric of racecraft—to become real by conditioning the ways spectators read the real world, its inhabitants, and their movements.

Understanding guineo as a kinetic style rather than a precisely codified dance helps us move beyond issues of labels and reconstruct this perceived kinetic style as much as possible by collecting information from different sites of performance.[22] Navarro García explains: "The most representative movements of guineo, executed on a very fast-paced rhythm, consisted in moving the hips with the body completely leaning forward."[23] Indeed, in *Premática del tiempo*, Francisco de Quevedo describes guineo as "leaning the whole body excessively, dangerously, disgustingly," and Sebastián de Villaviciosa's interlude *Entremés de los sones* describes the guineo-esque *zarambeque* as the dance that "leaps, dives, and skips more than all the sounds of guitar."[24] In a dance culture where the aristocratic upper body had to remain still and vertical while only the legs moved, such choreographies were marked as very lower class.[25] Moreover, these gestures indicate controlled patterns of balance loss and recovery foreign to most European dance traditions, playful shifts in gravity center location, and great energy. Contracts between the city of Seville and the dancing masters commissioned during Corpus Christi indicate that processional guineo dancers, performing in groups, often wore bells around their shins, which multiplied the importance of precisely synchronized leg movements, for bells mingled with "loud hollers, Moorish tambourines, guitars, and timbrels."[26] To make the bells around their shins ring rhythmically, the performers, male and female, must have jumped and stamped—body movements reserved, again, for the lower class.[27]

To the lower class belonged the lower bodily stratum. The guineo routine of Madrid-based Afro-Spanish dancer Francisco Menesez included "putting on a lot of bells" and "going out pulling a thousand different faces."[28] Making such faces was not unique to him: Fernando Palatín notes that guineo contained "violent movements and ridiculous gestures."[29] The hilarity that a zarambeque performance elicits from an embedded female spectator in Francisco Lanini's *Entremés de los gorrones* leaves no doubt as to the efficacy of those gestures.[30] During the *fiestas* celebrating the king's visit in Tortosa in December 1585, a white confraternity presented eight performers in black-up who would "stick their tongues out and give the finger in order to make viewers laugh."[31] The priapic nature of those gestures (especially the latter) signals the genital fixation that informed the vocabulary of black dances: "leaning forward completely" and "moving the hips," to return to Navarro García's description, could easily read as sexual. Thus, according to the *Diccionario de autoridades*, guineo featured "gestures that are ridiculous and indecent," and Luis Vélez de Guevara attributes the invention of that indecent dance to *el diablo cojuelo*, "the Limping Devil" himself.[32] Guineo deployed a script of blackness that construed Afro-descendants as energetic and hypersexual.

Paul Scolieri argues that, in early modern Spain, "dancing was a viable way to negotiate perceptions of social, cultural, and religious differences in an ever-expanding world," and he demonstrates how those negotiations, after affecting North African *moros*, started affecting native Americans in early modern Spanish eyes.[33] Sub-Saharan Afro-diasporic people too, I contend, must be inscribed in that long history of Spanish interracial kinetic negotiations. Guineo developed in Spain in the region of Andalusia where sub-Saharan Africans had been used as enslaved servants in urban areas since the late fifteenth century. A 1565 census had the enslaved Afro-diasporic population as approximately 13.5 percent of the total population in Seville; not surprisingly, the first recorded black dance is a dance for the 1576 Corpus Christi processions of Seville—"*La zambra de los negros*," designed by Hernando Manuel. Black dances became a staple of the Corpus Christi processions in the 1590s as the Afro-Spanish population kept increasing; around the same time, enslaved *negro* characters became a staple of the commercial stage, and so did black dances. Thus, early modern Spanish black dances are tied to the growth of black slavery. Conceptually, the two questions are inseparable, as Alonso de Sandoval suggested, when he wrote in 1627 that Cham "was born laughing, and it seems that his children have inherited his laughter, for even in their terrible condition as slaves, they always go laughing, singing, drumming, and dancing."[34] Black dances spoke to and about slavery: for white participants, *guineo* served to uphold the system of color-based slavery, while for Afro-Spaniards, *guineo* could be used to renegotiate one's condition in a slavery-based society.

One way of conceptualizing slavery is to think of it as an issue of mobility in the most capacious sense of the term: a mobility-based approach gets at politics, as Tim Creswell puts it, by "considering the fact of movement, the represented meanings attached to movement, and the experienced practice of movement."[35] Enslaved Afro-Spaniards were subjected to forced mobility as they were transported to the peninsula, and subjected to forced immobility upon purchase. They experienced forced immobility, crystalized in the image of shackles, on a daily basis as confinement to locations determined by their enslavers, and as a paucity of options for social advancement. Spanish society thus limited Afro-Spaniards' horizontal and vertical mobility. Tirso de Molina's interlude *El negro* (1635) captures the linkage between dance and horizontal mobility for Afro-Spaniards. Domingo spends the whole interlude trying to get musicians to play a danceable tune, and he eventually graces the stage with a black dance; meanwhile his presence in the streets of Madrid at night—which was forbidden to the enslaved both in Madrid and in Seville and was very harshly punished—manifests his willingness to break the law in order to move freely around the city.[36] Domingo's desire to dance encodes, at a fundamental level, his fearless desire for self-determined mobility.

Dance not only was a symbolic way of reclaiming mobility for Afro-Spaniards; it was a material way of doing so—and cultural productions reveal a strong awareness of this. Some enslaved Afro-Spaniards could make enough money by dancing to buy their own freedom. That was the case for Francisco Menesez, the above-mentioned Afro-Spanish dancer from Madrid whose story was recorded in a 1687 broadsheet ballad (*jácara*). In the ballad, the "mischievous" Francisco, bought by a tavern owner, gets drunk on his enslaver's wine one day, and when his enslaver starts beating him, he pleads:

I will pay you back, master
all that my drinking cost you
If you just let me walk
and dance all over the city.

The enslaver accepts, and Francisco dances the guineo through the city's streets:

> He would enter taverns
> and if there was any piper there,
> he would get a drink
> and get money too.

Francisco dances so well and so much that he earns enough money to buy his own freedom:

> He gave his master two *reales*
> every day, so that when he finally got
> his free papers, he left,
> and danced from town to town.

Francisco thus starts a professional dancing career as a free man of color.[37]

But his story does not end there. Capturing the potential of black dances for emancipation in the hands of Afro-Spaniards, the ballad also captures white perceptions of this push for Black mobility as a threat to the established order. The ballad shuts this threat down by manipulating basic white fantasies about Black masculinity, as it turns Francisco's triumphant mobility into an unchecked and destructive libidinal drive fueled by inebriation. Reaching Ciudad Real as a free man, Francisco sees a white peasant girl: "his blood turned / and he followed her, dancing and drumming." She runs away, but the athletic dancer runs faster:

> The shepherdess runs as much as she can
> but her breath comes short
> for the Ethiop was fast as lightning
> and there was a flaming volcano inside of him.[38]

The textbook scenario of interracial rape culminates with murder—the ballad has Francisco stab and bury the shepherdess. Francisco is arrested, his movement interrupted, his mobility abruptly stopped. The marvelous dancer was hanged in Peralvillo on June 6, 1687, the ballad says. With this final image of the black dancer's corpse hanged and immobilized ("con eso quedó colgado"), the ballad advertises what happens to Afro-Spaniards who claim too much horizontal and vertical mobility in late seventeenth-century Spanish society.

In this jácara, the containment of Afro-Spanish kinetic agency and mobility operates at the plot level, but also, and just as importantly, at the performative level. The *Diccionario de autoridades* gives six definitions for the musical genre of the jácara in the early modern period; the dynamic aggregation of those meanings reveals that jácaras were perceived as musical street performances.[39] The image that we get from this aggregation of interconnected meanings is that early modern jácaras were written to be sung by professional or amateur performers who often walked the streets at night—perhaps in a state of light inebriation—singing, playing music with "bows and strings," and dancing to accompany the ballad they sang, thereby disrupting the peace and quiet of the night in potentially troublesome ways. Might not the rowdy musicians who performed the jácara recounting the story of Francisco Menesez in 1687 have included some guineo moves in their peripatetic performance? Did not this jácara on Black mobility function as a script inviting savvy performers to do just that? If white performers answered the script's invitation by embodying kinetic blackness, they reclaimed the guineo that Menesez had used for self-emancipation as a medium to assert white dominance and quash Black mobility. The ballad's performance offers a replay of the racial struggle for control at the core of the ballad's plot. If Afro-Spanish musicians answered the script's invitation to perform kinetic blackness, depending on the context (that is, depending on who the spectators and patrons were each time), performers could choose to quash Menesez's mobility in their own bodies, resuscitate it, or do both simultaneously. Laying claim to that site of performative production was the key.

Francisco Menesez was neither the first nor the last Afro-Spaniard to use dance to move across Spanish social hierarchies. There were many professional Afro-Spanish dancers and dance teachers, to the point that Sevillian dancing master Juan de Esquivel Navarro bitterly lamented the competition of "a great number of *negros*" (tanta cantidad de negros) for men of his profession in his *Discursos sobre el arte del danzado* (1642).[40] Black Iberians laid claim early on to many of black dances' sites of production. Those included informal public performances such as those described around Santa Maria la Blanca in Seville by Cervantes, or around "all the town squares" of Evora, Portugal, according to Flemish visitor Nicholas Cleynaerts—and indeed, many Afro-Portingals can be seen dancing together, dancing for white people, and dancing *with* white people, in the late sixteenth-century painting of the Chafariz d'el Rey in the Alfama district of Lisbon (see Plate 10).[41] Those sites also included highly formal public performances linked to royal celebrations. For instance, as early as 1451, a German ambassador reports the involvement of Canarians and black-skinned dancers in the wedding celebrations of Eleanor of Portugal to the Holy Roman emperor Friedrich III in Lisbon; in 1497, all Afro-Sevillians were ordered to celebrate the queen's entrance into the city, and in 1599, in Valencia, "the anonymous chronicler of the celebration of Philip III's nuptials was similarly impressed by the appearance of a group of 'richly attired' dark-skinned Afro-Spaniards performing a dance *'en tono de Guinea.'*"[42]

A third and crucial public site of guineo production was religious processions. While we know that the black dances of Corpus Christi processions were sometimes performed by white dancers in black-up, evidence suggests that Afro-Spanish dancers were also employed on those occasions.[43] Commercial theatre registers the participation of Afro-Spaniards in those public dances: in the 1640 *mojiganga El registrador*, Juan de Quiros has the Sevillian alcalde in charge of organizing autos for Corpus Christi go from door to door and enlist an Afro-Spanish woman to dance the zarambeque.[44] Hernando de Rivera, the dancing master who produced more danzas de negros than any other maestro hired by the city between 1609 and 1639 may have been a key figure in that respect. Working against the grain of Lynne Brooks's point that there is only one recorded account of an Afro-Spanish dancer being contracted by the city (Juan Antonio de Castro, in 1693), I am adopting an approach closer to that championed by Imtiaz Habib in *Black Lives in the English Archives*, and I offer here a biographical *recording* of Rivera's life.[45] While early modern Spanish archives do not generally hide Afro-diasporic lives the way their English counterparts do, dance being a fraught site of contestation, we cannot trust Spanish dance archives to be neutral vis-à-vis racial identity. Thus, I wonder whether the *maestro de danza* Hernando de Rivera identified by Jean Sentaurens might have been Hernando de Rivera, the "negro captivo de Juan Francisco de Rivera" who married "Ysabel de Vega, negra captiva de Maria de la Vega" in 1601 in the parish of el Salvador, and then, as his various contracts with the city indicate, moved, either as a free man or as a *cortado* slave, to the parish of San Esteban, in one of the city's Afro-diasporic pockets, whose records register the death of an infant, "a little boy, son of Hernando de Rivera," in 1610.[46] If, as I record, Rivera was Black, then most probably, so was his professional network of dancers.

Black dances particularly empowered Afro-Spanish communities by empowering the Black confraternities, which often integrated dances into their own processional moves.[47] The extant archives of the Hermandad de los Negritos in Seville regularly include costs for hiring musicians on the occasion of various celebrations.[48] They leave no doubt as to the importance of music (and by extension dance) in the life of a confraternity that was "essential for the black community," providing "shelter in case of need, a space for expression that was more adapted to the culture of blacks, and a vector for black people that gave them a certain visibility and reinforced their cohesion as a way to prevent their disintegration and promote their rights."[49] *Negro* and *mulato* confraternities across Iberia used alms to provide a space for Black people to build community and solidarity across the freedom line, often stepping in to help community members negotiate delicate manumission cases with their enslavers.[50] Confraternities such as the Hermandad de los Negritos in Seville were strong formations that defended the interests of the Black community, and they were perceived as such: their mission was proudly advertised when the confraternity claimed horizontal and vertical mobility by moving throughout the streets of Seville during Holy Week processions on equal footing with white confraternities.[51]

In that sense, the 1604 attack led by the powerful confraternity of Nuestra Señora de la Antigua Siete Dolores on the Black confraternity's right to take part in the procession—which was not resolved until 1625, when Pope Urbano VIII ruled in favor of the Black confraternity—was an attack on one of the strongest symbols of early modern Black mobility. As Erin Rowe puts it, "we can measure the success of black confraternities by the amount of hostility they generated on the part of white Catholics."[52] The authorities' distrust of Black confraternities extended throughout the empire, as suggested by a 1612 royal letter sent to the *real audiencia* of Santo Domingo, Hispaniola, to inquire into the existence of a Black confraternity in the colony. The confraternity in question (named after Nuestra Señora de la Candelaria) was most probably involved in the "various games and inventions" (diversos juegos y invenciones) including black dances that accompanied Corpus Christi processions in Santo Domingo—which locals relished. The Spanish crown was anxious "to know what this confraternity is, who founded it, on whose permission, how many people joined it, whether there is any other black confraternity . . . and whether this confraternity might become inconvenient."[53] In short, authorities in Madrid, Seville, and Santo Domingo were wary of Black confraternities' push for mobility and closely surveilled them. For those confraternities, dance was simultaneously a symbol of mobility and collective agency and a public relations asset. Black dances performed by Afro-Spaniards garnered the support of spectators "enraptured to a degree that cannot be expressed," and Black confraternities knew it full well.

Black dances were a material and symbolic way of reclaiming physical, geographic, and social mobility for Afro-Spaniards; this manifests in the systemic pairing of black dances with Afro-diasporic weddings in early modern Spanish literature.[54] Indeed, "marriage was understood as a previous step to freedom, since the Church was favorable to the idea that married slaves should spend some time together—usually two or three days a week—, and also urged their masters not to sell couples separately.... Understandably, marriage could be seen by slaves as a way to resist their situation and improve their status."⁵⁵ Not surprisingly then, Afro-diasporic weddings were seen as sources of chaos in Spanish social imagination. Early modern commonplace sayings attest to this: the phrase *"negros' wedding"* (boda de negros) meant "chaos." In 1618, the Sevillian Juan de Mal Lara glossed the phrase as follows: "look what happens when *negros* get married: see how much noise they make, how much they chat, and how little they understand one another."⁵⁶ The pairing of black dances and of what had apparently become a synonym for chaos bears witness to the perceived disruptive nature of black dances.

The impulse to quash attempts at self-determination and social mobility inherent in Afro-diasporic marriages and their appended black dances is enacted in a ballad dating back to the beginning of the eighteenth century, the anonymous *Nueva relacion y curioso romance, en que se refiere la celebridad, galanteo y acaso de una Boda de Negros, que se executó en la Ciudad del Puerto de Sta. Maria*. In this ballad, Tomás Meló and his beloved Lucía are getting married after two years of courtship: during Easter week they invite

> all the *negros*
> of Cadiz, San Lucar,
> Xerez, Rota, and Puerto

to celebrate with them and enjoy a banquet in their Andalusian hometown of Puerto de Santa Maria.⁵⁷ Neither of them is enslaved; Lucía, the "daughter of good parents, although they were black," makes a living by selling "roasted chickpeas, shrimps, and doughnuts."⁵⁸ As for Tomás, although his profession is never disclosed, he does well enough for himself to pay for an abundant wedding feast, and to pay for musicians to play at Lucía's door every night for two years (Tomás himself may have been a musician or a dancer—the ballad does not say).

> After the religious ceremony,
> the reception took place
> And before having dinner, they started
> playing music instruments,
> Dancing tap dances,
> Minuets in the Guinean fashion,

and the Congolese chain dance
in which men and women cling on to one another.[59]

During those merriments, four masked white men crash the party: they steal the food prepared for the wedding feast unbeknownst to the Afro-Spanish dancers.

While the ballad does not disclose the thieves' motives, the specificity of the denouement suggests that they might participate in a larger and diffuse effort to punish the working-class Afro-Spanish newlyweds for the attempt at self-determination and social mobility driving their professional choices, their decision to marry each other, and, of course, their joyful dancing—which takes place behind closed doors, denying white spectators access to the "enrapturing" sight of authentic Afro-diasporic bodies in motion, and, perhaps, to authentic Afro-diasporic dances that did not result from kinetic code-switching. For their audacity, the newlyweds get an exemplary punishment: they are condemned to perpetual motionlessness. Indeed, once the Afro-Spanish wedding party finds out about the theft, they try to pursue the thieves into the streets, but they get arrested by a police patrol as they do so. The groom falls down the stairs and breaks his leg and skull, while the bride, suffering a nervous breakdown, is put to bed, and forced by an incompetent barber to drink a burning-hot toxic concoction that burns her and makes her eject part of her insides—the poor bride dies lying down in her own guts. The ballad's concluding verses home in on the economic and social imperatives driving this denouement:

> the bride kicked the bucket,
> the groom broke his skull
> and limped for a long time,
> and the *negros* lost
> the right to do business.[60]

Ultimately, what was at stake here, it seems, was the anxiogenic rise of a free Black working class claiming social mobility and joyfully dancing it out.

In one edition of this ballad, the broadside's frontispiece is adorned with a woodcut representing the black wedding dancers in motion (Figure 6). What is most striking about this image is not so much the nature of the movements performed by the Afro-Spanish dancers as the clearly theatrical setting of their performance. This theatricalized frontispiece—reframing authentic Afro-diasporic dances that are inaccessible to white viewers as accessible theatrical

NUEVA RELACION, Y CURIOSO ROMANCE, EN QUE
se refiere la celebridad, galanteo, y acaso de una Boda de
Negros, que se executó en la Ciudad de el Puerto
de Santa Maria. Sucedió el año passado.

Figure 6. "A Black Wedding in Andalusia" in *Nueva relacion y curioso romance*. Woodcut. Late seventeenth century. Biblioteca de Castilla y León.

black dances of a dubious ontological nature—points out, to a modern reader, the active and ambivalent participation of theatrical culture in the kinetic aspect of the racial struggle in early modern Spain. As we saw in the previous chapters of this book, theatre was, on the one hand, a site of racial impersonation that resisted the irruption of real Afro-European bodies for the most part more stubbornly than other sites of public performance; and, on the other hand, it was a site where the victories earned by Afro-Spaniards in the racial struggle registered most strongly.

For instance, in Simón Aguado's interlude *Los negros* (1602)—a canonical text in Hispanic early modern race studies—the enslaved celebrate Gasparillo and Dominga's triumph over their enslavers' initial refusal to let them marry with a spectacular dance: "enter as many *negros* as possible, in an orderly fashion: dancing a saraband with timbrels and jingles, they come and go across the stage."[61] This happy ending is antithetical with the denouement of the ballad of Tomás and Lucia, and linked to the fact that this specific interlude did let Afro-Spaniards onto the commercial stage for its final dance. Indeed, Aguado's interlude was created in Granada, Andalusia, and I agree with John Beusterien: the stage direction "as many *negros* as possible" suggests that real Afro-Spanish dancers might have been employed, if not to perform the lead parts of Gasparillo and Dominga, then at least to perform this final black dance.[62] When real Afro-Spaniards are given a chance to dance, they take ownership of the site of production: in *Los negros*, they took ownership of the kinetic discourse of blackness, and they altered it. Indeed, not only do Aguado's *negros* dance in an "orderly fashion" that departs from usual depictions of guineo; they choose a dance, the saraband, whose contested origins simultaneously evoke the racial hybridity of the American colonies and the Moorish heritage of Andalusia, a region that—given its eight centuries of Islamic rule—was always already African.[63] The *zarabanda* was a dance that destabilized neat identity categories and racial historiographies in early modern Granada. This choice on the Afro-Spanish dancers' part was not random.

In letting Black performers exercise their agency, Aguado's interlude is at odds with most of the early modern Spanish theatrical corpus of blackness—which, in performance, overwhelmingly relied but for a few exceptions on racial impersonation and resisted Black bids for control throughout the early modern period. Thus, I conclude this section with Aguado's *Los negros* not in an attempt to redeem theatre's role in the Spanish racial struggle by emphasizing what really was a quirky exception to the rule but, rather, to emphasize the difference between black dances and their cosmetic and sonic counterparts. Unlike black-up and blackspeak, black dances were often wielded, utilized, and hermeneutically reconfigured by Afro-Spaniards for strategic purposes. Afro-Spaniards' partial control over the sites of production of black dances perhaps explains to some extent why, even on the commercial stage, sexualizing Iberian black dances did not resort to the devastating script of black animalization so prevalent up north.

Dancing Like a Beast: Black Dances at the French Court

By contrast with Spain, in early modern France, the discourse of kinetic blackness was overwhelmingly constituted through racial impersonation. It is impossible to discuss European black dances without mentioning the highly popular *mauresque/moresque/morisque*, a dance that circulated fluidly between rural popular culture, court culture, and commercial theatre, and across national frontiers in Europe: one *danza de cascabeles* among many in Spain, it was known as moresque in France, *moresca* in Italy, and Morris dancing in England, among other countries. The transnational dimension of *moresque* archives has fueled an ongoing debate on the origins of the dance, the question being whether moresque was inspired by and imitative of Africanness (a thesis most convincingly

defended by Robert Hornback and Esther J. Terry), or whether it was, as tradi-
tionalists argue, an expression of nationally rooted folk culture and rural arche-
types.[64] The question has been whether moresque was a black dance or an
unruly white dance. I argue that the unruly dance became a black dance as it
moved across time and space, and I am less interested in pinning down a defini-
tive genealogy of moresque than in understanding how it conditioned the way
early modern Europeans thought about the sub-Saharan Africans with whom it
became associated.[65] My goal is to tease out the script of animalization that
moresque offered.

Moresque, like Spanish guineo, required elaborate "hand gestures" and
"postures conducive to laughter."[66] It often included sexual motifs and leg movements that led Arcangelo Tuccarro, the Neapolitan acrobat attached to the
court of Charles IX, to claim this dance as a part of his domain of expertise.[67]
Moresque required such "unholy footwork," to use K. Meira Goldberg's phrase,
that a farce from 1572 denied morisque dancers entrance to Paradise, for fear they
should break heaven's floor.[68] Margaret McGowan notes: "Mauresques are sometimes performed by local youth, as was the case in Aix and Marseille in 1516, but
most often, they are performed by professional dancers, for those dances, extremely vigorous and spectacular as they were, entailed jumps, caprioles, and
breathtakingly virtuosic acrobatics. . . . The dancer must have an exceptional
technique and be aware of his own virtuosity. The dancer must know the rules of
dancing well enough to put them aside and dance off beat, for instance."[69] The
vigor of those movements is captured in one of the illustrations of *Freydal: The
Book of Jousts and Tournament of Emperor Maximilian I* (ca. 1515), in which
white dancers wearing tight-fitting masks of black gauze plunge, stomp, adopt
angular postures, and cut low-gravity-center figures that require putting one's
hands on the ground (Figure 7).[70] About 150 years after the *Freydal* illustrations
were produced, French accounts still insisted on *moresque* dancers' elaborate
"foot and hand gestures" and on the "gesticulations of their whole bodies."[71]

The blackening of moresque coincided with its animalization. That mechanism is particularly visible in travel writings in which European travelers call
authentic sub-Saharan dances "moresques." For instance, in his *Cosmographie
universelle* (1575), André Thevet comments on the dance moves of Senegalese
women, whose "friskiness defies imagination," and he adds: "I am not surprised
that in France we call several dances mauresques, considering all the monkeying
around that they entail."[72] Thevet's description resembles other travelers' accounts, such as Pieter de Marees's *Description et récit historial du riche royaume
d'or de Gunea* (1606): de Marees, too, depicts dancing African women who "ex-

Figure 7. "A Moresque Dance" in *Freydal: Des Kaisers Maximilian I.
Turniere und Mummereien*. Drawing. Circa 1515. University of Tübingen,
University Library, Da 204.2 (p. 36), http://idb.ub.uni-tuebingen.de
/opendigi/Da204_fol_Text.

ert themselves monkeying around fabulously."[73] Thévet's chain of associations
implies that he perceives French moresque as a form of "monkeying around,"
which is congruent with Ingrid Brainard's observation that mauresque dancers
were sometimes dressed as apes.[74]

The same script of animalization affected another early modern black dance,
the *canarie*, a dance allegedly hailing from the Canary Islands, whose inhabitants were represented as dark skinned, and where Iberians first experimented
with sugar culture and plantation slavery in the fifteenth century.[75] Julia Sutton

and Pamela Jones describe it as "as a fiery wooing dance, marked by rapid heel-and-toe stamps, by noisy sliding steps with which the partners alternately advance and retreat."[76] According to early modern dance theorist Marin Mersenne, "Canary dance is very difficult and only danced by those who know it well and are light-footed. It entails several kinds of foot beats . . . half-caprioles, half-spins, and other turns both in the air and on the ground."[77] One of those foot beats was the *rus de vache*—"the cow's kick"—an extremely rare step consisting in raising one foot laterally, instead of forward or backward (as was the norm in baroque dancing). According to Arbeau, this step was used only for the canarie. In his view, canarie "moves are lively, and yet, they are strange, odd, and smack of savagery. . . . You will learn them from those who know them, and you can invent new ones yourself."[78] With this direction, Arbeau encouraged dancers to unleash their imagination and incorporate into the vocabulary of canarie whatever they identified as "savage" gestures.

Arbeau himself somehow knew that such animalizing black dances were inauthentic: "Some say this dance is commonly used in the Canary Islands, but others, whose opinion I favor, argue that this dance was born from a ballet composed for a mascarade in which the dancers were disguised as kings and queens of Mauretania, or as some *Sauvages*, with feathers dyed in various colors."[79] This suspicion did little to prevent the kinetic discourse of blackness from achieving its ideological work, and if dances such as the canarie could do ideological work particularly efficiently, it was because, as Arbeau makes clear, they looped between court culture and popular culture from their very inception. Keeping this circulation in mind heightens the stakes of studying black dances (and performative blackness more generally) at the French court.

Indeed, the virtuosic animalizing strangeness of the steps found in European social dances such as moresque and canarie found its fullest expression in the unlabeled black dances of burlesque French court ballets, which were particularly in vogue between 1620 and 1636, according to McGowan.[80] Black characters feature in at least thirty of them.[81] The animalistic inspiration behind black social dances is amplified in two French ballets for which we have very detailed records: *Ballet de Monseigneur le duc de Vandosme* (1610) and *Grand bal de la douairière de Billebahaut* (1626). *Ballet de Monseigneur le duc de Vandosme* opens with a scene in which Sir Gobbemagne, who governs Apes' Island in the name of the sorceress Alcine, metamorphoses into a young *More* with a specific purpose: "This *More*, having shown his agility as the violin played, went toward the forest with a golden wand in his hand in order to introduce two torch-bearing lackeys dressed as big green apes." Leaving those apes seated with jams and sweets, the *More*

> caprioled his way back to the forest in order to introduce three en-
> slaved violin players. . . . Ten big green apes entered, in pairs. Once
> they were all entered and aligned . . . fifteen violins started playing the
> ballet of the big green apes, which they danced in ten different ways,
> always on the beat, with various leaps, gambols, gestures, and grimaces.
> The *More* was in the middle of them, showing them what to do, and
> that way, he had them retire in a line into the forest, sometimes jump-
> ing on one foot, sometimes on the other, and sometimes on both feet
> at the same time.[82]

Showing the big green apes what gestures to make, the *More* shares a body language with them, and that body language (caprioles, leaps, gambols, gestures,
grimaces, and asymmetrical postures) blurs the distinction between blackness
and apeness. That the grave, white, and slow-footed Sir Gobbemagne should
turn into a young *More* in order to access that hybrid kinesis designates blackness as a privileged point of connection between humanity and animality. *Ballet de Monseigneur le duc de Vandosme* thus echoes the perception of sub-Saharan
dances as "monkeying around" peppered in travel writing, or found in Philibert
Monet's 1635 definition of a moresque dancer as a "mimicus saltator maurusius,"
that is, an athletic dancer sharing a strong propensity to mimicry with apes.[83]

In *Grand bal de la douairiere de Billebahaut* (1626), the animalization of
black dances is encoded in the costume of the African king called the "Grand
Cacique," who pays homage to the grotesque Dowager of Bilbao on the occasion
of her wedding. There is no extant choreographic information or stage direction
for this ballet, yet the king's costume design, which Daniel Rabel recorded in
his vivid illustrations of the ballet, suggests particularly interesting kinetic tensions. The African king enters seated on an elephant, a machine conveying the
heaviness of the pachyderm (see Plate 5). McGowan depicts him as "a massive
black figure, with a tusk-like white beard, dressed in a spiked gold tunic and red
cloak."[84] McGowan's observation that the king's beard is "tusk-like" likens the
dancer to his monumental elephant. Meanwhile, the shape of his gold tunic and
red cloak evokes gigantic feathers, turning the king into a human-sized exotic
firebird (see Plate 9)—an avian touch reinforced by the fact that the Cacique, as
we saw in Chapter 3, sounds like a bird: he "warbles and babbles."[85] The tension

between the heaviness of the elephant and the lightness of the firebird was likely to permeate the king's kinetic language, resulting in steps "lively, yet strange, odd, and smacking of savagery," in Arbeau's words. It is, after all, always in a tension between heaviness and lightness that the most dramatic leaps, plunges, and caprioles are formed. Costume design, as a script, invited the dancer to draw imaginatively on the energy of birds and elephants to fashion his movements and to perform blackness by animalizing his own kinesis.

Inspired by kicking cows, leaping apes, flying birds, and stomping elephants, French black dances racialized Afro-diasporic people by giving them a liminal position on the fringes of mankind. Movements were indeed routinely essentialized in a culture that believed, in the words of late seventeenth-century dance theorist Claude-François Ménestrier, that "ballet expresses movements that painting and sculpture can't, and doing so, it expresses the very nature of things and the soul's habits, which can only be apprehended by the senses through those movements."[86] Black dances construed black souls' "habits" in a French public sphere where dance moves were expected to express both one's inner truth and one's place in the world. Arbeau explicitly defines dance as a communicative modality: "Dance is, in a way, a silent rhetoric: the orator can speak with his movements, without a word, and still be understood."[87] What was communicated in black dances was the dancer's liminal status between human and animal. In the first decades of the seventeenth century, French black dances routinely downgraded sub-Saharan Africans in the Great Chain of Being—a hierarchy that established gradual, not absolute, difference between humans and animals in the first place.[88]

The peculiar popularity of black dances at the French court is in part the result of their topicality: namely, the fact that white aristocratic performers used them to address political issues they deemed urgent. Indeed, French aristocrats recuperated the popular tradition of animalizing black dances—palpable, for instance, in moresque dancing—in the first decades of the seventeenth century, turning those dances into vehicles for expressing political frustrations unique to that specific milieu, time, and place. French aristocrats repeatedly instrumentalized black dances to criticize the king's attack on their traditional prerogatives: as the crown increasingly leveraged nobility to reward its most faithful servants, aristocrats appropriated black dances in order to contest aspects of royal authority that they hyperbolically experienced as bondage, or as a form of exclusion from ownership and self-ownership. My use of the term *appropriation* here does not hinge on the notion of theft (since we cannot know whether French black dances shared any ontological kinship with authentic

sub-Saharan dances), but on the notion of property, in both its legal and its theatrical senses. Black dances were used by aristocrats as props to publicly address
the king's wrongdoings in relation to their own political, legal, and socioeconomic property. While it is hard for modern readers to think of overprivileged
white male aristocrats as oppressed, that group had no difficulty seeing itself as
victimized and no qualms about drawing a parallel between its own condition
and the condition of enslaved Afro-diasporic people in the French Caribbean.
The critique directed at the royal power came precisely from the callous analogy
between aristocrats and slaves. Aristocrats repurposed the racial discourse embedded in black dances to articulate a critique of their current condition.[89]

Indeed, as previously mentioned, black dances were the opposite of what
aristocratic dancing was supposed to look like, especially at a time when, as
Sarah Cohen points out, the epistemological crisis that affected the notion of
nobility made it even more urgent for aristocrats' body language to express, perform, and reify nobility.[90] François de Lauze, in *Apologie de la danse* (1623), considered that caprioles often "smack of street dancing," and forty-five years later,
dance theorist De Pure still wrote that what "we call the beautiful dance, which
consists in moving with simplicity, respecting the steps, and keeping the tempo
right and steady, is always more majestic—smacks more of nobility, and (even
more importantly) of modesty and virtue."[91] Caprioling their hearts away, aristocratic black dance performers—who, by virtue of the ballet performance
aesthetics, were always present on stage, recognizable under the mask of the
characters they performed—abjectly declassed their own bodies. They appropriated a racializing yet "enrapturing" kinesis that put them naturally at the
bottom of the social order in order to shock spectators, among whom the king
often sat.

It may be a testament to continued aristocratic resentment against the development of absolutist royal power that black dances remained a popular staple
of court performance culture throughout the seventeenth century. Or it may
simply be the case that the initial recuperation of black dances in the aristocratic kinetic repertoire during the baroque ballet era ensured the long-term
inscription of black dances into court performance culture. Either way, black
dances remained in vogue in court ballets at least as long as Louis XIV danced,
and they permeated many forms of commercial theatre that retained strong affinities with court culture in neoclassical France. For instance, Thomas Corneille's *L'inconnu* (1675), one of the last early modern pièce à machines, explicitly
embeds court ballet aesthetics by including an entry of *Mores* dancing with Cupids, as we saw in Chapter 2. The creation of the Académie Royale de Musique

under Lully's leadership in 1671 fostered a French operatic tradition of *tragédies en musique*, which often included black dances. Philippe Quinault's *Cadmus and Hermione* (1674), considered to be the first French opera, includes a scene in which nine "Affriquains" dance around "a great palm tree," while two others sing verses in the tradition of baroque ballet libretti.[92] Black dances also featured in operas of ancient Ethiopian inspiration, such as Philippe Quinault's *Persée* (1682), where Ethiopians "show their joy by singing and dancing," and Joseph-François Duché de Vancy's Heliodoric adaptation *Téagène et Cariclée* (1695), in which Ethiopian warriors dance.[93] Royal patronage granted the Académie Royale de Musique a quasi monopoly over the use of music and dance on stage and guaranteed that it would find aristocratic audiences. Thus, Lully's operatic audience was, to a large extent, an aristocratic audience attuned to and appreciative of the old race politics of court ballet culture.

The most famous commercial play to cannibalize the court tradition of black dances is *Le malade imaginaire* (1673), a comédie-ballet by Molière. Anyone who completed secondary school in the French education system studied this hypercanonical play at some point, yet most would be surprised to hear that the play includes black dances or performative blackness in any form, owing to the pathological averseness to racial inquiry and reckoning embedded in French national mythology and its appended pedagogical practices. Molière did use black dances in the interlude between act 1 and act 2: "The imaginary invalid's brother seeks to entertain him by bringing on stage several Egyptian men and women, dressed as *Mores*, who intersperse dances with songs.... All the *Mores* dance together; they brought apes with them: now they make the apes jump."[94] The songs sung by Moorish women are an exhortation for young women to enjoy their youth, to follow the ardors, transports, and whims of their hearts, surrendering to their beloveds even when those are unfaithful. This scene presents Orgon, the titular imaginary invalid, with an allegorical representation of his daughter Isabelle, who is in love with Léandre and, in the act preceding this interlude, has just rejected the ridiculous physician whom her inflexible father wants her to marry. By linking Isabelle to sensual blacked-up Moorish women, the play draws on the connections between blackness, eros, and slavery that were, as we saw in Chapter 2, ubiquitous in court performance culture, implicitly framing Isabelle's plight as a situation of exclusion from self-ownership resembling that of an enslaved Afro-diasporic woman. It is no coincidence that the interlude is introduced by Orgon's brother, who, in the opening lines of the following act, states that he fully supports his niece's right not to marry against her will and to dispose of herself. This interlude was part and parcel of the play.

The scene's appropriation of a racial imagery to critique Isabelle's exclusion from self-ownership finds its apex in its choreographic ending, as "Egyptian" dancers "make the apes jump." "Egyptiens" being a synonym for "Gypsies," the stage direction signals that Romani performers were cast in the role of the *Mores* for this interlude, perhaps because of the brownness of their skin, perhaps because of the liveliness and spectacular dimension of Romani dance traditions. In this interlude, Molière's spectators at the Versailles palace, where the play was performed in 1674, witnessed professional Romani entertainers perform sartorial, musical, and choreographic blackness. The production's striking use of Romani performers for Afro-diasporic roles speaks to the relational nature of racial formations, the connectedness of paradigms and subparadigms within the racial matrix, and, perhaps, to some experimental inclinations in court performance culture with relation to racial impersonation.[95] But more importantly, it speaks to the fact that the French conventions of choreographic blackness were strong enough by the 1670s to convey Africanist blackness on any non-sub-Saharan body, including nonwhite bodies.

Those conventions, hinging on the script of black animalization, are unmistakably present in the inclusion of apes in the Roma's Moorish act—a scene eerily reminiscent of the young *More*'s dance with the green big apes in *Ballet de Monseigneur le duc de Vandosme* some sixty-three years earlier. One might object that what first comes across in this Moorish act is the power of the human performer over the trained animal, and that this very power shores up the divide between humans and animals. But as Erica Fudge compellingly shows, across the Channel, performative situations that were supposed to demonstrate the absolute quality of that divide often ended up destabilizing it.[96] Such dynamics do not stop at borders. In *Le malade imaginaire*, the animalistic choreographic language used by performers destabilized the divide between humans and animals, even as the taming act they performed with apes shored it up. Molière did not script that animalistic black kinesis with stage directions, simply because it would have been superfluous at the time. By destabilizing the divide between animals and the Moorish characters used to allegorically code Isabelle in this phantasmatic interlude, the *Mores*' black dance associates the bourgeois Frenchwoman with a figure who is fully excluded from ownership and self-ownership—the ape. The indirect quality of this connection, doubly mediated by nonwhite figures (Moorish characters and Roma performers), allows the play to preserve the white woman's symbolic purity intact.

Undoubtedly, Molière was familiar with the practice—which had been in vogue in court ballets for decades—of appropriating black dances for the purposes of articulating a sociopolitical critique benefitting white people. In the same spirit as his aristocratic forebears, he recuperated that practice to articulate what we might recognize as a white feminist critique of patriarchal matrimonial practices. Only by reading Molière's last play in light of the long-lived and extremely influential yet understudied tradition of baroque court ballets can we take the full measure of Molière's antimisogynist engagement and of the complete absence of intersectionality in that engagement. Molière participated in the dissemination of the racial tropes and scripts that produced and were produced by the culture in which he lived, as color-based slavery boomed in the French colonies. The case study of *Le malade imaginaire* alerts us to the processes of whitewashing that have shaped canon formation in *dix-septièmiste* studies. Not only must we from now on teach *Le malade imaginaire* with its interludes; we must teach the entire canon of neoclassical drama within the larger culture of racial trafficking that shaped it.

What Mingo and Jack Knew, or, The English Crucible

Both French and Spanish articulations of kinetic blackness—as different as they were from one another, yet as similar in their configuration of black dance as a dancer's tool for political contestation and resistance to bondage— illuminate the hitherto unrecognized tradition of black dances that developed west of the Channel. Indeed, English performance culture was a crucible for various European traditions of kinetic blackness. In following the dissemination of the politics of black dances in that crucible, I first record the possibility that Queen Anne may have resorted to black dances when she performed *Masque of Blackness* (1605).[97] This masque is not necessarily representative of English performance culture in the first decade of the century, but it is an evocative case study that highlights English court performance culture's connections with its British and continental counterparts. By analyzing *Masque of Blackness* here, I aim to shift scholarly attention from the now well discussed cosmetic dimension of the masque to its untouched kinetic dimension. Scholars such as Kim F. Hall, Bernadette Andrea, Andrea Stevens, and Hardin Aasand have contributed to establishing the now common understanding of Queen Anne's deliberate self-presentation as exotic, unruly, and threatening by means of black-up in *Masque of Blackness* as a challenge to a potent strand of Jacobean ideology built on an intersectional oppression of women and non-white people.[98] Anne's use of cosmetic blackness constituted a form of resistance to the king's power. I suggest that the self-assertive and self-emancipatory dynamics of *Masque of Blackness* might have been conveyed not solely through black-up on bodies that happened to dance but also through dance itself, through the kinetic idiom of blackness that Anne and her ladies might have adopted for this performance.

At first glance, *Masque of Blackness* seems devoid of the kind of black dances encountered in this chapter. Almost nothing of the musical score of *Masque of Blackness* has survived; the only dances clearly invoked in Ben Jonson's account, "measures and corantos," can hardly be described as exotic; and the social dances of the revels did not include any dance imagined as African such as Canary or Saraband.[99] I would argue, however, that dance gave Anne and her ladies a window of opportunity for subversion during the second and fourth phases of the masque, which frame the revels: those dancing phases of transition, during which Niger's daughters move in formation from sea to land and back with remarkable coordination, upstage to downstage and back—those unnamed protean dances characterized by liminality, crossing, and decision making that Jonson, the king's poet and apologist, did not care to notate, leaving them for us to record.

This hypothesis hinges on the connectedness of early modern court performance cultures across the Channel and across Europe generally. Anne Daye has compellingly demonstrated the influence of late sixteenth-century French ballets on Stuart masque culture, and, more specifically, the influence of *Ballet comique de la reine* (1582) on Ben Jonson's *Masque of Queens* (1609), the very sequel to *Masque of Blackness*.[100] The existence of communication channels between French and English court performance cultures in the first decade of the seventeenth century opens possibilities: black dances were performed in at least two French court ballets in 1600–1601 (the lost *Ballet du roy des Maures Nègres*, and *Pour des masques assez hideux et sauvages*), so we may wonder whether the novelty trend of animalizing black dances in French ballets influenced the makers of *Masque of Blackness*. Traditions of black-up were not new to the English court in 1605; records signal their existence at the English court in the mid-sixteenth century, when Edward VI participated in *Mask of Young Moors* on Shrovetide 1548, for instance.[101] Thus, in 1605, French influence had only to rekindle a tradition of performative blackness that lay dormant, and give it new scripts.

In addition to the possible influence of French court culture on the English masquers' use of kinetic blackness, we must reckon with a very likely Scottish influence. Clare McManus, comparing *Masque of Blackness* to some of the royal

entertainments that featured both black-up and authentic Afro-diasporic performers in late sixteenth-century Scotland, claims that, in *Masque of Blackness*,
Anne appropriated in her own body the blackness that had surrounded her in
various Scottish entertainments prior to her arrival in London.[102] McManus
describes in very useful ways some of the black dances performed by those professional male performers during Anne's royal entry into Edinburgh in 1590.
Anne was then escorted by dozens of local young men in black-up led by "an
absolutely real and native Blackamoor" wielding a sword.[103]

A Danish account of the spectacular entry mentions that these performers
"had been assigned a particular and special gait in imitation of various sorts of
people."[104] "Unfamiliarity means that the Danish spectator went into greater
detail than most about the kind of movement he observed; some Moors danced
jerkily, some low to the ground, and some with their heads down in disregard of
their audience."[105] To be more specific, according to the Danish spectator,
"some [Moors] walked erect and defiant, so as if in a half dance, like storks in
the water with long high steps, some as if they were drunk and staggering from
side to side, some were bent low and hung their heads."[106] This description of
Scottish black dances by a Danish observer—replete as it is with explicit avian
animality, simian imitativeness, and breaches of decorum of all sorts—is reminiscent of French moresques, canaries, and other black ballet acts—most probably because the popular practice of animalizing black dances circulated across
Europe. Meanwhile, the fraught negotiations that must have been at the core of
the choreographic collaboration between the Afro-diasporic lead performer
and his white dancing crew (and are alas lost to us) probably had a lot in common with the negotiations surrounding the contested interracial production of
black dances in early modern Andalusia.

The moves observed in 1590 by the Danish spectator, I record, might have
informed the movements of the blacked-up Queen Anne and her train in 1605.
Indeed, as soon as Niger's daughters envision dancing with Britannia's inhabitants, the tenor voice that seeks in vain to recall them to the ocean calls them
"the syrens of the sea," and the beauty often associated with the figure of the
sirens cannot make us forget that sirens are hybrids of human and animal life
forms—animalized humanoids.[107] Not only does this term open the door for
thinking about the unscripted kinetic language of Queen Anne and her train as
potentially hybridized with the body language of aquatic life forms; Jonson's
own stage directions define that unscripted body language as essentially protean in that it obeys the logic of Proteus, the sea god of mutability. Indeed,
when the Ladies obey the Moon's injunction to come ashore and "Indent the

land, with those pure traces / They flow with, in their native graces," their dance involves a metachoreographic reflection. As the terse Jonsonian stage direction puts it, *"they danced on shore, every couple, as they advanced, severally presenting their fans: in one of which were inscribed their mixt names, in the other a mute hieroglyphic, expressing their mixed qualities."*[108] As Donald James Gordon remarks, the six specific hieroglyphic symbols chosen by Jonson, mostly drawn from Pierio Valeriano Bolzani's *Hieroglyphica* (1556), all express qualities classically associated with water: transparency, fluidity, purity, swiftness, cold, dampness, gentleness, fertilization, or the ability to extinguish fire.[109] I read the "syrens" of the sea's inclusion of water hieroglyphics within their choreographic act as a signal that the kinetic style chosen by the blacked-up dancers for that moment was itself as protean as water: fluid, versatile, and potentially open to Scottish and continental influxes.

Ultimately, if, as McManus argues, in *Masque of Blackness*, Queen Anne remembered and repurposed her encounter with performative blackness in 1590 Scotland fifteen years earlier, we should note that, for her, performative blackness involved kinesis. The kinetic blackness that Anne ushered into the English archives had strong English roots and yet was connected by transnational routes and sea routes to European performance practices. *Masque of Blackness* constitutes a case of English aristocratic appropriation of black dances for the purposes of self-emancipation. It reveals that the commonalities between early modern French and English black dances were not only aesthetic but also political, as black dances helped white aristocrats, men and women, protest what they saw as their exclusion from ownership or self-ownership, or a form of bondage, on either side of the Channel.

In the following decades, English commercial theatre seized upon black dances' potential as a site of racialized power play. While commercial plays would constantly rehearse the trans-European history of aristocratic appropriations of kinetic blackness, they would also turn those dances into a site of resistance and affirmation not only for white aristocrats but for fictional black characters—in line with the politics of black dances in the Spanish cultural context. Philip Massinger's *The Bondman*, performed by the Lady Elizabeth's Men at the Cockpit Theatre in London in 1623, was a turning point in that respect.[110] In this play, black dances animalize and debase the silent rhetoric of black kinesis while expressing shifting interracial power relations between enslavers and the enslaved.

Thomas C. Fulton places *The Bondman* in the stream of late Jacobean and early Caroline plays written in response to the Anglo-Spanish crisis of the

Thirty Years' War: he reads the Syracusan society of the play as a topical stand-in for English society, weakened by its dissolute spendthrift aristocrats, and about to be conquered by Spain/Carthage, were it not for the beneficial effect of the Dutch republican ideology wielded by the Corinthian general Timoleon.[111] I concur with Fulton that Syracuse is a reflection of English society in the early 1620s, but I insist on reckoning with the colonial situation of Syracuse, which, as part of the Kingdom of Sicily, had been under Spanish rule for a couple of centuries when Massinger wrote the play. A political laboratory, Massinger's Syracuse is a site where English and Spanish societies merge and English and Spanish traditions superimpose one another, producing dance forms and dance politics that seem to Anglicize Spanish black dances.

Massinger's play reflects what I see as the Hispanicization of black musical and choreographic culture in late Jacobean England. Professional Afro-diasporic musicians and dancers were not rare in early seventeenth-century metropolitan England, largely because of ongoing Anglo-Spanish diplomatic and commercial exchanges. Africans were perceived as natural entertainers; thus, as Kate Lowe notes, "a cluster of skilled occupations 'permitted' to sub-Saharan Africans in Renaissance Europe centered on music," and England was no exception.[112] Theatrical culture, as always, records the presence of those musicians in courtly circles: in *Love's Labor's Lost* (1598), for instance, the Muscovite masque that the gentlemen of the court of Navarre (a Spanish region) mean to perform for the French princesses is accompanied by "Blackamoors with music."[113] Imtiaz Habib notes that Jacobean musicians were "protected individuals who may 'not be arrested,' nor be chosen into any office, nor warned to attend at assises, nor be impaneled on juries, not to be charged with any contributions, taxes or payment but in courts only as other of his majesty's servants."[114] Afro-British musicians had a privileged status: music and, by extension, dance were ways of achieving some degree of mobility for Afro-Britons who lived otherwise in a legal vacuum and fell somewhere on the expansive spectrum ranging from de facto servitude to menial occupations in a free capacity. Over time, Afro-British entertainers became available for hire not only at the court but also in town: in Brome's previously cited city comedy *The English Moor* (1637), the London merchant Quicksands hires Moorish musicians and dancers for a private masque performance at his house on Market Lane. Like the lead Afro-Scottish performer in 1590 Edinburgh or Francisco Menesez in late seventeenth-century Spain, the Afro-British entertainers whom Quicksands hires are willing to "dance an antique in which they use actions of mockery and derision": they will perform racializing black dances for pay if it helps them make a living and achieve mobility.[115] They will, in the process, lay claim to the site of cultural production of English black dances.

This Hispanicization of the structures of production powering English black dances went hand in hand with English commercial theatre's metabolization of a popular choreographic discourse closely connected to the tradition of kinetic blackness we encountered in the French context. I refer to that discourse, as Richard Brome himself did, as black "antics." The first registered occurrence of black antics in commercial theatre occurs three years after *Masque of Blackness*, in John Mason's *The Turke* (1608), when Mulleasses exclaims:

> Be pleas'd ye powers of might, and bout me skip
> Your anticke measures: like to cole black moores,
> Dauncing their high Lavoltas to the Sun
> Circle me round.[116]

Lexicons from the period highlight the centrality of visual culture to the meaning of "antiques."[117] Antics are gargoyles "pulling faces and making gestures" (varios vultus et gestus exprimunt) in John Baret's *An Alveary or Triple Dictionary, in English, Latin, and French* (1574); an "anticke-work" is "a worke in painting or caruing, of diuers shapes of beasts, birds, flowers, etc. vnperfectlie mixt and made one out of another" in John Bullokar's *An English Expositor* (1616), and "a term in painting, or Carving, it being a disorderly mixture of divers shapes of men, birds" in Edward Philips's *The New World of English Words* (1658).[118] In 1612, master of arts Henry Peacham wrote the most elaborate extant definition of "antiques" in visual culture as delightful compositions where the borders between humans, animals, and vegetals become porous:

> The form of it is a general and (as I may say) unnaturall or unorderly
> composition for delight's sake, of men, beasts, birds, fishes, flowres, etc
> without (as we say) rime or reason, for the greater variety you shew in
> your invention, the more you please. . . . You may, if you list, draw na-
> ked boys riding and playing with their paper-mils or bubble-shels upon
> goates, eagles, dolphins, etc, the bones of a ram's head hung with
> streams of beads and ribands, Satyres, Trytons, Apes, and Cornuco-
> pias, Dogs yoakt etc., drawing cocumbers, cherries, and any kind of
> wild trail or vinet after your own invention, with a thousand such
> more idle toys, so that herein you cannot be too fantasticall.[119]

In early modern lexicons, when the noun or adjective forms of "antiques" do not refer to visual culture, they usually refer to movement.[120] "Antics" form a concept that moves between visual culture and kinetic culture, as we can see in the juxtaposition of both domains in the definition given in E.B.'s *A New Dictionary of the Canting Crew* (1699): "Antics: little Images on Stone, on the out side of old Churches. Antick postures or dresses, such as are odd, ridiculous and singular, the habits and motions of Fools, Zanies, or Merry-andrews, of Mountebanks, with Ribbands, mismatched colours and Feathers."[121] The inseparability of visual and kinetic culture here suggests that the definition of antics provided in the former domain has traction in the latter: Peacham's description of "antics" helps us understand the "antics" deployed in the realm of dance, where they are notoriously ill defined. "Antics" translate in the kinetic sphere as a hybridization of human body language with animal forms.

From this multimodal definitional process, antics emerge as a choreographic principle encouraging performers to unleash their imagination and animalize their own body language. Like blackspeak, it was modular in that it could function either as an autonomous entity, or as an add-on that would distort and animalize familiar domestic dance moves by degree.[122] Systematically used in antimasques to convey a sense of chaos, antics are typically performed in early modern English theatre by three groups: devils (or supernatural creatures), nonwhite people, (Moors, Native Americans, Turks, Roma), and baboons.[123] Baboons and devils share a clear physiological hybridity, as they combine anthropomorphic features with animal features. The association of Afro-diasporic people with such creatures through the same choreographic tradition construed them as hybrids on the fringes of mankind. Thus, the pre-Enlightenment association of Africans with apes that Kim F. Hall insightfully brought to light twenty years ago, as much as it registered in the scientific discourse exemplified by Topsell's *History of the Foure-Footed Beasts* in 1607, became part of mainstream popular English culture via dance and its theatrical instantiations.[124]

Massinger channeled that tradition in *The Bondman*. The play revolves around the enslaved's rebellion in Syracuse during the failed Carthaginian attempt at invading the island—foiled by the Corinthian Timoleon in 338 B.C. Longing for the time when bondage in Syracusan society followed a paternalistic model, "when lords were styled fathers of families / and not imperious masters" and when "each private house derived / the perfect model of a Commonwealth" (120), the enslaved take advantage of their enslavers' absence, as the latter fight the Carthaginians. They take over the city, "shake off their heavy yokes off" (120), rape the enslavers' wives and daughters, and perpetrate the same abuse that has been inflicted on them. When the enslavers come back, they defeat the "thick-skinn'd slaves" (113) and ultimately spare their lives in exchange for their submission.

The play articulates a keen reflection on the immorality of slavery. At the beginning of the play, Timoleon argues that, although he abhors tyranny as a political regime,

> such as have made forfeit of themselves
> By vicious courses, and their birthright lost,
> 'Tis no injustice they are marked for slaves,
> To serve the virtuous. (102)

Yet the play mercilessly debunks this rationale by showing how all its characters, both the enslaved and their enslavers, follow vicious courses of action. Slavery is not the punishment of vice: deprived of its moral justification, it is exposed as a pure exercise in power. In the same vein as the aristocratic appropriations encountered in French ballets, in *Le malade imaginaire*, and in *Masque of Blackness*, *The Bondman* consistently uses slavery as a metaphor to articulate critiques of oppressive political regimes and oppressive matrimonial practices leaving white women at the mercy of men: Cleora, for instance, will not "live enslaved to [her fiancé's] jealous humours" (125). It is fitting that she should ultimately marry Pisander, a Theban lord who disguises himself as a slave to pursue her, evoking the Petrarchan figure of the Blackamoor enslaved by love (114).

More specifically, this is a play about color-based slavery. Although the enslaved are never explicitly called Blackamoors, the alignment of the enslaved in Syracuse, the enemies from within, with the Carthaginian enemies from without (whose victory would enslave white Syracusans) points toward a Moorish identity. Onomastics confirms this: the lead female slave character is called Zanthia, and she shares that name not only with Zanthia, the "succuba" from *The Knight of Malta* (1618), but also with another woman whose Moorishness is clearly stated in a later play by Massinger, *Believe as You List* (1631).[125] In *The Parliament of Love*, written the same year as *The Bondman*, Massinger introduces yet another Moorish woman, whom he describes as having a "dark complexion," while declaring that people "of her country" typically have "thick lips" and "rough curl'd hair."[126] Thus Zanthia in *The Bondman* was very likely to be performed as a Blackamoor, in black-up. She was to be contrasted on stage with Cleora, whose "ivory forehead" is exalted throughout the play (107), and with her mistress Corisca, who is worried that the sun might "take her complexion off" (109). The ethnic ambiguity attached to the enslaved and their dances in the play should not be ignored, especially in the light of the commendatory verses attached to the original 1624 edition, in which William Basse refers to the "Gipsie jigges . . . drumming stuffe, and dances" of the play, thereby connecting black dances to Romani dances.[127] Nonetheless, the deployment of those ethnically ambiguous dances within the slavery-based society of Syracuse underlines their kinship with black dances, and, as we saw in the second interlude of Molière's *Le malade imaginaire*, association with Romani culture did not make black dances any less black across early modern Europe.

Massinger uses black dances as a powerful metaphorical platform to express the shifting power relations between enslaved Blackamoors and white enslavers throughout the play. When their enslavers come back victorious from the war, the enslaved state their demands and ask, in addition to a general pardon for their offenses, for

> Liberty
> To all such as desire to make return
> Into their countries; and, to those that stay,
> A competence of land freely allotted
> To each man's proper use, no lord acknowledged
> Lastly, with your consent, to choose them wives
> Out of your families. (121)

Those demands, immediately rejected by the enslavers, all express a desire for mobility: geographic mobility (leave to depart), social mobility (land ownership), and romantic mobility (interracial marriage)—they ask for freedom of movement in all the possible senses of the word. Dance encodes this desire for free movement, this yearning for mobility among the enslaved and, as such, becomes a form of political action throughout the play. In that sense, Massinger's black dances resemble Spanish guineo as a tool for the enslaved to renegotiate their condition.

When Marullo, the mutineers' leader, incites slaves to rebellion and asks what they are ready to do to conquer their freedom, Gracculo responds: "Anything! To burn a church or two, and dance by the light on't, were but a Maygame" (112). Mentioning dance and the early modern English tradition of May games so close to each other immediately would evoke Morris dancing in the spectators' minds and associate it with the image of a violent attack on the religious institution upholding the slavery-based system. Later on, when the rebellion Gracculo dreams of is carried out, it is danced out:

Hell, I think's broke loose
There's such variety of all disorders,
As leaping, shouting, drinking, dancing, whoring,
Among the slaves; answer'd with crying, howling,
By the citizens and their wives; such a confusion,
In a word, not to tire you, as I think,
The like was never read of. (113)

Gracculo sees revolution as a moment when the body politick dances a "leaping," chaotic, and violent convulsive dance.

Two scenes later, power dynamics get reversed, and the enslaved are now enslavers of all the Syracusans who stayed in the city instead of leaving for the front. Gracculo has his ridiculous former enslaver, Asotus, dance like a baboon, "in an ape's habit, with a chain about his neck." "Gracculo: What for the Carthaginians? [*Asotus makes mopes*] A good beast. What for ourself your lord? [*Dances.*] Exceeding well. There's your reward. [*Gives him an apple*]" (115). Forcing Asotus to pull faces, dance antics, and "caper like an ape" (125), Gracculo brings attention to the animalizing dimension of black dances: this animalization is exerted against the enslaver, but only as part of carnivalesque role reversal. Meanwhile Zanthia's former mistress, Corisca, who suffers the same fate as her stepson Asotus, is called a "Jane-of-Apes," the female version of a jackanapes. This term animalizes her and reasserts the political value of black dances, since "jackanape" also referred derogatively to a social upstart: someone who craves mobility. Zanthia is now Corisca's mistress, "in Corisca's clothes, she bearing up her train" (115), in a scene of inversion that makes Zanthia reminiscent of the famous "Black Lady" played by the African maidservant Ellen More in a disappearing act during a 1507 festivity at the court of James IV of Scotland.[128] Here again, the play demonstrates its familiarity with and cannibalization of a long trans-European history of aristocratic engagements with performative blackness. When, thanks to the revolution, Poliphron is able to marry his former mistress and lover Olympia, the Moorish community celebrates this interracial marriage and the mobility that it represents with a dance, a vengeful one—"Gracculo: I have thought of a most triumphant one, which shall express we are lords and these our slaves" (116). This dance signals that black-white power relations have not been abolished; they have been inverted temporarily for a brief carnival.

It is not surprising, then, that the final restoration of white power over the enslaved in Syracuse should take the form of a black dance. Gracculo, seeing that the fight against the victorious white enslavers is lost, is ready to be hanged with his fellows, yet he demands that they not be illegally executed twice, "at the gallows first, and after in a ballad / Sung to some villainous tune" (132). His concern evokes the black "Gypsy" Cleopatra's fear that "scald rhymers" might "ballad [her] out o' tune" in Rome in Shakespeare's play.[129] This fear is founded: as we know from the case of the marvelous dancer Francisco Menesez, the memory projects known as ballads are rarely neutral or innocuous for early modern Afro-European dancers. Gracculo states, with panache, "Let the state take order / For the redress of this abuse, recording / 'Twas done by my advice, and, for my part, / I'll cut as clean a caper from the ladder, / As ever merry Greek did" (132). In that scenario, Gracculo would caper into death, turning black dance into a defiant final claim of agency. But the play does not end thus, for black dances are ultimately recuperated to reassert white power:

> *Timoleon* Yet I think you would shew more activity to delight our
>   master for a pardon.
> *Gracculo* O! I would dance, As I were all air and fire. [*Capers.*]
> *Timoleon* And ever be obedient and humble?
> *Gracculo* As his spaniel, Though he kick'd me for exercise; and the
>   like promise for all the rest.
> *Timoleon* Rise then, you have it. (132)

Gracculo performs the last black dance of the play in a final act of submission to white power, participating in his own canine animalization, capering his way into oppression and survival. To save his own life, Gracculo gives to Timoleon what Sambo would refuse to give his own enslaver in the West Indian dialogue that Thomas Tryon would write some sixty years later.

In *The Bondman*, enslaved Moors yearn for mobility, use dance as a metaphor to describe political revolutions, and demonstrate their keen awareness that animalizing black dances—or antics—put anyone who dances them in a position of subjection. In short, in this play, kinesis is simultaneously the object, language, and instrument of power. Those dynamics are encapsulated in act 4, scene 2, when the enslavers triumph over the rebellious enslaved by virtue not of military might but of their own body language. Timoleon orders that "each man take a tough whip in his hand, such as you used to punish them with, as masters," and his plan works: "The senators shake their whips, the Slaves throw away their weapons, and run off" (121). The fight is won over the traumatic movement of white hands raising whips. This moment invites us to take seriously Asotus's earlier statement that

> Not all the catalogue
> Of conjurers or wise women bound together
> Could have so soon transform'd me, as my rascal
> Did with his whip; for not in outside only,
> But in my own belief, I thought myself
> As perfect a baboon.

Timoleon interrupts him and calls him "an ass ever," yet the play's insistence on the psychological power of kinesis does not allow us to dismiss Asotus's account of his experience performing black dances like Timoleon does (124). *The Bondman* powerfully draws attention to the mnemonic charge of kinesis, a charge equally attached to black dances and to the sight of raised whips in white fists.

The tradition of black "antics" would inform a number of late Jacobean and Caroline plays often—but not exclusively—connected to actor and theatrical impresario Christopher Beeston (such as Henry Shirley's *The Martyr'd Souldier* and Richard Brome's *The English Moor*).[130] A testament to the popularity of that tradition is the university play *Mr. Moore's Revels*, performed at Oxford in 1636, in which Blackamoors are juxtaposed with apes who seek to resemble them in all things, cosmetically and kinetically.[131] While, as Kim F. Hall points out, the play was connected to popular entertainments such as the Lord Mayor's pageants, *Mr. Moore's Revels* was a pastiche of court masques and might have simply spoofed the black dances that permeated court performance culture across the Channel—or it might have drawn on the antics tradition of commercial theatre.[132] The multiplicity of potential sources attests to the circulation of black dances in Caroline performance culture.

That legacy survived the closure of theatres in 1642. Tracing the tradition of black dances in Interregnum and Restoration England requires tracking "antics" while tempering philological zeal with an awareness that antics are not always labeled as such. For instance, in Thomas St. Serfe's comedy *Tarugo's Wiles* (1668), white discussants, marveling at a baboon that "imitates the music," decide to "have a dance, to see if he'll imitate us." Their curiosity is soon gratified: "they dance, where Pugge [the baboon] at the corner of the stage imitates with the Negro-girl" of the household.[133] *Tarugo's Wiles* shows us that the practice of animalizing black kinetic language did not require a label. Thus this practice might very well have informed theatrical moments such as the scene in Killigrew's *The Imperial Tragedy* (1669) when "seven Blackamore boys, in Turkish or Morisco habit, dance" and are compared to devils as they do so; the scene in Whitaker's *The Conspiracy* (1680) when "enter eight of ten Blackmoors, drest like fiends [who] dance an antic"; the scene when "enter four Black Women that dance to the same measure of the song" in Otway's *The Atheist* (1684); or the scene in Behn's *The Emperor of the Moon* (1688) when "Negroes dance and mingle in the chorus," among others.[134] That Elkanah Settle's Restoration spectacular *The Empress of Morocco* (1673), the first English play printed with engravings, includes a lively reproduction of a black dance by William Dolle is indicative of the striking effect of this technique on spectators, of the popular demand for it, and of the growing importance of black dances in English collective imagination at the dawn of the colonial era (Figure 8).[135]

The growing popularity of black dances in the archives of colonial England coincides with their growing Hispanicization. Indeed, the growing alignment between the politics of English black dances and their Spanish counterpart that we saw in *The Bondman* only strengthened over time—certainly not because English performance culture sought to imitate Spanish performance culture in any way but because growing interracial frictions around the notion of mobility in the colonial Anglophone world where color-based slavery was soaring created ideological needs that were best addressed through the medium of dance, as the Hispanic world had long known. This alignment is particularly noticeable in colonial dance politics. Indeed, the colonial literature that developed in the mid-seventeenth century on both sides of the Channel often evokes the plantation dances performed by the enslaved as sites of interracial power play. In 1658, some twenty-six years before Thomas Tryon had Sambo say it himself, Charles de Rochefort noted, "One could tell that, after they [the enslaved] had danced thus, they would work with more energy, not showing any sign of weariness, and better than if they had rested in their hut all night" on St. Christophe Island.[136]

That observation resembles those Zuñiga would make twenty years later about the historical function of black dances in Andalusia, or those made by the Dutch Zacharias Wagener about the role of *calenda* dances on the Brazilian plantations that he painted in 1640 (see Plate 11): "when the slaves have carried out their arduous duties for weeks on end, they are allowed to celebrate one Sunday as they please; in large numbers in certain places and with all manner of

Figure 8. "A Moorish Dance" in *The Empress of Morocco*. William Dolle. Engraving. 1673. Beinecke Rare Book and Manuscript Library, Yale University.

leaps, drums, and flutes, they dance from morning to night, all in a disorganized way, with men and women, young and old [...]"[137] As Frantz Fanon notes, those dances served as outlets, safety valves shrewdly put in place to let out the frustrations of the enslaved in the metropole and the colonies.[138] Yet because dance was also a space of resistance that Afro-diasporic people never relinquished, chroniclers like Jean-Baptiste Labat also insist on the subversive potential of black dances in the Caribbean: "Edicts were promulgated in the islands to forbid *calendas*, not only because of the indecent and lascivious movements of which this dance is made, but also in order to prevent *Nègres* from assembling: gathered so merrily and often drunk on liquors, crews of *Nègres* can rise, rebel, or go steal."[139] Dance encouraged the enslaved to get in formation and fight.[140]

As had been the case in Iberia for over a century, black dances became indissolubly tied to the issue of slavery in the Anglophone world. Since, in that configuration, black dances were conceptualized as a tool for self-emancipation in the hands of the enslaved, characters belonging to the African aristocracy never stoop to dancing in Restoration theatre. In Pierre Motteux's 1668 operatic version of *The Island Princess*, "enter an African Lady, with slaves who dance with timbrels; a negro lord makes love to her": the African aristocrats are involved in courtly courtship, and they leave the dancing to slaves.[141] In Thomas Southerne's 1695 stage adaptation of *Oroonoko*, "the scene drawn shews the slaves, Men, Women, and children upon the ground, some rise and dance, others sing the following song," but Oroonoko and Imoinda, the African aristocrats, do not dance. They observe the dance like the white enslavers do: they "enter as spectators."[142] Oroonoko and Imoinda are construed as characters whose nobility cannot be touched by the condition accidentally and wrongfully imposed upon them. When Oroonoko ultimately fights back, he leads an epic armed rebellion; what he does not care to do, however, is engage in the enslaved-enslaver power play of everyday life that was black dances.

Nowhere is the Hispanicization of black dances in English culture and society more clearly articulated than in Sir William Davenant's *The History of Sir Francis Drake* (1658), an operatic tableau, the hybrid nature of which allowed Davenant to circumvent the prohibition placed on staged plays under the Commonwealth.[143] The anti-Spanish propagandist nature of the piece too was designed to ingratiate it with the authorities: drawing on Philip Nichols's *Sir Francis Drake Revived* (1626), which recounts Drake's voyage to the West Indies and to the northeastern coast of South America in 1572, Davenant mustered Drake's status as an Elizabethan icon of English expansionism in support of

Cromwell's Western Design, which aimed at establishing a strong English presence in the Caribbean in order to weaken the Spanish Empire by disrupting its maritime trade routes from 1655 onward.[144] In this tableau, black kinesis is where Afro-descendants assert their own mobility and agency as they choose to rebel and form alliances with Englishmen against the Spaniards—yet it is also, ironically, a site where English racial culture morphs into its old nemesis: its Spanish counterpart. Davenant's black dances, as a medium, enable colonialist English racial culture to find itself through denial.

Davenant shows us Drake's men looting Spanish ships, and, ultimately, defeating Spanish armies in Panama. Yet before that, we see Drake make strategic alliances with "Peruvians" who welcome him as a liberating ally against the Spaniards, as well as dark-skinned "Symerons"—that is, cimarrones, Maroons— introduced in a stage direction as "Moorish people brought formerly to Peru by the Spaniards as their slaves, to dig in mines; and having lately revolted from them, did live under a government of a king of their own election" (8). Enslaved North Africans had long been banned from the Iberian colonies for fear they should introduce Islam to the New World; "Moor" is thus used here for Blackamoors.

Davenant construes Symerons as hypermobile figures. Brought on Iberian slave ships from across the Atlantic, they first experienced the Americas as the dual imposition of forced mobility and forced immobility. Having recovered their mobility by running away and standing up to the Spaniards, they celebrate "their own election" and their self-determined alliance with Drake in order "to afflict the Enemy" with a dance: as soon as the king of Symerons tells Drake "all my strengths are thine," "enter four Symerons who dance a Morisco for joy of the arrival of Sir Francis Drake" (13). Drake uses Symerons as fighters against the Spaniards, but before that, he has them serve as efficient scouts, "guides," and "conductors" sent ahead of the force to collect knowledge about topography and the enemy's movements: that function enlists, specifically, their kinetic mobility in the service of English expansionism (12). The black Morisco dance performed to a tune "sung by a chorus of [English] Marriners within" kinetically symbolizes the merger of English and Maroon interests. Similarly, in the final scene, which celebrates the Spanish debacle, "the grand dance begins, consisting of two [English] land-soldiers, two seamen, two Symerons, and a Peruvian, intimating by their several interchange of salutations their mutual desires of amity" (37).

Yet those interracial alliances are undermined by subterraneous resemblances between Englishmen and Spaniards that undercut official military

strategies. Those resemblances articulate themselves not so much in relation to
the Native "Peruvians" as to the Symerons. The kinship between Spanish and
English cultures is articulated most definitively at the expense of Symerons in a
scene of interracial rape fantasy. Just before the attack, one of Drake's men,
Rouse, brings to the camp the alarming news that Symeron scouts, moving freely
and without supervision at night, have surprised a Spanish wedding party,

> To whom the Symerons now,
> Much more than fury show
> For they have all those cruelties exprest
> That Spanish pride could ever provoke from them
> or Moorish malice can revenge esteem (27–28)

Specifically, Rouse is outraged at the "discovery of a beautiful [Spanish] lady
tied to a tree, adorn'd with the ornaments of a bride, with her hair disheveled
and complaining with her hands toward heaven; near her are likewise discerned
the Symerons who took her prisoner" (27). Dishevelment was a visual code for
sexual assault in early modern drama, and this cue is sufficient for Drake and his
men, aristocrats and common sailors alike, to wrongly infer that the mobile free
Afro-diasporic men have raped a white woman. Drake immediately breaks his
alliance with the Symerons and prepare to massacre them in the blink of an eye:

> though here these cruel Symerons exceed
> Our number, yet they are too few to bleed
> When honor must revengeful be
> For this affront to love and me. (28)

Pedro, the Symeron leader, ultimately fixes the situation by telling the truth:
"She is as free and as unblemisht too / As if she had a prisoner been to you" (29).
    Pedro's comparative syntax seeks to revive the grammar of English-Symeron
alliance established at the play's outset, but in vain. Drake sees his mistake, and
he backpedals just in time for his purposes, but this scene has exposed the pre-
cariousness of interracial alliances, the absolute primacy of shared whiteness
even among old enemies or colonial rivals, and the fears that unfettered Black
mobility could elicit from Davenant's audience in a heartbeat. Of course, this
fantasy episode is nowhere to be found in the source text *Drake Revived*: Davenant
dreamed it up, and it was made of the same stuff as the 1687 ballad of Francisco
Menesez was made on.

Davenant's play works through its own denial to acknowledge a subterraneous kinship between Englishmen and their Spanish enemies in the New World; that acknowledgement is inseparable from English anxieties about the black dances that had been initially set up as liberating and strategically beneficial. Those are palpable in the very aesthetic form Davenant chose to represent those dances on stage. Using the Spanish name "Morisco" to refer to the Symerons's dance rather than its English variant, "Morris dancing," Davenant chose, like several English lexicographers and commenters, to highlight the continuity between English and Spanish forms within a common European dance culture. By choosing the Morisco/Morris, Davenant conjured an animalizing black dance radically different from the dances described in his source text. Indeed, in *Sir Francis Drake Revived*, Symerons dance only once: in battle, when they attack the Spanish town with the English. In other words, their dances are war dances. "Symerons, although by terror of the shot continuing they were for the time step aside, yet as soone as they discerned by hearing that we marched onward, they all rusht forwards one after another, traversing the way with their Arrowes ready in their Bowes, and their manner of Country dance or leap, very lustily singing *Yó pehó Yó pehó*, and so got before us where they continued their leape and song after the manner of their owne Country warres till they and we overtooke some of the Enemie."[145] Nicholas describes dancing as fully integrated within African fighting techniques, which, wielded against the Spanish enslavers, are instruments of self-emancipation from slavery. While Englishmen in Davenant's play draw on the Symerons' military strength and mobility, the transformation of Afro-diasporic war dances into "Morisco" dances emolliates them by turning a kinesis of war into a kinesis of entertainment. The black Morisco dance is a medium that allows Symerons to assert their political mobility and simultaneously contains them, forcing them into a dance orchestrated, controlled, and observed by Drake himself. Contradiction exists only superficially here: it is the surface-level manifestation of deep desire and denial. Ultimately, the English aspired to replace and outperform the Iberians within a colonial framework that relied on color-based slavery—in 1658, Davenant's use of black dances revealed just that.

Conclusion: Black Resistance and the Archive

The Hispanicization of English black dances in the second half of the seventeenth century is allegorically captured in Wycherley's comedy *The Gentleman*

Dancing-Master (1673), a play inspired by Calderón de la Barca's own comedy *El maestro de danzar* (1664).[146] No more than the Spanish originals of Dryden's *An Evening's Love, or The Mock-Astrologer* and St. Serfe's *Tarugo's Wiles* does the Calderonian original of Wycherley's play contain black characters. Yet Wycherley, like Dryden and St. Serfe, must have found that writing a black character into his play was one of the most efficient ways to conjure up Spanish culture on stage. In Wycherley's play, then, Don Diego, a severe Englishman enamored with Spanish culture, who brought a "Spanish and Guiny force" back to his London household after spending fifteen years in Spain, forces his nephew, who is himself enamored with French culture, to embrace the Spanish ways.[147] Don Diego wants Mr. de Parris to learn how to move in the world like a Spaniard, and he orders one of his Spanish servants to train his nephew: "Come Sirrah-Black, now, do you teach him to walk with the *verdadero gesto, gracia,* and *gravidad* of a true Castilian. . . . Black struts about the stage, the Monsieur follows him, imitating awkerdly all he does."[148] Don Diego seems to know from experience that the surest way to have an Englishman behave like a Spaniard is to put him in the presence of black kinesis.

At the close of this chapter, what better figure to muse upon than Wycherley's nameless Afro-diasporic dancing master, who retreats backstage after imparting his firsthand knowledge of how early modern white men moved in the world? If Wycherley had given him more lines, what might we have learned about his life prior to his arrival in London? We might have recognized in him one of the many dancing masters whose competition Juan de Esquivel Navarro bitterly lamented in 1642 Seville. We might have recognized in him a member of a powerful confraternity bringing the art of Black formation to England. We might have recognized in him Mingo—short for Domingo, one of the most popular slave names in the early modern Hispanophone world—the Afro-diasporic dancer who fascinated Samuel Pepys in a London tavern on March 27, 1661. After dinner, "we made Mingo, Sir W. Batten's black, and Jack, Sir W. Pen's, dance, and it was strange how the first did dance with a great deal of seeming skill."[149] As Pepys notes, Mingos routinely danced with Jacks in Restoration England. The real counterparts of Wycherley's dancing master came from Spain, from the Iberian Americas, and from Anglophone colonies alike, yet they all brought with them a deep-seated knowledge of the racial politics and power embedded in black dances wherever color-based slavery exists.[150] Mingo and Jack knew that, no matter how much or how little they had in common, no matter how much or how little their diasporic, creolized, and code-switching dance moves resembled one another's, they simply had to get in formation.

Acknowledging the epistemological limitations of a kinetic archive entirely constituted by white subjectivity means accepting that we cannot tell whether any of the black dances encountered in this chapter in early modern metropolitan Europe were genealogically connected to authentic dances performed by the sub-Saharan African diaspora in early modern Africa, America, Europe, and Asia. The early modern period plays a key role in scholarly attempts at writing a narrative of continuity between African and Afro-diasporic dances. Those attempts often proceed from a desire to re-member dance as a powerful site for self-determined transmission that could resist the brutal processes of cultural dislocation, atomization, and erasure that slavery visited on Afro-diasporic subjects.[151] They proceed from a deeply rooted and powerful reparative drive. I do share that drive, and my contribution to the collective project of repair consists in locating Black resistance and agency not in a hypothetical retention of Africanness in early modern black dances for which I cannot make a compelling case, but, rather, in early modern Afro-Europeans' relentless efforts to take control of the cultural sites that produced early modern repertoires of kinetic blackness. White archives, especially dramatic ones, do register those efforts over and over again.

Those efforts were those of professional Afro-diasporic dancers like Francisco Menesez, who used dancing skills to buy their own freedom; of Black confraternities, which, aware of their precarious position relative to the authorities, used dance to ingratiate themselves with white spectators; of Afro-Europeans, such as the Granadine *negros* who took over the stage to dance a saraband in Aguado's interlude and who, while doing so, used theatrical settings to redefine what a black dance could be; of dancing masters, such as Hernando de Rivera, taking charge of Corpus Christi procession skits; of dancers leading and influencing white crews in Edinburgh, or moving to London and disseminating their knowledge of interracial power play, as in Wycherley's comedy; of dancers like Jack and Mingo, coordinating and getting in formation across diasporic lines.

Black agency fiercely expressed itself in early modern dance culture. If a dimension of authentic Afro-diasporic kinesis was, beyond a doubt, directly transmitted from the metropole to the colonies and back generation after generation, it is the deep-seated awareness that dance was and still is a privileged site of contestation and self-assertion. Whether it be in eighteenth-century plantations, in Harlem Renaissance choreographies, or in hip-hop culture around the Atlantic, dance has remained a crucial medium for Black radical political expression from the sixteenth century to this day. If, on both sides of the Channel, slave-owning aristocrats, men and women, did not hesitate in the seventeenth century to appropriate what they perceived as the kinetic identity of people who struggled to reclaim mobility and control over their own bodies in order to denounce their own predicaments, it is because, as early as the 1600s, Black bodies in movement were becoming a point of reference in Western political imagination for marking deprivation of mobility, exclusion from ownership and self-ownership, and indefatigable resistance to those.

Post/Script

Ecologies of Racial Performance

At the close of this book, I want to return to the question of the efficacy of scripts of blackness, and acknowledge that, on occasion, those collaborative hermeneutic acts of racialization may very well have failed. It will not have escaped readers that I do not share the critical inclination—common in literary and performance studies—to read drama, theatre, and performance culture as sites that automatically resist hegemonic ideological forces. In the majority of cases I have encountered in the archives, the conditions for resistance are not met. In that sense, Wallerstein's words resonate with what *Scripts of Blackness* does: "To be sure, there are all sorts of resistances, but we need to start by emphasizing, rather, the mechanisms, the constraints, the limits."[1] Certainly, the mechanisms, constraints, and limits of early modern racecraft were not absolute. Scripts of blackness may not have landed when there were so many moving pieces involved in their hermeneutic production, so many agents with different vested interests and perspectives interacting with performative blackness.

The historiography of early modern racecraft needs room for contingency, for potential failure, for bifurcated responses, and—yes—for occasional resistance, too. Readers should find that room in the realization that what this book has offered is only a map of early modern racecraft. I do not mistake the map for the territory, but I insist that the map matters. I tried in this book to delineate the deep riverbed where early modern performances of blackness flow. The river might overspill in emancipatory directions, unforeseen and refreshing rivulets might form here and there, the river might dry up sometimes—but its bed runs deep, and the river steadily flows in the same direction, the direction of racialization. Appreciation for the complexities of dramatic playtexts and for the emancipatory energies of live performance can complement but not substitute for that painful realization.

In *Scripts of Blackness*, I have consistently highlighted the genesis of racializing scripts of blackness at the intersection of material practices and literary tropes (demonizing, commodifying, excluding, animalizing, infantilizing, associative, and sexualizing tropes). It is only fitting that the book should, ultimately, reflect on its own historiographic metaphors. In writing this account of early modern scripts of blackness, I have endeavored to use historiographic poetics that might reconcile the critical drive toward freedom that is so deeply ingrained in our disciplinary ethos with the systemic nature of early modern racecraft and its ideological effects.[2] To do so, I have turned to ecological poetics, in an effort to use style to address a conceptual tension. In the Introduction to this book, I compared early modern Afro-diasporic subjectivity to the sun: we can hardly look at it, given the whiteness of the archives, but its light makes everything else visible in early modernity. That image launched a subdued but persistent ecological poetics of transnational racecraft. In Chapter 1, I described the history of black-up's secularization with the metaphor of a tree, as national traditions "branched out" of a core medieval episteme. In Chapter 2, invoking Susan Lanser, I described the recurrence of the oblique aesthetics of black women's desirability across those traditions during the high baroque phase as a "confluence" of "underground aquifers." In Chapter 3, I referred to the extant archives of early modern blackspeak as the waterline of an iceberg of performative practices lost to us. I would, at this point, describe the proliferation of black dances and their politics of contestation across Western Europe I studied in Chapter 4 as fungi whose spores are spread by transnational winds and grow only where something is rotten.

Taken together, these metaphors point toward the ecology of harm, or toward the garden of torments that was early modern racecraft. Ecological poetics foregrounds the ways in which a historiographic recording of racecraft must reconcile our critical drive toward freedom with the recognition that the early modern culture of racial impersonation functioned as a powerful system. For we grasp the environment in fragments; it strikes our consciousness in the form of accidents and surprises; we move in its midst with a perfectly well-founded sense of our own freedoms and responsibilities—yet we know that, as a system, it obeys an imperious internal logic, which operates across space and time and ultimately delimitates the possible.

*   *   *

It is always the same woman. You have been clicking through the pages of a late seventeenth-century French collection of engravings entitled *Recueil de modes de la cour de France*, and you suddenly notice that it is always the same woman who poses allegorically in multiple series (see Plate 12). Those series represent, in turn, the four elements, the four seasons, the four continents, the five senses, the four times of the day, the four cardinal directions, four virtues, six ancient divinities, five more virtues, four vices, and the twelve months of the year. They form a totalizing system of representation metaphorically capturing human life's embeddedness in natural cycles, natural sensoria, and naturalized behavioral patterns. The model is always the same: a Greek-nosed, button-mouthed white woman with bright eyes, round cheeks, light brown hair, and a slim waist. You stop clicking. In this engraving, she is posing as the allegory of Africa, for the second time now. She is standing not in a garden of torments, but in a desert. No trees, water sources, icebergs, or fungi in view, but the sun presides over the scene, shining its beams over a lion, a scorpion, and her—the pale-skinned allegory of Africa.

She holds in her right hand a full-face black mask with a closed, full-lipped mouth reminiscent of so many "thick-lipped" early modern black characters. Is that the kind of mask, material or internalized, that your formidable acting teacher thought might help you find your Africanness some thirteen years ago? The anonymous white model has excellent posture. Her feet are in first position, her baroque costume advantageously reveals her calves, and the shape of her wrap billowing in the air suggests that you might actually have caught her at the end of a kinetic sentence. She was dancing a second ago: she just landed in first position and took her mask off. Why? Her left hand is resting lightly on her chest. You know that technique, you learned it from your acting teacher: it allows you to feel soundwaves and modulate your voice accordingly. She will use her voice. She took her full-face mask off to speak—or maybe to sing a moresche? She is not looking at you, as you are not the person she speaks to or for. Black-up, blackspeak, black dances: this allegory mobilizes all the techniques of early modern performative blackness. In small characters, the caption below the engraving invokes the scripts of blackness that animated early modern performance culture: almost too predictably, that caption tries to distract the reader with the obfuscating nonquestion of Afro-diasporic women's erotic (un)desirability. The caption reads:

> To my mind, scorching climates
> Would seem preferable to others

if the awful monsters that live there
looked like this one.[3]

You click, you zoom out, and in the light of the piercing African sun that floods the engraving, the "awful monstrosity" of the virtuosic allegorical performer suddenly becomes visible.

Selection of Early Modern Plays Featuring
Black Characters

English Materials

English plays and masques are listed, whenever possible, under the dates provided by Alfred Harbage in *Annals of English Drama, 975–1700*. Otherwise, English plays and Lord Mayor's Pageants are listed under their first known year of publication, with the phrase "(pub.)."

French Materials

French ballets prior to 1652 are listed under the dates provided by Paul Lacroix in *Ballets et mascarades de cour de Henri III à Louis XIV (1581–1652)*, volumes 1 through 6.

French ballets after 1652 and all French plays are listed under their first known year of publication.

Spanish Materials

Corpus Christi dances, autos, and autos sacramentales performed in Seville are listed under the dates provided by Jean Sentaurens in *Séville et le théâtre: De la fin du Moyen Âge à la fin du XVIIe siècle*.

Lope de Vega's plays are listed, whenever possible, under the dates provided by Sylvanus Griswold Morley and Courtney Bruerton in *The Chronology of Lope De Vega's Comedias.*

All plays by dramatists other than Lope de Vega are listed under their first known year of publication, unless the year of composition can be guessed, in which case the play is listed under its presumed year of composition and the publication year is indicated as "(pub.)"

For chronology and attribution, I lean heavily on Héctor Urzáiz Tortajada's *Catálogo de autores teatrales del siglo XVII.*

The following abbreviations are used in this section:

L= this work is *likely* to have featured black Afro-diasporic characters.
LMP = this Lord Mayor's Pageant was performed in London.
SA = this Corpus Christi auto or auto sacramental was performed in Seville.
SCCD = this Corpus Christi Dance was performed in Seville.

For the sake of brevity, the bibliography at the end of this book provides complete bibliographic information only for the plays and performances that I discussed previously.

My selection builds capaciously on the selections of Black plays previously compiled by Sylvie Chalaye, John Lipski, Nicholas R. Jones, and Anthony Gerald Barthelemy.

Year	Spain	England	France
1500s		1507: Anonymous, Scottish, *Joust of the Wild Knight and the Black Lady* (lost)	
1520s	1521: Gil Vicente, *Cortes de Júpiter* 1523–49: Diego Sánchez de Badajoz, *Farsa teologal, Farsa de la hechizera, Farsa de la ventana, Farsa de la fortuna o hado, Farsa del moysen* 1525: Gil Vicente, *Fragoa d'amor* 1528–35: Jaime de Huete, *Tesorina* 1529: Hernán López de Yanguas, *La farsa dicha Turquesana contra el Turco muy galana*	1527: John Ritwise, *Dido* (lost) L.	
1530s	1536: Gil Vicente, *Floresta de engaños*		1536: Arnoul and Simon Greban, *Mystère des saints actes des Apôtres faite à Bourges*
1540s		1547: Anonymous, *A Mask of Prester John* (lost) 1548: Anonymous *A Mask of Young Moors* (lost)	1547: Marguerite de Navarre, *Comédie de l'adoration des trois rois mages*

(Continued)

Year	Spain	England	France
1550s	1550: Martín de Santander, *Comedia de Rosabella*	1550: Anonymous, *A Mask of Irishmen and Moors* (lost)	
	1554: Luis de Miranda, *Comedia pródiga* **Midcentury:** Juan Pastor, *Farsa de Lucrecia, tragedia de la castidad*; Anonymous, *Aucto de Thamar*	1551: Anonymous, *A Mask of Moors and Amazons* (lost) 1559: Anonymous, *A Mask of Moors* (lost)	
1560s	1560: Pedro de Medina, *Los tres reyes magos* (SCCD)	1563: W. Croston, *Aeneas and Queen Dido* (lost) L.	
	1564: Luis Nuñez, *Los negrillos* (SCCD)	1564: Edward Halliwell, *Dido* (lost) L.	
	1567: (pub.): Lope de Rueda, *Comedia de Eufemia; Comedia de los engañados; Colloquio de Tymbria; Colloquio de Gila*	1565: Anonymous, *Massinissa and Sophonisba* (lost) L.	
1570s	1571: Cristóbal Sánchez de Mendoza, *Visitacion de la reine Saba* (SCCD)	1572: Anonymous, *Theagenes and Chariclea* (lost) L.	
	1575 (?): Anonymous, *Códice de autos viejos* (SCCD)	1574: *Perseus and Andromeda* (lost) L.	
	1576: Juan Batista, *Los reyes magos* (SCCD); Hernando Manuel, *La zambra de los negros* (SCCD)	1578: Anonymous, *The Queen of Ethiopia* (lost) L.	
	1577: Juan Batista, *Los reyes magos* (SCCD)	1579: *A Morris Mask* (lost) L.	
	1550–1600 (?): Anonymous, *Egloga al Sanctísimo Sacramento sobre la figura de Melquisedec*		

(Continued)

(Continued)

Year	Spain	England	France
1580s	**1582:** Juan Batista de los Santos, *Convite del rey Salomon a la reina Saba* (SA)	**1583:** William Gager, *Dido* L.	
	1588: Hernando Franco, *La zambra de los negros* (SCCD)	**1585:** George Peele, *The Pageant Before Woolstone Dixie* LMP	
	1589: Pedro Guerrero, *La cachumba de los negros* (SCCD)	**1587:** Christopher Marlowe, *Tamburlaine, Part 1*	
		1588: Christopher Marlowe, *Tamburlaine, Part 2*	
		1588: Maurice Kyffin, *Eunuchus* (lost) L.	
		1589: Christopher Marlowe, *The Jew of Malta* L.	
		1589: George Peele, *The Battle of Alcazar*	

(Continued)

Year	Spain	England	France
1590s	**1597–1603:** Lope de Vega, *La corona derribada y vara de Moises*	**1591:** George Peele, *King Edward I*	
	1598 (?): Lope de Vega. *Los comendadores de Córdoba*	**1592:** Anonymous, *Mully Mollocco* (lost) L.	
	1599: Juan Bautista de Aguilar, *Indios y negros* (SCCD); Diego de Santander, *El arca de Noe* (SA) L.	**1594:** William Shakespeare, *Titus Andronicus*; Thomas Lodge, *The Wounds of Civil War* (pub.); Robert Greene, *The Historie of Orlando Furioso*	
	1599–1608: Lope de Vega, *El negro del mejor amo*	**1595:** William Shakespeare, *Love's Labour's Lost*	
		1596: William Shakespeare, *The Merchant of Venice*; George Chapman, *The Blind Beggar of Alexandria*	
		1598: Richard Bernard, *Eunuchus* L.; Thomas Dekker, *Phaeton* (lost) L.; Thomas Dekker, Michael Drayton, and Robert Wilson, *The Madman's Morris* (lost) L.; Anonymous, *Dido and Aeneas* (lost) L.	
		1599: Anonymous, *The Thracian Wonder* (pub. 1661)	

(Continued)

Year	Spain	England	France
1600s	1600: Hernando Franco, Indios y negros (SCCD) 1600 (?): Lope de Vega, El prodigio de Etiopia (pub. 1645) 1602: Simón Aguado, Los negros; Simón Aguado, Entremés del platillo; (?) Lope de Vega, El amante agradecido 1603: Lope de Vega, El arenal de Sevilla; Hernando Franco, Los reyes magos (SCCD) 1603–26 (?): Andrés de Claramonte, El mayor rey de los reyes 1604: Hernando Franco, La boda de la gata-tumba (SCCD) 1606: Martín de la Rumia, Las naciones de Guinea (SCCD) 1607: Lope de Vega, El sancto negro Rosambuco de la ciudad de Palermo; Juan de Madrid, Los negros de Guinea (SCCD) 1609: Anonymous, Los negros de Santo Tomé; Lope de Vega, La octava maravilla; Hernando de Rivera, El rey Bamba (SCCD); Miguel Jerónimo Punzón, La boda del rey de Guinea (SCCD); Martín de la Rumia, Los trajes y naciones (SCCD) 1609–15: Lope de Vega La vitoria de la honra	1600: William Boyle, Jugurth, King of Numidia (lost) L.; Thomas Dekker, Lust's Dominion 1601: Henry Chettle and Thomas Dekker, Sebastian King of Portugal (lost) L. 1604: William Shakespeare, Othello; Elizabeth Cary, Mariam the Fair Queen of Jewry 1605: Ben Jonson, Masque of Blackness; John Marston, The Wonder of Women; Anonymous, The Famous History of the Life and Death of Captain Thomas Stukeley (pub.) 1606: Anonymous, Solomon and the Queen of Sheba (lost) L. 1607: William Shakespeare, Antony and Cleopatra; Anonymous, Aeneas and Dido (lost) L.; Thomas Campion, Discription of a Maske in Honour of the Lord Hayes	1600: Anonymous, Ballet du roy des Maures Nègres; Anonymous, Pour des masques assez hideux et sauvages 1601: Alexandre Hardy, Les chastes et loyales amours de Théagène et Chariclée 1606: Anonymous, Ballet d'Andromède exposée au monstre marin (lost) 1608: Nicolas Chrétien des Croix Les Portugaiz infortunez 1609: Octave-César Genetay, L'Ethiopique, ou les chastes amours de Théagène et de Chariclée; Anonymous, Boutade des Maures esclaves d'amour delivrés par Bacchus

(Continued)

Year	Spain	England	France
1610s	1610–15: Lope de Vega, La madre de la mejor	1610: Thomas Heywood, The Fair Maid of the West, Part 1 (pub. 1631); Francis Beaumont and John Fletcher, Four Plays or Moral Representations	1610: Anonymous, Ballet de Monseigneur le duc de Vandosme
	1610–18: Lope de Vega, Servir a señor discreto	1611: William Shakespeare, The Tempest L.	1613: Anonymous, Tragédie francoise d'un More cruel envers son seigneur
	1612–18: Lope de Vega, El príncipe perfecto, primera parte	1612: John Webster, The White Devil	1616: Anonymous, Ballet des petits Maures (lost)
	1613: Cristobal Suárez, El convite del rey Baltazar (SA)	1613: Thomas Middleton, The Triumphs of Truth LMP	1617: René Bordier, Ballet de la délivrance de Renaud
	1613–15: Lope de Vega, Nacimiento de Cristo	1614: Thomas Campion, Somerset Masque	1618: Jean Boissin de Gaillardon, La Perséne, ou la délivrance d'Andromède
	1613–16: Lope de Vega, El capellán de la Virgen	1615 (ca.): John Fletcher, Monsieur Thomas; George Ruggle, Ignoramus	
	1613–18: Lope de Vega, El Antecristo	1616: Anthony Munday, Chrysanaleia LMP	
	1613–20: Lope de Vega, Los peligros de la ausencia	1617: John Webster, The Devil's Law Case	
	1614: Hernando de Rivera, La batalla de Guinea (SCCD)	1618: John Fletcher, Nathan Field, and Philip Massinger, The Knight of Malta	
	1615: Francisco Hernández, El rey Baltasar (SCCD); (C.) Cervantes, Entremés de los mirones	1619: William Rowley, All's Lost by Lust (pub. 1633)	
	1617: Hernando Mallén, El sarao de las naciones (SCCD)		
	1619: Francisco Hernández, Negros y indios (SCCD)		

(Continued)

Year	Spain	England	France
1620s	**1620:** Hernando de Rivera, *Los reyes de Etiopía* (SCCD)	**1622:** Anonymous, *The Black Lady* (lost) L.	**1620:** Anonymous, *Ballet de l'amour de ce temps*; Anonymous, *Comédie admirable intitulée la merveille* (C.)
	1621: Francisco Hernández, *Los negros* (SCCD)	**1623:** Philip Massinger, *The Bondman*	**1622:** Anonymous, *Ballet de Monsieur le Prince*
	1623: Lope de Vega, *La limpieza no manchada*; Francisco Hernández, *Los negros* (SCCD)	**1624:** Philip Massinger, *The Parliament of Love*	**1623:** Anonymous, *Ballet des Maures*
	1620–25 (?): Andrés de Claramonte, *El valiente negro en Flandes* (pub. 1638); Diego Jiménez de Enciso, *La comedia famosa de Juan Latino* (pub. 1652)	**1627:** Thomas Newman, *The Eunuch* L.	**1625:** Anonymous, *Ballet de la magnifique duchesse de Dendaye*
	1624–25: Lope de Vega, *El premio de bien hablar y volver por las mujeres*	**1629:** Thomas Dekker, *The White Moor* (lost) L.	**1626:** Anonymous, *Ballet des Maures adorant le soleil* (lost); Claude de l'Estoile, *Ballet du naufrage heureux*; René Bordier, *Grand bal de la douairière de Billebahaut*
	1624–35: Lope de Vega, *Amar, servir, y esperar*		**1627:** Anonymous, *Ballet de la tour de Babel*; Anonymous, *Entrée magnifique de Bacchus et de Madame Dimanche Grasse sa femme*; Anonymous, *Ballet de Monsieur le prince*; Vincent Borée, *Achille victorieux*
	1625: Hernando Mallén, *El rey Bamba* (SCCD); (?) Luis Vélez de Guevara, *Virtudes vencen señales y negro rey bandolero* (pub. 1640)		**1628:** Anonymous, *Les Jeunes Maures amoureux*
	1626: Hernando Mallén, *El rey Bamba* (SCCD)		
	1627: Ambrosio de Aguilar, *La conquista de Guinea* (SCCD)		
	1628: Ambrosio de Aguilar, *El sarao del rey de Guinea* (SCCD); (?) Felipe Godínez Manrique, *Coloquio segundo de los pastores de Belén* (pub. 1655)		
	1629: Ambrosio de Aguilar, *La conquista de Guinea* (SCCD); Ambrosio de Aguilar, *La conquista de las Indias* (SCCD)		

(Continued)

Year	Spain	England	France
1630s	1630: Ambrosio de Aguilar, La conquista de las Indias (SCCD)	1631: John Fletcher, The Fair Maid of the West, Part II; Philip Massinger, Believe as You List	1631: Anonymous, Ballet de l'extravagant; Anonymous, Ballet de l'almanach ou les prédictions véritables
	1631: Antonio Mira de Amescua, El negro del mejor amo; Ambrosio de Aguilar, Los negros (SCCD)	1632: Richard Brome, The Novella	1632: Anonymous, Grand bal des effets de la Nature
	1634: Francisco Hernández, La conquista de negros e indios (SCCD)	1633: Walter Montague, The Shepherds' Paradise	1633: Anonymous, Ballet de la puissance d'Amour
	1635: Juan Pérez de Montalban, Teagenes y Clariquea; Tirso de Molina, El negro, entremés; Felipe Godínez Manrique, San Mateo en Etiopia (SCCD); Lope de Vega, La siega, auto sacramental (pub. 1644)	1634: Philip Massinger and John Fletcher, A Very Woman	1634: Veronneau, L'impuissance
	1636: Tirso de Molina, Escarmientos para el cuerdo	1636: Thomas Killigrew, Claracilla; Anonymous, Moore's Mask	1635: Colletet, Ballet de la marine
	1637: Juan Félix de Moncada, Los negros (SCCD)	1637: Richard Brome, The English Moor, or The Mock-Marriage; Lodowick Carlell, The Fool Would Be a Favorite, or The Discreet Lover (pub. 1657); William Berkeley, The Lost Lady	1637: Anonymous, Boutade du temps perdu
	1638: Hernando de Rivera	1639: William Hemming, The Fatal Contract	1638: Desfontaines (Nicolas Mary), Orphise, ou la beauté persécutée
	Los negros (SCCD); Juan Félix de Moncada, El rey Salomón y la reina de Saba (SCCD)		
	1639: Hernando de Rivera, El regocijo de las naciones a San Juan (SCCD)		

(Continued)

(Continued)

Year	Spain	England	France
1640s	**1640:** Ana de Medina, *El sarao de las naciones* (SCCD) **1641:** Rodrigo Pacheco, *El negro del serafín San Antonio* (lost); Hernando de Rivera, *El engaño de Guinea* (SCCD) **1643:** Luis Vélez de Guevara, *El negro del serafín* **1644:** Ana de Medina, *El engaño de Guinea* (SCCD); Antonio de Rueda, *El arca de Noe* (L.) **1645:** (pub.) Luis Quiñones de Benavente, *Las dueñas*; (pub.) Luis Quiñones de Benavente, *Entremés del borracho*; Ana de Medina, *El casamiento del rey Bamba* (SCCD); Ana de Medina, *Los negros* (SCCD) **1646–56 (?):** Pedro Calderón de la Barca, *Las carnestolendas, entremés* (pub. 1661)	**1640:** (pub.) John Gough, *The Strange Discovery*; Samuel Harding, *Sicily and Naples* (pub.)	**1640:** Anonymous, *Mascarade du poinct du jour* (C.); Anonymous, *Ballet du bureau d'adresse* **1643:** M. de la Serre, *Ballet dansé en l'honneur du roi sur le sujet de ses triomphes* **1644:** Desfontaines (Nicolas Mary), *Alcidiane ou les quatre rivaux* **1647:** Anonymous, *Ballet des rues de Paris* **1649:** Jacques Bramereau, *Les divers entretiens de la fontaine de Vaucluse*

(Continued)

Year	Spain	England	France
1650s	**1651:** (pub.) Jerónimo de Cáncer y Velasco, *Jácara "Cantó de plano el mulato"* **1653:** (pub.) Jerónimo de Cáncer y Velasco, *Entremés del Portugues* **1654:** Ana de Medina, *Las fuerzas de Rengo* (SCCD) **1656:** Ana de Medina, *La fuerza de Rengo* (SCCD); Anonymous, *El mulato de Huescar* (SCCD) **1657:** Isidro de Herrera y Aguilar, *El engaño de Guinea* (SCCD) **1658:** Agustín Moreto, *Las fiestas del palacio*; Juan de Matos Fragoso, *El yerro del entendido: comedia famosa*; Manuel Coelho Rebelo, *O negro mais bem mandado*; Manuel Coelho Rebelo, *Los dos alcaldes y engaño a una negra, entremés*; Antonio de Solís y Ribadeneyra, *Entremés del niño cavallero* **1659 (?):** Pedro Calderón de la Barca, *Entremés de la rabia*	**1650:** Anonymous, *The White Ethiopian* **1658:** William Davenant, *The History of Sir Francis Drake*; John Tatham, *London's Tryumph, Presented by Industry and Honour* LMP **1659:** John Tatham, *London's Tryumphs* LMP	**1650:** Colletet, *Ballet des nations*; Pierre Corneille, *Andromède* **1651:** Anonymous, *Mascarade de la foire de Saint-Germain* **1656:** Bensérade, *Ballet royal de Psyché*; Molière, Beauchamps, et al., *Ballet dansé à Essaune pour le divertissement de la Reine de Suède* **1657:** Duc de Guise, *La mascarade des plaisirs troublés* **1658:** Bensérade, *Ballet d'Alcidiane et Polexandre*

(Continued)

(Continued)

Year	Spain	England	France
1660s	**1663:** Vicente Suárez de Deza y Ávila, *Mojiganga del Nuevo Mundo*; Vicente Suárez de Deza y Ávila, *El galeote mulato, baile*; Francisco de Avellaneda, *Los negros, baile entremésado*; Sebastián de Villaviciosa, *Baile de los sones*; Luis Quiñones de Benavente, *Entremés de los sacristanes burlados* **1664:** (pub.) Pedro Calderón de la Barca, *Los hijos de la fortuna: Teágenes y Clariquea*; Francisco de la Torre y Sevil and José de Bolea, *La azucena de Etiopía* (pub. 1676) **1668:** (pub.) Agustín Moreto, or Pedro Guerrero, *La negra por el honor*	**1661:** Richard Carpenter, *The Pragmatical Jesuit New Leavened*; Richard Flecknoe, *Erminia, or The Fair and Virtuous Lady*; John Tatham, *Londons Tryumphs LMP* **1662:** W.M.A., *The Marriage Broker, or The Pander*; Robert Codrington, *Ignoramus*; Ferdinando Parkhurst, *Ignoramus* **1663:** William Davenant, *The Playhouse to Be Let* **1664:** Edward Howard, *The Usurper* **1667:** William Davenant and John Dryden, *The Enchanted Island* **1668:** John Dryden, *An Evening's Love, or The Mock-Astrologer*; Thomas St. Serfe, *Tarugo's Wiles, or The Coffee House* **1669:** Thomas Killigrew, *The Imperial Tragedy*	**1661:** Anonymous, *Ballet royal de l'impatience* **1662:** Gabriel Gilbert, *Théagène* (lost); Boursault, *Le mort vivant*; Vallée, *Le fidelle esclave* **1662–64 (?):** Jean Racine, *Théagène et Chariclée* (lost) **1665:** Anonymous, *Ballet des proverbes* **1666:** Du Perche, *L'ambassadeur d'Affrique*; Bensérade, *Ballet royal des muses* **1667:** Molière, *Le Sicilien ou l'amour peintre*

(Continued)

Year	Spain	England	France
1670s	**1670:** (pub.) Pedro Francisco de Lanini y Sagredo, *El colegio de los gorrones* **1674:** (pub.) Juan Bautista Diamante, *El negro mas prodigioso*; (pub.) Gil López de Armesto y Castro, *El negro valiente y enamorador*; (pub.) Gil López de Armesto y Castro, *Entremés de los nadadores de Sevilla y de Triana*; Don Jerónimo de Cancer y Velasco, *El negro hablador, entremés*; Francisco Bernardo de Quirós, *Entremés del regidor* **1677:** Pedro Calderón de la Barca, *El arbol de mejor fruto, auto sacramental* **1672 (?):** Pedro Calderón de la Barca, *Mogiganga de la pandera* **1674 (?):** Don Jerónimo de Cancer y Velasco, *Entremés de las lenguas*	**1670:** Edward Howard, *The Women's Conquests* **1671:** Edward Howard, *The Six Days Adventure, or The New Utopia* **1672:** Anonymous, *Emilia*; Edward Ravenscroft, *The Citizen Turned Gentleman*; Thomas Jordan, *London Triumphant* LMP **1673:** Elkanah Settle, *The Empress of Morocco*; Thomas Jordan, *London in Its Splendor* LMP; William Wycherley, *The Gentleman Dancing-Master* **1674:** Elkanah Settle, *Love and Revenge*; Thomas Jordan, *The Goldsmiths' Jubile* LMP **1675:** John Crowne, *Calisto, or The Chaste Nymph*; Francis Fane, *Love in the Dark, or The Man of Bus'ness* **1676:** Aphra Behn, *Abdelazer, or The Moor's Revenge* **1677:** Edward Ravenscroft, *The English Lawyer* **1678:** Thomas Jordan, *The Triumphs of London* LMP	**1672:** Jean Racine, *Bajazet* **1673:** Molière, *Le malade imaginaire* **1675:** Thomas Corneille, *L'inconnu*

(Continued)

Year	Spain	England	France
1680s	**1680:** (pub.) Anonymous, *Entremés del sacristán hechicero*	**1679:** Edward Ravenscroft, *Titus Andronicus*; Edward Ecclestone, *Noah's Flood, or The Destruction of the World*; Thomas Jordan, *London in Luster* LMP	**1682:** Belisle, *Le mariage de la reine du Monomotapa*
	1681: Pedro Calderón de la Barca, *La sibila del Oriente y gran reyna de Saba*	**1680:** William Whitaker, *The Conspiracy*; Thomas Jordan, *London's Glory* LMP	**1687:** M. de La Poujade de Laroque-Lacusson, *Alphonce ou le triomphe de la foi*
		1681: Thomas Jordan, *London's Joy* LMP	**1688:** Anonymous, *Harlequin Grand Visir*
		1682: Elkanah Settle, *The Heir of Morocco, with the Death of Gayland*	
		1683: Thomas Otway, *The Atheist, or The Second Part of the Soldier's Fortune*	
		1686: Matthew Taubman, *London's Yearly Jubilee* LMP	
		1687: Aphra Behn, *The Emperor of the Moon*; Matthew Taubman, *London's Triumph, or The Gold-smiths' Jubile* LMP	
		1689: Aphra Behn, *The Widow Ranter, or The History of Bacon in Virginia*; John Dryden, *Don Sebastian King of Portugal*	

(Continued)

(Continued)

Year	Spain	England	France
1690s	1691: (pub.) Anonymous, *Entremés de las naciones*	1691: Elkanah Settle, *The Triumphs of London* LMP	1695: Joseph-Francois Douché de Vancy, *L'Ethiopique*
	Undated seventeenth century plays (published in the eighteenth century or extant only as manuscripts)	1692: Elkanah Settle, *The Triumphs of London* LMP	1696: Anonymous, *La foire St. Germain*
	Anonymous, *Jácara El mulato de Andújar*	1694: Lawrence Echard, *Eunuchus*	1697: Anonymous, *Harlequin comédien aux Champs Elysées*
	Anonymous, *Bayle de Paracumbé, à lo portugués* (pub. 1708)	1695: Thomas Southerne, *Oroonoko*	
	Anonymous, *Entremés de la negra lectora* (pub. 1735)	1697: A Young Lady, *The Unnatural Mother*	
	Pedro Calderón de la Barca, *La casa de los linajes, entremés* (pub. 1742)		
	Marcelo de Ayala y Guzmán, *El negro de cuerpo blanco y esclavo de su honra* (pub. 1763)		

NOTES

INTRODUCTION

1. For a clear and thoughtful unpacking of the *querelle des Suppliantes*, see Sylvie Chalaye, *Race et théâtre: Un impensé politique* (Arles: Actes Sud, 2020), 97–102.

2. Chalaye, *Race et théâtre*, 31. I provide in endnotes the original version of Spanish and French source-texts that I translate into English in the body of each chapter because access to original phrasing matters. For the sake of brevity, however, I only do so exceptionally for modern secondary sources.

3. My endowing the racial matrix with agency is part of the metaphorical conceit (the matrix is not an agent—people invoke it to cultivate practices). By using the matrix metaphor to model the inner workings of the concept of race, I depart from philosopher Elsa Dorlin, who uses the phrase "matrice de la race" to refer to the crucial role played by white mothers in the imagined transmission and preservation of French racial character in the Caribbean colonies and in the health of the French body politic at large starting in the eighteenth century. Elsa Dorlin, *La matrice de la race: Généalogie sexuelle et coloniale de la Nation française* (Paris: Découverte, 2006).

4. Timothy Harrison, *Coming To: Consciousness and Natality in Early Modern England* (Chicago: University of Chicago Press, 2020), 15.

5. Guillaume Aubert, "The Blood of France: Race and Purity of Blood in the French Atlantic World," *William and Mary Quarterly* 61, no. 3 (2004): 443.

6. Jean E. Feerick, *Strangers in Blood: Relocating Race in the Renaissance* (Toronto: University of Toronto Press, 2010), 6.

7. Ivan Hannaford, *Race: The History of an Idea in the West* (Baltimore: Johns Hopkins University Press, 1996), 175.

8. The racialization of religion through blood imagined since the late Middle Ages as able to pass on religion from one generation to the next despite conversion has been extensively studied in works such as Gil Anidjar, *Blood: A Critique of Christianity* (New York: Columbia University Press, 2014); Frédéric Schaub and Silvia Sebastiani, "Between Genealogy and Physicality: A Historiographical Perspective on Race in the 'Ancien Régime,'" *Graduate Faculty Philosophy Journal* 35, nos. 1–2 (2014): 23–51; and David Nirenberg, "Race and the Middle Ages," in *Rereading the Black Legend: The Discourses of Religious and Racial Difference in the Renaissance Empires*, ed. Margaret R. Greer, Walter D. Mignolo, and Maureen Quilligan (Chicago: University of Chicago Press, 2007), 71–87.

9. My use of the word paradigm is quite distinct from its uses in the history of science, where forward motion relies on termination in a continuous sequence of paradigm shifts. See

primarily Thomas Kuhn, *The Structure of Scientific Revolutions*, 2nd ed., enlarged (Chicago: University of Chicago Press, 1970).

10. Geraldine Heng, "The Invention of Race in the European Middle Ages: Race Studies, Modernity, and the Middle Ages," *Literature Compass* 8, no. 5 (2011): 324.

11. Stuart Hall, "Subjects in History: Making Diasporic Identities," in *The House That Race Built: Black Americans, U.S. Terrain*, ed. Wahneema Lubiano (New York: Pantheon Books, 1997), 290.

12. Etienne Balibar and Immanuel Maurice Wallerstein, *Race, Nation, Class: Ambiguous Identities* (New York: Verso, 1991), 33.

13. Ian Smith, *Race and Rhetoric in the Renaissance: Barbarian Errors* (New York: Palgrave Macmillan, 2009), 12.

14. Historians of ideas have often described concepts in disembodied technological terms. For instance, Peter De Bolla thinks of concepts as networked—"concepts are like subway or tube maps projected into multiple dimensions, consequently their geometry is complex"—and created though "ports and wirings." Peter De Bolla, *The Architecture of Concepts: The Historical Formation of Human Rights* (New York: Fordham University Press, 2013), 4. Lorraine Daston and Peter Galison turn to older technologies to describe the concept of objectivity: "If it is a pure concept, it is less like a bronze sculpture cast from a single mold than like some improvised contraption soldered together out of mismatched parts of bicycles, alarm clocks, and steam pipes." Lorrraine Daston and Peter Galison, *Objectivity* (New York: Zone Books, 2007), 51. My use of the organic matrix metaphor aligns, rather, with the organic imagery that Timothy Harrison uses to describe the emergence of the concept of consciousness in the mid-seventeenth century itself as a "birth" or a "hatching" in poetic accounts of natality. Harrison, *Coming To*, 4.

15. Ann Laura Stoler, "Racial Histories and Their Regimes of Truth," in *Race Critical Theories, Text and Context*, ed. Philomena Essed and David Theo Goldberg (Malden, Mass.: Blackwell, 2002), 375–76.

16. I follow in the footsteps of Patricia Akhimie in seeking to put to rest the counterproductive competition between race and class in accounts of early modern systems of difference and Othering. Patricia Akhimie, *Shakespeare and the Cultivation of Difference: Race and Conduct in the Early Modern World* (New York: Routledge, 2018).

17. *The Matrix*, dir. Lana Wachowski and Lilly Wachowski (Burbank, Calif.: Warner Bros., 1999); *Matrix Reloaded* and *Matrix Revolutions* dir. Lana Wachowski and Lilly Wachowski (Burbank, Calif.: Warner Bros., 2003).

18. *The Matrix* has, for instance, been co-opted by alt-right communities on the dark web, such as the subreddit RedPill, for whom the journey of liberation featured in the Wachowskis' movies symbolizes a liberation from the oppression to which feminism, antiracism, and social justice efforts allegedly subject white men in twenty-first-century America. Brian O'Flynn, "How the Matrix Was Adopted by 4chan and the Alt-Right," *Dazed*, March 24, 2017, https://www.dazeddigital.com/artsandculture/article/35251/1/how-the-matrix-was-adopted-by-4chan-and-the-far-right.

19. Although her case was dismissed in 2005, the centrality of Blackness and racial history to *The Matrix* cannot but remind us of the lawsuit that Sophia Stewart, a Black woman writer, brought against the Wachowskis, accusing them of having plagiarized a short story she had sent for their consideration a few years earlier.

20. See, for instance, Kwame Anthony Appiah, "Race, Culture, and Identity," Tanner Lectures on Human Values delivered at University of California at San Diego, October 27 and 28, 1994, 61; Stuart Hall, *The Fateful Triangle: Race, Ethnicity, Nation*, ed. Kobena Mercer (Cam-

bridge, Mass.: Harvard University Press, 2017), 45–46; and Karen E. Fields and Barbara J. Fields, *Racecraft: The Soul of Inequality in American Life* (New York: Verso, 2012).

21. Michael Omi and Howard Winant, *Racial Formation in the U.S.: From the 1960s to the 1980s* (New York: Routledge and Kegan Paul, 1987), 61.

22. Geraldine Heng, *The Invention of Race in the European Middle Ages* (Cambridge: Cambridge University Press, 2018), 42.

23. Cord J. Whitaker, *Black Metaphors: How Modern Racism Emerged from Medieval Race-Thinking* (Philadelphia: University of Pennsylvania Press, 2019), 6.

24. Whitaker, *Black Metaphors*, 197.

25. On Blackness and performance in early modern Dutch theatre, especially the drama of Gerbrand Bredero, see Anston Bosman's "'Best Play with Mardian': Eunuch and Blackamoor as Imperial Culturegram," *Shakespeare Studies* 34 (2006): 123–57; Nigel Smith's "Slavery, Rape, Migration: The View from the Amsterdam Stage, 1615," *Shakespeare Studies* 48 (2020): 80–86; and Nigel Smith's "Migration and Drama: Amsterdam 1617," in *Transnational Connections in Early Modern Theatre*, ed. M. A. Katritzky and Pavel Drábek (Manchester: Manchester University Press, 2020), 89–113.

26. Robert Stam and Ella Shohat, *Race in Translation: Culture Wars Around the Postcolonial Atlantic* (New York: New York University Press, 2012), xiv.

27. "Negro: el Etiope de color negra." Sebastián de Covarrubias Orozco, *Tesoro de la lengua castellana o española* (Madrid: Luis Sanchez, 1611), 562r.

28. "Color la que no es del todo negra, como la de los moros, de donde tomó nombre, o de mora." Covarrubias Orozco, *Tesoro de la lengua*, 555v.

29. "Asi de la provincia de Mauritania." Covarrubias Orozco, *Tesoro de la lengua*, 556r.

30. "La tierra de los negros, o Etiopes en Africa a donde contratan los Portugueses." Covarrubias Orozco, *Tesoro de la lengua*, 457v.

31. I am aware of only one exception: Cañeri in Diego Jiménez de Enciso's *Comedia famosa de Juan Latino* (Madrid: en la Imprenta Real, a costa de Antonio Ribero, 1652). Cañeri is defined in the dramatis personae as a "moro negro" wearing animal skins. He is the phantasmatic embodiment of Moorishness who tempts the white-passing morisco Don Fernando de Valor into rebelling against the king's authority during the Rebellion of the Alpujarras (1568–71) in response to the measures taken by the crown to enforce cultural genocide. Cañeri's phantasmatic nature might explain his merger of the *moro* and *negro* categories that usually remain separate.

32. William D. Phillips, *Slavery in Medieval and Early Modern Iberia* (Philadelphia: University of Pennsylvania Press, 2014); A.C. de C M. Saunders, *A Social History of Black Slaves and Freedmen in Portugal, 1441–1555* (New York: Cambridge University Press, 1982); Jerome Branche, *Colonialism and Race in Luso-Hispanic Literature* (Columbia: University of Missouri Press, 2006); Manuel F. Fernández Chaves and Rafael M. Pérez García, "Las redes de la trata negrera: Mercaderes portugueses y tráfico de esclavos en Sevilla (c. 1560–1580)," in *La esclavitud negroafricana en la historia de España: Siglos XVI y XVII*, ed. Aurelia Martín Casares and Margarita García Barranco (Granada: Comares, 2010), 5–34.

33. Qtd. in Emily Weissbourd, "Transnational Genealogies: Jews, Blacks and Moors in Early Modern English and Spanish Literature, 1547–1642" (Ph.D. diss., University of Pennsylvania, 2011), 142.

34. Manuel Lucena Salmoral, "Leyes para esclavos: El ordenamiento jurídico sobre la condición, tratamiento, defensa y represión de los esclavos en las colonias de la América española," in *Tres grandes cuestiones de la historia de Iberoamérica: Ensayos y monografías*, ed. José Andrés-Gallego (Madrid: Fundación MAPFRE Tavera, 2005), 662. Note that France would fol-

low Spain's lead at the end of the seventeenth century, as the first article of the *Code Noir*, meant to define the conditions of slavery in 1685, serves to expel Jews from the French Caribbean.

35. Antonio de Almeida Mendes, "The Foundations of the System: A Reassessment of the Slave Trade to the Spanish Americas in the Sixteenth and Seventeenth Centuries," in *Extending the Frontiers: Essays on the New Transatlantic Slave Trade Database*, ed. David Eltis and David Richardson (New Haven, Conn.: Yale University Press, 2008), 71.

36. Gustav Ungerer, "The Presence of Africans in Elizabethan England and the Performance of *Titus Andronicus* at Burley-on-the-Hill, 1595/96," *Medieval and Renaissance Drama in England* 21 (2008): 20.

37. Imtiaz Habib, *Black Lives in the English Archives, 1500–1677: Imprints of the Invisible* (Burlington, Vt.: Ashgate, 2008), 76.

38. Emily Weissbourd argues that those three warrants were less edicts of deportation than documents meant to "authorize the gift of blacks—as commodities—in reward for services rendered." Weissbourd, "'Those in Their Possession': Race, Slavery, and Queen Elizabeth's 'Edicts of Expulsion,'" *Huntington Library Quarterly* 78, no. 1 (2015): 2. For Weissbourd, those documents are "evidence both for the presence of enslaved blacks in England and for an emergent discourse in English culture that naturalized the enslavement of black Africans" (13).

39. For instance, John Minsheu defines *moro* as "a blacke Moor of Barbarie or a Neager that followeth the Turkish religion," and *negro* as "a blacke Moor of Aethiopia." John Minsheu, *A Dictionarie in Spanish and English, First Published into the English Tongue by Ric. Percivale Gentleman. Now Enlarged* (London: Edm. Bollifant, 1599), 172–75. Similarly, Randle Cotgrave translates the French *More* as "a Moor, Morian, Blackamore," the French *Moresse* as "a Mooress, a woman Moore, a black woman" and the French *Nègre* as "a Negro, a Moore." Randle Cotgrave, *A Dictionarie of the French and English Tongues* (London: Adam Islip, 1611), Nnn4v-Ppp2r.

40. George Peele's *The Battell of Alcazar Fought in Barbarie, Betweene Sebastian King of Portugall, and Abdelmelec King of Marocco. With the Death of Captaine Stukeley.* (London: By Edward Allde for Richard Bankworth, 1594), for instance, contrasts a black-skinned Muslim Moorish villain with white-skinned Muslim Moors. In the same vein, Robert Daborne's *A Christian Turn'd Turke: or The Tragicall Liues and Deaths of the Two Famous Pyrates, Ward and Dansiker* (London: Printed by Nicholas Okes for William Barrenger, 1612) and Philip Massinger's *The Renegado, a Tragaecomedie* (London: Printed by Augustine Mathewes for Iohn Waterson, 1630) famously stage white-skinned Muslim Moors.

41. For instance, César Oudin translates the Spanish "negro de la Guinea" as "un Nègre, ou More." César Oudin, *Tesoro de las dos lenguas francesa y española* (Paris: La Veuve Marc Orry, 1616), n.p. In 1636, Philibert Monet lumped all Africans into one group defined by its dark skin, regardless of geographic origin: "*Nègres*, all kinds of *Mores* and Ethiopians wherever they come from [Nègres, toutes sortes de Maures et Ethiopiens, de quel terroir que ce soit]: Ethiopians, *Nègres*, people with black skin, races with dark skin [hic Aethiopes, um. hi Nigri, orum. Nigra cute populi. Pullo colore gentes]." Monet, *Invantaire des deus langues françoise et latine, assorti des plus utiles curiositez de l'un et de l'autre idiome* (Lyon: chez Claude Obert, 1636), 589. Finally, in 1690, Antoine Furetière wrote that "*Mores* have a black face" (les Mores ont le visage noir). Furetière, *Dictionnaire universel contenant généralement tous les mots françois tant vieux que modernes, et les termes de toutes les sciences et des arts. Tome Second* (Den Haag & Rotterdam: Arnoud et Reinier Leers, 1690), *Y4r.

42. Simone Delesalle and Lucette Valensi, "Le mot 'Nègre' dans les dictionnaires français d'Ancien Régime: Histoire et lexicographie," *Langue française* 15 (1972): 84.

43. On the cultural conditioning explaining such historiographic lacunae, see Noémie Ndiaye, "Rewriting the *Grand Siècle*: Blackface in Early Modern France and the Historiography of Race," *Literature Compass* 18.10 (2021). e12603. 1–11. https://doi.org/10.1111/lic3.12603

44. Nicolas Médevielle notes that Africa did not inspire the same craze for travel writing in France that Brazil would a few decades later. Nonetheless, we do have a text written by the captain-trader-pirate Jean Alfonse de Saintonge (most likely born a Portuguese) documenting his travels around the world, including "Africa, Aethiopia, and Guinea" in *Les voyages auantureux du capitaine Ian Alfonce, Sainctongeois*. Médevielle reads this text in conversation with the Norman Vallard Atlas (1547), the illustrations of which depict Africans from the region of Guinea with a striking degree of realism. Médevielle underlines the fact that most of the documentation used to create the Vallard Atlas was Iberian, and he calls those documents "Luso-French." Nicolas P.A. Médevielle, "La Racialisation des Africains: Récits commerciaux, religieux philosophiques et littéraires 1480–1880" (Ph.D. diss., Ohio State University, 2006), 27–28.

45. Allison Blakely, *Blacks in the Dutch World: The Evolution of Racial Imagery in a Modern Society* (Bloomington: Indiana University Press, 1993), xvi.

46. Susanne Zantop uses the term "colonial fantasies" to "highlight two important aspects of those colonialist stories: their purely imaginary wish-fulfilling nature, and their unconscious subtext, which links sexual desire of the other with desire for power and control." Susanne Zantop, *Colonial Fantasies: Conquest, Family, and Nation in Precolonial Germany, 1770–1870* (Durham, N.C.: Duke University Press, 1997), 3. Zantop also shows the importance of Las Casas's *Brevíssima relación de la destruyción de las Indias* in German colonial fantasy writings, and emphasizes the impact of Las Casas's temporary support for the enslavement of black Africans onto non-Iberian colonial fantasies (24).

47. "Est proprement celuy ou celle qui sont de la province de Mauritanie en Affrique, *Maurus, Maurusius*. L'Espagnol et l'Italien disent aussi Moro, sont de couleur basanée, ou olivastre, differents du Negro, qu'on appelle, et met on pour enseigne aux hostelleries More: Mais c'est abusivement, car le Negro, que nous pouvons appeler noir, est de couleur parfaitement noire, pour le commun camus, et relevé de babines et grosses lèvres, payen et gentil de creance, residant en l'interieur de l'Affrique et en la coste exterieure d'icelle. Là où le More est de couleur tanée, de façon de visage commune, de creance Mahumetiste. Pour raison de laquelle religion Alcorane, le mot de More s'est estendu hors de ses premieres limites, à tous ceux presques qui sont de mesme foy, des Turcs en hors, lesquels retiennent le nom de Turcs, quoy qu'ils soyent Alcoranistes." Jean Nicot, *Thrésor de la langue francoyse, tant ancienne que moderne* (Paris: chez David Douceur, 1606), 418.

48. Catherine Cole, "American Ghetto Parties and Ghanaian Concert Parties: A Transnational Perspective on Blackface," in *Burnt Cork: Traditions and Legacies of Blackface Minstrelsy*, ed. Stephen Johnson (Amherst: University of Massachusetts Press, 2012), 224.

49. Sharon Patricia Holland, who refuses to decenter Blackness, sketches the landscape of that debate within critical race studies in *The Erotic Life of Racism* (Durham, N.C.: Duke University Press, 2012), 28–29. The movement toward globality and away from American parochialism in critical race studies is perhaps best represented in Denise Ferreira da Silva, *Toward a Global Idea of Race* (Minneapolis: University of Minnesota Press, 2007) and in David Theo Goldberg and Philomena Essed's introduction to *Race Critical Theories* (Malden, Mass.: Blackwell, 2002). In the field of early modern race studies more specifically, that movement is palpable in Martin Orkin and Alexa Alice Joubin, *Race* (New York: Routledge, 2019), in the recent work of Ania Loomba, and in various global Renaissance projects that touch on the notion of race.

50. Engaging with the work of Eric Swyngedouw, Loren Kruger glosses the term *glocal* as "the intersection of local and global concerns in cities that function both as national or regional capitals and as destinations for transnational migration of people, markets, and culture." Loren Kruger, "Seeing Through Race: Athol Fugard, (East) Germany, and the Limits of Solidarity," *Modern Philology* 100, no. 4 (2003): 622.

51. Katherine McKittrick and Clyde Woods, *Black Geographies and the Politics of Place* (Toronto: Between the Lines, 2007), 5.

52. Stuart Hall, "The Spectacle of the 'Other,'" in *Representation: Cultural Representations and Signifying Practices*, ed. Stuart Hall (London: Sage, 1997), 232.

53. Fields and Fields, *Racecraft*, 203.

54. "Once racecraft takes over the imagination, it shrinks well-founded criticism of inequality to fit crabbed moral limits, leaving the social grievances of white Americans without a language in which to frame them. . . . In the shadow of racecraft, 'discrimination' shoves 'unfairness' out of the vocabulary available for public debate." Fields and Fields, *Racecraft*, 286–87.

55. Fields and Fields, *Racecraft*, 6, 198.

56. Devika Sharma and Frederik Tygstrup, eds., *Structures of Feeling: Affectivity and the Study of Culture* (Berlin: De Gruyter, 2015), 25.

57. Stuart Hall, "The Work of Representation," in *Representation*, 7. In "Spectacle of the Other," Hall takes the sixteenth century to be the first of three "major moments when the 'West' encountered black people, giving rise to an avalanche of popular representations based on the marking of racial difference" (239). Yet his own analyses start only with readily available visual materials from the second "major moment," the colonization of Africa in the nineteenth century. This book provides a new archive of materials that can open the early modern period for media studies informed by Hall's approach.

58. Jonathan Xavier Inda, "Performativity, Materiality, and the Racial Body," *Latino Studies Journal* 11, no. 3 (2000): 88.

59. This approach draws on Dympna Callaghan's insight that early modern racial impersonation, taking place at a time when there was no dearth of potential Afro-European performers, was always informed by the necessity "to produce racial difference and to control it nevertheless." Dympna Callaghan, *Shakespeare Without Women: Representing Gender and Race on the Renaissance Stage* (New York: Routledge, 2000), 92.

60. Inda, "Performativity, Materiality, and the Racial Body," 89.

61. Judith Butler, *Gender Trouble: Feminism and the Subversion of Identity*, repr. (New York: Routledge, 2007), 192.

62. For Judith Butler, gender is an act "open to splittings, self-parody, self-criticism, and those hyperbolic exhibitions of 'the natural' that, in their very exaggeration, reveals its fundamentally phantasmatic status," and therein lies our chance to exercise political "agency" vis-à-vis oppressive fictions of gender. Judith Butler, *Gender Trouble*, 200–201. Similarly, for E. Patrick Johnson, although "performance may not fully account for the ontology of race," racial performance, "the process of doing blackness," allows "maladroit and skilled cultural workers to press blackness into service," thereby demonstrating "the fallibility of the question of authenticity," and providing "a space for meaningful resistance to oppressive systems" in a white supremacist culture. E. Patrick Johnson, *Appropriating Blackness: Performance and the Politics of Authenticity* (Durham, N.C.: Duke University Press, 2003), 8–16.

63. Diana Taylor, *The Archive and the Repertoire: Performing Cultural Memory in the Americas* (Durham, N.C.: Duke University Press, 2003), 19.

64. Taylor, *Archive and the Repertoire*, 19.

65. In that sense, I heed Robin Bernstein's invitation to "call into question the very model of archive and repertoire as distinct-but-interactive." Robin Bernstein, "Dances with Things: Material Culture and the Performance of Race," *Social Text* 27, no. 4 (2009): 89.

66. Ayanna Thompson, *Performing Race and Torture on the Early Modern Stage* (New York: Routledge, 2008), 19.

67. That tradition aligns with Diana Taylor's own conceptualization of the repertoire as a site of resistance to the cultural erasure of subalterns: "If performance did not transmit knowledge, only the literate and powerful could claim social memory and identity." Diana Taylor, *Archive and Repertoire*, xvii. The finest scholarship representing that tradition in early modern studies includes Jean E. Howard's idea that "in such a complex institutional setting [as commercial theatre], the ideological import of a dramatic fable and the ideological implications of the material conditions in which it was produced and consumed could conflict, interpellating subjects in contradictory ways that open space for change," and Gina Bloom's thesis that, given the vulnerability of English boy actors' cracking voices, "when performed plays underscore the ephemerality of the voice, they put pressure on one of the foundational ways gender difference [and hierarchy] was established in early modern England." Jean E. Howard, *The Stage and Social Struggle in Early Modern England* (London: Routledge, 1994), 13; Gina Bloom, *Voice in Motion: Staging Gender, Shaping Sound in Early Modern England* (Philadelphia: University of Pennsylvania Press, 2007), 8.

68. Michel Foucault, *The Archaeology of Knowledge*, translated by A. M. Sheridan Smith (New York: Routledge, 2002), 160–62.

69. Judith Butler, *Excitable Speech: A Politics of the Performative* (New York: Routledge, 1997), 15, 25.

70. Susan Bennett, *Theatre Audiences: A Theory of Production and Reception*, 2nd ed. (New York: Routledge, 1997), 156.

71. Jacques Rancière, *The Emancipated Spectator* (London: Verso, 2009), 13.

72. Howard, *Stage and Social Struggle*, 7.

73. Eric Lott, *Love and Theft: Blackface Minstrelsy and the American Working Class* (New York: Oxford University Press, 1993), 41, 4. I side with Saidiya Hartman: "While much is to be admired in Lott's deft and comprehensive examination, I take issue with his claim about cross-racial solidarity and the subversive effects of minstrelsy." Saidiya V. Hartman, *Scenes of Subjection: Terror, Slavery, and Self-Making in Nineteenth-Century America* (New York: Oxford University Press, 1997), 212.

74. See Anthony Gerard Barthelemy, *Black Face, Maligned Race: The Representation of Blacks in English Drama from Shakespeare to Southerne* (Baton Rouge: Louisiana State University Press, 1987); Eliot Tokson, *The Popular Image of the Black Man in English Drama 1550–1688* (Boston: G. K. Hall, 1982); Arthur L. Little, Jr., *Shakespeare Jungle Fever: National-Imperial Re-Visions of Race, Rape and Sacrifice* (Stanford, Calif.: Stanford University Press, 2000); Matthieu Chapman, *Anti-Black Racism in Early Modern English Drama: The Other "Other"* (New York: Routledge, 2017); Patricia Akhimie, *Shakespeare and the Cultivation of Difference: Race and Conduct in the Early Modern World* (New York: Routledge, 2018). Virginia Mason Vaughan's *Performing Blackness on English Stages, 1500–1800* (New York: Cambridge University Press, 2005) combines a traditional typological approach with a groundbreaking focus on the materiality of black-up in early modern England, and I see the present book as operating in direct conversation with Vaughan's, and with Ian Smith's forthcoming monograph on early modern textile black-up in early modern England, of which we get a glimpse in Smith, "The Textile Black Body: Race and 'Shadowed Livery' in *The Merchant of Venice*," in *The Oxford Handbook of Shakespeare and Em-*

bodiment: Gender, Sexuality, and Race, ed. Valerie Traub (Oxford: Oxford University Press, 2016), 170–85.

75. Eve Kosofsky Sedgwick, *Touching Feeling: Affect, Pedagogy, Performativity* (Durham, N.C.: Duke University Press, 2003), 140.

76. Sedgwick, *Touching Feeling*, 128.

77. Noémie Ndiaye, "Off the Record: Contrapuntal Theatre History," in *Companion to Theatre and Performance Historiography*, ed. Tracy C. Davis and Peter W. Marx (New York: Routledge, 2021), 229–48.

78. The verb "to record" meant "to sing," primarily for birds, and by extension, for humans (*OED*). Cotgrave translates the French verb *rossignoler* as "to record, or sing, like a Nightingale," and *regazouiller* as "to report, or to record, as birds, one another's warbling." Cotgrave *Dictionarie*, Hhhh3v, Eeee3v. When extended to humans, "recording" referred, specifically, to a singing technique particularly popular in the baroque age: John Fletcher contrasts "recording" with "maine singing" in *Monsieur Thomas, a Comedy* (London: Printed by Thomas Harper for John Waterson, 1639), G4v. And in Cotgrave's already mentioned *Dictionarie*, "to record in singing; to answer in the same note, or tune" is the phrase that serves to define the French verb *contrechanter*—to sing in counterpoint (Y2r).

79. The poles of the critical conversation around historiographic ethics are best illustrated by the work of Marisa J. Fuentes, for whom good historical scholarship is "a gesture toward redress," and the work of Stephen Best, who, by contrast, explores what he sees as the limits of the "impulse to redeem the past" offered by the recent "melancholic turn" in Black studies. Marisa J. Fuentes, *Dispossessed Lives: Enslaved Women, Violence, and the Archive* (Philadelphia: University of Pennsylvania Press, 2016), 12; Stephen Michael Best, *None Like Us: Blackness, Belonging, Aesthetic Life* (Durham, N.C.: Duke University Press, 2018), 65.

80. Saidiya Hartman, "Venus in Two Acts," *Small Axe: A Caribbean Journal of Criticism* 26 (2008): 11.

81. C. Riley Snorton, *Black on Both Sides: A Racial History of Trans Identity* (Minneapolis: University of Minnesota Press, 2017), 187.

82. Barbara Fuchs, "No Field Is an Island: Postcolonial and Transnational Approaches to Early Modern Drama," *Renaissance Drama* 40, no. 1 (2012): 125–33.

83. Sharon Marcus, "The Theatre of Comparative Literature," in *A Companion to Comparative Literature*, ed. Ali Behdad and Dominic Thomas (Chichester, West Sussex: Wiley-Blackwell, 2011), 137–38.

84. Louise Clubb defines "theatregrams" as "streamlined structures for svelte playmaking, and elements of high specific density, weighty with significance from previous incarnations." There are "theatregrams of persons" (stock characters), "theatregrams of association" (specific pairings of characters), "theatregrams of motion (actions and reactions with apposite speech, kinds of encounter, use of props, and parts of the set for hiding, meeting, attack, defense, seduction, deceit, and so forth), all of which produce variations of plot and character united in theatregrams of design, patterns of meaning expressed by a disposition of material reciprocally organizing the whole comedy and the spectator's perception of its form." Clubb, "Theatregrams." In *Comparative Critical Approaches to Renaissance Comedy*, ed. Donald Beecher and Massimo Ciavolella (Ottawa, Canada: Dovehouse Editions, 1986), 18, 20–21.

85. Baltasar Fra-Molinero, *La imagen de los negros en el teatro del Siglo de Oro* (Madrid: siglo veintiuno de españa editores, 1995); John Beusterien, *An Eye on Race: Perspectives from Theater in Imperial Spain* (Lewisburg: Bucknell University Press, 2006); Emily Weissbourd, "Transnational Genealogies: Jews, Blacks and Moors in Early Modern English and Spanish Literature, 1547–1642"

(Ph.D. diss., University of Pennsylvania, 2011); Nicholas R. Jones, *Staging Habla de Negros: Radical Performances of the African Diaspora in Early Modern Spain* (University Park: Pennsylvania State University Press, 2019); Aurelia Martín-Casares and Marga García Barranco, "The Musical Legacy of Black Africans in Spain: A Review of Our Sources," *Anthropological Notebooks* 15, no. 2 (2009): 51–60; Aurelia Martín-Casares and Marga G. Barranco, "Popular Literary Depictions of Black African Weddings in Early Modern Spain," *Renaissance and Reformation / Renaissance et Réforme* 31, no. 2 (2008): 107–21; Erin Rowe, *Black Saints in Early Modern Global Catholicism* (Cambridge: Cambridge University Press, 2019); Larissa Brewer-García, *Beyond Babel: Translations of Blackness in Colonial Peru and New Granada* (Cambridge: Cambridge University Press, 2020); Carmen Fracchia, *"Black but Human": Slavery and Visual Arts in Hapsburg Spain, 1480–1700* (Oxford: Oxford University Press, 2019).

86. Studies of eighteenth-century representations of Afro-diasporic people include Madeleine Dobie, *Trading Places: Colonization and Slavery in Eighteenth-Century French Culture* (Ithaca, N.Y.: Cornell University Press, 2010); Doris Garraway, *The Libertine Colony: Creolization in the Early French Caribbean* (Durham, N.C.: Duke University Press, 2005); Youmna Charara, ed., *Fictions coloniales du XVIIIe siècle* (Paris: L'Harmattan, 2005); Doris Y. Kadish, *Fathers, Daughters, and Slaves: Women Writers and French Colonial Slavery* (Liverpool: Liverpool University Press, 2012); and Julia Prest, "Pale Imitations: White Performances of Slave Dance in the Public Theatres of Pre-Revolutionary Saint-Domingue," *Atlantic Studies* 16, no. 4 (2019): 502–20.

87. Christian Biet, ed., *Théâtre de la cruauté et récits sanglants en France (XVIe–XVIIe siècle)* (Paris: Editions Robert Laffont, 2006); Sylvie Chalaye, *Du Noir au Nègre: L'image du Noir au théâtre, de Marguerite de Navarre à Jean Genet (1550–1960)* (Paris: L'Harmattan, 1998); Toby Wikström, "Law, Conquest and Slavery on the French Stage, 1598–1685" (Ph.D. diss., Columbia University, 2010).

88. Garraway, *Libertine Colony*, 3.

89. "Je décide d'être noire. Non pas de la manière dont l'histoire m'a définie et façonnée sur la base de mon corps. Je suis noire de la manière dont les corps qui ressemblent au mien ont réagi, combattu, contesté, résisté, et se sont soustraits à ces tentatives anciennes, répétées et organisées d'inféririsation. Dans ces résistance et affirmations de leur humanité, ces corps et esprits construits comme noirs ont offert au monde une multitude de trésors. Je me définis comme noire comme je le décide, précisément au vu de l'histoire. Il s'agit d'un choix. Par mon entrée consciente dans une communauté transnationale délimitée par les arts et les lettres, la spiritualité et si fermement ancrée dans les traditions intellectuelles que j'ai évoquées tout au long de cet ouvrage, je pose un acte de solidarité politique." Maboula Soumahoro, *Le triangle et l'hexagone: Réflexions sur une identité noire* (Paris: La Découverte, 2020), 146. Translation and capitalization my own.

90. Kim F. Hall, *Things of Darkness: Economics of Race and Gender in Early Modern England* (Ithaca, N.Y.: Cornell University Press, 1996), 8.

91. Stam and Shohat, *Race in Translation*, 58. For those foreign terms, I follow the rules of capitalization specific to each language: French capitalizes substantives expressing race, ethnicity, and nationality, while Spanish does not (unless said substantive opens a sentence or is deliberately capitalized by a Spanish author I cite).

92. All Shakespearean plays cited in this book are drawn from *The Norton Shakespeare*, Third Edition, edited by Stephen Greenblatt (general editor), Walter Cohen, Suzanne Gossett, Jean E. Howard, Katharine Eisaman Maus, and Gordon McMullan (New York: W. W. Norton, 2016).

93. Nicolas Chrétien des Croix, *Les Portugaiz infortunez: Tragédie*, in *Les tragédies de N. Chrétien Sieur des Croix, Argentenois* (Rouen: Théodore Reinsart, 1608), 1–126; *Tragédie francoize d'un More cruel envers son seigneur nommé Riviery, gentil homme espagnol, sa damoiselle et ses enfans* (Rouen: Abraham Cousturier, 1613); *Comédie admirable intitulée la merveille, où l'on voit comme un capitaine françois, esclave du Soldam d'Egypte, transporté de son bon sens, ce donne au Diable pour s'affranchir de servitude, lequel il trompe mesme subtillement tant qu'il fut contrainct luy rendre son obligation* (Rouen: Abraham Cousturier, ca. 1620).

94. Diego Sánchez de Badajoz, *Farsa teologal*, in *Recopilación en metro del bachiller Diego Sánchez de Badajoz, reimpresa del ejemplar único por el excmo señor D. V. Barrantes, Tomo I* (Madrid: Biblioteca de los bibliófilos—Fernando Fé, 1882), 85–136; *Farsa de la fortuna ó hado*, in *Recopilación en metro del bachiller Diego Sánchez de Badajoz, reimpresa del ejemplar único por el excmo señor D. V. Barrantes, Tomo II* (Madrid: Biblioteca de los bibliófilos—Fernando Fé, 1886), 77–87; *Farsa de la ventera*, in *Recopilación en metro del bachiller Diego Sánchez de Badajoz, reimpresa del ejemplar único por el excmo señor D. V. Barrantes, Tomo II* (Madrid: Biblioteca de los bibliófilos—Fernando Fé, 1886), 239–51; *Farsa del moysen*, in *Recopilación en metro del bachiller Diego Sánchez de Badajoz, reimpresa del ejemplar único por el excmo señor D. V. Barrantes, Tomo II* (Madrid: Biblioteca de los bibliófilos—Fernando Fé, 1886, 117–28; Diego Jiménez de Enciso, *Comedia famosa de Juan Latino* (Madrid: en la Imprenta Real, a costa de Antonio Ribero, 1652); Andrés de Claramonte y Corroy, *El valiente negro en Flandés* (Barcelona: en la Emprenta de Iayme Romeu, a costa de Iuan Sapera, 1638); Félix Lope de Vega Carpio, *El negro del mejor amo*, ed. José Fredejas Lebrero (Madrid: Universidad de Educación a Distancia, 1984), written 1599–1608; *El sancto negro Rosambuco de la ciudad de Palermo* (Barcelona: en casa de Sebastian de Cormellas... Vendese en Zaragoza: en casa de Iayme Gotar, 1612), written before 1607. Unless otherwise specified, in dating Lope de Vega's plays, I follow Sylvanus Griswold Morley and Courtney Bruerton, *The Chronology of Lope de Vega's Comedias: With a Discussion of Doubtful Attribution, the Whole Based on a Study of His Strophic Versification* (New York: Modern Language Association of America, 1940).

95. John Webster, *The White Devil*, ed. John Russell Brown (Cambridge, Mass.: Harvard University Press, 1960); John Dryden and William Davenant, *The Tempest, or The Enchanted Island, A Comedy* (London: Printed by J.M. for Henry Herringman, 1670).

96. Félix Lope de Vega Carpio, *El premio de bien hablar y volver por las mujeres* (Seville: Francisco de Leefdael, n.d.); *La vitoria de la honra* (Madrid, por la viuda de Alonso Martín, a costa de Diego Logroño, 1635); *Los peligros de la ausencia* (Zaragoza: por Pedro Verges, 1641); *Servir a señor discreto*, ed. Frida Weber de Kurlat (Madrid: Editorial Castalia, 1975).

97. Tirso de Molina, *El negro, entremés famoso*, in *Segunda parte de las comedias del maestro Tirso de Molina* (Madrid: en la Imprenta del Reino, 1635), 284r–285v; Luis Quiñones de Benavente, *El negrito hablador y sin color anda la niña*, in *Navidad y Corpus Christi, festejados por los mejores ingenios de España en diez y seis autos a lo divino, diez y seis loas, y diez y seis entremeses. Representados en esta corte y nunca hasta aora impressos. Recogidos por Isidro de Robles, natural de Madrid* (Madrid: por Joseph Fernández de Buendía. A costa de Isidro de Robles, 1664), 128–32; *Entremés de la negra lectora*, in *Arcadia de entremeses escritos por los ingenios más clásicos de España* (Madrid: Ángel Pasqual Rubio, 1723), 164–75.

98. Richard Brome, *The English Moor, or The Mock-Marriage*, modern text, ed. Matthew Steggle, in *Richard Brome Online*, http://www.dhi.ac.uk/brome, November 11, 2021, ISBN 978-0-9557876-1-4.

99. Nicolas du Perche, *L'ambassadeur d'Affrique: Comédie* (Moulins: Chez la veuve Pierre Vernoy et Claude Vernoy son fils, Imprimeur du Roy, 1666).

100. Francis Fane, *Love in the Dark, or The Man of Bus'ness, a Comedy* (London: Printed by T.N. for Henry Herringman, 1675).

101. Benjamin Jonson, *Masque of Blackness* (1605), in *The Routledge Anthology of Renaissance Drama*, ed. Simon Barker and Hilary Hinds (London: Routledge, 2003), 222–30.

102. Philip Massinger, *The Bondman* (1623), in *The Plays of Philip Massinger, from the Text of William Gifford*, ed. Francis Cunningham (London: Alfred Thomas Crocker, 1868), 99–132.

103. Molière, *Le malade imaginaire: Comédie en trois actes. Mélez de Danses et de Musique* (Amsterdam: Daniel Elzevir, 1674); William Davenant, *The History of Sir Francis Drake. The First Part* (London: Printed for Henry Herringman, 1659); William Wycherley, *The Gentleman Dancing-Master* (London: Printed by J.M. for Henry Herringman and Thomas Dring, 1673).

CHAPTER 1

1. Vaughan, *Performing Blackness*, 21. The epigraph is from John Ray, *A Collection of English Proverbs Digested into a Convenient Method for the Speedy Finding any one upon Occasion* (Cambridge: Printed by John Hayes, for W. Morden, 1678), 125.

2. Vaughan, *Performing Blackness*, 22.

3. Callaghan, *Shakespeare Without Women*, 78.

4. Farah Karim-Cooper, "The Materials of Race: Staging the Black and White Binary in the Early Modern Theatre," in *The Cambridge Companion to Shakespeare and Race,* ed. Ayanna Thompson (Cambridge: Cambridge University Press, 2021), 25–26.

5. "Le plus étonnant, ce fut le personnage de Lucifer, avec ses cornes sur le front, son visage barbouillé de noir charbon, sa queue déroulant ses longs anneaux." Qtd. in Raymond Lebègue, "Le Diable dans l'ancien théâtre religieux," *Cahiers de l'Association internationale des études françaises* 3–5, no. 1 (1953): 104.

6. Cantigas 82 and 47, qtd. in Peter Anthony Checca, *The Role of the Devil in Golden Age Drama* (Ph.D. diss., Pennsylvania State University, 1975), 31; Alfonso X (el Sabio) of Castile, *Las siete partidas del rey Don Alfonso el Sabio, cotejadas con varios códices antiguos por la Real Academia de la Historia. Tomo I, Partida primera* (Madrid: en la Imprenta Real, 1807), 276. A great example of theatre historians using *Las siete partidas* as evidence in the quasi-total absence of extent dramatic texts from the Middle ages is Bárbara Mujica, *A New Anthology of Early Modern Spanish Theater, Play and Playtext* (New Haven, Conn.: Yale University Press, 2014), 2. For a thorough discussion of the historiography of medieval theatricality in the peninsula, see Bruce R. Burningham, *Radical Theatricality: Jongleuresque Performance on the Early Spanish Stage* (West Lafayette, Ind.: Purdue University Press, 2007), 19–25.

7. In his still authoritative study of French medieval theatre performances, *La mise en scène dans le théâtre religieux francais du Moyen-âge* (Paris: Honoré Champion, 1906), 222, Gustave Cohen warns that hypotheses based on "the examination of miniatures are always suspect, because the artist could always follow his own fancy," but he also acknowledges that, prior to the fifteenth century, those are the only documents we have to imagine the conditions of performance (222).

8. *Nicholas Hilliard's Art of Limning*, transcribed by Arthur F. Kinney; ed. Linda Bradley Salamon; prefaced by Sir John Pope-Hennessy (Boston: Northeastern University Press, 1983).

9. Qtd. in John Cox, *The Devil and the Sacred in English Drama, 1350–1642* (New York: Cambridge University Press, 2000), 10. Mikhail Bakhtin reads the medieval stage devil as a carnivalesque comic monster "the gay ambivalent figure expressing the unofficial point of view, the

material bodily stratum. There is nothing terrifying or alien in him." Mikhail Bakhtin, *Rabelais and His World*, translated by Helene Iswolsky (Cambridge, Mass.: MIT Press, 1968), 41. Theatre historians such as Lebègue, however, remind us that "authors of mystery plays would never forget the original goal of stage devils: religious edification." Lebègue, "Le Diable," 104.

10. Cox, *Devil and the Sacred*, 18–19.

11. Callaghan, *Shakespeare Without Women*, 78. The 1525 receipt submitted to the Toledo Cathedral of the expenses incurred in the production of a black dance designed by Bautista de Valvidieso and Juan Correa during the procession of the Assumption is the oldest record of Spanish black-up that we have. Those wigs were, according to the record, almost twice as expensive as the masks. "Three little bonnets made of thin black ropes. For the leather and the rest: 2 *reales* and 10 *maravedis*" (De tres bonetillos de cordecitas negras, por Cuero y todo, 2 reales y 10 maradevises). Qtd. in Emilio Cotarelo y Mori, *Collección de entremeses, loas, bailes, jácaras y mojigangas, desde fines del siglo XVI á mediados del XVIII*, vol. 1 (Madrid: Casa Editorial Bailly-Baillière, 1911), clxxii.

12. The Spanish record from 1525 is illuminating here: "for painting the wagons and the 4 *negros'* masks, as well as for the blacking used to dye legs and arms, the painter took 1 ducat.... Eggs and oil used to attach the blacking to arms and legs: 3 *blancas* for 7 eggs, and 2 *maravedis* worth of oil, which makes a total of 14 *maravedis*" (Llevó el pintor por pintar los carros y cuatro máscaras de negros, y por el betún para teñir las piernas y los brazos, un ducado.... De huevos y aceite para sentar el betún negro en las piernas y brazos: siete huevos á 3 blancas, y 2 maravedises de aceite, que montan 14 maravedises). Cotarelo y Mori, *Collección*, clxxii. Africanized devil performers put masks on their faces, but they blackened the skin of their arms and legs black with a paste made of eggs, oil, and blacking. This technique differs from English practices of black-up, which dyed the face but covered legs, arms, and hands with cloth. Ian Smith, "Textile Black Body," 179–80.

13. For an account of a different narrative of performative blackness, see Ian Smith's work on the scripts of blackness conveyed by the tradition of textile black-up in late Tudor England in "Textile Black Body"; and "Othello's Black Handkerchief," *Shakespeare Quarterly* 64, no. 1 (2013): 1–25. Smith seeks to retrieve the ways in which the courtly tradition of textile black-up associated blackness with a discourse of commodification early on by highlighting the "thingness" of black skin. Smith's findings could be interestingly discussed in conversation with the commodifying paradigm that dominated early modern Spanish commercial theatre. While the textile imagery deployed around Othello or around Morocco in *The Merchant of Venice* that Smith brings to light gives the racial poetics of those plays a rich polyphonic dimension (and the presence of Spanish racial culture, incarnated, respectively, by Iago and the prince of Aragon, is probably not coincidental), diabolical cosmetic black-up was much more common than textile black-up in early modern English playhouses.

14. Peele, *Battell of Alcazar*, A2.

15. All quotations from *Othello* are drawn from the Norton E3 print edition, that is, from the folio version.

16. Christopher Marlowe, *Lusts Dominion, or The Lascivious Queen* (London: Printed for Francis Kirkman, 1657), C2v, C1r.

17. George Chapman, *The Blinde Begger of Alexandria Most Pleasantly Discoursing His Variable Humours in Disguised Shapes Full of Conceite and Pleasure* (London: Printed by J. Roberts for William Jones, 1598), F3v.

18. William Rowley, *A Tragedy Called All's Lost by Lust* (London: Thomas Harper, 1633), H4v, E4r.

19. Habib, *Black Lives in the English Archives*, 117, 63, 78, 116. Some have made much of the exceptions to the rule. Miranda Kaufmann in *Black Tudors: The Untold Story* (London: Oneworld, 2017) argues that racial difference did not influence the treatment of Africans in Tudor England based on ten biographical cases, only a couple of which present Afro-Britons in economically independent positions, which are not representative of the Afro-British population at large.

20. George Best, *A True Discourse of the Late Voyages of Discoverie for the Finding of a Passage to Cathaya* (London: Imprinted by Henry Bynnyman, 1578), 29. For a recapitulation of early modern natural philosophical discourse in Elizabethan England, see Lynda Boose, "The Getting of a Lawful Race: Racial Discourse in Early Modern England and the Unrepresentable Black Woman" in *Women, "Race," and Writing in the Early Modern Period*, ed. Margo Hendricks and Patricia Parker (London: Routledge, 1994), 42–45, and Kim F. Hall's *Things of Darkness*, 11–13.

21. Habib, *Black Lives in the English Archives*, 118.

22. Emily Bartels argues that in the last of the three decrees promulgated by Elizabeth to expel "Negroes and Blackamoors" from the kingdom, "the Queen's explicitly 'racist' language suggests that England's subjects had grown more inclined ideologically toward discrimination against 'blacks' as a subject group." Emily C. Bartels, "Too Many Blackamoors: Deportation, Discrimination, and Elizabeth I," *Studies in English Literature, 1500–1900* 46, no. 2 (2006): 319. Habib understands those decrees as the logical outcome of the hostility toward Africans.

23. Noémie Ndiaye, "Aaron's Roots: Spaniards, Englishmen, and Blackamoors in *Titus Andronicus*," *Early Theatre* 19, no. 2 (2016): 59–80.

24. For example, Aaron shows that he is aware of this law when he defends his son against Chiron and Demetrius: "Look how the black slave smiles upon the father, / As who should say, old Lad I am thine own. / Nay he is your brother by the surer side, / Of that self blood that first gave life to you, / And from your womb where you imprisoned were, / He is enfranchised, and come to light: / Although my seal be stamped in his face" (4.2.119–26). Here, when the baby "smiles upon his father," he is referred to as a "black slave," but when he is described coming out of his ultra-white mother's womb, he is "enfranchised." Using legal vocabulary, Aaron implies that Tamora's womb has the power to free her son twice.

25. Balibar and Wallerstein, *Race, Nation, Class*, 33. On the economic logic that informs the retention of Aaron and Tamora's mixed-race child in a subordinate position in imperial Roman society and in the early modern London anamorphically depicted in this play, see Noémie Ndiaye, "Shakespeare, Race, and Globalization: *Titus Andronicus*," in *Cambridge Companion to Shakespeare and Race*, ed. Ayanna Thompson (Cambridge University Press, 2021), 158–74.

26. At their apex, shortly before the Paris Parliament banned them, mystery plays started using black-up to represent dark-skinned Africans. In 1536, the procession of *Le Mystère des saints actes des Apôtres* in Bourges visually contrasted "six **white** Maures, with their arms and legs uncovered" (six Maures blancs, bras et jambes nus) with "a dozen more Maures, also uncovered" (douze Maures, aussi nuds) in emperor Nero's train. Jacques Thiboust, *L'Ordre de la triomphante et magnifique monstre du mystère des saints actes des Apostres faite à Bourges le dimanche dernier jour d'avril 1536*, in *Relation de la monstre du mystère des saints actes des Apostres et faits divers*, ed. M. Labouvrie (Bourges: Imprimerie en caractères et lithographie de Manceron, 1836), 68, emphasis mine. Similarly, Marguerite de Navarre, channeling trans-European painterly trends, introduced a Black Magus to the stage in *Comédie de l'adoration des trois roys à Iesus Christ*, in *Marguerites de la Marguerite des princesses, très illustre royne de Navarre* (Lyon: Jean de Tournes, 1547), 206–70.

27. Robin Blackburn, *The Making of New World Slavery: From the Baroque to the Modern, 1492–1800* (London: Verso, 1997), 279.

28. Georges Duhamel, *Acoubar ou la loyauté trahie:Tragédie. Tirée des amours de Pistion, et Fortunie en leur voyage de Canada* (Rouen: Raphaël du Petit Val, 1611).

29. For a thorough exploration of Rouen theatre's engagement with the lawfulness of colonization, see Wikström, "Law, Conquest and Slavery on the French Stage, 1598–1685."

30. Erick Noël, ed, *Dictionnaire des gens de couleur dans la France moderne: Paris et son bassin; Entrée par localité et par année (fin XVe siècle–1792), Paris suivi des provinces classées alphabétiquement* (Geneva: Droz, 2011), 364, 369.

31. François de Belleforest, *Second tome des histoires tragiques, extraites de l'italien de Bandel* (Paris: Pour Robert le Magnier, 1566).

32. See, for instance, *Lamentable Ballad of the Tragical End of a Gallant Lord and a Vertuous Lady: With the Untimely End of Their Two Children, Wickedly Performed by a Heathenish Black-a-Moor Their Servant; The Like Never Heard of Before* (London: Printed for W. Thackeray and T. Passinger, 1686–88).

33. Based on the performances recorded in Philip Henslowe's diary, attending shows at the Rose theatre during that time period, Cousturier could have seen Shakespeare's *The Merchant of Venice*, the cardiophagia motif of which resonates in *Tragédie mahommetiste ou l'on peut voir et remarquer l'infidélité commise par Mahumet, fils ayné du roy des Othomans nommé Amurat, à l'endroit d'un sien amy et son fidelle serviteur* (Rouen: Abraham Cousturier, 1612). He could have seen Turkish stereotypes in Marlowe's *1 Tamburlaine the Great* (London: Printed by Richard Ihones, 1590) and the lost play *Mahumet*—the Ottoman king in Cousturier's *Tragédie mahommetiste* is called "Mahumet," with this specific spelling. He could also have seen Marlowe's *The Tragicall History of D. Faustus* (London: Printed by V. Simmes for Thomas Bushell, 1604), which strongly resonates in *La merveille*. And he could have seen Thomas Heywood's *The Foure Prentises of London, with the Conquest of Ierusalem* (London: By Nicholas Okes for I. Wright, 1615), which Henslowe calls "2 pte of Godfrey of Bullen," a play that includes a "Sultan of Babylon" comparable to the sultan of *La merveille. Henslowe's Diary*, ed. Walter W. Greg (London: A. H. Bullen, 1904). He might also have caught a performance of a play about Hester and Assuerus (he published one himself later on), and a performance of Shakespeare's *The Taming of the Shrew*, which resonates in other publications of his such as *Ténèbres de mariage* (Rouen: Abraham Cousturier, date unknown) and *Discours facétieux des hommes qui font saller leurs femmes à cause qu'elles sont trop douces: Lequel se joue à cinq personnages* (Rouen: Abraham Cousturier, ca. 1600).

34. There are records of English traveling players in Rouen in 1598 and 1599. Unfortunately, the identity and repertory of those players led by Jehan Sehais are unknown. Sybile Chevallier Micki, "Tragédie et théâtre Rouennais, 1566–1640: Scénographies de la cruauté" (Ph.D. diss., Université Paris X–Nanterre, 2013), 13, 131. An English troupe leased L'Hôtel de Bourgogne in Paris during summer 1598, and Louis XIII's doctor, Héroard, reports that, as a boy, the king had been very impressed with Falstaff during a performance of *Henry IV* at Fontainebleau in September 1604. Frances A. Yates, "English Actors in Paris During Shakespeare's Lifetime," *Review of English Studies* 1, no. 4 (1925): 396. *Titus Andronicus* was an extremely popular play in England and abroad: we know that a German adaptation of *Titus Andronicus* was published in 1620 in Leipzig in a collection of plays performed by traveling English actors, and that Jan Vos adapted *Titus Andronicus* for the Amsterdam theatre in 1638. *Tito Andronico* (German *Tragedy of Titus Andronicus*), in *Shakespeare in Germany in the Sixteenth and Seventeenth Centuries: An Account of English Actors in Germany and the Netherlands and of the Plays Performed by Them During the Same Period*, ed. Albert Cohen, 162–236 (London: Asher,

1865). Jan Vos, *Aran en Titus, of Wraak en Weerwraak: Treurspel* (Amsterdam: Dominicus van der Stichel, 1641).

35. Sybile Chevallier Micki prefaces the most thorough study of the Rouen theatre industry and scenography to date with a telling disclaimer: "My reflection is based upon the rare engravings on the front page of the plays published by Abraham Cousturier, which Cousturier presumably engraved himself." Chevallier Micki, "Tragédie et théâtre Rouennais, 1566–1640," 279.

36. The lack of historical documentation regarding theatrical life in France and in Rouen in particular has prevented scholars to this day from determining whether *Le More cruel* was ever performed. Yet some internal dramaturgic components, such as the long reference to Medea, which is absent from Belleforest's novella, denote a familiarity with long-standing dramatic traditions. Similarly, the mise en abîme of audience dynamics in the scene when Riviery's choric hunters comment on the plot denotes an awareness of the audience's presence. Taken together, these elements suggest that the author of *Le More cruel* intended this play for the stage.

37. "Un serf natif de la Barbarie, et vrayement barbare comme assez il feist cognoistre par effect." Belleforest, *Second tome des histoires tragiques*, 327r.

38. The historical anecdote on which the play is based indicates that the original *moro* of Mallorca was a native of Maghreb, but no allusion to his skin tone is to be found in the first written account of the story: Giovanni Pontano, *De obediencia* (Naples, 1480–94, Universitat de València, Biblioteca Histórica BH Ms. 52). In the 1560s Bandello wrote a version of the story that does not contain any reference to dark skin either. Pontano and Bandello could easily have capitalized on the villain's dark skin: the fact that they did not suggests that phenotype was not part of the anecdote.

39. "L'heure assez tost viendra qu'il payera l'usure / Des maux que j'ay soufferts. Venez doncques Pluton, / Mégère, Tisiphone et sa soeur Allecton, / Hastez-vous vittement, tous tous je vous appelle / Pour me tenir escorte à ma juste querelle:/ Si je suis favory de vous, je vous requers / Qu'acourez vitement, et que foudre et esclairs / Accompagnent vos pas, sus Mégère puante / Tarde tu à venir avec ta torche ardante: / Venez à moi aussi, ô fantosmes hurlans, / Vous demons, vous esprits, vous chiens d'enfer hurlans!" (3.1.4–14). Lineation my own, based on the unpaginated original edition.

40. Thiboust, *L'ordre de la triomphante et magnifique monstre du mystère des saints actes des Apôtres*, 17–24.

41. "Hé quoy donc cet infait / Vivra il impuni d'un si lasche forfeit? / Quoy? Se vantera il en toute compagnie / De m'avoir fait souffrir si grande ignominie / Et ne m'en ressentir? Plutost je seray fait / Plus blanc et plus vermeil que le corail ou laict!" (3.1.33–38).

42. "O nous aveuglez gentishommes et seigneurs, / De tenir ces meschants Mores pour serviteurs / Desquels la cruauté est cent fois plus félonne / Que n'est celle d'un tigre ou de quelque lionne!" (5.1.309–12).

43. "The kingdom of France is blessed where we only recognize freedom, and where slaves are freed" (Bien-heureux pour vray le païs de France où la liberté est seule est recogneue et où les esclaves sont remis en leur pleine deliverance). Belleforest, *Second tome des histoires tragiques*, 329r.

44. "Il ne se faut fier qu'à ceux de nostre loy." 4.1.39.

45. "Le circuit de ce grand univers." *Merveille*, 10.

46. "Je fay de grosses tours, des pallais triomphans, / Des chasteaux sourcilleux, des Arsenacs, des Louvres." *Merveille*, 14.

47. Nicot, *Thrésor de la langue françoyse*, 272.

48. Antoine Le Roux de Lincy, *Le livre des proverbes français, Tome premier,* 2nd ed. (Paris: Adolphe Delahays, 1859), 10.

49. "Des voleurs qui ont la peau si blanche." "Ils viennent de pays fort eloignez d'ici / Pour emporter nos biens et nous domter aussi." Chrétien Des Croix, *Portugaiz infortunez,* 70, 24.

50. "Ha diabolique race / Engence de Pluton, de la terre excrément! . . . / Ha détestable gent! Race malitieuse! / Plus brutale cent fois qu'une ourse furieuse!" Chrétien Des Croix, *Portugaiz infortunez,* 99.

51. Michel de Montaigne, "Of Cannibals," in *The Complete Essays of Montaigne,* translated by Donald M. Frame (Stanford, Calif.: Stanford University Press, 1958), 150–59.

52. "Ils se mettent en fuite. / Qu'ils soient tous mis en blanc, courez, despeschez viste / Puis allons presenter leurs dépouïlles au Roy / Ce chastiment sera pour d'autres une loy." Chrétien Des Croix, *Portugaiz infortunez,* 100.

53. Christian Biet emphasizes Chrétien Des Croix's decision, informed by Montaigne and Las Casas, to represent Africans as similar to Europeans in nature: "That play cannot be faulted with either idealizing the Savage, or praising Christians: in the play, black and white people are both good and evil, for the behavior of black characters faithfully mimics that of white characters. Thus, the circumstances that befall those tragic characters becomes an analogy of the fight between European States, for cunning, violence, and self-interest are common to all." Christian Biet and Sylvie Requemora, "L'Afrique à l'envers ou à l'endroit des Caffres: Tragédie et récit de voyage au XVIIe siècle," in *L'Afrique au XVIe siècle: Mythes et réalités, Actes du VIIe Colloque du Centre International de Rencontres sur le XVIIe siècle, Tunis, 14–16 mars 2002,* ed. Alia Baccar Bournaz (Tübingen: Gunter Narr Verlag, 2003), 378.

54. Arthur Little, *Shakespeare Jungle Fever,* 98.

55. Loomba, *Shakespeare, Race, and Colonialism* (Oxford: Oxford University Press, 2002), 91.

56. In using the phrase "boy actress" rather than boy actor, I am following Roberta Barker in "The 'Play-Boy,' the Female Performer, and the Art of Portraying a Lady," *Shakespeare Bulletin* 33, no. 1 (2015): 83–97.

57. Callaghan, *Shakespeare Without Women,* 83.

58. Andrea Ria Stevens, *Inventions of the Skin: The Painted Body in Early English Drama, 1400–1642* (Edinburgh: Edinburgh University Press, 2013), 10.

59. Farah Karim-Cooper, *Cosmetics in Shakespearean and Renaissance Drama* (Edinburgh: Edinburgh University Press, 2006), 170–71.

60. Dennis Britton notes that Othello's complex recognition involves a dialectic between romance anagnorisis, in which "the hero correctly identifies another and then alters another's predicament," and tragic anagnorisis, in which "the hero identifies the self and his and or her present predicament." Dennis Britton, *Becoming Christian: Race, Reformation, and Early Modern English Romance* (New York: Fordham University Press, 2014), 124–25.

61. Ian Smith, "We Are Othello: Speaking of Race in Early Modern Studies," *Shakespeare Quarterly* 67, no. 1 (2016): 111.

62. Barthelemy, *Black Face, Maligned Race,* 162.

63. Smith, "We Are Othello," 112.

64. Qtd. in María Luisa Mateo Alcalá, "Máscaras y tocados para las figuras infernales del Códice de Autos Viejos," *Teatro de palabras, revista sobre teatro áureo* 5 (2011): 182.

65. "Bobo: Y diga señor ¿Donde nació? / Satan: ¿Porque lo preguntas? ¿Parézcote mal? / Bobo: Ni aún muy bien tampoco. Quemado venís / Del sol ó del aire, y ansina os sofrís / Andar sin camisa. / Satan: ¿Porque no, zagal? / Bobo: A fe, sois hermoso. ¡Qué corto vestis! / ¿Sois cortesano, ó sois de Guinea?" *Aucto de la paciencia de Job,* in *(Códice de autos viejos) Colección de autos*

sacramentales, loas y farsas del siglo XVI (anteriores a Lope de Vega) (Biblioteca Nacional de España. Ms. 14.711. ca. 1550–75), 464r.

66. "Bobo: ¿Y cómo se llama, señor? / Satan: Satanás. / Fool: Pulido es el nombre: y allá ¿dan librea? / Satan: Sírveme, hermano, que bien vestirás. / Bobo: ¿Mi hermano soís vos? Si tal ha parido / Mi madre, yo muera vestido y calzado. / Mi madre era blanca, vos sois tapetado; / La otra rodunda, vos boquicumplido. . . . / Señor Satanás, vivís engañado: / Más creo que soís hijo de gato rabon." *Aucto de la paciencia de Job*, 464r.

67. Mateo Alcalá, "Máscaras y tocados," 180.

68. *Farsa del triunfo del sacramento*, in *Códice de autos viejos* (Biblioteca Nacional de España. Ms. 14.711. ca. 1550–75).

69. Mateo Alcalá, "Máscaras y tocados," 181–82.

70. Teresa Ferrer Valls, "Las dos caras del Diablo en el teatro antiguo español," in *Convegno di studi: Diavoli e mostri in scena dal Medio Evo al Rinascimento (Roma, 30 giugno / 3 luglio 1988)*, ed. Maria Chiabó and Federico Doglio (Roma: Centro di Studi sul Teatro Medioevale e Rinascimentale, 1989), 323.

71. A shapeshifter, the Devil would take the appearance of whomever his victim was most likely to trust. He can appear as a beautiful woman, a hermit, a shepherd, a dead person, a confidant—but his most popular costume on the seventeenth-century stage seems to have been the costume of the *galán*, the tempter par excellence. Checca, *Role of the Devil in Golden Age Drama*, 129–34.

72. Arsenio Moreno Mendoza, "La figura del demonio en el teatro y la pintura del Siglo de oro español," *Atrio: Revista de historia del arte* 15–16 (2009): 149–54.

73. "Aquí viene una Negra, cantando y tañendo con su pichel al son del." Sánchez de Badajoz, *Farsa teologal*, 110.

74. "¡Oh sacro verbo divino! / ¡Oh misterios eternales! / Que áun a los negros bozales / Manifiestas tu camino." Sánchez de Badajoz, *Farsa teologal*, 111.

75. Note on glyphs: as discussed in the Introduction, in this book, the grammatical mistakes of blackspeak are signaled with a star symbol immediately preceding the grammatically accented word or word group, and the phonetic distortions of blackspeak are signaled with a hash symbol immediately preceding the translation of the accented word or word group.

76. "Past: tú eres cristiana? / Sold. Ni ella ni cuya es. / Cura. Hablar en eso conviene. / Súfrese tal barbarismo? / Sold. Soy un moro con bautismo, / Y ella no sé si lo tiene. / Cura. Pues cómo Dios os sostiene? . . . ¡No estar ésta bautizada! / Entre cristianos y mora! / Tú vístete rociar / Del lavatorio divino? / Neg. Nunca me raba con vino, / Mas con agua, sí rabar. / Cura: Conviene verificar / Esta cosa de cimiento, / Porque aqueste sacramento / dos veces no se ha de dar." Sánchez de Badajoz, *Farsa teologal*, 120–21.

77. "Que yo la haré aprender." Sánchez de Badajoz, *Farsa teologal*, 133.

78. Sánchez de Badajoz, *Farsa teologal*, 134.

79. In *Farsa de la ventera*, a *negra* is confronted with the Devil (whom she deeply fears) and contrasted with him in ways that neutralize the diabolical script of blackness (Sánchez de Badajoz, *Farsa de la ventera*, 250–51). In *Farsa de la fortuna ó hado*, an enslaved *negro* and a gentleman compare their lots and eventually reconcile, "Since God is Charity; / Let not the brotherhood among his Christian children / be disrupted" (Pues que Dios es caridad, / No se rompa la hermandad / Entre su hijos cristianos) (Sánchez de Badajoz, *Farsa de la fortuna ó hado*, 85). Similarly, in *Farsa del moysen*, a character declares that "God wants us all, white and black, rich and poor, healthy and lame, to remain brothers" (Dios a negros y blancos, / pobres, ricos, sanos, mancos, / nos tienen y quier hermandad) (Sánchez de Badajoz, *Farsa del moysen*, 126).

80. Berta Ares Queija, "La cuestión del bautismo de los Negros en el siglo XVII: La proyección de un debate Americano," in *Mirando las dos orillas: Intercambios mercantiles, sociales y culturales entre Andalucía y América*, ed. Enriqueta Vila Vilar and Jaime J. Lacueva Muñoz (Seville: Fundación Buenas Letras, 2012), 471.

81. Fra-Molinero points out that fifteenth-century Portuguese apologists such as Eanes de Zurara and Duarte Pacheco de Pereira already justified the slave trade with this religious argument. Fra-Molinero, *La imagen de los negros*, 11.

82. Alonso de Sandoval, *Naturaleza, policia sagrada i profana, costumbres i ritos, disciplina i catechismo evangelico de todos Etiopes* (Seville: por Francisco de Lira, 1627).

83. Alonso de Sandoval, *De instauranda aethiopum salute* (Madrid: por Alonso de Paredes, 1647).

84. "La estima grande que Christo señor nuestro hizo de semejante gente mostrandonos que de carbones frios sabe y puede su majestad hazer brasas incendidas, y que alumbren. . . . Pero como las almas de estos Negros y miserablse pecadores estan tan negras, que se pueden comparar muy bien con los carbones, parece que este resplandor y fuego divino se emprendio con mas fuerza y efficacia encendiendo y convirtiendo sus feos y obscuros carbones en finos carbuncos." Sandoval, *De instauranda aethiopum salute*, Prologo al Letor, paragraph 4.

85. "Tiznado no, mas lavado / De su sangre, de quien fui, / Aunque negro, rescatado / Hizóme Dios de carbón / Para que emprendiese luego / Más presto en mi corazón / Cualquier centella de fuego / De su santa inspiración." Vega Carpio, *El negro del mejor amo*, 94.

86. This metaphor circulated in other early modern hagiographies of Black saints, such as José Gómez de la Parra's account of Juana Esperanza de San Alberto's life. Rowe, *Black Saints*, 201.

87. "Castro y Quiñones's text is cited verbatim in the last chapter of the third book of Sandoval's 1627 treatise." Larissa Brewer-García, "Imagined Transformations: Color, Beauty, and Black Christian Conversion in Seventeenth-Century Spanish America," in *Envisioning Others: Race, Color, and the Visual in Iberia and Latin America*, ed. Pamela Anne Patton (Leiden: Brill, 2016), 126.

88. Ares Queija, "La cuestión del bautismo de los Negros en el siglo XVII," 480–81.

89. There are a few exceptions, which underline the existence of a residual association of blackness with the diabolical in the seventeenth century. In María de Zayas's novella *El prevenido engañado*, for instance, a negro is described as "so ugly and hideous . . . even more so than the Devil himself" (tan feo y abominable, que . . . le pareció que el demonio no podia serlo tanto). María de Zayas y Sotomayor, *Novelas ejemplares y amorosas de Doña María de Zayas y Sotomayor, natural de Madrid, Primera y segunda parte* (Paris: Baudry Librería Europea, 1847), 78. María de Zayas's holding on to an episteme that was already outdated in her own cultural moment manifests in another novella, *Tarde llega el desengaño*, which frames an enslaved black woman as diabolical: "a *negra* so dark that jet appeared white in comparison, and so beastly, Don Martín thought, that if she was not the Devil himself, she must have been his portrait" (una negra tan tinta que el azabache era blanco en su comparacion, y sobre esto tan fiera que juzgó Don Martín, que si no era el demonio, que debía ser retrato suyo). María de Zayas, *Tarde llega el desengaño*, in *Biblioteca de autores españoles, desde la formación del lenguaje hasta nuestros días: Novelistas posteriores a Cervantes*, Tomo segundo, 574–82 (Madrid: Imprenta Rivadeneyra, 1871), 576. Similarly, in Lope de Vega's *El prodigio de Etiopia*, the Afro-diasporic saint Filippo declares, in the dark phase of his life, "Woman, I am a devil" (un demonio soy, muger). Félix Lope de Vega Carpio, *El prodigio de Etiopia* (n.p.: n.p., 16??], 13.

90. The sheer number of adaptations of *El sancto negro* by later playwrights bears witness to the popularity of this play. Note that Mira de Amescua's play rewrote Lope's *El sancto negro*

while borrowing the title of Lope's first black saint play, *El negro del mejor amo*: this has been the source of much bibliographic confusion.

91. "Sin tanta tizne y tinta." Vega Carpio, *El sancto negro*, 305v.

92. "Ya dentro del pecho siento, / Nueuos gustos que me dan / Valor, animo, y aliento, / ¡A peruertido Alcoran! / Dexar tu fabula intento / Ya mi gloria solicito / Ya a ser cristiano me incite / Ya con esta ley me alegro / Blanca el alma, el cuerpo negro." Vega Carpio, *El sancto negro*, 308v.

93. "Aunque eres negro, aurá día / que estés bello, hermoso y blanco." Vega Carpio, *El sancto negro*, 310r.

94. Beusterien describes black-up in early modern Spain as a blank "denarrativized" mode of racialization as opposed a "narrativized" mode based on preexisting anti-Semitic and Islamophobic socioreligious discourses. Beusterien, *Eye on Race*, 101–2. By focusing on scripts of blackness and arguing that narratives were the animating force of performative blackness across early modern Europe, I radically depart from Beusterien's reading.

95. For instance, Sandoval dedicates an entire chapter to "the structure of Ethiops' faces, their hair, the ugliness of their limbs, and their color when they resurrect" (la composicion de la cabeza de los Etiopes, de sus cabellos, de la fealdad que se vè en sus miembros, y del color con que han de resucitar). Sandoval, *De instauranda*, 22.

96. "No podras / Negro tiznado modorro / Que de verte aqui me corro.... / Ni tú, ni el cielo, ni Dios, / No soys bastantes ¿No ven / El hocico de lechon, / El azabache, el tizón, / El aforro de sarten? / Nenglo Angola, de donzeya / Querar sacar ¡Toma higa!" Vega Carpio, *El sancto negro*, 217v. I translate "echar higas" as "to give the finger" for purposes of clarity, but the *Diccionario de autoridades*, the first dictionary published by the Real Academia Española, specifies that this gesture "is done with a closed fist, consisting in showing the tip of the thumb between the index and the major, in order to point out dumb or awful people, or to mock and ridicule them" (la acción que se hace con la mano cerrado el puño, mostrando el dedo pulgar por entre el dedo índice y el de enmedio, con la qual se señalaba a las personas infames y torpes, o se hacía burla y desprécio de ellas). "Higa," in *Diccionario de autoridades*, 1729–36. https://apps2.rae .es/DA.html Accessed November 13, 2021.

97. For instance, Erin Rowe argues that early modern hagiographers were instrumental in developing a discourse on Black sanctity and salvation in histories, hagiographies, and sermons "to help promote evangelization among enslaved populations throughout the latter half of the sixteenth and the early seventeenth centuries." That discourse hinged on the notion of "*candidez*, sometimes translated as 'whiteness' but meaning more accurately the dazzling brightness originating from the celestial kingdom, a unifying force that underscored the monogenetic origins of humanity." Rowe, "After Death, Her Face Turned White: Blackness, Whiteness, and Sanctity in the Early Modern Hispanic World," *American Historical Review* 121, no. 3 (2016): 728, 729. Through the lens of *candidez*, Rowe reads hagiographic discourse as a force that "pushed back against fixed ideas of race and natural slavery" (754). However, the discourse of candidez is absent from the stage's rendering of black saints' lives; in *El sancto negro*, when God promises to Benedict that his soul shall turn white as he enters Heaven, he uses the racial adjective *blanco*, not *candido*.

98. Rowe, "After Death, Her Face Turned White," 730.

99. "Aquel soberano mercader del Evangelio, cuya ansia y desseo es sacar en el Oriente y Occidente perlas de sumo valor (que son almas redimidas con su sangre) de las conchas broncas y feas de cuerpos negros y indias, ha puesto religiosos que como buzos se zabullen en la profundidad y mar de mil dificultades a sacarselas." Alonso de Sandoval, *Naturaleza, policia sagrada y profana*, 78v.

100. Larissa Brewer-García, "Hierarchy and Holiness in the Earliest Colonial Black Hagiographies: Alonso de Sandoval and His Sources," *William and Mary Quarterly* 76, no. 3 (2019): 478. The image is biblical: "The kingdom of heaven is like unto a merchant man, seeking goodly pearls: Who, when he had found one pearl of great price, went and sold all that he had, and bought it." *King James Bible* (London: Robert Barker, 1611), Matthew 13:45. Brewer-García points out the discrepancies, in particular, between Sandoval's Afro-diasporic hagiographies and some of his source texts produced in the Americas, and she rightfully reminds us that Sandoval's vision, though dominant in Iberia, was not necessarily hegemonic in the Americas.

101. Immanuel Wallerstein, *World-Systems Analysis: An Introduction* (Durham, N.C.: Duke University Press, 2004), 41.

102. Robert Hornback keenly perceives the link between "natural folly" and slavery: "these figures promoting blackface comic traditions popularized the belief that black people were less rational, hence, less human, and thereby rendered especially suited to inhumane servitude" Robert Hornback, *Racism and Early Blackface Traditions: From the Old World to the New* (New York: Palgrave, 2018), 25. My reflection here departs from Hornback's in its focus on dynamics of domestication and the heavy reliance of such dynamics on gender.

103. Erica Fudge, *Brutal Reasoning: Animals, Rationality, and Humanity in Early Modern England* (Ithaca, N.Y.: Cornell University Press, 2006), 54.

104. Antonio Santos Morillo, "Caracterización del negro en la literatura española del XVI," *Lemir* 15 (2011): 38.

105. The *negra*'s enslaver first states that "this *negra* belongs to the Devil" (esta Negra es del Diablo), and the shepherd, in a fit of exasperation at the *negra*'s slow catechumenal progress, shouts, "The Devil come get your face!" (doy al diablo el tu rostro). Sánchez de Badajoz, *Farsa teologal*, 113, 127. Finally, he declares, "The Devil himself could not teach her anything" (no la avezará el diabro) (133).

106. Sánchez de Badajoz, *Farsa teologal*, 113.

107. "Para reir sendos cachos, / ¿Quereis her una limosna? / Manteemos esta chozna." Sánchez de Badajoz, 135. Note on translation: here, I understand "chozna" as the Pastor's distortion for *chusma*.

108. "Mantear," in *Diccionario de autoridades*.

109. Sánchez de Badajoz, *Farsa teologal*, 136.

110. In his dialogue *Segunda comedia de Celestina* (1534), Feliciano da Silva created the character of Boruca (whose name is reminiscent of Boricua, the Taíno name for Puerto Rico, a major slave colony). Boruca makes a fugitive appearance, but the couple of lines she delivers suffice to animalize her: when a lady asks her about her suitor, the negro Zambrán, Boruca answers "*To the devil with him, #Lady, he *is a #scoundrel, for the #other day, he *jumped me and *wanted to get down like a dog" (Dar al diablo xeñora, que extar muy bellaco. Que aremeter a mí extotro día, a querer baxar como un perro). Feliciano de Silva, *Segunda comedia de Celestina*, in *Collección de libros españoles raros o curiosos, tomo noveno* (Madrid: Imprenta de Miguel Ginesta, 1874), 26. This description bestializes black sexuality. In *Tesorina* (ca. 1530) by Jaime de Huete, the *negra* Margarita has a rough exchange with two white men, when they fail to understand what she is saying. Increasingly frustrated by Margarita's accent, one of them calls her "your bitch-ship" (doña perra), and a few lines later exclaims, "What a beast! What a stupid and filthy animal!" (¡Qué bestial, / Quán çuzio y torpe animal!). Jaime de Huete, *Tesorina*, in *Tesorina, Vidriana*, ed. Ángeles Errazu (Zaragoza: Prensas universitarias de Zaragoza, Larumbe, Clásicos Aragoneses, 2002), 87–88. She is then called "your pig-ship" (doña puerca) (96), and "cockroach" (carabagenta) twice (98, 100).

111. "La papagayos para qu'enseña a fablar en jaula, y la mona para que la tengas yo a mi puertas como dueña de sablo." Lope de Rueda, *Comedia llamada Eufemia*, in *Las quatro comedias y dos coloquios pastoriles del excellente poeta y gracioso representante Lope de Rueda*, Dirigidas por Ioan Timoneda (Valencia: en casa de Ioan Mey, vendense en casa de Ioan Timoneda, 1567), 29v.

112. "Yo la pienso vender en el primer lugar, diziendo que es mi esclava." Lope de Rueda, *Comedia llamada Eufemia*, 30r.

113. Lope de Rueda, *Comedia llamada Eufemia*, 30r.

114. Lope de Rueda recycles the animalistic black imagery in many plays: In *Comedia de los engañados*, Guiomar is called the daughter of "a podenco dog" (un podenco) and "a basement cockroach" (cucaracha de sotanos). Lope de Rueda, *Comedia llamada de los engañados*, in *Las quatro comedias y dos coloquios pastoriles del excellente poeta, y gracioso representant Lope de Rueda*. Dirigidas por Ioan Timoneda . . . (Valencia: en casa de Ioan Mey, vendense en casa de Ioan Timoneda, 1567), 11v–11r. In *Colloquio de Tymbria*, Fulgencia is called "a bitch" (perra), a "greyhound bitch" (galga) (39v), "a crow" (cuerva) (41v), and an "owl" (lechuza) (41r) with "the face of a blackbird in a cage" (cara de mirla enjaulada) (39v), and "the face of the monkey" (la cara como ximia) (40r). Lope de Rueda, *Colloquio de Tymbria*, in *Las quatro comedias y dos coloquios pastoriles del excellente poeta, y gracioso representant Lope de Rueda*. Dirigidas por Ioan Timoneda . . . , 30r–54r (Valencia: en casa de Ioan Mey, vendense en casa de Ioan Timoneda, 1567).

115. "Cara de parago por remojar." Lope de Rueda, *Comedia llamada de los engañados*, 11r.

116. Tamar Herzog, "How Did Early-Modern Slaves in Spain Disappear? The Antecedents," *Republics of Letters: A Journal for the Study of Knowledge, Politics, and the Arts* 3, no. 1 (2012): 4. Seville sold an estimated fourteen hundred enslaved Afro-diasporic people per year at the beginning of the seventeenth century, as opposed to one thousand per year at the end of the sixteenth century (3). In that respect, the metropole had the same patterns of slave importation as the colonies: New Spain imported in the first four decades of the seventeenth century more enslaved black people than it had throughout the sixteenth century. Herman L. Bennett, *Africans in Colonial Mexico: Absolutism, Christianity, and Afro-Creole Consciousness, 1570–1640* (Bloomington: Indiana University Press, 2003), 23.

117. Gitanjali G. Shahani, *Tasting Difference: Food, Race, and Cultural Encounters in Early Modern Literature* (Ithaca, N.Y.: Cornell University Press, 2020), 2.

118. The play was printed in Madrid in 1652 but must have been written decades earlier, as Jiménez de Enciso died in 1634. Although the exact date of composition of this play is unknown, the allusions to Juan Latino that can be found in *El valiente negro in Flandés* have led several scholars to believe that Andrés de Claramonte's play came in the wake of Jiménez de Enciso's. This would place *Comedia famosa de Juan Latino* in the very early 1620s.

119. Born in 1518 in North Africa, Juan Latino was brought to Spain as a slave at the age of twelve. In Granada, he joined the household of the young Duke of Sesa, his lifelong enslaver. Juan studied at the cathedral's school, and he graduated from the University of Granada, where he excelled in Latin and Greek, which earned him his surname. A humanist scholar and a prolific writer, he acquired fame with his extensive epic poem *Austriadis Carmen*, which celebrates the victory at Lepanto. Jiménez de Enciso's play dramatizes Juan's rise in Spanish society and the obstacles he overcame. For a thorough account of the life, works, and racial struggle of the historical Juan Latino, see Elizabeth R. Wright's *The Epic of Juan Latino: Dilemmas of Race and Religion in Renaissance Spain* (Toronto: University of Toronto Press, 2016).

120. Castillo is punning on homophones: *vaya* means "jest," while *baya* means "berry."

121. "Escucha, protonegro / De todos los de tu casta; / Garrafa de tinto escucha, / Escucha, breva passada, / Escucha tinte de medias, / Escucha ciruela pasa, / Escucha escarpin Benito, /

Escucha mi vaya; y vaya / De joyu, aunque tu color / No es vaya sino castaña. . . . / Quenta el Maestro Capucho / En sus doctas Miscelaneas / Que un dia naturaleza / Tuvo ciertas combidadas / Diosas de aquellos contornos, / Que de camino passavan; / Era Sabado, y muy triste, / De no poder regalarlas, / Se puso a hazer un menudo, / Y aun dizen que era de baca. / Tomo una larga morcilla / La naturaleza sabia, / Y començo a echar en ella / Letras, lenguas, y escencias varias, / Nominativos, gerundios, / En fin toda la Gramatica, / La Teologia, y las artes; / Pero echo pimienta harta, / Que al cozer esta morcilla / Salio como una gualdrapa. / Minerva, diosa de la Guerra, / Viendo que es rey de las armas / El claro Duque de Sesa, / Embiosela a su casa. / Donde ha los años que veis / Que està al humero colgada, / Sin que la dè libertad, / Que aun ay morcillas esclavas. . . . / O chorizo de Latines!" Jiménez de Enciso, *Comedia famosa de Juan Latino*, 61v–62v.

122. Calderón's *La niña de Gómez Arias* dramatizes the repression of the *morisco* rebellion in the Alpujarras and includes a villainous black *moro* called Cañeri, modeled after the Cañeri from Jiménez de Enciso's *Juan Latino*. María Luisa Lobato, *Calderón: Teatro cómico breve* (Kassel: Edition Reichenberg, 1989), 430.

123. "(*Pónese mascarilla y bonete colorado.*) Gracioso: Agora sale el negrillo / requebrando aquestas damas, / con su cara de morcilla / y su bonete de grana." Pedro Calderón de la Barca, *Las carnestolendas*, in *Entremeses, jácaras y mojigangas*, edited by Evangelina Rodríguez y Antonio Tordera, 138–55 (Madrid: Editorial Castalia, 1983), 148.

124. "Que no tengan esclavas ni esclavos negros." Jiménez de Enciso, *Comedia famosa de Juan Latino*, 37r.

125. Héctor Urzáiz Tortajada, *Catálogo de autores teatrales del siglo XVII* (Madrid: Publicaciones de la Fundación Universitaria Española, 2002), 432.

126. "Jamás por tu color pardo / Ardo, que su tez picaña / Caña parece en aloque: / Ò què linda mermelada! / Tu cejas y tu cabello / Bello parece de rana / Ana, o Nise, y con teson / Son tus dos manos batatas [. . .] / Estos son los versos, que / Hice a tan bella Mulata / En tono de tiquis miquis, / Y en metro de taca maca." Juan de Matos Fragoso, *El yerro del entendido: Comedia famosa* (Valencia: en la Imprenta de Joseph y Thomàs de Orga, 1772), 18.

127. For instance, Sánchez de Badajoz already had the shepherd ironically call the *negra* "her ladyship of jet" (doña negra de azabache). Sánchez de Badajoz, *Farsa teologal*, 112.

128. Vega Carpio, *El sancto negro*, 306r; Luis Vélez de Guevara, *Virtudes vencen señales*, ed. William R. Manson and C. George Peale (Newark, Del.: Juan de la Cuesta, 2010), 86. Vega Carpio, *El negro del mejor amo*, 34. Pedro Calderón de la Barca, *La sibila del Oriente y gran reyna de Saba* (Madrid: por Francisco Sanz, 1682), 338.

129. For a striking example of black saint characters deploying the luxury script around themselves to counter the deployment of animal and foodstuff scripts by antagonists, see Luis Vélez de Guevara's *El negro del serafín*, ed. C. George Peale and Javier J. González Martínez (Newark, Del.: Juan de la Cuesta, 2012), 104–5.

130. *El valiente negro en Flandés* was published in 1638, but it must have been written before, as Claramonte died in 1626. Although the exact date of composition of the play is unknown, the focus of the play suggests that it was written in the early 1620s. The play revisits the successful operations led by the Duke of Alba to crush the early phase of the Dutch revolt in the 1560s and 1570s. This theme would have been particularly welcome on stage at some point between the end of the Twelve Years Truce, in 1621, and the death of military leader Maurice of Orange in 1625 (the play features a wish-fulfilling scene in which William of Orange, Maurice's father, is captured by the Spaniards). John Beusterien notes that the play relocates to Flanders the exploits of a historical Afro-Spanish soldier, Juan Valiente, who was key in the 1550 conquest of Chile

(Beusterien, *Eye on Race*, 114). The imperial propaganda in which it participates partly accounts for the play's immense popularity in the seventeenth century (114–15).

131. Claramonte y Corroy, *El valiente negro en Flandés*, 176v.

132. "Oyga, que discursos tiene, / filosoficos tambien / el negro embes de sarten." Claramonte y Corroy, *El valiente negro en Flandés*, 158r.

133. "Juan: Del sol nuestro orijen viene / que el nos abraza. Alfarez: Seran / carbon con alma." Claramonte y Corroy, *El valiente negro en Flandés*, 158r.

134. "Y carbón / que encendido en la ocasión / rayos da por chispas." Claramonte y Corroy, *El valiente negro en Flandés*, 158r.

135. "El azabache se aplica / a la garganta mas bella. . . . Negro es el porfido hermoso / y el evano. . . . Negra es la pentarbe piedra / contra el fuego riguroso." Claramonte y Corroy, *El valiente negro en Flandés*, 158r.

136. "Las excelencias sabemos / de lo negro, color vil / en presencia del marfil." Claramonte y Corroy, *El valiente negro en Flandés*, 158r.

137. "Juan: Por obedencia me siento / y sere entre dos cristales / negro azabache. Orange: Quisiera / mas, Capitan, su azabache / que el marfil que me engrandece." Claramonte y Corroy, *El valiente negro en Flandés*, 163v.

138. "Don Pedro: No reparays en los negros / que son notables figuras. / Don Francisco: Dos dias ha que los veo / en la antecamara assi. / Don Martín: Con que gravedad / el perro se passea! Y las pisadas / el paje le va midiendo. / Don Pedro: Bien valdran tres mil reales, / amo y paje." Claramonte y Corroy, *El valiente negro en Flandés*, 175r.

139. Fra-Molinero, *La imagen de los negros*, 186.

140. Cedric J. Robinson, *Black Marxism: The Making of the Black Radical Tradition* (Chapel Hill: University of North Carolina Press, 1983), 129.

CHAPTER 2

1. Boose, "Getting of a Lawful Race," 46. The epigraph is from William Shakespeare, *Antony and Cleopatra*, in *The Norton Shakespeare, Tragedies*, Third Edition, ed. Stephen Greenblatt (general editor), Walter Cohen, Suzanne Gossett, Jean E. Howard, Katharine Eisaman Maus, and Gordon McMullan, 971–1060 (New York: W. W. Norton, 2016), 1.5.27–29.

2. Joyce Green MacDonald, *Women and Race in Early Modern Texts* (Cambridge: Cambridge University Press, 2002), 10.

3. Joyce Green MacDonald, *Women and Race in Early Modern Texts*, 10.

4. Joyce Green MacDonald, "Black Ram, White Ewe: Shakespeare, Race, and Women," in *A Feminist Companion to Shakespeare*, ed. Dympna Callaghan (Malden, Mass.: Blackwell, 2000), 124–25.

5. "Oblique, adj., n., and adv." *OED Online*, June 2020, Oxford University Press, https://www-oed-com.proxy.uchicago.edu/view/Entry/129718?rskey=0KheBy&result=1&isAdvanced=false, accessed July 20, 2020.

6. Susan Peabody, *"There Are No Slaves in France": The Political Culture of Race and Slavery in the Ancien Régime* (New York: Oxford University Press, 1996).

7. René Bordier, *Grand bal de la douairière de Billebahaut*, in *Ballets et mascarades de cour de Henri III à Louis XIV (1581–1652), Tome troisième*, ed. Paul Lacroix (Geneva: Slatkine Reprints, 1968), 151–202.

8. Melinda Gough, "Courtly Comédiantes: Henrietta Maria and Amateur Women's Stage Plays in France and England," in *Women Players in England, 1500–1660: Beyond the All-Male Stage*, ed. Pamela Allen Brown and Peter Parolin, 193–215 (Burlington, Vt.: Ashgate, 2005), 198.

9. Giovanni Battista Andreini, *Lo schiavetto* (Venice: Giovanni Battista Ciotti, 1620).

10. Emily Wilbourne, "*Lo Schiavetto* (1612): Travestied Sound, Ethnic Performance, and the Eloquence of the Body," *Journal of the American Musicological Society* 63, no. 1 (2010): 26.

11. The Fedeli would return to France in 1622, and their success was such that Paris would be one of their regular performance venues for years. Wilbourne, "*Lo Schiavetto* (1612)," 3.

12. Helen Dewar, "Souveraineté dans les colonies, souveraineté en métropole: Le rôle de la Nouvelle-France dans la consolidation de l'autorité maritime en France, 1620–1628," *Revue d'Histoire de L'Amérique Française* 64, nos. 3–4 (2011): 67.

13. Philip B. Boucher, *France and the American Tropics to 1700: Tropics of Discontent?* (Baltimore: Johns Hopkins University Press, 2008), 81.

14. According to Boucher, a company is truly "colonial" and not simply "commercial" when it is involved in the production of the staple commodities that interests it. "In such cases, the state granted property rights, monopoly trading rights for a certain number of years, and other privileges, including the right to maintain private armies and navies. In turn, the company accepted royal sovereignty through the king's right to appoint a lieutenant general and, sometimes, judicial officials. Companies agreed to transport a specific number of colonists, to support missionaries, and to fight the king's wars if called upon." Boucher, *France and the American Tropics to 1700*, 67.

15. Richelieu was the most important associate of the St. Christophe Company: he contributed almost a quarter to the company's total capital stock. In 1627, he chartered the most important of all French colonial companies, La Compagnie de la Nouvelle France, which administered French North America. Helen Dewar has shown that, for all the seemingly autonomous administration of the Compagnie de la Nouvelle France, social structures were so clientelist in the first half of the seventeenth century that "despite the royal edict that granted some state powers to the company, in fact, Richelieu was the viceroy of New France, even if he did not bear that title." Dewar, "Souveraineté dans les colonies," 88.

16. Médevielle, "La racialisation des Africains," 116.

17. Boucher, *France and the American Tropics to 1700*, 155.

18. In 1630, Théophraste Renaudot, Louis XIII's physician, founded Le Bureau d'adresse in Paris. The Bureau was originally intended to put job seekers in touch with potential employers, but it soon developed additional functions. One of its core missions became the dissemination of scientific knowledge into popular culture beyond narrow academic circles. Starting in 1633 and for about a decade, every week, the Bureau organized public conferences in French where orators debated topics ranging from anthropology to medicine, philosophy, and more.

19. "La couleur qui ne se peut appeler accident aux Mores, mais une propriété inséparable qui les sépare des autres hommes et constitue la nature du Nègre." *Quatriesme centurie des questions traitées aux conférences du bureau d'adresse, depuis le 24 janvier 1639 jusqu'au 10 juin 1641* (Paris: Au bureau d'adresse, rüe de la Calandre, 1641), 321.

20. "Les Nègres n'ont pas la seule teinture de leur peau particulière, ils ont beaucoup d'autres propriétez qui les font distinguer des autres peuples: telles que sont les grosses lèvres, le nez enfoncé, les cheveux cotonnez, la tunique conjonctive de l'oeil et les dents plus blanches que le reste des hommes. . . . Sans parler des qualitez de leur esprit, qui est si ignorant, qu'ayant abondance de lin ils manquent de toile, pour ne le pouvoir mettre en oeuvre: des cannes à sucre et ils ne s'en servent point ni pour le traffic ni pour leur usage; et estiment le cuivre plus que l'or, au poids

duquel ils achètent le sel; abondent en gibier et ne vont point à la chasse; et sont du tout ignorants des Lois et de la médecine: laquelle ignorance rend les mesmes esprits plus bas et serviles que celui des autres peuples, et tellement nez à l'esclavage que les personnes libres d'entre les Abyssins, les personnes les plus considérables de toute l'Aethiopie, s'employant pour quelqu'un, ne trouvent point étrange qu'on les fouette à coups de nerfs de boeuf." *Quatriesme centurie des questions*, 322.

21. The proceedings of each public conference were published in weekly fascicles anonymizing the orators, and ultimately compiled into five *Centuries* volumes printed between 1634 and 1655. The popularity of those volumes is evidenced by the fact that they were translated into English and published in London in 1665.

22. *Ballet des rues de Paris*, in *Ballets et mascarades de cour de Henri III à Louis XIV (1581–1652), Tome VI,* ed. Paul Lacroix (Geneva: Slatkine Reprints, 1968), 140.

23. "La France, mère de liberté, ne permet aucuns esclaves." Erick Noël, "L'esclavage dans la France moderne," *Dix-huitième siècle* 39, no. 1 (2007): 363.

24. "Toutes personnes sont franches en ce royaume, et sitost qu'un esclave a atteint les marches d'icelui, se faizant baptizer, est affranchi." Antoine Loysel, *Institutes coustumieres: Ou manuel de plusieurs et diuerses reigles, sentences, et prouerbes tant anciens que modernes du droict coustumier et plus ordinaire de la France* (Paris: chez Abel L'Angelier, 1607), 3.

25. Richelieu's patronage took several forms. In 1629, he imposed his acting company to the Confrérie de la Passion, which owned the only fixed theatre in Paris, L'Hôtel de Bourgogne; in 1630, he turned one of the rooms of his palace into a theatre; in 1641, he inaugurated the Théâtre du Palais-Cardinal, which we know today as the Comédie Francaise. Paris became the theatrical hub of the country under the aegis of playwrights like Alexandre Hardy. The cardinal had a vision for French theatre. In 1635, he founded the Société des Cinq Auteurs (including Pierre Corneille who, emblematically, left Rouen for Paris on this occasion): the Société members expressed in dramatic forms the ideas and values that Richelieu championed. Abbé d'Aubignac explains in the preface to *La pratique du théâtre* (Paris: Antoine de Sommaville, 1657) that it is upon Richelieu's commission some twenty years earlier that he started writing the aesthetic manifesto underlying the tradition of classical French theatre.

26. Naturally, court ballets did not form in a vacuum: like Stuart court masques, baroque French ballets had their roots in the tradition of sixteenth-century courtly festivities and pageants celebrating aristocratic marriages and travels. To cite but one example, *Labyrinthe royal de l'Hercule gaulois triomphant* (Avignon: Jacques Bramereau, 1600), which celebrated the queen's arrival in Avignon in 1600, included two black *Mores* perched on elephants.

27. "Du couroux du vent et des eaux / Les richesses de mes vaisseaux / N'ont jamais pu estre sauvées; / Mais un plus grand bien m'est rendu / Et je croy vous ayant trouvées / Que j'ay plus gaigné que perdu. / Mon pilote et mes matelots / Et ceux qu'ils menaient sur les flots / Viendront bien tost vous rendre homage." Claude de L'Estoille, *Ballet du naufrage heureux* (1626), 3.

28. "Les Mores ont les cheveux courts et crespus, le visage et les mains noires, ils sont teste nue, à moins qu'on ne leur donnât un tourtil greslé de perles en forme de diadème; ils doivent porter des pendants d'oreille." Claude-François Ménestrier, *Des ballets anciens et modernes selon les règles du théâtre* (Paris: chez René Guignard, 1682) 251–52. Skeptics who might believe that black-up was limited to the "amateur" milieu of court performance will want to read commercial plays such as *Le fidelle esclave* (1659), in which a white character pretending to be Egyptian appears successively black and "unblackened" (dénoircy). While he is in disguise, a character "lifts his sleeve" and comments, "Whoever blackened your hand did not blacken your arm?" (*L'Infante [lui levant la manche]:* Qui vous noircit la main ne noircit pas le bras?) Jacques Vallée, *Le fidelle esclave: Comédie* (Paris: chez Jean Cochart, 1662), 47.

29. "Beautez à qui rien n'est pareil, / Vos yeux plus beaux que le soleil / Plus que luy nous ont fait d'outrages, / Cet astre a bien moins de rigueurs: / Il n'a noircy que nos visages, / Et vous avez bruslé nos coeurs." L'Estoille, *Ballet du naufrage heureux*, 9–10.

30. Mark Franko, *Dance as Text: Ideologies of the Baroque Body* (Cambridge: Cambridge University Press, 1993).

31. "Je fais distiller nuit et jour / des eaux pour faire des pomades / qui peuvent guérir nuit et jour / tous ceux qui n'en sont point malades." L'Estoille, *Ballet du naufrage heureux*, 10.

32. "Je veux fondre dans mes fourneaux / Ces pauvres amants misérables / Et rendray ces Mores plus beaux, / Qu'ils ne semblent désagréables. / Je veux que charmant tous les yeux / Ils soient vainqueurs de leurs maîtresses / Et bien qu'ils ne soient pas des dieux, / Ils possèderont ces déesses." L'Estoille, *Ballet du naufrage heureux*, 11.

33. "Portant ce charbon, je tremble à tous moments, / Et soudain tout plaisir loin de moi se recule; / Car ce charbon n'est fait que des coeurs des amants / Que l'amour a bruslé comme encore me brusle." L'Estoille, *Ballet du naufrage heureux*, 12.

34. The erotic hermeneutics of black-up can be traced back to earlier performances, such as *Pour des Masques assez hideux et sauvages* (1601), or *Boutade des Mores esclaves d'Amour delivrés par Bacchus* (1609), but only in the 1620s did such hermeneutics become a staple of court ballets. It can also be found in later pieces, at least as late as *Ballet des Proverbes*, which was performed at the Duke of Nancy's court in 1665. *Pour des masques assez hideux et sauvages*. In *Ballets et mascarades de cour de Henri III à Louis XIV (1581–1652), Tome premier*, edited by Paul Lacroix, 155–56 (Geneva: Slatkine Reprints, 1968). *Ballet des proverbes dancé par son altesse Monsieur de prince de Vaudémont* (Nancy: Claude Anthoine et Charles les Charlots, Imprimeurs ordinaires, 1665).

35. "Si cette couleur que je porte / Est aussi sombre qu'un cercueil; / C'est que mon corps porte le deuil / De ce que sa franchise est morte." *Grand bal des effets de la nature*, in *Ballets et mascarades de cour de Henri III à Louis XIV (1581–1652), Tome quatrième*, ed. Paul Lacroix (Genève: Slatkine Reprints, 1968), 206.

36. "Nous sommes trop heureux et nous aimons nos chaînes / Quand nous avons l'honneur de les porter pour vous." *Boutade des Mores esclaves d'Amour délivrés par Bacchus* (1609), 1.

37. Stuart Hall, "Spectacle of the 'Other,'" 266–67.

38. "It seems that the Blacks traded by *La Compagnie de Guinée* had become troubling enough for the world of entertainment and spectacle to avoid them. This is why we can observe an obvious reluctance to put on stage parts of authentic Africans. The *More* deliberately remains, in the realm of representation, a made-up image that people knew did not match reality." Chalaye, *Du Noir au Nègre*, 65. Chalaye's most recent book shows that her reading of that corpus has not changed over the last twenty years: for her, in ballets de cour and seventeenth-century comedies, "racial cross-dressing drew on exoticism, but it did not address slavery or relations of domination, for the subject had been censored." Chalaye, *Race et théâtre*, 90.

39. Dobie, *Trading Places*, 6, xii.

40. Julia Prest, *Theatre Under Louis XIV: Cross-Casting and the Performance of Gender in Drama, Ballet and Opera* (New York: Palgrave Macmillan, 2006), 83.

41. Thomas Corneille, *L'inconnu: comédie mêlée d'ornements et de musique* (Paris: chez Jean Ribou, 1675), ed. Paul Fièvre (Théâtre Classique, 2014), 81.

42. Corneille, *L'inconnu*, 82.

43. "Un Vulcan enfumé." Vincent Borée, *Achille victorieux* (Lyon: pour Vincent de Coeursilly, 1627), 307.

44. "Prendre un baiser du soleil qui me réduit en cendres"; "Humble esclavage." Borée, *Achille victorieux*, 256, 252.

45. "To make this deed even more memorable, / We will don Moorish garments, / And our faces will look like the faces / Of that people whom the sun darkens" (Pour rendre l'action plus mémorable encore / Nous nous présenterons en vestements de Mores, / Et nous aurons tous deux le visage pareil / A ce people noircy des rayons du soleil). Nicolas Mary, Sieur Desfontaines, *Orphise, ou la beauté persécutée: Tragi-comédie* (Paris: chez Antoine de Sommaville, 1638), 41. This moment of attempted interracial rape must have proved effective onstage, for Desfontaines recycled it four years later, in *Alcidiane ou les quatre rivaux*. François Parfaict, *Histoire du théâtre françois depuis son origine jusqu'à présent, Tome sixième* (Paris: Chez P. G. Le Mercier et Saillant, 1746), 194.

46. The blacked-up wooer's doomed aspirations to interracial romance feature prominently in neoclassical comedies such as Edmé Boursault's *Le mort vivant: Comédie* (Paris: Nicolas Pépingue, 1662) and Nicolas du Perche's *L'ambassadeur d'Affrique: Comédie* (Moulins: Chez la veuve Pierre Vernoy et Claude Vernoy son fils, Imprimeur du Roy, 1666). On interracial romance in this corpus, see Noémie Ndiaye, "The African Ambassador's Travels: Playing Black in Late-Seventeenth Century France and Spain," in *Transnational Connections in Early Modern Theatre*, ed. M. A. Katritzky and Pavel Drábek, 73–85 (Manchester: Manchester University Press, 2020).

47. Kim F. Hall, *Things of Darkness*, 65.

48. Jean-Baptiste Du Tertre, *Histoire générale des Antilles habitées par les François, Tome 2* (Paris: Thomas Iolly, 1667), 511.

49. "Leur teint poli d'ébène Noire / vaut bien un teint blanc comme Yvoire." *Les oeuvres de monsieur Scarron. Reveuës, corrigées et augmentées de nouveau, Tome Premier* (Rouen: Guillaume de Luyne, 1663), 33. Although this epistle was printed in 1663, several internal indications suggest that Scarron wrote it during the last decade of his life, in the 1650s.

50. Garraway, *Libertine Colony*, 25. As Guillaume Aubert has shown, although unions between Frenchmen and Afro-diasporic women in the colonies were overwhelmingly informal, those unions were sometimes consecrated as marriages. Aubert, "Blood of France," 461.

51. On the legal and fiscal measures adopted by the State to deter white men from engaging in interracial unions with Afro-diasporic women in the second half of the century, see Ndiaye, "African Ambassador's Travels," 76.

52. Felicity A. Nussbaum, *The Limits of the Human: Fictions of Anomaly, Race, and Gender in the Long Eighteenth Century* (Cambridge: Cambridge University Press, 2003), 172.

53. "Deux négresses d'une parfaite beauté avec de l'esprit et qui parlaient bien français." Noël, "L'esclavage dans la France moderne," 365. Noël also records the presence of male *négrillons* attached to aristocratic ladies in Paris starting in the 1650s (he numbers about forty recorded cases in extant archives between 1652 and 1715), in the *Dictionnaire des gens de couleur dans la France moderne.*

54. Louise Marie-Thérèse received attention and visits from members of the royal circle, including Madame de Maintenon—the king's second wife, who had raised his children—and the Grand Dauphin, heir to the throne, whom she once referred to as her own "brother." She received a pension of three hundred livres a year from the crown, and when the ever-sharp-tongued Voltaire saw her in 1716, he commented that she much resembled the late king. Shelby T. McCloy, "Negroes and Mulattoes in Eighteenth-Century France," *The Journal of Negro History* 30, no. 3 (1945): 282.

55. "Les femmes blanches ont petites les mammelles, / Que je taste pour voir si vous les avez telles, / En ce païs ici longues nous les avons, / Mais les vostres encor plus belles nous treuvons." Chrétien des Croix, *Portugaiz infortunez*, 84.

56. Octave-César Génetay, *L'Ethiopique: Tragicomédie des chastes amours de Théagène et Chariclée* (Rouen: Théodore Reinsart), 1609.

57. Alexandre Hardy, *Les chastes et loyales amours de Théagène et Cariclée, réduites du grec de l'histoire d'Héliodore en huict poëmes dramatiques ou théâtres consécutifs* (Paris: Jacques Quesnel), 1623.

58. Jean Boissin de Gallardon, *La Perséene, ou la délivrance d'Andromède*, in *Les tragédies et histoires sainctes de Jean Boissin de Gallardon*, 1–70 (Lyon: Simon Rigaud, 1618). On the deployment of racial thinking in those three plays, see Noémie Ndiaye, "'Everyone Breeds in His Own Image': Staging the *Aethiopica* Across the Channel," *Renaissance Drama* 44, no. 2 (2016): 157–85.

59. On the Ovidian tradition of African beauty in medieval and early modern French poetry, see the forthcoming work of Anna Klosowska. The exclusion of Afro-diasporic women from the dance of interracial desire in performance culture is perhaps best captured by Pierre Corneille, who decides, in the "Argument" prefacing the first edition of his wildly popular pièce à machines *Andromède* (1650), to turn Andromeda white because "of course, the blackest *Mores* too have their own kind of beauty, but it is not verisimilar that Perseus, who was a Greek born in Argos, should have fallen in love with Andromeda if she had been of that hue" (Ce n'est pas que les Mores les plus noirs n'ayent leur beauté à leur mode, mais il n'est pas vraysemblable que Persée qui était Grec et né dans Argos fut devenu amoureux d'Andromède si elle eût été de leur teint). Pierre Corneille, *Andromède: Tragédie représentée avec les machines sur le théâtre royal de Bourbon* (Rouen: Laurens Maurry, 1651). Afro-diasporic women would return to the stage in the 1730s, with characters such as "Négritte," the maid featured in Jean-Antoine Romagnesi, *Les Sauvages, parodie de la tragédie d'Alzire. De Messieurs Romagnesi et Riccoboni* (Amsterdam: chez J. Ryckhof Fils, 1736), and "Angolette," the protagonist in Alain-René Lesage et Jacques-Philippe d'Orneval, *La Sauvagesse, pièce d'un acte representée à la Foire St. Laurent, 1732*, in *Le théâtre de la foire, ou l'opéra comique, Tome IX*, 221–274 (Paris: Pierre Gandouin, 1737).

60. Olivia Bloechl, "Race, Empire, and Early Music," in *Rethinking Difference in Music Scholarship*, ed. Olivia Bloech, Melanie Lowe, and Jeffrey Kallberg (Cambridge: Cambridge University Press, 2015), 89.

61. Bordier, *Billebahaut*, 41.

62. "Je meure, ô merveille des cieux, / Si le plus grand orgueil d'une dame Africaine / Est propre devant vos beaux yeux / Qu'à servir de quaintaine." Bordier, *Billebahaut*, 42.

63. "Une troupe d'Afriquaines viennent attaquer les Afriquains avec leurs zagaies; mais les hommes, qui ne sont que sur la defensive tiennent à gentillesse le souffrir, et toute la caballe du cacique s'en retourne sur ses pas." Bordier, *Billebahaut*, 39–40.

64. Moya Bailey and Reina Gossett, "Analog Girls in Digital Worlds: Dismantling Binaries for Digital Humanists Who Research Social Media," in *The Routledge Companion to Media Studies and Digital Humanities*, ed. Jentery Sayers (New York: Routledge, 2018), 40.

65. Moya Bailey (Moyazb), "More on the Origins of Misogynoir," Tumblr, April 27, 2014, accessed July 17, 2018, http://moyazb.tumblr.com/post/84048113369/more-on-the-origin-of-misogynoir.

66. Bailey and Gossett, "Analog Girls in Digital Worlds," 40.

67. Philip Massinger, *A Very Woman, or The Prince of Tarent, a Tragi-comedy*. In *Three New Playes, viz The Bashful Lover, The Guardian, The Very Woman* (London: Printed for Humphrey Moseley, 1655), 40.

68. Elizabeth Cary, *The Tragedy of Mariam, the Fair Queen of Jewry*, in *The Routledge Anthology of Renaissance Drama*, ed. Simon Barker and Hilary Hinds (London: Routledge, 2003), 191–221; Benjamin Jonson, *Masque of Blackness*, in *The Routledge Anthology of Renaissance Drama*, ed. Simon Barker and Hilary Hinds (London: Routledge, 2003), 222–30; William

Shakespeare, *Antony and Cleopatra*. African female roles had already featured in a number of lost court masques prior to that date. Those include the well-known *Joust of the Wild Knight and the Black Lady* at the Scottish court in 1507, but also *A Masque of Egyptian Women* (1545), *Theagenes and Chariclea* (1572), and *The Queen of Ethiopia* (1578), among others. Those parts were presumably performed with textile black-up (veils or vizards).

69. Succubae often feature in continental representations of St. Anthony's temptation. Walter Stephens, *Demon Lovers: Witchcraft, Sex, and the Crisis of Belief* (Chicago: University of Chicago Press, 2002), 114. Stephens points out that early modern "witchcraft theorists... are usually more interested in women and incubi than in men and succubi." Stephens, *Demon Lovers*, 23.

70. I focus on plays that put black succubae on display, but a wider array of plays contains allusions to dark-skinned succubae. For instance, in George Ruggle's *Ignoramus* (1615), the titular character receives kisses from enslaved sex workers of various ethnicities (Greek, German, Hebrew, English, Spanish, French, Venetian, Persian, Turkish) yet refuses to be kissed by the Moorish one and singles her out as "the wife of the Divel." George Ruggle, *Ignoramus, a Comedy as It Was Several Times Acted with Extraordinary Applause Before the Majesty of King James . . . Written in Latine by R. Ruggles; And Translated into English by R.C.* (London: Printed for W. Gilbertson, 1662), D4r. Similarly, in *The Country Wit*, the rakish character Ramble lusts after a woman whom he imagines as having, among other attributes a "white little hand," yet he fears that this woman, whom he has never seen, might actually be the exact opposite: "for ought I know [she] may be only an old, ugly, leacherous *Succuba*." John Crown, *The Countrey Wit, a Comedy, Acted at the Dukes Theatren* (London: Printed by T.N. for James Magnes and Richard Bentley, 1675), 33. Such allusions are sprinkled over the early modern theatrical archive.

71. Philip Massinger and John Fletcher, *The Prophetess*, in *Comedies and Tragedies Written by Francis Beaumont and John Fletcher Never Printed Before* (London, Printed for Humphrey Robinson . . . and for Humphrey Moseley . . . , 1647), 35. The figure of the succuba was excised from this scene in Thomas Betterton's 1690 rewriting of the play.

72. Ludwig Lavater, *Of Ghostes and Spirites Walking by Nyght and of Strange Noyses, Crackes, and Sundry Forewarnynges, Whiche Commonly Happen Before the Death of Menne, Great Slaughters, [and] Alterations of Kyngdomes: One Booke, Written by Lewes Lauaterus of Tigurine and Translated into Englyshe by R.H.* (London: Henry Benneyman for Richard Vvatkyns, 1572), 6. The early moderns popularized but did not invent the succuban rape plot: thirteenth-century Franciscan Frier Bartholomeus Anglicus had already written: "in sleepe many are molested with *Ephialtes* and *Hvphialti*, that is *Iucubi* and *Succubi* . . . , night spirits: rather diuells, which I suppose to be wicked spirits who being not able to preuayle in the day, de defile the body in yᵉ night: yᵉ Phisitians do affirm, these are nothing els but a disease." Bartholomaeus Anglicus, *Batman Vppon Bartholome His Booke De Proprietatibus Rerum, Newly Corrected, Enlarged and Amended* (London: Thomas East, 1582), 84r.

73. Stephens, *Demon Lovers*, 13, 46. Stephens interprets the recurrence of demonic sex in records of witch trials as evidence that "the concept of sex with demons needed constant reinforcement," for witchcraft theorists saw in carnal knowledge precisely that, a form of *knowledge* helping them prove the existence of demons, angels, and spirits in their struggle against their own skepticism (7). While the significance of witch hunt and witch panic as an episode of social history trumps its significance as an episode in intellectual history, Stephens's account provides a useful context to understand the cultural rise of the figure of the succuba.

74. James I, *Daemonologie, in the Forme of a Dialogue, Divided into Three Books* (Edinburgh: Robert Walde-grave Printer to the Kings Majestie, 1597), 52.

75. James I, *Daemonologie*, 53.

76. Stephens, *Demon Lovers*, 333.

77. "De telle copulation il en vient quelquefois des enfants, qu'ils appellant Wechselkind, ou enfans changez." Jean Bodin, *De la démonomanie des sorciers* (Paris: chez Jacques Dupuys, 1587), 118.

78. James I, *Daemonologie*, 53.

79. Heinrich Kramer and James Sprenger, *Malleus maleficarum*, ed. and trans. by Montague Summers, repr. of the 1928 ed. (New York: Dover, 1971).

80. Reginald Scot, *The Discoverie of Witchcraft* (London: Printed by Henry Denham for William Brome, 1584), 75.

81. Although witches and wizards are represented as seeking demonic copulation, consent quickly becomes an issue: demonic copulation was "allegedly undertaken eagerly by the novice witch, but she—or he—, was often portrayed as enduring it with regret and even loathing after the initial trysts." Stephens, *Demon Lovers*, 14.

82. Qtd. in Ania Loomba and Jonathan Burton, *Race in Early Modern England: A Documentary Companion* (New York: Palgrave Macmillan, 2007), 61.

83. Peter Biller, "Black Women in Medieval Medical Thought," in *Black Skin in the Middle Ages / La Peau Noire au Moyen Âge*, ed. Agostino Paravicini Bagliani (Florence: Sismel, Edizzioni del Galluzzo, 2014), 144.

84. Gainsh qtd. in Loomba and Burton, *Race in Early Modern England*, 127; Leo Africanus qtd. in Barthelemy, *Black Face, Maligned Race*, 6.

85. Qtd. in Loomba and Burton, *Race in Early Modern England*, 212.

86. Qtd. in Loomba and Burton, *Race in Early Modern England*, 227.

87. Walter Stephens refers to succuban sex as "sexual slavery" for either the male or the female witch: "sexual submission to demons was defined as a ritual act, demonstrating the witch's servitude, in both body and soul, to the demonic familiar and to Satan, the archenemy of God." Stephens, *Demon Lovers*, 13.

88. John Marston, *The Wonder of Women, or The Tragedie of Sophonisba as It Hath Beene Sundry Times Acted at the Blacke Friers* (London: Printed by John Windet, 1606); Celia R. Daileader, *Racism, Misogyny, and the Othello Myth: Inter-Racial Couples from Shakespeare to Spike Lee* (Cambridge: Cambridge University Press, 2005), 31.

89. "Zanche: My dream most concern'd you. Lodovico: Shal's fall a dreaming? / Francisco: Yes, and for fashion sake I'll dream with her. / Zanche: Methought sir, you came stealing to my bed. / Francisco: Wilt thou believe me sweeting; by this light / I was a dreamt on thee too: for me thought / I saw thee naked. Zanche: Fy sir! as I told you, / Methought you lay down by me. Francisco: So dreamt I; / And least thou should'st take cold, I cover'd thee / with this Irish mantle. Zanche: Verily I did dream, / You were some what bold with me." John Webster, *The White Devil*, 5.3.224–34. If we are to take such dream talk at face value, the fact that Zanche too was dreaming when Mulinassar appeared to her and engaged in sexual intercourse suggests that, from her viewpoint, he could be an incubus. In that sense, this line anticipates Zanche's later rejection of the succuban script foisted on her.

90. "He comes. Hence petty thought of my disgrace, / I never lov'd my complexion till now, / Cause I may boldly say without a blush, / I love you." John Webster, *The White Devil*, 5.2.234–37. This statement makes sense for spectators only if Mulinassar—a "sun-burnt gentleman," in Flamineo's words—appears to be as dark skinned as Zanche, and vice versa.

91. John Webster, *The White Devil*, 1.2.204–5.

92. Johann Jacob Wecker, *Cosmeticks, or The Beautifying Part of Physick* (London: Thomas Johnson, 1660), 35.

93. Richard Blunt, "The Evolution of Blackface Cosmetics on the Early Modern Stage," in *The Materiality of Color: The Production, Circulation, and Application of Dyes and Pigments, 1400–1800*, ed. Andrea Feeser, Maureen Daly Goggin, and Beth Fowkes Tobin (Burlington, Vt.: Ashgate, 2012), 226, 224.

94. William Shakespeare, *The Merchant of Venice*, 3.5.35.

95. Theresa Bane, *Encyclopedia of Beasts and Monsters in Myth, Legend, and Folklore* (Jefferson, N.C.: McFarland, 2016), 130.

96. Antonio de Torquemada, *The Spanish Mandeuile of Miracles* (London: Printed by James Roberts for Edmund Matts, 1600), 84.

97. Francis Beaumont and John Fletcher, *Monsieur Thomas, a Comedy: Acted at the Private House in Blacke Fryers* (London: Printed by Thomas Harper for John Waterson, 1639).

98. Beaumont and Fletcher, *Monsieur Thomas*, I.r, I.v.

99. "He bargain'd with her; and for some large price / Shee yeilded to be his. But in the night / In the condition'd bed was laid a Moore; / A hideous and detested Blackamore, / Which he (demanding light to please his eye, / As old men use all motives) / Discoverd and inrag'd, forsooke the house; / Affrighted and asham'd to aske his coyne againe." Richard Brome, *The Novella, A Comedy*, modern text, ed. Richard Cave, *Richard Brome Online*. http://www.dhi.ac.uk/brome. November 11, 2021. ISBN 978-0-9557876-1-4, 2.1.627–34.

100. They promise Tota that when Spencer bosoms her, "he will think he enfolds his lovely Bess"; they promise Mullisheg that when Bess is in bed with him, she will "think she hugs her Spencer"; and they promise Mullisheg that they will shift in Spencer's bed "a certain Moor whom I have hired for money / Which (poor soul) [Spencer] entertains for Bess." Thomas Heywood, *The Fair Maid of the West, or A Girle Worth Gold: The Second Part*, in *The First and Second Parts of The Fair Maid of the West, or A Girl Worth Gold, Two Comedies by Thomas Heywood*, edited by J. Payne Collier (London: Printed for the Shakespeare Society, 1850), 110–13.

101. This theatregram recurs in plays such as John Webster, *The Devils Law-Case, or When Women Goe to Law, the Devill Is Full of Businesse, A New Tragecomoedy* (London: Printed by Augustine Mathewes for John Grismand, 1623); Philip Massinger, *The Parliament of Love*, in *The Plays of Philip Massinger, from the Text of William Gifford*, ed. Francis Cunningham, 166–93 (London: Alfred Thomas Crocker, 1868); Walter Montagu, *The Shepheards Paradise, A Comedy* (London: Printed for Thomas Dring, 1629); William Berkeley, *The Lost Lady, a Tragy-Comedy* (London: Printed by Jo. Okes, for John Colby, 1638); William Hemings, *The Fatal Contract, a French Tragedy* (Printed at London for J. M., 1653).

102. Francis Beaumont and John Fletcher, *The Knight of Malta*, in *Comedies and Tragedies Written by Francis Beaumont and John Fletcher Never Printed Before*, 71–95 (London: Printed for Humphrey Robinson . . . and for Humphrey Moseley . . . , 1647).

103. On the valorization of Afro-diasporic women's musical skills in early modern performance culture across Europe, see Ndiaye, "Off the Record," 233.

104. Zanthia shares a free spirit with her sister Zanche and calls Mountferrat out on his opportunistic mobilization of demonization: "If any thing cross ye, / I am the devil, and the devils heir, / All plagues, all mischiefs. . . . I have done too much, / Far, far too much, for such a thankless fellow, / If I be devil, you created me; / I never knew those arts, nor bloody practices / (—o'your cunning heart, that mine of mischief) / Before your flatteries won 'em into me." Beaumont and Fletcher, *Knight of Malta*, 90.

105. Just a few years after *The Knight of Malta* premiered, the English would annex St. Kitts, Barbados, and Nevis in the Caribbean, and in the 1630s they would found the colonies of Maryland, Rhode Island, and Connecticut. Despite their failure to seize Hispaniola, the English seized Jamaica in 1655. The colonial project would soon make further progress, with the annexation of the Bahamas and New York, and the foundation of Carolina in the 1660s.

106. That myth informs many of the foundational texts in early modern race studies. Margaret Ferguson first mentioned it, stating that "male English actors could appear in black-up, but actresses evidently could not" in her seminal essay "Juggling the Categories of Race, Class, and Gender: Aphra Behn's *Oroonoko*," in *Women, "Race," and Writing in the Early Modern Period*, ed. Margo Hendricks and Patricia Parker, 209–24 (London: Routledge, 1994), 220. Ferguson does not provide primary evidence of this convention and only footnotes Wylie Sypher's *Guinea's Captive Kings: British Anti-Slavery Literature of the XVIIIth Century* (Chapel Hill: University of North Carolina Press, 1942). Ferguson, "Juggling the Categories of Race, Class, and Gender", 346 (note 36). Yet Sypher herself, analyzing why Imoinda turns white in Southerne's play, focuses on audiences' racial sensibility and does not mention any acting conventions (Sypher, *Guinea's Captive Kings*, 121). Arthur Little echoes Ferguson (Little, *Shakespeare Jungle Fever*, 163). The same myth is recounted by Heidi Hutner, who states that "women could not wear blackface," without citing or footnoting evidence, in *Colonial Women: Race and Culture in Stuart Drama* (New York: Oxford University Press, 2001), 16. Ayanna Thompson echoes Hutner in *Performing Race and Torture on the Early Modern Stage* (New York: Routledge, 2008), 30–31. The myth snowballed further when Felicity Nussbaum wrote that, besides the court masque *Calisto* (1675), Afro-diasporic women did not feature in Restoration drama, for "a blackface white woman in a central serious dramatic role would have violated femininity," in *The Limits of the Human: Fictions of Anomaly, Race, and Gender in the Long Eighteenth Century* (Cambridge: Cambridge University Press, 2003), 158.

107. John Dryden, *An Evening's Love, or The Mock-Astrologer Acted at the Theatre-Royal, by His Majesties Servants* (London: Printed by T.N. for Henry Herringman, 1671); Thomas St. Serfe, *Tarugo's Wiles, or The Coffee House, A Comedy* (London: Printed for Henry Herringman, 1668); Edward Howard, *The Womens Conquest, a Tragicomedy: As It Was Acted by His Highness the Duke of York's Servants* (London: Printed by J.M. for H. Herringman, 1671); Elkanah Settle, *The Empress of Morocco, a Tragedy with Sculptures* (London: Printed for William Cademan, 1673); Thomas Otway, *The Atheist, or The Second Part of The Souldiers Fortune Acted at the Duke's Theatre* (London: Printed for R. Bentley, and J. Tonson, 1684).

108. *The White Devil* was revived by the King's Company in 1661, when Pepys saw it. *Diary of Samuel Pepys*, ed. G. Gregory Smith (London: Macmillan, 1920), 103. It was also revived at the Phoenix in Drury Lane in 1665, and in 1671. *All's Lost by Lust* was revived in 1660; *Monsieur Thomas* was revived in 1661; *The Bondman* was revived in 1661, 1662, and 1664; *The Knight of Malta* was allowed to the King's Company and revived in 1691. Lennep, William Van, ed. *The London Stage, 1660–1800: A Calendar of Plays, Entertainments and Afterpieces, Together with Casts, Box-Receipts and Contemporary Comment*. Part 1: 1660–1700 (Carbondale: Southern Illinois University Press, 1965).

109. Blackburn, *Making of New World Slavery*, 143.

110. Qtd. in Loomba and Burton, *Race in Early Modern England*, 229.

111. On the connections between the representation of the so-called "unrepresentable" Afro-diasporic women in the seventeenth-century colonial stage, with its emphasis on the Virginia plantation version of colonialism and the representation of Native American women in the same corpus, see Hutner, *Colonial Women*.

112. Jennifer L. Morgan, *Laboring Women: Reproduction and Gender in New World Slavery* (Philadelphia: University of Pennsylvania Press, 2004), 3. Derek Hughes correctly states that "Restoration tragedy often romanticized interracial marriage" and "almost every Restoration play portraying Europeans and non-Europeans favorably portrays love between them." Derek Hughes, "Race, Gender, and Scholarly Practice: Aphra Behn's Oroonoko," *Essays in Criticism* 52, no. 1 (2002): 5–6. Yet the specific features of the transatlantic slavery culture excluded Afro-diasporic women from such positive representations of interracial romances. Afro-diasporic women were not like other "non-European women" because the fruit of their womb occupied a very particular place central to the very survival of colonial societies.

113. Elizabeth Maddock Dillon, *New World Drama: The Performative Commons in the At-lantic World, 1649–1849* (Durham, N.C.: Duke University Press, 2014), 29. On the colonial politics of Restoration drama—mainly heroic drama—see Bridget Orr's *Empire on the English Stage, 1660–1714* (Cambridge: Cambridge University Press, 2001); Cynthia Lowenthal's *Performing Identities on the Restoration Stage* (Carbondale: Southern Illinois University Press, 2003); and the afterword of Gavin Hollis in *The Absence of America: The London Stage, 1576–1642* (Oxford: Oxford University Press, 2015).

114. John Dryden and William Davenant, *The Tempest, or The Enchanted Island, A Comedy* (London: Printed by J.M. for Henry Herringman . . . , 1670), 15.

115. Susan B. Iwanisziw, "The Shameful Allure of Sycorax and Wowski: Dramatic Precursors of Sartje, the Hottentot Venus," *Restoration and 18th Century Theatre Research* 16, no. 2 (2001): 10, 11. Dryden writes in the preface: "the comical parts of the saylors were [Davenant's] invention." Since Sycorax interacts only with Caliban and the sailors, she probably was the creation of the same misogynoir-prone playwright who had staged Western design fantasies in the 1650s and turned Cleopatra into a "Gypsy" harlot in the 1660s.

116. David Bevington, ed. *Shakespeare The Tempest* (New York: Bantam Books, 1988), xxviii.

117. Such characters include, among others, the nameless "female black slave" with whom English sailors have their way in the anonymous *The Sailor's Opera, or A Trip to Jamaica* (London: Printed for the author, 1745); Quasheba "the Negro girl" in Isaac Bickerstaff's opera *The Romp, A Musical Entertainment* (London: Printed for W. Lowndes and J. Barker, 1786); Wowski, who is in high danger of being sold into slavery in George Colman's opera *Inkle and Yarico, An Opera* (Glasgow: Printed for the booksellers, 1796); and Cubba in William Macready *The Irishman in London, or The Happy African, A Farce* (Dublin: Printed by G. Perrin, for the Company of Booksellers, 1793).

118. These lines were excised from the versions of the play printed after the original edition of 1670 (in 1674, 1676, 1690, and 1695).

119. Morgan, *Laboring Women*, 7, 36.

120. Morgan, *Laboring Women*, 135.

121. Iwanisziw, "Shameful Allure of Sycorax," 12. Although Iwanisziw mentions only eighteenth-century productions, the text supports the idea that the 1667 masculinized Sycorax could have been performed by a man—Michael Dobson and Elizabeth Maddock Dillon think so. Michael Dobson, *The Making of the National Poet: Shakespeare, Adaptation and Authorship, 1660–1769* (Oxford: Clarendon Press, 1992), 56; Maddock Dillon, *New World Drama*, 106. This makes it hard to know, when Pepys writes on May 11, 1668, that, backstage, he "had the pleasure to see the actors in their several dresses, especially the seamen and monster, which were very droll," whether he is referring to Caliban or to Sycorax. *Diary of Samuel Pepys*, 649.

122. Stephano, who is already married, had seduced Sycorax away from Trincalo by promising to take her to Europe, where "we'll ride into the country where [Liquor] grows . . . upon a

hackney-devil of thy Mother's" (64). That promise proves empty; neither Stephano nor Trincalo takes her to Europe, where she could have been manumitted.

123. Miguel Cervantes Saavedra, *Ocho comedias, y ocho entremeses nuevos, nunca representados* (Madrid: por la viuda de Alonso Martín: a costa de Iuan de Villarroel, 1615), fol. IIv.

124. Besides Sánchez de Badajoz's previously mentioned *Farsa de la fortuna o hado* and *Farsa del moysen*, black male characters feature, for instance, in Hernán López de Yanguas's *La farsa dicha Turquesana contra el Turco muy galana* (1529), ed. Julio F. Hernando and Javier Espejo (Textos Lemir, 2002) https://parnaseo.uv.es/Lemir/textos/FarsaTurquesana/Index.htm Accessed November 20, 2021; Juan Pastor's *Farsa de Lucrecia: Tragedia de la castidad de Juan Pastor, mitad del siglo XVI*, ed. Amy Sevcik (*Revista Lemir*, no. 3, 1999) https://parnaseo.uv.es/lemir/Textos/Lucrecia/Lucrecia.html Accessed 20 November 2021.; and Martín de Santander's *Comedia Rosabella de Martín de Santander*, ed. José Luis Canet, (*Revista Lemir*, no. 1, 1996–97) http://parnaseo.uv.es/lemir/textos/M_Santander.html Accessed November 20, 2021.

125. Snorton, *Black on Both Sides*, 126.

126. While my reading of the participation of theatrical culture in the racialization of blackness in early modern Iberia differs profoundly from his, nobody has written more eloquently about theatrical *negras'* sense of self-worth than Nicholas R. Jones in *Staging Habla de Negros*, 119–64.

127. Vega Carpio, *El negro del mejor amo*, 34.

128. "La reina de Etiopia / Saba, donde al azabache / negro dio espiritu brioso / el blanco Belga Timantes." Vélez de Guevara, *Virtudes vencen señales*, 86. Obviously, the ancient Greek painter Timanthes was not Belgian.

129. "Ebano y jaspe / Porque en la tez se parezca." Calderón de la Barca, *La sibila del Oriente y gran reyna de Saba*, 338.

130. "Agora te pones a enrubiar?" Lope de Rueda, *Comedia llamada Eufemia*, 28v. "Un poquito de mozaza, un poquito de trementinos . . . para hacer una muda para las manos" (Lope de Rueda, *Comedia llamada Eufemia*, 30r). For a different reading of Eulalla's desire for Eurocentric beauty, see Jones, *Staging Habla de Negros*, 125–45.

131. The laboring status of the *mulatas* encountered in comedias nuevas is palpable in contemporary visual culture, especially, in Velázquez's gorgeous *Cena de Emaús*, also known as *La mulata*, painted between 1620 and 1622, during the painter's stay in Seville.

132. "Una esclava mulatilla, / de semblante socarrón, / que ya sabes, que estos son / los lunares de Sevilla; / sin envidiar el marfil, / la tez de ébano lustrosa, / más limpia y más olorosa / que flor de almendro en abril. / Y más áspera que un rallo / al peligro inobediente, / con sombrerito en la frente / como antojo de caballo, / y su chinela briosa / que cubre el pie de nogal." Félix Lope de Vega Carpio, *Amar, servir, y esperar* (Madrid: por la viuda de Iuan Gonçalez, a costa de Domingo de Palacio y Villegas y Pedro Verges, 1635), 52 r.

133. "Y yo te daré un collar / de esmeraldas y berruecos, / que llamar puedas marfil / lo que hasta agora pescuezo." Vega Carpio, *Amar, servir, y esperar*, 56r. My translation emphasizes the animalizing connotations of the word "pescuezo": the term primarily refers to an animal's neck and only by extension to a human neck.

134. "Un tocadillo encajado en la cabeza de pelo negro rizo." Vega Carpio, *Servir a señor discreto*, 95.

135. "Sueltos en crespos rizos sus cabellos." Vega Carpio, *El premio de bien hablar y volver por las mujeres*, 13.

136. Vega Carpio, *La vitoria de la honra*, 200.

137. Ramón María Serrera Contreras ed., "Introduction," in *El Arenal de Sevilla de Lope de Vega* (Seville: Ayuntamiento de Sevilla, Colección "Sevilla lee," 2007), 151.

138. Tamar Herzog, "How Did Early Modern Slaves in Spain Disappear?" 3.

139. Jean Sentaurens, *Séville et le théâtre: De la fin du Moyen Âge à la fin du XVIIe siècle* (Lille: Atelier national de reproduction des thèses, Université de Lille III / Talence: Diffusion, Presses universitaires de Bordeaux, Université de Bordeaux III, 1984), 794.

140. "Mulata de quien estoy informado, / que corta en el aire un pelo." Vega Carpio, *Servir a señor discreto*, 93.

141. "Me parece dispuesta / si algun interes le inclina." Vega Carpio, *Los peligros de la ausencia*, 202r.

142. "Tienen el cuero muy suave." Vega Carpio, *Servir a señor discreto*, 128.

143. "Yo tengo por mi buen / mi color porque el Moreno / dicen que a los hombres mata." Vega Carpio, *Servir a señor discreto*, 119.

144. "El criado es un hombre / Asi de mi color y bien hablado" Vega Carpio, *Servir a señor discreto*, 229.

145. "Tan blanco es vuessa merced?" Vega Carpio, *Servir a señor discreto*, 287.

146. "Elvira: Dinero, dices? / Giron: Dinero. / Elvira: Pues con tan gran Caballero / Te ha faltado el dinerillo? / Giron: A el no, mas a mi si. / Elvira: Con el que puede faltarte? / Bien puedes tu regalarte / Con mi memoria. / Giron: Es ansi? / Elvira: Que lleves mi alma quiero. / Giron: Mejor tu cuerpo quisiera. / Que en efeto le vendiera / Y me valiera dinero." Vega Carpio, *Servir a señor discreto*, 185–86.

147. "Giron: ¡Negrita! / Elvira: Por mi desastre. / Deja esas necias porfias. / Cuélgame al cuello, y por Dios / Que parezcamos los dos / Tintero y escribanias. / Giron: Lindo azabache me cuelgo." Vega Carpio, *Servir a señor discreto*, 286–87.

148. "Yo callaré como si de bronze fuera." Vega Carpio, *Servir a señor discreto*, 232.

149. "Como al oro en el crisol / Giron, purifica el grano de Soliman." Vega Carpio, *Servir a señor discreto*, 138–39.

150. "Bien haya amén / El caballero que amó / Tu madre, pues engastó / Ebano en marfil tan bien." Vega Carpio, *Servir a señor discreto*, 143.

151. "Pedro: Plauto disculpa mejor / La lisonja de quien ama. / Que dize que hasta los perros / De sus damas lisonjean. / Pues como los perros sean / la disculpa de sus yerros, / Mira si alabo bien / la mulata. / Giron: Harto bien amas, / Pues que ya perra la llamas. / Pedro: Perra, y aun perla también." Vega Carpio, *Servir a señor discreto*, 140.

152. In that sense, Don Pedro echoes Motril who, in *La Otava maravilla* (1609), calls the *mulata* Inès "a nest of blue jays" (nido de grajos) and an "affected bitch" (galga relamida), following sixteenth-century conventions for characterizing stage *negras*. Félix Lope de Vega Carpio, *La otava maravilla* (Madrid: por la viuda de Alonso Martín de Balboa, a costa de Miguel de Siles, 1618), 159v.

153. "Y a mi tras el hollín de aquella perra, / perla quize decir." Vega Carpio, *Servir a señor discreto*, 194.

154. "Perra, perla, quería decir." Vega Carpio, *El premio de bien hablar y volver por las mujeres*, 11; *La vitoria de la honra*, 180v; *Los peligros de la ausencia*, 198r.

155. Vega Carpio, *Servir a señor discreto*, 128, 145, 97, 323.

156. "Amo, el Amor se ha embargado, / desde Guinea a Sevilla"; "por loarte consultara / a las Musas de Etiopia, / porque fuera cosa impropia / que las de España invocara." Vega Carpio, *Servir a señor discreto*, 141, 119.

157. "Suffrir no puedo / esas burlas por su vida. / Esto poco de vayeta / cortó de mi madre un sastre." Vega Carpio, *Servir a señor discreto*, 144.

158. "Elvira me fecit / porque ninguna bellaca, / ose hablar en su persona / en conociendo la marca." Vega Carpio, *Servir a señor discreto*, 161.

159. A masculine version of this *mulato* Black pride features in *Los comendadores de Córdoba* (1596–98), where Lope de Vega has the white servant Galindo recount how he got into a fight with a *mulato* cook. When the *mulato* asserts himself rhetorically (before using physical language), he defends the cause of the Afro-Spanish community at large, and it is, ironically, Galindo who reminds him that he is only half Black, by evoking the possibility that his mother might have been Jewish. Félix Lope de Vega Carpio, *Los comendadores de Córdoba* (Barcelona: en casa de Sebastian de Cormellas al Call, vendese en la mesma emprenta, 1611), Bb2r.

160. "Si tengo / hijos Axedrez seran, / pues seran blancos y negros." Vega Carpio, *Servir a señor discreto*, 323.

161. Vega Carpio, *Los peligros de la ausencia*, 198r.

162. Vega Carpio, *La dama boba*, [1st ed.], ed. Isidoro Montiel (Madrid: Ediciones Castilla, 1948), 135.

163. Mimma de Salvo, *La mujer en la prática escénica de los siglos de oro: La búsqueda de un espacio profesional* (Ph.D. diss., Universitat de València, Facultat de Filología Española, 2006), 192–93.

164. Vega Carpio, *Amar, servir, y esperar*, 34.

165. Vega Carpio, *Amar, servir, y esperar*, 34.

166. N. D. Shergold and Peter Ure, "Dryden and Calderón: A New Spanish Source for 'The Indian Emperour,'" *Modern Language Review* 61, no. 3 (1966): 370.

167. Dryden, *An Evening's Love*, 2.

168. Dryden, *An Evening's Love*, 45.

169. The sexual allure of *mulatas* in Hispanic societies was well known in England. In 1625, Thomas Gage visited Mexico city and remarked: "A Blackamoor or a tawny young maid and slave will make hard shift, but she will be in fashion with her neck-chain and bracelets of pearls and her earbobs of considerable jewels. The attire of this baser sort of Blackamoors and Mulattoes . . . is so light and their carriage so enticing that many Spaniards, even of the better sort (who are too too prone to venery) disdain their wives for them." Qtd. in Bennett, *Africans in Colonial Mexico*, 32.

170. Dryden, *An Evening's Love*, 52.

171. Dryden, *An Evening's Love*, 52.

172. Pedro Calderón de la Barca, *El astrólogo fingido*, in *Parte veynte y cinco de comedias recopiladas de diferentes autores è ilustres poetas de España* (Zaragoza: a costa de Pedro Escuer . . . , 1632), 193v–216r.

173. Baltasar Fra-Molinero, "Ser mulato en España y América: Discursos legales y otros discursos literarios," in *Negros, mulatos, zambaigos: Derroteros africanos en los mundos ibéricos*, ed. Berta Ares Queija and Alessandro Stella (Sevilla: Escuela de Estudios Hispano-Americanos, Consejo Superior de Investigaciones Científicas, 2000), 126.

174. Fra-Molinero, "Ser mulato en España y America," 127.

175. "La quintessencia / de toda la discreta picardía / que lo Moreno de esta tierra cría." Vega Carpio, *El premio de bien hablar y volver por las mujeres*, 8. La Chaves is not called a *mulata*, but she is called "comadre" in the play. Vicente Suárez de Deza y Avila, *Bayle entremesado del galeote mulato*, in *Parte primera de los donayres de Tersícore* (Madrid: por Melchor Sánchez, a costa de Mateo de la Bastida, 1663), 146v. Jonathan Schorsch notes that "in Inquisition testimony, slaves

seem to reserve the term *compadre* for other slaves or free *Mulatos / Mulatas.*" Schorsch, *Swimming the Christian Atlantic: Judeoconversos, Afroiberians and Amerindians in the Seventeenth Century* (Boston: Brill, 2009), 32.

176. Alessandro Stella, *Histoires d'esclaves dans la péninsule ibérique* (Paris: EHESS, 2000), 174.

177. Stella, *Histoires d'esclaves dans la péninsule ibérique*, 185.

178. Elio Antonio de Nebrija, *Vocabulario español-latino* (Salamanca, ca. 1495).

179. "Nombres nuevos para nombrar diversas generaciones." Garcilaso de la Vega, *Primera parte de los comentarios reales* (Lisbon: Pedro Crasbeeck, 1609), 255. In Peru, Garcilaso writes, Spaniards are called "españoles" or "castellanos," slaves brought from Africa are called "*negros*" or "*guineos*," Spaniards' children born in the Indies are called "criollos," just like the children of negros slaves born in the Indies. Children born from a "*negro*" and an "*indio*" are called "*mulatos*," and mulatos' children are called "*cholos*" (an injurious term, according to Garcilaso, who does not explain why *mulatos'* children are perceived so negatively). Meanwhile, children born from "castellanos" and "*indios*," such as Garcilaso himself, are called "*mestizos*"; children born from "castellanos" and "*mestizos*" are called "*quatralvos*," and children born from "*mestizos*" and "*indios*" are called "*tresalvos*" (255). Garcilaso's interests clearly lean—for obvious reasons—more toward Indian / Spanish *mestizaje* than African / Spanish *mestizaje*, but this short chapter suggests that, about a century before *pinturas de castas* boomed in New Spain, the racial classification of "nations" "mixed in all kinds of manners" was already on the rise in the empire, as a result of colonial expansion.

180. "Ay hombres blancos de muchas maneras de blancura, y negros de muchas maneras de negregura: y de blanco va a Bermejo por descolorido y rubio, y a negro por ceniciento, moreno, rojo, y leonado, como los Indios deste Nuevo mundo, los quales son todos en general como leonados, o membrillos cochos, atericiados, o castaños, lo qual tambien se verifica en los negros." Alonso de Sandoval, *De instauranda aethiopum salute*, 10.

181. "Amulatados, o del todo mulatos, pardos, zambos, de color bazo, loro, castaño o tostado, porque toda esta variedad y mucho mas colores tiene esta nacion entresi." Alonso de Sandoval, *De instauranda aethiopum salute*, 12.

182. In New Spain for instance, between 1570 and 1646, the creole population, mostly comprising free *mulatos*, grew fiftyfold despite the intensification of the slave trade. In 1646, there were 116,529 creoles, as opposed to 35,089 Novo-Spaniards born in Africa. Bennett, *Africans in Colonial Mexico*, 23.

183. "Y que como no conocen otros deudos sino los de sus madres, se juntan con ellos, de que andando el tiempo podria haber inconvenientes." Qtd. in Lucena Salmoral, "Leyes para esclavos," 179.

184. Joanne Rappaport, *The Disappearing Mestizo: Configuring Difference in the Colonial New Kingdom of Granada* (Durham, N.C.: Duke University Press, 2014), 4, 10, 70–81.

185. Lucena Salmoral, "Leyes para esclavos," 183.

186. Stuart Schwartz and Frank Salomon, "New Peoples and New Kinds of People: Adaptation, Readjustment, and Ethnogenesis in South American Indigenous Societies (Colonial Era)," in *The Cambridge History of the Native Peoples of the Americas, Volume 3: South America, Part 2*, ed. Frank Salomon and Stuart B. Schwartz (Cambridge: Cambridge University Press, 1999), 444.

187. Monica Styles, "Foreshadowing Failure: Mulatto and Black Oral Discourse and the Upending of the Western Design in Thomas Gage's *A New Survey* (1648)," *Hispania* 102, no. 4 (2019): 585.

188. Barbara Fuchs, *Passing for Spain: Cervantes and the Fictions of Identity* (Urbana: University of Illinois Press, 2003), 2.

189. Barbara Fuchs, "The Spanish Race," in *Re-Reading the Black Legend: The Discourses of Religious and Racial Difference in the Renaissance Empires*, ed. Margaret R. Greer, Walter D. Mignolo, and Maureen Quilligan (Oxford: Oxford University Press, 2008), 95.

190. Barbara Fuchs, "A Mirror Across the Water: Mimetic Racism, Hybridity, and Cultural Survival," in *Writing Race Across the Atlantic World*, ed. Philip D. Beidler and Gary Taylor (New York: Palgrave, 2005), 13.

191. Jean E. Feerick, *Strangers in Blood: Relocating Race in the Renaissance* (Toronto: University of Toronto Press, 2010).

192. Susan S. Lanser, *The Sexuality of History: Modernity and the Sapphic, 1565–1830* (Chicago: University of Chicago Press, 2014), 18.

CHAPTER 3

1. "Sahe o Negro da fragoa muito gentil Homem branco, porém a fala de negro. Nao se pode tirar na fragoa, e elle diz: Negro: Ja mao minha branco estai, / E aqui perna branco he, / Mas a mi fala guiné: / Se a mi negro falai, / A mi branco para que? / Se fala meu he negregado, / E nao fala Portugas, / Para que mi martelado? / Mercurio: No podemos haver mas, / Lo que pediste te han hecho." Gil Vicente, *Fragoa d'amor*, in *Obras de Gil Vicente, Tomo II*, edited by J. da S. Mendes Leal Junior and F.J. Pinheiro, 336–37 (Lisbon: Escriptorio da Bibliotheca Portugueza, 1852). The epigraph is from Branden Jacobs-Jenkins, *An Octoroon* (New York: Dramatists Service, 2015), 19.

2. Vicente, *Fragoa d'amor*, 338. I am grateful to Josiah Blackmore for bringing this text to my attention; my translation of this passage is indebted to his.

3. Jennifer Lynn Stoever, *The Sonic Color Line: Race and the Cultural Politics of Listening* (New York: New York University Press, 2016), 4–7.

4. "Cada uno de los años que su cofradia sale en la semana santa tienen pendencias unas veces con cofradías que concurren aquella noche de gente principal y otras veces con personas que hacen burlas dellos." Biblioteca Colombina AGAS, Caja 9885, expediente 1.

5. "Mucha gente silvaba y hacía otros ruidos afrentosos a los dichos negros, hablándoles en guineo y affrentándoles en grandes desonor de la procession y representación de la Pasión de nuestro Salvador, de lo cual los negros se corrían y respondían otras palabras, y juraban juramentos diciendo palabras afrentosas a los que les silvaban, de lo qual se seguía que parecía cosa de risa y entremés mas que procesión de Semana Santa." Isidoro Moreno Navarro, *La antigua hermandad de los negros de Sevilla: Etnicidad, poder y sociedad en 600 años de historia* (Seville: Universidad de Sevilla, Consejería de Cultura de la Junta de Andalucía, 1997), 86.

6. Most of the meticulous linguistic scholarship dedicated to habla de negros has sought to assess the distance between blackspeak and authentic early modern Afro-Spanish speech forms. Edmund de Chasca, "The Phonology of the Speech of the Negroes in Early Spanish Drama," *Hispanic Review* 14, no. 4 (1946): 322–39; John M. Lipski, *A History of Afro-Hispanic Language: Five Centuries, Five Continents* (Cambridge: Cambridge University Press, 2005); Antonio Salvador Plans, "Los lenguajes 'especiales' y de las minorías en el siglo de oro," in *Historia de la lengua española*, ed. Rafael Cano (Barcelona: Editorial Ariel, 2004), 771–97. Another focus has been to determine whether blackspeak replicated Afro-Iberian speech forms born in the Iberian peninsula or in Portuguese outposts on the African continent: Paul Teyssier, *La langue de Gil Vicente* (Paris: C. Klincksieck, 1959); Germán de Granda, *El español en tres mundos: Retenciones y contactos lingüísticos en América y África* (Valladolid: Universidad de Valladolid, Secretariado de Publicaciones, 1991). Another group of scholars, more literary, have focused on the

genealogy and evolution of blackspeak in the dramatic canon (Consolación Baranda Leturio, "Las hablas de negros. Orígenes de un personaje literario," *Revista de Filología Española* 69, nos. 3–4 [1989]: 311–33); on its comedic effect (Frida Weber de Kurlat, "Sobre el negro como tipo cómico en el teatro español del siglo XVI," *Romance Philology* 17, no. 2 [1963]: 380–91); on its parody of institutional discourses (Baltasar Fra-Molinero, *La imagen de los negros en el teatro del Siglo de Oro* [Madrid: siglo veintiuno de españa editores, 1995]); and on its channeling of authentic Afro-Spanish voices (Nicholas R. Jones, *Staging Habla de Negros: Radical Performances of the African Diaspora in Early Modern Spain* [University Park: Pennsylvania State University Press, 2019]).

7. Alain Fleischer, *L'accent, une langue fantôme* (Paris: Le Seuil, 2005).

8. Jennifer Linhart Wood, *Sounding Otherness in Early Modern Drama and Travel: Uncanny Vibrations in the English Archive* (Cham, Switzerland: Palgrave Macmillan, 2019), 2.

9. Jennifer Linhart Wood makes a similar distinction when she argues that "otherness is sounded through experimental performance, which could include unusual instruments and non-normative performance techniques on familiar instruments." Wood, *Sounding Otherness in Early Modern Drama and Travel*, 23.

10. "Chi linguacina bacu lapia clama gurgh." Orlando di Lasso, *Libro de villanelle, moresche, e altre canzoni* (Anversa: Pierre Phalèse et Jean Bellère, 1582), 11v. My translation is based on the translation offered by Eric Rice in Program of the Ensemble Origo concert "Motets, Madrigals and Moresche: Orlando di Lasso's Music for the Commedia dell'Arte at a 1568 Wedding," Italian Academy, Columbia University, October 2015. I amended Rice's translation in light of Gianfranco Salvatore's invitation to reckon with Kanuri linguistic imports in moresche lyrics. Gianfranco Salvatore, "Parodie realistiche. Africanismi, fraternità e sentimenti identitari nelle canzoni moresche del Cinquecento," *Kronos* 14 (Università del Salento, 2011): 97–130. "Lapia" was indeed a general blessing formula in Kanuri. Charles Henry Robinson, *Dictionary of the Hausa Language, Vol. 1. Hausa-English* (Cambridge: Cambridge University Press, 1913), 227.

11. Orlando di Lasso, *Libro de villanelle*, 11v.

12. George Orwell, *1984*, ed. Robert Icke and Duncan Macmillan (London: Oberon Books, 2014).

13. Fra-Molinero, *La imagen de los negros*, 3.

14. Stoever, *Sonic Color Line*, 7.

15. Luis Quiñones de Benavente, *Entremés cantado de las dueñas*, in *Ioco Seria: Burlas veras, o reprehension moral, y festiua de los desordenes públicos*, 168v–172v (Madrid: Por Francisco Garcia, a costa de Manuel Lopez, 1645).

16. For David Theo Goldberg, a relational account, rather than performing a simple "compare and contrast" analysis, "reveals through indicating how effects are brought about as a result of historical, political, or economic, legal or cultural links, the one acting upon the other. . . . A relational account connects materially and affectively, causally and implicatively." David Theo Goldberg, "The Comparative and the Relational: Meditations on Racial Methods," in *A Companion to Comparative Literature*, ed. Ali Behdad and Dominic Thomas (Chichester, U.K.: Wiley-Blackwell, 2011), 361–62.

17. Ian Smith, *Race and Rhetoric in the Renaissance*, 28.

18. Bruce Smith, *The Acoustic World of Early Modern England: Attending to the O-Factor* (Chicago: University of Chicago Press, 1999), 334.

19. Robert Hornback, *Racism and Early Blackface Comic Traditions*, 143, 169.

20. Jones, *Staging Habla de Negros*, 5, 19, 68.

21. Bruce Smith, *The Acoustic World of Early Modern England*, 47.

22. María Paz Calvo Lozano and Ursula de Luis-André Quattelbaum, "Dinámica de la población, 1560–1804," in *Madrid, Atlas historico de la ciudad, siglos IX–XIX*, ed. Virgilio Pinto Crespo and Santos Madrazo Madrazo (Barcelona: Fundación Caja de Madrid and Lunwerg Editores, 1995), 147.

23. Similarly, calle de las Negras (black women's street), which still exists today, just below the Liria palace, was apparently called so because there lay a pavilion hosting the enslaved who belonged to Christopher Colombus's nephews, the Dukes of Veragua. Pedro de Répide, *Las calles de Madrid,* edited by Federico Romero (Madrid: Afrodisio Aguado, S.A., 1971), 446.

24. For instance, Antonio Martínez, a costume maker, seller, and renter as well as a musician and choreographer (he designed the dances of the 1628 Corpus Christi procession in Seville), had his shop, his home, and possibly a couple of houses on this street. When Martínez and his wife, the actress Isabel de Cordoba, died, their daughters, actresses Sebastiana Martínez and María de Cordoba, inherited their parents' estate on calle de los Negros where they had grown up. Sebastiana and her husband, the playwright Luis de Toledo, still lived there in 1631. Another example: Luis de Monzón, a choreographer, costume maker, seller, and renter, a sometime actor and "lessor of the *corrales* in Madrid," conducted business on calle de los Negros while living on Plaza Mayor. In 1608, he bought from Ana Muñoz, who lived on calle de los Negros, the stock of theatre costumes she inherited from her late husband, Martín Gonzalez, who used to be a costume maker, seller, and renter; and in 1612, he provided actor and choreographer Gabriel Angel with a place to live on calle de los Negros so that Angel might look after his costume-renting shop for him. Teresa Ferrer Valls, ed., *Diccionario biográfico de actores del teatro clásico español (DICAT)* (Kassel: Reichenberger, 2008).

25. Mimma de Salvo, "La mujer en la prática escénica de los siglos de oro," 188.

26. Between 1647 and 1652, the Great Plague decimated the population of Seville, wreaking particular havoc on the most vulnerable communities, such as the Afro-Spanish communities in the suburbs extra muros (*arrabales*). Moreover, the emancipation of Portugal, which regained its independence from Spain in 1640, was a serious blow to the Iberian slave trade, for Portugal had been the exclusive purveyor of slaves in Spain for a century and a half under the system of the *asiento.* The interruption of this trade agreement abruptly cut supplies: the Afro-diasporic population that had been decimated in Seville could not be replenished. The situation was comparable in Madrid, where, starting in 1640, enslaved Afro-Spaniards saw their number drop and largely taken over by white Muslim slaves. Claude Larquié, "Les esclaves de Madrid à l'époque de la décadence, 1650–1700," *Revue Historique* 244, fasc. 1 (495) (1970): 57.

27. Aristocrats' taste for and patronage of entremeses was well known. María Luisa Lobato notes that entremeses and the other short pieces that accompanied comedia performances, such as *loas* or *mojigangas*, began to be published in collections, separately from comedia playtexts in 1640. It is "a sociological curiosity" that those collections "have dedications usually directed to members of the aristocracy." Lobato, "La edición de textos teatrales breves," in *La edición de textos, Actas del I congreso internacional de hispanistas del Siglo de Oro*, ed. Pablo Jauralde, Dolores Noguera, and Alfonso Rey (London: Tamesis Books, 1990), 292.

28. Between 1650 and 1700, 87 percent of enslaved Afro-Spaniards who received baptism belonged to aristocrats. Larquié, "Les esclaves de Madrid à l'époque de la décadence," 65.

29. To the extent that blackspeak was always meant to convey its own whiteness to auditors, attempts at measuring the distance—increasing or decreasing over time—between blackspeak and authentic Afro-Spanish speech forms give little insight into the ontology of that performance technique. Readers interested in those approaches, however, might want to consult the work of John M. Lipski, and Antonio Salvador Plans, who both note that "from the second half

of the seventeenth century onward, we face the gradual decadence of this genre, which becomes increasingly stereotypical." Antonio Salvador Plans, "Los lenguajes 'especiales' y de las minorías en el siglo de oro," 776. This evolution leads them to conclude that, in the second half of the seventeenth century, playwrights who used blackspeak imitated and caricatured earlier versions of blackspeak, drawing on a sedimented trope that had little relation to linguistic reality any longer.

30. "Venimo lo neglo, hermano, / A da oberencia a Reye, / Que son vassayo de leye, / Como branco cortezano. / Juran dioso sagaravo, / Y que sa Maria Hermosa, / Mas beya que brancun roza, / Y lo Niño soberano. / Gun gulum gua. / Cantando y bairando / Venimo adora, / Gungulum gun / Gungulun gua." *Villanzicos y chanzonetas que se cantaron en el coro de la santa Iglesia mayor de Sevilla, a la venida de los santos Reyes a Belen, recien nacido Iesu Christo. Celebrada esto año de 1644* (Seville: Simón Fajardo, 1644), n.p.

31. Lipski, *History of Afro-Hispanic Language*, 90.

32. Glenn Swiadon, "Los villancicos de negro: Breve introducción al género," *Dimensión Antropológica* 5, no. 14 (1998): 4.

33. Góngora's habla de negros poems include his Corpus Christi poem "En la fiesta del Santísimo sacramento," 1609; his Christmas poem "Al nacimiento de Cristo nuestro señor," 1615; and his Epiphany poem "En la fiesta de la adoración de los reyes," 1615—all of which mock the participation of Afro-Spaniards in the great Catholic feasts—as well as his sonnet "A la Jerusalen Conquistada de Lope de Vega," 1609. Horacio Jorge Becco, ed, *El tema del negro en cantos, bailes y villancicos de los siglos XVI y XVII* (Buenos Aires: Ollantay, 1951), 35–41. On Sor Juana Inés de la Cruz's use of blackspeak, see Nicholas R. Jones, "Hyperbolic Hybridities: *Habla de Negros* and the Economies of Race and Language in Early Modern Spanish Poetry and Theater" (Ph.D. diss., New York University, 2013; UMI: 3601670), 100–144.

34. Tirso de Molina, *El negro, entremés famoso,* in *Segunda parte de las comedias del maestro Tirso de Molina* (Madrid: en la Imprenta del Reino, 1635), 284r–285v.

35. "Guitarriya, a como suena, / no sé que diabro se tiene / este modo de instrumenta, / como li tengo aficion / todo en el alma me yeua / aqui embosado le escucho, / aunque el dia me amanesca." Tirso de Molina, *El negro,* 284v.

36. "Argales: Quieres callar? / Domingo: Si seor, / cayarè como vna dueña, / como monja en locutorio, / como una ochentona suegra, / como niño si le açotan, / como quien perdiendo juega, / como vn herrador vesino, / como gato, y perro en prensa, / como una muger de parto, / como quien trampas pleitea, / como vulgo si se enoja / en vna mala comedia; / de cayar como estos cayan, / juro an Dioso, y en mi cunciencia. / Argales: Viue Dios, que si no callas, / que te rompa la cabeça. / Domingo: Non puedo mas, señor mio, / Plunuiera an Dios, que quisiera / vn sapatero, a dos cabos / cuserme la boca, y luengua. / Pero de mi cundision / pienso, que aunque la cusiera, / que auia de hablar pur ojos, / pur las manos las orejas, / pur los pies, pur la rodilla, / pur los muslos, pur las piernas / pur las espaldas, y luego / pur otro ojo que me queda. / Gra.: Negro del diablo, si callas, / te haremos aqui vna fiesta. / Domingo: Cayarè, con cundision, / que tengo de entrar en eya, / que tambien sabo bailar." Tirso de Molina, *El negro,* 285v.

37. The obsession of black speech with the body often intersects with the comic physicality of blackspeak when phonetic distortions create sexual puns. For instance, one pun circulates in several texts in blackspeak: the distortion of the word *corazón* (heart) into *culazón* (a voluptuous behind). In Simón Aguado's 1602 interlude *Los negros,* Dominga declares to her future husband Gaspar how much she loves him, "como a la tela del culazón." She means "like the fabric of my heart," but, through blackspeak, audience members hear "like the fabric of my curvaceous behind." Simón Aguado, *Los negros, entremés,* in Cotarelo y Mori, ed., *Collección,* 232. In his re-

writing of Tirso de Molina's *El negro*, Luis Quiñones de Benavente made sure to alter the first line delivered by his black protagonist in order to repeat that pun. Quiñones de Benavente, *El negrito hablador y sin color anda la niña*, in *Navidad y Corpus Christi, festejados por los mejores ingenios de España, en diez y seis autos a lo divino, diez y seis loas, y diez y seis entremeses. Representados en esta corte y nunca hasta aora impressos. Recogidos por Isidro de Robles, natural de Madrid* (Madrid: por Joseph Fernández de Buendía, a costa de Isidro de Robles, 1664), 129.

38. "Comiera, plegueten Dioso, / para poder estar buena, / tuzino, baca, carnero, / ganyina, periz, coneja, / palonmino, ganso, pambo, / poyos, y poyas sin cresta; / capun de leche, churiso, / solomiyo, y su moyeja, / salchichone, longanisa, / y cubilete de peya. . . . Si vn amante te desvela, / a cada essequina ayaràs / amantes de mil maneras, / vno lo vigote rubio, / y la cabenyera negra: / otro muy gordo de cuerpo, / muy delgadito den pierna, / otro, que con la valona, / tanta nues echa den fuera, / que como a narise, puede / poner antojos en eya: / otro, que—" Tirso de Molina, *El negro*, 284v.

39. Carmen Fracchia studies the renderings of the miracle of the black leg in early modern Castilian iconography and their insistence on the pain of the African who has been amputated alive in order to provide a white man with a new leg. She convincingly reads this transformation of the black leg miracle motif as an aesthetic acknowledgement of "the exploitation and violent appropriation of the African body by the mighty imperial power of Spain." Fracchia, *"Black but Human,"* 153.

40. Sigmund Freud, *Jokes and Their Relation to the Unconscious*, in *The Standard Edition of the Complete Psychological Works of Sigmund Freud*, vol. 8, trans. and ed. James Strachey (New York: Norton, 1960), 194.

41. George Puttenham, *The Art of English Poesy*, ed. Frank Whigham and Wayne A. Rebhorn (Ithaca, N.Y.: Cornell University Press, 2007), 228.

42. Jones, "Hyperbolic Hybridities," 5.

43. Huete, *Tesorina*, 96.

44. Freud, *Jokes and Their Relation to the Unconscious*, 225.

45. Teyssier, *La langue de Gil Vicente*, 229.

46. Tirso de Molina, *El negro*, 285v.

47. Fra-Molinero, *La imagen de los negros*, 8.

48. Henri Bergson, *Le rire, essai sur la signification du comique* (Paris: Éditions Alcan, 1924), 16.

49. Freud, *Jokes and Their Relation to the Unconscious*, 249.

50. "No puedo (callar), juro an Christo, por mas que hago." Tirso de Molina, *El negro*, 285v.

51. Quiñones de Benavente, *El negrito hablador*, 128. Quiñones de Benavente's entremés is longer than Tirso's, it uses more specific indications (of location, and dance names, for instance), and its protagonist is much more stylized than Tirso's. These elements suggest that it was Benavente who reworked Tirso's entremés, not the reverse.

52. *Entremés de la negra lectora*, in *Arcadia de entremeses escritos por los ingenios mas clasicos de España*, 164–75 (Madrid: Ángel Pasqual Rubio, 1723).

53. "Quien les mete a las neglas / Ser tan sabidas, / Estudien solo en libros / De las cocinas." *Entremés de la negra lectora*, 175.

54. "Dizen que esta Morenilla / A leer, y a escribir la enseña / Manuel Perez Botijon, / Esse Maestro de escuela, / Y en saliendo los muchachos / Le viene a dar a la Negra / Leccion en vna cartilla; / Y como es Negra bozal, / Podrà nuestra diligencia / Engañarla fácilmente, / Que ella quiera, ò que no quiera; / Llevaremosle el Maestro, / Que la adoctrina, y enseña / Para que le de leccion / Y le enseñe nuestra lengua; / Y quando ella entretenida / Estè en su entretenimiento / El

menudillo, y los callos / Quitaremos a la perra, / Y luego los tres saldremos / Cada vno con su vihuela, / A celebrarle los dichos, / Y hazer burla de la treta, / diziendole algunos dichos / Que ella dezirlos no pueda, / Ni pronunciar." *Entremés de la negra lectora*, 164–65.

55. "Maestro: H. / Negra: Cache. / Maestro: H. / Negra (haziendo fuerza para pronunciar la letra): H. / Ahora todos tres de dar grandes estornudos, diziendo guachi en lugar de ache, con grande fiesta y bulla, y el Maestro tambien con ellos hará lo mismo, puesto enteojos. / Francisco: Ay, que bona lectora, / Esta la plima beyaca mandingola!" *Entremés de la negra lectora*, 172–73.

56. The few scholars who have promoted sound as an epistemic mode in early modern studies have often yielded to that temptation. For instance, Gina Bloom reads the difficulty that English boy actresses had in controlling their voices as a tool for emancipation: "When early modern texts highlight the difficulties of producing, tracking, and controlling inherently unmanageable vocal matter, they (paradoxically) lay the groundwork for a model of vocal agency that benefits those whose expressive acts were curtailed or marginalized," primarily women. Gina Bloom, *Voice in Motion: Staging Gender, Shaping Sound in Early Modern England* (Philadelphia: University of Pennsylvania Press, 2007), 6. Similarly, Jennifer Linhart Wood thinks of soundwaves in early modern playhouses as mediating and facilitating cross-cultural encounters in ways that eschew the typical violence of such encounters in early modernity: "the otherness of strange lands comes to resonate uncannily in and as the traveler's body," thereby problematizing "distinctions between inside and outside, subject and object, self and other, and . . . *heimlich* and *unheimlich*." Wood, *Sounding Otherness in Early Modern Drama and Travel*, 41, 37.

57. William Shakespeare, *The Tempest*, 1.2.357–58.

58. John Taylor, *All the Workes of John Taylor the Water-Poet* (London: Printed by Iohn Beale, Elizabeth Allde, Bernard Alsop, and Thomas Fawcet for Iames Boler, 1630), 253, 61.

59. Taylor, *All the Workes of John Taylor the Water-Poet*, 62.

60. Hornback, *Racism and Early Blackface Traditions*, 152; Taylor, *All the Workes of John Taylor the Water-Poet*, 63. On the literary context of Taylor's linguistic experiments, see Victor Skretkowicz, "Poems of Discovery: John Taylor's Barbarian, Utopian and Barmooda Tongues," *Renaissance Studies* 6, no. 3–4 (1992): 391–99.

61. Webster, *The White Devil*, 129, 5.1.96–98.

62. Massinger, *The Parliament of Love*, 173.

63. Bruce Smith, *The Acoustic World of Early Modern England*, 43; Cristina Paravano, *Performing Multilingualism on the Caroline Stage in the Plays of Richard Brome* (Newcastle-upon-Tyne: Cambridge Scholars, 2018), 9.

64. *The English Moor* has received critical attention over the last twenty years mostly for the emphasis it puts on the material conditions of black-up (Vaughan, *Performing Blackness*, 117–18), for its use of the racial rhetoric of English masques (Kim F. Hall, *Things of Darkness*, 166–75), and for its distinct focus on the Afro-British presence in London (Matthew Steggle, "Critical Introduction and Textual Introduction to *The English Moor, or The Mock-Marriage*," *Richard Brome Online*).

65. Paravano, *Performing Multilingualism on the Caroline Stage*, 9.

66. Steggle, "Critical Introduction and Textual Introduction to *The English Moor*," 57. Catalina, etymologically "the pure" or the "whitened" in the symbolic order of the time, was one of the most popular names for christened Black women in Iberia. Spanish dramatis personae attest to this, and so does Albrecht Durer's 1521 drawing of "Katharina," who was enslaved by the Portuguese consul in Antwerp. Paul H. D. Kaplan, "The Calenberg Altarpiece: Black African Christians in Renaissance Germany," in *Germany and the Black Diaspora: Points of Contact, 1250–1914*, ed. Mischa Honeck, Martin Klimke, and Anne Kuhlmann-Smirnov (New York: Berghahn Books, 2013), 23.

67. A manuscript version of the play, dating back to 1637, before the play was performed, is addressed to William Seymour, Marquis of Hertford, one of Brome's most generous aristocratic patrons, whose family had invested in African trading. Imtiaz Habib found a 1673 document showing Seymour's son, John Seymour, fourth Duke of Somerset, entering a deed with "Alice Long (daughter of a blackamoor, Britannia, a daughter of the king of Morocco), making provisions for her descendants." Habib, *Black Lives in the English Archives*, 215. The deed involves a significant amount of money, which Habib reads as indication that Alice was John Seymour's illegitimate mixed-race daughter (216).

68. At least one "John Matthews, a blackmoor lodging in the precinct next to the Tower servant to one Mr. Kellet in Market Lane," was buried in 1614. Steggle, "Critical Introduction and Textual Introduction to *The English Moor*," 60.

69. Habib, *Black Lives in the English Archives*, 123.

70. Jean E. Howard, *Theater of a City: The Places of London Comedy, 1598–1642* (Philadelphia: University of Pennsylvania Press, 2007), 3.

71. Susan Phillips, "Schoolmasters, Seduction, and Slavery: Polyglot Dictionaries in Pre-Modern England," *Medievalia et Humanistica: Studies in Medieval and Renaissance Culture* 34 (2008): 148–49.

72. The acoustic script of ethnic conjuration is not unique to England. Jerome Branche insists on the connection between Spanish blackspeak and *sayagués*, for instance. He states that "Guinean (guineo), 'black talk' (habla de negros), or 'half talk' (media lengua) replicated the comic effect of the *Sayagués* spoken by the pastores [shepherds] in the liturgical poetry of the late 1400s." Branche, *Colonialism and Race in Luso-Spanish Literature*, 67. Originally designating the Leonese romance dialect spoken by the inhabitants of Sayago, near Salamanca, a region famous for its geographic isolation, sayagués quickly became a class accent, the standard rustic jargon spoken by all peasants, fools, and pastors regardless of their geographic origins. While the phonetic distortions proper to sayagués are different from the distortions proper to blackspeak, both accents derived their comic force from the perception of their speakers as childish, intellectually deficient, and excessively physical. It is likely that the conjuration of sayagués informed Spanish receptions of blackspeak.

73. On that masque's rewriting of Heliodorus's *Aethiopika*, see Ndiaye, "'Everyone Breeds in His Own Image.'"

74. Wood, *Sounding Otherness in Early Modern Drama and Travel*, 4.

75. The numerous Spanish characters of English drama either speak unaccented Castilian—see Thomas Dekker's *The Pleasant Comedie of Old Fortunatus* (London: Printed by S. Stafford for William Aspley, 1600) and Ben Jonson's *The Alchemist* (London: Printed by Thomas Snodham for Walter Burre, 1612); or they simply weave a couple of well-known Spanish words into their unaccented English—see Don Armado in *Love's Labor's Lost*, or Beaumont and Fletcher's *Love's Pilgrimage*, in *Comedies and Tragedies Written by Francis Beaumont and John Fletcher Never Printed Before*, 1–26 (London: Printed for Humphrey Robinson . . . and for Humphrey Moseley . . . , 1647).

76. This may be the reason why Brome goes to conspicuous lengths in *The Northern Lass* to avoid having the mock-Spaniard Squelch speak either Spanish or a Spanish-accented English. Richard Brome, *The Northern Lass*. Modern text, J. Sanders, ed., in *Richard Brome Online*. See also William Haughton, *Englishmen for My Money, or a Pleasant Comedy called A Woman Will Have Her Will* (London: By W. White, 1616); Thomas Dekker, *The Shomaker's Holiday, or The Gentle Craft* (London: Valentine Sims, 1600).

77. Thomas Herbert, *A Relation of Some Yeares Travaile Begunne Anno 1626* (London: William Stansby and Iacob Bloome, 1634), 14.

78. Herbert, *Relation of Some Yeares Travaile*, 16.

79. David J. Baker, "'Wildehirissheman: 'Colonialist Representation in Shakespeare's 'Henry V,'" *English Literary Renaissance* 22, no. 1 (1992): 45.

80. Paula Blank, *Broken English: Dialects and the Politics of Language in Renaissance Writings* (New York: Routledge, 1996), 126; Michael Neill, "Broken English and Broken Irish: Nation, Language, and the Optic of Power in Shakespeare's Histories," *Shakespeare Quarterly* 45, no. 1 (1994): 15.

81. On the development of the New English discourse on Irish difference, see David J. Baker, *Between Nations: Shakespeare, Spenser, Marvell, and the Question of Britain* (Stanford, Calif.: Stanford University Press, 1997). For a detailed study of primary sources evidencing an obsession with the idea of racial degeneration and advocating for the destruction of Irish culture and language, see Michael Neill, "Broken English and Broken Irish." On the ambivalent effect of hearing the stage Irish accent on English spectators, see Paula Blank, *Broken English*. On the use of dialectal stereotypes on the English stage, see Erin Reynolds "Strange Accents or Ill Shapen Sounds: Dialect in Early Modern Drama," 2008, Thesis. http://homes.chass.utoronto.ca/~cpercy/courses/6362-ReynoldsErin.htm.

82. Kim F. Hall, *Things of Darkness*, 16.

83. Kim F. Hall, *Things of Darkness*, 19.

84. Blank, *Broken English*, 144–45, 147.

85. "Eudoxus: What is that you say, of so many as remayne English of them? Why are, not they that were once English, abydinge Englishe still? Irenius: No, for the most parte of them are degenerated and growen almost meare Irishe, yea, and more malicious to the Englishe then the very Irishe them selves." Edmund Spenser, *A View of the Present State of Ireland* (1596), ed. Risa S. Bear (University of Oregon, Renascence Edition, 1997), http://www.luminarium.org/renascence-editions/veue1.html, n.p. Davies qtd. in Bruce Smith, *The Acoustic World of Early Modern England*, 310.

86. Steggle, "Critical Introduction and Textual Introduction to *The English Moor*," 41.

87. Thomas Heywood, *An Apology for Actors* (London: Printed by Nicholas Okes, 1612), F3r.

88. Colonist Nathaniel Morton writes about "an Indian called Samòset" who spoke in March 1621 to a crew of Englishmen "in broken English." Nathaniel Morton, *New-Englands Memoriall* (Cambridge, Mass.: Printed by Samuel Green and Marmaduke Johnson for John Usher of Boston, 1669), 23. Similarly, William Bradford, mentions "a Savage . . . [who] saluted us in English, and bad us welcome for he had learned some broken English." William Bradford, *A Relation or Iournall of the Beginning and Proceedings of the English Plantation Setled at Plimoth in New England* (London: Printed by J. Dawson for Iohn Bellamie, 1622), 32. Native Americans speaking in "broken English" would later feature in Roger Williams's *A Key into the Language of America* (London: Printed by Gregory Dexter, 164), A7r, in John Eliot's *A Further Account of the Progress of the Gospel Amongst the Indians in New England* (London: John Macock, 1660), 1, and in Increase Mather's *Relation of the Troubles Which Have Hapned in New-England* (Boston, Mass.: Printed and sold by John Foster, 1677), 4, among other colonial works. The voice of Native American colonial subjects was phantasmatically introduced to the London stage a few years before *The English Moor*, in Philip Massinger's 1632 *The City-Madam*, where, following the logic of heightened artificiality that would inform blackspeak dramaturgy in England and in France, a group of English characters try to pass as Virginians, and, to that purpose, speak gibberish, or what is described in the play as "a heathen language" before switching to unaccented English, for, conveniently, they "have liv'd long in the English Colonie, and speak our language as their own Dialect." Philip Massinger, *The City-Madam, a Comedy* (London: Printed for Andrew Pennycuicke, 1659), 47.

89. Edward Terry, *The Merchants and Mariners Preservation and Thanksgiving* (London: Thomas Harper, 1649), 30.

90. On comparisons between Irish and Native American culture in early modern England, see Bruce Smith, *The Acoustic World of Early Modern England*, 325–26.

91. Edward Terry, *A Voyage to East-India* (London: Printed by T.W. for J. Martin and J. Allestrye, 1655), 20–21.

92. Terry, *A Voyage to East-India*, 20–21.

93. Sally McKee, "Domestic Slavery in Renaissance Italy," *Slavery and Abolition* 29, no. 3 (2008): 321.

94. In *Spain in Italy*, James Amelang acknowledges that Spain and Italy had close cultural exchanges, and yet the history of those exchanges with regard to theatre largely remains to be written. James S. Amelang, "Exchanges Between Italy and Spain: Culture and Religion," in *Spain in Italy: Politics, Society, and Religion 1500–1700*, ed. Thomas James Dandelet and John A. Marino (Leiden: Brill, 2007), 455. For the moment, we have to be content with clues and hypotheses pointing toward transnational influence. First, if Spanish Christmas carols written in blackspeak could reach South American cathedrals, they are likely to have reached the ears of a Neapolitan composer like Orlando di Lasso. Second, close reading one of the moresche songs of the *Motets, Madrigals and Moresche* composed by Lasso for the 1568 wedding of Renate of Lorraine to Wilhelm V, Natalie Operstein finds strong formal similarities between "Canta, Giorgia" and coplas written by Rodrigo de Reinosa at the end of the fifteenth century, *Coplas de como vna dama ruega a vn negro que cante en manera de requiebro: Y como el negro se dexa rogar en fin la señora vencida de su gracia le offrece su persona*. Natalie Operstein, "Golden Age *Poesía de Negros* and Orlando di Lasso's *Moresche*: A Possible Connection," *Romance Notes* 52, no. 1 (2012): 13–18. Third, according to Donna G. Cardamone, moresche developed through the collaboration of Orlando di Lasso with the Dentice singers—Donna G. Cardamone, "The Salon as Marketplace in the 1550s: Patrons and Collectors of Lasso's Secular Music," in *Orlando di Lasso Studies*, ed. Peter Bergquist (New York: Cambridge University Press, 1999), 64–90; and we know that the Dentice traveled to Spain in 1554 and 1559—Richard Wistreich, *Warrior, Courtier, Singer: Giulio Cesare Brancaccio and the Performance of Identity in the Late Renaissance* (Aldershot, U.K.: Ashgate, 2007).

95. Cardamone, "The Salon as Market Place," 1. Rice, Program of the Ensemble Origo concert, 3.

96. Hornback, *Racism and Early Blackface Traditions*, 35–65. For an account of *moresche*'s possible influence over English Renaissance drama via commedia dell'arte touring companies, see Ndiaye "Off the Record."

97. Africanese blackspeak existed in Iberia too, although it was not as common there as the black-accented vernacular version of blackspeak. The two versions coexist in plays such as Tirso de Molina, *Escarmientos para el cuerdo*, in *Quinta parte de comedias del maestro Tirso de Molina* (Madrid: en la Imprenta Real, a costa de Gabriel de Leon, 1636), 49v–72r.

98. "Le nez camus du récit des Africains se monstre en teste d'une escouadre de Basanez qui dansent devant l'élephant sur lequel le Grand Cacique se présente à ses peuples: Il cause en son ramage, et ses sujets luy respondent en si excellent jargon que l'on n'entend ni les uns ni les autres." Bordier, *Billebahaut*, 39.

99. "Jargon," *Trésor de la langue français*, July 20, 2020, ATILF-CNRS & Université de Lorraine, https://www.cnrtl.fr/definition/jargon. Accessed November 13, 2021.

100. "Langage vicieux et corrompu du peuple, de paysans, qu'on a de la peine à entendre. . . . Se dit aussi par extension en parlant des langues mortes ou estrangères." Furetière, *Dictionnaire universel*, 298–99.

101. Michèle Perret, *Introduction à l'histoire de la langue française* (Paris: SEDES, 1998), 69–70.

102. *Maistre Pierre Pathelin, de nouveau revu et mis en son naturel* (Paris: Pour Estienne Groulleau, 1564), Diiii–E.

103. Molière, *Monsieur de Pourceaugnac*, in *Les oeuvres de Monsieur de Molière, Tome VI* (Paris: chez Claude Barbin, 1673), 64.

104. "Langage imparfait et corrompu. . . . Il se dit aussi quelquefois des langues qu'on n'entend pas." *Dictionnaire de l'Académie française* (Paris: Chez la Veuve de Jean-Baptiste Coignard, Imprimeur ordinaire du Roy et de l'Académie Françoise, 1694), 82.

105. In Raymond Poisson's comedy *Les faux Moscovites*, stage directions indicate that a servant pretending to be Russian "barragouine" extensively before he appears on stage "jargonnant." Raymond Poisson, *Les faux Moscovites, comédie*, in *Les oeuvres de Monsieur Poisson* (Paris: Jean Ribou, 1679), 185, 186.

106. Edmé Boursault, *Le mort vivant, comédie* (Paris: Nicolas Pépingué, 1662). Nicolas du Perche, *L'ambassadeur d'Affrique, comédie* (Moulins: Chez la veuve Pierre Vernoy et Claude Vernoy son fils, Imprimeur du Roy, 1666).

107. Eight years prior to *L'ambassadeur d'Affrique*, Molière scripted a heavy German accent in French in *L'étourdi* (1658) and had a character label that technique "German jargon" (jargon allemand). Molière, *L'étourdi ou les contre-temps* (Paris: Gabriel Quinet, 1663; Publié par Paul Fièvre, Théâtre classique. http://theatre-classique.fr/pages/programmes/edition.php?t=.. /documents/MOLIERE_ETOURDI.xml#haut Accessed 11/13/2021 5.1.1808–19.

108. Du Perche, *L'ambassadeur d'Affrique*, 38.

109. "Crispin: Tirbautes. / Un valet en habit d'Affriquain: Ben d'harleK. / Crispin: Gooth dan kem cum vir, / Salkardy bucdemeK satir / Et voldrecam. Le docteur (à Lélie): Qu'est-ce qu'il chante par ces mots? / Lélie: Il s'impatiente / De ce qu'il ne voit point venir Lucresse / Et l'envoie quérir." Du Perche, *L'ambassadeur d'Affrique*, 37.

110. "Crispin: Détalez, ou Kamdem S Koreille / Horleam scanem tourtoury. / Le Docteur: Que dit-il? / Lélie: Il est fort marry de vous avoir vu tant d'audace / Et veut qu'à l'instant on vous chasse." Du Perche, *L'ambassadeur d'Affrique*, 31.

111. Jean Rotrou, *La soeur, comédie* (Paris: Augustin Courbe, 1647). Giambattista Della Porta, *La sorella*, in *Renaissance Comedy: The Italian Masters*, vol. 1, ed. Don Beecher, trans. Bruno Ferraro (Toronto: University of Toronto Press, 2008), 373–460; François Tristan L'Hermite, *Le parasite, comédie* (Paris: Augustin Courbe, 1654).

112. "Un faux jargon qui n'est point en usage." Rotrou, *La soeur*, 79. For an English translation of this passage attentive to the difference between lines written in mock-Turkish and in authentic Turkish, see Beecher, *Renaissance Comedy*. It is an open question whether a bourgeois Parisian audience in 1666 could hear the difference between authentic Turkish and Turkish jargon, and how performers helped linguistically incompetent spectators distinguish between the two.

113. Antoine de Montfleury, *L'école des jaloux, ou le cocu volontaire, comédie* (Paris: La Compagnie des Libraires, 1761).

114. "Que jargonne-t-il tant?" Montfleury, *L'école des jaloux*, 44. "Comment? En ma présence vous faites le railleur? Pour en tirer vengeance, *Biradam fourk dermak galera gourdini*!" Montfleury, *L'école des jaloux*, 30.

115. Molière, *Le bourgeois gentilhomme: Comédie-ballet* (Paris: n.p., 1688).

116. In 1654, Jean-Baptiste Dutertre transcribes a sentence delivered by a "sauvage" in French "baragoin" in *Histoire générale des isles de S. Christophe, de la Guadeloupe, de la Marti-*

nique et autres dans l'Amérique (Paris: Jacques Langlois, 1654), 43, 465. So does Rochefort in his *Histoire morale des îles Antilles de l'Amérique, Tome second* (Lyon: Christofle Fourmy, 1667), which contains a short French-Carib lexicon including some words in accented or distorted French labeled "baragoin" (673 and 676). Du Tertre references the "baragoin" and "jargon" spoken by "Nègres" in his *Histoire générale des Antilles habitées par les François, Tome 2* (Paris: Thomas Iolly, 1667), 510. Pierre Besnier writes about "le jargon des Nègres et des Sauvages" in *La réunion des langues, ou l'art de les apprendre toutes par une seule* (Paris: Sébastien Mabre-Cramoisy, 1674), 13. Mère Marie de l'Incarnation mentions, from Québec, "le baragoin des Nègres" in Martinique in 1670 in *Lettres* (Paris: Louis Billaine, 1681), 285.

117. Francis Fane, *Love in the Dark, or The Man of Bus'ness, a Comedy* (London: Printed by T.N. for Henry Herringman), 1675.

118. Allusions to Webster's *The White Devil* are peppered throughout the play, as in the scene in which Intrigo pretends to be afraid of Cornanti's whitefaced wife, Bellinganna, for "in their Countrey the Devil's painted White, and their Beauties are all Blacks." Fane, *Love in the Dark*, 31. See also M.W., M.A., *A Comedy Called The Marriage Broker, or The Pander* (London: n.p., 1662); Aurelio Aureli, *Emilia* (London: Printed for the author, 1672). On the racial dynamics at play in *The Marriage Broker, or The Pander*, see Noémie Ndiaye, "Black Roma: Afro-Romani Connections in Early Modern Drama (and Beyond)," *Renaissance Quarterly* 75, no. 4 (2022), forthcoming.

119. Thomas Middleton, *No Wit [No] Help Like a Womans: A Comedy* (London: Printed for Humphrey Moseley, 1657).

120. Marjorie Rubright, *Doppelganger Dilemmas: Anglo-Dutch Relations in Early Modern English Literature and Culture* (Philadelphia: University of Pennsylvania Press, 2014), 89–109.

121. Peter Fryer, *Staying Power: The History of Black People in Britain* (London: Pluto, 2010), 25, 33.

122. Cotgrave, *Dictionarie of the French and English Tongues*, L4v.

123. "Gibberish," in John Wilkins, *An Alphabetical Dictionary*, in *An Essay Towards a Real Character and a Philosophical Language* (London: Printed for Sa. Gellibrand, and for John Martyn, 1668), Ggg3v.

124. Cotgrave, *Dictionarie of the French and English Tongues*, Ppp1r.

125. I further explore the mechanisms through which this association between Africans and Romani people worked in performance in Noémie Ndiaye, "'Come Aloft, Jack-Little-Ape': Race and Dance in *The Spanish Gypsie*," *English Literary Renaissance* 51, no. 1 (Winter 2021): 121–51.

126. J. P. Vander Motten, 2008, "Fane, Sir Francis (d. 1691), Playwright," in *Oxford Dictionary of National Biography*, https://www.oxforddnb.com/view/10.1093/ref:odnb/9780198614128 .001.0001/odnb-9780198614128-e-913 Accessed November 21, 2021.

127. Edward Ravenscroft, *The Citizen Turn'd Gentleman, a Comedy Acted at the Duke's Theatre* (London: Printed for Thomas Dring, 1672). Another element suggesting that *Love in the Dark* drew some of its inspiration from *The Citizen Turn'd Gentleman* and its Turkish spectacles is the almost gratuitous antimasque performed by the ghosts of Turkish bashaws defeated by Sforza. Fane, *Love in the Dark*, 51–52.

128. Ravenscroft, *The Citizen Turn'd Gentleman*, 85.

129. Cotgrave, "Chattering," in *Dictionarie of the French and English Tongues*, E2r.

130. Anthony Julius, *Trials of the Diaspora: A History of Anti-Semitism in England* (Oxford: Oxford University Press, 2010), 117.

131. David West Brown, *English and Empire: Literary History, Dialect, and the Digital Archive* (Cambridge: Cambridge University Press, 2018), 139. On 1760s as a turning point, see also

Roxann Wheeler, "Sounding Black-Ish: West Indian Pidgin in London Performance and Print," *Eighteenth-Century Studies* 51, no. 1 (2017): 63–87; and David Paisey, "Black English in Britain in the Eighteenth Century," *Electronic British Library Journal* (2015) https://www.bl.uk/eblj /2015articles/article12.html. They note the existence of a few precursors, including Daniel Defoe. Interestingly, the most (in)famous eighteenth-century English play to use blackspeak, Isaac Bickerstaff's *The Padlock, a Comic Opera* (New York: Charles Wiley, 1825), was based on a novella by Cervantes, *El celoso extremeño*. The published English translation that Bickerstaff used as source text did not contain blackspeak for the character that inspired his enslaved Afro-Spaniard Mungo—yet Cervantes's novella did. In other words, the most famous English piece of blackspeak constitutes an unwitting palimpsest of early modern Spanish blackspeak, which had been lost in translation. Miguel de Cervantes Saavedra, *El celoso extremeño*, in *Novelas ejemplares*, edited by Jorge García López, 325–70 (Barcelona: Crítica, 2001).

132. The French plays include, among others, Pierre-Yves Barré and Jean-Baptiste Radet, *La Négresse, ou le pouvoir de la reconnaissance, comédie* (Paris: Imbault, 1787); Jean-Baptiste Radet, *Honorine, ou la femme difficile à vivre, comédie* (Paris: n.p., 1797); Larivallière, *Les Africains ou le triomphe de l'humanité, comédie* (Paris: Meurant, 1794); and Citoyen B***, *La liberté générale, ou les colons à Paris, comédie* (Cap-Français: P. Roux, imprimeur de la commission, 1796), a play written, printed, and first performed in Haiti.

133. In act 4, scene 2, Intrigo, still in black-up, has been taken to prison. Sforza, looking for his love interest, Parhelia, takes him to be Parhelia with her vizard on. He is, however, struck by the sound of Intrigo's voice, which is deeper than Parhelia's, and resolves: "I, to be hurry'd and hall'd away by force, / And mew'd up in a kind of inchanted Castle. / The Lady has caught cold by her voice." Fane, *Love in the Dark*, 61.

CHAPTER 4

1. Thomas Tryon, *Friendly Advice to the Gentlemen-Planters of the East and West Indies* (London: Andrew Sowle, 1684), 147–48. The epigraph is from Beyoncé Knowles-Carter, "Formation." On *Lemonade*. Parkwood Columbia, 2016.

2. The first recorded slave ship dance in the Anglophone Atlantic dates back to 1664. Geneviève Fabre, "The Slave Ship Dance," in *Black Imagination and the Middle Passage*, ed. Maria Diedrich, Henry Louis Gates Jr., and Carl Pedersen (New York: Oxford University Press, 1999), 34.

3. Saidiya V. Hartman, *Scenes of Subjection: Terror, Slavery, and Self-Making in Nineteenth-Century America* (New York: Oxford University Press, 1997), 42, 50, 8. Scholarship underlining the ambivalence of slave dances in the Atlantic world after 1660 focuses primarily on slave ship and plantation dances. Besides Hartman, it includes but is not limited to Katrina Hazzard-Gordon's *Jookin': The Rise of Social Dance Formations in African-American Culture* (Philadelphia: Temple University Press, 1990) and Rodreguez King-Dorset's *Black Dance in London, 1730–1850: Innovation, Tradition and Resistance* (Jefferson, N.C.: McFarland, 2008).

4. Christopher W. Marsh, *Music and Society in Early Modern England* (New York: Cambridge University Press, 2010), 331.

5. Margaret M. McGowan, *Dance in the Renaissance: European Fashion, French Obsession* (New Haven, Conn.: Yale University Press, 2008), 9.

6. Julia Sutton et al., "Dance," *Grove Music Online, Oxford Music Online*, Oxford University Press https://doi-org.proxy.uchicago.edu/10.1093/gmo/9781561592630.article.45795. Accessed 11/22 /2021.; McGowan, *Dance in the Renaissance*, 2.

7. Jennifer Nevile, *The Eloquent Body: Dance and Humanist Culture in Fifteenth-Century Italy* (Bloomington: Indiana University Press, 2004), 15–16.

8. Baldesar Castiglione, *The Book of the Courtier by Count Baldesar Castiglione*, trans. Leonard Eckstein Opdycke (New York: Charles Scribner's Sons, 1903), 38. Decorum determined "who danced with whom, the order of the dancing, what dances should be performed in public, and those allowed for private entertainment." McGowan, *Dance in the Renaissance*, 21. In practice there seems to have been much more porosity than dance treatises suggest, so that, as Christopher Marsh puts it, "dance simultaneously revealed and concealed the major dividing lines within English culture and society." Marsh, *Music and Society in Early Modern England*, 389.

9. "Deux eunuques, esclaves de l'empereur des terres qui ne sont pas découvertes, et qui, par un fol caprice de la nature, naissent demy-blancs demy-noirs, attendans la venue de leur maître, firent une entrée si divertissante, avec des pas et des postures si peu connus en ces régions que les spectateurs restèrent dans un ravissement que l'on ne peut exprimer." *Ballet des divers entretiens de la fontaine de Vaucluse* (1649), in *Ballets et mascarades de cour de Henri III à Louis XIV (1581–1652), Tome VI*, ed. Paul Lacroix (Geneva: Slatkine Reprints, 1968), 203.

10. Illuminating readings of black cosmetics in *Masque of Blackness* include Kim F. Hall, *Things of Darkness*; Vaughan, *Performing Blackness on English Stages*; Stephen Orgel's *The Jonsonian Masque* (Cambridge, Mass.: Harvard University Press, 1965); Clare McManus, *Women on the Renaissance Stage: Anna of Denmark and Female Masquing in the Stuart Court, 1590–1619* (Manchester: Manchester University Press, 2002); Mary Floyd Wilson's "Temperature, Temperance, and Racial Difference in Ben Jonson's 'The Masque of Blackness,'" *English Literary Renaissance* 28, no. 2 (1998): 183–209; Hardin Aasand, "'To Blanch an Ethiop, and Revive a Corse': Queen Anne and *The Masque of Blackness*," *Studies in English Literature, 1500–1900* 32, no. 2 (1992): 271–85; Andrea Stevens, "Mastering Masques of Blackness: Jonson's 'Masque of Blackness,' the Windsor Text of 'The Gypsies Metamorphosed,' and Brome's 'The English Moor,'" *English Literary Renaissance* 39, no. 2 (2009): 396–426; and Bernadette Andrea, "Black Skin, the Queen's Masques: Africanist Ambivalence and Feminine Author(ity) in the Masques of 'Blackness' and 'Beauty,'" *English Literary Renaissance* 29, no. 2 (1999): 246–81. On the reception of Native American dances, see Paul A. Scolieri, *Dancing the New World: Aztecs, Spaniards, and the Choreography of Conquest* (Austin: University of Texas Press, 2013); Olivia A. Bloechl, *Native American Song at the Frontiers of Early Modern Music* (Cambridge: Cambridge University Press, 2008); and Gavin Hollis, *The Absence of America*.

11. Sylvie Chalaye, *Du Noir au Nègre*. Ballet scholarship focusing on Native American dances and Turqueries include Ellen Welch's "The Specter of the Turk in Early Modern French Court Entertainments," *Esprit Créateur* 53, no. 4 (2013): 84–97; and "Dancing the Nation: Performing France in the Seventeenth-Century 'Ballets des nations,'" *Journal for Early Modern Cultural Studies* 13, no. 2 (2013): 3–23; as well as Margaret M. McGowan, *La danse à la Renaissance: Sources livresques et albums d'images* (Paris: Bibliothèque Nationale de France, 2012); and V. K. Preston, "Un/Becoming Nomad: Marc Lescarbot, Movement, and Metamorphosis in *Les Muses de la Nouvelle France*," in *History, Memory, Performance*, ed. David Dean, Yana Meerzon, and Kathryn Prince, 68–82 (London: Palgrave Macmillan, 2015). Michel Paquot barely pays attention to sub-Saharan Africans in his problematic yet foundational *Les étrangers dans les divertissements de la cour, de Beaujoyeulx à Molière (1581–1673): Contribution à l'étude de l'opinion publique et du théâtre en France* (Bruxelles: Palais des Académies, 1932). In "Pale Imitations: White Performances of Slave Dance in the Public Theatres of Pre-Revolutionary Saint-Domingue," *Atlantic Studies: Literary, Cultural, and Historical Perspectives* 16, no. 4 (2019): 502–20, Julia Prest investigates the power dynamics of dance in the theatre of late eighteenth-century colonial Saint-

Domingue. She argues that racial impersonation by kinetic means was an attempt on white colonials' part to reframe, emolliate, and defang slave dances that were perceived as dangerous, such as vodou. I offer a metropolitan genealogy of those dynamics.

12. On processions in Seville, see Jean Sentaurens, *Séville et le théâtre*, and Lynn Matluck Brooks, *The Dances of the Processions of Seville in Spain's Golden Age* (Kassel: Reichenberger, 1988). Studies of danzas de negros on stage include the work of Aurelia Martín-Casares and Marga G. Barranco: see their cowritten articles "The Musical Legacy of Black Africans in Spain: A Review of Our Sources," *Anthropological Notebooks* 15, no. 2 (2009): 51–60, and "Popular Literary Depictions of Black African Weddings in Early Modern Spain," *Renaissance and Reformation / Renaissance et Réforme* 31, no. 2 (2008): 107–21; as well as Marcella Trambaoioli, *"Apuntes sobre el guineo o baile de negros: Tipologías y funciones dramáticas,"* in *Actas del VI Congreso de la Asociación Internacional Siglo de Oro*, ed. María Luisa Lobato and Francisco Domínguez Matito (Madrid: Iberoamericana-Vervuert, 2004), 1773–83; and Nicholas R. Jones, *Staging Habla de Negros*.

13. Jones, *Staging Habla de Negros*, 50–51.

14. Judith Butler, *Excitable Speech: A Politics of the Performative* (New York: Routledge, 1997), 14.

15. "Les Noirs meinent une bonne vie … et s'étudient de tout leur pouvoir à se donner tous les plaisirs de quoy ils se peuvent aviser, à se réjouyr en danses, et le plus souvent, en banquets, convis, et ébas de diverses sorte … ayans meilleur temps que tout le reste des autres peuples lesquels demeurent en Afrique." Leo Africanus, *Historiale description de l'Afrique, tierce partie du monde* (Lyon: Jean Temporal, 1556), 43. *Description of Africa* was not translated into Castilian until the twentieth century, but Italian, French, and Latin versions circulated in Spain from the 1550s onward.

16. Kate Lowe, "The Stereotyping of Black Africans in Renaissance Europe," in *Black Africans in Renaissance Europe*, ed. Kate Lowe and T. F. Earle (Cambridge: Cambridge University Press, 2005), 41.

17. "Santa Maria la Blanca en cuya placetilla suele juntarse infinidad de negros y negras." Miguel Cervantes Saavedra, *Entremés de los mirones* (1615?), in *Varias obras inéditas de Cervantes*, ed. Don Adolfo de Castro (Madrid: A. de carlos é Hijo, Editores, 1874), 229.

18. "Los negros eran tratados con benignidad desde los tiempos de don Henrique Tercero, permitiéndoles juntarse a sus bailes y fiestas en los días feriados, con que acudían gustosos al trabajo y toleraban mejor el cautiverio." Diego Ortiz de Zúñiga, *Anales eclesiásticos y seculares de la muy noble y muy leal ciudad de Sevilla* (Madrid: Imprenta real, 1677), 374.

19. "Yo me voy tras ellos / que gusto me dan." Simón Aguado, *El platillo, entremés* (1602), in Cotarelo y Mori, ed., *Collección*, 230.

20. "Guineo, o el negro de Guinea, es una cierta danza de movimientos prestos y apresurados; pudo ser fuesse trayda de Guinea, y que la danzassen primero los negros, y puede ser nombre griego del verbo kineo, moveo, incitor, por la agilidad y presteza de la danza." Covarrubias, *Tesoro de la lengua*, 458.

21. "Aunque disfrazada vengas, / te conozco, Andaluzia." Félix Lope de Vega Carpio, *La limpieza no manchada*, in *Parte diecinueve y la mejor parte de las comedias de Lope de Vega Carpio* (Madrid: por Juan González: a costa de Alonso Pérez, 1624), 216.

22. I am not alone in reading *guineo* as an umbrella term for a variety of dances (*zarambeque, paracumbé, ye-ye, cachumba, gurumbe*, and more). In the absence of extant choreographic information in the city archives of Seville, Lynn Matluck Brooks posits that guineo inspired the "compositional framework and movement style" used in the "danzas de negros" of Corpus

Christi processions. Similarly, although the name of the dance performed during the Afro-Spanish street dance scene in *La vitoria de la honra* is not specified, Marcella Trambaioli assumes that it is a guineo. Brooks, *The Dances of the Processions of Seville*, 226; Trambaioli, "Apuntes sobre el guineo o baile de negros," 1779–83.

23. José Luis Navarro García, *Semillas de ébano: El elemento negro y afroamericano en el baile flamenco* (Seville: Portada Editorial, 1990), 91.

24. "Haciendo el Guineo, inclinando con notable peligro y asco todo el cuerpo demasiado." Francisco de Quevedo, "Premática del tiempo," in *Obras de Francisco de Quevedo Villegas, Tomo primero* (Amberes: por Henrico y Cornelio Verdussen, 1699), 532. "El zarambeque que salta, / pica y brinca mas que todos / los sones de la guitarra." Sebastián de Villaviciosa, *Entremés de los sones*, in *Tardes apacibles de gustoso entretenimiento: Repartidas en varios entremeses, y bayles entremesados, escogidos de los mejores ingenios de España*, edited by Don Lope Gaspar de Figueroa Guzman y Velasco (Madrid: por Andrés García de la Iglesia, a costa de Iuan Martín Merinero, 1663), 137.

25. Lynn Matluck Brooks, "Text and Image as Evidence for Posture and Movement Style in Seventeenth-Century Spain," *Imago Musicae* 13 (1998): 55.

26. "Salen con grande grita negros, y negras con adufes, guitarras, y sonajas." Vega Carpio, *La vitoria de la honra*, 184r.

27. Brooks, "Text and Image as Evidence," 56.

28. "Le puso de cascaveles / un remate y con esto / salio haciendo mil visages / con la danca del guineo." *Famosa xacara nueva en que se da quenta y declara el mas fiero delito que se ha visto en nuestros tiempos . . . este año de 1687* (BNE, signatura VE/114/20), n.p.

29. Fernando Palatín, *Diccionario de música: Sevilla 1818* (Oviedo: Universidad de Oviedo, 1990), 68.

30. Francisco Lanini, *Los gorrones*, in *Migaxas del ingenio y apacible entretenimiento, en varios entremeses, bayles, y loas, escogidos de los mejores ingenios de España* (Zaragoza: Diego Dormer . . . a costa de Iuan Martínez de Ribera Martel, ca. 1670), 20.

31. "O sacaban la lengua, o echaban higas para mover a los que estaban presente al riso." Cotarelo y Mori, *Collección*, clxxiv.

32. Luis Vélez de Guevara, *El diablo cojuelo* (Madrid: Imprenta Real, a costa de Alonso Pérez, 1641), fol. 5v.

33. Scolieri, *Dancing the New World*, 14.

34. "Salió al mundo riendo se (risa que parece heredaron sus hijos, pues aun en lo terrible de su esclavitud, siempre se andan riendo, cantando, tañendo, y bailando)." Sandoval, *De instauranda aethiopum salute*, 26.

35. Tim Creswell, "Toward a Politics of Mobility," *Environment and Planning: Society and Space* 28 (2010): 22.

36. Moreno Navarro, *La antigua hermandad de los negros de Sevilla*, 73.

37. "Yo te pagaré señor / todo el caudal que te cuesto / con que me dejes andar / baylando por todo el pueblo. . . . Entravase en las tavernas / y si hallaba algun gaytero / no solo el vino tomaba / sino ganava dinero. . . . Dava al amo cada dia / dos reales, con que en teniendo / la carta de horro se fue / baylando de pueblo en pueblo." *Famosa xacara nueva*, n.p.

38. "Alteróse la sangre / y fue danzando y tañendo / tras ella. . . . Corre mucho la pastora / mas era corto su aliento / que era el Etiope un rayo, / y lleva un volcan de fuego." *Famosa xacara nueva*, n.p.

39. Read synthetically, the articles from the *Diccionario de autoridades* define a *jácara* as "1) A poetic composition using the metrical form of the *romance* that often refers to a strange or pe-

culiar event. Often sung by the people we call Xaque*s*, whence, perhaps, it took its name ["Xaque*s*" is a synonym for ruffians, according to Covarrubias]. 2) Also refers to the music played to accompany singing or dancing. 3) A type of dance designed for the music or sound proper to jácara*s*. 4) Also refers to the group of lads and joyful people that walk the streets at night, singing and making noise, because, often, they sing a jácara. 5) Informally, it means nuisance and discomfort in reference to the noise made by those who sing jácaras in the streets at night. 6) It also means a lie or a cock-and-bull story, since that is usually what jácaras are about." (Composicion Poética, que se forma en el que llaman Romance, y regularmente se refiere en ella algun sucesso particular, ò extraño. Usase mucho el cantarla entre los que llaman Xaques, de donde pudo tomar el nombre. Se toma tambien por el tañido que se toca para cantar, ò bailar. Se llama assimismo una especie de danza; formada al tañido, ù son proprio de la xácara. Se toma tambien por la junta de mozuelos, y gente alegre, que de noche anda metiendo ruido, y cantando por las calles. Dicese, porque por lo comun andan cantando alguna xácara. En estilo familiar se toma por molestia, ò enfado, tomada la alusion del que causan los que andan de noche cantando xácaras. Se toma tambien por mentira, ò patraña: tomado de que las mas veces lo es el sucesso, que en ella se refiere.) "Jácara." *Diccionario de autoridades*, 1729–36.

40. Juan de Esquivel Navarro, *Discursos sobre el arte del danzado y sus excelencias y primer origen, reprobando las acciones deshonestas* (Seville: por Juan Gomez de Blas, 1642), 24. In his novella *El celoso extremeño*, Cervantes confirms the presence of Afro-Spanish professionals in the world of music and dance in Seville when a character, posing as a white musician claims: "I teach *morenos* and poor people how to drum: I have already taught three *negros* who belong to the city's most important officials so well that they can sing and drum in any ball and any tavern, and they paid me well for it" (Enseño a tañer a algunos morenos y a otra gente pobre; y ya tengo tres negros, esclavos de tres veinticuatros, a quien he enseñado de modo que pueden cantar y tañer en cualquier baile y en cualquier taberna, y me lo han pagado muy rebién). Miguel Cervantes Saavedra, *El celoso extremeño*, 338.

41. Jorge Fonseca, "Black Africans in Portugal During Cleynaerts's Visit (1533–1538)," in Lowe and Earle, *Black Africans in Renaissance Europe*, 115. Lowe, "Stereotyping of Black Africans in Renaissance Europe," 41.

42. Saunders, *A Social History of Black Slaves and Freedmen in Portugal*, 105; Luis Méndez Rodríguez, *Esclavos en la pintura sevillana de los Siglos de Oro* (Universidad de Sevilla / Ateneo de Sevilla, 2011), 28, 49; Debra Blumenthal, "La Casa dels Negres: Black African Solidarity in Late Medieval Valencia," in Lowe and Earle, *Black Africans in Renaissance Europe*, 242.

43. An account of the 1617 feast for the Immaculate Conception in Seville evidences the use of black-up: "The negroes were whites made into blacks with such shining faces." Brooks, *Dances of the Processions of Seville*, 164. The contracts I consulted in Seville's city archive are mute on the subject of the performers' ethnicity in the danzas de negros of Corpus Christi processions. While they painstakingly detail the clothes that black characters were to wear, they do not contain any reference to makeup. There is no reason, however, why the cross-racial performance practice used during the 1617 Immaculate Conception should have been limited to that celebration.

44. Maria José Moreno Muñoz, "La danza teatral en el siglo XVII" (Ph.D. diss., Servicio de Publicaciones de la Universidad de Córdoba, 2010), 379.

45. Moreno Muñoz, "La danza teatral en el siglo XVII," 279.

46. I formulate this biographical hypothesis, which illustrates the historiographic method I called "recording" in this book's Introduction, based on my findings in various Sevillian archives: the contract between the city of Seville and Hernando Rivera (Sección II, Archivo de Contaduría y Junta de Propios, Carpeta 2, documento 24—Archivo Municipal), the marriage record for

Hernando Rivera (*Bodas: 1601–1609*, AGAS Fundo paroquial del Salvador, I, 2, 1, Libro 06—Biblioteca Colombina), and the death certificate of Hernando de Rivera's son (Book 1, fol. 169. Parish registers of San Esteban, 1609). Thanks go to Nazario Aguilar Montes, the volunteer archivist of San Esteban Church, who painstakingly digitized the data of his voluminous parish records and granted me access to both archives and digital catalogue.

47. For instance, at the end of Epiphany Mass, the Black confraternity of Jaén performed a dance in front of their icon: "After a few dance steps within the church, the images went out in a procession preceded by the dancers and the banners. . . . The same procession was repeated for Corpus Christi." Moreno Navarro, *La antigua hermandad de los negros de Sevilla*, 55. Moreno Navarro also connects some costs recorded in the registers of the Sevillian Black confraternity for repairing "jingles" in the early seventeenth century to this type of dances (54).

48. I am grateful to Alfredo Montilla Carvajal for letting me access the confraternity's private archives.

49. Aurelia Martín-Casares and Christine Delaigue, "The Evangelization of Freed and Slave Black Africans in Renaissance Spain: Baptism, Marriage, and Ethnic Brotherhoods," *History of Religions* 52, no. 3 (2013): 235. For a fuller account of the ways in which confraternities undertook to defend free Afro-Iberians, see Saunders, *Social History of Black Slaves and Freedmen in Portugal*, 155.

50. Saunders, *Social History of Black Slaves and Freedmen in Portugal*, 154; Blumenthal, "La Casa dels Negres," 233–37.

51. As we know from Góngora's poem "En la fiesta del Santísimo Sacramento" (1609), spectators during those processions included Afro-Spaniards who could move freely in the city on such occasions. Becco, ed., *El tema del negro*, 35–37.

52. Rowe, *Black Saints*, 87.

53. "Quiero saber que cofradia es esta, quien la fundo y con que orden y licencia, y que numero se junta y si hay otra alguna de negro os mando que en la primera occasion me informese de todo muy particularmente, avisandome si se os ofrece inconveniente en que las aya." *Real Cédula Cofradías de negros en la iglesia de Santo Domingo*, Santo_Domingo, 869, L.6, F.154V: *Archivo de Indias*, Seville. On Corpus Christi celebrations in Santo Domingo, see *Real Cédula*, Santo_Domingo, 868, L.2, F.322V: *Archivo de Indias*, Seville.

54. Examples of this pairing include Quevedo's poem "Boda de negros" (1626), in Becco, ed., *El tema del negro*, 43–46; Francisco Avellaneda de la Cueva y Guerra, *Bayle entremesado de los negros*, in *Tardes apacibles de gustoso entretenimiento: Repartidas en varios entremeses, y bayles entremesados, escogidos de los mejores ingenios de España*, ed. Don Lope Gaspar de Figueroa Guzman y Velasco, 67r–70r (Madrid: por Andrés García de la Iglesia, a costa de Iuan Martín Merinero, 1663), which ends with a gurumbe dance; and several wedding-themed danzas de negros performed in Sevillian Corpus Christi processions such as "La boda de la gatatumba" (1604), designed by Hernando Franco; "La boda del rey de Guinea" (1609), designed by Miguel Jeronimo Punzón; and "El casamiento del rey Bamba" (1645), designed by Ana de Medina. Sentaurens, *Séville et le théâtre*, 1171–1225.

55. Martín-Casares and Delaigue, "The Evangelization of Freed and Slave Black Africans," 230. Similar dynamics existed in Portugal, where "several masters tried to stop the marriages, since they claimed that they would not be able to sell a slave who was married." Saunders, *Social History of Black Slaves and Freedmen in Portugal*, 104.

56. "Quien ha bien mirado lo que pasa quando los negros se casan, vera el ruydo que traen, lo mucho que hablan, y lo poco que se entiende." Juan de Mal Lara, *La filosofía vulgar de Juan de*

Mal Lara, vezino de Sevilla, in *Refranes o proverbios en romance . . . y la filosofía vulgar de Juan de Mal Lara* (Madrid: por Juan de la Cuesta, 1619), 182.

57. *Nueva relación y curioso romance en que se refiere la celebridad, galanteo y acaso de una Boda de Negros, que se executó en la Ciudad del Puerto de Santa María* (Seville: Por Joseph Padrino, 18??, Fundación Joaquín Díaz, signatura: PL 689), n.p.

58. "Vende garbanzos tostados / camarones y buñuelos, / Es hija de buenos padres / aunque todos fueron negros." *Nueva relación*, n.p.

59. "Despues de las oraciones, / Se hizo el recebimiento / Y antes de cenar empiezan / A tocar los instrumentos, / A baylar zapateados, / Minuetes a lo Guineo, / Y la Cadena de Congo / que es pegarse ellas con ellos." *Nueva relación*, n.p.

60. "La novia largó el pellejo / el novio se abrió los cascos / y cojo por mucho tiempo / y a los negros los quitaron / del despacho los derechos." *Nueva relación*, n.p.

61. "Van entrando todos los negros que puedan en orden, danzando la zarabanda, con tamboriles y sonajas, y dan una vuelta al teatro." Simón Aguado, *Los negros, entremés* (1602), in Cotarelo y Mori, ed., *Collección*, 234.

62. Beusterien, *Eye on Race*, 102.

63. Ralph P. Locke, *Music and the Exotic from the Renaissance to Mozart* (Cambridge: Cambridge University Press, 2015), 126.

64. Hornback, *Racism and Early Blackface Traditions*; Esther J. Terry, "Belonging While Black: A Choreography of Imagined Silence in Early Modern African Diasporic Dances" (Ph.D. diss., University of Pittsburgh, 2016). On Morris dancing, see Robert Hornback's "'Extravagant and Wheeling Strangers': Early Blackface Dancing Fools, Racial Impersonation, and the Limits of Identification," *Exemplaria* 20, no. 2 (2008): 197–222; Sujata Iyengar's "Moorish Dancing in the *Two Noble Kinsmen*," *Medieval and Renaissance Drama in England* 20 (2007): 85–107; Dennis A. Britton, "From the Knight's Tale to the Two Noble Kinsmen: Rethinking Race, Class and Whiteness in Romance," *Postmedieval: A Journal of Medieval Cultural Studies* 6, no. 1 (2015): 64–78; and John Forrest, *The History of Morris Dancing, 1458–1750* (Toronto: University of Toronto Press, 1999).

65. Germanic iconography suggests that moresque was not perceived as a black dance in continental Europe at the beginning of the sixteenth century. In his *Trachtenbuch* (Germanisches Nationalmuseum Nürnberg, Hs. 22474, 1535), Christoph Weiditz includes an illustration of *moriscos* dancing, and the difference in skin tone, physiognomy, habit, and mobility between the *moriscos* dancing a moresque and the shackled dark-skinned slaves on another page dissociates the *moriscos'* dance from blackness. Similarly, a late fifteenth-century engraving by Israel van Meckenem representing white moresque dancers features movements similar to those depicted in *Freydal*, but sans black-up (on *Freydal*, see Footnote #70). Finally, the series of statues representing moresque dancers that sculptor Erasmus Grasser produced circa 1480 numbers only one black-skinned dancer amidst nine white-skinned dancers. Thus, the practice of dancing the moresque in black-up so vividly depicted in *Freydal* was not hegemonic from the start—it became so. In 1538, when Strasbourg bakers danced a moresque throughout the city, "they were all painted black like the Moors, and had black painted caps on." Qtd. in Locke, *Music and the Exotic from the Renaissance to Mozart*, 117. Similarly, records from 1530s Siena, Italy, refer to moresca as "a dance in the Ethiopian style" (un ballo a uso di Etiopia). Frank A. D'Accone, *The Civic Muse: Music and Musicians in Siena During the Middle Ages and the Renaissance* (Chicago: University of Chicago Press, 1997), 645. The turn is visible at the end of the sixteenth century, when moresque's archival presence intensifies. Claire Sponsler, "Writing the Unwritten: Morris Dance and

Theatre History," in *Representing the Past: Essays in Performance Historiography*, ed. Charlotte M. Canning and Thomas Postlewait (Iowa City: University of Iowa Press, 2010), 91. Most famously, in 1596, Thoinot Arbeau defined morisque as a slightly obsolete thumping-based dance performed by "a boy with his face smeared and blackened, with white or yellow taffeta around his forehead, and many bells on his shins." Thoinot Arbeau, *Orchésographie* (Langres: Jehan des Preyz, 1596), 94. Blackened moresque found its way into court ballets such as the *Ballet de la tour de Babel* (1627), which, to illustrate the diversity of nations and languages, has two *Mores* dancing the moresque in black-up. *Ballets et mascarades de cour de Henri III à Louis XIV (1581–1652), Tome III*, ed. Paul Lacroix (Geneva: Slatkine Reprints, 1968), 205–25.

66. "Faisans divers gestes des mains selon la matière qu'ils trattoyent; postures qu'à la vérité tout à coup excitoyent à rire, ayant semblance d'une dance moresque." Antoine Domayron, *Histoire du siège des muses* (Lyon: Simon Rigaud, 1610), 146.

67. Hornback, *Racism and Early Blackface Traditions*, 207. "Une façon de sauter que l'on appelle aujourd'hui la Moresque." Arcangelo Tuccaro, *Trois dialogues*. (Tours: chez Georges Griveau, 1616), 38.

68. K. Meira Goldberg, *Sonidos Negros: On the Blackness of Flamenco* (Oxford: Oxford University Press, 2019), 37; *Troys galans et un badin: Farce*, 1572, *Manuscrit La Vallière* (BnF, ms. fr. 24341), l.176. Facsimile: Slatkine Reprints, 1972. https://sottiesetfarces.wordpress.com/2018/10/06/troys-galans-et-un-badin/.

69. "Les mauresques sont parfois exécutées par les jeunes gens du cru, comme ce sera le cas à Aix et à Marseille en 1516. Mais le plus souvent, ce sont des professionnels qui les exécutent: ces danses, extrêmement vigoureuses et spectaculaires, impliquent en effet la pratique de sauts, de cabrioles, et d'acrobaties d'une virtuosité à couper le souffle." Margaret McGowan, *La danse à la Renaissance*, 39.

70. *Freydal: Des Kaisers Maximilian I. Turniere und Mummereien*. Circa 1515. http://idb.ub.uni-tuebingen.de/opendigi/Da204_fol_Text.

71. "On faisait donc dans les danses des Romains des postures des pieds et des mains et des gesticulations de tout le corps, comme font les basteleurs ou les danseurs de Morisques." *Extraordinaire du Mercure Galant: Quartier d'avril 1680, Tome X* (Paris: G. de Luyne, 1680), 300.

72. "Des gestes les plus folastres que vous sçauriez penser. Je ne m'esbahis pas si encore en France on appelle plusieurs danses les Moresques, veu les singeries qu'ils font en dansant." André Thevet, *Cosmographie universelle d'André Thevet, cosmographe du roy, Tome premier* (Paris: Guillaume Chaudière, 1575), 94.

73. "Elles font des terribles démenées et singeries." Pieter de Marees, *Description et récit historial du riche royaume d'or de Gunea* (Amsterdam: chez Cornille Claesson, 1605), 71–72. Esther Terry also detects animalizing rhetoric in English travel writings, namely, in Captain William Towerson's log of his first voyage to Guinea in 1555 and in Jobson's *The Golden Trade*. Terry, "Belonging While Black," 203–6, 219–20.

74. Qtd. in Locke, *Music and the Exotic from the Renaissance to Mozart*, 117.

75. On the perception of Canary people as dark-skinned, see the illustration representing a man from Tenerife in Leo Africanus's *Historiale description de l'Afrique*, 406. On the development of plantation slavery in the Canary Islands (and other islands such as Madeira), see Lawrence Clayton, "Bartolomé de las Casas and the African Slave Trade," *History Compass* 7, no. 6 (2009), 1527.

76. Julia Sutton and Pamela Jones, "Canary," *The International Encyclopedia of Dance*. Oxford University Press. https://www.oxfordreference-com.proxy.uchicago.edu/view/10.1093/acref/9780195173697.001.0001/acref-9780195173697-e-0317. Accessed 22 November 2021.

77. "La Canarie est grandement difficile et ne se danse que par ceux qui sont très bien instruits dans cet exercice, et qui ont le pied fort prest. Elle est composée de plusieurs batteries de pied ... et de demie-caprioles, de demi-pirouettes, et d'autres tours tant en l'air et par en haut, que ... terre à terre." Marin Mersenne, *Harmonie universelle, contenant la théorie et la pratique de la musique* (Paris: Sébastien Cramoisy, 1636), 174.

78. "Lesdits passages sont gaillards et néanmoins étranges, bizarres, et resentent fort le sauvage. ... Vous les apprendrez de ceulx qui les savent et vous pourrez en inventer vous-mêmes de nouveaux." Arbeau, *Orchésographie*, 95v.

79. "Aulcuns dient qu'és isles des Canaries, on use de cette dance, et qu'elle leur est ordinaire: aultres, de l'opinion desquels j'aymerais mieux estre, soutiennent qu'elle a pris source d'un ballet composé pour une mascarade, où les danseurs étaient habillés en roys et roynes de Mauritanie, ou bien en forme de Sauvages, avec plumaches teintes de diverses couleurs." Arbeau, *Orchésographie*, 95v.

80. I register here my disagreement with Ralph Locke's statement that "dark-skinned characters were rare in courtly ballets." Locke, *Music and the Exotic from the Renaissance to Mozart*, 140. Locke's surprising reluctance to give sub-Saharan African characters their due in his otherwise fairly comprehensive study of exotic others in early modern European musical and choreographic culture relies on a truncated reading of the archives.

81. In *Ballet de la magnifique duchesse de Dendaye* (1625), for instance the grotesque duchess of Dendaye (Garlic-Breath) wants to get married. "She does not want to be won by blood but through dance" and she rejects the king of France and the Great Turk for the king of Ethiopia, who seduces her "through the lovely effects of his turns" (double cadence). *Ballet de la magnifique duchesse de Dendaye* (1625), in *Ballets et mascarades de cour de Henri III à Louis XIV (1581–1652), Tome III,* ed. Paul Lacroix (Geneva: Slatkine Reprints, 1968), 83–84. The excellence of the African king at dancing is confirmed by his countrymen's performances. In *Ballet de l'almanach ou les prédictions véritables* (1631), the arrival of summer is represented by four black *Mores:* "Their color, tawny and black, could horrify you, but the gentleness of their steps, the diversity of their postures, and their talent for dance, dispelling your aversion for their color, will make you applaud and confess that their dance is one of the most pleasant things you have ever seen." (Leur couleur basanée et noire pourrait vous donner de l'horreur; mais la gentillesse de leurs pas, la diversité de leurs postures, et la disposition avec laquelle ils danseront, vous ostant toute l'aversion que vous pourriez avoir de cette couleur, vous porteront à un applaudissement et un aveu que leur balet sera une des plus agréables choses que vous avez encore vues.) *Ballet de l'almanach ou les prédictions véritables* (1631), in *Ballets et mascarades de cour de Henri III à Louis XIV (1581–1652), Tome IV,* ed. Paul Lacroix (Geneva: Slatkine Reprints, 1968), 153.

82. "Lequel More, au son desdits violons, ayant fait quelque tour de souplesse, une baguette dorée en la main, s'en allait vers ladite forêt faire entrer deux pages porte-flambeaux vêtus en Magots verts ... [le More] s'en retournant à capriole vers ladite forêt en faisait sortir trois autres violons esclaves. ... Et les dix magots verts porte-flambeaux entraient ensemble deux à deux, puis estans tous entrés et rangés ... les quinze violons commençaient à sonner ensemble le bal des magots verts, lequel ils dansaient en dix façons, toujours en cadence, avec saults, gambades, gestes et grimaces différentes. Ledit More, étant au milieu d'eux, leur faisant signe de ce qu'ils devaient faire, et en cette façon il les faisait retirer après lui file à file vers la forêt, tantost sautant sur un pied, tantost sur un autre, tantost sur les deux ensemble." *Ballet de Monseigneur le duc de Vandosme* (1610), in *Ballets et mascarades de cour de Henri III à Louis XIV (1581–1652), Tome I,* ed. Paul Lacroix (Geneva: Slatkine Reprints, 1968), 243–44.

83. Philibert Monet, *Invantaire des deus langues françoise et latine,* 572.

84. Margaret M. McGowan, *The Court Ballet of Louis XIII: A Collection of Working Designs for Costumes, 1615–1633* (London: Victoria and Albert Museum in association with Hobhouse and Morton Morris, 1986), no. 75.

85. Bordier, *Billebahaut*, 39.

86. "Le ballet exprime les mouvements que la peinture et la sculpture ne sauraient exprimer, et par ces mouvements, il va jusqu'à exprimer la nature des choses et les habitudes de l'âme, qui ne peuvent tomber sous les sens que par ces mouvements." Ménestrier, *Des ballets anciens et modernes*, 41. For an exploration of this belief both in humanist writings and in the writings of dance masters, see Nevile, *Eloquent Body*, 91–92.

87. "La dance est une espèce de rhétorique muette, par laquelle l'orateur peut par ses mouvements, sans parler un seul mot, se faire entendre." Arbeau, *Orchésographie*, 5v.

88. As Keith Thomas puts it, "It was because the separateness of the human race was thought so precarious, so easily lost, that the boundary had to be so tightly guarded." Keith Thomas, *Man and the Natural World: A History of the Modern Sensibility* (New York: Pantheon Books, 1983), 135.

89. Mark Franko sees the burlesque ballet as "an attempt to establish a legibility for dance independent of verbal means," a deeply politicized practice, in which dancing aristocrats tried to emancipate themselves from the yoke of the Crown by having their bodies emancipate themselves from text and textuality, the old "metaphor for autocratic power" that had traditionally informed the aesthetics of ballet since the 1580s. Franko, *Dance as Text*, 5, 6. In that sense, "burlesque ballet had represented a form of veiled protest in its curious autonomy, and an obvious critique through its satire," and "the most satiric of burlesque ballets were in dialogue with the monarch and society at large over nobiliary rights versus royal power" (11, 68). Franko reads the blacked-up aristocrats' expressions of abject servility—which I conceptualize as central to the script of black enslavement to love—as an ironical submission of white aristocrats to absolutist royal power. Here, I extend to black dances themselves the dynamics that Franko identifies regarding the aristocratic recuperation of performative blackness.

90. Sarah R. Cohen, *Art, Dance, and the Body in French Culture of the Ancien Régime* (Cambridge: Cambridge University Press, 2000), 3–4.

91. "Qui sentent par trop son baladin." François de Lauze, *Apologie de la danse, et la parfaite méthode de l'enseigner tant aux cavaliers qu'aux dames* (1623), 46. "La danse que l'on nomme la belle, qui consiste en simples démarches, à bien observer les pas, et à garder des temps réguliers et justes, est toujours plus majestueuse et sent mieux sa personne de qualité, et ce qui vaut, beaucoup mieux encore, la modestie et la vertu." Michel de Pure, *Idée des spectacles anciens et nouveaux* (Paris: chez Michel Brunet, 1668), 279.

92. Philippe Quinault, *Cadmus et Hermione: Tragédie représentée par l'Académie royale de musique* (Paris: René Baudry, 1674), 18–20.

93. "Les Éthiopiens descendent des rochers, et témoignent leur joie en chantant et en dansant." Philippe Quinault, *Persée: Tragédie représentée par l'Académie royale de musique* (Paris: Christophe Ballard, 1682), 49; Joseph-François Duché de Vancy, *Téagène et Chariclée : Tragédie en musique, représentée par l'Académie royale de musique* (Amsterdam: Antoine Schelte, 1695), 21.

94. "Le frère du malade imaginaire lui amène pour le divertir plusieurs Egyptiens et Egyptiennes vestus en Mores, qui font des danses entremeslées de chansons. . . . Tous les Mores dansent ensemble et font sauter des singes qu'ils ont amenez avec eux." Molière, *Le malade imaginaire*, 26–30.

95. Olivia Bloechl notes, "Although I have not yet found any record of their serving in any particular court spectacles, the 'fifty-four Moors, genuine Africans' whom the King 'purchased'

in 1680 were intended to serve on the Grand Canal, the site of many such performances." Bloechl, "Race, Empire, and Music," 87.

96. "When human power over animals is represented, it often undercuts humanity as a separate category.... To assert human supremacy, writers [and performers] turn to discuss animals, but in this turning they reveal the frailty of the supremacy which is being asserted." Erica Fudge, *Perceiving Animals: Humans and Beasts in Early Modern English Culture* (New York: St. Martin's, 2000), 4.

97. Benjamin Jonson, *Masque of Blackness*.

98. Scholars often connect that decision to the foreign Catholic queen consort's estrangement from James I and to her general unhappiness at the English court. Aasand, "To Blanch an Ethiop, and Revive a Corse," 276–80; Kim F. Hall, *Things of Darkness*, 10. Anne claimed political agency not only by commissioning a masque and performing it herself—an act of self-display that, in a country that did not admit of female performers on the commercial stage, was sufficient to "blacken" the queen's reputation—but also by performing it in cosmetic black-up, a demand from which playwright Ben Jonson distances himself as much as possible in his published account of the masque. Andrea, "Black Skin, the Queen's Masques," 264–65. As Bernadette Andrea explains: "from the perspective of Jacobean patriarchy, black(ened) femininity encodes loathsomeness, strangeness, and dishonesty. From the oppositional position of the Queen and her ladies, however, black(ened) femininity functions as a polysemic site of resistance" (281). In other words, the queen's deliberate self-presentation as exotic, unruly, and threatening by means of black-up challenged the strand of Jacobean ideology built on an intersectional oppression of women and non-white people. As Kim F. Hall argues, the liberating dynamics of black-up in *Blackness* are short-lived, for Ben Jonson's libretto, hinging on Ethiopian princesses' desire to turn white and the promise once made to them that the sun of Britannia would whiten them, promotes King James's ability to contain, subdue, and erase female blackness. Kim F. Hall, *Things of Darkness*, 11–12.

99. Sarah Schmalenberger, "Hearing the Other in the *Masque of Blackness*," in *Blackness in Opera*, ed. Naomi Andre, Karen Bryan, and Eric Saylor (Urbana: University of Illinois Press, 2012), 36; Benjamin Jonson, *Masque of Blackness*, 230, l.306. Saraband and Canary were well known among the English aristocracy: "Toward the end of the sixteenth century,... the sarabande and the canary confirmed a preoccupation with foreign exoticism and strange encounters. The sarabande, supposedly invented by the Saracens, was a sinuous, gliding dance accompanied by guitar and castanets, so in vogue that even little children (of gentle birth) knew it: the duchess of Buckingham proudly wrote to the duke that their infant daughter 'loves dancing extremely, and when the sarabande is played, she will set her thumb and finger together, offering to snap.'" Howard Skiles, *The Politics of Courtly Dancing in Early Modern England* (Amherst: University of Massachusetts Press, 1998), 113.

100. Anne Daye, "The Role of *Le Balet comique* in Forging the Stuart Masque: Part 1, The Jacobean Initiative," *Dance Research* 32, no. 2 (2014): 185–88.

101. Smith, "Textile Black Body," 172–73.

102. McManus, *Women on the Renaissance Stage*, 70.

103. McManus, *Women on the Renaissance Stage*, 75.

104. David Stevenson, ed., *Scotland's Last Royal Wedding: The Marriage of James VI and Anne of Denmark. With a Danish Account of the Marriage Translated by Peter Graves* (Edinburgh: John Donald, 1997), 109.

105. McManus, *Women on the Renaissance Stage*, 77.

106. Stevenson, ed., *Scotland's Last Royal Wedding*, 109.

107. Jonson, *Masque of Blackness*, 230, l.305.

108. Jonson, *Masque of Blackness*, 229, l.265–69.

109. Donald J. Gordon, *The Renaissance Imagination: Essays and Lectures* (Berkeley: University of California Press, 1975), 138–41.

110. Philip Massinger, *The Bondman* (1623), in *The Plays of Philip Massinger, from the Text of William Gifford*, ed. Francis Cunningham, 99–132 (London: Alfred Thomas Crocker, 1868).

111. Thomas C. Fulton, "'The True and Naturall Constitution of That Mixed Government:' Massinger's 'The Bondman' and the Influence of Dutch Republicanism," *Studies in Philology* 99, no. 2 (2002): 156–57.

112. Lowe, "Stereotyping of Black Africans in Renaissance Europe," 35.

113. Shakespeare, *Love's Labor's Lost*, 5.2.157.

114. Habib, *Black Lives in the English Archives*, 136.

115. Brome, *The English Moor*, 4.5.805–6.

116. John Mason, *The Turke, a Worthie Tragedie* (London: Printed by Edward Allde for John Busbie, 1610), G1v.

117. Those lexical entries were retrieved through the Lexicons of Early Modern English project: http://leme.library.utoronto.ca/.

118. John Baret, *An Alveary or Triple Dictionary in English, Latin, and French* (London: Henry Denham, 1574), n.p.; John Bullokar, *An English Expositor Teaching the Interpretation of the Hardest Words Used in our Language* (London: Printed by Iohn Legatt, 1616) n.p.; Edward Philips, *The New World of English Words, or A General Dictionary Containing the Interpretations of Such Hard Words as Are Derived from Other Languages* (London: Printed by E. Tyler for Nathaniel Brooke, 1658), C2.

119. Henry Peacham, *The Gentleman's Exercise, or An Exquisite Practise, as Well for Drawing All Manner of Beasts in Their True Portraitures* (London: Printed for Iohn Browne, 1612), 39–45.

120. "Antick'd" is a synonym for "disguised" in both Edmund Coote's *The English Schoole-Maister Teaching All His Scholers the Order of Distinct Reading, and True Writing Our English Tongue* (London: Printed by the widow Orwin for Ralph Jackson and Robert Dextar, 1596), 75; and Robert Cawdry's *A Table Alphabeticall Contayning and Teaching the True Writing and Understanding of Hard Usuall English Wordes* (London: Printed by T.S. for Edmund Weauer, 1609), n.p. The term is used to define a "mascarade" as "an anticke dance of disguised persons" in John Wilkins's *An Alphabetical Dictionary*, Kkk3r; it is used to define the "Pimpompet" dance as "a kind of antick dance wherein three hit each other on the bum with one of their feet" in Edward Philips's *The New World of English Words*, HHv; and to define the "Matachin" dance as "an antick or morrice dance" in Elisha Coles's *An English Dictionary* (London: Printed by Samuel Crouch, 1676), A2.

121. E.B., *A New Dictionary of the Canting Crew in Its Several Tribes of Gypsies, Beggers, Thieves, Cheats, etc.* (London: Printed for W. Hawes, P. Gilbourne, and W. Davis, 1699), B.E. B2v.

122. In early modern lexicons, even in (the rare) performative contexts that are not kinetic, the term "antics" connote animalization. For instance, we encounter "anticke musicke counterfeiting the voyces of birds" in Henry Shirley, *The Martyr'd Souldier* (London: Printed by I. Okes, 1638), 3.

123. Too many plays feature antick-dancing devils for me to list them here, but plays featuring ethnic anticks include Aphra Behn's *The Widdow Ranter, or the History of Bacon in Virginia, a Tragicomedy* (London: James Knapton, 1690), 14, which contains Native American antics; the various translation of Corneille's *Pompey* in the 1660s (which contain Romani antics); and Ra-

venscroft's *The Citizen Turn'd Gentleman*, 86–87 (which contains Turkish antics), among others. Baboons dance "delightful anticks" in Chapman's *The Memorable Maske of the Two Honorable Houses or Innes of Court: The Middle Temple and Lyncolns Inne* (London: Printed by G. Eld, for George Norton, 1613), C4r; and "a Boy drest like a Baboon . . . making mouths and antick postures" eighty years later, in Roger Boyle of Orrery's *Guzman, a Comedy* (London: Printed for Francis Saunders, 1693), 18.

124. Kim F. Hall, "'Troubling Doubles': Apes, Africans, and Blackface in Mr. Moore's Revels," in *Race, Ethnicity, and Power in the Renaissance*, ed. Joyce Green MacDonald (Madison, N.J.: Fairleigh Dickinson Press, 1997), 125–26.

125. Philip Massinger, *Believe as You List* (1631), in *The Plays of Philip Massinger, from the Text of William Gifford*, edited Francis Cunningham, 595–625 (London: Alfred Thomas Crocker, 1868).

126. Philip Massinger, *The Parliament of Love*, 166–93, 172, 167.

127. For a thorough analysis of the "Gypsy" genealogy of antics and their Africanization in the late Jacobean and Caroline period, see Ndiaye, "Come Aloft, Jack-Little-Ape."

128. I am grateful to Kim F. Hall for drawing my attention to the echo between Zanthia's drag scene and the Black Lady's performance. On the latter, see MacDonald, *Women and Race in Early Modern Texts*, 1–20.

129. Shakespeare, *Antony and Cleopatra*, 4.2.210–11.

130. Shirley, *Martyr'd Souldier*. John Forrest notes that the tradition of staging Morris dances in commercial theatre "had a vogue of only about thirty-five years, from 1589 to 1623." Forrest, *History of Morris Dancing*, 215–19. The rise of black antics in commercial theatre precisely in 1623, in the wake of *The Bondman*, might help explain that decline.

131. John R. Elliott Jr., "Mr. Moore's Revels: A 'Lost' Oxford Masque," *Renaissance Quarterly* 37, no. 3 (1984): 411–20. Although, according to Elliott, the only dances the libretto of *Mr. Moore's Revels* mentions are "country dances" and "French dances" (417), patterns of animalization and mimicry suggest that performers resorted to antics, all the more since the epilogue delivered during the second performance of the masque alludes to that tradition: "whilst your goodness blest us with a smile, / our frisking soules danc't Anticke all the while" (419).

132. Kim F. Hall, *Things of Darkness*, 123.

133. Thomas St. Serfe, *Tarugo's Wiles*, 14. This play was based on Agustín Moreto y Cavana's *No puede ser el guardar una mujer*, in *Parte quarenta y una de famosas comedias de diferentes autores*, 179–224 (Pamplona: por Ioseph del Espiritu Santo, [1675?]).

134. William Killigrew, *The Imperial Tragedy Taken Out of a Latin Play, and Very Much Altered* (London: Printed for Will. Wells and Rob. Scott, 1669), 44; William Whitaker, *The Conspiracy, or The Change of Government, a Tragedy* (London: Printed for William Cademan, 1680), 5; Thomas Otway, *The Atheist*, 66; Aphra Behn, *The Emperor of the Moon, a Farce* (London: Printed by R. Holt for Joseph Knight and Francis Saunders, 1687), 60.

135. Elkanah Settle, *The Empress of Morocco, a Tragedy, with Sculptures* (London: Printed for William Cademan, 1673).

136. "On remarquait qu'après qu'ils s'étoyent divertis de cette sorte, ils travailloient de beaucoup meilleur courage, sans témoigner aucune lassitude, et mieux que s'ils eussent reposé en leur cabane tout le long de la nuit." Jean Rochefort, *Histoire naturelle et morale des îles Antilles de l'Amérique* (Rotterdam: Chez Arnout Leers, 1658), 322. In the American colonies, masters did more than allow those dances: "It was not uncommon for slave owners to participate in the frolics [slaves] organized. They indulged the slaves with whiskey, sang and danced with them, served as musicians, and frequently were spectators." Hartman, *Scenes of Subjection*, 45. Beyond Sunday

dances, Hartman has shown how black dances were part and parcel of the plantation economy, from slave ship decks to the market places, to the sugar cane fields, where black bodies moved to the sound of music: "innocent amusements supplemented other methods of managing the slave body" (43).

137. Qtd. in Kenneth Mills, William B. Taylor, and Sandra Lauderdale Graham, eds., *Colonial Latin America: A Documentary History* (Wilmington, Del.: Scholarly Resources, 2002), 164.

138. For Frantz Fanon, dance's function as an outlet for frustrations serves to maintain an oppressive social order and is thus a problematic fixture of colonial societies: "The native's relaxation takes precisely the form of a muscular orgy in which the most acute aggressivity and the most impelling violence are canalized, transformed, and conjured away. The circle of the dance is a permissive circle: it protects and permits. . . . When they set out, the men and women were impatient, stamping their feet in a state of nervous excitement; when they return, peace has been restored to the village; it is once more calm and unmoved. . . . Now the problem is to lay hold of this violence which is changing direction." Frantz Fanon, *The Wretched of the Earth* (1963), trans. Richard Philcox (New York: Grove, 2004), 56–57.

139. "On a fait des ordonnances dans les isles pour empêcher les calendas non seulement à cause des postures indécentes et tout-à-fait lascives dont cette danse est composée, mais encore pour ne pas donner lieu aux trop nombreuses assemblées des Nègres, qui, se trouvant ainsi ramassez dans la joie et le plus souvent avec de l'eau de vie dans la tête, peuvent faire des révoltes, des soulèvements, ou des parties pour aller voler." Jean-Baptiste Labat, *Nouveau voyage aux isles de l'Amérique, Tome Second* (La Haye: P. Husson et al, 1724), 53.

140. On the various prohibitions set on calenda in the French Caribbean, see Garraway, *Libertine Colony*, 253, 355n30. Virtually anywhere a big slave population existed, dance gatherings were strictly regimented because of their galvanizing effect. For instance, in Palermo, Italy, as early as 1440, Africans were forbidden from carrying drums, tambourines, and weapons; and in Cartagena, Colombia, a 1573 edict stipulated that Afro-diasporic people, both free and unfree, could meet only on Sundays if and where the town council authorized them to do so (only during daytime). Lowe, "Stereotyping of Black Africans in Renaissance Europe," 39–40; Méndez Rodríguez, *Esclavos en la pintura sevillana de los Siglos de Oro*, 52.

141. Pierre Motteux, *The Island Princess, or the Generous Portuguese made into an opera* (London: Printed for Richard Wellington, 1699), 42.

142. Thomas Southerne, *Oroonoko, a Tragedy* (London: Printed for H. Playford, B. Tooke, and S. Buckley, 1696), 30.

143. William Davenant, *The History of Sir Francis Drake. The First Part* (London: Printed for Henry Herringman, 1659).

144. Philip Nichols, *Sir Francis Drake Reviv'd* (London: Printed for Nicholas Bourne, 1628), in *Documents Concerning English Voyages to the Spanish Main, 1569–1680*, 2nd ser., no. 71, ed. Irene A. Wright, 247–326. London: Hakluyt Society, 1932.

145. Nichols, *Sir Francis Drake Reviv'd*, 307.

146. Nora Rodríguez Loro hypothesizes that Wycherley saw performances of Calderonian plays during his stay in Madrid in 1664 in the service of the English ambassador and theatre enthusiast Richard Fanshawe. Presumably, he then purchased a copy of the *Tercera parte de las comedias de Calderón*, published that very year, which influenced his first two comedies, *Love in a Wood* and *The Gentleman Dancing-Master*. Nora Rodríguez Loro, "Falsos maestros de danzar: Análisis comparativo de la comedia El Maestro de danzar de Lope de Vega y las obras homónimas

de Calderón de la Barca y Wycherley" M.A. Thesis (Universidad de Sevilla, Facultad de Filología, Departamento de Literatura Española, 2014), 27–28.

147. William Wycherley, *The Gentleman Dancing-Master, a Comedy* (London: Printed by J.M. for Henry Herringman and Thomas Dring, 1673), 83.

148. Wycherley, *The Gentleman Dancing-Master*, 59.

149. Qtd. in Habib, *Black Lives in the English Archives*, 179.

150. Rodreguez King-Dorset has shown that, in the early eighteenth century, "most of the blacks making up the London community arrived from the Caribbean" and that, for them, dance was a means for community building. King-Dorset, *Black Dance in London*, 83, 103.

151. For examples of such scholarly attempts, see Nicholas R. Jones's *Staging Habla de Negros*; Mark Knowles's *The Early History of Tap Dancing* (Jefferson, N.C.: McFarland, 2002); Lynne Fauley Emery's *Black Dance from 1619 to Today* (Princeton, N.J.: Princeton Book, 1988); Sonjah Stanley-Niaah's *Dancehall: From Slave Ship to Ghetto* (Ottawa: University of Ottawa Press, 2010); and Edward Thorpe's *Black Dance* (Woodstock, N.Y.: Overlook Press, 1990). Narratives of choreographic continuity that hinge on early modern black dance descriptions also severely underestimate the changes that African dances—like any dances around the globe—have undergone since the early modern period. As Esther Terry puts it, "the overarching compositional and narrative choices in Black dance history, that is, the survival of Africanist esthetics despite the brutality of the trans-Atlantic slave trade . . . preemptively freezes sub-Saharan Africans in isolated stasis." Esther J. Terry, "Choreographies of Trans-Atlantic Primitivity: Sub-Saharan Isolation in Black Dance Historiography," in *Early Modern Black Diaspora Studies: A Critical Anthology*, ed. Cassander L. Smith, Nicholas R. Jones, and Miles P. Grier (New York: Palgrave Macmillan, 2018), 66.

POST/SCRIPT

1. Balibar and Wallerstein, *Race, Nation, Class*, 230.

2. The critical drive toward freedom is perhaps most clearly instantiated in Foucault's decision to switch from history of ideas to archeology in an effort to escape teleology: "the essential task was to free the history of thought from its subjection to transcendence. . . . My aim was to analyse this history, in the discontinuity that no teleology would reduce in advance; to map it in a dispersion that no pre-established horizon would embrace; to allow it to be deployed in an anonymity on which no transcendental constitution would impose the form of the subject; to open it up to a temporality that would not promise the return of any dawn." Michel Foucault, *The Archaeology of Knowledge*, trans. A. M. Sheridan Smith (New York: Routledge, 2002), 223–24.

3. "A mes yeux, les climats bruslés / Aux autres régions paroistroient préférables / Si les monstres affreux dont ils sont habités / Estoient à celuy-ci semblables." Nicolas Arnoult et al., *Recueil de modes de la cour de France, Tome 2* (Paris: 1750), n.p.

BIBLIOGRAPHY

PRIMARY SOURCES

Africanus, Leo. *Historiale description de l'Afrique, tierce partie du monde*. Lyon: Jean Temporal, 1556.

Aguado, Simón. *El platillo, entremés* (1602). In *Collección de entremeses, loas, bailes, jácaras y mojigangas, desde fines del siglo XVI á mediados del XVIII*, vol. 1, edited by Emilio Cotarelo y Mori, 226–31. Madrid: Casa Editorial Bailly Bailliére, 1911.

———. *Los negros, entremés* (1602). In *Collección de entremeses, loas, bailes, jácaras y mojigangas, desde fines del siglo XVI á mediados del XVIII*, vol. 1, edited by Emilio Cotarelo y Mori, 231–35. Madrid: Casa Editorial Bailly Baillière, 1911.

Alfonso X (el Sabio) of Castile. *Las siete partidas del rey Don Alfonso el Sabio, cotejadas con varios códices antiguos por la Real Academia de la Historia. Tomo I, Partida primera*. Madrid: en la Imprenta Real, 1807.

Andreini, Giovanni Battista. *Lo schiavetto*. Venice: Giovanni Battista Ciotti, 1620.

Anglicus, Bartholomaeus. *Batman Vppon Bartholome His Booke De Proprietatibus Rerum, Newly Corrected, Enlarged and Amended*. London: Thomas East, 1582.

Arbeau, Thoinot. *Orchésographie*. Langres: Jehan des Preyz, 1596.

Arnoult, Nicolas, et al. *Recueil de modes de la cour de France, Tome 2*. Paris: 1750.

Aubignac, Abbé de. *La pratique du théâtre*. Paris: Antoine de Sommaville, 1657.

Aucto de la paciencia de Job. In *(Códice de autos viejos) Colección de autos sacramentales, loas y farsas del siglo XVI (anteriores a Lope de Vega)*. Biblioteca Nacional de España. Ms. 14.711. ca. 1550–75.

Aureli, Aurelio. *Emilia*. London: Printed for the author, 1672.

Auto de los reyes magos. In *Textos medievales españoles*, 171–77. Madrid: Espasa Calpe, 1976.

Avellaneda de la Cueva y Guerra, Francisco. *Bayle entremesado de los negros*. In *Tardes apacibles de gustoso entretenimiento: Repartidas en varios entremeses, y bayles entremesados, escogidos de los mejores ingenios de España*, edited by Don Lope Gaspar de Figueroa Guzman y Velasco, 67r–70r. Madrid: por Andrés García de la Iglesia, a costa de Iuan Martín Merinero, 1663.

Ballet de l'almanach ou les prédictions véritables (1631). In *Ballets et mascarades de cour de Henri III à Louis XIV (1581–1652), Tome IV*, edited by Paul Lacroix, 123–54. Geneva: Slatkine Reprints, 1968.

Ballet de la magnifique duchesse de Dendaye (1625). In *Ballets et mascarades de cour de Henri III à Louis XIV (1581–1652), Tome III*, edited by Paul Lacroix, 81–100. Geneva: Slatkine Reprints, 1968.

Ballet de la tour de Babel (1627). In *Ballets et mascarades de cour de Henri III à Louis XIV (1581–1652), Tome III*, edited by Paul Lacroix, 205–25. Geneva: Slatkine Reprints, 1968.

Ballet de Monseigneur le duc de Vandosme (1610). In *Ballets et mascarades de cour de Henri III à Louis XIV (1581–1652), Tome I*, edited by Paul Lacroix, 236–39. Geneva: Slatkine Reprints, 1968.

Ballet des divers entretiens de la fontaine de Vaucluse (1649). In *Ballets et mascarades de cour de Henri III à Louis XIV (1581–1652), Tome VI*, edited by Paul Lacroix, 192–223. Geneva: Slatkine Reprints, 1968.

Ballet des rues de Paris. In *Ballets et mascarades de cour de Henri III à Louis XIV (1581–1652), Tome VI*, edited by Paul Lacroix, 129–40. Geneva: Slatkine Reprints, 1968.

Ballet des proverbes dancé par son altesse Monsieur de prince de Vaudémont. Nancy: Claude Anthoine et Charles les Charlots, Imprimeurs ordinaires, 1665.

Bandello, Matteo. *La terza parte de le novelle del Bandello*. Lucca: per il Busdrago, 1554.

Baret, John. *An Alveary or Triple Dictionary in English, Latin, and French*. London: Henry Denham, 1574.

Barré, Pierre-Yves, and Jean-Baptiste Radet. *La Négresse, ou le pouvoir de la reconnaissance, comédie*. Paris: Imbault, 1787.

Beaumont, Francis, and John Fletcher. *The Knight of Malta*. In *Comedies and Tragedies Written by Francis Beaumont and John Fletcher Never Printed Before*, 71–95. London: Printed for Humphrey Robinson . . . and for Humphrey Moseley . . . , 1647.

———. *Love's Pilgrimage*. In *Comedies and Tragedies Written by Francis Beaumont and John Fletcher Never Printed Before*, 1–26. London: Printed for Humphrey Robinson . . . and for Humphrey Moseley . . . , 1647.

Behn, Aphra. *The Emperor of the Moon, a Farce*. London: Printed by R. Holt for Joseph Knight and Francis Saunders, 1687.

———. *The Widdow Ranter, or the History of Bacon in Virginia, a Tragicomedy*. London: James Knapton, 1690.

Belleforest, Francois de. *Second tome des histoires tragiques, extraites de l'italien de Bandel*. Paris: Pour Robert le Magnier, 1566.

Berkeley, William. *The Lost Lady, a Tragy-Comedy*. London: By Jo. Okes, for John Colby, 1638.

Besnier, Pierre. *La réunion des langues, ou l'art de les apprendre toutes par une seule*. Paris: Sébastien Mabre-Cramoisy, 1674.

Best, George. *A True Discourse of the Late Voyages of Discoverie for the Finding of a Passage to Cathaya*. London: Imprinted by Henry Bynnyman, 1578.

Bickerstaff, Isaac. *The Padlock, a Comic Opera*. New York: Charles Wiley, 1825.

———. *The Romp, A Musical Entertainment*. London: Printed for W. Lowndes and J. Barker, 1786.

Bodin, Jean. *De la démonomanie des sorciers*. Paris: chez Jacques Dupuys, 1587.

———. *Les six livres de la République*. Paris: chez Jacques du Puys, 1577.

Boissin de Gallardon, Jean. *La Perséene, ou la délivrance d'Andromède*. In *Les tragédies et histoires sainctes de Jean Boissin de Gallardon*, 1–70. Lyon: Simon Rigaud, 1618.

Bordier, René. *Grand bal de la douairière de Billebahaut*. In *Ballets et mascarades de cour de Henri III à Louis XIV (1581–1652), Tome troisième*, edited by Paul Lacroix, 151–202. Geneva: Slatkine Reprints, 1968.

———. *Grand bal de la douairière de Billebahaut, Ballet dansé par sa majesté* (Paris: 16??)

Borée, Vincent. *Achille victorieux*. Lyon: pour Vincent de Coeursilly, 1627.

Boursault, Edmé. *Le mort vivant, comédie*. Paris: Nicolas Pépingué, 1662.

Boutade des Mores esclaves d'Amour délivrés par Bacchus. 1609.

Bradford, William. *A Relation or Iournall of the Beginning and Proceedings of the English Plantation Setled at Plimoth in New England.* London: Printed by J. Dawson for Iohn Bellamie, 1622.

Brome, Richard. *The Damoiselle, or The New Ordinary.* London: Printed by T.R. for Richard Marriott and Thomas Dring, 1653.

———. *The English Moor, or The Mock-Marriage.* Modern text, edited by Matthew Steggle. In *Richard Brome Online.* http://www.dhi.ac.uk/brome. November 11, 2021. ISBN 978-0-9557876-1-4.

———. *The Northern Lass.* Modern text, edited by J. Sanders. In *Richard Brome Online.* http://www.dhi.ac.uk/brome. November 11, 2021. ISBN 978-0-9557876-1-4.

———. *The Novella, A Comedy.* Modern text, edited by Richard Cave. In *Richard Brome Online.* http://www.dhi.ac.uk/brome. November 11, 2021. ISBN 978-0-9557876-1-4.

Bullokar, John. *An English Expositor Teaching the Interpretation of the Hardest Words Used in Our Language.* London: Printed by Iohn Legatt, 1616.

Calderón de la Barca, Pedro. *El astrólogo fingido.* In *Parte veynte y cinco de comedias recopiladas de diferentes autores è ilustres poetas de España,* 193v–216r. Zaragoza: a costa de Pedro Escuer . . . , 1632.

———. *Las carnestolendas.* In *Entremeses, jácaras y mojigangas,* edited by Evangelina Rodríguez y Antonio Tordera, 139–55. Madrid: Editorial Castalia, 1983.

———. *La sibila del Oriente y gran reyna de Saba.* Madrid: por Francisco Sanz, 1682.

Cary, Elizabeth. *The Tragedy of Mariam, the Fair Queen of Jewry.* In *The Routledge Anthology of Renaissance Drama,* edited by Simon Barker and Hilary Hinds, 191–221. London: Routledge, 2003.

Castiglione, Baldesar. *The Book of the Courtier by Count Baldesar Castiglione.* Translated by Leonard Eckstein Opdycke. New York: Charles Scribner's Sons, 1903.

Cawdry, Robert. *A Table Alphabeticall Contayning and Teaching the True Writing and Understanding of Hard Usuall English Wordes.* London: Printed by T.S. for Edmund Weauer, 1609.

Cervantes Saavedra, Miguel de. *El celoso extremeño.* In *Novelas ejemplares,* edited by Jorge García López, 325–70. Barcelona: Crítica, 2001.

———. *Entremés de los mirones* (1615?). In *Varias obras inéditas de Cervantes,* edited by Adolfo de Castro, 23–88. Madrid: A. de Carlos é Hijo, Editores, 1874.

———. *Ocho comedias, y ocho entremeses nuevos, nunca representados.* Madrid: por la viuda de Alonso Martín, a costa de Iuan de Villarroel, 1615.

Chapman, George. *The Blinde Begger of Alexandria Most Pleasantly Discoursing His Variable Humours in Disguised Shapes Full of Conceite and Pleasure.* London: Printed by J. Roberts for William Jones, 1598.

———. *The Memorable Maske of the Two Honorable Houses or Innes of Court: The Middle Temple and Lyncolns Inne.* London: Printed by G. Eld, for George Norton, 1613.

Chrétien des Croix, Nicolas. *Les Portugaiz infortunez: Tragédie.* In *Les tragédies de N. Chrétien Sieur des Croix, Argentenois,* 1–126. Rouen: Théodore Reinsart, 1608.

Citoyen B***. *La liberté générale, ou les colons à Paris, comédie.* Cap-Français: P. Roux, imprimeur de la commission, 1796.

Claramonte y Corroy, Andrés de. *El valiente negro en Flandés.* Barcelona: en la Emprenta de Iayme Romeu, a costa de Iuan Sapera, 1638.

Code noir (Ordonnance de mars 1685 sur les esclaves des îles de l'Amérique). Versailles, 1685.

Coles, Elisha. *An English Dictionary*. London: Printed by Samuel Crouch, 1676.

Colletet, Guillaume. *Ballet de la marine*. Paris: A. de Sommaville, 1635.

Colman, George. *Inkle and Yarico, An Opera*. Glasgow: Printed for the booksellers, 1796.

Comédie admirable intitulée la merveille, où l'on voit comme un capitaine françois, esclave du sol- dam d'Egypte, transporté de son bon sens, ce donne au Diable pour s'affranchir de servitude, lequel il trompe mesme subtillement tant qu'il fut contrainct luy rendre son obligation. Rouen: Abraham Cousturier, ca. 1620.

Contract Between the City of Seville and Hernando Rivera. Sección II (Archivo de Contaduría y Junta de Propios), Carpeta 2, documento 24. Archivo Municipal de Sevilla.

Coote, Edmund. *The English Schoole-Maister Teaching All His Scholers the Order of Distinct Reading, and True Writing Our English Tongue*. London: Printed by the widow Orwin for Ralph Jackson and Robert Dextar, 1597.

Corneille, Pierre. *Andromède: Tragédie représentée avec les machines sur le théâtre royal de Bour- bon*. Rouen: Laurens Maurry, 1651.

Corneille, Thomas. *L'inconnu: Comédie mêlée d'ornements et de musique*. Paris: chez Jean Ribou, 1675. Edited by Paul Fièvre. Théâtre Classique, 2014.

Cotgrave, Randle. *A Dictionarie of the French and English Tongues*. London: Adam Islip, 1611.

Covarrubias Orozco, Sebastián de. *Tesoro de la lengua castellana o española*. Madrid: Luis San- chez, 1611.

Crown, John. *The Countrey Wit, a Comedy, Acted at the Dukes Theatre*. London: Printed by T.N. for James Magnes and Richard Bentley, 1675.

Daborne, Robert. *A Christian Turn'd Turke: or The Tragicall Liues and Deaths of the Two Famous Pyrates, Ward and Dansiker*. London: Printed by Nicholas Okes for William Barrenger, 1612.

Davenant, William. *The History of Sir Francis Drake. The First Part*. London: Printed for Henry Herringman, 1659.

Death Certificate of Hernando de Rivera's Son. Book 1, fol. 169. Parish registers of San Esteban, Seville, 1609.

Dekker, Thomas. *The Pleasant Comedie of Old Fortunatus*. London: Printed by S. Stafford for William Aspley, 1600.

———. *The Shomaker's Holiday, or The Gentle Craft*. London: Valentine Sims, 1600.

Della Porta, Giambattista. *La sorella*. In *Renaissance Comedy: The Italian Masters*, vol. 1, edited by Don Beecher, translated by Bruno Ferraro, 373–460. University of Toronto Press, 2008.

Diccionario de autoridades. Dictionary of the Real Academia Española. https://apps2.rae.es/DA .html. Accessed November 13, 2021.

Dictionnaire de l'Académie française. Paris: chez la Veuve de Jean-Baptiste Coignard, Imprimeur ordinaire du Roy et de l'Académie Françoise, 1694.

Discours facétieux des hommes qui font saller leurs femmes à cause qu'elles sont trop douces: Lequel se joue à cinq personnages. Rouen: Abraham Cousturier, ca. 1600.

Domayron, Antoine. *Histoire du siège des muses*. Lyon: Simon Rigaud, 1610.

Dryden, John. *An Evening's Love, or The Mock-Astrologer Acted at the Theatre-Royal, by His Maj- esties Servants*. London: Printed by T.N. for Henry Herringman, 1671.

Dryden, John, and William Davenant. *The Tempest, or The Enchanted Island, A Comedy*. Lon- don: Printed by J.M. for Henry Herringman . . . , 1670.

Duché de Vancy, Joseph-François. *Téagène et Cariclée: Tragédie en musique, représentée par l'Académie royale de musique*. Amsterdam: Antoine Schelte, 1695.

Duhamel, Georges. *Acoubar ou la loyauté trahie: Tragédie. Tirée des amours de Pistion et Fortunie en leur voyage de Canada*. Rouen: Raphaël du Petit Val, 1611.

E.B. *A New Dictionary of the Canting Crew in Its Several Tribes of Gypsies, Beggers, Thieves, Cheats, etc.* London: Printed for W. Hawes, P. Gilbourne, and W. Davis, 1699.

Edward, Terry. *The Merchants and Mariners Preservation and Thanksgiving.* London: Thomas Harper, 1649.

———. *A Voyage to East-India.* London: Printed by T.W. for J. Martin and J. Allestrye, 1655.

Eliot, John. *A Further Account of the Progress of the Gospel Amongst the Indians in New England.* London: John Macock, 1660.

Entremés de la negra lectora. In *Arcadia de entremeses escritos por los ingenios más clásicos de España*, 164–75. Madrid: Ángel Pasqual Rubio, 1723.

Entremés septimo: Los negros de Santo Tomé. In *Collección de entremeses, loas, bailes, jácaras y mojigangas, desde fines del siglo XVI á mediados del XVIII*, vol. 1, edited by Emilio Cotarelo y Mori, 136–38. Madrid: Casa Editorial Bailly Bailliére, 1911.

Esquivel Navarro, Juan de, *Discursos sobre el arte del danzado y sus excelencias y primer origen, reprobando las acciones deshonestas.* Seville: por Juan Gomez de Blas, 1642.

Extraordinaire du Mercure Galant: Quartier d'avril 1680, Tome X. Paris: G. de Luyne, 1680.

Famosa xacara nueva en que se da quenta y declara el mas fiero delito que se ha visto en nuestros tiempos . . . este año de 1687. BNE, signatura VE/114/20.

Famous Historye of the Life and Death of Captaine Thomas Stukeley. London: Printed by William Jaggard for Thomas Pauyer, 1605.

Fane, Francis. *Love in the Dark, or The Man of Bus'ness, a Comedy.* London: Printed by T.N. for Henry Herringman, 1675.

Farsa del triunfo del sacramento. In *Códice de autos viejos.* Biblioteca Nacional de España. Ms. 14.711. ca. 1550–75.

Fletcher, John. *Monsieur Thomas, a Comedy: Acted at the Private House in Blacke Fryers.* London: Printed by Thomas Harper for John Waterson, 1639.

Freydal: Des Kaisers Maximilian I. Turniere und Mummereien. Circa 1515. http://idb.ub.uni -tuebingen.de/opendigi/Da204_fol_Text

Furetière, Antoine. *Dictionnaire universel, contenant généralement tous les mots françois tant vieux que modernes, et les termes de toutes les sciences et des arts. Tome Second.* Den Haag and Rotterdam: Arnoud et Reinier Leers, 1690.

Génetay, Octave-César. *L'Ethiopique: Tragicomédie des chastes amours de Théagène et Chariclée.* Rouen: Théodore Reinsart, 1609.

Góngora, Luis de. "En la fiesta del Santísimo Sacramento" (1609). In *El tema del negro en cantos, bailes y villancicos de los siglos XVI y XVII*, edited by Horacio Jorge Becco, 35–37. Buenos Aires: Ollantay, 1951.

———. "En la fiesta de la adoración de los reyes" (1615). In *El tema del negro en cantos, bailes y villancicos de los siglos XVI y XVII*, edited by Horacio Jorge Becco, 37–40. Buenos Aires: Ollantay, 1951.

———. "Al nacimiento de Cristo nuestro señor" (1615). In *El tema del negro en cantos, bailes y villancicos de los siglos XVI y XVII*, edited by Horacio Jorge Becco, 40–41. Buenos Aires: Ollantay, 1951.

Gouges, Olympe de. *L'esclavage des Noirs, ou l'heureux naufrage.* Paris: Veuve Duchesne, Veuve Bailly, chez les Marchands de Nouveauté, 1792.

Grand bal des effets de la nature. In *Ballets et mascarades de cour de Henri III à Louis XIV (1581–1652), Tome quatrième*, edited by Paul Lacroix, 191–206. Geneva: Slatkine Reprints, 1968.

Hardy, Alexandre. *Les chastes et loyales amours de Théagène et Cariclée, réduites du grec de l'histoire d'Héliodore en huict poëmes dramatiques ou théâtres consécutifs.* Paris: Jacques Quesnel, 1623.

Haughton, William. *Englishmen for My Money, or a Pleasant Comedy called A Woman Will Have Her Will*. London: By W. White, 1616.

Hemings, William. *The Fatal Contract, a French Tragedy*. Printed at London for J. M., 1653.

Henslowe's Diary. Edited by Walter W. Greg. London: A. H. Bullen, 1904.

Herbert, Thomas. *A Relation of Some Yeares Travaile Begunne Anno 1626*. London: William Stansby and Iacob Bloome, 1634.

Heywood, Thomas. *An Apology for Actors*. London: Printed by Nicholas Okes, 1612.

———. *The Fair Maid of the West, or A Girle Worth Gold: The Second Part*. In *The First and Second Parts of The Fair Maid of the West, or A Girl Worth Gold, Two Comedies by Thomas Heywood*, edited by J. Payne Collier, 83–182. London: Printed for the Shakespeare Society, 1850.

———. *The Foure Prentises of London, with the Conquest of Ierusalem*. London: By Nicholas Okes for I. Wright, 1615.

Hilliard, Nicholas. *Nicholas Hilliard's Art of Limning*. Transcribed by Arthur F. Kinney. Edited by Linda Bradley Salamon. Prefaced by Sir John Pope-Hennessy. Boston: Northeastern University Press, 1983.

Howard, Edward. *The Six Days Adventure, or The New Utopia, a Comedy*. London: Printed for Thomas Dring, 1671.

———. *The Womens Conquest, a Tragicomedy: As It Was Acted by His Highness the Duke of York's Servants*. London: Printed by J.M. for H. Herringman, 1671.

Huete, Jaime de. *Tesorina, Vidriana*, edited by Ángeles Errazu, 1–107. Zaragoza: Prensas universitarias de Zaragoza, Larumbe, Clásicos Aragoneses, 2002.

Jacobs-Jenkins, Branden. *An Octoroon*. New York: Dramatists Service, 2015.

James I. *Daemonologie, in the Forme of a Dialogue, Divided into Three Books*. Edinburgh: Robert Walde-grave Printer to the Kings Majestie, 1597. Project Gutenberg Ebook.

Jiménez de Enciso, Diego. *Comedia famosa de Juan Latino*. Madrid: en la Imprenta Real, a costa de Antonio Ribero, 1652.

Jonson, Benjamin. *The Alchemist*. London: Printed by Thomas Snodham for Walter Burre, 1612.

———. *The Irish Masque at Court*. Edited by Kristen McDermott. In *Masques of Difference: Four Court Masques*, 133–40. Manchester: Manchester University Press, 2007.

———. *Masque of Blackness*. In *The Routledge Anthology of Renaissance Drama*, edited by Simon Barker and Hilary Hinds, 222–30. London: Routledge, 2003.

Joust of the Wild Knight and the Black Lady. Scottish Court, 1507. (Lost play.)

Killigrew, William. *The Imperial Tragedy Taken Out of a Latin Play, and Very Much Altered*. London: Printed for Will. Wells and Rob. Scott, 1669.

King James Bible. London: Robert Barker, 1611.

Kramer, Heinrich, and James Sprenger. *Malleus maleficarum*. Edited and translated by Montague Summers. Reprint of the 1928 edition. New York: Dover, 1971.

Labat, Jean-Baptiste. *Nouveau voyage aux isles de l'Amérique, Tome Second*. La Haye: P. Husson et al., 1724.

Labyrinthe royal de l'Hercule gaulois triumphant. Avignon: Jacques Bramereau, 1600.

Lamentable Ballad of the Tragical End of a Gallant Lord and a Vertuous Lady: With the Untimely End of Their Two Children, Wickedly Performed by a Heathenish Black-a-Moor Their Servant: The Like Never Heard of Before. London: Printed for W. Thackeray and T. Passinger, 1686–88.

Lanini, Francisco. *Los gorrones*. In *Migaxas del ingenio y apacible entretenimiento, en varios entremeses, bayles, y loas, escogidos de los mejores ingenios de España*, 10v–14v. Zaragoza: Diego Dormer . . . a costa de Iuan Martínez de Ribera Martel, ca. 1670.

Larivallière. *Les Africains, ou le triomphe de l'humanité, comédie.* Paris: Meurant, 1794.

Lasso, Orlando di. *Libro de villanelle, moresche, et altre canzoni.* Anversa: Pierre Phalèse et Jean Bellère, 1582.

Lauze, François de. *Apologie de la danse, et la parfaite méthode de l'enseigner tant aux cavaliers qu'aux dames,* 1623.

Lavater, Ludwig. *Of Ghostes and Spirites Walking by Nyght and of Strange Noyses, Crackes, and Sundry Forewarnynges, Whiche Commonly Happen Before the Death of Menne, Great Slaughters, [and] Alterations of Kyngdomes: One Booke, Written by Lewes Lauaterus of Tigurine and Translated into Englyshe by R.H.* London: Henry Benneyman for Richard VVatkyns, 1572.

La Vega, Garcilaso de. *Primera parte de los comentarios reales.* Lisbon: Pedro Crasbeeck, 1609.

Lesage, Alain-René, and Jacques-Philippe d'Orneval. *La Sauvagesse, pièce d'un acte representée à la Foire St. Laurent, 1732.* In *Le théâtre de la foire, ou l'opéra comique. Tome IX,* 221–74. Paris: Pierre Gandouin, 1737.

L'Estoille, Claude de. *Ballet du naufrage heureux.* 1626.

Ligon, Richard. *A True and Exact History of the Island of Barbados.* London: Humphrey Moseley, 1657.

L'Incarnation, Marie de. *Lettres.* Paris: Louis Billaine, 1681.

López de Yanguas, Hernán. *La farsa dicha Turquesana contra el Turco muy galana.* 1529. Edited by Julio F. Hernando and Javier Espejo. Textos Lemir, 2002. https://parnaseo.uv.es/Lemir /textos/FarsaTurquesana/Index.htm Accessed November 20, 2021.

Loysel, Antoine. *Institutes coustumieres: Ou manuel de plusieurs et diuerses reigles, sentences, et prouerbes tant anciens que modernes du droict coustumier et plus ordinaire de la France.* Paris: chez Abel L'Angelier, 1607.

Macready, William. *The Irishman in London, or The Happy African, A Farce.* Dublin: Printed by G. Perrin, for the Company of Booksellers, 1793.

Maistre Pierre Pathelin, de nouveau revu et mis en son naturel. Paris: Pour Estienne Groulleau, 1564.

Mal Lara, Juan de. *La filosofía vulgar de Juan de Mal Lara, vezino de Sevilla.* In *Refranes o proverbios en romance . . . y la filosofía vulgar de Juan de Mal Lara.* Madrid: por Juan de la Cuesta, 1619.

Marees, Pieter de. *Description et récit historial du riche royaume d'or de Gunea.* Amsterdam: chez Cornille Claesson, 1605.

Marguerite de Navarre. *Comédie de l'adoration des trois roys à Iesus Christ.* In *Marguerites de la Marguerite des princesses, la très illustre royne de Navarre,* 206–70. Lyon: par Jean de Tournes, 1547.

Marlowe, Christopher. *The Famous Tragedy of the Rich Jew of Malta.* London: Printed by John Beale for Nicholas Vavasour, 1633.

———. *Lusts Dominion, or The Lascivious Queen, a Tragedie.* London: Printed for Francis Kirkman, 1657.

———. *Tamburlaine the Great.* London: Printed by Richard Ihones, 1590.

———. *The Tragicall History of D. Faustus.* London: Printed by V. Simmes for Thomas Bushell, 1604.

Marmol Carvajal, Luis de. *Rebellión y castigo de los Moriscos del Reino de Granada* (1600). In *Biblioteca de autores españoles desde la formación del lenguaje hasta nuestros dias, historiadores de sucesos particulares, Tomo primero,* edited by Don Cayetano Rosell, 123–356. Madrid: Imprenta y esterotipía de M. de Ribadenevra, 1852.

Marriage Record for Hernando Rivera. Bodas: 1601–1609. AGAS Fundo paroquial del Salvador, I, 2, I, Libro 06. Biblioteca Colombina, Seville.

Marston, John. *The Wonder of Women, or The Tragedie of Sophonisba as It Hath Beene Sundry Times Acted at the Blacke Friers.* London: Printed by John Windet, 1606.

Mary, Nicolas, Sieur Desfontaines. *Orphise, ou la beauté persécutée: Tragi-comédie.* Paris: chez Antoine de Sommaville, 1638.

Mason, John. *The Turke, a Worthie Tragedie.* London: Printed by Edward Allde for John Busbie, 1610.

Masque of Egyptian Women. English Court, 1545. (Lost play.)

Massinger, Philip. *Believe as You List* (1631). In *The Plays of Philip Massinger, from the Text of William Gifford,* edited Francis Cunningham, 595–625. London: Alfred Thomas Crocker, 1868.

———. *The Bondman* (1623). In *The Plays of Philip Massinger, from the Text of William Gifford,* edited by Francis Cunningham, 99–132. London: Alfred Thomas Crocker, 1868.

———. *The City-Madam, a Comedy.* London: Printed for Andrew Pennycuicke, 1659.

———. *The Parliament of Love.* In *The Plays of Philip Massinger, from the Text of William Gifford,* edited by Francis Cunningham, 166–93. London: Alfred Thomas Crocker, 1868.

———. *The Renegado, a Tragaecomedie.* London: Printed by Augustine Mathewes for Iohn Waterson, 1630.

———. *A Very Woman, or The Prince of Tarent, a Tragi-comedy.* In *Three New Plays, viz The Bashful Lover, The Guardian, The Very Woman,* 1–103. London: Printed for Humphrey Moseley, 1655.

Massinger, Philip, and John Fletcher. *The Prophetess.* In *Comedies and Tragedies Written by Francis Beaumont and John Fletcher Never Printed Before,* 25–46. London: Printed for Humphrey Robinson . . . and for Humphrey Moseley, 1647.

Mather, Increase. *Relation of the Troubles Which Have Hapned in New-England.* Boston, Mass.: Printed and sold by John Foster, 1677.

Matos Fragoso, Juan de. *El yerro del entendido: Comedia famosa.* Valencia: en la Imprenta de Joseph y Thomas de Orga, 1772.

Ménestrier, Claude-François. *Des ballets anciens et modernes selon les règles du théâtre.* Paris: chez René Guignard, 1682.

Mersenne, Marin. *Harmonie universelle, contenant la théorie et la pratique de la musique.* Paris: Sébastien Cramoisy, 1636.

Middleton, Thomas. *No Wit [NO] Help Like a Womans: A Comedy.* London: Printed for Humphrey Moseley, 1657.

Minsheu, John. *A Dictionarie in Spanish and English, First Published into the English Tongue by Ric. Percivale Gentleman. Now Enlarged.* London: Edm. Bollifant, 1599.

Miracles de Nostre Dame par personnages. Ms. 819–20. Bibliothèque Nationale de France. 14th century.

Molière. *Le bourgeois gentilhomme: Comédie-ballet.* Paris: n.p., 1688.

———. *Le malade imaginaire: Comédie en trois actes. Mélez de Danses et de Musique.* Amsterdam: Daniel Elzevir, 1674.

———. *L'étourdi ou les contre-temps.* Paris: Gabriel Quinet, 1663. Publié par Paul Fièvre, Théâtre classique. http://theatre-classique.fr/pages/programmes/edition.php?t=../documents/MOLIERE_ETOURDI.xml#haut. Accessed November 13, 2021.

———. *Monsieur de Pourceaugnac.* In *Les oeuvres de Monsieur de Molière, Tome VI,* 1–90. Paris: chez Claude Barbin, 1673.

Molina, Tirso de. *El negro, entremés famoso*. In *Segunda parte de las comedias del maestro Tirso de Molina*, 284r–285v. Madrid: en la Imprenta del Reino, 1635.

———. *Escarmientos para el cuerdo*. In *Quinta parte de comedias del maestro Tirso de Molina*, 49v–72r. Madrid: en la Imprenta Real, a costa de Gabriel de Leon, 1636.

Monet, Philibert. *Invantaire des deus langues françoise et latine, assorti des plus utiles curiositez de l'un et de l'autre idiome*. Lyon: chez Claude Obert, 1636.

Montagu, Walter. *The Shepheards Paradise, A Comedy*. London: Printed for Thomas Dring, 1629.

Montaigne, Michel de. "Of Cannibals." In *The Complete Essays of Montaigne*, translated by Donald M. Frame, 150–59. Stanford, Calif.: Stanford University Press, 1958.

Montfleury, Antoine de. *L'école des jaloux, ou le cocu volontaire, comédie*. Paris: La Compagnie des Libraires, 1761.

Moreto y Cavana, Agustín. *No puede ser el guardar una mujer*. In *Parte quaranta y una de famosas comedias de diferentes autores*, 179–224. Pamplona: por Ioseph del Espiritu Santo, [1675?].

Morton, Nathaniel. *New-Englands Memoriall*. Cambridge, Mass.: Printed by Samuel Green and Marmaduke Johnson for John Usher of Boston, 1669.

Motteux, Pierre. *The Island Princess, or the Generous Portuguese made into an opera*. London: Printed for Richard Wellington, 1699.

M.W., M.A. *A Comedy Called The Marriage Broaker, or The Pander, Written by M.W., M.A.* London: n.p., 1662.

Mystère du jour du jugement. Bibliothèque municipale de Besançon BM MS.579. 1326–50.

Navarre, Marguerite de. *Comédie de l'adoration des trois rois à Jésus-Christ: Marguerites de la Marguerite des princesses, très illustre Royne de Navarre*. Lyon: Jean de Tournes, 1647.

Nebrija, Elio Antonio de. *Vocabulario español-latino*. Salamanca, ca. 1495.

Nichols, Philip. *Sir Francis Drake Reviv'd*. London: Printed for Nicholas Bourne, 1628. In *Documents Concerning English Voyages to the Spanish Main, 1569–1680*, 2nd ser., no. 71, edited by Irene A. Wright, 247–326. London: Hakluyt Society, 1932.

Nicot, Jean. *Thrésor de la langue francoyse, tant ancienne que moderne*. Paris: chez David Douceur, 1606.

Nueva relación y curioso romance en que se refiere la celebridad, galanteo y acaso de una Boda de Negros, que se executó en la Ciudad del Puerto de Santa María, sucedió el año pasado. Seville: Por Joseph Padrino, 18??. Fundación Joaquín Díaz, signatura: PL 689.

Orrery, Roger Boyle, Earl of. *Guzman, a Comedy*. London: Printed for Francis Saunders, 1693.

Ortiz de Zúñiga, Diego. *Anales eclesiásticos y seculares de la muy noble y muy leal ciudad de Sevilla*. Madrid: Imprenta real, 1677.

Otway, Thomas. *The Atheist, or The Second Part of The Souldiers Fortune Acted at the Duke's Theatre*. London: Printed for R. Bentley, and J. Tonson, 1684.

Oudin, César. *Tesoro de las dos lenguas francesa y española*. Paris: La Veuve Marc Orry, 1616.

Pastor, Juan. *Farsa de Lucrecia: Tragedia de la castidad de Juan Pastor, mitad del siglo XVI*, edited by Amy Sevcik. *Revista Lemir*, no. 3 (1999). https://parnaseo.uv.es/lemir/Textos/Lucrecia /Lucrecia.html Accessed November 20, 2021.

Peacham, Henry. *The Gentleman's Exercise, or An Exquisite Practise, as Well for Drawing All Manner of Beasts in Their True Portraitures*. London: Printed for Iohn Browne, 1612.

Peele, George. *The Battell of Alcazar Fought in Barbarie, Betweene Sebastian King of Portugall, and Abdelmelec King of Marocc., With the Death of Captaine Stukeley*. London: By Edward Allde for Richard Bankworth, 1594.

Pepys, Samuel. *Diary of Samuel Pepys*. Edited by G. Gregory Smith. London: Macmillan, 1920.

Perche du, Nicolas. *L'ambassadeur d'Affrique, comédie*. Moulins: chez la veuve Pierre Vernoy et Claude Vernoy son fils, Imprimeur du Roy, 1666.

Petition Addressed to the Archbishop of Seville by the Nuestra señora de la antigua siete Dolores Brotherhood Against the Black Brotherhood of Nuestra señora de los Angeles. Manuscript. Seville. Biblioteca Colombina, ACS, Caja 9885, Expediente 1. 1604.

Philips, Edward. *The New World of English Words, or A General Dictionary Containing the Interpretations of Such Hard Words as Are Derived from Other Languages*. London: Printed by E. Tyler for Nathaniel Brooke, 1658.

Poisson, Raymond. *Les faux Moscovites, comédie*. In *Les oeuvres de Monsieur Poisson*, 165–91. Paris: Jean Ribou, 1679.

Pontano, Giovanni. *De obediencia*. Naples, 1480–94. Universitat de València, Biblioteca Històrica BH Ms. 52. Valencia, Spain.

Pour des masques assez hideux et sauvages. In *Ballets et mascarades de cour de Henri III à Louis XIV (1581–1652), Tome premier*, edited by Paul Lacroix, 155–56. Geneva: Slatkine Reprints, 1968.

Pure, Michel de. *Idée des spectacles anciens et nouveaux*. Paris: chez Michel Brunet, 1668.

Puttenham, George. *The Art of English Poesy*. Edited by Frank Whigham and Wayne A. Rebhorn. Ithaca, N.Y.: Cornell University Press, 2007.

Quatriesme centurie des questions traitées aux conférences du bureau d'adresse, depuis le 24 janvier 1639 jusqu'au 10 juin 1641. Paris: Au bureau d'adresse, ruë de la Calandre, 1641.

The Queen of Ethiopia. Howard's at Bristol, 1578. (Lost play.)

Quevedo, Francisco de. "Boda de negros" (1626). In *El tema del negro en cantos, bailes y villancicos de los siglos XVI y XVII*, edited by Horacio Jorge Becco, 43–46. Buenos Aires: Ollantay, 1951.

———. *Premática del tiempo*. In *Obras de Francisco de Quevedo Villegas, Tomo primero*, 530–37. Amberes: por Henrico y Cornelio Verdussen, 1699.

Quinault, Philippe. *Cadmus et Hermione: Tragédie représentée par l'Académie royale de musique*. Paris: René Baudry, 1674.

———. *Persée: Tragédie représentée par l'Académie royale de musique*. Paris: Christophe Ballard, 1682.

Quiñones de Benavente, Luis. *Entremés cantado de las dueñas*, in *Ioco seria. Burlas veras, o reprehension moral, y festiua de los desordenes públicos*, 168v–172v. Madrid: Por Francisco Garcia, a costa de Manuel Lopez, 1645.

———. *El negrito hablador y sin color anda la niña*. In *Navidad y Corpus Christi, festejados por los mejores ingenios de España, en diez y seis autos a lo divino, diez y seis loas, y diez y seis entremeses. Representados en esta corte y nunca hasta aora impressos. Recogidos por Isidro de Robles, natural de Madrid*, 128–32. Madrid: por Joseph Fernández de Buendía, a costa de Isidro de Robles, 1664.

Rabelais, Francois. *Le quart livre des faicts et dicts héroïques du bon Pantagruel*. Paris: Michel Fezeandar, 1552.

Radet, Jean-Baptiste. *Honorine, ou la femme difficile à vivre, comédie*. Paris: n.p., 1797.

Ravenscroft, Edward. *The Citizen Turn'd Gentleman, a Comedy Acted at the Duke's Theatre*. London: Printed for Thomas Dring, 1672.

Ray, John. *A Collection of English Proverbs Digested into a Convenient Method for the Speedy Finding any one upon Occasion*. Cambridge: Printed by John Hayes, for W. Morden, 1678.

Real cédula. Cofradías de negros en la iglesia de Santo Domingo. Archivo General de Indias, Seville. Signature: Santo_Domingo, 869, L.6, F.154V.

Real cédula. Corpus Christi Celebrations in Santo Domingo. Signatura: Santo_Domingo, 868, L.2, F.322V Archivo General de Indias, Seville.

Reynosa, Rodrigo de. *Comienzan unas coplas a los negros y negras y de como se motejavan en Sevilla un negro de gelofe mandinga contra una negra de guinea*. Burgos, Juan de Junta, ca. 1535.

Rochefort, Jean. *Histoire morale des îles Antilles de l'Amérique, Tome Second*. Lyon: Christofle Fourmy, 1667.

———. *Histoire naturelle et morale des îles Antilles de l'Amérique*. Rotterdam: chez Arnout Leers, 1658.

Romagnesi, Jean-Antoine. *Les Sauvages, parodie de la tragédie d'Alzire. De Messieurs Romagnesi et Riccoboni*. Amsterdam: chez J. Ryckhof Fils, 1736.

Rotrou, Jean. *La soeur, comédie*. Paris: Augustin Courbe, 1647.

Rowley, William. *A Tragedy Called All's Lost by Lust*. London: Thomas Harper, 1633.

Rueda, Lope de. *Comedia llamada Eufemia*. In *Las quatro comedias y dos coloquios pastoriles del excellente poeta, y gracioso representante Lope de Rueda*. Dirigidas por Ioan Timoneda..., 3r–33v. Valencia: en casa de Ioan Mey, vendense en casa de Ioan Timoneda, 1567.

———. *Comedia llamada de los engañados*. In *Las quatro comedias y dos coloquios pastoriles del excellente poeta, y gracioso representante Lope de Rueda*. Dirigidas por Ioan Timoneda..., 3r–33r. Valencia: en casa de Ioan Mey, vendense en casa de Ioan Timoneda, 1567.

———. *Colloquio de Tymbria*. In *Las quatro comedias y dos coloquios pastoriles del excellente poeta, y gracioso representante Lope de Rueda*. Dirigidas por Ioan Timoneda..., , 30r–54r. Valencia: en casa de Ioan Mey, vendense en casa de Ioan Timoneda, 1567.

Ruggle, George. *Ignoramus a Comedy as It Was Several Times Acted with Extraordinary Applause Before the Majesty of King James ... Written in Latine by R. Ruggles ... ; And Translated into English by R.C.* London: Printed for W. Gilbertson, 1662.

The Sailor's Opera, or A Trip to Jamaica. London: Printed for the author, 1745.

Sánchez de Badajoz, Diego. *Farsa de la fortuna ó hado*. In *Recopilación en metro del bachiller Diego Sánchez de Badajoz, reimpresa del ejemplar único por el excmo señor D. V. Barrantes, Tomo II*, 77–87. Madrid: Biblioteca de los bibliófilos—Fernando Fé, 1886.

———. *Farsa de la ventera*. In *Recopilación en metro del bachiller Diego Sánchez de Badajoz, reimpresa del ejemplar único por el excmo señor D. V. Barrantes, Tomo II*, 239–51. Madrid: Biblioteca de los bibliófilos—Fernando Fé, 1886.

———. *Farsa del moysen*. *Recopilación en metro del bachiller Diego Sánchez de Badajoz, reimpresa del ejemplar único por el excmo señor D. V. Barrantes, Tomo II*, 117–28. Madrid: Biblioteca de los bibliófilos—Fernando Fé, 1886.

———. *Farsa teologal*. In *Recopilación en metro del bachiller Diego Sánchez de Badajoz, reimpresa del ejemplar único por el excmo señor D. V. Barrantes, Tomo I*, 85–136. Madrid: Biblioteca de los bibliófilos—Fernando Fé, 1882.

Sandoval, Alonso de. *De instauranda aethiopum salute*. Madrid: por Alonso de Paredes, 1647.

———. *Naturaleza, policia sagrada i profana, costumbres i ritos, disciplina i catechismo evangelico de todos Etiopes*. Seville: por Francisco de Lira, 1627.

Santander, Martín de. *Comedia Rosabella de Martín de Santander*. Edited by José Luis Canet. *Revista Lemir*, no. 1 (1996–97). http://parnaseo.uv.es/lemir/textos/M_Santander.html Accessed November 20, 2021.

Scarron, Paul. *Les oeuvres de monsieur Scarron. Reveuës, corrigées et augmentées de nouveau, Tome Premier*. Rouen: Guillaume de Luyne, 1663.

Scot, Reginald. *The Discoverie of Witchcraft*. London: Printed by Henry Denham for William Brome, 1584.

Settle, Elkanah. *The Empress of Morocco, a Tragedy, with Sculptures*. London: Printed for William Cademan, 1673.

Shakespeare, William. *Antony and Cleopatra*. In *The Norton Shakespeare, Tragedies*, Third Edition, edited by Stephen Greenblatt (general editor), Walter Cohen, Suzanne Gossett, Jean E. Howard, Katharine Eisaman Maus, and Gordon McMullan, 971–1060. New York: W. W. Norton, 2016.

——. *Henry the Fifth*. In *The Norton Shakespeare, Histories*, Third Edition, edited by Stephen Greenblatt (general editor), Walter Cohen, Suzanne Gossett, Jean E. Howard, Katharine Eisaman Maus, and Gordon McMullan, 779–858. New York: W. W. Norton, 2016.

——. *King Lear*. In *The Norton Shakespeare, Tragedies*, Third Edition, edited by Stephen Greenblatt (general editor), Walter Cohen, Suzanne Gossett, Jean E. Howard, Katharine Eisaman Maus, and Gordon McMullan, 587–840. New York: W. W. Norton, 2016.

——. *Love's Labor's Lost*. In *The Norton Shakespeare, Comedies*, Third Edition, edited by Stephen Greenblatt (general editor), Walter Cohen, Suzanne Gossett, Jean E. Howard, Katharine Eisaman Maus, and Gordon McMullan, 323–94. New York: W. W. Norton, 2016.

——. *The Merchant of Venice*. In *The Norton Shakespeare, Comedies*, Third Edition, edited by Stephen Greenblatt (general editor), Walter Cohen, Suzanne Gossett, Jean E. Howard, Katharine Eisaman Maus, and Gordon McMullan, 455–521. New York: W. W. Norton, 2016.

——. *The Most Lamentable Tragedy of Titus Andronicus*. In *The Norton Shakespeare, Tragedies*, Third Edition, edited by Stephen Greenblatt (general editor), Walter Cohen, Suzanne Gossett, Jean E. Howard, Katharine Eisaman Maus, and Gordon McMullan, 135–98. New York: W. W. Norton, 2016.

——. *The Taming of the Shrew*. In *The Norton Shakespeare, Comedies*, Third Edition, edited by Stephen Greenblatt (general editor), Walter Cohen, Suzanne Gossett, Jean E. Howard, Katharine Eisaman Maus, and Gordon McMullan, 197–268. New York: W. W. Norton, 2016.

——. *The Tempest*. In *The Norton Shakespeare*. In *The Norton Shakespeare, Romances and Poems*, Third Edition, edited by Stephen Greenblatt (general editor), Walter Cohen, Suzanne Gossett, Jean E. Howard, Katharine Eisaman Maus, and Gordon McMullan, 387–448. New York: W. W. Norton, 2016.

——. *The Tragedy of Othello, the Moor of Venice*. In *The Norton Shakespeare, Tragedies*, Third Edition, edited by Stephen Greenblatt (general editor), Walter Cohen, Suzanne Gossett, Jean E. Howard, Katharine Eisaman Maus, and Gordon McMullan, 501–86. New York: W. W. Norton, 2016.

Shirley, Henry. *The Martyr'd Souldier*. London: Printed by I. Okes, 1638.

Shirley, James. *The Triumph of Peace, a Masque*. London: Printed by John Norton for William Cooke, 1633.

Silva, Feliciano de. *Segunda comedia de Celestina*. In *Collección de libros españoles raros o curiosos, tomo noveno*. Madrid: Imprenta de Miguel Ginesta, 1874.

Southerne, Thomas. *Oroonoko, a Tragedy*. London: Printed for H. Playford, B. Tooke, and S. Buckley, 1696.

Spenser, Edmund. *A View of the Present State of Ireland* (1596). Edited by Risa S. Bear. University of Oregon, Renascence Edition, 1997. http://www.luminarium.org/renascence-editions /veue1.html.

St. Serfe, Thomas. *Tarugo's Wiles, or The Coffee House, A Comedy*. London: Printed for Henry Herringman, 1668.

Suárez de Deza y Ávila, Vicente. *Bayle entremesado del galeote mulato*. In *Parte primera de los donayres de Tersícore*, 146r–148v. Madrid: por Melchor Sánchez, a costa de Mateo de la Bastida, 1663.

Taylor, John. *All the Workes of John Taylor the Water-Poet*. London: Printed by Iohn Beale, Elizabeth Allde, Bernard Alsop, and Thomas Fawcet for Iames Boler, 1630.

Ténèbres de Mariage. Rouen: Abraham Cousturier, date unknown.

Terry, Edward. *The Merchants and Mariners Preservation and Thanksgiving*. London: Thomas Harper, 1649.

———. *A Voyage to East-India*. London: Printed by T.W. for J. Martin and J. Allestrye, 1655.

Tertre, Jean-Baptiste du. *Histoire générale des Antilles habitées par les François, Tome 2*. Paris: Thomas Iolly, 1667.

———. *Histoire générale des isles de S. Christophe, de la Guadeloupe, de la Martinique et autres dans l'Amérique*. Paris: Jacques Langlois, 1654.

Theagenes and Chariclea. English Court, 1572. (Lost play.)

Thevet, André. *Cosmographie universelle d'André Thevet, cosmographe du roy. Tome premier*. Paris: Guillaume Chaudière, 1575.

Thiboust, Jacques. *L'ordre de la triomphante et magnifique monstre du mystère des saints actes des Apostres faite à Bourges le dimanche dernier jour d'avril 1536*. In *Relation de la monstre du mystère des saints actes des Apostres et faits divers*, edited by M. Labouvrie, 17–74. Bourges: Imprimerie en caractères et lithographie de Manceron, 1836.

Tito Andronico. (German *Tragedy of Titus Andronicus*.) In *Shakespeare in Germany in the Sixteenth and Seventeenth Centuries: An Account of English Actors in Germany and the Netherlands and of the Plays Performed by Them During the Same Period*, edited by Albert Cohen, 162–236. London: Asher, 1865.

Torquemada, Antonio de. *The Spanish Mandeuile of Miracles*. London: Printed by James Roberts for Edmund Matts, 1600.

Tragédie françoize d'un More cruel envers son seigneur nommé Riviery, gentil homme espagnol, sa damoiselle et ses enfans. Rouen: Abraham Cousturier, 1613.

Tragédie mahommetiste ou l'on peut voir et remarquer l'infidélité commise par Mahumet, fils ayné du roy des Othomans nommé Amurat, à l'endroit d'un sien amy et son fidelle serviteur. Rouen: Abraham Cousturier, 1612.

Troys galans et un badin: Farce. 1572. Manuscrit La Vallière (BnF, ms. fr. 24341). Facsimile: Slatkine Reprints, 1972. https://sottiesetfarces.wordpress.com/2018/10/06/troys-galans-et-un -badin/.

Tristan L'Hermite, François. *Le parasite, comédie*. Paris: Augustin Courbe, 1654.

Tryon, Thomas. *Friendly Advice to the Gentlemen-Planters of the East and West Indies*. London: Andrew Sowle, 1684.

Tuccaro, Arcangelo. *Trois dialogues*. Tours: chez Georges Griveau, 1616.

Vallée, Jacques. *Le fidelle esclave: Comédie*. Paris: chez Jean Cochart, 1662.

Vega Carpio, Lope Félix de. *Amar, servir, y esperar*. Madrid: por la viuda de Iuan Gonçalez, a costa de Domingo de Palacio y Villegas y Pedro Verges, 1635.

———. *Arte nuevo de hacer comedias en este tiempo: Rimas de Lope de Vega Carpio; Aora de nuevo imprimidas con el nuevo arte de hazer comedias deste tiempo*. Milan: por Ieronimo Bordon librero, 1611.

———. *El negro del mejor amo*. Edited by José Fredejas Lebrero. Madrid: U.N.E.D., 1984.

———. *El premio de bien hablar y volver por las mujeres*. Seville: Francisco de Leefdael, n.d.

———. *El prodigio de Etiopia*. N.p.: n.p., 16??.

———. *El sancto negro Rosambuco de la ciudad de Palermo*. Barcelona: en casa de Sebastian de Cormellas . . . Vendese en Zaragoza: en casa de Iayme Gotar, 1612.

———. *La dama boba*. [1st ed.], edited by Isidoro Montiel. Madrid: Ediciones Castilla, 1948.

———. *La limpieza no manchada*. In *Parte diecinueve y la mejor parte de las comedias de Lope de Vega Carpio*. Madrid: por Juan González, a costa de Alonso Pérez, 1624.

———. *La otava maravilla*. Madrid: por la viuda de Alonso Martín de Balboa, a costa de Miguel de Siles . . . , 1618.

———. *La vitoria de la honra*. Madrid, por la viuda de Alonso Martín, a costa de Diego Logroño, 1635.

———. *Los comendadores de Córdoba*. Barcelona: en casa de Sebastian de Cormellas al Call, vendese en la mesma emprenta, 1611.

———. *Los peligros de la ausencia*. Zaragoza: por Pedro Verges, 1641.

———. *Servir a señor discreto*. Edited by Frida Weber de Kurlat. Madrid: Editorial Castalia, 1975.

Vélez de Guevara, Luis. *El diablo cojuelo*. Madrid: Imprenta Real, a costa de Alonso Pérez, 1641.

———. *El negro del serafín*. Edited by C. George Peale and Javier J. González Martínez. Newark, Del.: Juan de la Cuesta, 2012.

———. *Virtudes vencen señales*. Edited by William R. Manson and C. George Peale. Newark, Del.: Juan de la Cuesta, 2010.

Veronneau. *L'impuissance: Tragicomédie pastorale*. Paris: Toussaint Quinet, 1634.

Vicente, Gil, *Fragoa d'amor*. In *Obras de Gil Vicente, Tomo II*, edited by J. da S. Mendes Leal Junior and F. J. Pinheiro, 321–46. Lisbon: Escriptorio da Bibliotheca Portugueza, 1852.

Villanzicos y chanzonetas que se cantaron en el coro de la santa Iglesia mayor de Sevilla, a la venida de los santos Reyes a Belen, recien nacido Iesu Christo. Celebrada esto año de 1644. Seville: Simón Fajardo, 1644.

Villaviciosa, Sebastián de. *Entremés de los sones*. In *Tardes apacibles de gustoso entretenimiento: Repartidas en varios entremeses, y bayles entremesados, escogidos de los mejores ingenios de España*, edited by Don Lope Gaspar de Figueroa Guzman y Velasco, 134r–137v. Madrid: por Andrés García de la Iglesia, a costa de Iuan Martín Merinero, 1663.

Vos, Jan. *Aran en Titus, of Wraak en Weerwraak: Treurspel*. Amsterdam: Dominicus van der Stichel, 1641.

Webster, John. *The Devils Law-Case, or When Women Goe to Law, the Devill Is Full of Businesse, A New Tragecomoedy*. London: Printed by Augustine Mathewes for John Grismand, 1623.

———. *The White Devil*. Edited by John Russell Brown. Cambridge, Mass.: Harvard University Press, 1960.

Wecker, Johann Jacob. *Cosmeticks, or The Beautifying Part of Physick*. London: Thomas Johnson, 1660.

Weiditz, Christoph. *Trachtenbuch*. Germanisches Nationalmuseum Nürnberg, Hs. 22474. 1535.

Whitaker, William. *The Conspiracy, or The Change of Government, a Tragedy*. London: Printed for William Cademan, 1680.

Wilkins, John. *An Alphabetical Dictionary*. In *An Essay Towards a Real Character and a Philosophical Language*. London: Printed for Sa. Gellibrand, and for John Martyn, 1668.

Williams, Roger. *A Key into the Language of America*. London: Printed by Gregory Dexter, 1643.

Wycherley, William. *The Gentleman Dancing-Master, a Comedy*. London: Printed by J.M. for Henry Herringman and Thomas Dring, 1673.

Zayas y Sotomayor, María. *Novelas ejemplares y amorosas de Doña María de Zayas y Sotomayor, natural de Madrid: Primera y segunda parte*, 70–96. Paris: Baudry Librería Europea, 1847.

———. *Tarde llega el desengaño*. In *Biblioteca de autores españoles, desde la formación del lenguaje hasta nuestros días: Novelistas posteriores a Cervantes, Tomo segundo*, 574–82. Madrid: Imprenta Rivadeneyra, 1871.

SECONDARY SOURCES

Aasand, Hardin. "'To Blanch an Ethiop, and Revive a Corse:' Queen Anne and *The Masque of Blackness*." *Studies in English Literature, 1500–1900* 32, no. 2 (1992): 271–85.

Akhimie, Patricia. *Shakespeare and the Cultivation of Difference: Race and Conduct in the Early Modern World*. New York: Routledge, 2018.

Almeida Mendes, Antonio de. "The Foundations of the System: A Reassessment of the Slave Trade to the Spanish Americas in the Sixteenth and Seventeenth Centuries." In *Extending the Frontiers: Essays on the New Transatlantic Slave Trade Database*, edited by David Eltis and David Richardson, 63–94. New Haven, Conn.: Yale University Press, 2008.

Amelang, James S. "Exchanges Between Italy and Spain: Culture and Religion." In *Spain in Italy: Politics, Society, and Religion 1500–1700*, edited by Thomas James Dandelet and John A. Marino, 433–55. Leiden: Brill, 2007.

Andrea, Bernadette. "Black Skin, the Queen's Masques: Africanist Ambivalence and Feminine Author(ity) in the Masques of 'Blackness' and 'Beauty.'" *English Literary Renaissance* 29, no. 2 (1999): 246–81.

Anidjar, Gil. *Blood: A Critique of Christianity*. New York: Columbia University Press, 2014.

Appiah, Kwame Anthony. "Race, Culture, and Identity." Tanner Lectures on Human Values, delivered at University of California at San Diego, October 27 and 28, 1994.

Ares Queija, Berta. "La cuestión del bautismo de los Negros en el siglo XVII: La proyección de un debate Americano." In *Mirando las dos orillas: Intercambios mercantiles, sociales y culturales entre Andalucía y América*, edited by Enriqueta Vila Vilar and Jaime J. Lacueva Muñoz, 469–85. Seville: Fundación Buenas Letras, 2012.

Aubert, Guillaume. "The Blood of France: Race and Purity of Blood in the French Atlantic World." *William and Mary Quarterly* 61, no. 3 (2004): 439–78.

Bailey, Moya (Moyazb). "More on the Origins of Misogynoir." Tumblr, April 27, 2014. Accessed July 17, 2018. http://moyazb.tumblr.com/post/84048113369/more-on-the-origin-of-misogynoir.

Bailey, Moya, and Reina Gossett. "Analog Girls in Digital Worlds: Dismantling Binaries for Digital Humanists Who Research Social Media." In *The Routledge Companion to Media Studies and Digital Humanities*, edited by Jentery Sayers, 33–43. New York: Routledge, 2018.

Baker, David J. *Between Nations: Shakespeare, Spenser, Marvell, and the Question of Britain*. Stanford, Calif.: Stanford University Press, 1997.

———. "'Wildehirissheman': Colonialist Representation in Shakespeare's 'Henry V.'" *English Literary Renaissance* 22, no. 1 (1992): 37–61.

Bakhtin, Mikhail. *Rabelais and His World*. Translated by Helene Iswolsky. Cambridge, Mass.: MIT Press, 1968.

Balibar, Etienne, and Immanuel Maurice Wallerstein. *Race, Nation, Class: Ambiguous Identities*. London: Verso, 1991.

Bane, Theresa. *Encyclopedia of Beasts and Monsters in Myth, Legend, and Folklore*. Jefferson, N.C.: McFarland, 2016.

Baranda Leturio, Consolación. "Las hablas de negros. Orígenes de un personaje literario." *Revista de Filología Española* 69, nos. 3–4 (1989): 311–33.

Barker, Roberta. "The 'Play-Boy,' the Female Performer, and the Art of Portraying a Lady." *Shakespeare Bulletin* 33, no. 1 (2015): 83–97.

Bartels, Emily C. "Too Many Blackamoors: Deportation, Discrimination, and Elizabeth I." *Studies in English Literature, 1500–1900* 46, no. 2 (2006): 305–22.

Barthelemy, Anthony Gerard. *Black Face, Maligned Race: The Representation of Blacks in English Drama from Shakespeare to Southerne*. Baton Rouge: Louisiana State University Press, 1987.

Becco, Horacio Jorge, ed. *El tema del negro en cantos, bailes y villancicos de los siglos XVI y XVII*. Buenos Aires: Ollantay, 1951.

Bennett, Herman L. *Africans in Colonial Mexico: Absolutism, Christianity, and Afro-Creole Consciousness, 1570–1640*. Bloomington: Indiana University Press, 2003.

Bennett, Susan. *Theatre Audiences: A Theory of Production and Reception*. 2nd ed. London: Routledge, 1997.

Bergson, Henri. *Le rire, essai sur la signification du comique*. Paris: Éditions Alcan, 1924.

Bernstein, Robin. "Dances with Things: Material Culture and the Performance of Race." *Social Text* 27, no. 4 (2009): 67–94.

Best, Stephen Michael. *None Like Us: Blackness, Belonging, Aesthetic Life*. Durham, N.C.: Duke University Press, 2018.

Beusterien, John. *An Eye on Race: Perspectives from Theater in Imperial Spain*. Lewisburg: Bucknell University Press, 2006.

Bevington, David, ed. *Shakespeare The Tempest*. New York: Bantam Books, 1988.

Biet. Christian, ed. *Théâtre de la cruauté et récits sanglants en France (XVIe–XVIIe siècle)*. Paris: Editions Robert Laffont, 2006.

Biet, Christian, and Sylvie Requemora, "L'Afrique à l'envers ou à l'endroit des Cafres: Tragédie et récit de voyage au XVIIe siècle." In *L'Afrique au XVIIe siècle: Mythes et réalités, Actes du VIIe Colloque du Centre International de Rencontres sur le XVIIe siècle, Tunis, 14–16 mars 2002*, edited by Alia Baccar Bournaz, 371–403. Tübingen: Gunter Narr Verlag, 2003.

Biller, Peter. "Black Women in Medieval Medical Thought." In *Black Skin in the Middle Ages / La Peau Noire au Moyen Âge*, edited by Agostino Paravicini Bagliani, 135–50. Florence: Sismel, Edizzioni del Galluzzo, 2014.

Blackburn, Robin. *The Making of New World Slavery: From the Baroque to the Modern, 1492–1800*. London: Verso, 1997.

Blakely, Allison. *Blacks in the Dutch World: The Evolution of Racial Imagery in a Modern Society*. Bloomington: Indiana University Press, 1993.

Blank, Paula. *Broken English: Dialects and the Politics of Language in Renaissance Writings*. New York: Routledge, 1996.

Bloechl, Olivia A. *Native American Song at the Frontiers of Early Modern Music*. Cambridge: Cambridge University Press, 2008.

———. "Race, Empire, and Early Music." In *Rethinking Difference in Music Scholarship*, edited by Olivia Bloech, Melanie Lowe, and Jeffrey Kallberg, 77–107. Cambridge: Cambridge University Press, 2015.

Bloom, Gina. *Voice in Motion: Staging Gender, Shaping Sound in Early Modern England*. Philadelphia: University of Pennsylvania Press, 2007.

Blumenthal, Debra. "La Casa dels Negres: Black African Solidarity in Late Medieval Valencia." In *Black Africans in Renaissance Europe*, edited by Kate Lowe and T. F. Earle, 225–46. Cambridge: Cambridge University Press, 2005.

Blunt, Richard. "The Evolution of Blackface Cosmetics on the Early Modern Stage." In *The Materiality of Color: The Production, Circulation, and Application of Dyes and Pigments, 1400–1800*, edited by Andrea Feeser, Maureen Daly Goggin, and Beth Fowkes Tobin, 217–34. Burlington, Vt.: Ashgate, 2012.

Boose, Lynda. "The Getting of a Lawful Race: Racial Discourse in Early Modern England and the Unrepresentable Black Woman." In *Women, "Race," and Writing in the Early Modern Period*, edited by Margo Hendricks and Patricia Parker, 35–54. London: Routledge, 1994.

Bosman, Anston. "'Best Play with Mardian': Eunuch and Blackamoor as Imperial Culturegram." *Shakespeare Studies* 34 (2006): 123–57.

Boucher, Philip B. *France and the American Tropics to 1700: Tropics of Discontent?* Baltimore: Johns Hopkins University Press, 2008.

Boulle, Pierre. *Race et esclavage dans la France de l'ancien régime.* Paris: Perrin, 2007.

Branche, Jerome. *Colonialism and Race in Luso-Spanish Literature.* Columbia: University of Missouri Press, 2006.

Brewer-García, Larissa. *Beyond Babel: Translations of Blackness in Colonial Peru and New Granada.* Cambridge: Cambridge University Press, 2020.

———. "Hierarchy and Holiness in the Earliest Colonial Black Hagiographies: Alonso de Sandoval and His Sources." *William and Mary Quarterly* 76, no. 3 (2019): 477–508.

———. "Imagined Transformations: Color, Beauty, and Black Christian Conversion in Seventeenth-Century Spanish America." In *Envisioning Others: Race, Color, and the Visual in Iberia and Latin America*, edited by Pamela Anne Patton, 111–41. Leiden: Brill, 2016.

Britton, Dennis A. *Becoming Christian: Race, Reformation, and Early Modern English Romance.* New York: Fordham University Press, 2014.

———. "From the Knight's Tale to the Two Noble Kinsmen: Rethinking Race, Class and Whiteness in Romance." *Postmedieval: A Journal of Medieval Cultural Studies* 6, no. 1 (2015): 64–78.

Brooks, Lynn Matluck. *The Dances of the Processions of Seville in Spain's Golden Age.* Kassel: Reichenberger, 1988.

———. "Text and Image as Evidence for Posture and Movement Style in Seventeenth-Century Spain." *Imago Musicae* 13 (1998): 39–61.

Brown, David West. *English and Empire: Literary History, Dialect, and the Digital Archive.* Cambridge: Cambridge University Press, 2018.

Burningham, Bruce R. *Radical Theatricality: Jongleuresque Performance on the Early Spanish Stage.* West Lafayette, Ind.: Purdue University Press, 2007.

Butler, Judith. *Excitable Speech: A Politics of the Performative.* New York: Routledge, 1997.

———. *Gender Trouble: Feminism and the Subversion of Identity.* Reprint. New York: Routledge, 2007.

Callaghan, Dympna. *Shakespeare Without Women: Representing Gender and Race on the Renaissance Stage.* New York: Routledge, 2000.

Calvo Lozano, María Paz, and Ursula de Luis-André Quattelbaum. "Dinámica de la población, 1560–1804." In *Madrid, Atlas historico de la ciudad, siglos IX–XIX*, edited by Virgilio Pinto Crespo and Santos Madrazo Madrazo, 146–49. Barcelona: Fundación Caja de Madrid and Lunwerg Editores, 1995.

Cardamone, Donna G. "The Salon as Marketplace in the 1550s: Patrons and Collectors of Lasso's Secular Music." In *Orlando di Lasso Studies*, edited by Peter Bergquist, 64–90. New York: Cambridge University Press, 1999.

Chalaye, Sylvie. *Du Noir au Nègre: L'image du Noir au théâtre, de Marguerite de Navarre à Jean Genet (1550–1960)*. Paris: L'Harmattan, 1998.

———. *Race et théâtre: Un impensé politique*. Arles: Actes Sud, 2020.

Chapman, Matthieu. *Anti-Black Racism in Early Modern English Drama: The Other "Other."* New York: Routledge, 2017.

Charara, Youmna, ed. *Fictions coloniales du XVIIIe siècle*. Paris: L'Harmattan, 2005.

Chasca, Edmund de. "The Phonology of the Speech of the Negroes in Early Spanish Drama." *Hispanic Review* 14, no. 4 (1946): 322–39.

Checca, Peter Anthony. "The Role of the Devil in Golden Age Drama." Ph.D. diss., Pennsylvania State University, 1975.

Chevallier Micki, Sybile. "Tragédie et théâtre Rouennais, 1566–1640: Scénographies de la cruauté." Ph.D. diss., Université Paris X–Nanterre, 2013.

Clayton, Lawrence, "Bartolomé de las Casas and the African Slave Trade." *History Compass* 7, no. 6 (2009): 1526–41.

Clubb, Louise G. "Theatregrams." *Comparative Critical Approaches to Renaissance Comedy*, edited by Donald Beecher and Massimo Ciavolella, 15–33. Ottawa, Canada: Dovehouse Editions, 1986.

Cohen, Gustave. *La mise en scène dans le théâtre religieux francais du Moyen-âge*. Paris: Honoré Champion, 1906.

Cohen, Sarah R. *Art, Dance, and the Body in French Culture of the Ancien Régime*. Cambridge: Cambridge University Press, 2000.

Cole, Catherine. "American Ghetto Parties and Ghanaian Concert Parties: A Transnational Perspective on Blackface." In *Burnt Cork: Traditions and Legacies of Blackface Minstrelsy*, edited by Stephen Johnson, 223–58. Amherst: University of Massachusetts Press, 2012.

Cotarelo y Mori, Emilio. *Collección de entremeses, loas, bailes, jácaras y mojigangas, desde fines del siglo XVI a mediados del XVIII*. Vol. 1. Madrid: Casa Editorial Bailly-Baillière, 1911.

Cox, John D. *The Devil and the Sacred in English Drama, 1350–1642*. New York: Cambridge University Press, 2000.

Creswell, Tim. "Toward a Politics of Mobility." *Environment and Planning: Society and Space* 28 (2010): 17–31.

D'Accone, Frank A. *The Civic Muse: Music and Musicians in Siena During the Middle Ages and the Renaissance*. Chicago: University of Chicago Press, 1997.

Daileader, Celia R. *Racism, Misogyny, and the Othello Myth: Inter-Racial Couples from Shakespeare to Spike Lee*. Cambridge: Cambridge University Press, 2005.

Daston, Lorraine, and Peter Galison, *Objectivity*. New York: Zone Books, 2007.

Daye, Anne. "The Role of *Le Balet comique* in Forging the Stuart Masque: Part 1, The Jacobean Initiative." *Dance Research* 32, no. 2 (2014): 185–207.

De Bolla, Peter. *The Architecture of Concepts: The Historical Formation of Human Rights*. New York: Fordham University Press, 2013.

Delesalle, Simone, and Lucette Valensi. "Le mot 'Nègre' dans les dictionnaires français d'Ancien régime: Histoire et lexicographie." *Langue française* 15 (1972): 79–104.

Dewar, Helen. "Souveraineté dans les colonies, souveraineté en métropole: Le rôle de la Nouvelle-France dans la consolidation de l'autorité maritime en France, 1620–1628." *Revue d'Histoire de L'Amérique Française* 64, nos. 3–4 (2011): 63–92.

Dobie, Madeleine. *Trading Places: Colonization and Slavery in Eighteenth-Century French Culture*. Ithaca, N.Y.: Cornell University Press, 2010.

Dobson, Michael. *The Making of the National Poet: Shakespeare, Adaptation and Authorship, 1660–1769*. Oxford: Clarendon Press, 1992.

Dorlin, Elsa. *La matrice de la race: Généalogie sexuelle et coloniale de la Nation française*. Paris: Découverte, 2006.

Elliott, John R., Jr. "Mr. Moore's Revels: A 'Lost' Oxford Masque." *Renaissance Quarterly* 37, no. 3 (1984): 411–20.

Emery, Lynne Fauley. *Black Dance from 1619 to Today*. Princeton, N.J.: Princeton Book, 1988.

Fabre, Geneviève. "The Slave Ship Dance." In *Black Imagination and the Middle Passage*, edited by Maria Diedrich, Henry Louis Gates Jr., and Carl Pedersen, 33–46. New York: Oxford University Press, 1999.

Fanon, Frantz. *The Wretched of the Earth*. 1963. Translated by Richard Philcox. New York: Grove Press, 2004.

Feerick, Jean E. *Strangers in Blood: Relocating Race in the Renaissance*. Toronto: University of Toronto Press, 2010.

Ferguson, Margaret W. "Juggling the Categories of Race, Class, and Gender: Aphra Behn's *Oroonoko*." In *Women, "Race," and Writing in the Early Modern Period*, edited by Margo Hendricks and Patricia Parker, 209–24. London: Routledge, 1994.

Fernández Chaves, Manuel F., and Rafael M. Pérez García. "Las redes de la trata negrera: Mercaderes portugueses y tráfico de esclavos en Sevilla (c. 1560–1580)." In *La esclavitud negroafricana en la historia de España: Siglos XVI y XVII*, edited by Aurelia Martín Casares and Margarita García Barranco, 5–34. Granada: Comares, 2010.

Ferrer Valls, Teresa, ed. *Diccionario biográfico de actores del teatro clásico español (DICAT)*. Kassel: Reichenberger, 2008.

———. "Las dos caras del Diablo en el teatro antiguo español." In *Convegno di studi: Diavoli e mostri in scena dal Medio Evo al Rinascimento (Roma, 30 giugno / 3 luglio 1988)*, edited by Maria Chiabò and Federico Doglio, 303–24. Roma: Centro Studi sul Teatro Medioevale e Rinascimentale, 1989.

Fields, Karen E., and Barbara J. Fields. *Racecraft: The Soul of Inequality in American Life*. New York: Verso, 2012.

Fleischer, Alain. *L'accent, une langue fantôme*. Paris: Le Seuil, 2005.

Floyd-Wilson, Mary. "Temperature, Temperance, and Racial Difference in Ben Jonson's *The Masque of Blackness*." *English Literary Renaissance* 28, no. 2 (1998): 183–209.

Fonseca, Jorge. "Black Africans in Portugal During Cleynaerts's Visit (1533–1538)." In *Black Africans in Renaissance Europe*, edited by Kate Lowe and T. F. Earle, 113–21. Cambridge: Cambridge University Press, 2005.

Forrest, John. *The History of Morris Dancing, 1458–1750*. Toronto: University of Toronto Press, 1999.

Foucault, Michel. *The Archaeology of Knowledge*. Translated by A. M. Sheridan Smith. New York: Routledge, 2002.

Fracchia, Carmen. *"Black but Human": Slavery and Visual Arts in Hapsburg Spain, 1480–1700*. Oxford: Oxford University Press, 2019.

Fra-Molinero, Baltasar. *La imagen de los negros en el teatro del Siglo de oro*. Madrid: siglo veintiuno de españa editores, 1995.

———. "Ser mulato en España y América: Discursos legales y otros discursos literarios." In *Negros, mulatos, zambaigos: Derroteros africanos en los mundos ibéricos*, edited by Berta Ares Queija and Alessandro Stella, 123–47. Seville: Escuela de Estudios Hispano-Americanos, Consejo Superior de Investigaciones Científicas, 2000.

Franko, Mark. *Dance as Text: Ideologies of the Baroque Body*. Cambridge: Cambridge University Press, 1993.

Freud, Sigmund. *Jokes and Their Relation to the Unconscious*. In *The Standard Edition of the Complete Psychological Works of Sigmund Freud*, vol. 8, translated and edited by James Strachey. New York: Norton, 1960.

Fryer, Peter. *Staying Power: The History of Black People in Britain*. London: Pluto, 2010.

Fuchs, Barbara. "A Mirror Across the Water: Mimetic Racism, Hybridity, and Cultural Survival." In *Writing Race Across the Atlantic World*, edited by Philip D. Beidler and Gary Taylor, 9–26. New York: Palgrave, 2005.

———. "No Field Is an Island: Postcolonial and Transnational Approaches to Early Modern Drama." *Renaissance Drama* 40, no. 1 (2012): 125–33.

———. *Passing for Spain: Cervantes and the Fictions of Identity*. Urbana: University of Illinois Press, 2003.

———. "The Spanish Race." In *Re-Reading the Black Legend: The Discourses of Religious and Racial Difference in the Renaissance Empires*, edited by Margaret R. Greer, Walter D. Mignolo, and Maureen Quilligan, 88–98. Oxford: Oxford University Press, 2008.

Fudge, Erica. *Brutal Reasoning: Animals, Rationality, and Humanity in Early Modern England*. Ithaca, N.Y.: Cornell University Press, 2006.

———. *Perceiving Animals: Humans and Beasts in Early Modern English Culture*. New York: St. Martin's, 2000.

Fuentes, Marisa J. *Dispossessed Lives: Enslaved Women, Violence, and the Archive*. Philadelphia: University of Pennsylvania Press, 2016.

Fulton, Thomas C. "'The True and Naturall Constitution of That Mixed Government': Massinger's 'The Bondman' and the Influence of Dutch Republicanism." *Studies in Philology* 99, no. 2 (2002): 152–77.

Garraway, Doris. *The Libertine Colony: Creolization in the Early French Caribbean*. Durham, N.C.: Duke University Press, 2005.

Goldberg, David Theo. "The Comparative and the Relational: Meditations on Racial Methods." In *A Companion to Comparative Literature*, edited by Ali Behdad and Dominic Thomas, 357–68. Chichester, U.K.: Wiley-Blackwell, 2011.

Goldberg, K. Meira. *Sonidos Negros: On the Blackness of Flamenco*. Oxford: Oxford University Press, 2019.

Gordon, Donald J. *The Renaissance Imagination: Essays and Lectures*, edited by Stephen Orgel. Berkeley: University of California Press, 1975.

Gough, Melinda. "Courtly Comédiantes: Henrietta Maria and Amateur Women's Stage Plays in France and England." In *Women Players in England, 1500–1660: Beyond the All-Male Stage*, edited by Pamela Allen Brown and Peter Parolin, 193–215. Burlington, Vt.: Ashgate, 2005.

Granda de, Germán. *El español en tres mundos: Retenciones y contactos lingüísticos en América y Africa*. Valladolid: Universidad de Valladolid, Secretariado de Publicaciones, 1991.

Habib, Imtiaz. *Black Lives in the English Archives, 1500–1677: Imprints of the Invisible*. Burlington, Vt.: Ashgate, 2008.

Hall, Kim F. *Things of Darkness: Economics of Race and Gender in Early Modern England*. Ithaca, N.Y.: Cornell University Press, 1995.

———. "'Troubling Doubles': Apes, Africans, and Blackface in Mr. Moore's Revels." In *Race, Ethnicity, and Power in the Renaissance*, edited by Joyce Green MacDonald, 120–44. Madison, N.J.: Fairleigh Dickinson University Press, 1997.

Hall, Stuart. *The Fateful Triangle: Race, Ethnicity, Nation,* edited by Kobena Mercer. Cambridge, Mass.: Harvard University Press, 2017.

———. *Representation and the Media.* Produced and directed by Sut Jhally. Northampton, Mass.: Media Education Foundation, 1997.

———. "Subjects in History: Making Diasporic Identities." In *The House That Race Built: Black Americans, U.S. Terrain,* edited by Wahneema Lubiano, 289–99. New York: Pantheon Books, 1997.

———. "The Spectacle of the 'Other.'" In *Representation: Cultural Representations and Signifying Practices,* edited by Stuart Hall, 225–90. London; Thousand Oaks, CA.: Sage, 1997.

———. "The Work of Representation." In *Representation: Cultural Representations and Signifying Practices,* edited by Stuart Hall, 1–47. London; Thousand Oaks, CA.: Sage, 1997.

Hannaford, Ivan. *Race: The History of an Idea in the West.* Baltimore: Johns Hopkins University Press, 1996.

Harbage, Alfred. *Annals of English Drama, 975–1700.* London: Methuen, 1964.

Harrison, Timothy M. *Coming To: Consciousness and Natality in Early Modern England.* Chicago: University of Chicago Press, 2020.

Hartman, Saidiya V. *Scenes of Subjection: Terror, Slavery, and Self-Making in Nineteenth-Century America.* New York: Oxford University Press, 1997.

———. "Venus in Two Acts." *Small Axe: A Caribbean Journal of Criticism* 26 (2008): 1–14.

Hazzard-Gordon, Katrina. *Jookin': The Rise of Social Dance Formations in African-American Culture.* Philadelphia: Temple University Press, 1990.

Heng, Geraldine. *The Invention of Race in the European Middle Ages.* Cambridge: Cambridge University Press, 2018.

———. "The Invention of Race in the European Middle Ages: Race Studies, Modernity, and the Middle Ages." *Literature Compass* 8, no. 5 (2011) 315–31.

Herford, C. H., Percy Simpson, and Evelyn Simpson, eds. *Ben Jonson.* Vol. 10. *Play Commentary: Masque Commentary.* Oxford: Oxford University Press, 1950.

Herzog, Tamar. "How Did Early-Modern Slaves in Spain Disappear? The Antecedents." *Republics of Letters: A Journal for the Study of Knowledge, Politics, and the Arts* 3, no. 1 (2012): 1–7.

Holland, Sharon Patricia. *The Erotic Life of Racism.* Durham, N.C.: Duke University Press, 2012.

Hollis, Gavin. *The Absence of America: The London Stage, 1576–1642.* Oxford: Oxford University Press, 2015.

Hornback, Robert. "'Extravagant and Wheeling Strangers': Early Blackface Dancing Fools, Racial Impersonation, and the Limits of Identification." *Exemplaria* 20, no. 2 (2008): 197–222.

———. *Racism and Early Blackface Traditions: From the Old World to the New.* New York: Palgrave, 2018.

Howard, Jean E. *The Stage and Social Struggle in Early Modern England.* London: Routledge, 1994.

———. *Theater of a City: The Places of London Comedy, 1598–1642.* Philadelphia: University of Pennsylvania Press, 2007.

Howard, Skiles. *The Politics of Courtly Dancing in Early Modern England.* Amherst: University of Massachusetts Press, 1998.

Hughes, Derek. "Race, Gender, and Scholarly Practice: Aphra Behn's Oroonoko." *Essays in Criticism* 52, no. 1 (2002): 1–22.

Hutner, Heidi. *Colonial Women: Race and Culture in Stuart Drama.* New York: Oxford University Press, 2001.

Inda, Jonathan Xavier. "Performativity, Materiality, and the Racial Body." *Latino Studies Journal* 11, no. 3 (2000): 74–99.

Iwanisziw, Susan B. "The Shameful Allure of Sycorax and Wowski: Dramatic Precursors of Sartje, the Hottentot Venus." *Restoration and 18th Century Theatre Research* 16, no. 2 (2001): 3–23.

Iyengar, Sujata. "Moorish Dancing in the *Two Noble Kinsmen*." *Medieval and Renaissance Drama in England* 20 (2007): 85–107.

Johnson, E. Patrick. *Appropriating Blackness: Performance and the Politics of Authenticity*. Durham, N.C.: Duke University Press, 2003.

Jones, Nicholas. "Hyperbolic Hybridities: *Habla de Negros* and the Economies of Race and Language in Early Modern Spanish Poetry and Theater." Ph.D. diss., New York University, 2013. UMI: 3601670.

———. *Staging Habla de Negros: Radical Performances of the African Diaspora in Early Modern Spain*. University Park: Pennsylvania State University Press, 2019.

Jones, Rosalind, and Peter Stallybrass. "Dismantling Irena: The Sexualizing of Ireland in Early Modern England." In *Nationalisms and Sexualities*, edited by Andrew Parker, Mary Russo, Doris Sommer, and Patricia Yaeger, 157–74. London: Routledge, 1992.

Julius, Anthony. *Trials of the Diaspora: A History of Anti-Semitism in England*. Oxford: Oxford University Press, 2010.

Kadish, Doris Y. *Fathers, Daughters, and Slaves: Women Writers and French Colonial Slavery*. Liverpool: Liverpool University Press, 2012.

Kaplan, Paul H. D. "The Calenberg Altarpiece: Black African Christians in Renaissance Germany." In *Germany and the Black Diaspora: Points of Contact, 1250–1914*, edited by Mischa Honeck, Martin Klimke, and Anne Kuhlmann-Smirnov, 21–37. New York: Berghahn Books, 2013.

Karim-Cooper, Farah. *Cosmetics in Shakespearean and Renaissance Drama*. Edinburgh: Edinburgh University Press, 2006.

———. "The Materials of Race: Staging the Black and White Binary in the Early Modern Theatre." In *The Cambridge Companion to Shakespeare and Race,* edited by Ayanna Thompson, 17–29. Cambridge: Cambridge University Press, 2021.

Kaufmann, Miranda. *Black Tudors: The Untold Story*. London: Oneworld, 2017.

King-Dorset, Rodreguez. *Black Dance in London, 1730–1850: Innovation, Tradition and Resistance*. Jefferson, N.C.: McFarland, 2008.

Knowles, Mark. *The Early History of Tap Dancing*. Jefferson, N.C.: McFarland, 2002.

Knowles-Carter, Beyoncé. "Formation." On *Lemonade*. Parkwood Columbia, 2016.

Knutson, Roslyn L. "A Caliban in St. Mildred Poultry." In *Shakespeare and Cultural Traditions: The Selected Proceedings of the International Shakespeare Association World Congress* (Tokyo, 1991), edited by Tetsuo Kishi, Roger Pringle, and Stanley Wells, 110–26. Newark: University of Delaware Press, 1994.

Kruger, Loren. "Seeing Through Race: Athol Fugard, (East) Germany, and the Limits of Solidarity." *Modern Philology* 100, no. 4 (2003): 619–51.

Kuhn, Thomas. *The Structure of Scientific Revolutions*. 2nd ed., enlarged. Chicago: University of Chicago Press, 1970.

Lanser, Susan S. *The Sexuality of History: Modernity and the Sapphic, 1565–1830*. Chicago: University of Chicago Press, 2014.

Larquié, Claude. "Les esclaves de Madrid à l'époque de la décadence, 1650–1700." *Revue Historique* 244, fasc. 1 (495) (1970): 41–74.

Lebègue Raymond. "Le Diable dans l'ancien théâtre religieux." *Cahiers de l'Association internationale des études françaises* 3–5, no. 1 (1953): 97–105.

Lennep, William Van, ed. *The London Stage, 1660–1800: A Calendar of Plays, Entertainments and Afterpieces, Together with Casts, Box-Receipts and Contemporary Comment.* Part 1: 1660–1700. Carbondale: Southern Illinois University Press, 1965.

Le Roux de Lincy, Antoine. *Le livre des proverbes français, Tome premier.* 2nd ed. Paris: Adolphe Delahays, 1859.

Lipski, John M. *A History of Afro-Hispanic Language: Five Centuries, Five Continents.* Cambridge: Cambridge University Press, 2005.

Little, Arthur. *Shakespeare Jungle Fever: National-Imperial Re-Visions of Race, Rape and Sacrifice.* Stanford, Calif.: Stanford University Press, 2000.

Lobato, María Luisa. *Calderón: Teatro cómico breve.* Kassel: Reichenberg, 1989.

———. "La edición de textos teatrales breves." In *La edición de textos: Actas del I congreso internacional de hispanistas del Siglo de Oro*, edited by Pablo Jauralde, Dolores Noguera, and Alfonso Rey, 287–94. London: Tamesis Books, 1990.

Locke, Ralph P. *Music and the Exotic from the Renaissance to Mozart.* Cambridge: Cambridge University Press, 2015.

Loomba, Ania. *Shakespeare, Race, and Colonialism.* Oxford: Oxford University Press, 2002.

Loomba, Ania, and Jonathan Burton. *Race in Early Modern England: A Documentary Companion.* New York: Palgrave Macmillan, 2007.

Lott, Eric. *Love and Theft: Blackface Minstrelsy and the American Working Class.* New York: Oxford University Press, 1993.

Lowe, Kate. "The Stereotyping of Black Africans in Renaissance Europe." In *Black Africans in Renaissance Europe*, edited by Kate Lowe and T. F. Earle, 17–47. Cambridge: Cambridge University Press, 2005.

Lowenthal, Cynthia. *Performing Identities on the Restoration Stage.* Carbondale: Southern Illinois University Press, 2003.

Lucena Salmoral, Manuel. "Leyes para esclavos: El ordenamiento jurídico sobre la condición, tratamiento, defensa y represión de los esclavos en las colonias de la América española." In *Tres grandes cuestiones de la historia de Iberoamérica: Ensayos y monografías*, edited by José Andrés Gallego, 1–1384. Madrid: Fundación MAPFRE Tavera: Fundación Ignacio Larramendi, 2005.

MacDonald, Joyce Green. "Black Ram, White Ewe: Shakespeare, Race, and Women." In *A Feminist Companion to Shakespeare*, edited by Dympna Callaghan, 206–25. Malden, Mass.: Blackwell, 2000.

———. *Women and Race in Early Modern Texts.* Cambridge: Cambridge University Press, 2002.

Maddock Dillon, Elizabeth. *New World Drama: The Performative Commons in the Atlantic World, 1649–1849.* Durham, N.C.: Duke University Press, 2014.

Marcus, Sharon. "The Theatre of Comparative Literature." In *A Companion to Comparative Literature*, edited by Ali Behdad and Dominic Thomas, 136–55. Chichester, West Sussex: Wiley-Blackwell, 2011.

Marsh, Christopher W. *Music and Society in Early Modern England.* New York: Cambridge University Press, 2010.

Martín-Casares, Aurelia, and Marga García Barranco. "The Musical Legacy of Black Africans in Spain: A Review of Our Sources." *Anthropological Notebooks* 15, no. 2 (2009): 51–60.

———. "Popular Literary Depictions of Black African Weddings in Early Modern Spain." *Renaissance and Reformation / Renaissance et Réforme* 31, no. 2 (2008): 107–21.

Martín-Casares, Aurelia, and Christine Delaigue. "The Evangelization of Freed and Slave Black Africans in Renaissance Spain: Baptism, Marriage, and Ethnic Brotherhoods." *History of Religions* 52, no. 3 (2013): 214–35.

Mata Carriazo y Arroquia, Juan de. "Negros, esclavos y extranjeros en el barrio sevillano de San Bernardo, 1617–1629." Archivo personal, Biblioteca de la Universidad de Sevilla, Caja 043, folio 68. Later published in *Archivo hispalense: Revista histórica, literaria y artística* 20, no. 64–65 (1954): 121–33.

Mateo Alcalá, María Luisa. "Máscaras y tocados para las figuras infernales del Códice de Autos Viejos." *Teatro de palabras, revista sobre teatro áureo* 5 (2011): 163–95.

McCloy, Shelby T. "Negroes and Mulattoes in Eighteenth-Century France." *Journal of Negro History* 30, no. 3 (1945): 276–92.

McGowan, Margaret M. *The Court Ballet of Louis XIII: A Collection of Working Designs for Costumes, 1615–1633.* London: Victoria and Albert Museum in association with Hobhouse and Morton Morris, 1986.

———. *Dance in the Renaissance: European Fashion, French Obsession.* New Haven, Conn.: Yale University Press, 2008.

———. *La Danse à la Renaissance: Sources livresques et albums d'images.* Paris: Bibliothèque Nationale de France, 2012.

McKee, Sally. "Domestic Slavery in Renaissance Italy." *Slavery and Abolition* 29, no. 3 (2008): 305–26.

McKittrick, Katherine, and Clyde Woods. *Black Geographies and the Politics of Place.* Toronto: Between the Lines, 2007.

McManus, Clare. *Women on the Renaissance Stage: Anna of Denmark and Female Masquing in the Stuart Court, 1590–1619.* Manchester: Manchester University Press, 2002.

Médevielle, Nicolas P. A. "La racialisation des Africains: Récits commerciaux, religieux, philosophiques et littéraires 1480–1880." Ph.D. diss., Ohio State University, 2006.

Méndez Rodríguez, Luis. *Esclavos en la pintura sevillana de los Siglos de Oro.* Seville: Universidad de Sevilla / Ateneo de Sevilla, 2011.

Mills, Kenneth, William B. Taylor, and Sandra Lauderdale Graham, eds. *Colonial Latin America: A Documentary History.* Wilmington, Del.: Scholarly Resources, 2002.

Moreno Mendoza, Arsenio. "La figura del demonio en el teatro y la pintura del Siglo de oro español." *Atrio: Revista de historia del arte* 15–16 (2009): 149–54.

Moreno Muñoz, María José. "La danza teatral en el siglo XVII." Ph.D. diss., Servicio de Publicaciones de la Universidad de Córdoba, 2010.

Moreno Navarro, Isidoro. *La antigua Hermandad de los Negros de Sevilla: Etnicidad, poder y sociedad en 600 años de historia.* Seville: Universidad de Sevilla / Consejería de Cultura de la Junta de Andalucía, 1997.

Morgan, Jennifer L. *Laboring Women: Reproduction and Gender in New World Slavery.* Philadelphia: University of Pennsylvania Press, 2004.

Morley, Sylvanus Griswold, and Courtney Bruerton. *The Chronology of Lope de Vega's Comedias: With a Discussion of Doubtful Attribution, the Whole Based on a Study of His Strophic Versification.* New York: Modern Language Association of America, 1940.

Motten, J. P. Vander. 2008 "Fane, Sir Francis (d. 1691), Playwright." *Oxford Dictionary of National Biography.* https://www.oxforddnb.com/view/10.1093/ref:odnb/9780198614128.001.0001/odnb-9780198614128-e-913 Accessed November 21, 2021.

Mujica, Bárbara. "Introduction." In *A New Anthology of Early Modern Spanish Theater, Play and Playtext,* edited by Bárbara Mujica, 1–22. New Haven, Conn.: Yale University Press, 2014.

Navarro García, José Luis. *Semillas de ébano: El elemento negro y afroamericano en el baile fla-menco*. Seville: Portada Editorial, 1990.

Ndiaye, Noémie. "Aaron's Roots: Spaniards, Englishmen, and Blackamoors in *Titus Androni-cus*." *Early Theatre* 19, no. 2 (2016): 59–80.

———. "Black Roma: Afro-Romani Connections in Early Modern Drama (and Beyond)." *Re-naissance Quarterly* 75, no. 4 (2022), forthcoming.

———. "'Come Aloft, Jack-Little-Ape': Race and Dance in *The Spanish Gypsie*." *English Literary Renaissance* 51, no. 1 (Winter 2021): 121–51.

———. "'Everyone Breeds in His Own Image': Staging the *Aethiopica* Across the Channel." *Re-naissance Drama* 44, no. 2 (2016): 157–85.

———. "Off the Record: Contrapuntal Theatre History." In *Companion to Theatre and Perfor-mance Historiography*, edited by Tracy C. Davis and Peter W. Marx, 229–48. New York: Routledge, 2021.

———. "Rewriting the *Grand Siècle*: Blackface in Early Modern France and the Historiography of Race." *Literature Compass, 18.10 (2021)*. e12603. 1-11. https://doi.org/10.1111/lic3.12603.

———. "Shakespeare, Race, and Globalization: *Titus Andronicus*." In *The Cambridge Compan-ion to Shakespeare and Race*, edited by Ayanna Thompson, 158–74. Cambridge: Cambridge University Press, 2021.

———. "The African Ambassador's Travels: Playing Black in Late Seventeenth-Century France and Spain." In *Transnational Connections in Early Modern Theatre*, edited by M. A. Ka-tritzky and Pavel Drábek, 73–85. Manchester: Manchester University Press, 2020.

Neill, Michael. "Broken English and Broken Irish: Nation, Language, and the Optic of Power in Shakespeare's Histories." *Shakespeare Quarterly* 45, no. 1 (1994): 1–32.

Nevile, Jennifer. *The Eloquent Body: Dance and Humanist Culture in Fifteenth-Century Italy*. Bloomington: Indiana University Press, 2004.

Nirenberg, David. "Race and the Middle Ages." In *Rereading the Black Legend: The Discourses of Religious and Racial Difference in the Renaissance Empires*, edited by Margaret R. Greer, Wal-ter D. Mignolo, and Maureen Quilligan, 71–87. Chicago: University of Chicago Press, 2007.

Noël, Erick, ed. *Dictionnaire des gens de couleur dans la France moderne: Paris et son bassin; En-trée par localité et par année (fin XVe siècle-1792), Paris suivi des provinces classées alphabé-tiquement*. Geneva: Droz, 2011.

———. "L'esclavage dans la France moderne." *Dix-huitième siècle* 39, no. 1 (2007): 361–83.

Nussbaum, Felicity A. *The Limits of the Human: Fictions of Anomaly, Race, and Gender in the Long Eighteenth Century*. Cambridge: Cambridge University Press, 2003.

O'Flynn, Brian. "How the Matrix Was Adopted by 4chan and the Alt-Right." *Dazed*, March 24, 2017. https://www.dazeddigital.com/artsandculture/article/35251/1/how-the-matrix-was -adopted-by-4chan-and-the-far-right.

Omi, Michael, and Howard Winant. *Racial Formation in the U.S.: From the 1960s to the 1980s*. New York: Routledge and Kegan Paul, 1987.

Operstein, Natalie. "Golden Age *Poesía de Negros* and Orlando di Lasso's *Moresche*: A Possible Connection." *Romance Notes* 52, no. 1 (2012): 13–18.

Orgel, Stephen. *The Jonsonian Masque*. Cambridge, Mass.: Harvard University Press, 1965.

Orkin, Martin, and Alexa Alice Joubin. *Race*. Abingdon, New York: Routledge, 2019.

Orr, Bridget. *Empire on the English Stage, 1660–1714*. Cambridge: Cambridge University Press, 2001.

Orwell, George, *1984*, edited by Robert Icke and Duncan Macmillan. London: Oberon Books, 2014.

Paisey, David. "Black English in Britain in the Eighteenth Century." *Electronic British Library Journal* (2015). https://www.bl.uk/eblj/2015articles/article12.html.

Palatín, Fernando. *Diccionario de música: Sevilla, 1818.* Oviedo: Universidad de Oviedo, 1990.

Paquot, Michel. *Les étrangers dans les divertissements de la cour, de Beaujoyeulx à Molière (1581– 1673): Contribution à l'étude de l'opinion publique et du théâtre en France.* Bruxelles: Palais des Académies, 1932.

Paravano, Cristina. *Performing Multilingualism on the Caroline Stage in the Plays of Richard Brome.* Newcastle-upon-Tyne: Cambridge Scholars, 2018.

Parfaict, François. *Histoire du théâtre françois depuis son origine jusqu'à présent, Tome sixième.* Paris: chez P. G. Le Mercier et Saillant, 1746.

Peabody, Susan. *"There Are No Slaves in France": The Political Culture of Race and Slavery in the Ancien Régime.* New York: Oxford University Press, 1996.

Perret, Michèle. *Introduction à l'histoire de la langue française.* Paris: Editions SEDES, 1998.

Phillips, Susan. "Schoolmasters, Seduction, and Slavery: Polyglot Dictionaries in Pre-Modern England." *Medievalia et Humanistica: Studies in Medieval and Renaissance Culture* 34 (2008): 129–58.

Phillips, William D. *Slavery in Medieval and Early Modern Iberia.* Philadelphia: University of Pennsylvania Press, 2014.

Plans, Antonio Salvador. "Los lenguajes 'especiale's y de las minorías en el siglo de oro." In *Historia de la lengua española,* edited by Rafael Cano, 771–97. Barcelona: Editorial Ariel, 2004.

Prest, Julia. "Pale Imitations: White Performances of Slave Dance in the Public Theatres of Pre-Revolutionary Saint-Domingue." *Atlantic Studies: Literary, Cultural, and Historical Perspectives* 16, no. 4 (2019): 502–20.

———. *Theatre Under Louis XIV: Cross-Casting and the Performance of Gender in Drama, Ballet and Opera.* New York: Palgrave Macmillan, 2006.

Preston, Virginia K. "Un/Becoming Nomad: Marc Lescarbot, Movement, and Metamorphosis in *Les Muses de la Nouvelle France.*" In *History, Memory, Performance,* edited by David Dean, Yana Meerzon, and Kathryn Prince, 68–82. London: Palgrave Macmillan, 2015.

Quéruel, Danielle. "Des gestes à la danse: L'exemple de la 'Morisque' à la fin du Moyen-Âge." In *Le geste et les gestes au Moyen-âge,* 499–517. Aix-en-Provence: CUER MA, Université de Provence (Centre d'Aix), 1998.

Rancière, Jacques. *The Emancipated Spectator.* London: Verso, 2009.

Rappaport, Joanne. *The Disappearing Mestizo: Configuring Difference in the Colonial New Kingdom of Granada.* Durham, N.C.: Duke University Press, 2014.

Répide de, Pedro. *Las calles de Madrid,* edited by Federico Romero. Madrid: Afrodisio Aguado, S.A., 1971.

Reynolds, Erin. "Strange Accents or Ill Shapen Sounds: Dialect in Early Modern Drama." 2008. Thesis. http://homes.chass.utoronto.ca/~cpercy/courses/6362-ReynoldsErin.htm.

Rice, Eric. Program of the Ensemble Origo concert "Motets, Madrigals and Moresche: Orlando di Lasso's Music for the Commedia dell'Arte at a 1568 Wedding." Italian Academy, Columbia University, October 2015.

Robinson, Cedric J. *Black Marxism: The Making of the Black Radical Tradition.* Chapel Hill: University of North Carolina Press, 1983.

Robinson, Charles Henry. *Dictionary of the Hausa Language. Vol. 1. Hausa-English.* Cambridge: Cambridge University Press, 1913.

Rodríguez Loro, Nora. *Falsos maestros de danzar: Análisis comparativo de la comedia El Maestro de danzar de Lope de Vega y las obras homónimas de Calderón de la Barca y Wycherley*. M.A. Thesis. Universidad de Sevilla. Facultad de Filología. Departamento de Literatura Española, 2014.

Rowe, Erin. "After Death, Her Face Turned White: Blackness, Whiteness, and Sanctity in the Early Modern Hispanic World." *American Historical Review* 121, no. 3 (2016): 727–54.

———. *Black Saints in Early Modern Global Catholicism*. Cambridge: Cambridge University Press, 2019.

Rubright, Marjorie. *Doppelganger Dilemmas: Anglo-Dutch Relations in Early Modern English Literature and Culture*. Philadelphia: University of Pennsylvania Press, 2014.

Salvatore, Gianfranco. "Parodie realistiche: Africanismi, fraternità e sentimenti identitari nelle canzoni moresche del Cinquecento." *Kronos* 14 (Università del Salento, 2011): 97–130.

Salvo, Mimma de. *La mujer en la prática escénica de los siglos de oro: La búsqueda de un espacio profesional*. Ph.D. diss., Universitat de València, Facultat de Filología Española, 2006.

Santos Morillo, Antonio. "Caracterización del negro en la literatura española del XVI." *Lemir* 15 (2011): 23–46.

Saunders, A.C. de C.M. *A Social History of Black Slaves and Freedmen in Portugal, 1441–1555*. New York: Cambridge University Press, 1982.

Schaub, Frédéric, and Silvia Sebastiani. "Between Genealogy and Physicality: A Historiographical Perspective on Race in the 'Ancien Régime.'" *Graduate Faculty Philosophy Journal* 35, nos. 1–2 (2014): 23–51.

Schmalenberger, Sarah. "Hearing the Other in the *Masque of Blackness*." In *Blackness in Opera*, edited by Naomi Andre, Karen Bryan, and Eric Saylor, 32–54. Urbana: University of Illinois Press, 2012.

Schorsch, Jonathan. *Swimming the Christian Atlantic: Judeoconversos, Afroiberians and Amerindians in the Seventeenth Century*. Boston: Brill, 2009.

Schwartz, Stuart, and Frank Salomon. "New Peoples and New Kinds of People: Adaptation, Readjustment, and Ethnogenesis in South American Indigenous Societies (Colonial Era)." In *The Cambridge History of the Native Peoples of the Americas, Volume 3: South America, Part 2*, edited by Frank Salomon and Stuart B. Schwartz, 443–501. Cambridge: Cambridge University Press, 1999.

Scolieri, Paul A. *Dancing the New World: Aztecs, Spaniards, and the Choreography of Conquest*. Austin: University of Texas Press, 2013.

Sedgwick, Eve Kosofsky, and Frank, Adam. *Touching Feeling: Affect, Pedagogy, Performativity*. Durham, N.C.: Duke University Press, 2003.

Sentaurens, Jean. *Séville et le théâtre: De la fin du Moyen Âge à la fin du XVIIe siècle*. Lille: Atelier national de reproduction des thèses, Université de Lille III / Talence: Diffusion, Presses universitaires de Bordeaux, Université de Bordeaux III, 1984.

Serrera Contreras, Ramón María, ed. "Introduction." In *El Arenal de Sevilla de Lope de Vega*, 149–67. Seville: Ayuntamiento de Sevilla, Colección "Sevilla lee," 2007.

Shahani, Gitanjali G. *Tasting Difference: Food, Race, and Cultural Encounters in Early Modern Literature*. Ithaca, N.Y.: Cornell University Press, 2020.

Sharma, Devika, and Frederik Tygstrup. *Structures of Feeling: Affectivity and the Study of Culture*. Berlin: De Gruyter, 2015.

Shergold, N. D., and Peter Ure. "Dryden and Calderón: A New Spanish Source for 'The Indian Emperour.'" *Modern Language Review* 61, no. 3 (1966): 369–83.

Silva, Denise Ferreira da. *Toward a Global Idea of Race*. Minneapolis: University of Minnesota Press, 2007.

Skretkowicz, Victor. "Poems of Discovery: John Taylor's Barbarian, Utopian and Barmooda Tongues." *Renaissance Studies* 6, no. 3–4 (1992): 391–99.

Smith, Bruce R. *The Acoustic World of Early Modern England: Attending to the O-Factor*. Chicago: University of Chicago Press, 1999.

Smith, Ian. "Othello's Black Handkerchief." *Shakespeare Quarterly* 64, no. 1 (2013): 1–25.

———. *Race and Rhetoric in the Renaissance: Barbarian Errors*. New York: Palgrave Macmillan, 2009.

———. "The Textile Black Body: Race and 'Shadowed Livery' in *The Merchant of Venice*." In *The Oxford Handbook of Shakespeare and Embodiment: Gender, Sexuality, and Race*, edited by Valerie Traub, 170–85. Oxford: Oxford University Press, 2016.

———. "We Are Othello: Speaking of Race in Early Modern Studies." *Shakespeare Quarterly* 67, no. 1 (2016): 104–24.

Smith, Nigel. "Migration and Drama: Amsterdam 1617." In *Transnational Connections in Early Modern Theatre*, edited by M. A. Katritzky and Pavel Drábek, 89–113. Manchester: Manchester University Press, 2020.

———. "Slavery, Rape, Migration: The View from the Amsterdam Stage, 1615." *Shakespeare Studies* 48 (2020): 80–86.

Snorton, C. Riley. *Black on Both Sides: A Racial History of Trans Identity*. Minneapolis: University of Minnesota Press, 2017.

Sommerville, C. John. *The Secularization of Early Modern England: From Religious Culture to Religious Faith*. Oxford: Oxford University Press, 1992.

Soumahoro, Maboula. *Le triangle et l'hexagone: Réflexions sur une identité noire*. Paris: La Découverte, 2020.

Sponsler, Claire. "Writing the Unwritten: Morris Dance and Theatre History." In *Representing the Past: Essays in Performance Historiography*, edited by Charlotte M. Canning and Thomas Postlewait, 84–113. Iowa City: University of Iowa Press, 2010.

Stam, Robert, and Ella Shohat. *Race in Translation: Culture Wars Around the Postcolonial Atlantic*. New York: New York University Press, 2012.

Stanley-Niaah, Sonjah. *Dancehall: From Slave Ship to Ghetto*. Ottawa: University of Ottawa Press, 2010.

Steggle, Matthew. "Critical Introduction and Textual Introduction to *The English Moor, or The Mock-Marriage*." *Richard Brome Online*. http://www.dhi.ac.uk/brome. November 11, 2021. ISBN 978-0-9557876-1-4.

Stein, Louise K. "Eros, Erato, Terpsíchore, and the Hearing of Music in Early Modern Spain." *Musical Quarterly* 82, nos. 3–4 (1998): 654–77.

Stella, Alessandro. *Histoires d'esclaves dans la péninsule ibérique*. Paris: EHESS, 2000.

Stephens, Walter. *Demon Lovers: Witchcraft, Sex, and the Crisis of Belief*. Chicago: University of Chicago Press, 2002.

Stevens, Andrea Ria. *Inventions of the Skin: The Painted Body in Early English Drama, 1400–1642*. Edinburgh: Edinburgh University Press, 2013.

———. "Mastering Masques of Blackness: Jonson's 'Masque of Blackness,' The Windsor Text of 'The Gypsies Metamorphosed,' and Brome's 'The English Moor.'" *English Literary Renaissance* 39, no. 2 (Spring 2009): 396–426.

Stevenson, David, ed. *Scotland's Last Royal Wedding: The Marriage of James VI and Anne of Denmark. With a Danish Account of the Marriage Translated by Peter Graves.* Edinburgh: John Donald, 1997.

Stoever, Jennifer Lynn. *The Sonic Color Line: Race and the Cultural Politics of Listening.* New York: New York University Press, 2016.

Stoler, Ann Laura. "Racial Histories and Their Regimes of Truth." In *Race Critical Theories, Text and Context,* edited by Philomena Essed and David Theo Goldberg, 369–91. Malden, Mass.: Blackwell, 2002.

Styles, Monica. "Foreshadowing Failure: Mulatto and Black Oral Discourse and the Upending of the Western Design in Thomas Gage's *A New Survey* (1648)." *Hispania* 102, no. 4 (2019): 583–600.

Sutton, Julia, et al. "Dance." *Grove Music Online. Oxford Music Online.* Oxford University Press. https://doi-org.proxy.uchicago.edu/10.1093/gmo/9781561592630.article.45795. Accessed November 22, 2021.

Sutton, Julia, and Pamela Jones. "Canary." *The International Encyclopedia of Dance.* Oxford University Press. https://www-oxfordreference-com.proxy.uchicago.edu/view/10.1093/acref/9780195173697.001.0001/acref-9780195173697-e-0317. Accessed November 22, 2021.

Swiadon, Glenn. "Los villancicos de negro: Breve introducción al género." *Dimensión Antropológica* 5, no.14 (1998): 133–47.

Sypher, Wylie. *Guinea's Captive Kings: British Anti-Slavery Literature of the XVIIIth Century.* Chapel Hill: University of North Carolina Press, 1942.

Taylor, Diana. *The Archive and the Repertoire: Performing Cultural Memory in the Americas.* Durham, N.C.: Duke University Press, 2003.

Terry, Esther J. "Belonging While Black: A Choreography of Imagined Silence in Early Modern African Diasporic Dances." Ph.D. diss., University of Pittsburgh, 2016.

———. "Choreographies of Trans-Atlantic Primitivity: Sub-Saharan Isolation in Black Dance Historiography." In *Early Modern Black Diaspora Studies: A Critical Anthology,* edited by Cassander L. Smith, Nicholas R. Jones, Miles P. Grier, 65–82. New York: Palgrave Macmillan, 2018.

Teyssier, Paul. *La langue de Gil Vicente.* Paris: C. Klincksieck, 1959.

Thomas, Keith. *Man and the Natural World: A History of the Modern Sensibility.* New York: Pantheon Books, 1983.

Thompson, Ayanna. *Performing Race and Torture on the Early Modern Stage.* New York: Routledge, 2008.

Thorpe, Edward. *Black Dance.* Woodstock, N.Y.: Overlook Press, 1990.

Tokson, Eliot. *The Popular Image of the Black Man in English Drama 1550–1688.* Boston: G. K. Hall, 1982.

Trambaioli, Marcella. "Apuntes sobre el guineo o baile de negros: Tipologías y funciones dramáticas." In *Actas del VI Congreso de la Asociación Internacional Siglo de Oro,* edited by María Luisa Lobato and Francisco Domínguez Matito, 1773–83. Madrid: Iberoamericana-Vervuert, 2004.

Trésor de la langue Française informatisé. ATILF-CNRS and Université de Lorraine. http://www.atilf.fr/tlfi. Accessed November 13, 2021.

Ungerer, Gustav. "The Presence of Africans in Elizabethan England and the Performance of *Titus Andronicus* at Burley-on-the-Hill, 1595/96." *Medieval and Renaissance Drama in England* 21 (2008): 19–55.

Urzáiz Tortajada, Héctor. *Catálogo de autores teatrales del siglo XVII*. Madrid: Publicaciones de la Fundación Universitaria Española, 2002.

Vaughan, Virginia Mason. *Performing Blackness on English Stages, 1500–1800*. New York: Cambridge University Press, 2005.

Wachowski, Lana, and Lilly Wachowski, directors. *The Matrix*. Burbank, Calif.: Warner Bros., 1999.

———. *Matrix Reloaded*. Burbank, Calif.: Warner Bros., 2003.

———. *Matrix Revolutions*. Burbank, Calif.: Warner Bros., 2003.

Wallerstein, Immanuel. *World-Systems Analysis: An Introduction*. Durham, N.C.: Duke University Press, 2004.

Weber de Kurlat, Frida. "Latinismos arrusticados en el sayagués." *Nueva Revista de Filología Hispánica* 1, no. 2 (1947): 166–70.

———. "Sobre el negro como tipo cómico en el teatro español del siglo XVI." *Romance Philology* 17, no. 2 (1963): 380–91.

Weissbourd, Emily. "'Those in Their Possession': Race, Slavery, and Queen Elizabeth's 'Edicts of Expulsion.'" *Huntington Library Quarterly* 78, no. 1 (2015): 1–19.

———. "Transnational Genealogies: Jews, Blacks and Moors in Early Modern English and Spanish Literature, 1547–1642." Ph.D. diss., University of Pennsylvania, 2011.

Welch, Ellen. "Dancing the Nation: Performing France in the Seventeenth-Century 'Ballets des nations.'" *Journal for Early Modern Cultural Studies* 13, no. 2 (2013): 3–23.

———. "The Specter of the Turk in Early Modern French Court Entertainments." *Esprit Créateur* 53, no. 4 (2013): 84–97.

Wheeler, Roxann. "Sounding Black-Ish: West Indian Pidgin in London Performance and Print." *Eighteenth-Century Studies* 51, no. 1 (2017): 63–87.

Whitaker, Cord J. *Black Metaphors: How Modern Racism Emerged from Medieval Race-Thinking*. Philadelphia: University of Pennsylvania Press, 2019.

Wikström, Toby. "Law, Conquest and Slavery on the French Stage, 1598–1685." Ph.D. diss., Columbia University, 2010.

Wilbourne, Emily. "*Lo Schiavetto* (1612): Travestied Sound, Ethnic Performance, and the Eloquence of the Body." *Journal of the American Musicological Society* 63, no. 1 (2010): 1–43.

Wistreich, Richard. *Warrior, Courtier, Singer: Giulio Cesare Brancaccio and the Performance of Identity in the Late Renaissance*. Aldershot, U.K.: Ashgate, 2007.

Wood, Jennifer Linhart. *Sounding Otherness in Early Modern Drama and Travel: Uncanny Vibrations in the English Archive*. Cham, Switzerland: Palgrave Macmillan, 2019.

Wright, Elizabeth R. *The Epic of Juan Latino: Dilemmas of Race and Religion in Renaissance Spain*. Toronto: University of Toronto Press, 2016.

Yates, Frances A. "English Actors in Paris During Shakespeare's Lifetime." *Review of English Studies* 1, no. 4 (1925): 392–403.

Zantop, Susanne. *Colonial Fantasies: Conquest, Family, and Nation in Precolonial Germany, 1770–1870*. Durham, N.C.: Duke University Press, 1997.

INDEX

ACKNOWLEDGMENTS

None of my work (past, present, future) would be possible without Jean E. Howard. For welcoming me into the fold of American academia, for listening to me, for believing in me and my crazy project from the very start, for guiding me superbly and supporting me indefatigably through years of thinking and up to this very moment—I cannot thank her enough. Jean has read more drafts of this book than anyone should ever have to, yet my debt goes even further. With her strength, wisdom, and generosity, Jean has been a beacon of light and a force for good in early modern studies and beyond. Not a week passes by that I don't wonder, "What would Jean Howard do?"—and that the answer does not bring me clarity. Thank you for everything, Jean. And "Onward!" indeed.

None of my work (past, present, future) would be any good without Kim F. Hall. For welcoming me into the fold of early modern critical race studies, for inspiring me by her example to aim higher and to persist in the face of scholarly resistance, for providing such constructive feedback on my work through the years and pushing me to think ever more capaciously, more ambitiously, and more politically—I am forever grateful to her. Thank you, Kim, for showing us what it means and what it takes to grow into one's own power and to grow a field "without losing one's soul."

My project significantly benefited from the insights and suggestions of many other folks at Columbia University during my graduate school years there: Madeleine Dobie—who taught me, among other things, that if I can convince a French eighteenth centuryist, I can convince anyone—and Patricia Grieve—whose course on Siglo de Oro drama, taught in English for inclusive purposes, was pivotal to my scholarly growth, as it introduced me to the archives of early modern Spanish drama and convinced me to learn Spanish. Thinking back on my graduate school years, I am grateful to Julie Stone Peters for her continued support, to Alan Stewart for granting me archival research funding as department chair, to Pierre Force and Toby Wikström for providing me with invaluable bibliographic information, and to the various members of the Early Modern

Colloquium and the Theatre Colloquium—faculty and graduate students—
who responded to my chapter drafts from 2014 to 2017. My dissertation and the
archival research it required in Seville, Madrid, and Paris were funded by Columbia University and by the Mellon/ACLS Dissertation Completion Fellow-
ship program. I am very grateful to the English Departments at Carnegie
Mellon University (2017–19) and at the University of Chicago (2019–present)
for granting me the course releases and the time necessary to write and revise
this book.

As I embarked upon my journey as a graduate student, I was lucky to meet
senior scholars willing to support my research: Barbara Fuchs, the late Christian Biet, Enrique García Santo Tomas, Valerie Traub, and Josiah Blackmore
read various chapter drafts and were kind enough to share their expertise, questions, and advice with me early on. Similarly, the members of the research collaborative Theatre Without Borders provided useful feedback on my project
through its various stages. I am especially grateful to Susanne Wofford, whose
generous mentoring has been unwavering as years have gone by, and to Pavel
Drábek, who kindly read most of the book manuscript. During my years in
Pittsburgh after graduation, conversations with the marvelous Kristina Straub
and Mame-Fatou Niang fed my soul. I am also grateful to Andreea Ritivoi,
Richard Purcell, Stephen Wittek, Chris Warren, Kathy Newman, Marian
Aguiar, and Jennifer Waldron, who all supported my project in different ways.
Recently, new accomplices have entered my life, whose friendship, trust, and il-
luminating conversation are a great source of joy and growth for me: among
them, let me name Urvashi Chakravarty, Patricia Akhimie, Lia Markey, Lisa
Freeman, Emily Weissbourd, S. J. Zhang, Hoda El Shakry, Liza Blake, and
Tracy C. Davis.

At the University of Chicago, I have been blessed with the smartest and
most generous colleagues one could ask for—they have enriched this book more
than I can say. Heartfelt thanks go to my colleagues in early modern English
studies: Ellen MacKay—the best listener and dazzling wordsmith, who returned
my argument to me wrapped in a luminousness I never knew it could have; the
brilliant Tim Harrison—who read and responded to my work with his unique
insightfulness, curiosity, and love of conceptual history; and Joshua Scodel—
who kindly put his erudition and keen editorial eye in service of my project.
This project greatly benefitted from the feedback of Adrienne Brown (who
helped me find nothing less than the title of the book), C. Riley Snorton (who
helped me find my way into Black studies), S. J. Zhang (who inspired me to
keep thinking about the relation between my archives, the Caribbean, and the

capaciousness of the early modern), Julie Orlemanski (who helped me see with greater clarity the place of whiteness in my project), John Muse (who helped me articulate my own definition of the performative), Loren Kruger (who encouraged me to emancipate myself vis-à-vis various theorists' authority), Tim Campbell (the image wizard who helped locate the beautiful 1626 Cacique drawing), and Kenneth Warren (who prompted me to think through the relation between race and class, and what it means to use the word *Black*). In the Department of Romance Languages and Literature, I am grateful to Larissa Brewer-García, Larry Norman, and Noel Blanco Mourelle for their smart suggestions and their continued intellectual companionship. Let me also thank the graduate students, colleagues, and friends in the Renaissance Workshop and the Early Modern Mediterranean Workshop who provided valuable feedback on sections of this book. I am spoiled to have joined such a wonderful intellectual community.

Working with the University of Pennsylvania Press has been a great experience. I am infinitely grateful to Jerry Singerman for seeing the value of my project early on and shepherding my book manuscript toward publication with the utmost care, enthusiasm, and determination. And I could not have asked for better series editors than Geraldine Heng and Ayanna Thompson. I am delighted to be able to acknowledge by name Virginia Mason Vaughan and Baltasar Fra-Molinero, who peer-reviewed this manuscript and decided to green-light it: I am grateful for the diligence and critical generosity that their suggestions evidenced. I also want to thank Amy Sherman, the line editor who did great work on this manuscript and helped me see that what I study in this book is indeed "a hermeneutic war," as well as Kavita Mudan Finn, the incredibly perceptive and creative indexer who helped me draw paths and itineraries across the thick archives of this book. I could not have located the materials I needed without the help of librarians and archivists, among whom Candice Kail, Alfredo Montilla Carvajal, and Nazario Aguilar Montes deserve particular recognition. Writing can be lonely: let me acknowledge here the amazing writing buddies with whom I worked over the years—Erica Richardson, Anais Maurer, Rosa Schneider, Taarini Mukherjee, Andy Crow, Akua Banful, Ernesto Matos Gutiérrez, Anna Winterstein, and Daniel Makonnen, as well as the teachers from my salad days who inspired me in their own way to do this work: Elisabeth Angel-Perez and Chantal Brière.

Finally, I want to thank my family and the loved ones who patiently listened to my ideas about racial formations, theatre, and early modern performance culture over the years. They witnessed the joy, the anger, the exhilaration, and the exhaustion of it all. All too often, they had to compete with "The Book" for my time and attention, and for that, I remain in their debt. Special mentions to my grandmother Marie-Claire Reltgen, the actress at heart who taught me how to love method, how to make a good plan, and stick to it; to my mother, Lucie Reltgen, the beautiful mind who taught me how to love theatre, think critically, and value freedom above anything else; and to my late father, Babacar Ndiaye, the absent-present who found a way to teach me how to cross oceans and move mountains. Last but not least, heartfelt thanks go to Nigel Ridgeway, who taught me how to *take a break* and make time for happiness.

A section from Chapter 4 was published in the article "'Come Aloft, Jack-Little-Ape': Race and Dance in *The Spanish Gypsie,*" *English Literary Renaissance* 51, no. 1 (2021), 121–51, © 2020 by English Literary Renaissance, Inc. A section from Chapter 2 was published in the article "Rewriting the *Grand Siècle*: Blackface in Early Modern France and the Historiography of Race," *Literature Compass* 18.10 (2021). e12603. 1-11. https://doi.org/10.1111/lic3.12603 Those essays are reprinted here with permission.

Printed in the USA
CPSIA information can be obtained
at www.ICGtesting.com
JSHW081913160224
57534JS00003B/6